Thomas Lindall Winthrop
= Elizabeth Bowdoin Temple

Robert Charles Winthrop
= (1) Elizabeth Cabot Blanchard

Robert Charles Winthrop, Jr.
= (2) Elizabeth Mason

Margaret Tyndal Winthrop
= James Grant Forbes

Frederic Winthrop   =   Angela Elizabeth Forbes

THE DESCENDANTS OF

Robert Winthrop

of NEW YORK

THE DESCENDANTS OF

Robert Winthrop

of NEW YORK

by Scott C. Steward and Chip Rowe

Newbury Street Press
Boston 2017

Explanatory text for back endpapers:

The Forbes children in Gstaad in 1929

From left to right: *James Grant[10] Forbes, Jr.; John Winthrop Forbes; Griselda Margaret Forbes (later Mrs. Warren Delano Martineau); Angela Elizabeth Forbes (later Mrs. Frederic[10] Winthrop); Rosemary Isabel Forbes (later Mrs. Richard John Kerry); Eileen Mason Forbes (later Mme. Francis Tailleux); Monica Ethel Forbes (later Mrs. Dunstan Michael Carr Curtis and Mrs. John Sleigh Pudney); Alastair Cameron Forbes; Ian Archibald Forbes; Iris Decima Forbes (later Mrs. Terence Edward Armstrong); and Fiona Deirdre Forbes (later Mme. Alain-Gauthier Lalonde).*

A Winthrop union

Gardner Cox's fanciful mural of Squerryes Court in Westerham, Kent, where the wedding reception following the marriage of Frederic[10] Winthrop and Angela Elizabeth[10] Forbes was held in July 1933. Their wedding marked the union of three branches of the Winthrop family, two represented by the groom and one by the bride.

Wedding party of Frederic[10] Winthrop and Angela Elizabeth[10] Forbes

From left to right: *The bride's brothers Alastair and Jock Forbes; her sister Iris Forbes; their brother James Forbes; their sister Eileen Forbes; the best man, Morton Eustis; the bride; the bride's sister Fiona Forbes; the groom; the bride's sister Rosemary Forbes; the groom's cousin William A. Coolidge; the bride's sister Monica Forbes; Moses Williams; and the bride's brother Ian Forbes.*

ISBN-13: 978-0-88082-361-6
Library of Congress Control Number: 2017941655

NEWBURY STREET PRESS
imprint of New England Historic Genealogical Society
Boston, Massachusetts
AmericanAncestors.org

TABLE OF CONTENTS

INTRODUCTION

DURING the seventeenth and early eighteenth centuries, the Winthrop family of Massachusetts produced three colonial governors in three generations; if the third was less potent than the first two, this feat must still be considered remarkable. The family, having reached a kind of apogee by 1700, did not—as would so many early New England families—then fade away. One line drifted south, to Connecticut, and then settled in New York City in the late eighteenth century. It was this branch of the Winthrop family to which Robert[8] Winthrop belonged, and by the time he was born in 1833 the family was well-established in Manhattan.

The New York Winthrops remained connected with their Boston cousins: the descendants of Robert's great-aunt Anne Winthrop Sears and great-uncle Thomas Lindall Winthrop were prominent in nineteenth-century Massachusetts, and indeed the Sears line would provide a spouse for Robert's son; a descendant of the T. L. Winthrop branch married Robert's grandson.

I was struck, in preparing to write this Introduction, by the lives of the distaff Winthrops, the wives and sisters and daughters of the family. It is they, as much as the Winthrop men, who have done much to establish the family's distinction. If it was Adam[B] Winthrop who made the initial family fortune as a London clothier, it was his wife Agnes Sharpe whom their son described as "a woman adorned with splendid gifts." The spirited "Besse" Fones, Adam and Agnes' great-granddaughter, married her first cousin Henry[2] Winthrop; she would become Anya Seton's "Winthrop Woman," a headache to her relations in the hidebound New England wilderness but a romantic figure to our later generation.

Elizabeth Reade, second wife of John[2] Winthrop, was the step-daughter of the regicide Hugh Peter, making for a startling connection between Boston and London at a time when choosing the wrong side could end in execution. In the nineteenth and early twentieth centuries, Kate Wilson Taylor, Robert[8] Winthrop's wife, multiplied her inheritance several-fold while appearing to do nothing of the kind: in the words of her granddaughter, Dorothy Winthrop Bradford, "When she was about 35 years old, she retired, put on a little lace cap and sat by the fire. . . . They had lovely little coke fires in those days, and she'd sit by the fireplace, next to the coke fire, lace cap on her head—and invest."[1]

Kate's daughter-in-law, Melza Riggs Wood, was beloved within the family—and honored for her success as wife of Puerto Rico's governor. Melza's sisters-in-law included Katharine Winthrop Kean, wife of Senator Hamilton Fish Kean of New Jersey, and Albertina Winthrop van Roijen, wife of the Dutch Minister to the United States. Their nieces, stalwarts within the family, included Theodora Ayer Winthrop and Margaret Stone Winthrop (wives of Robert[10]), Dorothy Winthrop Bradford, Angela Elizabeth[10] Forbes (the wife of Frederic[10] Winthrop, she died as recently as 2011 at the age of 99), Eleanor Beane Winthrop (second wife of Nathaniel Thayer[10] Winthrop), and Katharine Winthrop McKean.

The posterity of Robert and Kate Winthrop includes their son Beekman[9] Winthrop ("Governor of Porto Rico" and then a cabinet undersecretary in the Roosevelt and Taft administrations); their grandsons Robert Winthrop[10] Kean (a Congressman from New Jersey 1938–58) and Jan Herman[10] van Roijen (Dutch Ambassador to the United States 1950–64); granddaughter Kay[10] Winthrop (later McKean), U.S. woman's indoor singles tennis champion in 1944; Thomas Howard[11] Kean, Governor of New Jersey 1982–90; David[11] McKean, U.S. Ambassador to Luxembourg 2016–17; actors David Anthony[12] Lansbury and Ally Sheedy; Thomas Howard[12] Kean, Jr., a New Jersey state senator since 2003; Robert Farrell[12] Bonnie, a U.S. Undersecretary for Agriculture 2013–17; novelist Elizabeth Hartley[12] Winthrop; Matthew Winthrop[12] Barzun, U.S. Ambassador to Sweden 2009–11 and to Great Britain 2013–17; and Emmy-winning producer Lucy[12] Barzun.

Added to the trio of Winthrop governors—John[1] Winthrop, John[2] Winthrop, and "Fitz John"[3] Winthrop—and to Thomas Lindall[6]

---

[1]   Dorothy B. Wexler, *Reared in a Greenhouse: The Stories—and Story—of Dorothy Winthrop Bradford* (New York and London: Garland Publishing, 1998), 68.

Winthrop (Lieutenant Governor of Massachusetts 1826–33) and his son Robert Charles[7] Winthrop (Speaker of the House of Representatives and briefly Senator from Massachusetts), this modern group of Winthrops continues the family tradition of intelligence and drive. Blessed by good fortune and, at times, riven by tragedy, this line of the Winthrop clan now sprawls across the United States and Europe. Members of the thirteenth generation in America are poised to make their mark—and no doubt it will be an interesting one.

Scott C. Steward
May 2017

ACKNOWLEDGMENTS

ALMOST two generations have passed since 1948 and the publication of Lawrence Shaw Mayo's magisterial *The Winthrop Family in America*. Members of a new generation of the Winthrop family have been born and grown up in the years since, so this 2017 genealogy of the family of Robert[8] Winthrop will cover much that is new since the earlier book appeared. Its focus is not as limited as the title might suggest, since Robert's Winthrop line is covered back to 1498, and three lines descending from John Still[5] Winthrop are treated in some detail before, with the generation of Robert[8] Winthrop's children, all of his progeny is treated in full.

Three members of the Winthrop family have proven invaluable in their support of this project. The authors are grateful to John[11] Winthrop and his sister Serita[11] Winthrop, and to their cousin Jonathan[11] Winthrop, for reviewing the manuscript before publication. In addition, they supported the production of the book through the New England Historic Genealogical Society's Family History Fund, as did their kinsmen Matthew Winthrop[12] Barzun, Theodora[11] Winthrop Hooton, Dorothy[11] Bradford Wexler, Frederic[11] Winthrop, Grant Forbes[11] Winthrop, Katharine[11] Winthrop, Stephen Van Rensselaer[11] Winthrop, and Robert[11] Winthrop, 2nd.

Claire Vail of the Society's web team photographed a number of family portraits in Boston and at "Groton House" in Ipswich, as well as the cover portrait (of Robert[8] Winthrop) and Daniel Huntington's portrait of Robert Dudley[9] Winthrop; we thank her—and Jonathan and Grant Winthrop—for help in corralling this group of images, scattered from Massachusetts to South Carolina. We also owe an enormous debt to Dotty Wexler, whose *Reared in a Greenhouse: The Stories—and Story—of Dorothy Winthrop Bradford* was a treasure trove of information and images about the Winthrop family, and who generously shared many of her photographs with us to illustrate this book.

Many other members of the family filled out paper or online questionnaires for the book, and their contributions are noted on the page(s) where their work is quoted; our thanks to you all.

At the New England Historic Genealogical Society, thanks are due to D. Brenton Simons, the Society's president and C.E.O.; to Ted MacMahon, vice president and Director of Development and Member Services; and to Senior Philanthropy Officer Steven L. Solomon for their tireless support of the Winthrop project. Publishing Director Sharon Inglis, Assistant Publishing Director Cécile Engeln, and Publications Design Manager Ellen Maxwell each provided expert assistance throughout the development and production phases of the book, carefully editing (Sharon), collecting permissions and overseeing the creation of the index (Cécile), and amassing the images—and securing the credits—to be found in the photo section (Ellen).

A list of text credits and photography and art credits appear elsewhere in the book, but we are also grateful to Martha Bustin for copy editing the book; to Anne Lenihan Rolland for composing the book's interior; to Steve Csipke for providing the index; to Ellen Maxwell for designing the dust jacket, and to Claire Vail for providing the cover image; and to former Publishing Director Penny Stratton for her support during the first three years of the project.

Scott C. Steward
Chip Rowe
May 2017

LIST OF CHARTS

Part I

The Winthrop Family in England

Robert[8] Winthrop's Descent from Adam[C] Winthrop

Adam Winthrop = Joan Burton

Adam Winthrop = (2) Agnes Sharpe

Adam Winthrop = (2) Anne Browne

John Winthrop = (1) Mary Forth

John Winthrop = (2) Elizabeth Reade

Waitstill Winthrop = (1) Mary Browne

John Winthrop = Anne Dudley

John Still Winthrop = (1) Jane Borland

Francis Bayard Winthrop = (2) Phebe Taylor

Thomas Charles Winthrop = Georgiana Maria Kane

Robert Winthrop = Katharine Wilson Taylor

THREE GENERATIONS

"The name Winthrop . . . existed in Nottinghamshire, England, as long ago as the year 1086." A settlement known as Wimunthorp and belonging to the Bishop of Lincoln, "in the course of time [it] became the present parish of Winthorpe."[1]

> Toward the end of the thirteenth century men bearing the name of Winthrop or its equivalent are mentioned in the records of Yorkshire. Presumably they or their ancestors came from the villages of Winthrop [in Lincolnshire and Nottinghamshire]. There was, for instance, a Richard de Wymthorpe, who served on a board of inquiry (inquisition) at Pokelington in 1279; and there was a Thomas de Wimpethorpe, of Baynton, who performed a similar governmental duty "at the Cross near Beverle," in the spring of 1296. In other entries Thomas's name is spelled Wymerthorpe, Wymundthorpe, and, in 1301, Wynthorpe. More or less contemporary with them and likewise living in Yorkshire were an Adam de Wyrunthorpe and a Robert de Wyrinthorp.[2]

---

[1]   Lawrence Shaw Mayo, *The Winthrop Family in America* (Boston: The Massachusetts Historical Society, 1948), 3.

[2]   Mayo, *The Winthrop Family in America*, 3, citing *The Yorkshire Archaeological and Topographical Association Record Series*, 12 [1892]: 194, 21 [1897]: 35, 165, 23 [1898]: 86, 134, 171, 29 [1901]: 213, 194.

The earliest recorded forebear of the Winthrop family in America was

1. **ADAM**^C **WINTHROP** of Lavenham, Suffolk,[3] who married **JOAN BURTON** by 1498.[4] Both were perhaps dead by 1515,[5] although by one account, Joan's second husband was John Ponder, a clothworker of Lavenham, and she was the Johane mentioned in his will of 5 June 1520, in which he asked that she "see my [minor] children honestly kept."[6]

---

[3] Joseph James Muskett, ed. (with Robert C. Winthrop, Jr.), *Evidences of the Winthrops of Groton, co. Suffolk, England, and of families in and near that county, with whom they intermarried* (Boston: privately printed, 1894–96), 25, Vol. 1 of *Suffolk manorial families, being the county visitations and other pedigrees, with extensive additions*, 4 vols. (Boston and Exeter: 1894–1910), reported that it appeared a copyist had erroneously identified Adam^C Winthrop as being of the first of Groton, rather than his son, Adam^B Winthrop. "The third Adam W. must have known that the manor of Groton was acquired by his father, and not by his grandfather," Muskett wrote. "There is no proof that the first Adam W. was of Groton, or that he was entitled to be styled *armiger*. A pedigree dated 1742 called him 'Serjeant-at-law,' but there is no evidence of this, and it is very improbable." Mayo, *The Winthrop Family in America*, 3, noted that Lavenham, located about 55 miles northeast of London, is pronounced "Lannam."

[4] "Latin Pedigree, 1498–1623," in Muskett, *Evidences of the Winthrops of Groton*, 3. "Anno domini . . . Adamus Winthropus uxorem duxit Joane Burton filia D: Burton," followed by a record for the birth of their son Adam in 1498. (In a footnote on the same page, Muskett noted that an "unreliable" 1742 pedigree identified Joane as the widow of D: Burton and dau. and co-heir of D: Burnell.) The "Emblazoned Pedigree" of 1610 transcribed in *Evidences of the Winthrops of Groton*, 9, gives Adam Winthrop as married to Jane Burton. Of the "Latin Pedigree," believed to date to 1705, Muskett wrote that "internal evidence" showed it "to have been chiefly copied by the third Adam Winthrop (d. 1623). . . . The original record is not in existence, but the following is taken from a copy, in the handwriting of John Winthrop, F.R.S., when a young man." Francis J. Bremer, *John Winthrop: America's Forgotten Founding Father* (New York: Oxford University Press, 2003), 13, noted that while little is known of this first Winthrop and his wife, "it is believed that the couple lived in a building that still stands, on what is now called Barn Street in Lavenham. . . . Portions of the fifteenth-century home survive, most notably a carved wooden frieze, dating from the time of the Winthrops, on which are carved shields embossed with the letter W, angels, an image of Christ crucified, and a figure thought to represent St. Edward the Confessor."

[5] "Latin Pedigree," in Muskett, *Evidences of the Winthrops of Groton*, 4. The pedigree notes their deaths ("Anno domini. . . . Adamus Winthrop cum gravissimo morbo expiravit" and "Anno domini . . . Joane Winthrop uxor Adami Winthrop vitâ excessit"), but does not give dates. The next entry (for Adam Winthrop's apprenticeship) is dated 1515.

[6] Will of John Pondyr, proved 4 July 1520, transcribed in Muskett, *Evidences of the Winthrops of Groton*, 35, citing P.C.C. 30 Ayloffe. Ponder, who included a request "to be buryed in the churchyard by the Crosse next to my wif in launeh³m aforesaid," mentioned his children William, Eme, Johane, Roger, John, and Symon, all under age 21. John Ponder was buried at St. Peter and Paul's Church in Lavenham; see *Findagrave.com* 146020260. Muskett asserts at 25 that Joane Winthrop was the

"As a clothier, Adam would have been an organizer and financier, providing capital for the purchase of wool, generally from Lincolnshire, Northamptonshire or elsewhere, because Suffolk wool was not rated highly," writes historian Francis J. Bremer, who has written extensively on the Winthrops. "He would have recruited and paid dyers, weavers, fullers, and other craftsmen who produced the broad cloths for which the region was noted, and then sold them, often at London's Blackwell Hall, to members of the city trade guilds who would export them abroad."[7]

Child of Adam[C] and Joan (Burton) Winthrop:[8]

2   i.   ADAM[B] WINTHROP, b. at Lavenham 9 Oct. 1498; m. (1) 16 Nov. 1527, ALICE HUNNE; m. (2) 20 July 1534, AGNES SHARPE.

Joane in this will, apparently based on the 1557 will of Simon Ponder of London in which he mentions his "brother Wyntroppe and his wief," possibly his stepbrother Adam[B] Winthrop (Muskett, *Evidences of the Winthrops of Groton*, 36, citing P.C.C. 37 Noodes).

[7] Bremer, *John Winthrop: America's Forgotten Founding Father*, 13.

[8] "Latin Pedigree" in Muskett, *Evidences of the Winthrops of Groton*, 3.

The Kinship Between Robert[8] Winthrop
and Sarah, Duchess of York

Adam Winthrop = (2) Agnes Sharpe

Alice Winthrop
= Sir Thomas Mildmay

William Mildmay
= Margaret Hervey

Carew Hervey Mildmay
= Dorothy Gerard

Francis Hervey Mildmay
= (2) Mathew Honywood

Carew Hervey Mildmay
= Anne Barrett

Humphrey Hervey Mildmay
= Letitia Mildmay

Carew Mildmay
= Mary Pescod

Jane Mildmay
= Sir Henry Paulet St. John-Mildmay, 3rd Bt.

Judith Anne St. John-Mildmay
= William Pleydell-Bouverie, 3rd Earl of Radnor

Hon. Edward Pleydell-Bouverie
= Elizabeth Anne Balfour

Walter Pleydell-Bouverie
= Mary Bridgeman Simpson

Sybil Pleydell-Bouverie
= Mervyn Richard Wingfield, 8th Viscount Powerscourt

Hon. Doreen Julia Wingfield
= FitzHerbert Wright

Susan Mary Wright
= (1) Ronald Ivor Ferguson

Sarah Margaret Ferguson
= HRH The Prince Andrew, Duke of York

Adam Winthrop
= (2) Anne Browne

John Winthrop
= (1) Mary Forth

John Winthrop
= (2) Elizabeth Reade

Waitstill Winthrop
= (1) Mary Browne

John Winthrop
= Anne Dudley

John Still Winthrop
= (1) Jane Borland

Francis Bayard Winthrop
= (2) Phebe Taylor

Thomas Charles Winthrop
= Georgiana Maria Kane

Robert Winthrop
= Katharine Wilson Taylor

2. **ADAM**[B] **WINTHROP** (*Adam*[C]) was born at Lavenham, Suffolk 9 October 1498,[9] died at Groton, Suffolk 9,[10] and was buried there 12 November 1562.[11] He married, first, at London, Middlesex 16 November 1527, **ALICE HUNNE**, "honestis parentibus natam" [born of honest parents],[12] who died at London 25 January 1533[/34],[13] perhaps the daughter of Richard Hunne[14] and Alice (_____) Hunne.[15] Adam Winthrop married

---

9   "Latin Pedigree" in Muskett, *Evidences of the Winthrops of Groton*, 3. "Anno domini 1498 et anno Regni regis Henriei Septimi decimo quarto, die nono Octob[r] in oppido Lannamiae in comitatu Suffolciae, Adamus filius suus primogenitus natus fuit, viz., uno anno post preliii apud Blackheath field."

10   "Latin Pedigree" in Muskett, *Evidences of the Winthrops of Groton*, 5. "Anno domini 1562 nono die novembri et anno regni Elizabethae Reginae quarto, dictus Adamus Winthrop cum gravissimo morbo laborasset et anno aetatis suae sexagesimo quarto e vita excessit, et in paroehiae Ecclesia de Groton consepultus est. Vir pius et verae religionis amans." See also *Pond's Almanack for 1603*, transcribed in *Winthrop Papers*, 6 vols. (Boston: Massachusetts Historical Society, 1929–92), 1: 154, in which his son Adam entered, "November 9. Adam Winthrop my father died. 1562. Eliz. 4. 41 yeres synce." And later, in *Hopton's Almanack for 1614*: "9 [Nov.] my owne father died. 1562. 52 y[eres] since" (*Winthrop Papers*, 1: 178). (Despite the 68 boxes and 126 volumes of Winthrop family papers at the Massachusetts Historical Society, the historian Missy Wolfe found a note among them that reads, "The eating teeth of time devour all things. / A hogshead of ancient papers of value to our family, lost at Ipswich in New England. / A barrelful of papers &c. burnt in a warehouse in Boston.")

11   Transcription from Groton parish register by Richard Almack in James Savage, "Gleanings for New England History," *Collections of the Massachusetts Historical Society*, 3rd series, 8 [1843]: 297. "1562. Adam Winthrop the elder Esq. was buryed the 12th day of November."

12   "Latin Pedigree" in Muskett, *Evidences of the Winthrops of Groton*, 4. "Anno domini 1527 decimo sexto die novembris et amio regni regis Henrici octavi decimo nono, uxorem primam duxit Aliciam Henny honestis parentibus natam."

13   "Latin Pedigree" in Muskett, *Evidences of the Winthrops of Groton*, 4. "Eodem anno 1533 vicessimo quinto die januarij et anno regni regis Henrici octavi vicessimo quinto, Alicia uxor ejus, exquâ illi nati sunt filii quatuor et una filia, Londini obijt. Vixit cum iliâ sex annos duos menses et quinq: dies."

14   Bremer, *John Winthrop: America's Forgotten Founding Father*, 389. Hunne was a Protestant tailor in Whitechapel, Middlesex, who refused to pay the standard mortuary fee in 1511 to the Catholic priest following the death of his five-week-old son. The priest banished Hunne, who sued for slander. Accused of heresy, Hunne was imprisoned on 2 December 1514; two days later, he was found hanged in his cell. See W.R. Cooper, "Richard Hunne," *Reformation* 1 [1996]: 221–51, online at *tyndale.org/reformj01/cooper.html*. Bremer considers evidence that Alice (Hunne) Winthrop was a daughter of Richard Hunne to be "circumstantial but persuasive." He notes that the primary account of Hunne's martyrdom, published in 1563 by John Foxe in *Actes and Monuments of these Latter and Perillous Days, Touching Matters of the Church*, was based in large part on hearsay, and that William Winthrop, son of Adam[B] and Alice (Hunne) Winthrop, was known to have provided information to Foxe on various topics.

15   In his 1562 will (transcribed in Muskett, *Evidences of the Winthrops of Groton*, 11–14), Adam[B] Winthrop mentioned Richard Burde of Ipswich and "my syster his wife." Other records suggest she was not Adam's sister but a stepsister of his first wife. See Muskett's

second, at London 20 July 1534, **AGNES SHARPE**, who was born ca. 1516,[16] daughter of Robert and Elizabeth (_____) Sharpe of Islington, Middlesex, and granddaughter of William Sharpe of that place.[17] She married, second, 7 June 1563, William Mildmay.[18] Agnes Mildmay, remembered by her son Adam Winthrop as "a woman adorned with splendid gifts," died at Springfield, Essex 13 May 1565[19]; William Mildmay died in February 1570.[20]

Adam was apprenticed in 1515, when he was about 17, to Edward Altham,[21] a member of the Fullers Company of London. Bremer writes:[22]

---

analysis in *Evidences of the Winthrops of Groton*, 165–66, in which he cites a 1571 chancery proceeding (*Hunne c. Burd*) and the wills of John Cely (1557) and his widow Alice (_____) (Hunne) Cely (1558). See also Joseph James Muskett, ed., "Goodwin of Bull's Hall," *Suffolk Manorial Families: Being the County Visitations and Other Pedigrees*, 2 vols. (Exeter: William Pollard & Co., 1900–8), 1: 223. John and Alice Cely's son, William, may be the William Cely who married Adam[B] Winthrop's daughter Mary.

[16] "Sharpe of Islington, Co. Middlesex" in Muskett, *Evidences of the Winthrops of Groton*, 41, says she was 18 at time of marriage.

[17] "Latin Pedigree" in Muskett, *Evidences of the Winthrops of Groton*, 4. "Anno domini 1534 vicesimo die julij anno regni regis Henrici octavi vicessimo sexto Adamus Winthrop anno aetatis suae tricessimo sexto, Agnetem Sharpe filia D: Roberti Sharpe de Islingtona in comitatu Middlesexiae generosi, puellam annum decimum octavum agentem, in uxorem secundam duxit." See also the Sharpe pedigree in *Evidences of the Winthrops of Groton*, 41.

[18] Groton parish register, *Collections of the Massachusetts Historical Society*, 3rd series, 8 [1843]: 297. "1563. Willm Mildmaye Esq. and Annis Winthropp widow was married the 7th daie of June—Thomas his son, and Alice her daughter the 12th of same Month." See also note 19.

[19] "Latin Pedigree" in Muskett, *Evidences of the Winthrops of Groton*, 5. "Anno domini 1565 decimo tértio die Maij, anno regni Reginae Elizabethae septimo et anno aetatis suae quadragesimo octavo, Agnes uxor secuudus Adami Winthrop in Springfield in comitatu Essexiae obijt et in chancell: de ecclesia Springfield consepulta est. Post mortem Adami Winthrop nupta fuisset Gulielmo Mildmay de Springfield in comitatu Essexiae geueroso. Foemina preclaris condecorata donis." See also *Pond's Almanack for 1603*, transcribed in *Winthrop Papers*, 1: 153, in which her son Adam entered, "13 [May]. My owne mother died. 1565. Eliz. 7." Later, an entry by Adam in *Hopton's Almanack for 1614*, transcribed at 1: 176, reads, "Foemina praeclaris condecorat donis. My owne mother died 1565. 49 y[eres] since."

[20] Will of William Mildmay of Springfield, 13 February 1570, transcribed in Muskett, *Evidences of the Winthrops of Groton*, 42, citing P.C.C. 10 Holney. It was proved 24 February 1570.

[21] "Latin Pedigree" in Muskett, *Evidences of the Winthrops of Groton*, 4. "Anno quinto decimo supra millessimum quingentessimum et anno regni Regis Henrici octavi nono, Adamus Winthrop Londinum venit et se apprenticum cum Edwardo Altam per decimum obligavit."

[22] Bremer, *John Winthrop: America's Forgotten Founding Father*, 14, citing Barbara Hanawalt, *Growing Up in Medieval London* (New York: Oxford University Press, 1993), 139–41. Bremer appears to accept Muskett's conclusion that Joan (Burton) Winthrop married (2) John Ponder.

John Ponder would have paid a fee for apprenticing his stepson, and though the records do not survive, that fee would have been registered by the company. Under Altham young Adam would learn the skills of cleansing and thickening cloth to prepare it for finishing. On arriving in London in 1515 Adam would have been examined by the wardens of the guild, who dressed in the livery of the Fuller, would then have administered an oath to the young man. Within a year Altham was also required to bring the apprentice before the municipal officials, perhaps on one of the set guild days, to have his contract officially enrolled. Each of these ceremonies had its own rituals and was designed to underline the importance of the occasion as the young man was launched on the path to company membership and city citizenship.

Adam would have lived with Altham's other apprentices and eaten meals with the family; a typical contract in London would have made him agree not to "commit fornication nor contract matrimony," play "cards, dice, tables or any other unlawful games," or "haunt taverns nor playhouses."[23] After an eleven-year indenture, Adam accompanied Altham in September 1526 to the Fullers Company Hall on Fenchurch Street, where he swore an oath and was admitted as a member. A few days later he went to the Guild Hall, where he was enrolled as a citizen of London.[24] A year after he married in 1527, the Fullers merged with the Shearsmen to form the Clothworkers Company.[25] Adam rose rapidly from journeyman to householder before 1531, and to be a member of the livery in 1536, a status which only one in four members achieved.

He was caught bending the rules on occasion, Bremer notes. In 1530, he was fined 15 shillings for resisting a search of his goods by company inspectors and for two cloths that failed to meet quality

[23] Steven Rappaport, *World within Worlds: The Structure of Life in Sixteenth-Century London* (Cambridge: Cambridge University Press, 1988), 234.

[24] "Latin Pedigree" in Muskett, *Evidences of the Winthrops of Groton,* 4. "Anno domini 1526 Adamus Winthrop admissus fuit in libertatem civitatis London: et juratus tempore Johannis Allein majoris et Johannis Husae camerarii ejusdem civitatis, viz., nono Septembr anno regni Regis Henrici octavi decimo octavo et anno aetatis suae vicessimo octavo."

[25] William Herbert, *History of the Twelve Great Livery Companies*, 2 vols. (London: the author, 1836), 2: 644.

standards. He also would be fined in 1537, 1542, and 1543[26] (when he was briefly imprisoned, apparently for negotiating with foreigners for the sale of cloth; he was released after paying £600[27]). It is also true that in 1531 he was given permission to take on apprentices of his own. In 1537, with Altham as the master of the company, he was chosen as a steward and in 1543 voted renter warden. In 1546, Adam became prime warden, and in 1551, he was elected master, the highest office in the company[28]; soon after, he sat for his portrait.[29]

During the 1540s, Adam Winthrop owned at least one ship, the *Mary Flower*, and three-quarters interest in another, the *John* of London, Bremer writes, which brought him to the High Court of Admiralty six times as a defendant and seven times as a plaintiff in disputes over debts and the loss of goods.[30] Nevertheless, by 1541 "Adam Wynthrope" was the third wealthiest individual in his parish of St. Peter, Cornhill.[31] In 1544, his son William was admitted to the Clothworkers and joined his father in business.[32] That same year Adam bought Groton Manor from the government for £408. Located a few miles south of Lavenham, it had belonged to the Abbey of Bury St. Edmunds,[33] one of many

---

26 Bremer, *John Winthrop: America's Forgotten Founding Father*, 18, citing Clothworkers Company, Court Orders, 1536–1558, CM I and CM II, manuscripts in the Archives of the Clothworkers Company.

27 "Latin Pedigree" in Muskett, *Evidences of the Winthrops of Groton*, 5. "Hoc anno 1543 Adamus Winthrop incarceratus est in le fleete, eo quod cum alienigenis negotiatus fuerit contra Regis edictum, ibiq: detentus donee 600ᵇ ad fiscam regiam solutus sit." Bremer, *John Winthrop: America's Forgotten Founding Father*, 18, noted that records in John Roche Dasent, ed., *Acts of the Privy Council of England*, 43 vols. (London, 1890), 1: 92, 102 (see *british-history.ac.uk/acts-privy-council/vol1/pp76-100*) and James Gairdner and R.H. Brodie, eds., "Henry VIII: February 1543, 26–28," *Letters and Papers, Foreign and Domestic, Henry VIII*, Vol. 18, Part 1 (London, 1901), item 212 (see *british-history.ac.uk/letters-papers-hen8/vol18/no1/pp114-134*), appear to confirm the imprisonment, although the first record refers to "_____ Wyntrop" and the latter to Thomas Wynthroppe.

28 Bremer, *John Winthrop: America's Forgotten Founding Father*, 18, citing Clothworkers Company Court Orders and Renter Warden Accounts in the Archives of the Clothworkers Company.

29 Bremer, *John Winthrop: America's Forgotten Founding Father*, 21.

30 Bremer, *John Winthrop: America's Forgotten Founding Father*, 19, citing public and Admiralty records.

31 "1541 London Subsidy Roll: Bishopsgate Ward," in R.G. Lang, ed., *Two Tudor Subsidy Rolls for the City of London 1541 and 1582*, vol. 29 (London Record Society Publications, 1993), 22, at *british-history.ac.uk/london-record-soc/vol29/pp21-25*. He paid £5 tax on £200 in property.

32 Bremer, *John Winthrop: America's Forgotten Founding Father*, 21.

33 For the 1544 grant of Groton Manor to Adam Wynthroppe, in Latin, see Muskett, *Evidences of the Winthrops of Groton*, 14–16, citing Patent Roll 35 Hen. VIII, part 14, Memb. 5 (31). See also *The Statutes of the Realm*, 3: 575–78, 13: 733–39.

monasteries seized by Henry VIII between 1536 and 1541 after he broke with Rome.[34] In 1548, King Edward VI granted Adam a coat of arms and the rank of gentleman, and thereafter he became "Lord of the Manor, and Patron of the Church" in Groton.[35] When Mary Tudor became queen in 1553 following the death of Edward VI, she "took steps to restore Catholicism" as the official state religion, and many reformers were jailed or executed. "The sympathies of men such as the Winthrops were closely watched," Francis Bremer writes. At the family church in London, the priest was replaced by John Hodgkins, who was clearly eager to root out Protestantism.

"As a leader of one of the great city companies, Adam had a role to play in civic ceremonies and was looked to to provide leadership," Bremer notes. "Should Hodgkins have reported him as a non-participant in the restored Catholic worship, he would likely have ended in prison with other godly merchants. So Adam decided at this time to leave London and retire to his country manor in Groton . . . where the incumbent in the parish rectory was his own appointee."[36] He might have gone sooner, but he had to wait for a twenty-year lease the monks had issued in 1533 to expire.[37] (During those ten years, he expanded the rectory on the property into a dwelling he referred to as the "mansion house."[38]) His eldest son, William, remained in the city to manage the family business.[39]

In his will, dated 20 September 1562 and probated 10 January 1562/63, Adam Wyntrope left Groton Manor and other rental property to Agnes and his son John. He also mentioned son Adam and daughters Alice, Bridget, Mary, and Susan. He left son William his clothing and his

---

[34] Bremer, *John Winthrop: America's Forgotten Founding Father*, 43, notes that Adam would have gone to Thomas Mildmay, auditor of the Court of Augmentations, to purchase the abbey, "and this perhaps initiated family contacts that later led to [his brother] William's rapid courtship of Adam's widow": they were married seven months after Adam's death.

[35] Mayo, *The Winthrop Family in America*, 4.

[36] Bremer, *John Winthrop: America's Forgotten Founding Father*, 31.

[37] A reference to the lease appears in William Dugdale, *Monasticon Anglicanum: A New Edition*, 6 vols. (London: James Bohn, 1846), 3: 126 (item 95). "De manerio de Grotone, 8 Jan. 24 Hen. VIII, fol. 69b." See also Lilian J. Redstone, "'First Ministers' Account' of the Possessions of the Abbey of St. Edmund," *Proceedings of the Suffolk Institute of Archaeology and Natural History* 13 [1909]: 333, which notes the lease was for twenty years.

[38] Bremer, *John Winthrop: America's Forgotten Founding Father*, 40, 43.

[39] Bremer, *John Winthrop: America's Forgotten Founding Father*, 31. When Queen Mary died in 1558, Queen Elizabeth took the throne and began a restoration of Prostestanism.

London home in St. Michael's, Cornhill, although Agnes was to have free rein there with her friends and servants, as well as full use of the pewter, brass, bedding, and other "necessaries and implements." Adam named Richarde Burde of Ipswiche as executor and bequeathed to "my syster, his wief, xx[s] [20 shillings] to make her a Ringe. And to my sister Whiting other xx[s]."[40]

Children of Adam[B] and Alice (Hunne) Winthrop:

    i.   THOMAS WINTHROP, b. 8 Nov. 1528 and d. in April 1529.[41]

    ii. WILLIAM WINTHROP, clothworker of London, b. 12 Nov. 1529[42] and d. at London 1 March 1581[/82].[43] He m. ELIZABETH NORWOOD, who d. in Kent 2 June 1578, and had issue,[44] including Adam Winthrop of London (and later Bandon, Cork), who married Joan Hilles.[45] William was remembered by his half-brother Adam as "a good man, without harm, and a lover of piety."[46]

    iii. BRIDGET WINTHROP, b. 9 Jan. 1530[/31][47] and d. in Jan. 1536[/37].[48]

---

[40] *Evidences of the Winthrops of Groton,* 11–14, citing P.C.C. 2, Cayre. These were very likely sisters of his wife or wives. See note 14.

[41] "Latin Pedigree" in Muskett, *Evidences of the Winthrops of Groton,* 4. "Anno domini 1528 octavo die novembris Thomas suus filius primogenitus natus fuit, qui obiit mense Aprilis anni proxime sequentis."

[42] "Latin Pedigree" in Muskett, *Evidences of the Winthrops of Groton,* 4. "Anno domini 1529 decimo secundo die novembris Wilhelmus filius ejus secundus natus fuit."

[43] "Latin Pedigree" in Muskett, *Evidences of the Winthrops of Groton,* 6. "Anno domini 1581 primo die Martij Wilhelmus Winthrop filius Adanii Winthrop et Aliciae uxor ejus primus, Loudini obiit anno regni Reginae Elizabethae vicesimo quarto. Vir sine fraude bonus et pietatis amans." See also *Pond's Almanack for 1603,* transcribed in *Winthrop Papers,* 1: 151, in which Adam[A] Winthrop entered, "March 1 William Wynthrop my brother died 1581. Eliz. 23, 22 y[eres] since." And later, an entry by Adam in *Hopton's Almanack for 1614,* transcribed at 1: 175, reads, "1 [Mar.] This day my brother Wm. W. died. 1581. 32 y[eres] since."

[44] "Latin Pedigree" in Muskett, *Evidences of the Winthrops of Groton,* 5. "Anno domini 1578 secundo die junij Elizabetha uxor Wilhelmus Winthrop in Kent obijt, ex qua illi nati sunt 3 filii et 2 filiae, nomina Joshua, Adam, William, Elizabeth and Sarah." Muskett noted in a footnote that "unless some portion of the record is missing, the writer [Adam[B] Winthrop] omitted to enter the marriage of his brother William, whose wife is stated to have been the dau. of ____ Norwoode of Kent."

[45] Her mother, Joan (Browne) Hilles, was a sister of Anne Browne, who married Adam[A] Winthrop.

[46] "Latin Pedigree" in Muskett, *Evidences of the Winthrops of Groton,* 6. "Vir sine fraude bonus et pietatis amans."

[47] "Latin Pedigree" in Muskett, *Evidences of the Winthrops of Groton,* 4. "Anno domini 1530 Brigitta filia sua primogenita vero die januarii nata fuit."

[48] "Latin Pedigree" in Muskett, *Evidences of the Winthrops of Groton,* 4. "Anno domini 1536 mense vero januarij anno regni regis Henrici octavi vicessimo octavo Brigitta filia sua postquam annum sextum aetatis suae appulisset, obijt."

iv. CHRISTOPHER WINTHROP, b. at London 4 Jan. 1531[/32] and d. at Stoke, Essex ca. Sept. 1532.[49]

v. THOMAS WINTHROP, b. at London 20 June 1533[50] and d. at Islington in 1537.[51]

Children of Adam[B] and Agnes (Sharpe) Winthrop:

vi. ALICE WINTHROP, b. 15, bp. at St. Peter's Church, Cornhill 16 Nov. 1539,[52] and d. at Springfield, Essex 8 Nov. 1607, about a week after a fall at home. She was bur. at Springfield 12 Nov. 1607.[53] She m. at Groton 12 June 1563,[54] her stepbrother THOMAS MILDMAY of Barnes in Springfield parish, who was born in 1539, son of William and Elizabeth (Paschall) Mildmay, and had issue.[55] Thomas served as Sheriff of Essex in 1597[56] and was knighted in the Royal

---

49 "Latin Pedigree" in Muskett, *Evidences of the Winthrops of Groton,* 4. "Anno domini 1531 quarto die januarii Christoferus filius ejus tertius Londini natus fuit, et obiit in parochia de Stocke in comitatu Essexiae cum nonum mensem aetatis suae appuliset, anno regni regis Henrici octavi vicessimo tertio."

50 "Latin Pedigree" in Muskett, *Evidences of the Winthrops of Groton,* 4. "Anno domini 1533 vicesimo die junij anno regni regis Henrici octavi vicessimo quinto et pentecostes feria secunda, Thomas secundus ejus nominis et quartus filius suus natus fuit Londini, quo vero die D. Anna Bollena Regina Angliae coronata est."

51 "Latin Pedigree" in Muskett, *Evidences of the Winthrops of Groton,* 4. "Anno domini 1537 et anno regni regis Henrici octavi vicessimo nono Thomas ejus 4: filius postquam annum quartum aetatis suae complevisset, Islingtonae obijt."

52 "Latin Pedigree" in Muskett, *Evidences of the Winthrops of Groton,* 4. "Anno domini 1539 decimo quinto die Novembris et anno regni regis Henrici octavi tricessimo primo, Alicia filia sua primogenita ex Agnete uxore sua cum jam illi annos quinos quinq: menses et octo dies nupta fuisset, nata est."

53 "Latin Pedigree" in Muskett, *Evidences of the Winthrops of Groton,* 7. "Anno domini 1607 octavo die novembris Alicia filia Adami Winthrop et Agnetae uxor ejus secundus anno aetatis suae sexagesimo octavo obijt. Cujus erat vita vitae medulla meae. Nupta fuisset 1563: Thomae Mildmaye Eq: Aurat: ex quá illi nati sunt William, Francis, George, Henrie, Tomas." An entry by Adam[A] Winthrop in *Hopton's Almanack for 1614,* transcribed in *Winthrop Papers,* 1: 178, reads, "8 [Nov.] My sister Mildmay died. 1607. *Cuius erat vita vitae medulla meae.* [Her life was the marrow of my soul.]" He also wrote in his diary, "On fryday the 30th of Octobre [1607] my sister Mildemaye had a fall in her chamber where of she died the viijth of November followinge. The 2 of Novem[b]er I did ryde to Springfild and retourned the 7th and the 11 I did ryde thither againe to hir Buriall the which was on the xvth of November" (1: 96).

54 Groton parish register, *Collections of the Massachusetts Historical Society,* 3rd series, 8 [1843]: 297. "1563. Willm Mildmaye Esq. and Annis Winthropp widow was married the 7th daie of June—Thomas his son, and Alice her daughter the 12th of same Month."

55 "Latin Pedigree" in Muskett, *Evidences of the Winthrops of Groton,* 47. See also note 53.

56 Charles Mosley, ed., *Burke's Peerage, Baronetage & Knightage, 107th ed.,* 3 vols. (Wilmington, Del.: Burke's Peerage Ltd., 2003), 3: 3491.

Garden at Whitehall on 23 July 1603 with some 325 other country
gentlemen prior to the coronation of King James VI.[57] Sir Thomas
d. 15 Dec. 1612[58]; his will, dated 14 Nov. 1612, was proved 30 Jan.
1612/13.[59]

vii.   BRIDGET WINTHROP, b. 3 May 1543[60] and d. at Therfield, Hertfordshire
4 Nov. 1614.[61] She m. 26 April 1567, ROGER ALABASTER of Hadleigh,
Suffolk, and had issue (including the dramatist William Alabaster).[62]

In his journal of the time, her brother Adam[A] Winthrop noted
that on 16 June 1595 "my brother Winthrop departed from my
house towards Ireland, and my brother [Roger] Alibaster went
with him."[63] About three weeks later, on 7 July, Adam wrote that
"my brother Roger Alibaster, and my sister his wife with their iij
sons, George, John and Thomas, and Sarah, their daughyter, tooke
their journey from Hadleigh to goe into Irelande. That same day

---

57   William A. Shaw, *The Knights of England: A Complete Record from the Earliest Time to
the Present Day of the Knights in all the Orders of Chivalry*, 2 vols. (London: Sherratt
and Hughes, 1906), 2: 115, which gives the list of men who owned more than
£40 of property who accepted an invitation to become Knights Bachelor—that
is, they were not given membership in one of the Orders of Chivalry but received
the equivalent of the knighthoods today bestowed on British entertainers, e.g., Sir
Paul McCarthy. The list includes both "Thomas Mildmay of Essex" and his cousin,
"Thomas Mildmay of Co. Hereford (Moulsham, Essex)." Adam[A] Winthrop made
note of the honor in his diary: "The 23th daye of July my brother Mildmay was
made Knight at Whighthall" (*Winthrop Papers*, 1: 82). Others knighted that day included John Tyndal, father of Margaret (Tyndal) Winthrop, and Francis Bacon.

58   Mosley, *Burke's Peerage, Baronetage & Knightage*, 3: 3491.

59   Will of Sir Thomas Mildmaye of Barnes, Springfield, transcribed in Muskett,
Evidences of the Winthrops of Groton, 44, citing P.C.C. 1 Capell.

60   "Latin Pedigree" in Muskett, *Evidences of the Winthrops of Groton,* 4. "Anno domini
1543 Brigitta filia sua altera ex Agnete uxore genita, tertio die Maij ascentionis domini festo celebrato anno regni regis Henrici octavi tricessimo quinto, nata fuit." An
entry by Adam[A] Winthrop in *Hopton's Almanack for 1614*, transcribed in *Winthrop
Papers* 1: 176, reads, "4 [May] This day anno 1543, being holy Thursday, my sister
Briget was borne. 71 y[eres] since. The 4. of No[vember] 1614 obijt [died]." The 3
May 1543 was a Thursday under the Julian calendar.

61   "Latin Pedigree" in Muskett, *Evidences of the Winthrops of Groton,* 7. "Anno domini
1614 quarto die novembris Brigitta filia Adami Winthrop et Agnetae uxor ejus
secundus in Tharfield in Hertfordshire obijt anno aetatis suae septuagesimo secundo. Nupta fuisset D: Rogerio Alibaster ex qua illi nati sunt George, John, Tomas,
Sara, Wilham." See also previous note. An entry by Adam[A] Winthrop in *Hopton's
Almanack for 1614*, transcribed in *Winthrop Papers* 1: 177, reads, "The same day and
yere [4 Nov. and year when a cousin's wife died, not given] my sister Alibaster died
at Tharfield in Herfordshire."

62   "Alabaster of Hadleigh" in Muskett, *Evidences of the Winthrops of Groton,* 55.

63   *Winthrop Papers,* 1: 68. At 139 he wrote that John left for Ireland 2 April 1595 and
that "my b[rother] Alibaster and my sister took ther farewell of me the iiijth of July
1595 when they went to Ireland."

it Thundred, hailed and Rayned very sore. Willm Alibaster their eldest soonne departed from my house towards Cambrige the ixth of July, malcontent."[64] On 13 Dec., "I received a letter from my brother Alibaster written from Tenby in Wales concernynge his ill success in his Irisshe journy."[65]

viii. MARY WINTHROP, b. 1 March 1544[/45][66] and living 24 May 1605.[67] She m. (1) before 13 Feb. 1570, WILLIAM CELY/SELYE of London[68]; m. (2) ABRAHAM VESEY, son of Laurence and Alice (_____) Vesey of Hadleigh,[69] and had issue by both husbands.

ix. JOHN WINTHROP, twin, b. 20 Jan. 1546[70] and d. in Ireland 26 July 1613.[71] He m. (1) 6 Feb. 1566/67,[72] ELIZABETH RISBY, dau. of Robert and Margery (Rosse) Risby of Thorpe Morieux, Suffolk,[73] from whom he apparently separated after 19 June 1608.[74] She m.

---

64   *Winthrop Papers*, 1: 65.

65   *Winthrop Papers*, 1: 66.

66   "Latin Pedigree" in Muskett, *Evidences of the Winthrops of Groton*, 5. "Anno domini 1544 primo die martij et anno regni regis Henrici octavi tricessimo sexto Mariam tertiam filiam uxor illi peperit."

67   In his journal, Adam^A Winthrop noted that "the same day [the viijth of May 1605] my sisater Veysye came to me and departed on 24 of Maye" (*Winthrop Papers*, 1: 89).

68   He may have been the son of John Cely and the son or stepson of Alice (_____) (Hunne) Cely. See note 18.

69   "Vesey of Holton" in Muskett, *Evidences of the Winthrops of Groton*, 63.

70   "Latin Pedigree" in Muskett, *Evidences of the Winthrops of Groton*, 5. "Anno domini 1546, vicessimo die januarij anno regni regis Henrici octavi tricessimo octavo et anno aetatis suae quadragessimo octavo, Johannem et Adamum gemellos uno partu uxor peperit quoq: junior infra 6: menses objit." See also In *Pond's Almanack for 1603*, transcribed in *Winthrop Papers*, 1: 151, Adam^A Winthrop entered, "20 [Jan.] my brother John Winthrop was born 1546."

71   "Latin Pedigree" in Muskett, *Evidences of the Winthrops of Groton*, 7. "Anno domini 1613 vicesimo sexto julij Johannes Winthrop filius Adami Winthrop et Agnetae uxor ejus secundus in Ireland objit, anno aetatis suae sexagesimo sexto et 7: menses. Qui sibi neque mihi utilis vitâ fuit, qui mihi frater durus tempore mortis erat. Nuptus fuisset 1566: Elizabethae Rysby filia D: Roberti Rysby de Thorpe in comitatu Suffolciae." An entry by Adam^A Winthrop in *Hopton's Almanack for 1614*, transcribed in *Winthrop Papers*, 1: 176, reads, "July 26, my brother John died in Irelande 1613, of the age of 66 y[eres] and 7 months." John's will, dated 28 March 1613 and apparently probated 31 Jan. 1613/14, was extracted by Muskett in *Evidences of the Winthrops of Groton*, 18.

72   "Latin Pedigree" in Muskett, *Evidences of the Winthrops of Groton*, 7, gives "Nuptus fuisset 1566: Elizabethae Rysby filia D: Roberti Rysby de Thorpe in comitatu Suffolciae." *Winthrop Papers*, 1: 14fn, gives the specific date.

73   See also the Risby Pedigree (Harl. MS. 1774), reprinted in Muskett, *Evidences of the Winthrops of Groton*, 66.

74   Adam^A Winthrop in his diary indicated John and Elizabeth Risby were still married 19 June 1608 (*Winthrop Papers*, 1: 98). "The xixth of June my brother [John] served

(2) (license dated at London 8 July 1617) Reynold Braunch[75] and d. at Southwark, Surrey before 11 April 1637.[76] John Winthrop m. (2) (prob. bigamously) ELIZABETH POWLDEN,[77] dau. of Thomas Powlden of Rathgogan, Cork, and had issue by both wives. Elizabeth m. (2) Thomas Nott and d. before 1638.[78]

Of John Winthrop's unhappy first marriage, Francis Bremer notes that "depositions from a much later lawsuit contain John's charges that 'Elizabeth his wife had eloped from him, and lived a most lewd and wicked life to his great great grief and discontent,' while Elizabeth maintained that 'he did neglect and cast [her] off by reason that his affections were set upon other women.' "[79] Elizabeth gave birth to a son, Benjamin Winthrop, in 1582,[80] but on 14 June 1584 John agreed to pay her £24 per quarter for the remainder of her life.[81] He may have been persuaded of the benefits of Irish

---

a citation on his wife [Elizabeth] out of the Arches and the same day she came to Groton." The Court of Arches was the ecclesiastical court of appeal for Canterbury. Adam also recorded that on 8 June 1608, his brother John had "departed from Groton towardes Ireland" after a family visit.

[75] "Winthrop of Groton" in Muskett, *Evidences of the Winthrops of Groton*, 25. In a foot-note at 7, Muskett noted the license was issued by the Bishop of London's Court. The license does not appear in Joseph Foster, ed., *London Marriage Licences 1521–1869* (London: Bernard Quaritch, 1887), which was said to include extracts of the Bishop of London's Office records through 1828, although there is an entry at 173 for Reinold Branch who married the widow Prudence Kirke of Westminster on 16 February 1636/37.

[76] Brampton Gurdon to John Winthrop, Jr., 11 April 1637, *Winthrop Papers*, 3: 88. "I latly doo hear that your aunt Winthrop who liued in Suthworck is latly dede."

[77] "Latin Pedigree" in Muskett, *Evidences of the Winthrops of Groton*, 7, gives only one marriage for John Winthrop of Ireland (see note 74), but in his 1613 will he left "Elixabeth my nowe Wyfe daughter of Thomas Powlden deceased all my houses, goods and chattels whatsoever" (18). Muskett noted that the validity of the marriage was "doubtful" (25).

[78] "Winthrop of Groton" in Muskett, *Evidences of the Winthrops of Groton*, 25.

[79] Bremer, *John Winthrop: America's Forgotten Founding Father*, 44–45, citing Nott c. Winthrop Public Records Office C 33/145/526.

[80] "Parish Registers for St. Andrew Undershaft Church, London, 1558–1901," index, *familysearch.org*, referencing Family History Library film 1374,408. "Beniamyn Wintrop or Wyntrop, 23 July 1582, son of John Wintrop or Wyntrop."

[81] Bremer, *John Winthrop: America's Forgotten Founding Father*, 45, noted that "such a judicial separation 'from bed and board' granted by church courts was the only way that a couple could legally live apart in England." He added (397) that "the actual indenture does not survive, but the details are spelled out in Elizabeth's Chancery suit undertaken three years later to enforce the agreement," citing Public Records Office C 2/JasI/230/91.

living by the fact he could remarry there[82]; he also was "engaged in constant quarrels with his Groton neighbors," Bremer notes, including a case where the churchwardens sued him for seizing "a cottage in the churchyard that had been built by the parish to house a poor man charged with ringing the church bells."[83] He also failed a number of times to make maintenance payments to Elizabeth, who had to petition the Lord Chancellor for assistance.[84] John had a pious affinity for Ireland and apparently visited there often before his move; his brother Adam Winthrop wrote in his journal on 16 June 1595 that "my brother Winthrop departed from my house towards Ireland, and my brother [Roger] Alibaster went with him."[85]

In 1594, John obtained a license to "alienate" the Groton estate,[86] which would allow him to sell his life interest, a legal move that allowed him to move to Ireland and lease the manor to his brother Adam. "He also used the threat of a sale to extort funds from his brother," Bremer writes. "Then, as the decade came to a close, John used the leverage that he had by virtue of the license to alienate in order to pressure his brother into buying the manor," which Adam did, but only after lengthy negotiations to have John sell it to Adam's son John.[87] John settled on Munster Plantation in June 1596, although Bremer notes his lands would have been overrun in the Tyrone Rebellion in 1598 when, within a forty-eight-hour period, "Irish chieftains swept away many of the English settlements in the southwest," forcing many refugees into the city of Cork.[88]

---

[82] By 1634, Bremer notes in *John Winthrop: America's Forgotten Founding Father*, 73, such marriages had become such common practice that the Irish Parliament felt compelled to make bigamy a felony.

[83] Bremer, *John Winthrop: America's Forgotten Founding Father*, 72, citing Thomas Kedbye and John Stockton, churchwardens of Groton, c. John Winthrop, Adam Winthrop, and Edward Stowe in the Court of Requests (Public Records Office REQ 2/231/4).

[84] Bremer, *John Winthrop: America's Forgotten Founding Father*, 98, citing Winthrop c. Munning, Public Records Office C 2/JasI/230/91.

[85] *Winthrop Papers*, 1: 68.

[86] See "Alienation of Groton Manor, 1594," in Muskett, *Evidences of the Winthrops of Groton*, 17, citing Patent Roll 36 Elizabeth, Part 13, Memb. 31.

[87] Bremer, *John Winthrop: America's Forgotten Founding Father*, 99–100. He notes that a sticking point was any claim Elizabeth (Risby) Winthrop might have on the estate. John promised to set aside £1,000 as a pledge that he would properly divorce Elizabeth or pay any claim she made, although it is not clear that he did either.

[88] Bremer, *John Winthrop: America's Forgotten Founding Father*, 98–99.

John returned to England, but in Aug. 1602 again departed for Ireland[89] and eventually settled in Aghadown in Cork.[90]

In his will, dated 28 March 1613 at Aghadown, he mentioned his cousin Adam Winthrop (who had left London for Bandon), his daughter Anne, and his (second) wife Elizabeth, whom he appointed executor.[91] When Adam received news of his brother's death, he commented in Latin that John "was neither useful to himself or me in his life; who was a hard brother to me at the time of his death."[92]

    x. ADAM WINTHROP, JR., twin, b. 20 Jan. 1546 and d. at the age of 6 months.[93]

3   xi. ADAM[A] WINTHROP, b. at London 10 Aug. 1548, m. (1) 16 Dec. 1574, ALICE STILL; m. (2) 20 Feb. 1579/80, ANNE BROWNE.

    xii. KATHARINE WINTHROP, b. 17 May 1550[94] and d.y. (not mentioned in her father's will).

---

[89] Adam Winthrop journal, *Winthrop Papers*, 1: 76.

[90] Bremer, *John Winthrop: America's Forgotten Founding Father*, 99. "The ruins of Aghadown House, which may have been his home, still sit on an elevated site overlooking verdant fields."

[91] Will of John Winthrop of Aghadowne, transcribed in *Winthrop Papers*, 1: 172–73.

[92] Adam Winthrop journal, *Winthrop Papers*, 1: 176–77. After noting his brother's death ("July 26. my brother John died in Irelande 1613. of the age of 66 y[eres] and 7 months"), Adam wrote on the bottom of the page: "Qui sibi, neque mihi, vtilis, vita fuit. Qui mihi frater durus, tempore mortis erat."

[93] "Latin Pedigree" in Muskett, *Evidences of the Winthrops of Groton,* 5. See note 73.

[94] "Latin Pedigree" in Muskett, *Evidences of the Winthrops of Groton,* 5. "Anno domini 1550 decimo septimo die maij et anno regni regis Edwardi sexti quarto Katherina quarta ejus filia nata fuit."

xiii.   Susanna Winthrop, b. 10,[95] bp. at St. Peter's Church 11 Dec. 1552,
and d. at Coventry, Warwickshire 9 Aug. 1604.[96] She m. _____
Cotta/Cottie.[97]

[95]   "Latin Pedigree" in Muskett, *Evidences of the Winthrops of Groton,* 5. "Anno domini
1552 decimo die decembris Susanna quinta ejus filia nata fuit anno regis Edwardi
sexti sexto."

[96]   "Latin Pedigree" in Muskett, *Evidences of the Winthrops of Groton,* 6. "Anno domini
1604 nono die augusti Susanna filia Adami Winthrop et Agnetae uxor ejus secundus in Coventry obijt, anno aetatis suae quinquagesimo secundo. Nupta fuisset D:
Cottie." See also *Pond's Almanack for 1603,* transcribed in *Winthrop Papers,* 1: 153,
in which her brother Adam entered, "9 [Aug.] my Sister Susan died in Coventry.
1604." And later, an entry by Adam in *Hopton's Almanack for 1614,* transcribed at
1: 177: "9 [Aug.] my sister Cottie died. 1604. 10 y[eres] since." Also in his diary,
transcribed at 1: 86: "The xijth day of september I first head of the death of my
sister Cottye who died the ixth day of August last being of the age of 51 yeres, 9
monethes and [blank] days."

[97]   Robert C. Winthrop, *Life and Letters of John Winthrop, Governor of the Massachusetts-
Bay Company at Their Emigration to New England, 1630,* 2 vols. (Boston: Ticknor and
Fields, 1864), 1: 43fn, identified her husband as possibly being John Cotta, noting a
tract in the collection of the Massachusetts Historical Society entitled *The Infallible
True & Assured Witch: or The Second Edition of the Tryall of Witchraft, by John Cotta,
Doctor in Physicke, London, 1624* and "an old family memorandum" that identified
the Cottie or Cotta who married Adam's sister "as having written a book on witchcraft." However, Peter Elmer, writing in the *Oxford Dictionary of National Biography*
(*oxforddnb.com*), identifies John Cotta as a son born about 1575 to Peter Cotta (who
was identified in his 1619 will as a "professor of Phisicke" in Coventry) and "most
probably" Susanna Winthrop, suggested by her brother Adam's references to the
Cottas of Coventry in his personal writings. In Adam's copy of the first edition of
Cotta's book, published in 1616, he scribbled a note that John Cotta was "the sonne
of Peter Cotta an Italian" but made no specific mention of a relationship between
the families. See Frederic Clark, "Annotations and Generations," blog entry, *Journal
of the History of Ideas,* 9 February 2015, at *jhiblog.org/2015/02/09.*

The Kinship Between Robert[8] Winthrop
and Presidents John Adams and John Quincy Adams

Adam Winthrop = (2) Anne Browne

John Winthrop
= (1) Mary Forth

John Winthrop
= (2) Elizabeth Reade

Waitstill Winthrop
= (1) Mary Browne

John Winthrop
= Anne Dudley

John Still Winthrop
= (1) Jane Borland

Francis Bayard Winthrop
= (2) Phebe Taylor

Thomas Charles Winthrop
= Georgiana Maria Kane

Robert Winthrop
= Katharine Wilson Taylor

Lucy Winthrop
= Emanuel Downing

Lucy Downing
= William Norton

John Norton
= Mary Mason

Elizabeth Norton
= John Quincy

Elizabeth Quincy
= William Smith

Abigail Smith
= John Adams

John Quincy Adams
= Louisa Catherine Johnson

3. **Adam**[A] **Winthrop** (*Adam*[B-C]) was born in St. Peter's parish, "in the street which is called Gracious" (Gracechurch), London, Middlesex 10 August 1548[98] and was buried at Groton, Suffolk 28 March 1623.[99] He married, first, 16 December 1574, **Alice Still**, daughter of William Still of Grantham, Lincolnshire.[100] She died in childbirth on 24 December 1577 and was buried at Hadleigh, Suffolk.[101] Adam married, second, at Groton on 20 February 1579/80,[102] **Anne Browne**, who

---

98   "Latin Pedigree" in Muskett, *Evidences of the Winthrops of Groton*, 5. "Anno domini 1548 decimo die augusti anno regni regis Edwardi sexti secundo, Adamus alter filius ejus natus fuit in Londini urbem in parochia S[t] Peters in via vocata gracious [Gracechurch], quo vero anno Adamus Winthrop ab Edwardo rege armigerum regio suo scripto et sigillo inscribitur." Muskett noted that in the margin of this entry are inserted the words "on fryday." Adam also entered his date of birth in a number of almanacs, e.g., *Pond's Almanack for 1603* ("10 [Aug.] Being fryday I Adam Winthrop was borne. 1548. 55. Yeres since") and *Allestree's Almanack for 1621* ("August 10. Dies natalis mei AW sen: 1548, aet. 73"). See *Winthrop Papers,* 1: 153, 216, 245, 258.

99   Groton parish register, *Collections of the Massachusetts Historical Society,* 3rd series, 8 [1843]: 297. "1623. Adam Winthropp Gent. was buried the 28th of Marche." Mayo, *The Winthrop Family in America,* 9, gives this as death date.

100   "Latin Pedigree" in Muskett, *Evidences of the Winthrops of Groton,* 5. "Anno domini 1574 decimo sexto die decembris et anno regni Reginae Eliz: decimo sexto, aetatis suae vicesimo sexto et quarto menses, Adamus Winthrop nuptus fuit Aliciae Still uxor ejus primus, filia D: Johannis Still de Lincolnshire et soror Doctoris Johannes Still magister, collegii sanctae trinitatis Cantabrigiae." See also *Pond's Almanack for 1603,* transcribed in *Winthrop Papers,* 1: 154, in which Adam entered, "16 [Dec.] I was maryed to Alice my first wife. 1574." See *Evidences of the Winthrops of Groton,* 76, for a Still pedigree. Alice was a sister of Dr. John Still, who at the time of her marriage was Master of Trinity College, Cambridge; he was later named Bishop of Bath and Wells. In *Life and Letters,* Robert C. Winthrop wrote, "Adam's diary shows that his relations to the bishop continued to be intimate as long as they both lived, frequent letters passing between them, and frequent visits being interchanged by their children, and the name of Still has been preserved in the Winthrop Family, in memory of this connection, for many succeeding generations" (47).

101   "Latin Pedigree" in Muskett, *Evidences of the Winthrops of Groton,* 5. "The saide Alice died in childbed, being delivered of a sonne which was born dead the 24 day of december an: 1577, in the 20 yere of Qu: Eliz: and lieth buried in Hadley churche." See also *Pond's Almanack for 1603,* transcribed in *Winthrop Papers,* 1: 154, in which her Adam Winthrop entered, "27 [Dec.] Alice my wife died in Childbed. 1577" and an entry by Adam in *Hopton's Almanack for 1614,* transcribed at 1: 178: "23 [Dec.] Alice my first wife died in childebed, 1577. 37 y[eres] synce. Protinus aeterno mittit vtrumque deo [Immediately the eternal God sends them on]." The "Emblazoned Pedigree" of 1610 in *Evidences of the Winthrops of Groton,* 9, says Adam and Alice "had no issue."

102   Groton parish register, *Collections of the Massachusetts Historical Society,* 3rd series, 8 [1843]: 297. "1579. Adam Winthrop Gent. & Anne Browne were married the 20th daie of Februarie." The "Latin Pedigree" in Muskett, *Evidences of the Winthrops of Groton,* 6, has: "1579. Adam Winthrop was married to Anne my seconde wife, the danghter of Henry Browne, of Edwardston, clothier, the 20: day of ffebruary 1579."

was born ca. 1560, the daughter of Henry and Agnes (_____) Browne of Edwardston, Suffolk.[103] She died at Groton 19 April 1629.[104]

As a young man, Adam was sent to study at Ipswich Grammar School under a Protestant translator named John Dawes, who, like Adam[B] Winthrop, was a Marian regime refugee. While there, Adam caught the attention of Roger Kelke, the town's preacher and president of Magdalene College, Cambridge, and he enrolled there in 1567.[105] In 1574, he was admitted to the Inner Temple of the Inn of Court in London. Bremer described the typical student's life there:[106]

> Education at the Inns was most intense during the law terms, when the central courts met at Westminster Hall, though residence and study were required in some vacations between terms. The routine was similar in many respects to college life. Members of the Inner Temple lived together in chambers, attended daily chapel and took dinner and supper in a common dining hall during terms. They learned the law from lectures or readings that followed the meals in hall, from attendance in the morning at the sessions of the courts in Westminster, and from their own readings of law reports and early published compilations.

Muskett noted in a footnote that "the words 'my seconde wife' and similar expressions later on seem clearly to establish the authorship of the third Adam W., who probably copied many of the earlier entries from his father's papers." See also *Pond's Almanack for 1603*, transcribed in *Winthrop Papers*, 1: 151, in which Adam entered, "20 [Feb.] I was maryed to Anne my 2 wife. 1579," and later, in *Hopton's Almanack for 1614* (1: 175): "20 [Feb.] This day I was maried to Anne my 2 wife. 1579. 34 y[eres] since."

[103] In his will, dated 23 June 1593 and proved 27 January 1596, Henry Browne left £50 to John Wynthropp and £50 each to Anne and Jane Wynthropp at age 24 or marriage. He also named Adam Wynthropp executor. See Muskett, *Evidences of the Winthrops of Groton*, 77–78, citing P.C.C. 2 Cobham; see 82 for a Brown pedigree. Henry Browne died 8 January 1596, age 76 (*Winthrop Papers*, 1: 69) and Agnes Brown died 17 December 1590, as noted by their son-in-law Adam Winthrop (*Winthrop Papers*, 1: 154, 178).

[104] Groton parish register, *Collections of the Massachusetts Historical Society*, 3rd series, 8 [1843]: 297. "1629. Mrs. Winthropp Senr. April the 19th." Given the context, this date is possibly that of her burial. John[1] Winthrop alludes to his mother's death in a letter to his wife dated 8 May 1629, noting he plans to "take a tyme to conferre with my sister Dow[ning] about thy clothes she weares no mourning apparel but I and my man are in it" [*Winthrop Papers*, 2: 87].

[105] Bremer, *John Winthrop: America's Forgotten Founding Father*, 45.

[106] Bremer, *John Winthrop: America's Forgotten Founding Father*, 49, citing various histories by Wilfrid R. Prest of the Inns of Court under Queen Elizabeth.

On 15 March 1575, Adam was appointed as steward of manors owned by St. John's College in Kent and Berkshire and as receiver of rents for Berkshire. No doubt he landed both positions through family connections: he had married Alice Still in December 1574, and six months earlier her brother John Still had been appointed Master of St. John's.[107] (In 1592, after John Still had been appointed Master of Trinity College, Cambridge, he had Adam hired as its auditor, and once a year until 1610 Adam would travel to Cambridge to check the books and socialize.[108])

After Alice died in childbirth in 1577, Adam married Anne Browne. A letter survives written by Anne to her husband in London about 1581:[109]

> I haue reseyued (Right deere and welbelouid) frome you this weeke a letter, though short, yet verye sweete, whiche gaue me a lyuelye tast of those sweete and comfortable wordes, whiche alwayes when you be present withe me, are wonte to flowe most aboundantlye from youre louinge hart, wherbye I perseyue that whether you be present with me, ore absent from me, you are euer one towardes me, and your hart remayneth allwayes with me. . . .
>
> In the meane tyme I will remayne as one hauing a greate inheritaunce, ore riche treasure, and it beinge by force kept from him, ore hee beinge in a strange contry, and cannot enjoye it longethe contynuallye after it, sithinge and sorrowinge that hee is so long berefte of it, yet rejoyseth that hee hathe so greatt tresure pertayninge to him, and hoppethe that one daye the tyme will com that hee shalle injoye it, and haue the wholle benyfytt of it. . . .
>
> I send you this weke by my fathers man a shyrte and fyve payer of hoses. I pray sell all thes, if ye wold any for your owne weryng I haue mor a knyttynge. I pray send me a pound of starche by my fathers man. You may uery well send my bible if it be redye.[110]

---

[107] Bremer, *John Winthrop: America's Forgotten Founding Father*, 48–49, citing St. John's College Archives, Think Black Book, C7.14, 65–66. In 1574, Dr. John Still married Adam's niece, Anne Alabaster.

[108] Bremer, *John Winthrop: America's Forgotten Founding Father*, 68.

[109] *Winthrop Papers*, 1: 29–31. It does not have a date, but Robert C. Winthrop noted it mentions no children, so it was probably soon after their marriage in 1580 (Winthrop, *Life and Letters*, 1: 48).

[110] Bremer, *John Winthrop: America's Forgotten Founding Father*, 71, notes it was probably being bound.

> If my brother [John] Wintropp be at Londone I pray
> forgett not to saye my very hartye commendacions vnto
> him.

On 9 February 1583/84, Adam was admitted to the bar as an "utter [junior] barrister" on the recommendation of Robert Dudley, the Earl of Leicester.[111] He would have been expected to continue his studies at the Inner Temple for another three years but now could give advice, plead cases in smaller courts, and draw up documents. Adam remained in good standing with the Inns of Court for the next decade,[112] but in the early 1590s he began to manage Groton Manor for his brother John, who had moved to Ireland.[113] At this point Adam gave up his membership in the Inner Temple to move his family to Groton Place, "the mansion house."[114] Bremer writes that he "settled his accounts with the chief butler and, shortly thereafter [in June 1595], having refused to serve as steward for a reader's dinner as was expected of him, was expelled."[115] That would not have prevented Adam from practicing law—he provided legal counsel to his brother, John, and brother-in-law, John Still, and wrote up indentures for neighbors[116]—but he had to give up any hope of arguing before London's high courts.[117]

A journal Adam kept from about 1594 until 1610 survives.[118] He also filled almanacks from 1603, 1614, 1617, 1620, and 1621 with dates and memoranda about family and friends, as well as news of the royal

---

[111]   F.A. Inderwick, ed., *A Calendar of the Inner Temple Records,* 3 vols. (London, 1896–1919), 1: 329.

[112]   Bremer, *John Winthrop: America's Forgotten Founding Father,* 50.

[113]   After much legal wrangling, John would later sell the manor to his nephew John[1] Winthrop (Bremer, *John Winthrop: America's Forgotten Founding Father,* 98).

[114]   See "Alienation of Groton Manor, 1594," in Muskett, *Evidences of the Winthrops of Groton,* 17, citing Patent Roll 36 Elizabeth, Part 13, Memb. 31.

[115]   Bremer, *John Winthrop: America's Forgotten Founding Father,* 50, citing Inderwick, *A Calendar of the Inner Temple Records,* 1: 406. The Temple used the phrasing "shall be from henceforth put out of this House and be disadmitted thereof for ever."

[116]   Bremer, *John Winthrop: America's Forgotten Founding Father,* 68, citing a list of legal fees Adam collected in 1593 in *Winthrop Papers,* 1: 135.

[117]   Bremer, *John Winthrop: America's Forgotten Founding Father,* 50.

[118]   "Diary of Adam Winthrop," *Winthrop Papers,* 1: 39–144. Before his death, the family historian Robert C. Winthrop lent Muskett the original sixty-seven-page journal (plus eight loose pages) to transcribe and edit. Muskett never got around to the task and in 1906 donated the document to the British Museum (Add. Manuscript 37, 419). The diary remained unpublished until transcribed and annotated by Lilian J. Redstone and her father Vincent Burrough Redstone for the Massachusetts Historical Society. She suggested the journal probably had been a mostly empty daybook owned by Adam's father-in-law, Henry Browne, and appropriated by Adam.

family that he apparently culled from news accounts (e.g., "His Majesty came to the Cyttye of Yorke"). His more personal entries noted money and books lent,[119] rents collected, grandchildren born, siblings lost, and visits from friends and family. Some selections:

- "The vijth [7] of Marche [1596] I was robbed by false kks [knaves] and iij [3] dayes before Mr. [Henry] Sandes was robbed."[120]
- "The 27 day [of April 1596] my sister Hilles came to my howse for that her husbande had beaten her face and Armes grevouslye."[121]
- "The vth of June [1600] Mr. Powle did shewe me an Infamous libel written in Ryming verses."[122]
- "The 14 of July [1600] my cosyn [William] Alibast[er] was removed out of the Tower into Framingham Castle."[123]
- "The v. [of August 1600] I sent my Auditt Accoumpt to Ipswich to Tho[mas] Laster to be ingrossed by him in parchm[en]t."[124]
- "The 23 of Decembre [1600] I felt an Erthquake."[125]
- "The ixth day [of August 1601] my sister [Bridget] Alib[aster] and my sister [Mary] Veysye came to my house, where fyve of vs that are bretheren and systers mett and made merry, which we had not doonne in xvj yeres before."[126]
- "The xxjth [of October 1602] my sister [Margerie] Weston came to my house, and she and my wife parted the lynnen which my sister [Joan] Hilles did give to her ij Daughters."[127]
- "The xxjth day [of December 1602] my brother [Roger]

---

[119] In his bookkeeping accounts he noted, "The man is blest that hath not lent" (*Winthrop Papers*, 1: 138).

[120] *Winthrop Papers*, 1: 69.

[121] *Winthrop Papers*, 1: 70. Joan (Browne) Hilles ("my wife's natural sister") and William Hilles both died later in the year (1: 71). Their daughter Jane Hilles married Adam Winthrop (son of William Winthrop and grandson of Adam[B] Winthrop) in 1599. Muskett, *Evidences of the Winthrops of Groton*, 25, 102.

[122] *Winthrop Papers*, 1: 73.

[123] *Winthrop Papers*, 1: 73. William Alabaster was sent to the Tower of London for publishing a controversial tract. Adam noted on 20 September 1603 that William "came to my howse and shewed me his pardon" (1: 83). However, in June 1604, he wrote, "My Cosen Wm Alibaster was committed againe to prison for popery."

[124] *Winthrop Papers*, 1: 73. Adam was the auditor of Trinity College, Cambridge.

[125] *Winthrop Papers*, 1: 75.

[126] *Winthrop Papers*, 1: 76.

[127] *Winthrop Papers*, 1: 77.

Alibaster came to my house and toulde me that he made certayne inglishe verses in his sleepe, which he recited vnto me, and I lent him xl *s*."[128]

- "The last of June [1603] Mr. Alyston vicar of Aton borrowed of me the Remes Testament in Englishe."[129]
- "The xth of October [1603] Hornebyes daughter was deliuered of a Childe which she destroied."[130]
- "The xijth of Marche [1604] John Speede came to Groton and tould me that he should marry his M[ist]res and I paid him x *li*. of his grandfathers legacie."[131]
- "The xxxth of August [1604] Johane Bettes my maide did wounde John Wailley my man in the hed with her patten for which she was very sory."[132]
- "The 26 [June 1605] it thundred and lightened wonderfullye."[133]
- "The iiijth of Aug. [1605] Johane Cooke was d[eliuere]d of a girl Abigail an Hermaphrodite."[134]
- "The vth [of September 1605] I was sworne at Stowe before Sir William Waldegrave and other Commissioners for to inquire of Recusantes landes and goodes."[135]
- "The xviijth of octobre [1605] I changed a barrowe hogge for a sowe with John Rawlyng and she furrowed xij pigges the next night."[136]
- "The vjth of Novembre [1605] my brother Alib[aster] came to me and bownde Thomas his sonne for a yere from the i of the same monethe with Cook the Sherman of B[oxford]. iiij *li*. per annum."[137]
- "The iijd of Maye [1606] I putt xlv younge piegeons into my nue Dovehouse."[138]

---

[128] *Winthrop Papers*, 1: 78.

[129] *Winthrop Papers*, 1: 81.

[130] *Winthrop Papers*, 1: 83.

[131] *Winthrop Papers*, 1: 84. Speed was a nephew of Anne (Browne) Winthrop, the son of her sister Margerie by her first husband (*Evidences of the Winthrops of Groton*, 82).

[132] *Winthrop Papers*, 1: 86.

[133] *Winthrop Papers*, 1: 89.

[134] *Winthrop Papers*, 1: 90.

[135] *Winthrop Papers*, 1: 90. This occurance was under the act of 5 July 1604, "for the due Execution of the Statutes againste the Jesuits Seminarie Preists Recusantes etc." (*The Statutes of the Realm*, 4, Part 2: 1020–22). The act reaffirmed the late Queen Elizabeth's various anti-Catholic sedition laws and made some more severe.

[136] *Winthrop Papers*, 1: 91.

[137] *Winthrop Papers*, 1: 91.

[138] *Winthrop Papers*, 1: 92.

- "The 26 [of May 1606] my soonne and his wife with their soonne did ride to Hadley."[139]
- "The first of Sept. [1606] I did give an estate to my soonne in the house and lande called Wrightes in the Fenne."[140]
- "The viijth of Jan: [1607] father Smyth of Toppesfild came to me and brought me a fatt Capon and James Bett[es] a bottle of secke. Also Mris. Alston sent me a fatt goose and a bottle of muskadine on nueyeres daye."[141]
- "The 22 of July [1608] I was sworne one of the grande Jury at thassises then holden at Bury bfore my L[ord] Coke. . . . The 23 Miles the Informer stoode on the pillory and the next daye Bowman a promoter [a professional informer]. Also Wyles a merchant of Ipswich was arrayned and condemned for poysonynge one Aldriche his wives first husband who denied the fact at the time of his deathe 27 Julii 1607."[142]
- "The 4 of Feb. [1608/9] I went to Hadley to see my sister Alib[aster]. The same day John Wynthrop hurt his forhed with a fall."[143]
- "The xiiijth [of March 1608/9] Ailwardes youngest Daughter was searched by women and fownde with Childe which she confessed and that Francis the Vinteners man was the Father thereof."[144]
- "The first of Octobre [1609] I had a swelling and payne in my right hande."[145]
- "The 22 and 23 [of January 1609/10] Mr. Dr. Meriton came to speake to me about the resiginge of my office at Trinity college to Mr. Brookes. The xiiijth of Marche I dyned at Dr. Meritons in Hadley and Received of him a xx *li.* for my Auditorshipp. . . . The 27 I surrendered my Auditorship in Trinitye College to the Master fellowes and schollers before a pub[lic] notary. . . . On Munday the xvjth of Aprill [1610] Mr.

---

[139] *Winthrop Papers,* 1: 92. He is here referring to John[1] Winthrop and his wife Mary Forth, with their newborn son John[2] Winthrop.

[140] *Winthrop Papers,* 1: 93.

[141] *Winthrop Papers,* 1: 94.

[142] *Winthrop Papers,* 1: 95.

[143] *Winthrop Papers,* 1: 100.

[144] *Winthrop Papers,* 1: 101.

[145] *Winthrop Papers,* 1: 103.

Rich. Brooke the nue Auditor of Trinity College was at my
house in Groton to whom I d[elivere]d diuers [other] papers
bookes and Roles touchinge his office."[146]

- "17 [October 1621] my wife had 2 of her great teeth pulled
  out."[147]

- "12 [November 1621] my sonnes nurse being 76 yeres olde
  came to Groton, vnto him."[148]

Adam was an attentive and voracious reader, as seen in the many
annotations he left in the books from his library.[149] The marginalia he
added to one title offers particular insight into his personality, Mayo
observed:[150]

> One item, now in the library of the Massachusetts
> Historical Society, indicates clearly that he was a
> painstaking reader; it is a tract by George Wilson, printed
> at London in 1607 and entitled *The Commendation of
> Cockes, and Cock-fighting, Wherein is shewed, that Cocke-
> fighting was before the coming of Christ*. On the margins of

---

[146] *Winthrop Papers*, 1: 103–5.

[147] *Allestreet's Almanack for 1621*, transcribed in *Winthrop Papers*, 1: 259.

[148] *Allestreet's Almanack for 1621*, transcribed in *Winthrop Papers*, 1: 260. This was likely
son John[1] Winthrop, then 33 years old.

[149] Frederic Clark, "Annotations and Generations," blog entry, *Journal of the History of
Ideas*, 9 February 2015, at *jhiblog.org/2015/02/09*. "How did Adam, the family patriarch, annotate?" Clark asked. "He often began by fixing both a book and its author in
context. He was aided in this task by the massive encyclopedic bibliographies of the
sixteenth century, especially John Bale's *Catalogus* of British writers. For instance, in
his copy of the Tudor-era polemic *The Complaint of Roderyck Mors*, Adam discovered
that Bale had identified the true author of this pseudonymous work as one Henry
Brinklow. Accordingly, he wrote this out front and center on the title page, remarking
'Mr. Bale maketh mention of the author of this booke in the end of his Centuries.'"
For a discussion of the annotations made by John[2] Winthrop, Jr., to his grandfa-
ther's books after they had been transported to the Massachusetts Bay Colony, see
Clark's "Annotations and Generations (II)" at *jhiblog.org/2015/02/11*. See also Clark,
"Erudition and Encyclopedism: Adam Winthrop Reads Conrad Gesner's *Mithridates*,"
blog entry, 20 March 2015, New York Society Library, at *nysoclib.org/blog*.

[150] Mayo, *The Winthrop Family in America*, 7. The author remarked that the intense
Puritanism of Adam's grandson John Winthrop appears from this instance not to
have come down from the Winthrops. The Browne family was far more pious, and
Henry Browne once wrote Adam to insist that Christ would not have been a patron of the arts. Mayo wonders if Browne might have been reacting to a stone pot
given to Adam by his sister in 1607 that depicted the Fall of Adam with Adam and
Eve "appearing the absolute minimum of apparel." The heirloom passed through
the family for two hundred years before being given to the American Antiquarian
Society (8–9, citing *AAS Proceedings*, New Series, 15 [1902–3]: 173).

its pages are many notes in Winthrop's hand; some are in Latin, some in English, some in prose, and some in verse. As good Puritans frowned on cock-fighting and similar unedifying diversions, we may have in these notes an indication of the extent to which Squire Winthrop shared their attitude of mind.

Curiously enough, neither the cruelty to the birds nor the demoralizing effect on the spectators evoked any marginal comments from Adam Winthrop. What interested him were the references to roosters and hens made by ancient writers and the somewhat doubtful information about their habits. To these data he added some facts and fancies he had acquired from other reading—and let it go at that. It is safe to say that if he had been a Puritan of any hue he could not have perused the little book with anything like such complete objectivity.

Adam also wrote the occasional verse, although Lawrence Shaw Mayo, in his 1948 genealogy of the family, noted that while the attempts at "versification" were not all bad, "the verses he dedicated to his neighbor, Lady Mildmay, on the birth of her son Henry [in 1619] make the reader wonder whether Adam Winthrop might not have spent his time more profitably in some other way." The opening lines are:[151]

> *I sing not like the swan, that ready is to die;*
> *But with the Phoenix I rejoice, when she in fire doth fry.*

That same year Adam wrote another poem to an unnamed friend that began:[152]

> *The sweetenes of your Loue,*
> *Which I did lately taste,*
> *Doothe make me to affecte the same,*
> *euen with a mynde most chaste. . . .*

---

[151] Mayo, *The Winthrop Family in America*, 6. For the complete poem, see *Winthrop Papers*, 1: 241–42.

[152] Transcribed in *Winthrop Papers*, 1: 233–34 and perhaps written to his new daughter-in-law, Margaret (Tyndal) Winthrop, after her marriage to his son John in 1618. It was signed "your loving and assured frende alwaies." Mayo, *The Winthrop Family in America*, 6, noted that one of his contemporaries did enjoy the poems enough to include them in an anthology (Harleian Manuscripts, No. 1598).

Much less is known about Adam's second wife, Anne Browne. Her father, briefly the rector at Groton, was a landowner who made sure his daughter received a superior education; she could speak a number of languages and was deeply religious.[153] An account of a family dispute by Adam reveals some of her personality. In 1603, the wife of Adam's nephew Joshua Winthrop fled London with her young son after some marital strife. She lodged with Paul Powle, "an attorney who was a thorn in the side of the Winthrops," Bremer noted.[154] Hearing she was in Groton, Adam invited her to visit. She came by after church on 9 October, but when Anne Winthrop criticized "her expenses in apparel etc., she departed in displeasure." A few weeks later, on 30 October, "she went not to Church neither in the forenoone or afternoon," and when Anne Winthrop "did friendly reprove her, she fell out with her in bitter woordes." A week later she returned to her husband in London.[155]

Child of Adam[A] and Alice (Still) Winthrop:

    i.   STILLBORN SON, b. and d. 24 Dec. 1577; bur. at Hadleigh.[156]

Children of Adam[A] and Anne (Browne) Winthrop:

    ii.   ANNE WINTHROP, b. 5 and d. 20 Jan. 1581[/82].[157]

    iii.   ANNE WINTHROP, b. at Edwardston 16 Jan. 1585/86[158] and d. 16 May 1619[159]; bur. at St. Sepulchre's Church, London. She m. at Groton 25

---

153 Bremer, *John Winthrop: America's Forgotten Founding Father*, 70.

154 Bremer, *John Winthrop: America's Forgotten Founding Father*, 71.

155 "Memorialls of my Cosen Josua Winthrop his wifes behavior since she came to dwell in Groton viz. the 24 of Septembre Anno 1603," transcribed in *Winthrop Papers*, 1: 105. Joshua and Anne later emigrated to Ireland.

156 "Latin Pedigree" in Muskett, *Evidences of the Winthrops of Groton*, 5. See note 101.

157 "Latin Pedigree" in Muskett, *Evidences of the Winthrops of Groton*, 6. "1581. Anne the first daughter of Adam Winthrop & Anne his wife was born on fryday being the 5 daie of January anno 1581 in the 24: yere of Qu: Eliz: and died the 20 daie of the same month." Milton Rubicam, "A Winthrop-Bernadotte Pedigree," *The New England Historical and Genealogical Register* 103 [1949]: 247, gives 1580/81; Mayo, *The Winthrop Family in America*, 9, gives 1581.

158 "Latin Pedigree" in Muskett, *Evidences of the Winthrops of Groton*, 6. "1585. Anne the second daughter of Adam Winthrop and Anne his wife was born in Edwardston on Sunday aboute 10 of the clocke in the evenynge beinge the 16 daye of January anno 1585 in the 28 yere of the reigne of Qu: Eliz: & in the 37 yere of my age." See also *Pond's Almanack for 1603*, transcribed in *Winthrop Papers*, 1: 151, in which Adam entered, "16 [Jan.] my daughter Anna was borne. 1585." And later, *Hopton's Almanack for 1614* (1: 175): "16 [Jan.] This day my daughter Anne was borne. 28 y[eres] since. 1585."

159 Groton parish register, *Collections of the Massachusetts Historical Society*, 3rd series, 8 [1843]: 297. "1604. Thomas Jones [*sic*] and Anna Winthropp were married the 20th daie of Februarie—She died the 16th daie of Maie Anno 1619." See "Latin

Feb. 1604/5, THOMAS FONES,[160] son of Thomas Fownes of Dedford in Bromsgrove, Worcestershire. Thomas was an apothecary (i.e., general medical practioner) in London at the sign of the "Three Fawnes" in the Old Bayley.[161] They had issue, including Elizabeth Fones, who m. Henry[2] Winthrop, and Martha Fones, who m. John[2] Winthrop.

In a journal entry dated 3 May 1617, Anne's father Adam noted that "my daughter Fones and her children came from London to Groton" for the summer, with her husband arriving on 15 July and the family departing on 25 Aug.[162] Following Anne's death, Thomas m. (2) at London 28 Aug. 1621, Priscilla (Burgess) Sherman.[163] He d. at London 15 April 1629.[164] In his will, dated 14 and proved on 29 April, Thomas wrote that because he had already given most of his estate to his children and wife, he did:[165]

> Hereby commit the tuition, education, care and tutelage of
> my son Samuel Fones during his minority unto his uncle

Pedigree" in Muskett, *Evidences of the Winthrops of Groton,* 7, for some verse in Latin by Thomas Fones in memory of his wife, although Muskett noted it was "imperfectly copied." Rubicam, *Register* 103 [1949]: 247, gives 16 May 1618.

[160] Groton parish register, *Collections of the Massachusetts Historical Society,* 3rd series, 8 [1843]: 297. "1604. Thomas Jones [*sic*] and Anna Winthropp were married the 20ᵗʰ daie of Februarie." See also *Pond's Almanack for 1603,* transcribed in *Winthrop Papers,* 1: 151, in which her father entered, "25 [Feb.] Anna my daughter was maried to Th Fones. Anno 1604." See also diary entry at 1: 88: "The xxiijth [of Feb.] TF came to Groton and was maried to my daughter Anne the xxvth and they departed toward London the xxvijth day of February 1604."

[161] "Fones of Suffolk" in Muskett, *Evidences of the Winthrops of Groton,* 87.

[162] Entries in *Bretnor's Almanack for 1617,* transcribed in *Winthrop Papers,* 1: 216–17. Adam also noted in his diary the birth and christening at Groton of the couple's first child, Dorothy, on 24 October 1608, and the family's departure for London on 19 December (1: 99–100).

[163] "Fones of Suffolk" in Muskett, *Evidences of the Winthrops of Groton,* 87. "She was the dau. of John Burgess, rector of Sutton Coldfield, Warwickshire." See Winthrop, *Life and Letters,* 359–61, for letters from Priscilla Fones to John Winthrop (including her reaction to "the heavi nuse of your going for new England") and John Winthrop, Jr., in 1630, 1631, and 1637. Priscilla married (1) Bezaleel Sherman and (3) Henry Painter. In *Allestree's Almanack for 1621,* transcribed in *Winthrop Papers,* 1: 259, Adam Winthrop noted, "28 [Aug.] my son Fones was married at London" and "28. [Sept] my son Fones and wife came to Groton."

[164] "Fones of Suffolk" in Muskett, *Evidences of the Winthrops of Groton,* 87. "Diary of Adam Winthrop," *Winthrop Papers,* 1: 143, reprints a list dated 1629 titled "Brothʳ Fones Debts," and "debtes owinge to the Testator at the tyme of his death." See "Remarks by Mr. R.C. Winthrop, Jr.," *Proceedings of the Massachusetts Historical Society* 32 [1898]: 146–48.

[165] Will of Thomas Fones, transcribed in Muskett, *Evidences of the Winthrops of Groton,* 84, citing P.C.C. 28 Ridley.

> John Wynthrop of Groton, Esq. . . . John White of the
> Middle Temple London, Esq., and James Thurlby, citizen
> and grocer of London, and do earnestly desire these my
> loving friends to have a special care that he be brought
> up in learning in the fear of God and knowledge of his
> ways, and do charge my sons, upon my blessing to subject
> himself unto them and be ruled by them in all things. And
> the tuition and education of my daughters Elizabeth and
> Martha I do commit unto my said loving brother John
> Wynthropp until they shall be married or attain their full
> age of one and twenty years. The tuition of my youngest
> daughter Mary I commit to my loving wife her mother.

4   iv.   JOHN[1] WINTHROP, b. at Edwardston 12 Jan. 1587/88; m. (1) 16 April
              1605, MARY FORTH; m. (2) 6 Dec. 1615, THOMASINE CLOPTON; m.
              (3) in April 1618, MARGARET TYNDAL; m. (4) (after 20 Dec. 1647),
              MARTHA (RAINSBOROUGH) COYTMORE.

       v.   JANE WINTHROP, b. at Edwardston between 1 and 2 a.m. on 14 or
              16,[166] bp. 17 June 1592,[167] and d. after 15 Feb. 1663.[168] She m. at
              Groton 5 Jan. 1612/13,[169] THOMAS GOSTLIN,[170] who was bp. at

---

[166] "Latin Pedigree" in Muskett, *Evidences of the Winthrops of Groton*, 6. "Jane the thirde
       daughter of Adam Winthrop and Anne his wife was borne in Edwardston on
       Wednesday betwene the houres of one and two in the morninge, beinge the 14:
       daie of June anno 1592 and the 34: yere of Queene Elizabeth. In the yere 1612, 5
       of January, she was married to Thomas Gostlin by whome she had sons & daughters
       nominatim: Anne, Jane, Steven, Mary." An entry by Adam[A] Winthrop in *Hopton's
       Almanack for 1614*, transcribed in *Winthrop Papers*, 1: 176, gives "16 [June] Jane my
       daughter was borne. 1591 [1592] 22 y[eres] since."

[167] Groton parish register, *Collections of the Massachusetts Historical Society*, 3rd series, 8 [1843]:
       296. "1592. Jane the daughter of Adam Winthrop was baptised the 17th daie of June."

[168] Lucy Downing to John Winthrop, Jr., 15 February 1663, *Collections of the
       Massachusetts Historical Society*, 5th series, 1 [1871]: 59–60. "My son Peters wrote
       mee word lately, that not long since hee had seen Captaine Gozlin, & yt my sister
       & all are well at Stratford [presumably in Suffolk], & yt my nephew [Benjamin
       Gostlin] had lately made a purchase an hundred pounds p An, neer Groton; yt hee
       & his wife, & children were purposed to goe and liue in that, that my sister and one
       of her daughters should continue in his house, wher he now liues at Stratford."

[169] Groton parish register, *Collections of the Massachusetts Historical Society*, 3rd series, 8
       [1843]: 297. "1612. Thomas Golsine and Mrs. Jane Winthrop were married the 5th
       day of January." See also entry by Adam[A] Winthrop in *Hopton's Almanack for 1614*,
       transcribed at *Winthrop Papers*, 1: 175. "5 [Jan.] my daughter Jane was maried 1612
       to Tho: Goslin." Mayo, 9, gives 15 Jan. 1613. Muskett, *Suffolk Manorial Families*, 1:
       389, gives 6 January 1612.

[170] "Latin Pedigree" in Muskett, *Evidences of the Winthrops of Groton*, 6. Some records
       give Gostling.

Groton 2 March 1588, son of Philip and Alice (_____) Gostlin,[171] and had twelve children.[172] Thomas Gostlin d. after 26 March 1649.[173]

In a letter dated 2 March 1639 from Groton to his brother-in-law, John[1] Winthrop, Thomas explained why he and Jane had not yet emigrated to New England: his wife was convinced they could not afford it. They had "a great desyer to send you your godson, our Sonn John, to be imployed by you, & indeed we had sent him now but for want of meanes."[174]

vi. LUCILLA/LUCY WINTHROP, b. at Groton 9,[175] bp. 20 Jan. 1600/1,[176] and d. 19 April 1679.[177] She m. at Groton 10 April 1622,[178] as his second wife, EMMANUEL DOWNING, who was bp. at St. Lawrence's Church, Ipswich, Suffolk 12 Aug. 1585, son of George Downing of Ipswich, and d. at Edinburgh about 1660.[179] Their children

---

[171] See Muskett, *Evidences of the Winthrops of Groton*, 90, for a transcription of the 1626 will of Philip Gostlyn of Groton (citing Arch. Sudbury. Liber "Pearle," folio 622), in which he leaves his son Thomas a house, land, and rental properties. Philip was co-founder in 1595 of the Boxford Grammar School.

[172] Their births are recorded in parish registers and Adam Winthrop's diary.

[173] Thomas Gostlin to John Winthrop, Jr., undated, *Winthrop Papers*, 6: 1. "I am hartely sorowfull for the losse of my deere Brother," he wrote, referring to John[1] Winthrop, who died 26 March 1649.

[174] Thomas Gostlin to John Winthrop, 2 March 1639/40, *Winthrop Papers* 4: 212. Muskett noted that John Gostlin apparently never came to New England, as his father wrote to John Winthrop, Jr., about 1650 that "we have lost many of our family since your departure [1644]: my sonn Willis, my sonn John, my daughter Mary, my sonn Wolfe— these are all gone" (see previous note). Apparently at least one child, Margaret Gostlin, did emigrate about 1639. For extracts of letters between another child, Captain Benjamin Gostlin, and his Winthrop uncles and cousins, see Muskett, *Evidences of the Winthrops of Groton*, 92–94. Captain Gostlin wrote his uncle John[1] Winthrop in March 1640 that "I shold be verry gladd of some good Occation to come to Newe England that I might inioy your sweete sosiety" (*Winthrop Papers*, 4: 216).

[175] "Latin Pedigree" in Muskett, *Evidences of the Winthrops of Groton*, 6. "Lucy my 4 daughter was borne in Groton on fryday in the morninge: 9: of January anno 1600 and in the 43: yere of Qu: Eliza: and in the 52: yere & 5 month of my age and in the 41: yere of the age of Anne her mother." Adam Winthrop's diary (*Winthrop Papers*, 1: 72) gives "the ixth Day my wife Deliuered of her fowrth daughter, Lucilla. . . . The same day [xxjth] Luce went home to her Nurse."

[176] Adam Winthrop's diary, transcribed in *Winthrop Papers*, 1: 72, gives "the xxth my daughter was Christened." The Groton parish register transcription in *Collections of the Massachusetts Historical Society*, 3rd series, 8 [1843]: 296, has "Lucie Winthrop the daughter of Adam Winthropp Gent. and Mrs. Anna his wife was baptised the 27th of January."

[177] "Downing of Gamlingay" in Muskett, *Evidences of the Winthrops of Groton*, 99.

[178] Groton parish register, *Collections of the Massachusetts Historical Society*, 3rd series, 8 [1843]: 297. "1622. Immanuell Downinge and Luce Winthropp Gent. were married the 10th of Aprile."

[179] "Downing of Gamlingay" in Muskett, *Evidences of the Winthrops of Groton*, 99. George Downing, who entered Queen's College, Cambridge, in 1569, was master

included Sir George Downing, 1st Baronet, for whom Downing Street in London was named; his grandson, Sir George Downing, 3rd Baronet, founded Downing College at Cambridge University.

Emmanuel Downing was a member of the Inner Temple. The Downings resided in Salem, Massachusetts Bay, from 1638 to 1654, then returned to London and later Edinburgh.[180] Many of Lucy Downing's letters—written from 1626 to 1674 to her brother John, sister-in-law Margaret, and nephew John Winthrop, Jr., among other relatives—have been preserved.[181]

---

of the grammar school at Ipswich 1607–10. His will, dated 14 January 1610, was proved by his daughter Nohomie on 3 October. George may have married a "dau. of Bellamy" buried at St. Lawrence's Church, Ipswich, in 1610.

[180] "Downing of Gamlingay" in Muskett, *Evidences of the Winthrops of Groton*, 99.

[181] See *Collections of the Massachusetts Historical Society*, 5th series, 1 [1871]: 3–63.

Part II

The Winthrop Family in America

The Kinship Between Robert[8] Winthrop and the 11th Marquess of Lothian, British Ambassador to the United States 1939–40

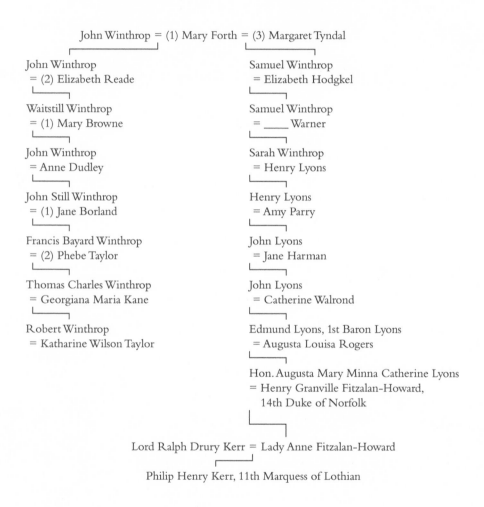

John Winthrop = (1) Mary Forth = (3) Margaret Tyndal

John Winthrop
= (2) Elizabeth Reade

Waitstill Winthrop
= (1) Mary Browne

John Winthrop
= Anne Dudley

John Still Winthrop
= (1) Jane Borland

Francis Bayard Winthrop
= (2) Phebe Taylor

Thomas Charles Winthrop
= Georgiana Maria Kane

Robert Winthrop
= Katharine Wilson Taylor

Samuel Winthrop
= Elizabeth Hodgkel

Samuel Winthrop
= _____ Warner

Sarah Winthrop
= Henry Lyons

Henry Lyons
= Amy Parry

John Lyons
= Jane Harman

John Lyons
= Catherine Walrond

Edmund Lyons, 1st Baron Lyons
= Augusta Louisa Rogers

Hon. Augusta Mary Minna Catherine Lyons
= Henry Granville Fitzalan-Howard,
    14th Duke of Norfolk

Lord Ralph Drury Kerr = Lady Anne Fitzalan-Howard

Philip Henry Kerr, 11th Marquess of Lothian

THE FIRST GENERATION

4. JOHN[1] WINTHROP (*Adam*[A-C]) was born at Edwardston, Suffolk at about 5 a.m. on 12 January 1587/88[182] and baptized at Groton, Suffolk on 16 January.[183] He died at Boston, Massachusetts 26 March 1649[184] and was buried at what is now called King's Chapel Burying Ground.[185] He married, first, at Great Stambridge, Essex 16 April

---

[182] Latin Pedigree" in Muskett, *Evidences of the Winthrops of Groton,* 6. "John the only sonne of Adam Winthrop & Anne his wife was borne in Edwardston aforesaide on Thursday about 5 of the clocke in the morning, the 12 daie of january 1587 in the 30 yere of the reigne of Qu: Eliz:" Edwardston is a village adjoining Groton. There are two entries in the pedigree for John's birth, one in Latin and one in English, and Muskett noted in a footnote that this dual notation suggests "the copyist of 1705 may have had two documents before him, one of them perhaps an almanac. There exist 13 almanacs containing entries by the third Adam W., but the earliest is of 1599." In *Pond's Almanack for 1603,* transcribed in *Winthrop Papers,* 1: 151, Adam entered, "12 [Jan.] my sonne John was born. 1587." Another entry in *Hopton's Almanack for 1614* (1: 175) has "12 [Jan.] This day my sonne John was b. 1587, 26 yeres since." And *Bretnor's Almanack for 1617* (1: 215) gives "12 [Jan]. This day JW the elder is 29 yeares olde."

[183] Groton parish register transcription, *Collections of the Massachusetts Historical Society,* 3rd series, 8 [1843]: 296. "1587. John Winthrop the sonne of Adam Winthropp and Anna his wife was baptised the 16th January."

[184] John Hull, "Some Passages of God's Providence," *Archaeologia Americana: Transactions and Collections of the American Antiquarian Society* 3 [1857]: 173.

[185] Thomas Bridgman, *Memorials of the Dead in Boston* (Boston: Benjamin B. Mussey & Co., 1853), 15. "John Winthrop, Gov. of Massachusetts, died 26 March, 1649, ae 61." At 27, Bridgman gives inscription as "John Winthrop, Governor of Massachusetts, Died 1649."

1605,[186] **MARY FORTH,** who was born 1 January 1583/84,[187] daughter of John and Thomasine (Hilles) (Crymble) (Bode) Forth.[188] She was buried at Groton 26 June 1615.[189] John married, second, at Groton 6 December 1615,[190] **THOMASINE CLOPTON,** who was baptized at Groton 18 February 1582, daughter of William and Margery (Waldegrave)

---

[186] "Latin Pedigree" in Muskett, *Evidences of the Winthrops of Groton,* 7. "Anno domini 1605 decimo sexto aprilis Johannes Winthrop in uxorem primam duxit Mariam filia unigenita Johannis fforthe de Magna Stambridge in comitatu Essexiae sexᵗus filius Gulielmi fforthe de Butley abbey in Suffolke." See also *Pond's Almanack for 1603,* transcribed in *Winthrop Papers,* 1: 152, in which John's father entered, "17 [April] my soonne was maried to Mary Forthe 1605." In his diary, Adamᴬ Winthrop noted that on xxviijth March 1605, "my soonne was sollemly contracted to Mary Foorth by Mr. Culverwell, minister of Great Stambridge in Exxes cum consentu parentum. The xvjth of Aprill he was maryed to her at Stambridge in Essex by Mr. Culverwell" (1: 88). Later, he wrote that "on viijth of Maye my soonne and his wife came to Groton from London and the ixth I made a marriage feaste which Sir Thomas Mildmay and his lady my sister were present. The same day my sister Vessye came to me and departed on fryday the 24 of Maye" (1: 89). The page on which the marriage would have been recorded in the parish register of St. Mary and All Saints Church is missing in a scan of the original (D/P 218/1/1) at *essexcc.gov.uk.*

[187] "Diary of Adam Winthrop," *Winthrop Papers,* 1: 43. "Mary Forth the wife of John Winthrop was borne on Wednesday the first day of January 1583."

[188] The "Emblazoned Pedigree" of March 1610 transcribed by Muskett in *Evidences of the Winthrops of Groton,* 9, gives her parents as "John forth of Stanbridge in Essex ye 6ᵗʰ sone of Will. Forth of Hadley in Com. of Suff., Maried Thomasine the Daughter of Hilles in the Com. of Essex & had issue one onely Daughter." According to the pedigree, John Forth was the son of William and Elizabeth (Powell) Forth of Hadley and grandson of Robert Forth of Hadley, who m. "ye Daughter of Odiam of London." John Forth was bailiff for the Rich family lands in Rochford Hundred. An entry by Adamᴬ Winthrop in *Hopton's Almanack for 1614,* transcribed in *Winthrop Papers,* 1: 176, noted on 15 May, "John Forth, my sonnes wifes father, died 1613. Vir pietate clarus [A man renowned for his piety]." In John Forth's will, probated 4 June 1613, transcribed in *Evidences of the Winthrops of Groton,* 113 (citing Wills, Arch. Essex, Aº 1613, No. 63), he left land to Henry Winthrop, "seconde sonne of John Winthrop and Mary his wife my daughter" and "fforthe Winthrop, the thirde sonne." He also left £240 to granddaughter Mary Winthrop, at age 18 or marriage, and appointed John and Mary Winthrop as executors. The document was witnessed by Adam Winthrop.

[189] Groton parish register, *Collections of the Massachusetts Historical Society,* 3rd series, 8 [1843]: 296. "1615. Mrs. Mary Winthropp the first wife of John Winthrope Esq. was buryed the 26ᵗʰ day of June." Rubicam, *Register* 103 [1949]: 247, gives this as the death date.

[190] Groton parish register, *Collections of the Massachusetts Historical Society,* 3rd series, 8 [1843]: 297. "1615. John Winthrop Esq. and Thomasinge Clopton was married the 6ᵗʰ day of Decr." For a transcription of their marriage settlement, in Latin, see Muskett, *Evidences of the Winthrops of Groton,* 22–23, citing Patent Roll, 13 Jas., 28ᵗʰ part, No. 21.

Clopton.[191] She died 8 December 1616, nine days after giving birth to a daughter who lived for three days, and was buried in Groton Chancel on 11 December.[192] John Winthrop married, third, at Great Maplestead, Essex in April 1618,[193] **MARGARET TYNDAL**, who was born about 1591 and died at Boston 14 June 1647,[194] daughter of Sir John Tyndal and Anne (Egerton) (Deane), Lady Tyndal[195]; and, fourth (marriage contract

---

[191] Groton parish register, *Collections of the Massachusetts Historical Society*, 3rd series, 8 1843]: 296. "1582. Teomasing Clopton the daughter of Mr. Willm Clopton Gent. and of Mistress Margery his wife was baptized the 18th day of February." See also "Clopton of Groton" in Muskett, *Evidences of the Winthrops of Groton*, 144.

[192] Groton parish register, *Collections of the Massachusetts Historical Society*, 3rd series, 8 [1843]: 297. "Mtrs. Thomasin Winthrope the 2d wife of John Winthrop Esq. was buried the 11thd ay of December." See also the "Death of Thomasine Clopton Winthrop 1616," from *Experiencia*, in which John wrote: "On Saturdaye beinge the last of November 1616, Thomasine, my deare and loving wife, was delivered of a daughter, which died the mundaye following in the morning. She tooke the deathe of it with that patience that made us all to merveile." Later, "When I tould hir that the daye before was 12 monthes she was maried to me, and now this day she should be maried to Christ Jesus, who would embrace her with another manner of love than I could, 'O husband (said she, and spake as if she were offended, for I perceived she did mistake me) I must not love thee as I love Christ'" (*Winthrop Papers*, 1: 182–90).

[193] Adam Winthrop in *Bretnor's Almanack for 1617*, transcribed in *Winthrop Papers*, 1: 218. "That on fryday the 24th of Aprill 1618 my sonnes 3 wife came first to Groton. She was maried to him the [29]th day of the same moneth at greate Maplested in Essex. Anno 1618." However, the same entry transcribed in Winthrop, *Life and Letters of John Winthrop*, 1: 437 gives "the [torn] day," so the source of 29 April is not clear, although often repeated, e.g., *Register* 33 [1879]: 237. In another entry, Adam noted that 17 September 1617 "my son rid first to maplested," the home of Margaret Tyndal (1: 217). On 31 March 1618, Adam wrote Margaret a letter that began: "I am, I assure yow (Gentle Mris. Margaret) alredy inflamed with a fatherly Loue and affection towardes yow: the which at the first, the only report of your modest behauiour, and mielde nature, did breede in my heart; but nowe throughe the manifest tokens of your true loue, and constant minde, which I perceyue to be setteled in yow towardes my soonne, the same is exceedingly increased in mee" (1: 220–21).

[194] James Savage, ed., *The History of New England from 1630 to 1649, by John Winthrop, Esq.*, 2 vols. (Boston: Little, Brown & Co., 1853), 2: 378–79. "14, (4.) [14th of 4th mo. (June)] An epidemical sickness was through the country among Indians and English, French and Dutch. It took them like a cold, and a light fever with it. Such as bled and used cooling drinks died; those who took comfortable things, for most part recovered, and that in a few days. . . . In this sickness the governour's wife, daughter of Sir John Tindal, Knight, left this world for a better, being about fifty-six years of age; a woman of singular virtue, prudence, modesty and piety, and specially beloved and honored of all the country." On 30 August 1647, Samuel Winthrop wrote his father from the West Indies, "By mr. Payton I receiued the sad newes of my mothers death, which I thought could haue born with a great deale more patience then now I finde I canne" (*Winthrop Papers*, 5: 180).

[195] Will of Sir John Tyndal, proved 2 December 1616, transcribed in *Winthrop Papers*, 1: 179–81, citing P.C.C. 126 Cope. Will of Anne Tyndal, 14 June 1620, proved 2

dated 20 December 1647[196]), his daughter-in-law's sister[197] **MARTHA RAINSBOROUGH**, who was baptized at St. Mary's Church, Whitechapel (London), Middlesex 20 April 1617[198] and died at Boston ca. 24 October 1660,[199] widow of Thomas Coytmore, and daughter of Captain William and Judith (Hoxton) Rainsborough.[200] She married, third, 10 March 1651/52, John Coggan, and had further issue.[201]

November 1620, transcribed at 1: 251, citing P.C.C. 94, Soame. Lady Tyndal left "to my daughter Winthorp [*sic*] my Tuftafeta Gowne and my Cabinett which her father gave me. I give her my greene velvett box with tills and all such things as be in them at the time of my death." Further, "Adam Winthrop's Note on Adam and Stephen Winthrop" calls Steven and Adam Winthrop, the sons of John[1] Winthrop, the grandchildren of "Sir John Tindal knight" and "the Ladye Anne Tindal" (1: 256).

[196] Nathaniel B. Shurtleff, ed., *Records of the Governor and Company of the Massachusetts Bay in New England, 1628–1686*, 5 vols. in 6 (Boston: W. White, printer to the Commonwealth, 1853–54), 2: 234–35. In March 1647/48, the General Court recorded a marriage indenture dated 20th of the 10th mo. [December] 1647 between John Winthrop and "Martha Coytemore, the relict of Thom: Coytemore." Wyman's *Genealogies and Estates of Charletown* and Pope's *Pioneers of Massachusetts* and other sources err with 4 December 1647, prob. a misreading an early record that indicated he married his fourth wife in December 1647.

[197] Martha's sister Judith Rainsborough had married, about 1644, Stephen[2] Winthrop, who became her stepson.

[198] Martha Raynsborow baptismal record, 20 April 1617, dau. Willm. Raynsborow, indexed at *familysearch.org* from Parish Registers of St. Mary's Church, Whitechapel, 1558–1687 (Family History Library film 094,691).

[199] Robert Charles Anderson, *The Winthrop Fleet: Massachusetts Bay Company Immigrants to New England, 1629–1630* (Boston: New England Historic Genealogical Society, 2012), 689. She committed suicide, according to a letter dated 27 of 9th mo. [November] 1660 from the Rev. John Davenport to John Winthrop, Jr., transcribed in *Collections of the Massachusetts Historical Society*, 3rd series, 10 [1849]: 45. "Sir, what I wrote, in my former [letter, now lost], concerning Mrs. Coghen, I had it from Anth. Elcock, who received in the Baye, viz. that she was discontented that she had no suitours, and that had encouraged her Farmer, a meane man, to make a motion to her for marriage, which accordingly she propounded, prosecuted and proceeded in it so farr that, afterwards, when she reflected what she had done, and what a change of her outward condition she was bringing herselfe into, she grew discontented, despaired and tooke a great quantity of ratts bane, and so died: Fides sit penes Authorem [Let the author be trusted]." Davenport's previous letter to Winthrop that has been preserved, dated 17th of 8th mo. [September] 1660, made no mention her death.

[200] In William Rainsborough's 1638 will, transcribed in Muskett, *Evidences of the Winthrops of Groton*, 156–57, he left £700 to his daughter "Martha Coytmore, the wife of Thomas Coytemore, now in New England . . . if she be alive at the tyme of my death." Thomas Coytemore, a mariner, died 27 December 1644, when he was shipwrecked on a voyage to Málaga in southern Spain, per James Savage, *A Genealogical Dictionary of the First Settlers of New England*, 4 vols. (Boston: Little, Brown & Co., 1860–62), 1: 467–68. For more on this family, see Henry F. Waters, *Genealogical Gleanings in England*, 3 vols. (Boston: New England Historic Genealogical Society, 1901), 1: 159–71.

[201] George E. McCracken, "Early Cogans English and American," *Register* 111 [1957]: 13–14.

On 2 December 1602, at age 14, John rode with his father from Groton to Trinity College, Cambridge, where Adam Winthrop conducted the annual audit. On 8 December John was admitted to the college,[202] although it was not until around Easter that he was officially enrolled as a "pensioner," meaning his family paid his tuition.[203] According to a short memoir John wrote in 1636 ("in the 49th year of my age just compleat"[204]), he had been indifferent to religion[205] until he fell deathly ill at school soon after his arrival and experienced a spiritual reckoning. Once healthy, however, he returned to his worldly ways. "My lusts were so masterly as no good could fasten upon me," he recalled. "I cared for nothing but how to satisfy my voluptuous heart."[206] John left Trinity at age 17 to marry 21-year-old Mary Forth. They had met the year before while he and a friend, William Forth, were visiting Forth's kinsman, John Forth, his wife Thomasine, and their daughter Mary at Great Stambridge in Essex. By January 1605, John Forth had ridden to Groton to meet Adam and Anne Winthrop, and by 28 March both parents had given their consent.[207]

As a young man John came to see God, and the devil, at work in his life. A private notebook[208] he kept between 1606 and 1636 describes his continuing "conflicts between the flesh & the Spirit."[209] On 20

---

[202] Adam Winthrop journal, *Winthrop Papers*, 1:78. "The 2d of December [1602] I rode to Cambridge and the 4th of the same moneth I was sore payned with the Collick and the stone for iiij howres. . . .The viijth day John my soonne was admitted into Trinitie College."

[203] Bremer, *John Winthrop: America's Forgotten Founding Father*, 79–80.

[204] "Governor John Winthrop's (the elder) Christian Experience," dated 12th of 11th mo. [January] 1636, transcribed in Winthrop, *Life and Letters of John Winthop*, 1:174.

[205] He was not without guilt, however. As he recalled in *Experiencia*: "When I was a boye I was at a house, where I spied 2 small books lye cast aside, so I stole them, and brought them awaye with me; and since when they have come to miy minde I have grieved at it, and would gladly have made restitution, but that shame still leted me . . . until I did (through Gods direction) finde a meanes to make satisfaction, which done, I had peace" (*Winthrop Papers*, 1: 193).

[206] "Governor John Winthrop's (the elder) Christian Experience," transcribed in Winthrop, *Life and Letters of John Winthop*, 1: 165–66.

[207] Bremer, *John Winthrop: America's Forgotten Founding Father*, 89–91. "Numerous questions about this marriage remain unanswered," Bremer wrote. "At a time when men of his status usually did not wed until their late twenties, John was seventeen. Mary was also young, twenty-one rather than the average twenty-six. By choosing marriage, John abandoned his Cambridge studies and thus any plans to enter the ministry. . . . Everything about the union seems rushed." Bremer admits to "speculation that the two were swept up by a strong physical attraction that forced their families to agree to the hasty march to the altar."

[208] A catalog of "sinnes" was written partly in cipher. See *Winthrop Papers*, 1: 163fn.

[209] *Winthrop Papers*, 1: 161–69.

April 1606, for instance, when he was just a year into his marriage and barely 18 years old, John promised God he would change his "pride, covetousnesse, love of this worlde, vanitie of minde, unthankfulnesse, slouth," etc.[210]—what historian Everett Emerson labeled a "typical Puritan" list of sins.[211] John also recorded moments throughout his life where he felt God had intervened, such as when on 15 December 1611, "my wife taking upp a messe of porridge, before the children or anybodye had eaten of it, she espied therein a greate spider."[212] In 1628, by God's grace, an arrow shot by his son Forth at a target a great distance away narrowly missed his son Adam. Soon after, his son Deane fell backward from a high stool and could easily have broken his neck, "but through Gods mercye, he had no harme."[213]

As Francis Bremer noted, John's journals includes only perfunctory references to his first wife. No letters he wrote to her survive, and the one surviving letter from Mary to John deals only with household affairs, though she did sign off as "thine euer Louing wife tel dethe."[214] Bremer observed:[215]

> John much later mentioned "looking over some letters of kindness that has passed between my first wife and me," but the phrase "letters of kindness" does not suggest deep

---

[210]   *Winthrop Papers*, 1: 162–63. As Samuel Eliot Morison pointed out in *Massachusettensis de conditoribus, or Builders of the Bay Colony* (Boston: Houghton Mifflin, 1930), 60, John's journals were far more religious than his father Adam's had been. "His ideal was to devote every waking moment to God, when not engaged in his calling, or in reasonable recreation," Morison wrote. "It was a matter of self-congratulation that his horseback journeys to London could be employed in praying, singing and meditation. . . . These soul-searching records were common among sincere puritans of that time [but] they could easily be carried to a morbid excess. . . . John Winthrop's *Experiencia* is often tiresome, and even ludicrous in one instance, where he gives his reasons for giving up shooting birds out of season: (1) it is illegal; (2) it offends his neighbors; (3) 'it wastes great store of tyme'; (4) 'it toyles a man's bodye overmuche'; [etc.] . . . (9) after he has gone shooting . . . he often returned with an empty bag! One may suspect that the last reason, which would suffice for most men, was really the first."

[211]   Everett Emerson, "John Winthrop," *American Colonial Writers, 1606–1734*, vol. 24 of *Dictionary of Literary Biography* (Chicago: Gale, 1984), 354.

[212]   *Winthrop Papers*, 1: 165.

[213]   *Winthrop Papers*, 1: 405.

[214]   Bremer, *John Winthrop: America's Forgotten Founding Father*, 98, citing Mary Winthrop to John Winthrop, transcribed in *Winthrop Papers*, 1: 161, undated but probably ca. 1607.

[215]   Bremer, *John Winthrop: America's Forgotten Founding Father*, 98, citing *Winthrop Papers*, 1: 202.

emotional union, and while he recorded that, in reviewing these letters, he found his heart "accepting" the "scribbling hand, the mean congruity, the fast orthography, & broken sentences, &c," it seems clear that while Mary lived he held feelings of superiority that frayed their relationship.

For his part, Lawrence Shaw Mayo believed that "Mary Winthrop never really understood her husband's religious preoccupation and intensity, and she was too honest to pretend that she did. . . . One comes away with the feeling that Mary was more patient than religious, and that from our point of view she was the more normal human being of the two."[216]

John received land at Great Stambridge from John Forth as a dowry,[217] and in 1608 the couple moved there.[218] He was greatly influenced in his wife's hometown by an Oxford-educated Puritan minister named Ezekiel Culverwell, although in 1609 Culverwell was removed from his post for refusing to observe the ceremonies of the Church of England.[219] In 1613, after the deaths of his uncle John Winthrop in Ireland and his father-in-law, John Forth, in Great Stambridge, John moved his family to Groton Manor.[220] He was admitted at about the same time to Gray's Inn, a professional association in London for aspiring barristers and judges that dates to the fourteenth century.[221] Although he was never called to the bar,[222] in 1615 he was appointed as a justice of the peace in Suffolk and in 1616 named to the Suffolk and Essex sewer commission, which oversaw the repair of bridges, channels, and causeways.[223]

---

[216] Mayo, *The Winthrop Family in America*, 13. John did write, probably following Mary's death, that while his wife did not share his spiritual fervor, "she proved after a right godly woman" (*Winthrop Papers*, 1: 163).

[217] Emerson, "John Winthrop," *American Colonial Writers, 1606–1734*, 24: 354.

[218] Adam Winthrop journal, *Winthrop Papers*, 1: 99. "The xth of octobre [1608] my soonne and his wyfe departed from Groton to dwell at Stambridge in Essex."

[219] Francis J. Bremer and Tom Webster, eds., *Puritans and Puritanism in Europe and America*, 2 vols. (Santa Barbara, Calif.: ABC Clio, 2006), 1: 69.

[220] Bremer, *John Winthrop: America's Forgotten Founding Father*, 101–2.

[221] Bremer, *John Winthrop: America's Forgotten Founding Father*, 101. Bremer notes that one register says John was admitted to the Inn of Court on 25 October 1613, but that his name also appears on a list of members dated 1611. There is no explanation as to why John chose Gray's Inn instead of the Inner Temple, where his father had studied (413).

[222] Bremer, *John Winthrop: America's Forgotten Founding Father*, 101.

[223] Bremer, *John Winthrop: America's Forgotten Founding Father*, 121, citing Public Record Office C 181/2.

After the deaths, due to complications of childbirth, of his first and second wives within eighteen months of each other, in 1618 John married Margaret Tyndal of Great Maplestead (about a half day's ride from Groton[224]); her father had been the Master of Chancery before he was ambushed in his office and shot to death two years earlier by a disgruntled defendant.[225] When some members of Margaret's family argued that John wasn't sufficiently well-to-do, he replied that piety was more important to a successful marriage than net worth.[226]

In 1626, John was among those who lobbied for the selection of Robert Naunton as a knight for the shire; in return, Naunton, who was Master of the Court of Wards and Liveries, appointed John as an attorney there in 1627.[227] He had close friendships with several members of Parliament and, as a result, was asked to draft bills such as one designed to combat "the loathsome vice of drunkenness and other disorders in Alehouses."[228]

But life was expensive, and John apparently was becoming disenchanted with his position in London. He lost money on his son Henry's scheme to grow tobacco in the West Indies ("I have disbursed a great deale of money for you, more then my estate will beare," he wrote Henry after one request for funds. "I have many other children that are vnprovided"),[229] he was paying for two sons in college—John

---

[224] Bremer, *John Winthrop: America's Forgotten Founding Father*, 112.

[225] Rosemary Fithian Guruswamy, "Margaret Tyndal Winthrop," *American Women Prose Writers to 1820*, vol. 200 of *Dictionary of Literary Biography* (Detroit: Gale, 1999), 414. The killer had been ruined financially by one of Tyndal's rulings. See *Winthrop Papers*, 1: 220–21 for a 1618 letter from Adam Winthrop to Margaret assuring her of a warm welcome to the family. See also 1: 221–29 for two 1618 letters to Margaret from her new husband, e.g, "My onely beloued spouse, my most sweet freind, and faithfull companion of my pilgrimage, the happye and hope full supplie (next Christ Jesus) of my greatest losses, I wishe thee a most plentifull increase of all true comfort in the loue of Christ, with a large, and prosperous addition of whatsoever happynesse the sweet estate of holy wedlocke, in the kindest societye of a lovinge husbande may afford thee" (1: 226). Bremer, *John Winthrop: America's Forgotten Founding Father*, 114, calls John's early letters to Margaret "sermons more than love letters."

[226] Bremer, *John Winthrop: America's Forgotten Founding Father*, 113–14.

[227] Bremer, *John Winthrop: America's Forgotten Founding Father*, 144–45. Bremer notes that the records show that John and his brother-in-law, Emmanuel Downing, also an attorney with the court, "clearly engaged in dubious practices" to enrich themselves, but "that with his strict conscience [John] found it difficult to negotiate through the corridors of power." In December 1628 he suffered a serious illness that Bremer suggests may have "reflected his inner turmoil."

[228] *Winthrop Papers*, 1: 371–74.

[229] John Winthrop to Henry Winthrop, 30 January 1628[/29], transcribed in *Winthrop Papers*, 2: 67.

Jr. at Trinity and Forth at Emmanuel College, Cambridge—and in June 1629 in his "Generall considerations for the plantation in New England" made reference to "the unsupportable chardge"[230] of tuition as one more reason to emigrate.[231]

John had reasons to be concerned for his spiritual well-being as well. In March 1629 King Charles I dissolved Parliament, which Puritans such as the Winthrops viewed as the last, best hope to ensure their right to worship freely. Soon after, John left his job at the court; it is not clear if he quit because he had a grander plan or was fired for his beliefs. He had grown pessimistic about the spiritual future of England. In May he wrote his wife in Groton to say he was convinced that "God will bringe some heauye Affliction vpon this lande, and that speedylye."[232]

Believing the church in Protestant Ireland to be in close relationship to God, John had considered leaving England as early as 1622, at the time when his uncle departed and settled in Aghadown in Cork. (In April 1623, John had written to his son John, then in Dublin, "I wish oft God would open a waye to settle me in Ireland, if it might be for his glorye."[233]) Now he peered across the Atlantic. He had suffered a "dangerous, hot, malignant fever"[234] in December 1628 that brought him near death, and when he recovered, he found his faith even stronger. He wrote his wife in May 1629 that "if the Lord seeth it willbe good for vs, he will prouide a shelter and hidinge place,"[235] and about that time he helped organize the Massachusetts Bay Company.[236] By August he was circulating a paper among potential investors listing a variety of reasons they should found a plantation in New England.[237] (His argument included, cynically, the observation that "God hath consumed" the natives" with a great plague, making room for the settlers, although there was already "more then

---

[230] "General Observations," *Winthrop Papers*, 2: 118.

[231] Bremer, *John Winthrop: America's Forgotten Founding Father*, 132–35. John was earning £120 annually from Groton Manor and paying £40 of that to Elizabeth (Powlden) Winthrop. In his 1621 suit filed in Dublin against Elizabeth and her second husband, Thomas Nott, John sought to recover the 1,000 marks his uncle had promised as security against any dower claims. The Notts alleged in their counterclaim that Adam[A] Winthrop had tricked his brother into agreeing to the security. The Irish Chancery Court ruled for the Winthrops in 1630.

[232] John Winthrop to Margaret Winthrop, 15 May 1629, *Winthrop Papers*, 2: 91.

[233] John Winthrop to John Winthrop, Jr., 20 April 1623, *Winthrop Papers*, 1: 280–81.

[234] "Experiencia," *Winthrop Papers*, 1: 412–13.

[235] John Winthrop to Margaret Winthrop, 15 May 1629, *Winthrop Papers*, 2: 91.

[236] Bremer, *John Winthrop: America's Forgotten Founding Father*, 157.

[237] "General Observations for the Plantation of New England," *Winthrop Papers*, 2: 111–14.

enough [land] for them and vs."[238]) The group agreed to embark on 1 March 1630.[239] They also agreed to take the company charter with them, which proved prescient: without it, the power over their affairs would have stayed with a committee in London.[240] In October 1629 John was appointed governor of the company; he would serve twelve more one-year terms over the next twenty years.[241]

On 8 April 1630, the governor led a group of some seven hundred colonists to Massachusetts Bay aboard a fleet of eleven ships. He left his pregnant wife behind; the couple agreed to think of each other between 5 and 6 p.m. each Monday and Friday.[242] (Margaret would follow aboard the *Lyon*, arriving 2 November 1631. Their toddler daughter, Anne, died en route.)[243] John took three of his sons, likely Stephen, 11, and Adam, 10, and certainly Henry, 22 (whose pregnant wife awaited a later ship),[244] although the hapless Henry was left behind during a trip ashore

---

[238] *Winthrop Papers*, 2: 113.

[239] "The Agreement at Cambridge," *Winthrop Papers*, 2: 151–52.

[240] Emerson, "John Winthrop," *American Colonial Writers, 1606–1734,* 24: 354.

[241] He served 1629–33, 1637–40, 1642–44, and 1646–49.

[242] John Winthrop to Margaret Winthrop, 26 February 1629/30, *Winthrop Papers*, 2: 211. Robert C. Winthrop, in *Life and Letters*, 1: 378, noted the Winthrops may have borrowed this idea from Shakespeare's *Cymbeline*, first performed in 1609 and published in 1623, in which Imogen vows to think of her beloved at these same times.

[243] Savage, *The History of New England from 1630 to 1649*, 1: 76–77. "November 2. The ship *Lyon*, William Peirce, master, arrived at Natascot. There came in her the governour's wife, his eldest son, and his wife, and others of his children, and Mr. Eliot, a minister, and other families, being in all about sixty persons, who all arrived in good health, having been ten weeks at sea, and lost none of their company but two children, whereof one was the governour's daughter Ann, about one year and a half old, who died about week after they came to sea."

[244] John Winthrop to Margaret Winthrop, from aboard the *Arbella* at Cowes, 28 March 1630, *Winthrop Papers*, 2: 224. "Our boyes are well and cheerfull, and haue no minde of home, they lye both with me, and sleepe as soundly in a rugge (for we vse no sheets heer) as euer they did at Groton, and so I doe my selfe (I prayse God)." J. Gardner Bartlett, "Leaders in the Winthrop Fleet, 1630," *Register* 75 [1921]: 236, shares a list retrieved from the Colonial Office Papers, Vol. 5, No. 78, at the Public Record Office in London of the "principal understakes for the plantation of the Mattachusetts bay in Newwe England" that includes "Mr. Joh: Winthroppe Esqr: Governor, and three of his sonnes." Charles Edward Banks, *The Winthrop Fleet of 1630* (Boston, 1930, rep. Baltimore: Genealogical Publishing Co., 1999), 98, gave Henry, Stephen, and Samuel as passengers, but the latter was not yet three years old and Adam seems the more likely passenger. Banks also said John Winthrop brought eight servants (unnamed in his assembled passenger list), citing a letter written in Boston from John to Margaret dated 29 November 1630 (*Winthrop Papers*, 2: 320) in which John noted he had "lost 12: of my family, viz. Walters and his wife and 2: of his children: mr. Gager and his man: Smith of Buxall and his wife and 2; children: the wife of Taylor of Hauerill and their childe: my sonne H: makes the 12." In a

for livestock and had to complete his journey in another ship.[245] John tried to sell Groton Manor before he left, but the property was tied up in a family legal dispute. The sale had to be completed by Margaret.[246]

It was during the two-month journey of the *Arbella* that John Winthrop delivered what has been called the clarion call for American exceptionalism. In "Christian Charitie: A Modell Hereof" (commonly called "A Modell of Christian Charity"), Winthrop appealed to his fellow passengers to consider themselves an example for mankind, "a Citty upon a Hill; the eies of all people" upon them:[247]

---

letter dated 9 September 1630, John Winthrop reported "my seruant, old Waters of Neyland" had been among those who died (*Winthrop Papers*, 2: 312–13).

[245] Savage, *The History of New England from 1630 to 1649*, 1: 9. "The day we set sail from the Cowes, my son Henry Winthrop went on shore with one of my servants to fetch an ox and ten wethers …They sent the cattle abroad, but returned not themselves.… We were very sorry they had put themselves upon such inconvenience, when they were so well accommodated in our ship." Clearly irritated, John added a dig: "I must add here one observation, that we have many young gentlemen in our ship, who behave themselves well, and are conformable to all good orders."

[246] Bremer, *John Winthrop: America's Forgotten Founding Father*, 168. For a discussion of the disposal of John Winthrop's property in England, see 427–30. Emerson, "John Winthrop," *American Colonial Writers, 1606–1734*, 24: 354, noted that "because John and Margaret were frequently separated, first by his work in London, later for a time by the Atlantic Ocean, they created a correspondence,' a celebrated one, that gives a most engaging insight into their love and devotion to each other." See Joseph Hopkins Twichell, ed., *Some Old Puritan Love Letters: John and Margaret Winthrop, 1618–1638* (New York: Dodd, Mead, 1893).

[247] *Winthrop Papers*, 2: 294–95. For a modernized version of the sermon, see Richard S. Dunn and Laetitia Yeandle, eds., *The Journal of John Winthrop, 1630–1649* (Cambridge, Mass.: Belknap Press of Harvard University, 1996), 1–11. They note that while there is no doubt John Winthrop is the author, the only known seventeenth-century manuscript, owned by the New-York Historical Society, is not in his hand. In 1999, the chaplain of Harvard College would observe that "what runs through his sermon is an honest realization that the seductions of self-interest and ambition are as dangerous to the common good as famine and pestilence" (Peter J. Gomes, "Best Sermon: Pilgrim's Progress," *The New York Times Magazine*, 18 April 1999). Bremer, in his profile of Winthrop in the *Dictionary of Literary Biography* series, notes that his beliefs are an example of "Christian organicism," i.e., "he accepted the fact of inequality in society, justifying it as a demonstration of the variety of God's creation, as encouraging the exercise of charity, and as necessitating mutual dependence within a community" (Francis J. Bremer, "John Winthrop, *American Historians, 1607–1865*, vol. 30 of *Dictionary of Literary Biography* [Farmington, Mich.: Gale, 1984], 342). The practical result was a colony that had a mix of democracy and aristocracy. For those who challenged the system, "the only freedom was that to live elsewhere." John Winthrop considered democratic rule "the meanest and worst of all forms of government" (*Winthrop Papers*, 4: 383). Eighteenth- and nineteenth-century progressive thinkers such as Nathaniel Hawthorne (*The Scarlet Letter*) and H.L. Mencken campaigned against Winthrop's legacy, but the historian Matthew Holland is a bit more forgiving, calling Winthrop "at once a significant founding father of some of America's best and worst impulses" (Matthew Holland, *Bonds of Affection* [Washington, D.C.: Georgetown University Press, 2007], 2).

> We must vphold a familiar Commerce together in all
> meekenes, gentlenes, patience and liberality, wee must
> delight in eache other, make each others Condicions our
> owne, reioyce together, mourne together, labour and suffer
> together, allwayes hauing before our eyes our Commission
> and Community in the worke.

After the *Arbella* had anchored at Salem on 12 June 1630, John
and his deputy, Thomas Dudley, decided to redirect their charges to the
Shawmut Peninsula, where they founded what is today Boston. Some
two hundred colonists died in those first months,[248] including Henry
Winthrop (who drowned the day after his arrival), and in the spring of
1631 about a hundred returned to England.[249]

John wrote his wife at Groton in September that the colony had
suffered "much mortality, sickness and trouble," but, on a positive
note, God had "purged our corruptions, and healed the hardnesse and
error of our heartes, and stripped vs of our vaine confidence in this
arme of flesh, and he may haue us relye wholy vpon himselfe."[250] John
apparently tried to lead by example. One observer noted that upon
landing in New England, Winthrop "fell to worke with his owne hands,
& thereby soe encouradged the rest that there was not an Idle person
then to be found in the whole Plantation."[251] John was granted a tract

---

[248] Governor Thomas Dudley's letter to the Countess of Lincoln, March 1631, in Peter
Force, ed., *Tracts and Other Papers Relating Principally to the Origin, Settlement and
Progress of the Colonies in North America*, 4 vols. (Washington, privately printed, 1838;
rep. New York: Peter Smith, 1947), 2: 10. "And of the people who came over with
vs from the time of their setting saile from England in Aprill 1630, vntill December
followinge there dyed by estimacon about 200 at the least." John Winthrop wrote
his wife Margaret from Boston on 29 November 1630 that "we conceiue that this
disease grewe from ill diet at sea and proued infectious" (*Winthrop Papers*, 2: 320).

[249] *Winthrop Papers*, 2: 9. "Insomuch that the shipps being now vppon their returne,
some for England some for Ireland, there was as I take it not much less than an
hundred (some think many more) partly out of dislike of our government which
restrained and punished their excesses, and partly through feare of famine not seeing other means than by their labour to feed themselves."

[250] John Winthrop to Margaret Winthrop, *Winthrop Papers*, 2: 312–13.

[251] "Narrative concer[n]ing the Settlement of New England," dated 1629, transcribed
from a copy in the Public Record Office, London, for Winthrop, *Life and Letters*,
2: 30. Its unknown author says three- to four-hundred servants had been sent to
the colony to build and plant corn two years prior to the arrival of the Winthrop
Fleet, but "through Idleness & and ill Government," neglected their duties, which
prompted Winthrop to dig in as soon as he landed.

on the Mystic River, which he named Ten Hills Farm.[252] He owned one
of the colony's first boats, the three-masted *Blessing of the Bay*, using it
as a packet up and down the northern coast.[253]

In 1632, after the magistrates attempted to collect a tax from
each town to pay for mutual fortifications, a group demanded to see
the company charter. This document revealed that the governor was
supposed to be elected by the colony freemen (of which there were
116 in May 1631[254]), rather than be appointed by the magistrates.
Many felt Winthrop had assumed too much power, and they demanded
written laws, rather than simply the governor's judgment of the merits
of each case.[255] (Dudley especially felt Winthrop was too lenient.[256])
Issues of governance would cause recurring struggles over the next
twenty years. In 1645, after his acquittal of a charge of abuse of power,
John Winthrop provided in his defense the circular reasoning that
guided his views:[257]

> It is yourselves who have called us to this office, and being
> called by you, we have our authority from God, in way of
> an ordinance, such as hath the image of God eminently
> stamped upon it, the contempt and violation whereof
> hath been vindicated with examples of divine vengeance. I
> entreat you to consider, that when you choose magistrates,
> you take them from among yourselves, men subject like
> passions as you are. Therefore when you see infirmities
> in us, you should reflect upon your own, and that would

---

[252] Deed of John Winthrop to John Winthrop, Jr., 22nd of 7th mo. [September] 1643,
transcribed in *Winthrop Papers*, 4: 416, which includes a copy of a map sketched in
1637. See Bremer, *John Winthrop: America's Forgotten Founding Father*, 248–49. John
also owned the land that became Billerica, Governor's Island (named for him but
sold by the family in 1808 and now the site of Logan Airport), and Prudence Island
in Narragansett Bay.

[253] Savage, *The History of New England from 1630 to 1649*, 1: 69. "July 4 [1631:] The
governor built a bark at Mistick, which was launched this day, and called the *Blessing
of the Bay*." Later, on 31 August: "The governour's bark, called the *Blessing of the
Bay*, being of thirty tons, went to sea" (1: 72). See Bremer, *John Winthrop: America's
Forgotten Founding Father*, 252–53.

[254] Bremer, *John Winthrop: America's Forgotten Founding Father*, 209.

[255] In 1634, the General Court passed laws that banned smoking and the wearing of
lace, gold, embroidery, silver girdles, beaver hats and "new fashions, long hair or
anything of like nature" (Bremer, 246, citing John Noble, ed., *Records of the Court of
Assistants of the Colony of the Massachusetts Bay, 1630–1692*, 3 vols. [Boston: County
of Suffolk, 1901], 1: 126).

[256] Bremer, *John Winthrop: America's Forgotten Founding Father*, 216, 245.

[257] Savage, *The History of New England from 1630 to 1649*, 2: 228.

make you bear the more with us, and not be severe
censurers of the failings of your magistrates.

One reason Winthrop despaired of democracy was his desire to
hold the colony together. Almost from its founding, it exploded with
new arrivals. Some three thousand disembarked in 1638 alone, and by
1640, eighteen towns had been organized.[258] Many of these emigrants
were not "converted"; if they were believers, they did not share the
Puritanical belief that following religious laws, rather than God's grace,
was necessary for salvation. There were also disagreements between
those who wanted a clean break from the Church of England and others,
like Winthrop, who preferred to maintain ties. John clashed in particular
with Roger Williams (who felt the magistrates got their power from
the people, not God), although the two men liked and respected each
other and would maintain a lifelong correspondence. Williams was able
to flee to Rhode Island in 1635 after being warned by Winthrop that
he was about to be put on the next ship to England.[259]

Winthrop was less considerate of another new resident, Anne
Hutchinson, who in 1634 had moved in across the street from the
Winthrops. She had almost immediately begun criticizing the colony's
ministers as "legalists" who put too much emphasis on Old Testament
rules. In 1636, one of her admirers, a 23-year-old man who had only
recently arrived in New England, was elected governor. When Winthrop
was re-elected in 1637, he led the prosecution against Hutchinson,
whom he dismissed as an "American Jesabel." Hutchinson proved a
worthy intellectual adversary, and it was only when she claimed God
spoke to her directly that the court banished her from the Colony. After
her departure, a law was quickly passed requiring new community
members to be first approved by the magistrates.[260]

In February 1649, soon after the birth of a son with his fourth wife,
John Winthrop fell ill and was confined to bed with a fever and cough.
He died on 26 March and was buried on 13 April in the public cemetery
adjacent to what is now King's Chapel in Boston.[261] He had been forced in
1645 to sell much of his property after a manager he had hired to oversee

---

[258] Emerson, "John Winthrop," *American Colonial Writers, 1606–1734,* 24: 359.
[259] Francis Bremer, "John Winthrop (1588–1649)," *Oxford Dictionary of National Biography* (Oxford: Oxford University Press, 2004), online at *oxforddnb.com.*
[260] Emerson, "John Winthrop," *American Colonial Writers, 1606–1734,* 24: 357-58.
[261] Bremer, "John Winthrop (1588–1649)," *Oxford Dictionary of National Biography,* online at *oxforddnb.com.*

Ten Hills Farm put him £2,600 in debt,[262] so an inventory taken on 17 April 1649 values his possessions at only £103, with no real estate.[263] John did leave forty books to the library at Harvard College (founded in 1636) and a silver communion cup to the First Church in Boston.[264]

A contemporary, John Hull, lauded the late governor in his diary as "a man of great humility and piety, and excellent statesman, well skilled in the law, and of a public spirit."[265] In 1636, after John had briefly fallen out of favor and been voted out as governor, Israel Stoughton wrote to his brother in England that while Winthrop was "a godly man, & a worthy magistrate," the governor was "but a man, & some say they have idolized him, & do now confess their error."[266] More recently, Francis Bremer has argued that Winthrop was more flexible than his subsequent reputation. "While insisting on unity, he did not demand absolute uniformity in belief and practice, accepting a creative conversation on how the religious and secular goals of the society could best be accomplished," Bremer wrote. "His charity was not always evident, most notably in his dealings with Anne Hutchinson, but he was more understanding than many of his contemporaries of the need to adapt principles to the realities of the New World."[267]

---

[262] Bremer, *John Winthrop: America's Forgotten Founding Father*, 317. The overseer, James Luxford, had been convicted in 1639 of bigamy and in 1640 of "forgery, lying and other foul offenses."

[263] *Winthrop Papers*, 4: 147. On 25th of 4th mo. [June] 1641, he filed a codicil that read, "My estate becoming much decayed through the vnfaithfullness of my servant Luxford, so as I have been forced to sell some of my lands allrady, and must sell more for satisfaction of 2600*li* debts whereof I did not knowe of more than 300*li* when I intended this for my Testament, I am now forced to revoke it." He never wrote another and died intestate; an inventory was taken on 17th of 2nd mo. [April] 1649 (first transcribed in *Proceedings of the Massachusetts Historical Society*, 2nd series, 7 [1891]: 140–43 and reprinted in *Winthrop Papers*, 5: 333–37) and his widow and son Adam granted administration on 9th of the 3rd mo. [May] 1649 to "pay so farr as the estate will go." An earlier will dated at Groton on 10 May 1620 mentioned his wife Margaret, parents Adam and Anne Winthrop, and sons John, Adam, Henry, Forthe, and Stephen. Among other bequests, he left property to his wife, a legacy to his daughter Mary to be held by her grandfather Forthe until she turned 18, and £120 to his sister Luce Winthrop (*Winthrop Papers*, 1: 249-51). The names of his parents and sister had been partly erased, likely due, the editor noted, "to changes that had occurred in the six or seven years after the will was made" (1: 250–51fn).

[264] The books were destroyed when Harvard Hall burned in 1764. The cup, which measures nearly a foot high, is still owned by the church and on display in the American Wing at the Museum of Fine Arts in Boston.

[265] Hull, *Archaeologia Americana* 3 [1857]: 173.

[266] Capt. Israel Stoughton to Dr. Stoughton, undated, *Proceedings of the Massachusetts Historical Society*, 1st series, 5 [1861]:141.

[267] Bremer and Webster, *Puritans and Puritanism in Europe and America*, 1: 283.

In addition to his 1630 sermon aboard the *Arbella*, Winthrop is best remembered for the three-volume journal of some two hundred thousand words he began on the voyage[268] and continued until his death in 1649. His chronicle of the daily life of the settlement, for better or worse, became the basis for many early histories,[269] although it was not published until 1790, when Noah Webster offered a transcription of the first two volumes as *A Journal of the Transactions and Occurrences in the Settlement of Massachusetts and the Other New-England Colonies*. Bremer said of the diary:[270]

> Winthrop believed that the story of the Bay colony was one of success, and he narrates it as such. The wilderness is subdued, dissidents expelled, Indian plots circumvented, and threats from the royal government blunted. Yet the journal is not merely an apologia. Winthrop is aware of human frailty and is ready to admit it in himself and in other magistrates. Like other Puritan historians, he believed that since all happenings were the will of God, covering up events would be presumptuous and sinful.

The third volume, thought be lost, was discovered in 1816 in the Old South Church in Boston[271] and published with the first two by James Savage in 1825 and 1826 as *The History of New England from 1630–1649*.[272] The second notebook was destroyed by a fire in 1825

---

[268] Its first entry, dated 29 March 1630, begins, "Easter Monday. Riding at the Cowes near the Isle of Wight in the *Arbella*, a ship of 350 tons whereof Captain Peter Milborne was mater, being manned with 52 seamen and 28 pieces of ordnance." He expected to sail the next day but rough seas delayed the departure a week. See Dunn and Yeandle, *The Journal of John Winthrop, 1630–1649*, 13.

[269] Emerson, "John Winthrop," *American Colonial Writers, 1606–1734*, 24: 356.

[270] Bremer, "John Winthrop," *American Historians, 1607–1865*, 30: 343.

[271] Bremer, "John Winthrop," *American Historians, 1607–1865*, 30: 343. In 1755, the pastor of the church, Thomas Prince, borrowed the volumes from the Winthrop family to write his *Annals of New England,* but he apparently only returned the first two. The third was discovered fifty-eight years later among his papers (*Winthrop Papers*, 1: vii). See also *Proceedings of the Massachusetts Historical Society* 12 [1872]: 233–35.

[272] Mayo, *The Winthrop Family in America*, 293, commented: "Mr. Savage, a gentleman of wealth and position, was a tremendous worker; he needed to be, for the task he had set himself was prodigious. Winthrop's handwriting alone was enough to discourage any ordinary mortal; and in Savage's time it was not so easy as it is today to find biographical data for footnotes about the many individuals mentioned in the text." He was assisted in his task by James Bowdoin, formerly James Bowdoin[7] Winthrop.

in Savage's office, but the first and third survive at the Massachusetts Historical Society.[273]

Children of John[1] and Mary (Forth) Winthrop:

5   i. JOHN[2] WINTHROP, b. at Groton 12 Feb. 1605/6; m. (1) 8 Feb. 1630/31, MARTHA FONES; m. (2) 6 July 1635, ELIZABETH READE.

        ii. HENRY WINTHROP, b. 10,[274] bp. at Groton 19 Jan. 1607/8,[275] and drowned at Salem, Massachusetts Bay Colony 2 July 1630 attempting to retrieve an Indian canoe he and his companions had spotted on the opposite shore of a river.[276] Two weeks later, when his father relayed the tragic news in a letter to Groton,[277] he lamented,

---

[273] *Winthrop Papers*, 1: viii. See also Malcolm Freiberg, "The Winthrops and Their Papers," *Proceedings of the Massachusetts Historical Society* 80 [1969]: 59–60, who noted that Savage had transcribed the second volume and edited but not corrected his manuscript, meaning "we can never check the accuracy of his transcription."

[274] Entry by Adam[A] Winthrop in *Hopton's Almanack for 1614*, transcribed in *Winthrop Papers*, 1: 175: "10 [Jan.]. This day Henry W[inthrop] was borne 6 yeeres since. Anno 1607."

[275] Groton parish register, *Collections of the Massachusetts Historical Society*, 3rd series, 8 [1843]: 296. "1607. Hennery Winthropp the sonne of John Winthropp and of Mary his wife was baptised the 19th day of Januarye." In his diary, Adam Winthrop gives "The xxth of Jan. [1607/8] my soonnes second sonne Henry was Christened at Groton. Mr. [Henry] Sands and my b[rother John] Snelling were his godfathers" (*Winthrop Papers*, 1: 97). He was almost certainly named for Sands, who was a preacher at Boxford (Mayo, *The Winthrop Family in America*, 59).

[276] Savage, *The History of New England from 1630 to 1649*, 1: 29. "Friday, 2. The *Talbot* arrived there. She had lost fourteen passengers. My son Henry Winthrop was drowned at Salem." Some sources say Henry arrived on the *Talbot*, which may be a misreading of John Winthrop's 2 July entry. His 1 July entry read: "The *Mayflower* and the *Whale* arrived safe in Charlton harbor. Their passengers were all in health, but most of their cattle dead (whereof a mare and horse of mine" [Savage, *The History of New England from 1630 to 1649,* 1: 29]). The details of Henry's death were recorded in a commonplace book now in the Winthrop Family Papers at the Massachusetts Historical Society (reel 39). Early in the eighteenth century, John Still[5] Winthrop copied an account written by his father John[4] Winthrop: "He mett with his Fate the very day he went on Shore at New England, for arriving at Salem, he and the Principal Officers, passengers on the Ship went on Shoar and walked up near a Place now called by the Salemites Northfield to View the Indian Wigwams, and to see the manners, Customs, ways of living, and when they came there, they saw the other side of the River, that goes up to town, a Small Canoe, he would have one of the Company swim over and fetch the Canoe to carry them all on together, rather than walk several Miles on foot it being very hott weather and they Drowsy and fat, just coming from Tea, but none of the Company could swim but he, and rather than walk in the heat, striped himself and went to swim over the River was taken with a cramp a few rodds from the Shoar & drowned."

[277] Bremer, *John Winthrop: America's Forgotten Founding Father*, 433–34, noted it was possible John had not learned of Henry's death for a week, "since there is no mention of it in a letter to Margaret dated 8 July and the grief that spills forth in his letter of eight days later seems fresh."

"My sonne Henry, my sonne Henry, ah, poore child."[278] Henry had
m. at London 25 April 1629,[279] his first cousin ELIZABETH FONES,
who was b. at Groton 21 Jan. 1609/10, dau. of Thomas and Anne
(Winthrop) Fones.[280] The couple had one child, Martha Johanna[3]
Winthrop, bp. at Groton 9 May 1630.[281]

In his journal, John[1] Winthrop recalled that when Henry was
13, they were entering Boxford when the coachman was thrown
off, and the horses "ranne throughe the towne over logges and
highe stumpes untill they came upon the causye [causeway] right
against the Churche, and there were snarled in the logges, etc." The
coach was "broken into peeces toppe, botom and sides, yet by Gods
more mercifull providence we were all safe: blessed be his holy
name."[282]

Henry seems to have been the wildest of the brothers; Bremer
notes that his spelling and grammar suggest he alone did not
apply himself to his studies.[283] In Dec. 1626, at age 20, Henry
accompanied an English expedition to the West Indies, urged by
his family to "learn experience in mariner's affairs."[284] Arriving in
Feb. 1627, he found himself among "but three score of Christians
and 40 slaves of Negroes and Indians"[285] and agreed to stay for three
years in exchange for £100 annually and playments for whatever
servants he could bring to the islands. He found Barbados to be
"the pleasantest island in all the West Indies,"[286] and he expected
that he would soon send home five hundred pounds of tobacco,

[278] John Winthrop to Margaret Winthrop, 16 July 1630, *Winthrop Papers*, 2: 302.
[279] John Winthrop to Margaret Winthrop, 28 April 1629, *Winthrop Papers*, 2: 84. "They
        were married on Saturday last, and intende to staye with thee [in Groton] till to-
        wards the ende of the [Easter] Terme," which ended 18 May.
[280] Rubicam, *Register* 103 [1949]: 247. In his will of 14 April 1629, Thomas Fones
        committed the tuition for his son Samuel "unto his uncle John Wynthropp of
        Groton, Suffolk, Esq." and the tuitions of his daughters Elizabeth and Martha "unto
        my said loving brother John Wynthropp" (*Register* 50 [1896]: 397–98).
[281] Alicia Crane Williams, *Early New England Families, 1641–1700, Vol. 1* (Boston: New
        England Historic Genealogical Society, 2015), 110, 328. Martha[3] Winthrop later married
        Thomas Lyon. See Robert C. Winthrop, "Thomas Lyon, His Family and Connections,"
        Proceedings of the Massachusetts Historical Society, 2nd series, 6 [1890]: 1–38.
[282] "Experiencia," *Winthrop Papers*, 1: 237.
[283] Bremer, *John Winthrop: America's Forgotten Founding Father*, 129.
[284] Henry Winthrop to Emmanuel Downing (?), 22 August 1627, *Winthrop Papers*, 1:
        356–57. The letter is addressed to "most loving Vnkell."
[285] Henry Winthrop to John Winthrop, 15 October 1627, *Winthrop Papers*, 1: 361–62.
[286] Henry Winthrop to Emmanuel Downing (?), 22 August 1627, *Winthrop Papers*, 1:
        356–57.

or maybe even a thousand.[287] At Henry's request, John recruited several young men to go to Barbados as indentured servants and sent clothes, shoes, tools, knives and other supplies.[288] By Jan. 1629, his father's patience was running thin, as the promised tobacco (to be sold to pay for the supplies he had sent) was of poor quality and had been used to pay other creditors first. John said he could send no more money.[289]

Henry returned home, staying in London with his uncle, Thomas Fones, where he soon made a nuisance of himself, overrunning the house with his friends, including a "papist," and treating the home "like an Inne." Further, Henry's "hart I see is much too bigg for his estates," and he had purchased on credit "a skarlet suit and cloke which is lined through with plush." He also had "wooed and wonne" his cousin Elizabeth "Besse" Fones, and "they both pretend to have proceeded so far that there is no recalling of yt at least promise of Mariage and all without my knowledge or consent what grief this is to me. . . . I am weak and cannot I see now be master in myne owne howse."[290] Conveniently for the young lovers, Thomas Fones died soon after, and on 25 April 1629, just ten days after his funeral, the couple was married in London. John, who had come to London to sort out the family dramas but now had to stay for business, sent the newlyweds to Groton. He wrote his wife (Henry's stepmother) to tell her to "labour to keepe my sonne at home as much as thou canst, especially from Hadleigh," the nearest large town.[291] Over the summer Henry became interested in the Massachusetts Bay Company; he was going to make a trip to Barbados to close his affairs, but his father and John Jr. dissuaded him.[292] So in the spring of 1630 Henry was on his way to Boston with his father and at least one of his brothers.[293]

---

[287]   Henry Winthrop to John Winthrop, 15 October 1627, *Winthrop Papers*, 1: 361–62.

[288]   John Winthrop to John Winthrop, Jr., *Winthrop Papers*, 1: 381–82.

[289]   John Winthrop to Henry Winthrop, 30 January 1628/29, *Winthrop Papers*, 2: 67.

[290]   Thomas Fones to John Winthrop, 2 April 1629, *Winthrop Papers*, 2: 78–79.

[291]   John Winthrop to Margaret Winthrop, 28 April 1629, *Winthrop Papers,* 2: 84.

[292]   John Winthrop, Jr., to John Winthrop, 5 October 1629, *Winthrop Papers* 2: 155–56. "His Voyage will but gaine him Expenses and bee to noe purpose." Also, John Winthrop to John Winthrop, Jr., 9 October 1629, *Winthrop Papers*, 2: 156.

[293]   John Winthrop to Margaret Winthrop, 28 March 1630, *Winthrop Papers*, 2: 224. See note 254.

After Henry's death, his widow Elizabeth (Fones) Winthrop apparently stayed with her mother-in-law before traveling with her and 18-month-old Martha Johanna Winthrop to Boston in Nov. 1631. By 27 Jan. 1631/32,[294] Elizabeth had married Robert Feake, a former London goldsmith and an early proprietor of Watertown, who in 1640 moved his family to Greenwich, Connecticut (then under Dutch rule), where he was a joint owner.[295] In 1647, Feake left for an extended trip to England, leaving his family and affairs with William Hallett. Thomas Lyon wrote John[1] Winthrop on 14 April 1648 to report that, his "Father[in-law] beeing destracted" (i.e., suffering from mental illness), "thare were som complaints made Against them" about "their Liuing together" and that his mother-in-law "confesd senc she came here openly she is Maried to him [Hallett], is with Child by him."[296] John Winthrop, Jr., had to use his influence to clear up the situation, convincing the Governor of New Netherland to allow the couple, who had been summoned to Hartford to answer charges of adultery, to return to Dutch-controlled Greenwich.[297] Elizabeth (Fones) (Winthrop)

---

[294]   Savage, *The History of New England from 1630 to 1649,* 1: 68–69. In a journal entry on that date, he wrote, "Thence they came another high pointed rock, having a fair ascent on the west side, which they called Mount Feake, from one Robert Feake, who had married the governour's daughter-in-law."

[295]   Winthrop, *Proceedings of the Massachusetts Historical Society,* 2nd series, 6 [1890]: 3. After Feake returned to Watertown in 1642, and detained there by poor health, he left his estate under the care of Captain Daniel Patrick. Soon "a painful sensation was created in New England" when rumors circulated that Patrick and Mrs. Feake were having an affair. Captain Patrick was killed by a Dutch soldier in 1643, after which Lucy (Winthrop) Downing wrote to her nephew John Winthrop asking that he look after "my poor cosen Feakes" for "I haue not had opertunity to writ to her since she leeft the Bay, nor haue I heard of her but by others; and that only wich was no like to be for her good, or our comfort" (Lucy Downing to John Winthrop, 24 February 1642/43, *Winthrop Papers,* 4: 444).

[296]   Thomas Lion [Lyon] to John Winthrop, 14 April 1648, *Winthrop Papers,* 5: 214–15.

[297]   Robert C. Winthrop, Jr., in "Remarks on Thomas Lyon, his Family and Connections," *Proceedings of the Massachusetts Historical Society,* 2nd series, 6 [1890]: 3, claimed Elizabeth's situation caused a scandal in part because William Hallet "was inferior in station." However, the historian Missy Wolfe, in *Insubordinate Spirit: A True Story of Life and Loss in Earliest America, 1610–1665* (Guilford, Conn.: Globe Pequot, 2012), 136–37, notes the complex legal issues of Elizabeth's marital status caused havoc in the "infantile judicial systems" of the colonies. On 21 July 1648, Connecticut's governor, Theophilus Eaton, reported to John Winthrop, Jr.: "It is possible that William Hallett and she that was mr. Feakes his wife, are maryed, though not onely the lawfulnes and validitie of such a mariage, but the reallity and truth is by some questioned" (*Winthrop Papers,* 5: 238). John asked Eaton to assist Elizabeth in her claims on Robert Feake's estate (her brother-in-law Toby Feake and son-in-law Thomas Lyon were seeking administrative control) and in reply Eaton expressed sympathy

(Feake) Hallett was living on 10 Jan. 1652/53, the date of her last surviving letter to John Winthrop, Jr.,[298] and had died by 9 June 1669, as on that date William Hallett had a wife named Susannah.[299]

iii.   FORTH(E) WINTHROP, b. at Stambridge, Essex 30 Dec. 1609,[300] bp. at Great Stambridge 10 Jan. 1609/10,[301] and bur. at Groton 23 Nov. 1630.[302]

Forth attended the grammar school in Bury St. Edmunds; two letters survive that he wrote from Groton in 1622 to his brother John, Jr., then attending university in Dublin.[303] In 1626,

---

for her situation but added a complaint about her "injurious writings" to him "desiring God may give her true repentance for greater miscariages" (*Winthrop Papers*, 5: 300), noting that, earlier, she had allowed her children to be "if not naked, very vnsatisfyingly apparraled" (*Winthrop Papers*, 3: 239). With the couple each facing arrest by Connecticut authorities for adultery, John persuaded the governor of New Netherland, Peter Stuyvesant, to allow the Hallets to return to Dutch-controlled Greenwich. Stuyvesant may have allowed the couple to marry under Dutch law, but it seems more likely John, Jr., a magistrate, quietly united them in New London before they fled. In an undated letter to John "from abord the vessell," written about June 1649, Elizabeth signed herself as "Elizabeth Hallett"; the letter was endorsed by John Winthrop as from "Sister Feakes" (*Winthrop Papers*, 5: 348). She next wrote him on 6 August 1649 from Greenwich; John endorsed this letter "Mrs. Hallett." (5: 358–59). In an undated letter to Stuyvesant, John described William Hallett as "industrious and carefull," by which perhaps he meant discreet (*Winthrop Papers*, 5: 338). See also George E. McCracken, "The Feake Family of Norfolk, London, and Colonial America," *Record* 86 [1955]: 212–20, and Donald Lines Jacobus, "That Winthrop Woman Again!" *Record* 97 [1966]: 131–34.

298   *Winthrop Papers*, 6: 239–40.

299   Williams, *Early New England Families, 1641–1700*, 1: 100; McCracken, *Record* 86 [1955]: 219–20. See also John Ross Delafield, *Delafield: The Family History of Brig. Gen. John Ross Delafield*, 2 vols. (New York: Privately printed, 1945), 2: 483–86.

300   Adam Winthrop journal, *Winthrop Papers*, 1: 103. "The xxxth day of Decembre my sonnes third sonne was born at Stambridge in Essex." A later entry by Adam in *Hopton's Almanack for 1614* (1: 178), gives "30 [December] Forthe Winthrop was borne 1609." The page on which his baptism would have been recorded in the parish register of St. Mary and All Saints Church is missing in a scan of the original (D/P 218/1/1) at *essexcc.gov.uk*.

301   Robert Charles Anderson, "Even the Best of Families . . .," *Great Migration Newsletter* 4 [1993]: 1, citing Great Stambridge parish register. "Remarkably, these baptisms, whose location is so clearly pointed to by Adam Winthrop, do not appear in Mayo [*The Winthrop Family in America*] or in any other published account of the Winthrop family so far encountered." The pages on which the baptisms would have been recorded in the parish register of St. Mary and All Saints Church are missing in a scan of the original (D/P 218/1/1) at *essexcc.gov.uk*.

302   Groton parish register, *Collections of the Massachusetts Historical Society*, 3rd series, 8 [1843]: 297. "Mrs. [*sic*] Forth Wintropp buried 23d November." In a footnote, James Savage noted that because "we had never heard before of the marriage of Forth Winthrop," the prefix was a transcription error.

303   Forthe Winthrop to John Winthrop, Jr., 2 September 1622, *Winthrop Papers*, 1: 273–74.

Forth enrolled at Emmanuel College at Cambridge. He hoped
to study theology and "began writing to his brother John and
father in Latin and referred to the 'hallowed halls and chapels' of
the university," Bremer noted.[304] But his father's perception that
he might be waffling about the ministry and, more seriously, the
family's shortage of funds, led Forth to withdraw in the summer of
1629.[305] About the same time he fell in love with Ursula Sherman,
whose mother was the second wife of Gov. Winthrop's brother-
in-law, close enough that the two called each other "cousin." They
apparently planned to marry and emigrate to New England,[306] but
Forth fell suddenly ill and died at Groton in Nov. 1630, only a
few months after his older brother Henry had drowned in New
England.

   "I did not expect the ende of his dayse had bine so neere,"
Margaret Winthrop wrote to John, Jr. "If I had I would haue sent
for you, to haue taken your last leaue of him."[307] A letter dated 18
June 1631 survives from Ursula Sherman in response to John, Jr.,
who had written to say he planned to repay some of the money
collected from well-wishers in London for their marriage. Her
words were gracious but pleading. Although her "much desired
match with your dearest brother" was not to be, she wrote, and
"though the Lord should greatly increase your estate by the loss of
my dearest friend . . . yet I shall never think my love ill settled upon
me, that loved me so dearly, though he could leave me nothing

---

After a lengthy discourse about God's love and salvation, he added, "But I shall
forget to wright to you of the things which I haue to write: for as concerning your
wrighting to me about my going to bury: I am not yet gone thither but I purpose
by gods grace for to goe about next Ester it may be sooner or later." In a subsequent
letter dated the same month he thanked his brother for his encouragement "to goe
on in the corse of learning, and shewed me the reason off it: *nam sine doctrina vita
est quasi mortis imago* ['Without learning, life is but the image of death.'—Dionysius
Cato]." See *Winthrop Papers*, 1: 329–30, for a short note from Forth in Cambridge
to John "at his fathers house in Groton" dated in July 1626, in which he apologizes
for not having written.

[304] Bremer, *John Winthrop: America's Forgotten Founding Father*, 131, citing Forth
Winthrop to John Winthrop, Jr. [1628], *Winthrop Papers*, 1: 392–94.

[305] Bremer, *John Winthrop: America's Forgotten Founding Father*, 131, citing John Winthrop
to Margaret Winthrop, 5 June 1629, *Winthrop Papers*, 2: 94–95. "I receiused a letter
from Forthes Tutor, wherein he complaynes of his longe absence, which he fines
doth him much hurte, both in his learning and manners. . . . If he intendes not the
ministerye, I haue no great minde to sende him any more."

[306] Mayo, *The Winthrop Family in America*, 62.

[307] Margaret Winthrop to John Winthrop, Jr., about 29 November 1630, *Winthrop
Papers* 2: 321–22.

but his prayers." She documented how the money already sent had
been quickly spent. Not to worry, she said, because she was putting
her faith in "the will of God," and "I do not mention any of this to
press you, good brother."[308]

    iv. MARY WINTHROP, bp. at Great Stambridge 19 Feb. 1611/12[309]
and d. at Salisbury, Mass. 12th of 2nd mo. [April] 1643. (Her son
Samuel, then about four years old, d. five days later.)[310] She m. by 14
Oct. 1632 (when she was identified as "Mary, the wife of Samuel
Dudley" in the membership records of the First Church, Boston)[311]
SAMUEL DUDLEY, who was bp. at All Saints' Church, Northampton,
Northamptonshire 30 Nov. 1608, son of Thomas and Dorothy
(Yorke) Dudley,[312] with whom she had five children.[313] Samuel d.
at Exeter, N.H. before 10 Feb. 1682/83, when the inventory was
taken on his estate,[314] and, by one account, "was probably interred

---

[308] Ursula Sherman to John Winthrop, Jr., 18 June 1631, *Winthrop Papers*, 3: 39–40.

[309] Anderson, *Great Migration Newsletter*, 4: 1, citing Great Stambridge parish register.
Williams, *Early New England Families, 1641–1700*, 1: 73, has 19 January 1611/12.
The page on which her baptism would have been recorded in the parish register of
St. Mary and All Saints Church is missing in a scan of the original (D/P 218/1/1)
at *essexcc.gov.uk*.

[310] *Vital Records of Salisbury, Massachusetts, to the End of the Year 1849* (Topsfield, Mass.:
Topsfield Historical Society, 1915), 550.

[311] Robert J. Dunkle and Ann S. Lainhart, *Records of the First Church in Boston* (CD-
ROM) (Boston: New England Historic Genealogical Society, 2001), 3, online at
americanancestors.org. In a letter received by John Winthrop, Jr. on 12 October 1632,
Edward Howes sent his regards to "Mr. Dudley and his beloued" (*Winthrop Papers*,
3: 85).

[312] Robert Charles Anderson, *The Great Migration Begins: Immigrants to New England,
1620–1633*, 3 vols. (Boston: New England Historic Genealogical Society, 1995), 1:
584. Thomas Dudley (1576–1653) served as deputy governor of Massachusetts Bay
Colony under John[1] Winthrop and as governor in 1634, 1640, 1645, and 1650. He
removed to Ipswich about 1634 and raised his grandsons John and Thomas Dudley,
sons of Samuel and Mary (Winthrop) Dudley, after their mother's death. In his will,
dated 26 April 1652, Thomas left Samuel's children part of his mill, house, and acreage at Watertown. But in a codicil dated 13 April 1653, he wrote that "whereas my
sonne Samuell Dudley, hath beene importunate with me to mayntaine his sonne
Thomas at ye colledge at Cambridge" until August 1654, he would do so, but that
the education of his younger children compelled him to revoke the Watertown bequest as well as £20 to Thomas and £45 to John. However, "because it is not equall
that John Dudley aforesaid (who hath been servisable to me) should lost any thing
by my benefycence to his brother," he gave John the interest in the Watertown
property (*Register* 5 [1851]: 295–97).

[313] Williams, *Early New England Families, 1641–1700*, 1: 77–78.

[314] Albert Stillman Batchellor, ed., *Probate Records of the Province of New Hampshire, Vol.
1, 1635–1717*, vol. 31 of *[New Hampshire] State Papers Series*, 40 vols. (1867–1943),
262. Elizabeth Dudley, widow of Mr. Samuel Dudley, testified on 1 March 1682/83
that she had "agreed with the Children of the Said dudly for my dowery" and re-

in the burial ground west of the road from the court-house to New-Market."[315]

Samuel Dudley had come to New England in 1630, at age 21, in the Winthrop Fleet with his parents, brother, and four sisters. On 5 Aug. 1633, shortly after he and Mary Winthrop were married, he was granted (at 1½ acres in the cow yards and subsequently received 4 acres of meadow and 3 acres between "Charls Town Path and the Comon Pales";[316] by 10 Oct. 1635, he owned a house and five parcels.[317] He was among the founders of Ipswich (1635) and, in 1638, of Colchester (later Salisbury).[318]

A series of letters from early 1636 from Mary (Winthrop) Dudley in Ipswich to her stepmother Margaret Winthrop in Boston survive in which Mary, then with two boys under age three, complained of the troubles she was having with a disobedient maid whom her parents had apparently hired for her:[319]

> At her first comminge to me she carried her selfe dutifully as became a servant; but since through mine and my husbands forebearance towards her for small faults, shee hath got such a head and is growen soe insolent, that her carriage towards vs especially myselfe is vnsufferable. If I bid her doe a thing shee will beid me to do it mys selfe.... If I should write to you of all the reviling speeches, and filthie language shee hath vsed towards me I should but greiue you. My husband hath vsed all meanes for

---

fused administration in favor of her "sonn in Lawe" Theophilus Dudley. The value of the estate was £641.12.

[315] J. Farmer and J.B. Moore, eds., *Collections, Historical and Miscellaneous: and Monthly Literary Journal*, 3 vols. (Concord, N.H., 1823), 2: 238. The site "has for many years past been improved as a pasture, or for tillage; the ancient monuments having been broken down, and probably converted to what was considered valuluble purposes, as a neighbor to the ground informed an inquirer that 'they make excellent whet-stones.'" Writing in 1856, the unnamed author of "Governor Thomas Dudley and His Descendants," *Register* 10 [1856]: 135, noted there "yet stands an old table tombstone supposed to have been his; but the inscription is gone," and that "a fragment of it, with the syllable 'Sam' still legible," was owned by a relative in 1848.

[316] *The Records of the Town of Cambridge (formerly Newtowne) Massachusetts, 1630–1703* (Cambridge, 1901), 5, 13, 16.

[317] *The Register Book of the Lands and Houses in the "New Towne" and the Town of Cambridge* (Cambridge, Mass., 1896), 31.

[318] Joseph B. Felt, *History of Ipswich, Essex and Hamilton* (Cambridge, Mass.: Charles Folsom, 1934), 72; Shurtleff, *Records of the Governor and Company of the Massachusetts Bay in New England, 1628–1686*, 1: 237, 277.

[319] Mary Dudley to Margaret Winthrop, ca. January 1635/36, *Winthrop Papers*, 3: 221.

to reforme her, reasons and perswasions, but shee doth professe that her heart and her nature will not suffer her to confesse her faults. If I tell my husband of her behauiour towards me, vpon examination shee will denie all that shee hath done or spoken, so that we know not how to proceede against her: but my husband now hath hired another maide and is resolved to put her away the next weeke.

It appears the servant agreed to leave, as Mary wrote Margaret on 15 Jan. to say she would need a new maid by the first week of that month, as "myne is then to goe away." In the same letter, Mary reported she had been ill with a toothache and asked for Margaret to send five yards of flowered holland, tape to bind it, and fine thread.[320] Mary wrote her brother John, Jr., on 26 Feb. to thank him for the sugar he sent and "pray thanke my father for my parsnips and pray my mother to send me as much cloth as will make [her son] John 3 shirtes."[321] On 28 March she wrote Margaret to remind her about the maid,[322] and prodded again in early April, asking that her stepmother locate "a good lusty seruant that hath skille in a dairy" and to let her know how much in wages she and her father were willing to pay. She added, "I would pray you to send me a childs chaire for I can get none made hear . . . John [then about nine months old] begins to brake out with heat. I would pray you send me that that you think fit will do him good: he hath two teeth already."[323]

Mary wrote a few weeks later, on 28 April, to say "I shall continue to be a troublesome suter to you, in the behalf of a mayd. . . . I am ashamed of my boldness . . . I desire the mayd that you provide me may be one that hath been vused to all kind of work, and must refuse none."[324] In a letter from about June 1636, she did not mention the maid (who apparently had been procured), but did ask

[320] Mary Dudley to Margaret Winthrop, 15 January 1635[/36], *Winthrop Papers*, 3: 222–23. Kathleen A. Staples and Madelyn Shaw, *Clothing through American History: The British Colonial Era* (Santa Barbara, Calif.: Greenwood, 2013), 275, note, "the use of flowered holland suggests that the garment was for informal wear."

[321] Mary Dudley to John Winthrop, Jr., 26 February 1635/36, *Winthrop Papers*, 3: 228–29.

[322] Mary Dudley to Margaret Winthrop, 28 March 1636, *Winthrop Papers* 3: 239.

[323] Mary Dudley to Margaret Winthrop, ca. April 1636, *Winthrop Papers*, 3: 242.

[324] Mary Dudley to Margaret Winthrop, 28 April 1636, *Winthrop Papers*, 3: 257.

Margaret to send fabric and sugar, adding, "I am ashamed to be thus continually troublesome to you but your readinesse to fulfill my desires imboldens me thus to do." In a postscript she wrote, "I pray you send me some sope. I can get none in this towne, and some fruit. My child growes but not very fast."[325] (Both John[3] Dudley and his elder brother Thomas survived their mother but died as young adults, unmarried.) After Mary's death, Samuel m. (2) prob. by Feb. 1644 (first child bp. 31st of 8th mo. [Oct.] 1644), Mary Byley/Biley.[326] In 1650, he was invited to become the minister in Exeter for £40 per year in corn and English commodities and the use of a house, parcel, and an old cow-house.[327] He m. (3) by 1651, Elizabeth _____, who was b. about 1628[328] and died after 16 Nov. 1702, when she was called "Mother Dudley" in a deed that said she was living with the family of her son-in-law, Moses Leavitt.[329]

   v.   ANNE WINTHROP, b. 3, bp. at Groton 8,[330] and d. 17 Aug. 1614.[331]

  vi.   ANNE WINTHROP, bp. at Groton 26[332] and bur. there 29 June 1615, three days after her mother.[333]

---

[325] Mary Dudley to Margaret Winthrop, ca. June 1636, *Winthrop Papers*, 3: 263.

[326] J. Henry Lea, "The English Ancestry of the Families of Batt and Byley of Salisbury, Mass.," *Register* 52 [1898]: 50.

[327] Charles H. Bell, *History of the Town of Exeter, New Hampshire* (Exeter, 1888), 158–59.

[328] She was 43 in 1671, according to Sybil Noyes, Charles T. Libby, and Walter G. Davis, *Genealogical Dictionary of Maine and New Hampshire* (Portland, Me.: The Southward Press, 1928), 209. See also Marston Watson, *Royal Families: Americans of Royal and Noble Descent*, 3 vols., 2nd ed. (Baltimore: Genealogical Publishing Co., 2002–7), 1: 5. "She may have been the daughter of a Richard Smith, but the evidence is lacking."

[329] Williams, *Early New England Families, 1641–1700*, 1: 72–73. On 1 March 1682/83, she notified the Governor of New Hampshire that she had "agreed with the Children of Said dudly for my dowery."

[330] Groton parish register, *Collections of the Massachusetts Historical Society*, 3rd series, 8 [1843]: 297. "1614. Anna Winthropp the daughter of John Winthrop Esqre. was baptised the 8th day of August."

[331] Adam Winthrop, in *Hopton's Almanac for 1614*, transcribed in *Winthrop Papers*, 1: 177. "17 [Aug.] Anna W died. 14 d olde." A transcription of Groton parish register in *Collections of the Massachusetts Historical Society*, 3rd series, 8 [1843]: 297, gives a burial date of 26 June 1614.

[332] Groton parish register, *Collections of the Massachusetts Historical Society*, 3rd series, 8 [1843]: 296. "1615. Anna Winthropp the daughter of John Winthbrop Esq. was baptised the the [sic] 26th of June." Mayo, 32, has a birth of 26 June.

[333] Groton parish register, *Collections of the Massachusetts Historical Society*, 3rd series, 8 [1843]: 297. "1615. Mrs. Mary Winthropp the first wife of John Winthrope Esq. was buryed the 26th day of June. Anna Winthrop her daughter was buryed the 29th day of June."

Child of John¹ and Thomasine (Clopton) Winthrop:

vii. DAUGHTER, b. at Groton 30 Nov. and bur. there 2 Dec. 1616.³³⁴ After Thomasine (Clopton) Winthrop died on 8 Dec., the infant was "taken up" and reburied on 11 Dec. with her mother.³³⁵

Children of John¹ and Margaret (Tyndal) Winthrop:

viii. COLONEL STEPHEN/STEVEN² WINTHROP, M.P., b. 24 March 1618/19,³³⁶ bp. at Groton 31 March 1619,³³⁷ and d. at London, Middlesex between 3 May (date of will) and 19 Aug. 1658 (will probated).³³⁸ He m. by 7 Nov. 1644 (birth in Boston of the eldest of at least eight children),³³⁹ JUDITH RAINSBOROUGH, who was bp. at Wapping, Middlesex 14 Sept. 1614, dau. of William and Judith (Hoxton) Rainsborough.³⁴⁰ She d. after 14 April 1657, when Stephen mentioned her in a letter to his brother John, Jr.³⁴¹

---

³³⁴ Groton parish register, *Collections of the Massachusetts Historical Society*, 3rd series, 8 [1843]: 297. "1616. A younge child of John Winthrop Esq. was buried the second of December." John Winthrop, in "Death of Thomasine Clopton Winthrop, 1616," *Winthrop Papers*, 1: 190, calls the child "a daughter."

³³⁵ "Death of Thomasine Clopton Winthrop, 1616," *Winthrop Papers*, 1: 190.

³³⁶ "Experiencia," *Winthrop Papers*, 1: 235. "On Wensdaye the 24th of Marche 1618[/19] Margaret my wife was delivered of a sonne, whereof I desire to leave this testimonye of my thankfulnesse unto God, that she being above 40 houres in sore travayle, so as beganne to be doubtful of hir life, yet the Lord sent hir a safe deliverance. Heerby I had occasion to finde the great power and benefite of prayer." Adam Winthrop, in his "Note on Adam and Stephen Winthrop," *Winthrop Papers*, 1: 256, calls Steven the elder brother of Adam. "The Ladye Anne Tindal was their grandmother. . . . Shee was godmother vnto Steuen, and Mr. Steuen Egerton her brother, and Mr. Deane Tindal her sonne were his godfathers."

³³⁷ Groton parish register, *Collections of the Massachusetts Historical Society*, 3rd series, 8 [1843]: 296. "1619. Steven the son of John Winthrop Esqre. and Margaret his 3d wife was baptised the last daie of March."

³³⁸ Will of Stephen Winthrop, 1658, transcribed in Muskett, *Evidences of the Winthrops of Groton*, 20–21, citing P.C.C. 418 Wotton. He names wife Judith (then pregnant); daughters Margarett, Johanna, and Judith; nephew Adam Winthrop, son of his brother Adam; brother Deanes and Samuel and half-brother John Winthropp; and "cousins" [nieces by marriage] Mary Raineborowe and Judith Chamberlaine. He also left £100 to the poor of Boston "upon condition that the Inhabitants of Boston aforesaid doe build and erect a Tombe or Monument . . . for my deceased father and Mother upon their grave or graves of £50 value at the least, who now lyeth att Boston aforesaid."

³³⁹ Mayo, *The Winthrop Family in America*, 67.

³⁴⁰ Waters, *Genealogical Gleanings in England*, 1: 170.

³⁴¹ Stephen Winthrop to John Winthrop, Jr., 14 April 1657, *Collections of the Massachusetts Historical Society*, 5th series, 8 [1882], 217–18. "I thanck God my wife and & all of vs are indifferent well at this time, though I have not my health longe together here. [The] eyre is two moist for me & breeds rumes & coughes." He also mentioned an

In a daybook Adam[A] Winthrop kept in 1621, he noted his grandson, then about two-and-a-half, had fallen into a fire but "had had no hurt."[342] In a letter written when Stephen was nearly 11, his father John described him and his brother Adam as "lusty trauaylers [travelers]."[343] But Mayo observed that Stephen appears to have suffered with the same introspection that dogged his father as a young man. When Stephen was nearly 14, his father would recount that "Satan buffeted him" with temptations and "blasphemous and wicked thoughts."[344] He was saved by prayer, and on 16 March 1634, just a few days before his fifteenth birthday, he was admitted to the Boston church.[345] In the spring of 1636 he spent time at Saybrook, Conn., visiting his half-brother John. Soon after he returned to England, then came back to New England in the summer of 1638 (presumably staying with his aunt and uncle Downing). He arrived in early Oct. and before winter set in had established himself as a merchant in Boston; soon after 28 Dec. he left for a trading voyage to Bermuda aboard the *Sparrow*.[346]

He had returned by 9 Sept. 1639, when the General Court in Boston noted that "Mr. Steven Winthrope was chosen to record things."[347] His duties were described by a contemporary: "Master Stephen Winthrop is Recorder, whose office is to record all Judgments, Mariages, Births, Deaths, Wills and Testaments, Bargaines and Sales, Gifts, Grants and Mortgages."[348] In Oct. 1640, perhaps because Stephen had been grumbling about his

---

unnamed son, who is "yet but a litle one, not above two monthes old." The letter was endorsed "Col. Steven Winthrop."

[342] "Allestree's Almanack, 1621," *Winthrop Papers*, 1: 259.

[343] John Winthrop to Margaret Winthrop, 27 February 1629/30, *Winthrop Papers*, 2: 212.

[344] Savage, *The History of New England from 1630 to 1649*, 1: 125 (entry dated 7 March 1633).

[345] Justin Winsor, ed., *The Memorial History of Boston*, 4 vols. (Boston: James R. Osgood & Co., 1881), 1: 568. "The 16th of ye same [first] Moneth [March] [1634], Stephen Winthrop, of ye sonnes of our brother John Winthrop, Governor."

[346] J. Hammond Trumbull, ed., "Note-book Kept by Thomas Lechford, Esq., Lawyer, in Boston, Massachusetts Bay," *Archaeologia Americana* 7 [1885]: 46. In a document dated 20 December 1638 (and translated here by Trumbull from the original Latin), Governor John Winthrop gave license to Stephen Winthrop, merchant, and William Goose, commander of the *Sparrowe*, 50 tons' burden with seven crew members, "to sail to those Islands called the Summers Islands, otherwise Bermudas, and there do business with the inhabitants of that region."

[347] Shurtleff, *Records of the Governor and Company of the Massachusetts Bay in New England, 1628–1686*, 1: 276.

[348] J. Hammond Trumbull, ed., *Plain Dealing or News from New England, by Thomas Lechford* (Boston: J.K. Wiggin & Wm. Parsons Lunt, 1867), 86 (page 38 of 1642 original).

workload, the Court assigned the registration of deeds to offices at Ipswich and Salem. In 1641, he joined the Military Company of Massachusetts and in spring 1644, at age 25, became a regular member of the General Court, representing Strawberry Bank (now an historic district in Portsmouth, N.H.).[349]

By the winter of 1644–45, Stephen had returned to London, where an alderman, unhappy with a court decision made in Massachusetts Bay, ordered him arrested. Alderman Berkeley insisted that Winthrop and Capt. Joseph Weld, who had been a member of the jury, produce sureties of £4,000 "to answer him in the court of admiralty." Stephen attempted to get the General Court in Boston to reimburse his expenses, without luck. By the summer of 1645, he was back in New England and in June bought 1,500 acres in Lynnfield and Danvers, which included what is today known as Suntaug Lake.[350] Writing to his mother from London, he commented on stern measures during Mass in dealing with Baptists: "It doth discourage any people from coming to us for fear they should be banished if they dissent from us in opinion."[351] When his father died in 1649, he inherited the Boston homestead that would become the site of the Old South Meeting-house and half of Prudence Island in Narragansett Bay, although he would never return to see either. In 1654, Roger Williams described him as being "eminent for maintaining the Freedome of Conscience as to matters of Beliefe, Religion and Worship."[352]

He returned to England once more, this time with his brother Samuel, his sixth and final voyage overseas. After a year, he was ready to return, but his business ventures had not gone as planned and his creditors would not allow him to leave. He sent word to his wife to come to London.[353] In the meantime, he kept company with his brother-in-law, Colonel William Rainsborow, who had lived in Massachusetts Bay but was now the Governor of Worcester

[349] Shurtleff, *Records of the Governor and Company of the Massachusetts Bay in New England, 1628–1686,* 3: 1–2.

[350] Mayo, *The Winthrop Family in America,* 65.

[351] Stephen Winthrop to Margaret Winthrop, ca. 1645, *Collections of the Massachusetts Historical Society,* 5th series, 8 [1882]: 200.

[352] Roger Williams to John Winthrop, Jr., 12 July 1654, *Winthrop Papers,* 6: 402.

[353] Stephen Winthrop to John Winthrop, 29 July 1647, *Winthrop Papers,* 5: 174. "It hath pleased God to [thwart] all my purposes and endeavors to come back to N.E. at present. Neither my vnckle nor myself cann find out any means to sattisfie our creditors though they are not many."

in England. "Partly because he believed in the cause and partly because it would provide him with a living, he joined Cromwell's army and was made 'captain of a troop of horse,'" Mayo wrote.[354] In the summer of 1648, Stephen found himself fighting the Scots in the north of England. By September he was back in London, where both of his two young sons had recently died.[355] A few months earlier, when Deal Castle was surprised by the Royalists, his wife and "all their children" fled to Harwich "and so to Ipswich, and then to London, for fear of Goring's army."

Stephen still planned to take his family back to New England. In a letter to his brother John dated 14 July 1650, he wrote, "I expect not to setle in England but to returne Amongst you when I may not be burdensome, but rather helpfull."[356] Of England, he said in 1653 that his "much lying in ye wet feilds vppon the grownd" during military campaigns had left him with "extremely troubled with the *zeatica*" and that he was on his way to Bath to seek relief: "It makes my life very vncomfortable."[357] In 1657, he complained that the "eyre is two moist for me, & breeds rumes & coughes"[358] Yet his memories of the winters in Boston were not encouraging, and he admitted in in March 1655, "I doe not give over thoughts of N.E."[359] About 1654, Stephen, who lived with his family on James Street in Westminster, became a colonel, and in 1656 he was elected to represent Banff and Aberdeen in Parliament, although he

---

[354] *Ibid.* "Providence opening a way of imployment in the Army, I have accepted of it seeing noe dore open to me any else of being serviceable in my generation." In a letter from John Winthrop to John, Jr., dated 28th of 8th mo. [October] 1646, he reported that "your brother hath sent againe for his wife, and it seemes means to stay in Engl. with his brother Rainsb[orough] who is gou[ernou]r of Worster, and he is Capt. of a Troope of horse: the Army intended for Ireland, is putt off, I suppose it is vpon the Kings refusing to Comply with the Parl[ia]ment which is all the newes we have, except that the sicknesse beganne to spread much in London" (*Winthrop Papers,* 5: 114).

[355] Elizabeth French, "Winthrop," *Register* 69 [1915]: 188, citing burial records from the 1648 register of St. Dunstan's Church, Stepney, Middlesex: "John son of Steven Winthropp of Ratcliff, gent., and wife Judith buried 9 August" and "Steven son of Steven Winthropp of Ratcliff, gent., and wife Judith buried 14 August." Ratcliff was on the Thames, about 2 miles southeast of St. Paul's, London. Mayo (*The Winthrop Family in America,* 67) gives Stephen as born at Boston 7 November 1644 and John born at Boston 24 May 1646; he attributed their deaths to smallpox.

[356] Stephen Winthrop to John Winthop, Jr., 14 July 1650, *Winthrop Papers,* 6: 50.

[357] Stephen Winthrop to John Winthrop, Jr., 2 August 1653, *Winthrop Papers,* 6: 317–18.

[358] Stephen Winthrop to John Winthrop, Jr., 14 April 1657, *Collections of the Massachusetts Historical Society,* 5th series, 8 [1882]: 218.

[359] Stephen Winthrop to John Winthrop, Jr., 11 March 1654/55, *Collections of the Massachusetts Historical Society,* 5th series, 8 [1882]: 216.

would only serve two years before his early death, when he was not yet 40.[360]

ix.   ADAM WINTHROP, b. at Groton about 1 a.m. on 7[361] and bp. there 9 April 1620.[362] He d. at Boston 24 Aug. 1652.[363] Adam m. (1) shortly before 10 Oct. 1642,[364] ELIZABETH GLOVER, dau. of the Rev. Joseph/Josse Glover of Sutton, Surrey, and Sarah (Owfield) Glover.[365] Elizabeth d. 14 Sept. 1648[366] at Governor's Island in Boston Harbor, which had been a wedding present to Adam from

---

[360]   Mayo, *The Winthrop Family in America*, 66.

[361]   "Experiencia," *Winthrop Papers*, 1: 237. 1620: "Aprill 7: beinge frydaye. About one of the clocke in the morninge Adam my sonne was borne. I have cause for ever to remember the goodnesse of the Lo: and the power of prayer, for my wife beinge in longe and very difficult travaile I humbled my selfe in earnest prayer to God for hir, and beinge in the next chamber, as I arose from prayer I heard the child crye." See also Adam Winthrop entry in *Allestree's Almanack, 1620*, transcribed in *Winthrop Papers*, 1: 244, which he may have prepared as a gift for his grandson, John² Winthrop, then about 14 years old. "[April] 7. Adam Winthrop was borne. 9. This day he was baptized and his brother Steuen weaned." In "Adam Winthrop's Note on Adam and Stephen Winthrop," *Winthrop Papers*, 1: 256, he calls Adam his "second soonne" and says he was born in Groton on Friday, 7 April 1620, and "baptised by Mr. Nicholson the parson of Groton and named Adam by Adam Wintrop his grandfather, Philip Goslin the elder, Jane Goslin his fathers sister and Mary Cole the wife of Joseph Cole, who were his godfathers and godmothers." He added that "Margaret their mother nursed the younger, and not the elder." In *Allestree's Almanack for 1621* (transcribed in *Winthrop Papers*, 1: 258), grandfather Adam noted that on 7 May "Adam Winthrop was weaned."

[362]   Groton parish register, *Collections of the Massachusetts Historical Society*, 3rd series, 8 [1843]: 297. "1620. Adam the sonne of John Winthropp Esquire was baptised the 9ᵗʰ of April."

[363]   *A Report of the Record Commissioners Containing Boston Births, Baptism, Marriages and Deaths, 1630-1699*, Report of the Record Commissioners, Vol. 9 (Boston: Rockwell and Churchill, 1883), 37. "Adam Winthropp Esq. died 24ᵗʰ of 6ᵗʰ mo. [1652]"

[364]   Adam Winthrop to John Winthrop, Jr., 10 October 1642, *Winthrop Papers*, 4: 357–58. "I suppose by this time yyou have heard of my mariage with Mrs. Elizabeth Glouer."

[365]   Anna Glover, *Glover Memorials and Genealogies: An Account of John Glover of Dorchester and His Descendants* (Boston: David Clapp & Son, 1867), 560–63, 567. When he emigrated to New England during the summer of 1638 with his family, the Rev. Jose Glover brought with him the first printing press set up in any of the British-American colonies. Unfortunately he was never able to use it, as he died during the journey. See Glover, 561, for a discussion of his name, which is sometimes rendered as José or Josse. See also John W. Dean, "Rev. Joseph or Josse Glover," *Register* 23 [1869]: 135–36. His widow married (2) the Rev. Henry Dunster, first president of Harvard College.

[366]   Mayo, *The Winthrop Family in America*, 69, without citation. Muskett, *Evidences of the Winthrops of Groton*, 26, gives only the year. Glover, *Glover Memorials and Genealogies*, 567, says Elizabeth died at Boston but her "date of death [is] not ascertained."

his father.[367] The couple had one son, Adam[3] Winthrop, b. in 1647,
whose grandson was the astronomer John[5] Winthrop.[368] Adam[2]
Winthrop m. (2) 7 May 1649, ELIZABETH HAWKINS, who was b.
8 and bp. at St. Dunstan's Church, Stepney, Middlesex 14 May
1629, dau. of Capt. Thomas and Mary (Welles?) Hawkins[369] and the
widow of Nathaniel Long.[370] After Adam died in 1652 (the couple
had no children), Elizabeth received a third interest in the proceeds
of Governor's Island and also was named (with four others) as a
guardian during her widowhood of the now orphaned Adam[3]
Winthrop, then about five years old.[371]

---

[367] W. B. Trask et al., eds., *Suffolk Deeds,* 14 vols. (Boston, 1880–1906), Liber 1, No. 25 (pages unnumbered). The island, known as "the Governour's Garden in the Massachuetts
Baye" was deeded on 1st day of the 12th mo. [February] 1641[/42] by "John Winthrop
Esq. & Margarett his wife & Adam theire sonne" for the use of "sayd Adam and wife
Elizabeth Glover & the heires of theire two bodyes," although Governor Winthrop and
his wife reserved for their own use "one third part of all such Apples, peares, grapes,
plumes as shalbe yearly growinge vpon the sayd Illand." Most of the island remained
in the family until 1833, when it was taken over by the U.S. Government (Mayo, *The
Winthrop Family in America,* 69). A letter survives from Elizabeth (Hawkins) Winthrop
to John Winthrop, Jr., dated 1 February 1653/54 with news and thanks "for your con-
tined remebrans of me by leters" (*Winthrop Papers,* 6: 356).

[368] Glover, *Glover Memorials and Genealogies,* 567–68, 572.

[369] Wayne H.M. Wilcox, "Captain Thomas Hawkins, Shipwright, of London and
Dorchester, Massachusetts and Three Generations of Descendants," *Register* 151
[1997]: 193, citing Greater London Record Office, Ms. P93/DUN/256. "1629
May. Elizabeth, daughter of Thomas Hawkins of Wappingwall shipwright & Mary
ux ye 14 day at 6 days old." Wilcox notes at 194 that Thomas was probably the
Thomas Hawkins of Wapping, Middlesex, shipwright, who was married at St.
Dunstan's 19 August 1628 to Mary Welles.

[370] *A Volume Relating to the Early History of Boston Containing the Aspinwall Notarial Records
from 1644 to 1651* (Boston: Municipal Printing Office, 1903), 225. "I granted a certificate that Mr. Adam Winthrop & Mrs. Elisab. The late wife of Nath: Long were lawfully
marryed the 7 (3) 1649." Long's death is noted by John Winthrop in a letter dated 9
November 1648: "The plague is still hott at Barbados; mr. Parker the minister, and mr.
Longe, who married Capt Hawkins daughter, are dead there" (*Winthrop Papers,* 5: 267).

[371] Shurtleff, *Records of the Governor and Company of the Massachusetts Bay in New England,
1628–1686,* 3: 292. A petition dated 19 October 1652 identified her as "second wife
to Adam Winthropp, deceased" and appointed Henry Dunster, Edward Rawson,
Captain Thomas Clarke, and Captain Richard Davenport as guardians with her
of Adam, then about 5 years old, "to take care of his education, & also of all his
estate." Elizabeth (Hawkins) Winthrop was a guardian for Adam for only about 18
months, as she married (3) on 3rd of 3rd mo. [May] 1654, John Richards (*A Report
of the Record Commissioners Containing Boston Births, Baptism, Marriages and Deaths,
1630–1699,* 9: 48. "John Richards & Elizabeth Winthrop widow were married 3rd
–3rd month by William Hibbins").

In a journal entry from Jan. 1632, John[1] Winthrop recalled
exploring with others the banks of the Charles River for about 8
miles above Watertown. Not far from the foot of Prospect Hill in
Waltham, John Winthrop wrote, "they went to a great rock, upon
which stood a high stone, cleft in sunder, that four men might go
through, which they called Adam's Chair, because the youngest of
their company was Adam Winthrop."[372] Mayo commented: "Could
anything have pleased an 11-year-old boy more?" After their
marriage, Adam and Elizabeth lived near her parents at the foot of
Clark Street in the North End of Boston.[373] Following Adam's death
in 1652, his uncle Emanuel Downing wrote John Winthrop, Jr.:[374]

> Yesterday your brother Adam Winthrop was buryed,
> who dyed the third day before, hauing layne sick fiue or
> six dayes, but in such as manner as neither himselfe nor
> any freind about him suspected his death scarce halfe an
> howre before he departed, who neither made will nor
> gave any word of directions concerning his estate though
> in perfect memorie, and wise men about him, he dying in
> the Elders armes. His wife and others your nere relatives
> here doe earnestly entreat your speedly repayre hither,
> because the ordering of the buisines about his wife, child
> and the rest is refered to your coming.

x.   DEANE WINTHROP,[375] b. 16[376] and bp. at Groton 23 March 1622/23.[377]
He d. at Pulling Point [now Winthrop], Mass. near dawn on

---

[372] Savage, *The History of New England from 1630 to 1649,* 1: 68. E.G. Chamberlain,
       "Gov. Winthrop's Outing to Doublet Hill in 1631," *Appalachia* 13 [1914]: 142, de-
       scribes it as a "boulder about four feet high, split in halves, which are separated
       about eight feet and make the arms of the chair."

[373] Mayo, *The Winthrop Family in America,* 69.

[374] Emmanuel Downing to John Winthrop, Jr., 28th of the 6th mo. [August] 1652,
       Collections of the Massachusetts Historical Society, 4th series, 6 [1863]: 79. Mayo, 70,
       notes that a Bible that belonged to Adam, passed down to him from his grandfather,
       Adam Winthrop, and then to his father, who brought it from Groton aboard the
       Arbella, remained in the family until 1825. "After that it went out of the family for
       a few years, but ultimately came into the possession of Robert C. Winthrop," and
       from there to the Massachusetts Historical Society.

[375] Named for his mother's half-brother, Sir John Deane (Mayo, *The Winthrop Family in
       America,* 70–71).

[376] William H. Whitmore, "Notes on the Winthrop Family and Its English Connections
       Viz: The Family of Forth, Clopton, Tyndale and Fones," *Register* 18 [1864]: 183.

[377] Groton parish register, *Collections of the Massachusetts Historical Society,* 3rd series, 8
       [1843]: 297. "1622. Deane Winthropp the sonne of John Winthroppe Esqre was
       baptised the 23d of Marche."

16 March 1703/4, his 81st birthday,[378] the last surviving child of
John[1] Winthrop. (He also outlived his nine children.[379]) He was
buried at Rumney Marsh Burial Ground in what is now Revere,
Mass.[380] Deane Winthrop m. (1) about 1648,[381] SARAH GLOVER, dau.
of the Rev. Joseph/Josse and Sarah (Owfield) Glover, and sister of
Elizabeth Glover, who m. Adam[2] Winthrop. They had at least three
children.[382] Sarah had died and Deane remarried by 6 June 1684,
when his second wife, MARTHA _____, b. ca. 1630,[383] the widow of
Capt. John Mellowes,[384] signed a receipt as Martha Winthrope.[385] She
d. at Boston 22 Jan. 1716.[386]

Deane, then about eight, stayed behind when his father and older
brothers emigrated in 1630, and also when his mother followed
in 1631. He attended school until 1635, but then came to New

---

[378] "Diary of Samuel Sewell, Vol. 2, 1699/1700–1714," *Collections of the Massachusetts Historical Society*, 5th series, 6 [1879]: 96. On 16 March 1703/4, Sewall wrote, "Mr. Dean Winthrop, of Pulling Point, dies upon his Birth-day, just about the Breaking of it."

[379] "Diary of Samuel Sewell, Vol. 2," *Collections of the Massachusetts Historical Society*, 5th series, 6 [1879]: 96. "He is the last of Govr. Winthrop's children." See also Waitstill Winthrop to Fitz-John Winthrop, 18 November 1702, *Collections of the Massachusetts Historical Society*, 6th series, 5 [1892]: 117. "My poor vncle has lost all his children: Cousin José and his other daughter, [Mercy] Hoffe, dyed of the small pox since my last to you."

[380] *Findagrave.com* (memorial 19078500). "Here lyeth buried ye body of Mr. Deane Winthrop of Pullin Point Aged 81 Years who departed this life March the 16 1703/4." See also stone HF1242 at Farber Gravestone Collection (*davidrumsey.com/farber*).

[381] Muskett, *Evidences of the Winthrops of Groton,* 26.

[382] Glover, *Glover Memorials and Genealogies,* 568–69.

[383] Thomas Amory Lee, "Old Boston Families, Number Six: The Lee Family," *Register* 76 [1922]: 198fn. Martha said in a deposition given 30 January 1673/4 that she was about 43. Lee described her as "a kinswoman of Rev. John Cotton."

[384] Williams, *Early New England Families, 1641–1700,* 1: 231, 240; Donald Lines Jacobus, "James, Mellowes and Ingoldsby Family Connections," *The American Genealogist* 11 [1934]: 28. See also a deed dated 22 January 1703/4 in Suffolk Registry Book 21: 457–60 that named Thomas Messenger and his wife Elizabeth, "one of the Daughters of John Mellows, late of Boston" and noted that Elizabeth was to inherit land "immediately after the Decease of Martha Winthrop wife of Deane Winthrop of Pullen Point and mother of the s[d] Elizabeth" (*Familysearch.org*> Massachusetts Lands Records, 1620–1986 > Suffolk > Deeds 1698–1704 vol. 19–21 > images 789–90 of 909).

[385] Lee, *Register* 76 [1922]: 199fn, citing *Suffolk Deeds,* Liber 20, folio 501. The receipt was for £50 due to her son John Mellows under his father's will.

[386] Mayo, *Winthrop Family in America,* 73. She was living 6 May 1706 when she was identified in a court document as "Martha Winthrope Executrix of the Last Will of her former Husband . . . John Mellows Senr" (Lee, *Register* 76 [1922]: 199, citing *Suffolk Deeds,* Liber 23, folio 3).

England at age 11 aboard the *Abigail* with his half-brother John, who had returned to England on business, and John's new wife.[387] Six years later Deane went to sea but, as Mayo recounted, liked it so little he had himself put ashore at "Maligo" [Malaga] and returned to England and then Massachusetts Bay.[388] In 1642, at age 20, Deane fell in love with a young woman from Salem but gave up his pursuit "apon hir manifestation that she could not set her affections apon him," according to his aunt Lucy Downing, who admitted she viewed the rejection "as a thing from providence."[389] In 1644, Deane joined the Artillery Company.[390] In the fall of 1646, he migrated with his brother John to Fisher's Island near New London, but by the following summer had returned to Boston.[391] In Nov. 1647, when he was 24, Deane's father deeded him a 200-acre farm at Pullen Point (now the southeastern part of the town of Winthrop, bordered on the east by the ocean and on the west by Boston Harbor).[392]

Deane first established himself at the Point Shirley end of the farm and later in a wood-frame home that still stands today at 34 Shirley Street.[393] He also invested in other land: before he inherited Pullen Point, he and brother Adam had purchased 1,000 acres about 17 miles west of Boston,[394] and in 1655 Deane was among a group that received a tract about 8 miles wide in the Nashua River Valley that was christened Groton, perhaps at Deane's suggestion. He claimed in a petition in May 1656 that he intended to live there but likely instead saw it as an investment.[395] He did flirt over the years with ideas of moving from Pullen Point, such as when he

---

[387] "Founders of New England," *Register* 14 [1860]: 320. "x [10] July 1635. In the Abigall . . . John Wynthropp, 27, Elizabeth Winthropp, 19, Deane Winthropp, 11."

[388] Deane Tyndale to John Winthrop, 7 April 1641, *Winthrop Papers*, 4: 329.

[389] Lucy Downing to John Winthrop, 24 February 1643/44, *Winthrop Papers*, 4: 444–45.

[390] Zachariah G. Whitman, *The History of the Ancient and Honorable Artillery Company*, 2nd ed. (Boston: John H. Eastburn, 1842), 142.

[391] Deane Winthrop [from Boston] to John Winthrop, Jr., 1 November 1648, *Winthrop Papers*, 5: 278.

[392] *Suffolk Deeds,* Liber 1, No. 86, 16th of 9th mo. [November] 1647 (pages unnumbered). Mayo, *The Winthrop Family in America*, 72, explained that Pullen or Pulling was so named because "it was a struggle to row against the tide that ran between it and Deer Island or because the early settlers preferred to go ashore there and haul their boats rather than row against the strong current."

[393] Since 1903, the house has been owned by the Winthrop Improvement and Historical Association.

[394] Shurtleff, *Records of the Governor and Company of the Massachusetts Bay in New England, 1628–1686,* 2: 189.

[395] Mayo, *The Winthrop Family in America*, 72–73.

wrote his brother John on 16 Dec. 1662 to say that "I haue some thoughts of remouing from the place that I now liue in into your coloni, if I cold lit of a convanet pleace. The please that I now liue in is too litel for me—mi chilldren now groueing up."[396]

On 11 July 1699, Judge Samuel Sewall recorded in his diary that he had visited Pulling Point with a minister friend, Mr. Willard, who had been asked to officiate the wedding of one of Deane's now-grown children, his daughter Mercy:[397]

> Between one and two, Mr. Williard married Atherton Haugh and Mercy Winthrop.... Gave very good Advice and Exhortation; especially most solemnly charged them never to neglect family Prayer. Between 3 and four Major Gen[l]. and Mr. Adam Winthrop[398] came and many with them, when we had almost din'd. Sang a Psalm together, I set St. David's Tune: Sung part of two Psalms, concluded with the 4 last verses of the 115. When Mr. Willard ask'd Mr. Winthrop's consent, he also complemented me respecting Atherton Haugh: I said I was glad that had found so good a Family and so a good a wife. And after, when saw the Bridegroom and Bride together after the Wedding; I praid God to bless them, and give them such an Offspring wherein the Name of Haugh and Winthrop might flourish. Mr. Dean Winthroop liv'd there in his fathers days, and was wont to set up a Bush [signal] when he saw a ship coming in; He is now 77 years old. In his Fathers time, his house stood more toward Dear Island.

---

[396] Deane Winthrop to John Winthrop, Jr., 16 December 1662, *Collections of the Massachusetts Historical Society*, 5th series, 8 [1882]: 232–33.

[397] "Diary of Samuel Sewall, Vol. 1, 1674–1729," *Collections of the Massachusetts Historical Society*, 5th series, 5 [1878]: 499.

[398] This is almost certainly a reference to the bride's cousins Waitstill[3] Winthrop and Adam[3] Winthrop, the latter the only son of Adam[2] Winthrop (*see above*). See Whitman, *The History of the Ancient and Honorable Artillery Company*, 224, 226.

When Deane Winthrop died five years later, Sewall wrote:[399]

> He was Taken at eight aclock the evening before, as
> he sat in his chair, sunk first, being set up, he vomited,
> complain'd of his head, which were almost his last words.
> Hardly spake anything after his being in bed. 81 years
> old. He is the last of Gov[r] Winthrop's children—*statione
> novissimus exit* [Ovid]. March, 20, is buried at Pulling
> Point by his son and Three Daughters. Bearers Russel,
> Cooke; Hutchinson, Sewall; Townsend, Paige. From the
> House of Hasey. Scutcheons on the Pall. I help'd to lower
> the Corps onto the Grave. Madam Paige went in her
> Coach. Maj[r] Gen[l] and Capt Adam Winthrop had Scarvs,
> and led the widow. Very pleasant day; Went by [the]
> Winisimet [ferry].

In his will, dated 29 Dec. 1702 and probated 27 April 1704,
Deane left his wife Martha £20 annually and use of his Negro
woman Moreah (spelled Marrear in the inventory). His grandson
Iotham Grover received £5 "because he is under the care &
Tuition of his Grandmother Kent." Grandsons Deane Grover
and John Grover (who he noted were "fatherless"), the sons of
his daughter Margaret, and granddaughters Priscilla Adams and
Priscilla Haugh received the remainder of the estate when the
youngest of them turned 21 or was married. If the girls died before
the division, each of their fathers ("my sons-in-law Eliah Adams
and Atherton Haugh") would receive £150, with the remainder to
his two grandsons. Two appraisers, in an inventory taken 28 April
and presented 2 Sept. 1704, valued the estate at £1,166, with the
house, barn, and 300 acres of Pulling Point accounting for £1,000.
Deane also owned "one Negro man, by name Primas," valued at
£30. Moreah and "a Boy, by name Robbin," were valued together
at £30. The livestock included two oxen, two steers, three cows, a

---

[399] "Diary of Samuel Sewall, Vol. 2, 1699/1700–1714," *Collections of the Massachusetts
Historical Society*, 5th series, 6 [1879]: 96. Mellen Chamberlain, in *A Documentary
History of Chelsea*, 2 vols. (Boston: Massachusetts Historical Society, 1908), 1: 262,
commented that "Sewall's statement that Winthrop was buried at Pullen Point is
remarkable, for his gravestone is still seen at Revere, more than a mile away from
Pullen Point and Winthrop's residence. So was Hasey's house. And yet Sewall, who
lowered the corpse into the grave, says it was at Pullen Point. This seems decisive;
and if so, then Winthrop's remains must have been transferred to Rumney Marsh,
where they now lie."

bull, two yearlings, 141 sheep, thirty-three lambs, and three sows, a boar, and sixteen summer shoats (weaned piglets). He also owned three muskets and a "very old" feather bed. The appraisers found £43 cash in a chest and records for two tracts of vacant land on either side of the Merrimack River.[400]

xi.   NATHANIEL WINTHROP, bp. at Groton 20 Feb. 1624/25[401] and prob. d.y.[402]

xii. CAPT. SAMUEL WINTHROP, bp. at Groton 26 Aug. 1627[403] and died in Antigua, presumably at his estate Groton Hall, after 8 Dec. 1672 (when he made his will[404]) and before 11 Dec. 1675 (when his wife Elizabeth noted in her own will that she was a widow[405]). He m. at Rotterdam, the Netherlands 8 July 1648, ELIZABETH HODGKEL,[406] who died after 11 Dec. 1675.[407]

Samuel left Groton for New England with his mother in the fall of 1631.[408] Like his siblings, he was well educated. "His letters show a trained mind and a cultivated style," observed Mayo. "He was almost as much at home in Latin as in English, and his occasional use of a Latin phrase never seems pendantic."[409] A year or two before he graduated from Harvard College in 1646, he and a classmate

---

[400] Transcribed in Chamberlain, *A Documentary History of Chelsea*, 1: 262–66, citing Suffolk Probate Records, Liber L, 15, folio 273–74.

[401] Groton parish register, *Collections of the Massachusetts Historical Society*, 3rd series, 8 [1843]: 297. "1624. Nathaniel Winthroppe the sonne of John Winthroppe Esquire was baptised the 20th of Februarie."

[402] James Savage, *Collections of the Massachusetts Historical Society*, 3rd series, 8 [1843]: 298fn.

[403] Groton parish register, *Collections of the Massachusetts Historical Society*, 3rd series, 8 [1843]: 297. "1627. Samuell the sonne of John Winthroppe Esqre. & Margaret his wife August the 26th."

[404] Vere Langford Oliver, *The History of the Island of Antiqua*, 3 vols. (London: Mitchell and Hughes, 1899), 3: 251, gives 1674 as the year of death. He also provides 8 December 1672 as the date of Samuel's will but says it is "not on record."

[405] Oliver, *The History of the Island of Antiqua*, 3: 251.

[406] DTB Rotterdam Stadstrouw [Rotterdam City Archive Weddings], online at *digitalestamboom.nl*. "Samuel Winthrop, jongeman, van Engelwonders In Nieu Engelant, wonend Op De Gelderse Kaeij; Elisabet Hodgkel, jongedochter, van Rotterdam, wonend In Engels Brouwerij. Bruidegom wonende ten huijse van Mr Jan Charleton." Anderson, *The Great Migration Begins*, 3: 2041, indicates 8 July 1648 is the New Style date. Samuel wrote his father from Rotterdam on 7 August 1648 and noted "My wife presents her humble dutie to yoᵣ selfe" (*Collections of the Massachusetts Historical Society*, 5th series, 8 [1882]: 240).

[407] Oliver, *The History of the Island of Antiqua*, 3: 251.

[408] Savage, *The History of New England from 1630 to 1649*, 1: 76–77.

[409] Mayo, *The Winthrop Family in America*, 75. A number of Samuel's letters are reprinted in *Collections of the Massachusetts Historical Society*, 5th series, 8 [1882]: 234–65.

and two tutors bought three-quarters of an acre of what is now the College Yard and planted apple trees. They called it *Pomarium Sociorum*, or the Fellows' Orchard, with the idea it would a place for the teachers to relax.[410] Sometime after 1 Nov. 1645, when the charges for his Harvard room ceased, Samuel dropped his studies and left for England with his brother Stephen.

"One of the pioneers in the trade between New England and the eastern Atlantic wine islands, Stephen shipped a cargo of grain, fish, beef, pork and pipe staves on John Wall's *Dolphin* in October for the Canary Islands," noted historian Larry Gragg. "He and Samuel followed on the *Defence* of Boston."[411] The brothers had a stopover at Tenerife, the leading wine island of the Canary Islands, where Samuel announced he would stay and work for a merchant named Ferdinando Bodge.[412] He explained to his father, "Here is as great a likelyhood for the raising my outward estate as in any place, considering the troubles of this age."[413] Samuel remained there for two-and-a-half years, then traveled to Barbados and St. Christophers [St. Kitts], where he nearly died of fever.[414] After recovering, he continued to Holland, where in 1648 he married Elizabeth Hodgkel.

---

[410] Samuel Eliot Morison, *The Founding of Harvard College* (Cambridge, Mass.: Harvard University Press, 1935), 290–91.

[411] Larry D. Gragg, "A Puritan in the West Indies: The Career of Samuel Winthrop," *The William and Mary Quarterly* 50 [1993]: 769, citing Aspinwall, *A Volume Relating to the Early History of Boston*, 397. "Exported by the Dolphin of London John Wall Mʳ Stephen Winthrop merchᵗ for the Account of Roger Kilvert Edward Parks & David Davison seven thousand bushels of graine, viz*. Wheat rye pease: one thousand Kintalls of fish: 12 thousand pipe staves: 40 hhd beefe & porke; & 40 hhs. Markrell & red herring for Canaries. The Master gave mee this Account of the pticulars."

[412] Stephen Winthrop to John Winthrop, Jr., 1645, *Collections of the Massachusetts Historical Society*, 5th series, 8 [1882]: 202–3. "We had not beene longe heare before my brother Samuell expressed to me some thoughts he had of staying here, wᵗʰ some merchᵗ to be perfected in yᵗ calling (wᶜʰ was yᵗ wᶜʰ he seemed most to close wᵗʰ all); & resoluing not to trust to his study for his future mainainance, did thinke it his best cource to setle to some setled calling; wᶜʰ reason I confesse I could not overthrow.... The man yᵗ now he shalbe wᵗʰ all is one Mr. Ferdinando Bodge, who is by all yᵗ know him reputed honest & relidgious."

[413] Samuel Winthrop to John Winthrop, 5 April 1646, *Winthrop Papers*, 5: 74.

[414] Samuel Winthrop to John Winthrop, 10 January 1647[/48], *Winthrop Papers*, 5: 195–96. "Since that, Mr. Starkie our merchant comeing downe to receiue what goods I had there reddy was taken away in the Sickness and the next day after his buriall my Selfe fell Sicke of the same desease whic was so extreme then in the Iland that Scarce a young man Scaped it. If they rubed out 3 dayes for the most part they recovered. Myne continued ten dayes in such extremity that everyone despayred of my health, not only, but expected when I should depart to another world."

Their eldest son was born in Rotterdam and his siblings in Antigua or St. Kitts.[415] Samuel wrote his brother John, Jr., soon after his marriage to say he hoped to return to the colonies for a visit before moving from Rotterdam to the West Indies.[416] Samuel later would write his half-brother John to report that he planned to send his two eldest sons to Harvard.[417]

In 1666, after Samuel had lived in Antigua for nearly twenty years, the French invaded, and Capt. Winthrop was among the six men chosen to negotiate a surrender for the British residents. (He shipped his wife and children to safety in Nevis early in the conflict.) As Samuel told it, just as the agreement was ready to be signed, "a party of Barbadian souldiers, inflamed wth wine" interrupted the proceedings. The French left but returned two weeks later to complete negotiations and to raise a French flag over Samuel's house. The British residents were persuaded to take an oath to the King of France; Samuel wrote that "all present, except 4 or 5 of those called Quakers," complied.[418] The soldiers took twenty-four of Samuel's slaves ("ye rest escaped") and destroyed most of his livestock.[419]

---

[415]   Mayo, *The Winthrop Family in America*, 78–79. See also Oliver, *The History of the Island of Antiqua*, 3: 251.

[416]   Samuel Winthrop [from Rotterdam] to John Winthrop, 7 August 1648, *Winthrop Papers*, 5: 243. "I informed yow per my last that I purposed to go to Barbadoes and setle there, but since I am resolued to come and present yow my duty first in New England, and take your Counsell therein, which shalbe verry suddaynly."

[417]   Samuel Winthrop to John Winthrop, Jr., undated, *Collections of the Massachusetts Historical Society*, 5th series, 8 [1882]: 254. "I purpose to continue my sonnes still in New England, & I thinke by this time they may be fitt for ye Colledge, & I shall giue order for their goeing thither, & doe heartily request ye President may receiue yor recomiends on their behalfe." Henry or Joseph Winthrop do not appear in the first three volumes (through 1689) of John Langdon Sibley et al., *Biographical Sketches of Graduates of Harvard University,* 18 vols. (Cambridge and Boston, Mass.: 1873–1999). Oliver, *The History of the Island of Antiqua*, 3: 250–51, says only that the brothers were "educated in New England."

[418]   For religious reasons, Quakers refused to take oaths. Samuel would later become a Quaker. Mayo, *The Winthrop Family in America*, 78, noted that as early as 1667 Samuel began to use the pronouns *thou* and *thee* in letters to John Winthrop, Jr., although he made no attempt to convert his half brother. About 1672 Samuel met George Fox, "the greatest Quaker of them all," when the latter visited Barbados.

[419]   Gragg, *The William and Mary Quarterly* 50 [1993]: 774, noted that Samuel complained that the French left him only with "land and 12 working Negroes," but when he died seven years later, he owned 1,100 acres, a quarter of the small island of Barbuda, and 67 slaves.

After seven days, the French departed again,[420] and within a year the island had been restored to British rule by the Treaty of Breda. Samuel became the chief deputy to the new government of the Leeward Islands, serving as deputy governor, register, and president of the council.[421] In 1665, his cousin Margaret (Gostlin) Heathcote, who lived for the time with her husband in Antiqua, described Samuel to John, Jr., as "a reall Winthrop and truely noble to all."[422] Her son, George Heathcote, wrote on 21 March 1667/68 that he had heard from his parents that "thy brother Samuel was Commander-in-chief, and that he said he did intent to give up his Commission, for it was a thing as it were in a manner forced upon him."[423]

Still, Samuel often expressed in his letters the hope he might return to Massachusetts, and in 1660 he asked his brother John if he might be able to purchase Ten Hills, the 600-acre farm on the Mystic River that had been granted John[1] Winthrop in 1631. The governor had sold part of the farm to cover the losses of his overseer and gave the rest to John, Jr., who later repurchased the lots his father sold. John, Jr., insisted he couldn't sell it because of complicated trust agreements.[424] "Crushed, Samuel nonetheless reacted to this lost opportunity to return home with the same deference he had shown his father," noted Larry Gragg.[425] Samuel wrote to John, Jr., "I am sorry you should take so much paines to giue me satisfaction touching yo' non capacity to sell yo' farm."[426]

---

[420] Samuel Winthrop to John Winthrop, Jr., undated, *Collections of the Massachusetts Historical Society*, 5th series, 8 [1882]: 255–58. See also Bryan Edwards, *The History, Civil and Commercial, of the British Colonies in the West Indies*, 3rd ed., 3 vols. (London: John Stockdale, 1801), 1: 474. "In 1666 a French armament from Martinico, co-operating with a body of Charaibes, invaded the island, and ravaged the country with fire and sword. All the negroes that could be found, were taken away; and the inhabitants, after beholding their houses and estates in flames, were plundered even to the clothes on their backs and the shoes on their feet, without regard to sex or age."

[421] Oliver, *The History of the Island of Antiqua*, 3: 251–53.

[422] Margaret Heathcote to John Winthrop, Jr., 27 June 1665, *Proceedings of the Massachusetts Historical Society*, 2nd series, 5 [1889]: 105–6.

[423] George Heathcote to John Winthrop, Jr., 21 March 1667/68, quoted in Oliver, *The History of the Island of Antiqua*, 3: 252, as communicated by Robert C. Winthrop, Jr.

[424] John Winthrop, Jr. to Samuel Winthrop, 24 May 1660, *Collections of the Massachusetts Historical Society*, 5th series, 8 [1882]: 60–61.

[425] Gragg, *The William and Mary Quarterly* 50 [1993]: 777.

[426] Samuel Winthrop to John Winthrop, Jr., 20 October 1660, *Collections of the Massachusetts Historical Society*, 5th series, 8 [1882]: 248–49. Nine years later, John sold Ten Hills to a Boston merchant (*Suffolk Deeds*, 6: 137–40).

In her will of 1675, Elizabeth (Hodgkel) Winthrop left son Henry "my part of Barbuda & all the stock there," while Samuel received "all monies in Urope" and Long Island, the land and storehouse at St. John's, and her gray horse. She also named her daughters Elizabeth Williams (£6 to buy a tankard), Sarah Jones (£10,000 and her mother's silver tankard), and Rebecca Winthrop (£40,000 at age 16, plus her mother's sidesaddle and two Negroes). Elizabeth left £4,000 and her "great bible" to Jonas Langford in gratitude for his looking after her during her final sickness. Her son Stephen received "my part of Groaten Hall plantation by my dear husband Saml Winthrop, dec^d, by his will given to me, he to pay legacies"; Samuel was to manage the estate until Stephen turned 17. Elizabeth appointed three Friends, "ye true ministers of ^{e} gospel whom ye world in scorn call quakers," including Langford, as executors and guardians of Rebecca and Stephen.[427]

xiii.   ANNE WINTHROP, bp. at Groton 29 April 1630[428] and d. aboard the *Lyon* en route to New England about the first week of Sept. 1631.[429]

xiv.   WILLIAM WINTHROP, b. 20, bp. at First Church, Boston 26th of 6th mo. [Aug.] 1632,[430] and d.y.

xv.   SARAH WINTHROP, bp. at First Church, Boston 29 June 1634[431] and d.y.

---

[427]   Oliver, *The History of the Island of Antiqua*, 3: 251, citing Folio 134, Book of Protests, Secretary's Office, 8 August 1679, proved 5 January 1675/76.

[428]   Groton parish register, *Collections of the Massachusetts Historical Society*, 3rd series, 8 [1843]: 297. "1630. Ann Winthrop daughter of John Esqre. and Margaret his 3d wife baptised Aprill 29th."

[429]   Savage, *The History of New England from 1630 to 1649*, 1: 76–77. Her father said she had died about a week after the *Lyon* left England for a ten-week voyage that ended 2 November 1631.

[430]   Richard D. Pierce, ed., "The Records of the First Church of Boston, 1630–1868," *Publications of the Colonial Society of Massachusetts,*39 [1961]: 278. "The 26th of the same sixth Moneth 1631 [*sic*] Willyam the sonne of our brother John Winthrope Governor." Savage, *The History of New England from 1630 to 1649*, 1: 88. "[August 1632:] The governour's wife was delivered of a son, who was baptized by the name of William. The governour himself held the child to baptism, as others in the congregation did use. William signifies a common man, &c." Anderson, *Great Migration Newsletter* 4 [1993]: 2, notes: "There is nothing surprising about this apparent 12-day gap between birth and baptism, for in the young colony the requirement to bring a child in for baptism on the next Sunday was soon relaxed. Surprisingly, though, inspection of the original of Winthrop's journal (for another entry on the same page) revealed that Savage, usually a meticulously accurate transcriber, had omitted the day of the month for this entry. Thus, the correct reading is that William Winthrop was born on 20 Aug. 1632, the record being the only item recorded by his father under that date."

[431]   Pierce, *Publications of the Colonial Society of Massachusetts* 39: 279. "The 29th of the 4 Moneth 1624. Sarah the Daughter of our Brother John Winthrop the Elder."

Child of John[1] and Martha (Rainsborough) (Coytmore) Winthrop:

xvi.   JOSHUA[2] WINTHROP, b. 12, bp. at First Church, Boston 17 Dec. 1648,[432] and d. 11th of 11th mo. [Jan.] 1651/52.[433]

---

[432]   Pierce, *Publications of the Colonial Society of Massachusetts* 39: 313. "The 17th Day of the 10th Moneth 1648 by our Pastor. Joshua Winthropp the Sonne of our brother Mr. John Winthropp Governor being about 5 Dayes old."

[433]   *A Report of the Record Commissioners Containing Boston Births, Baptism, Marriages and Deaths, 1630–1699*, 9: 34. "Joshua youngest son of the late John Winthropp Esq. died 11th–11th month [1651/52]." Mayo, *The Winthrop Family in America*, 32, errs with 11 January 1651.

The Kinship Between Robert[8] Winthrop
and Charles William Eliot, President of Harvard University
1869–1909

John Winthrop = (2) Elizabeth Reade

Elizabeth Winthrop
= (1) Antipas Newman

John Newman
= Ruth Emerson

Anne Newman
= David Plummer

Ruth Plummer
= Isaac Lyman

Theodore Lyman
= (2) Lydia Williams

Mary Lyman
= Samuel Atkins Eliot

Charles William Eliot

Waitstill Winthrop
= (1) Mary Browne

John Winthrop
= Anne Dudley

John Still Winthrop
= (1) Jane Borland

Francis Bayard Winthrop
= (2) Phebe Taylor

Thomas Charles Winthrop
= Georgiana Maria Kane

Robert Winthrop
= Katharine Wilson Taylor

The Second Generation

5. John[2] **Winthrop** (*John*[1]) was born at Groton, Suffolk 12[434] and baptized there 23 February 1605/6.[435] He died at Boston, Massachusetts 5 and was buried 10 April 1676 at the King's Chapel Burying Ground with his father in the Winthrop family tomb.[436] He married, first, at Groton 8 February 1630/31,[437] his first cousin **Martha Fones**, who was born 21 January 1608/9,[438] daughter of Thomas and Anne (Winthrop) Fones, and sister of Elizabeth Fones, who married his brother Henry[2] Winthrop.[439] She died at Agawam (Ipswich), Massachusetts, probably

---

[434] "Latin Pedigree" in Muskett, *Evidences of the Winthrops of Groton,* 7. "Anno domini 1605 duodecimo die febra: Joahnnes filius suus primogenitus in Groton in comitatu Suffolciae natus fuit quarto die septimanie circa 5: horologii in mane, et baptizatus fuit vicesimo tertio die sequente." See also *Pond's Almanack for 1603,* transcribed in *Winthrop Papers,* 1: 151, in which his grandfather Adam entered, "February 12. John Winthrop the youngest was borne. 1605." He also noted in his diary (*Winthrop Papers,* 1: 91): "On Wedensday in the morning the 12 of Feb. my soonnes first soonne was borne in Groton" and that on 26 March 1607, "John Wynthrop was weaned . . ." (1: 94). See also 1: 175, 216.

[435] Groton parish register, *Collections of the Massachusetts Historical Society,* 3rd series, 8 [1843]: 296. "1605. John Winthropp the sonne of John Winthropp and of Marie his wife was baptised the 23d of February." Adam Winthrop wrote: "The 23 of Feb: beinge sunday my soonnes first soonne was baptized and named John" (*Winthrop Papers,* 1: 91).

[436] Robert J. Dunkle and Ann S. Lainhart, *Inscriptions and Records of the Old Cemeteries of Boston* (Boston: New England Historic Genealogical Society, 2000), 796. "John Winthrop, Gov. of Conn., died 5 April 1676, AE 70." His death and burial were noted by Samuel Sewall in his diary (*Collections of the Massachusetts Historical Society,* 5th series, 5 [1878]: 12): "April 5, Wednesday, Governour Winthrop dyes. Interred old Burying place Monday following." Thomas Franklin Waters, *A Sketch of the Life of John Winthrop the Younger, Founder of Ipswich, Massachusetts, in 1633,* in *Publications of the Ipswich Historical Society* 7 [1889]: 59, reported that he "was laid beside his father in what is now King's Chapel grave-yard."

[437] Groton parish register, *Collections of the Massachusetts Historical Society,* 3rd series, 8 [1843]: 297. "1630. John Winthrope and Martha Jones [*sic*] were married Februarie the 8[th]."

[438] "Diary of Adam Winthrop," *Winthrop Papers,* 1: 104. "1609. One sundaie the 21th of January my daughter [Anne] Fones was d[dliuere]d of her seconde daughter."

[439] "Fones of Suffolk" in Muskett, *Evidences of the Winthrops of Groton,* 87.

soon after 20 July 1634,[440] and was buried at the Old North Burying Ground, likely with an infant daughter.[441] John married, second, at the Church of St. Matthew, Friday Street, London, Middlesex 6 July 1635,[442] **ELIZABETH READE**, who was baptized at St. Catherine's Church, Wickford, Essex 27 November 1614,[443] daughter of Edmund and Elizabeth (Cooke) Reade.[444] She died at Hartford, Connecticut 24 November 1672[445] and was buried there at Center Church-yard.[446]

---

[440] On 20 July 1634, John, Jr., wrote to his father from Ipswich and closed with greetings from himself and his wife (*Winthrop Papers*, 3: 170). Waters, *A Sketch of the Life of John Winthrop the Younger*, 8–9, asserts that Martha died with her infant daughter in the months following, "probably in the latter part of August or early in September." John, Jr., had departed for London by 6 November 1634, when his father wrote a letter addressed to him there.

[441] Waters, *A Sketch of the Life of John Winthrop the Younger*, 8–9, reported that Martha and her infant daughter "were laid away somewhere in the Old Burying ground." He added that "the Records of Boston contain no reference to this child, who is believed to have been born in Ipswich not long before her mother's death" On 30 August 2000, in an article titled "Burial site of first settler may be revealed," the *Ipswich Chronicle* reported: "The former owner of a home abutting Highland Cemetery on High Street has revealed what could be the best-kept secret in town. Some 30 years ago, when Rupert Kilgour, then of 61 High St., had a contractor excavate the driveway there, the backhoe hit something unexpected. 'As they were digging with a machine they hit and removed the corner of a sarcophagus,' Kilgour wrote in a recent letter to the Zoning Board of Appeals. A brick and stone mason who looked at the material at the time said the bricks looked like ballast from the early 1600s and seemed to be from England. Kilgour took it upon himself to investigate the grave. 'In the grave were the remains of a woman and child,' Kilgour wrote. 'After doing some checking, it was 99 percent certain that the remains were Mrs. John Winthrop and her small child.'. . . 'The grave is located in the corner of the cemetery nearest the town. At that time, it is where the first grave would be located,' he wrote." The grave was not found during a subsequent excavation. See *ipswich.wordpress.com/2014/ 08/30/john-winthrop-jr.*

[442] A.M. Bruce Bannerman, ed., "The Register of St. Matthew, Friday Street, London, 1538 to 1812," *The Publications of the Harleian Society, Register Series*, 63: 53, "1635. July 6. John Winthropp & Eliz: Reade."

[443] Register of Baptisms, Marriages and Burials, St. Catherine's, Wickford, scan of original at Essex Record Office, D/P 70/1/1, accessed at *essexcc.gov.uk.* "[1614] Elizabeth Read, daughter of Mr. Edmund Read was baptized Novemb. 27." She was 19 when she sailed on the *Abigail* in October 1635, according to James Camden Hotten, *The Original List of Persons of Quality* (London, 1874, rep. Boston: New England Historic Genealogical Society, 2012), 100.

[444] "Winthrop of New London" in Muskett, *Evidences of the Winthrops of Groton,* 27, gives her father's name. Her mother remarried to the Rev. Hugh Peter, who had arrived with John Winthrop at Boston in 1635. Peter returned to England in 1641 and became an advisor to Oliver Cromwell. He was executed at the Tower of London on 16 October 1660 as a regicide for his role in the execution of Charles I. See Raymond Phineas Stern, *The Strenuous Puritan: Hugh Peter, 1598–1660* (Urbana, Ill.: The University of Illinois, 1954), 152–53, 415–19.

[445] "Winthrop of New London" in Muskett, *Evidences of the Winthrops of Groton,* 27.

[446] Sherry S. Stancliff, "The Elizabeth Reade Winthrop Tombstone Affair (or the Tale of Three Tombstones)," *The Connecticut Nutmegger* 31 [1998]: 209–17.

The historian Richard Dunn, in his celebrated 1962 book, *Puritans and Yankees: The Winthrop Dynasty of New England, 1630–1717,* introduced John Winthrop, Jr., in this way:[447]

> Among second-generation New Englanders, there was no more attractive figure than John Winthrop, Jr. Founder of three towns, industrialist, scientist, doctor, governor, diplomat, farmer, land speculator, he reflected almost every aspect of his burgeoning society. Religion framed his life, but he did not experience his father's crusading zeal. He was energetic and public spirited but preferred science to politics. Whereas the elder Winthrop wrote didactic tracts and diaries of religious meditations, the son kept medical and alchemical notebooks. . . .

John would not settle down in one place until he was more than 50 years old, Dunn noted,[448] and his travels began with his education. He attended the Free Grammar School in Bury St. Edmunds, but his father then sent him to Trinity College, Dublin, where his uncle Emmanuel Downing, who lived in the city, helped ensure the young man would not become "ensnared with the lustes of youth which are comonly covered vnder the name of recreations," as his father warned.[449] John, Jr., was admitted as a barrister of the Inner Temple in February 1624/25, but had "an inclination for the sea"[450] and in 1627 sailed as a secretary to a ship's captain with the forces of George Villiers, the first Duke of Buckingham, who on 12 July landed with 100 ships and 6,000 soldiers in an attempt to aid rebellious French Protestants besieged at the port city of La Rochelle by the royal forces of Louis XIII and Cardinal

---

[447] Richard S. Dunn, *Puritans and Yankees: The Winthrop Dynasty of New England, 1630–1717* (Princeton, N.J.: Princeton University Press, 1962), 59. The author noted that while the subject signed himself as "John Winthrop," many of his correspondents addressed their letters to "John Winthrop, Junior." Anderson, in *The Great Migration Begins,* 3: 2042, called Dunn's book one of the two "most informative and perceptive of the modern studies" of Governor Winthrop; the other is Darrett B. Rutman, *Winthrop's Boston: A Portrait of a Puritan Town, 1630–1649* (Chapel Hill, N.C.: University of North Carolina Press, 1965).

[448] Dunn, *Puritans and Yankees,* 50.

[449] John Winthrop to John Winthrop, Jr., 16 October 1622, *Winthrop Papers,* 1: 276.

[450] Joshua Downing to John Winthrop, 24 April 1627, *Winthrop Papers,* 1: 347–48. "Concerning Mr. John Wenthrops inclinacion to the Sea, I will vse my best endeavours for hym; but I have no parte in any shipping that goes For Turkie, and the marchantes who are owners, doe comonly place their owne servauntes for pursers; but if he pleaseth, to goe alonge in those ships as a passenger to see the contries."

Richelieu.[451] After three months attempting to capture the French fortress of Saint-Martin-de-Ré, Buckingham was forced to retreat; by some accounts he lost some five thousand of his seven thousand men.

After surviving this ordeal, John decided to see the world. He thought about going to New England,[452] but instead traveled in Europe for fourteen months, with stops in Padua, Venice (where he was quarantined for a month to make sure he didn't have the plague), Constantinople, and Holland, although he missed a chance to visit Jerusalem.[453] He returned to London on 13 August 1629.[454] He found his father there, preparing to emigrate to New England, and offered to accompany him but, as Dunn observed, "If the journey to New England was a pilgrimage in his father's eyes, it was an odyssey to John." Instead, John would stay behind with the women and children and work to sell Groton Manor.[455] He also helped draw up plans for the colony's defense and acted as an agent in London for the emigrants.[456]

In February 1631, John, Jr., married his first cousin, Martha Fones, who had been his father's ward. Although Martha was 22 (and John 25), the Court of Alderman in London fined John five marks for marrying a close relative who was a minor without consent.[457] The

---

[451] On 31 August 1627, Emmanuel Downing reported to John Winthrop that "there is noe newes from the Duke only this that the Fort is neither taken nor releived" (*Winthrop Papers*, 1: 358). See 1: 359–60 for a battlefield letter written in September 1627 from John, Jr., to his father: "Our army lieth still the most part at St. martins some few Garrisons in other partes of the Iland." In an undated letter later that year, Margaret Winthrop wrote to her husband that she had heard of the "bad sucsese of the Duke" and "I am glad that theare is hope that John is safe" (1: 365).

[452] John Winthrop acknowledged his son's wanderlust, writing from Groton to London on 7 April 1628 that although he was suffering at that moment from a finger injury that had become infected with gangrene, as soon as he was able to "stirre aboute the house I will looke oute those Geometricall instruments and books" (*Winthrop Papers*, 1: 386). In a reply dated 11 April 1628, John mentions "my voyage to new England" (1: 387).

[453] Dunn, *Puritans and Yankees*, 61. For letters from John, Jr., to his father during his travels, see *Winthrop Papers* 1: 402–3, 408–11, and 417–18, and 2: 69–70, 72–77, and 103–5.

[454] John Winthrop, Jr., to John Winthrop, 14 August 1629, *Winthrop Papers*, 2: 149. "I am (God be thanked) yesterday safely arrived in London."

[455] As Richard Dunn notes (*Puritans and Yankees*, 63), this wasn't easy. The elder John Winthrop valued the estate at £5,760 but John, Jr., found it difficult to get £4,200 for it (*Winthrop Papers*, 3: 27). John, Jr., surrendered his title to the estate and reinvested £1,500 of the proceeds for his stepmother Margaret Winthrop and her young children. He also had to raise £3,000 to pay bills sent by his father from New England.

[456] Dunn, *Puritans and Yankees*, 62.

[457] Dunn, *Puritans and Yankees*, 63. On the day she arrived at Groton from London in May 1631, Martha wrote her new husband in London to report that she had heard "such strange newes: it is credibly reported all over the countrey that thou

couple's relationship had its rocky moments, apparently; in a letter to her husband written in early April 1631, Martha assured him of her love despite previous "pasions and weaknes" that had caused him doubt.[458] In November John and his wife were aboard the *Lyon* headed for New England leading a group that included his stepmother Margaret (Tyndal) Winthrop, his half-brother Adam, his half-sister Anne (then about 18 months old; she would die a week into the ten-week journey), and the widow and infant daughter of his brother Henry.[459] They also brought several hundred barrels of luggage, meal, beef, cheese, butter, two hogsheads of books, a supply of chemical glassware, and seeds for an herbal and medicinal garden.[460] The ship was greeted at Boston Harbor on 4 November 1631 with an honor guard, gun vollies, and a feast.[461]

Within a few months John, Jr., had been named a freeman (3 April 1632[462]) and was elected to the first of seven terms as an assistant on the

---

wert taken up at the court like a very boy and the reason was 1. because wee were neere a kine 2ly becaus wee maried without consent 3ly because I was under age" (*Winthrop Papers*, 3: 35). He replied on 28 May 1631 in cipher: "For those reports thou wrightest of let them not trouble the[e]. Thou maiest maist [*sic*] satisfi them that it is al false but I prethe doe not tel any that I doe not meane to pay the fine of fiue marke for I feare it may be the same tatling tonges be spread abroad and come to some of the aldermans ears with additions" (3: 37).

[458] Martha Winthrop to John Winthrop, Jr., ca. 5 April 1634, *Winthrop Papers*, 3: 23. She asked John "to bee perswaded of my loue to three notwithstanding my pasions and weaknes which formerly haue caused thee to thinke the contrary."

[459] Waters, *A Sketch of the Life of John Winthrop the Younger*, 4. See also Charles Edward Banks, *The Planters of the Commonwealth* (Boston: Houghton Mifflin, 1930), 94.

[460] Dunn, *Puritans and Yankees*, 63, citing *Winthrop Papers*, 3: 41–49.

[461] Savage, *The History of New England from 1630 to 1649,* 1: 70–71. November 2: "The ship *Lyon,* William Peirce master, arrived at Natascot. There came in her the governor's wife, his eldest son, and his wife, and others of his children, and Mr. Eliot, a minister, and other families, being in about sixty persons, who all arrived in good health, having been ten weeks at sea, and lost none of their company but two children, whereof one was the governor's daughter Ann, about a year and a half old, who died about a week after they came to sea." On 3 November they could not come ashore because of the winds. November 4: "The governor, his wife and children, went on shore, with Mr. Peirce, in his ship's boat. The ship gave them six or seven pieces. At their landing, the captains, with their companies in arms, entertained them with a guard, and divers vollies of shot, and three drakes; and divers of the assistants and most of the people, of the near plantations, came to welcome them, and brought and sent, for divers days, great store of provisions, as fat hogs, kids, venison, poultry, geese, partridges, etc., so as the like joy and manifestation of love had never been seen in New England."

[462] Shurtleff, *Records of the Governor and Company of the Massachusetts Bay in New England, 1628–1686,* 1: 367.

General Court,[463] although he only attended about half the sessions.[464] In 1633, he made the first of many moves around the colony when he was given charge of twelve men to build an outpost at Agawam (now Ipswich), about 25 miles north of Boston and 10 miles from any other settlers. He left for Agawam in March 1633 and by winter had finished a two-story house for his wife. It had four rooms, a "cabinet of Sugerie" in the parlor, and a chemical lab in the storehouse. He also began to clear a farm, although by October, after the sudden death of his wife and infant child, he was on his way to England. "This was merely the first of many occasions in which John left others to carry on a project he had started," Dunn notes,[465] although another historian argued John had simply become disillusioned with the Massachusetts Bay colony and justifiably hoped to secure funding for a fresh start elsewhere.[466]

John left for Barnstaple in winter, "in a small and weak ship" that was driven by bad weather and through "many desperate dangers" to Galway, on the western coast of Ireland. From there he continued to Dublin, Antrim, into Scotland and England, "and all the way he met with persons of quality, whose thoughts were towards New England, who observed his coming among them as a special providence of God."[467] He was advised by his uncle Emannuel Downing to be careful when visiting London, where the atmosphere was hostile toward the Massachusetts Bay settlers, sending word that "you should walk waryly and close because there be some that laye wayte to Attach [attack] you."[468]

Ten weeks later, in October 1635, John returned to Boston aboard the *Abigail* with his new wife Elizabeth and 11-year-old half-brother Deane.[469] He carried a commission from a group of wealthy Londoners

[463] Shurtleff, *Records of the Governor and Company of the Massachusetts Bay in New England, 1628–1686,* 1: 95. In 1634, he and his father were each granted permission to "intertaine an Indean a peece, as a howseholde serv'; John, Jr., also received approval "to imploy his Indean with a peece, to shoote att fowle" (1: 127).

[464] Dunn, *Puritans and Yankees,* 64. The author notes that between 1632 and 1641, John attended forty-five of the eighty-two court sessions where attendance was recorded, but he often lived far from Boston or was away in England. (His father did not miss a single meeting.) In June 1638 he and three others were each fined 5 shillings "for their absence when the Court was called" (Shurtleff, *Records of the Governor and Company of the Massachusetts Bay in New England, 1628–1686,* 1: 230).

[465] Dunn, *Puritans and Yankees,* 64–65.

[466] Arthur Percival Newton, *The Colonising Activities of the English Puritans* (New Haven, Conn.: Yale University Press, 1914), 176.

[467] Savage, *The History of New England from 1630 to 1649,* 1: 172–73.

[468] Emmanuel Downing to John Winthrop, Jr., 25 March 1635, *Winthrop Papers* 3: 195.

[469] Hotten, *The Original List of Persons of Quality,* 100. "In the *Abigail* Richard Hacwell Mr p Cert: from the Minsters & Justice of Peace of his conformitie to the Church

to claim a grant at Saybrook in the Connecticut colony. He was instructed to build a fort near the river and homes on the adjoining 1,500 acres of farm land for the proprietors "such houses as may receive men of qualitie." John also would serve as governor of the claim for one year after his return.[470] The sponsors soon abandoned their plan. They found it difficult, as prominent Puritans, to sneak away from England[471]; John also discovered the land had already been largely claimed by settlers of Hartford, Windsor, and Wethersfield. Finally, the colony leaders were not keen on newcomers who issued "certain proposals made by Lord Say, Lord Brooke and other Persons of Quality, as conditions of their removing to New-England," that included the creation of a hereditary class and a system of voting based on property ownership.[472]

In 1638, John paid £20 to Masconnomet, sagamore of Aggawam, for his rights to the land in the "Bay of Aggawan, alias Ipswich, being so called now by the English."[473] When he contemplated moving to Boston in 1637 to be captain of a fort, the authorities in Ipswich gave him a parcel that had been set aside to become the town common. It didn't keep him there, as he moved 10 miles south to Salem and staked a claim to Fisher's Island at the entrance to the Long Island Sound.[474] John decided to build an ironworks and in August 1641 sailed

---

of England & that he is no Subsedy Man. John Wynthropp, 27, Elizabeth Winthropp, 19, Deane Winthropp, 11." Elizabeth's stepfather, the Rev. Hugh Peter, was also aboard. "Here arrived two great ships, the *Defence* and the *Abigail* with . . . amongst others, Mr. Peter, pastor of the English church in Rotterdam" (Savage, *The History of New England from 1630 to 1649,* 1: 169).

[470] "Agreement of the Saybrook Company with John Winthrop, Jr.," *Winthrop Papers,* 3: 198–99.

[471] Philip Nye to John Winthrop, Jr., 21 September 1635, *Winthrop Papers,* 3: 211. "Some of the Gentlemen of the North who lay som 3 or 4 Monthes in London transacting these affaires did thinke that their would haue been no notice of their purposes and therevpon assumed to vs vp servants but when they came down found the Countrie full of the reports of their going."

[472] Dunn, *Puritans and Yankees,* 68, citing Thomas Hutchinson, *The History of the Colony of Massachuset's Bay,* Second Edition (London, 1765), 410–13.

[473] Shurtleff, *Records of the Governor and Company of the Massachusetts Bay in New England, 1628–1686,* 1: 252: "Maschanomete, the sagamore of Agawam, acknowledged that hee had received 20ᵗ of Mʳ John Winthrope, Junior, for all his land in Ipswich, for wᶜʰ hee acknowledged himselfe fully satisfied." In 1683, Wait Winthrop presented the bill of sale to be recorded (5: 381).

[474] Dunn, *Puritans and Yankees,* 70, citing J. Hammond Trumbull, ed., *The Public Records of the Colony of Connecticut,* 15 vols. (Hartford: Brown & Parsons, 1850), 1: 64–65. "Vppon Mr. Wyntrops motion to the Courte for Fyshers Iland, It is the mynd of the Courte, that so farre as yt hinders not the publike good of the Country, ether for fortifeing for defence, or setting vppe a trade of fisheing or salt & such like, he shall haue liberty to pʳceed therein."

again for England to secure capital and skilled workers.[475] He returned two years later, in May 1643, and, after managing the ironworks for a year, founded a third town known as Pequot, claiming land around the present town of Niantic based on a verbal agreement with an Indian sachem in 1636, when he was involved with the Saybrook settlement.[476]

On 22nd of the 7th month [September] 1643, his father, to pay back a loan from his son following his devastating losses to the fraud of his overseer, deeded John, Jr., his 1,200-acre farm on the Concord River plus 60 acres of meadow, and his 30 acres in Charleston known as Ten Hills.[477] Earlier that year, John had written his son with some practical advice:[478]

> You are the Chief of Two Families; I had by your Mother Three Sons and Three Daughters, and I had with her a Large Portion of outward Estate. These now are all gone; Mother gone; Brethren and Sisters gone; you only are left to see the Vanity of these Temporal things, and learn Wisdom thereby, which may be of more use to you, through the Lord's Blessing, than all that Inheritance which might have befallen you.

John, Jr., bought the remainder of Ten Hills back from his father's creditors and about 1646 made a deed of trust as "John Winthrop, the younger, of Charlestowne," to his wife and children by giving Ten Hills, then about 600 or 700 acres, to three friends with the understanding that after his death the rent would provide income for his family and then for his son Fitz-John and his heirs.[479]

In June 1644 John, Jr., asked the Massachusetts General Court for permission to build a plantation on Fisher's Island, and although the land lay outside its charter, the court generously agreed.[480] Thus began years of

---

[475] Dunn, *Puritans and Yankees*, 70. See also Waters, *A Sketch of the Life of John Winthrop the Younger*, 30.

[476] Dunn, *Puritans and Yankees*, 72. See Ebenezer Hazard, ed., *Historical Collections; Consisting of State Papers and Other Authentic Documents, Intended as Materials for an History of the United States of America*, 2 vols. (Philadelphia: T. Dobson, 1794), 2: 93–94, in which John, who has no written deed, lays claim to a "greate quantity of land at Nyanticott by purchase from the Indians" based on "the testimony of their Indians."

[477] *Suffolk Deeds*, Liber 1, item 45 (no page numbers).

[478] John Winthrop to John Winthrop, Jr., 12 April 1643, *Winthrop Papers*, 4: 366.

[479] *Winthrop Papers*, 5: 59–60.

[480] Dunn, *Puritans and Yankees*, 72–73. See Shurtleff, *Records of the Governor and Company of the Massachusetts Bay in New England, 1628–1686*, 1: 304. "Mr. John Winthrope,

discord between authorities in Connecticut and Massachusetts over the town, even over its name: John and others wanted to call it London, while a Connecticut court insisted on Fair Harbor. When John, Jr., became Governor of Connecticut ten years later, he officially changed the name of the town of Pequot to New London.[481] The house he had built there was ready by the fall of 1646, and he moved part of his family to it, including his brother Deane. Four of John's children remained in Boston.[482]

When his father died in 1649, John considered returning to Massachusetts. Roger Williams was recruiting him to move to Rhode Island, and the Dutch also suggested he relocate to their territory on Long Island. He was in demand in part because of his reputation as a political leader but also as a physician.[483] Dunn wrote:[484]

> John liked to call himself a student, especially a student of physic. Medicine as generally practiced in the seventeenth century was not a branch of science. . . . John Winthrop the elder was [an] amateur herb doctor, who medicated his friends and neighbors. . . . A new style of chemical therapy was evolving, using drugs compounded out of minerals. Much of the work of this school was bogus, chemistry intermingled with magic, but it was the embryo of modern medical practice.
>
> [John, Jr.] was a self-trained physician who considered medicine always as a side line. . . . Two crammed volumes of his medical records for the years 1657–1669 reveal an astonishingly active medical practice.[485] When he lived in New Haven, and for the first year or so in Hartford, John examined from two to a dozen or more patients every day. . . .

Junior, is granted Fishers Iland, against the mouth of Pecoit Ryver, so far as is in o͞r power, reserving the right of Conectecot & Seybrooke."

[481] Dunn, *Puritans and Yankees*, 74. See Frances Manwaring Caulkins, *History of New London* (New London, Conn.: the author, 1852), 58–59, 118–19.

[482] Caulkins, *History of New London*, 47. On 28th of 8th mo. [October] 1646 his father wrote him a letter addressed to "Mr. Jo: Winthrop at Fisher's Iland, on Pequod Riuer" (*Winthrop Papers*, 5: 114).

[483] Dunn, *Puritans and Yankees*, 75–76.

[484] Dunn, *Puritans and Yankees*, 80–82. After 1657 John began traveling all over the colony as a visiting doctor. "Something like half the inhabitants of Connecticut and New Haven colonies in these years [1657–1660] came to him for help," Dunn observed. "No wonder he was uncommonly beloved by his people" (83).

[485] Dunn, *Puritans and Yankees*, 80–82, citing Winthrop MSS XXa (1657–1660); XXb (1660–1669).

There were not many surgical cases. Measles or the ague
were frequently John's diagnoses; the general complaint was
of internal pains. . . . The sovereign Winthrop medicine for
curing almost anything, which his son Wait continued to
administer after John's death, was a reddish powder chiefly
compounded of niter and antimony which he called *rubila.*

John became so well known as a physician that he could not keep
up with demand. The historian Walter Woodward wrote:[486]

New London became a hospital town to which patients
came from all over New England seeking cures for a host
of medical conditions. To help meet the New England-
wide demand for his medicines, Winthrop distributed
them through a network of female practitioners, elite
wives who incorporated Winthrop's color-coded packets
of medicines into their own healing services. Both
Winthrop and the elite wives distributed the medicines
as a Christian service, without expectation of payment,
a form of benevolence that distinguished them from the
male and female doctors who healed for payment, acts of
benevolence that further reinforced their families' status
as community social and political leaders.

John moved to New Haven Colony in 1656, enticed by the new
ironworks there.[487] He was offered a house rent-free (he would buy it
in 1657 for £100 worth of goats from Fisher's Island),[488] but didn't join
the church. In June 1657, the town of Pequot began wooing him back:
"We are as naked without you, yea, indeed we are as a body without
a head."[489] The General Court in Hartford elected him Governor of
Connecticut, which he accepted after three invitations and the promise

---

[486] Walter W. Woodward, *Prospero's America: John Winthrop, Jr. and the Creation of New England Culture, 1606–1676* (Chapel Hill, N.C.: University of North Carolina Press, 2010), 6.

[487] Dunn, *Puritans and Yankees*, 77.

[488] Franklin Bowditch Dexter, ed., *Ancient Town Records, New Haven Town Records, 1649–1769*, 3 vols. (New Haven: New Haven Colony Historical Society, 1917), 1: 241, 313–14.

[489] Jonathan Brewster to John Winthrop, Jr., 14 June 1656, *Collections of the Massachusetts Historical Society*, 4th series, 7 [1865]: 73. At the same time, Brewster worried news of John's discovery of the "Elixer, fitt for medicine, & healing of all maladyes" would bring throngs of people to town (78, 80).

of the previous governor's house and lands in Hartford.[490] His proposed conditions (perhaps never presented) included that he "may have liberty at any tymes to be absent about my necessary occasions without any blame."[491] The Connecticut Fundamental Orders of 1638 placed a two-year term limit on the position; the freeman revoked the clause in 1660 and proceed to re-elect John every year until his death sixteen years later.[492]

Besides his work as a physician, John also attempted to introduce new industries to New England, which relied mostly on farming, fishing, and fur trading.[493] His expertise was alchemy, but rather than chase riches, he prayed his skills could save the world. "From the initiation of his alchemical studies in the 1620s, which he began with Edward Howes, his friend and fellow law student at London's Inner Temple, Winthrop was committed to the use of alchemy as a means of rendering Christian service and as a key to unlocking the hidden mysteries of nature," Woodward wrote.[494]

Alchemy was also a popular pursuit in the early seventeenth century, Woodward noted, because of the possibility that while serving Christ and mankind you also might make a tidy profit.[495] John saw his opportunity in salt, which was scarce in Massachusetts, even with several domestic producers attempting to keep up with demand.[496] On 16 November 1646, John Winthrop wrote to John, Jr., to report that "heer arived yesterday a Dutch Shippe of 300 tuns with 250 tuns of Salt. . . . We looke at it as a singular providence, and testimony of the Lords care of vs."[497] In March 1647/48, he pitched the idea of "making of salt out of meer salt wat'" to the Massachusetts General Court, and the colony leaders agreed to pay him in bushels of wheat upon delivery of "so many bushels of good white salt at Boston, Charles Towne, Salem,

---

490   Dunn, *Puritans and Yankees*, 78. See Trumbull, *The Public Records of the Colony of Connecticut*, 1: 208, 301, 306.

491   Dunn, *Puritans and Yankees*, 78, citing an undated statement among his papers at Winthrop MSS 5: 208.

492   Waters, *A Sketch of the Life of John Winthrop the Younger*, 53.

493   Dunn, *Puritans and Yankees*, 83.

494   Woodward, *Prospero's America*, 3. See Chapter 7 for an account of Winthrop's intervention in a number of cases of women accused of witchcraft, "based not on a lack of belief in magic, but rather on the knowledge – confirmed by his study of alchemy, natural magic, and other occult philosophies – that manipulation of the occult was complex and difficult and that most charges of witchcraft were unfounded" (7).

495   Woodward, *Prospero's America*, 2.

496   J. Leander Bishop, *A History of American Manufactures from 1608 to 1860*, 2 vols. (Philadelphia: Edward Young & Co., 1864), 1: 282–83.

497   *Winthrop Papers* 5: 119.

Ipswich & Salsberry."[498] In May 1648, the court granted him 3,000 acres of the Pequot land to set up a saltwork that would produce a hundred tons of salt over three years.[499] In May 1656, Winthrop claimed he had discovered a method to make salt, "never before devised or practiced," and essentially asked for patent protection for a period of twenty-one years, which was granted.[500] He established a saltworks on the seashore in what is now Beverly, Massachusetts.[501] He also pursued other elements. In May 1651, John was given approval to search for mines that produced lead, copper, and tin or antimony, vitriol, black lead, allum, stone salt, or salt springs; if he found anything he would receive title to everything within three miles, provided it hadn't already been settled.[502]

In 1661, John was assigned to travel to London to use his reputation and connections to obtain the Royal Charter for Connecticut from King Charles II.[503] Prior to what would be his last trip overseas, John wrote a will on 12 July 1661.[504] He left his wife £100 a year from rents at Fisher's Island or the Mill at New London, as well as the farm in Mistick that was already in trust. She was to have the use of the homes at Ten Hills and New London and of a rental at Hartford. She was also to receive all of

---

[498] Shurtleff, *Records of the Governor and Company of the Massachusetts Bay in New England, 1628–1686,* 2: 229.

[499] Shurtleff, *Records of the Governor and Company of the Massachusetts Bay in New England, 1628–1686,* 2: 241.

[500] Shurtleff, *Records of the Governor and Company of the Massachusetts Bay in New England, 1628–1686,* 3: 400.

[501] Dunn, *Puritans and Yankees,* 83–84. The author noted that because the colonists had to import English salt to preserve their meat and pack fish, they were happy to give John free wood to fuel the saltworks.

[502] Benjamin Trumbull, in *A Complete History of Connecticut,* 2 vols. (New Haven, Conn.: Maltby, Goldsmith & Co., 1818), 1: 195.

[503] Woodward, *Prospero's America,* 254–55. The author notes that although there was a patent from 1632, "no one seemed to possess an original copy of it." Trumbull, in *A Complete History of Connecticut,* 1: 248, related the story that "Mr. Winthrop had an extraordinary ring, which had been given his grand father by King Charles the first, which he presented to the king. This, it is said, exceedingly pleased his majesty, as it had been once the property of a father most daer to him. Under these circumstances, the petition of Connecticut was presented, and was received with uncommon grace and favor." Waters commented in *A Sketch of the Life of John Winthrop the Younger,* 55, that "in sober fact, Winthrop's grandfather was a quiet Suffolk squire, of scholarly tastes and strong Puritan leanings, whose duties as a county magistrate did not require his attendance at Court, who died at a good old age two years before Charles I came to the throne, and who would seem to have been one of the last persons to have attracted the favor that monarch when Prince of Wales."

[504] Waters, *A Sketch of the Life of John Winthrop the Younger,* 69–72, transcribed from the unpublished original in the Winthrop Family Papers.

the household goods at Hartford, New Haven, New London, Mistick, or Boston to distribute to the children, along with six cows, five mares, the great gray horse, ten sheep, and the use of the Negro called Strange (alias "Kaboôder"[505]) for half his time, "but the other halfe I allow to himself during his life, if his mistris consent to it."[506]

His daughters Elizabeth Newman and Lucy, Margaret, Martha, and Anne Winthrop each received land, livestock, or both; in addition, the three youngest were given £300 each. Son Wait was to get three horses, a sawmill, half a lead mine, a third of the net rent from Fisher's Island, and other property. The rest of the estate went to son Fitz-John. John appointed his wife, two sons, son-in-law Antipas Newman, and daughter Lucy as executors.

He would live another fifteen years. Mayo noted that John tried to resign as governor in 1667 but was rebuffed by the General Court, which exempted him from property taxes and threw in £110 cash.[507] He tried again in 1670, citing an impending voyage to England or, barring that, his need to stay in Massachusetts longer than he expected; the court this time responded by giving him a raise to £150 annually and some valuable land.[508] "Probably what Winthrop most desired was leisure in which to pursue various scientific interests,"[509] wrote Mayo, "for during this period he wrote many letters to his associates in the Royal Society[510] which indicate that almost everything under the sun aroused his curiosity—tides in the Bay of Fundy and at Hell Gate, 'some new notions about finding the longitude at sea,' waterspouts, swarming insects, comets, minerals, the depth of the ocean, a variety of Indian corn 'which may probably ripen in England, if planted there,' the effects of lightning, new ways of making salt and tar, and 'a way of trade and bank without money.'" He also owned a three-and-a-half-foot telescope "with which he saw, or thought he saw, a fifth satellite of Jupiter.[511]

---

[505] Also spelled Caboonder or Kabooner.

[506] That is, he should work for her three days a week and "the rest of the tyme to make the best of it for himself" in short-term labor. At her death, he was to be freed. Kaboôder also received 20 acres of land and a heifer or cow.

[507] Trumbull, in *A Complete History of Connecticut*, 1: 316–17.

[508] Trumbull, in *A Complete History of Connecticut*, 1: 321. See also Trumbull, *The Public Records of the Colony of Connecticut*, 2: 145n.

[509] See John Winthrop, Jr., to Henry Oldenburg (Secretary of the Royal Society), 12 November 1668, *Collections of the Massachusetts Historical Society*, 5th series, 8 [1882]: 134.

[510] He had been elected as a fellow of the Royal Society of London for Improving of Natural Knowledge during his previous trip to England. See *The Record of the Royal Society of London* (London: Oxford University Press, 1912), 18.

[511] Mayo, *The Winthrop Family in America*, 52–3. See John Winthrop, Jr., to Sir Robert

Elizabeth Winthrop, his wife of thirty-seven years, died in November 1672, and John was feeble and heavily in debt.[512] He had been struggling for years; between 1665 and 1667 he lost several thousand pounds in cargo to enemy privateers in the Dutch war. "Though he held title to many thousand acres of land in Connecticut and Massachusetts, most of it was either undeveloped or leased at low rents to tenant farmers," wrote Dunn. "John had difficulty converting his wealth in to cash, because the land could only sold at a ruinous loss. Year after year his grain crop failed, and most of his revenue (apart from his salary as governor) came from stock farming on Fisher's Island." He used the island as collateral on a £1,500 loan in 1663 but could not raise the cash when it came due six years later, even when the creditor knocked £300 off the bill.[513]

After King Philip's War broke out in 1675, John traveled to Boston for a session of the Commissioners of the United Colonies. In March 1676, preparing for his return to Connecticut, he caught cold and died soon after, at the age of 70.[514] A new will, dated 3 April, two days before he died, and probated 25 July 1676, split his estate between his children, with his sons each receiving a double portion. He noted that the overseers should consider that he had already given his daughters Elizabeth and Lucy "good farms." The children were named executors, and he named three men from Connecticut and three from Boston to act as overseers.[515] An inventory taken at Hartford on 5 September

---

Moray, 27 January 1664[/65], *Collections of the Massachusetts Historical Society*, 5th series, 8 [1882]: 93. John noted that in a previous letter he had "omitted to acquaint your Honor what now I will be bold to add: that having looked upon Jupiter wth a telescope, upon the 6th of August last, I saw 5 satellites very distinctly about that planet." In fact, there is a fifth satellite to Jupiter, although it would not be documented for another 228 years (E.S. Holden, "The Fifth Satellite of Jupiter," *Publications of the Astronomical Society of the Pacific* 4 [1892]: 262).

[512] Dunn, *Puritans and Yankees*, 83–84. In 1674, the Connecticut Assembly threw him a lifeline by agreeing to reimburse him for expenses he had incurred during his trip to London to procure its charter.

[513] Dunn, *Puritans and Yankees*, 201.

[514] Waters, *A Sketch of the Life of John Winthrop the Younger*, 59.

[515] Wait reported this information to his brother Fitz in a letter from Boston dated 15 May 1676: "Mr. Richards promised to send me a copye of it [the will] by this vessel, which I suppose he will. Least he should faile, I will write all I remember, which is, that yourself and I, with all my sisters, maryed and unmaryed, are left executors, and that after all debts are paide the rest to be diuided equally amongst us all; only yourself and I to haue as much more as any of the rest, which we neede not boast of" (*Collections of Massachusetts Historical Society*, 5th series, 8 [1882]: 404–5).

totaled £73.[516] The brothers sold Ten Hills Farm for £3,300,[517] and two warehouses and a wharf in Boston for £345.[518] They then paid £1,150 to redeem the mortgage on Fisher's Island[519] and give their two unmarried sisters £1,000 each.[520] They gave smaller amounts to two of their married sisters[521] and nothing to Lucy (Winthrop) Palmes and her husband Edward, who quarreled with them over the slight for the next forty years.[522]

Child of John[2] and Martha (Fones) Winthrop:

    i.   DAUGHTER, d. in infancy in 1634.

Children of John[2] and Elizabeth (Reade) Winthrop:

    ii.   ELIZABETH/BETTY[3] WINTHROP, bp. at First Church, Boston 3 July 1636[523] and bur. 4 Dec. 1716 in the Winthrop tomb at King's Chapel Burying Ground in Boston.[524] She m. (1) at Wenham, Mass. 10 Nov. 1658,[525] ANTIPAS NEWMAN,[526] who became the town's second

---

516 Charles William Manwaring, *A Digest of the Early Connecticut Probate Records, Vol. 1, Hartford District, 1635–1700* (Hartford: R.S. Peck: 1904), 257.

517 Deed of sale of Ten Hills Farm to widow Elizabeth Lidgett of Boston, 15 May 1677, transcribed in *Collections of Massachusetts Historical Society*, 6th series, 3 [1889]: 453–56.

518 Dunn, *Puritans and Yankees*, 203.

519 *Suffolk Deeds,* 10: 163–65 of original (pages unnumbered in transcript), payment to John Harwin for Fisher's Island to John Harwin, 5–6 February 1662.

520 *Suffolk Deeds,* 10: 167, £1,000 to Martha and Anne, "fully paid & Satisfied," 12 September 1677; 192–93, £100 to Elizabeth Newman, 9 October 1677.

521 *Suffolk Deeds,* 10: 102–4, £200 to John Curwin and wife, 17 May 1677; 192–93, £100 to Elizabeth Newman, 9 October 1677.

522 Dunn, *Puritans and Yankees*, 203, citing Winthrop Family Papers, Massachusetts Historical Society.

523 *A Report of the Record Commissioners Containing Boston Births, Baptism, Marriages and Deaths, 1630–1699*, 9: 4. "1636, First Church: Elizabeth of John Winthrop the younger, 3 day, 5 mo." A town record on the same page gives "Elizabeth of Mr. John & Elizabeth Winthrop born 24th–5th month," but editors of the *Winthrop Papers*, at 3: 266n, note that three letters to John Winthrop, Jr., one dated 3 July 1636 (3: 283), and the others 5 July 1636 (3: 287–88), make no mention of a newborn daughter.

524 "Diary of Samuel Sewall," *Collections of the Massachusetts Historical Society*, 5th series, 7 [1882]: 113. Entry for 7 December 1716: "Friday [4 December], Madam Elizabeth Endicott alias Winthrop, buried from her son Edwards': put into Gov. Winthrop's Tomb. . . . Was 80 years and 5 moneths old."

525 *Vital Records of Wenham, Massachusetts to the Year 1849* (Salem, Mass.: The Essex Institute, 1904), 149, citing Essex County court record. Mayo, 56, gives 12 November.

526 Sylvanus Chace Newman, *Rehoboth in the Past: An Historical Oration Delivered on the Fourth of July 1860* (Pawtucket, R.I.:, Robert Sherman, 1860), 62, gives Antipas Newman as born 15 October 1627 at Midhope in the parish of Ecclesfield in the West Riding of Yorkshire, son of the Rev. Samuel Newman of Rehoboth, but

pastor after being ordained in Dec. 1663.[527] He d. at Wenham on
15 Oct. 1672.[528] The couple had five children.[529] She m. (2) in
1677 or 1678,[530] ZERUBBABEL ENDICOTT, a physician in Salem, and
was admitted to the church there on the recommendation of the
Wenham church on 4 Aug. 1678.[531] Zerubbabel was b. at Salem in
1635,[532] d. after 23 Nov. 1683 (will) and before 27 March 1684 (will
probated at Salem), and was bur. at the Endicott Burying Ground
in what is now Danvers, Mass.[533] He was the son of John Endicott,
who served a total of sixteen years as governor of the Massachusetts
Bay Colony, and Elizabeth (Cogan) (Gibson) Endicott.[534]

iii.   JOHN ("FITZ-JOHN") WINTHROP, b. at Boston (or possibly Ipswich)
       14 March 1638[535] and d. at Boston 27 Nov. 1707. He was buried at

---

without citation. The index and a digital scan of the Yorkshire Bishops' Transcripts
of Baptisms at *findmypast.com* show only Hannah, daughter of Samuell Newman,
baptized at Ecclesfield 28 October 1627.

[527]   John Farmer, *A Genealogical Register of the First Settlers of New England* (Lancaster,
Mass.: Carter, Andrews & Co., 1829), 205.

[528]   *Vital Records of Wenham, Massachusetts to the Year 1849*, 213, citing Essex County
Court Record. See also Samuel Sewall, "New England Chronology," *Register* 7
[1853]: 206. "Antipas Newman, pastour of Wenham church, d. 15: 8. 1672";
"Bradstreet's Journal," *Register* 8 [1854]: 328. "Octob. 15. Mr Newman pas^t of y^e
chh of Wenham dyed"; C. Edward Egan, Jr., "The Hobart Journal," *Register* 121
[1967]: 192. "October [1]5 Mr Antipas Neuman dyed."

[529]   William C. Endicott, *Memoir of Samuel Endicott with a Genealogy of His Descendants*
(Boston, 1924), 79.

[530]   Endicott, *Memoir of Samuel Endicott*, 77, gives after 4 November 1677 and before 1
January 1678, without citation. They were certainly married after 24 April 1677,
when Elizabeth was identified in a probate record as "Mrs. Newman" (*The Probate
Records of Essex County, Massachusetts*, 3 vols. [Salem: The Essex Institute, 1920], 3:
133) and before 4 August 1678, when "Mrs. Endicott, formerly Newman" was admitted to the church in Salem by recommendation from Wenham Church (Joseph
B. Felt, *The Annals of Salem from Its First Settlement* [Salem, Mass.: W. & S. B. Ives,
1827], 261).

[531]   Felt, *The Annals of Salem from Its First Settlement*, 261.

[532]   Endicott, *Memoir of Samuel Endicott*, 76.

[533]   *Ibid.* See also Felt, *Annals of Salem*, 276. "27th [March 1684]. Zerubabel Endicott
died recently. He was son of Gov. John Endicott. His second wife, Elizabeth, the
widow of Rev. A. Newman and daughter of Governor Winthrop, survived him."

[534]   See Anderson, *The Great Migration Begins*, 1: 639–46.

[535]   *A Report of the Record Commissioners Containing Boston Births, Baptism, Marriages
and Deaths, 1630–1699*, 9: 6. "Fitz-John, Son of Mr. John & Elizabeth Winthrop
Winthrop, born 14th–1st month." Governor John Winthrop wrote John, Jr., "at
Ipswich" on 22 January 1637/38: "We have appointed the General Court the 12 of
the 1st moneth [12 March]. We shall expect you here before the Court of Assistants."
(*Winthrop Papers*, 4: 9–10), Waters, *A Sketch of the Life of John Winthrop the Younger*,
24–25, observes "that he took his wife with him when he started to attend this
Court of Assistants seems clear from the fact that his first son . . . was born two days

King's Chapel Burying Ground.[536] Called "Fitz" or "Fitz-John" to distinguish him from his father, he probably m. ELIZABETH TONGUE, who was b. 20 Oct. 1653,[537] dau. of George and Margery (_____) Tongue.[538] Elizabeth d. at New London 25 April 1731 and was buried there.[539]

The early legal status of their relationship is not clear; sometime in the 1670s she bore him a daughter, Mary, and Elizabeth signed a release of dower. Years later, a political rival would accuse Fitz of having "lived in open adultries in despight of your [Connecticut] lawes,"[540] while in his 1702 will Fitz referred to Elizabeth not as his wife but as "my Daughters Mother, Mrs Elizabeth Winthrop,"[541]

---

after the General Court met. A family tradition of uncertain date assigns this birth to Ipswich," but his birth was recorded at Boston.

[536] Dunkle and Lainhart, *Inscriptions and Records of the Old Cemeteries of Boston*, 797. "John Winthrop, Gov. of Conn., died 27 Nov. 1707, Æ 68."

[537] Caulkins, *History of New London*, 290.

[538] Caulkins, *History of New London*, 289–90. "The early records have his name written Tongue, but the orthography used by himself is given above [George Tonge]. . . . Nothing is known until he appears in New London about 1652. His marriage is not recorded." He died in 1674, and the Winthrop's neighbor, Joshua Hempstead, in his diary (*Collections of the New London County Historical Society* 1 [1901]: 31), noted on 22 December 1713 the burial of "Goode Tong," almost certainly George's widow, as "no other family of the name appears among the inhabitants. The inn so long kept by George Tonge and his widow and heirs stood on the bank between the present Pearl and Tilley Streets."

[539] See photo of stone 3642 at Farber Gravestone Collection (*davidrumsey.com/farber*). "Here lyeth the body of Madam Elizabeth Winthrop, the wife of the Honourable Governour Winthrop who died April ye 25th 1731, in her 79th Year."

[540] Jacob Leisler to Connecticut Assembly, 30 September 1690, in which he outlined the "unaccountable and unchristian behavior of Major Winthrop," reprinted in E.B. O'Callaghan, *The Documentary History of the State of New-York*, 4 vols. (Albany: Weed, Parsons & Co., 1849), 2: 300–3.

[541] Will of Fitz-John Winthrop, New London Probate District, No. 5790, scan at *ancestry.com* > Connecticut, Wills and Probate Records, 1609–1999, Hartford, Probate Packets, Wiley, I.-Wood, Erastus, 1675–1850 > images 1013–1152. Mayo, *The Winthrop Family in America*, 95, noted that Robert C. Winthrop, in a copy of his own book, *Short Account of the Winthrop Family*, made a manuscript notation that reads: "According to gossip, he did not marry Elizabeth Tongue until after his father's death in 1676 and had previously had a child by her." Mayo said he (Mayo) had been "informed" by an unnamed correspondent that "she still signed deeds up until—and including—1698 as Elizabeth Tongue, also letters." Dunn, 204, citing various manuscripts in the Winthrop Family Papers, wrote that "years passed before even Fitz's closest correspondents deigned to ask after 'Mrs. Elizabeth' or "Mrs. Betty' in their letters. Wait never did accept the lady as his sister-in-law. When necessary, he referred to her stiffly as 'Madam Winthrop,' in what we may take to be a double-entendre." When the couple's daughter, Mary Winthrop, caught the eye of John Livingston, and John's father Robert Livingston expressed concern about her status, Duncan Campbell, who was negotiating the marriage for the Winthrops,

with Winthrop written over the name Tongue.[542]

When Fitz was 16 his father tried to get him admitted to Harvard, without success.[543] Instead, he was tutored in Cambridge by a first cousin, the Harvard graduate and fellow Thomas Dudley, who wrote of Fitz to his uncle that "his mind seems not altogether adverse to what may seem for the present to be out of his reach, but willing to its utmost."[544] A year later, after Thomas Dudley died unexpectedly, Fitz himself fell sick (or homesick), ended his schooling, and went home.[545] Richard Dunn observed that at the time, a young man could become a minister, a merchant, or a farmer, but none of those prospects were appealing. In 1657, Fitz instead sailed for England, where he presented himself to his uncle Stephen Winthrop and expressed a desire to join Cromwell's army. When his uncle died soon after (as did Cromwell), Fitz turned to another uncle, Colonel Thomas Reade, who happened to have a place for a lieutenant in his regiment in Scotland, commanding about 50 men. By Nov. 1660, when he was 22, the government was disbanding its standing army, and Fitz was back in London, running up debts.[546] His father came to the city later that year on business

----

assured Livingston that Fitz-John and Elizabeth were "man and wife Although itt was not so publick att first . . . as itt is now." He added that the senior Livingston "need not scruple giving your consent to your son to marey so vertious & sober [a] young lady" (Lawrence H. Leder, *Robert Livingston, 1654-1728, and the Politics of Colonial New York* [Chapel Hill, N.C.: University of North Carolina Press, 1961], 159, citing Campbell to Livingston, 2 December 1700, Livingston-Redmond Manuscripts, Franklin D. Roosevelt Library, Hyde Park, N.Y.). For his part, Fitz-John wrote to his old friend Robert Livington that "I am much Surprized when I understood your Sons Affection to my Daughter" (*Ibid.*, Winthrop to Livingston, 9 December 1700). Mary (Winthrop) Livingston died 8 January 1713, without issue, "on the Livingston farm at Mohegan, seven miles from town [New London]. The weather being at the time intensely cold and the snow several feet deep, she was not buried until th 17th, when a crust being formed on the snow, the remains were brought into town upon a bier, by a procession of men in snow shoes" (Frances Manwaring Caulkins, "Ancient Burial Ground at New London, Conn.," *Register* 11 [1857]: 25).

[542] Will of Fitz-John Winthrop, New London Probate District, No. 5790, scan at *ancestry.com* > Connecticut, Wills and Probate Records, 1609–1999, Hartford, Probate Packets, Wiley, I.-Wood, Erastus, 1675–1850 > image 1014.

[543] Mayo, *The Winthrop Family in America*, 81. "President Dunster, having put the boy through an examination, could not stretch his conscience to that extent."

[544] Thomas Dudley, Jr., to John Winthrop, Jr., 3 October 1654, *Collections of the Massachusetts Historical Society*, 6th series, 3 [1889]: 424–25.

[545] Dunn, *Puritans and Yankees*, 194. See also Mayo, *The Winthrop Family in America*, 82.

[546] He apparently was something of a libertine. Mayo, *The Winthrop Family in America*, 83fn, noted that Robert C. Winthrop, on the Table of Contents of what was then

and suggested Fitz find a wife, but his son wanted to "spend som few yeares more in travell."[547] He sailed back to New England with his father and brother Wait in April 1663.[548] He would be drawn back to the military life in 1672, when he was given command of the New London county militia; in 1673, he was named sergeant major of British forces on Long Island that were resisting Dutch rule there.[549]

In 1686, Gov. Edmund Andros was sent from London to serve as royal governor of New England. Fitz and his brother Wait were among the twenty-seven members of his council, with Fitz as the only representative of the Connecticut colony.[550] In 1689, after Andros was pushed out, the Connecticut colony reverted to the liberal charter that John Winthrop, Jr., had procured in 1663. Fitz was elected an assistant and agreed in 1690 to help lead an effort by the New England and New York governments to conquer French Canada. Fitz took command of the overland attack upon Montreal, with the first third of the journey by land and the remainder by water.[551] He reached at Albany on 21 July 1690 for a rendevous with Indian allies, found "all in confusion" due to lack of Indian and New York soldiers and an outbreak of smallpox,[552] and continued north on 1 Aug. The men stopped to make canoes but found the bark would not come off the trees because it was too late in the season.[553]

Vol. 6 of the Winthrop Manuscripts (since disbound), had written, "Several love-letters addressed to F.J.W. in London by a lady named Von Limburg (?) have been destroyed as too confidential."

A note on Mayo's citations: When he wrote his genealogy in 1948, the family papers were in bound volumes. They were later disbound, arranged chronologically and microfilmed, filling 53 reels. A finding aid is located at *masshist.org/collection-guides/view/fa0294*, and a card catalog can be used to cross-reference Mayo's cites to the reels. The commonplace book, which was started in 1700 by John[4] Winthrop and later expanded by John Still[5] Winthrop and Francis Bayard[6] Winthrop, was kept intact.

[547] Fitz-John Winthrop to John Winthrop, Jr., 23 December 1661, *Collections of the Massachusetts Historical Society*, 5th series, 8 [1882]: 270–71.

[548] Dunn, *Puritans and Yankees*, 195.

[549] Dunn, *Puritans and Yankees*, 200–1.

[550] Mayo, *The Winthrop Family in America*, 86.

[551] Dunn, *Puritans and Yankees*, 289–90.

[552] Fitz-John Winthrop to the Governor and Council of Connecticut, 29 July 1690, *Collections of the Massachusetts Historical Society*, 5th series, 8 [1882]: 308.

[553] Dunn, *Puritans and Yankees*, 292. See "Journal of the Expedition to Canada," *Collections of the Massachusetts Historical Society*, 5th series, 8 [1882]: 312.

On 15 Aug., Fitz sent forty settlers and a hundred Indians (enough men to fill the ten birch canoes they had managed to assemble) toward Montreal to harass the enemy while he and the remaining troops returned to Albany.[554] There, a provincial captain named Jacob Leisler accused him of deliberately scuttling the invasion as part of a plot against William III and had him imprisoned.[555] He was freed after a few days by a delegation of Indians that happened to be Albany. After an enraged Leisler tried to get Fitz to pledge he would return to New York for trial, Fitz wrote his brother Wait: "Never did I see such a pittifull beastly fellow; assure yourself noething can Appeare Against me. . . . Man could not doe more then I did."[556]

Fitz seemed to be largely indifferent to political office. He was elected as a magistate in 1689 but did not attend a single council meeting (and was not re-elected). In 1693, he was elected to the Connecticut council but didn't bother taking the oath.[557] When a royal governor who arrived in New York in the summer of 1692 claimed his commission gave him control of the Connecticut milita, the assembly on 2 Sept. 1693 assigned Fitz to travel to London to appeal to William and Mary. The assembly assessed a tax of a penny on every pound of ratable estate to raise the £500 for his expenses.[558] He was sent with twenty-five documents and would spend the next four years overseas securing the charter.[559] He also performed some personal tasks, including attempting to retrieve his brother's Negro, Kinch, who had been kidnapped and pressed into service aboard a royal warship (Fitz found he had died),[560] and securing a new bell for the New London church to replace one that melted in a 1694 fire.[561]

On the eve of his return to New England in 1697, Fitz made a pilgrimage to the Winthrop ancestral home at Groton Hall "with

---

[554] "Journal of the Expedition to Canada," *Collections of the Massachusetts Historical Society*, 5th series, 8 [1882]: 317.

[555] Dunn, *Puritans and Yankees*, 293–94. See also Trumbull, in *A Complete History of Connecticut*, 1: 384.

[556] Fitz-John Winthrop to Wait Winthrop, undated, Winthrop Family Papers (reel 13, box 24). When a new royal governor took charge of New York the following spring, the rebellious Leisler was tried and executed for treason.

[557] Dunn, *Puritans and Yankees*, 298.

[558] Dunn, *Puritans and Yankees*, 299.

[559] Dunn, *Puritans and Yankees*, 302.

[560] Dunn, *Puritans and Yankees*, 313, citing Winthrop Family Papers.

[561] "Petition to the Lord Justices," *Collections of the Massachusetts Historical Society*, 5th series, 8 [1882]: 339. See also Caulkins, *History of New London*, 200.

greet Duty and affection to visit the tomb of my Ancestors," he wrote on 1 Sept. to his second cousin Charles Downing. "My Great Grandfather who was yr great Grandfather lyes there. . . . He had one son who was my Grandfather that went into New Engl: and 4 daughters of wch yr Grandmother Downing was one." Fitz said he had copied the inscription he found on Adam Winthrop's tomb.[562] He returned to Connecticut "something of a popular hero," Dunn wrote,[563] and on 12 May 1698, the freeman elected him governor.[564] It had been a dramatic turnaround; in 1690, he had "seemed destined to spend his declining years among the sheep and goats on Fisher's Island," Dunn observed. "During the 1690s Fitz himself had changed. His visit to the mother country taught him what his grandfather and father had never had to learn, that in England he was an outsider. Fitz's snobbery and awe of the King was counterbalanced by his love of New England real estate and his identity with the local colonial society."[565] He was undermined as governor, says Dunn, because rather than settling his personal differences quietly, he used the weight of his office to prosecute and humiliate his enemies, who retaliated, including appealing to the King for justice.[566]

Toward the end of May 1707 Fitz wrote his brother Wait, "I am now very sick, & weary of my life such as it is."[567] He gathered his strength to travel to Boston that fall when Wait remarried on 13 Nov. after seventeen years as a widower. But he became seriously ill afterward and died on 27 Nov. Seven days later, Judge Sewall wrote, "Mr. C. Mather preaches a very good Funeral sermon.[568] Govr Winthrop is buried from the Council Chamber. Foot-Companies in Arms, and Two Troops. Armor carried, a Led Horse. . . . Father, Son and Grandson ly together in one Tomb in the old burying place. Was a vast concourse of People."[569] His will, dated in March 1702, left all

---

[562] Fitz-John Winthrop to Charles Downing, 1 September 1697, Winthrop Family Papers (reel 14, box 25).

[563] Dunn, *Puritans and Yankees*, 316.

[564] Charles J. Hoadly, ed., *The Public Records of the Colony of Connecticut*, 15 vols. (Hartford: Case, Lockwood and Brainard, 1868), 4: 244.

[565] Dunn, *Puritans and Yankees*, 318–19.

[566] Dunn, *Puritans and Yankees*, 328.

[567] Fitz-John Winthrop to Wait Winthrop, 29 May 1707, *Collections of the Massachusetts Historical Society*, 6th series, 3 [1889]: 385.

[568] It was published in Boston in 1708 under the title *Winthropi Justa*.

[569] "Diary of Samuel Sewall," *Collections of the Massachusetts Historical Society*, 5th series,

the real estate he had inherited from his father to his brother Wait on the condition he give £100 to each of their four sisters. He also gave £100 to the "Collegiate School" (Yale) but only if it stayed in Saybrook;[570] the school moved to New Haven before his estate was settled. During administration, a deed was discovered from about eighteen months earlier in which Fitz had deeded all his property to Wait's son John Winthrop. This "created complications," Mayo noted, but the parties reached an amicable arrangement.[571]

iv. LUCY/LUCE WINTHROP, b. 28th of 11th mo. [Jan.] 1639/40,[572] d. 24 Nov. 1676,[573] and apparently bur. at the old burying ground in New London.[574] She m. about 1660,[575] EDWARD PALMES, who was b. about 1638, son of Andrew Palmes of Sherborn, Hampshire.[576] The brothers Edward and Guy Palmes were traders as early as 1659 in New Haven, but by Dec. 1660 Edward had relocated to New London.[577] He was a freeman there in 1667, a representative from 1671 to 1674, and a major in King Philip's War as a volunteer from New London Co.[578]

One narrative recounted that in April 1676, "Maj. Palmer [*sic*], having been scouring the Narragansets Country, brought in 30 of the Enemy, and 60 of Ninnicrofts People, which were about 30 fighting Men, who delivered up themselves to our Protection. We kept their Wives and Children safely, as Hostages, and made the Men go abroad with our Parites, who did us great Service in

---

6 [1879]: 204–5. The elaborate service cost Wait £611 (Dunn, *Puritans and Yankees,* 354).

570   *Collections of the Massachusetts Historical Society,* 6th series, 3 [1889]: 413–16.

571   Mayo, *Winthrop Family in America,* 93.

572   *A Report of the Record Commissioners Containing Boston Births, Baptism, Marriages and Deaths, 1630–1699,* 9: 8. "Luce daughter of John & Elizabeth Winthrop born 28th – 11th month."

573   "Bradstreet's Journal," *Register* 8 [1854]: 330. "1676. Nov. 24. Mrs. Lucy Palmes daughter to Jno. Winthrop, Esq. Govᵗ of this Colony dyed. She was aged about 36 a virtuous young Gentlewoman."

574   Caulkins, *Register* 11 [1857]: 28. "She sleeps near her husband, but only fragments of stone have been found at the head of her supposed grave." Savage, *A Genealogical Dictionary of the First Settlers of New England,* 3: 343, says they had no children; Caulkins, *History of New London,* 360, attributes to them a daughter Lucy who married (1) Samuel Gray and (2) Samuel Lynde of Saybrook.

575   "Winthrop of New London" in Muskett, *Evidences of the Winthrops of Groton,* 27.

576   John Nichols, *The History and Antiquities of the County of Leicester,* 4 vols. (London, 1795–1811), 2: 295. The pedigree describes Edward as "in New England, 1681, and married there."

577   Caulkins, *History of New London,* 360.

578   George Madison Bodge, *Soldiers in King Philip's War* (Boston: the author, 1906), 442–44.

clearing the Woods."[579] Edward, who m. (2) Sarah (Farmer) Davis, widow of William Davis of Boston,[580] d. 21 March 1714/15, age 77, and was buried at the old burying ground at New London.[581]

6   v.   WAITSTILL WINTHROP, b. at Boston 27 Feb. 1641/42; m. (1) before 18 Feb. 1678, MARY BROWNE; m. (2) 13 Nov. 1707, KATHARINE (BRATTLE) EYRE.

    vi.   MARY WINTHROP, bp. at Boston 15 Sept. 1644[582] and probably d. shortly before 27 July 1653, when a friend comforted John Winthrop, Jr., on the death of his child.[583]

   vii.   MARGARET WINTHROP, b. ca. summer 1646,[584] d. 29 Nov.,[585] and bur. at King's Chapel, Boston 3 Dec. 1711.[586] She m. at Salem in

---

[579]   Charles H. Lincoln, ed., *Narratives of the Indian Wars, 1675–1699* (New York: Charles Scribner's Sons, 1913), 89.

[580]   Samuel Forbes Rockwell, *Davis Families of Early Roxbury and Boston* (North Andover, Mass: Andover Press, 1932), 212, citing *Suffolk Deeds*, Liber 25, 10, dated 1695–96, recorded 1709.

[581]   Caulkins, *Register* 11 [1857]: 28. "Here Lyes Interred The Body of Major Edward Palmes who departed this life March Ye 21ˢᵗ. Anno Dom. 1714/15 in the 78ᵗʰ year of his age." "Diary of Joshua Hempstead," *Collections of the New London County Historical Society* 1 [1901]: 44. "Tuesd. 22d. . . . Majr Edward Palmes died Sudently being well last night & dead in 2 ½ hours. . . . Sat. Raw Cold. Wedensd 23. fair most of ye day. I was at ye funeral of Majr Edwd Palmes in ye foren & Capt Prentts in ye aftern. both buried in arms."

[582]   *A Report of the Record Commissioners Containing Boston Births, Baptism, Marriages and Deaths, 1630–1699,* 9: 19. "Mary of John Winthropp jun aged about 9 days [on] 15 day 7 mo."

[583]   William Parke to John Winthrop, Jr., 27 July 1653, *Winthrop Papers,* 4: 316. "But sorry we were to hire of the deth of your Child." The child is not named, however, and Mayo, *The Winthrop Family in America,* 56, says only that Mary "died young— probably in the early summer of 1653."

[584]   *Winthrop Papers,* 5: 94n. "The exact date of the birth of Margaret, fourth daughter of John and Elizabeth Winthrop, is not known, but subsequent references indicate that she was in her early infancy in the autumn of 1646." Also, John Jones to John Winthrop, Jr., 5 March 1646[/47]: "with loue to all your little ones and little Margaret." (*Winthrop Papers,* 5: 133). Also 13 May 1647, from Jones, "loue to your son and pretty Margaret" (5: 159–60).

[585]   "Diary of Samuel Sewell," *Collections of the Massachusetts Historical Society,* 5th series, 6 [1879]: 327, dated 30 November 1711: "Mrs. Margaret Corwin died last night," which was Thanksgiving Day. "Winthrop of New London" in Muskett, *Evidences of the Winthrops of Groton,* 27, gives 30 November; Lemuel Shattuck, "Genealogical Memoir of the Descendants of Edward Winslow, Governor of Plymouth Colony," *Register* 4 [1850]: 301, errs with 28 September 1697.

[586]   "Diary of Samuel Sewell," *Collections of the Massachusetts Historical Society,* 5th series, 6 [1879]: 327–28 dated 3 December 1711: "Mrs. Margaret Corwin, Mr. Jnᵒ Corwin's widow, Maiden name Winthrop, is buried in Govr Winthrop's tomb. . . . Neither Govr Dudley, nor Govr Saltonstall there [at service]. They came to give me a visit, and were here when the Time call'd me to the Funeral, upon account of which I was oblig'd to go away. Govr said What Funeral?"

May 1665,[587] JOHN CORWIN, who was b. 25 July 1638, son of Capt. George and Elizabeth (Herbert) (White) Corwin, and had issue.[588] John d. 12 July 1683.[589]

viii. MARTHA WINTHROP, b. before 14 Aug. 1648[590] and d. at Boston 27 Sept. 1712.[591] She m., as his third wife, before 29 June 1678 (baptism of eldest child[592]), RICHARD WHARTON, who d. at the home of his sister Dorothy Pack in London 14 May 1689,[593] four days after making a will from a copy of a previous one dated 10 July 1687.[594]

---

587 Shattuck, *Register* 4 [1850]: 301.

588 Wait Winthrop to Fitz-John Winthrop, 22 June 1680, *Collections of the Massachusetts Historical Society*, 5th series, 8 [1882]: 421. "My sister Curwin I heard yesterday was prety well, haueing bin brought to bed of a girle about a weeke since. Mat and Ann are both with her." See also Craig Partridge, "Elizabeth Herbert, Wife of (1) John White and (2) George Corwin," *Register* 150 [1996]: 193–95.

589 Shattuck, *Register* 4 [1850]: 301.

590 John Winthrop [from Boston] to John Winthrop, Jr., 14th of 6th mo. [August] 1648 (*Winthrop Papers*, 5: 245) replied "some two hours after I received yours": "My Good Sonne, I blesse the Lorde and reioyce with three in the safe deliuery of my deare daughter, and the Comfort of your little Martha." Also, Joseph Cooke to John Winthrop, Jr., 21st of 8th mo. [October] 1648, said glad to hear that "god hath soe comfortably Raysed vpp my Cousen your wyfe from her Childbed sorrowes and adding another branch of his blessing vnton your stock" (5: 272).

591 "Diary of Samuel Sewall," *Collections of Massachusetts Historical Society*, 5th series, 6 [1879]: 363. "7th 27th [27 September]. . . . Madam Wharton died last night, 2 hours past midnight."

592 Robert J. Dunkle and Ann S. Lainhart, "Records of the Old South Church in Boston," in *Records of the Churches of Boston* (Boston: New England Historic Genealogical Society, 2002), 89 (510 of original), accessed at *americanancestors.org*. "Anne daughter of Richard & Martha Wharton, [baptized] 29 June 1678." Wait Winthrop to Fitz-John Winthrop, 2 June 1679, noted that "we are all well (which I suppose Mr. Wharton informes you, as alsoe of your young neese, by his wife)" (*Collections of the Massachusetts Historical Society*, 5th series, 8 [1882]: 419). Further, Wait Winthrop to Fitz-John Winthrop, 24 October 1682, "My sister Wharton was the last night brought of bed of a girle, and is in a likely way to get up againe" (430–31). And Wait Winthrop to Fitz-John Winthrop, 17 October 1684, "Sister Wharton has got a boy and is almost up againe" (445).

593 Richard Wharton married (1) Bethia Tyng and (2) Sarah Higginson and had issue by both wives, per *Collections of the Massachusetts Historical Society*, 6th series, 3 [1889]: 466–67fn. Sarah (Higginson) Wharton died in 1676; see "Diary of Samuel Sewell," *Collections of Massachusetts Historical Society*, 5th series, 5 [1878]: 12, entry for 25 April 1676 ["Mrs. Wharton dyes"] and Wait Winthrop to Fitz-John Winthrop, 15 May 1676 ["Mrs. Wharton dyed last weeke"], 5th series, 8 [1882]: 405.

594 William M. Sargent, "Richard Wharton," *Notes and Queries*, 5th series, 12 [1885]: 447–48. Sargent noted one source gives Dorothy Hacke. He wrote: "It is from this lady's testimony at the probating of her brother's will that a clue is found to the English origin of the family. Dorothy Pack desposes that she is a widow, of Kirby

"Richard Wharton was a very active man," noted one history, "who at different periods was concerned in trade with the West Indies, with mining operations, and with land speculations in Maine and in the Narragansett country. He was a member of the council of Sir Edmund Andros, but, becoming one of the later's strongest opponents, went to England in 1687 to complain of him."[595] On 29 May 1689, the colonial administrator Edward Randolph, sitting in the Boston jail after a popular uprising against Gov. Andros, wrote to the Lords of Trade and Plantations to report (with some justification) that the rebellion's ringleaders had been motivated purely by personal finances because the governor had cracked down on piracy and the private minting of money. "Mr. Richard Wharton was a great undertaker for pirates and promoter of irregular trade," Randolph claimed, and the ability to coin money attracted pirates who brought their plate to be minted. "Mr. Sewell, who, as well as Mr. Wharton, is now an agent in England, was master of the mint, and a great loser by its abolition."[596] Randolph was not aware that Wharton had died two weeks earlier in London, with his affairs in what James Savage would characterize as a "much embarrassed" state.[597]

Street, Hatton Garden, co. Middlesex, where she had dwelt 12 years, was born in the parish of Warcupp, in county Westmoreland, and that Richard Wharton was her brother." She may be the Dorothye Wharton, dau. of Humfray, baptized at Warcop 30 May 1638. There is also Richard, son of Richard, baptized at Warcop 21 February 1637. Richard Wharton and his first wife Bethiah (Tyng) Wharton had sons Richard (1664) and Humphrey (1666).

[595] *Collections of the Massachusetts Historical Society*, 6th series, 3 [1889]: 465–67. In commenting on a letter from Richard Wharton to Waite Winthrop dated 16 July 1683 (5th series, 9 [1885]: 113fn), Charles Deane noted that while James Savage, in *A Genealogical Dictionary of the First Settlers of New England*, 4: 494–95, had entries for two Richard Whartons, one with two wives and the second married to Margaret Winthrop, they are almost certainly the same man.

[596] John R. Brodhead, ed., *Documents Relative to the Colonial History of the State of New-York*, 15 vols. (Albany: Weed, Parsons and Co., 1853), 3: 582.

[597] Savage, *A Genealogical Dictionary of the First Settlers of New England*, 4: 494. Sargent, *Notes and Queries*, 5th series, 12 [1885]: 447–48, noted that "because of the disturbances of the Indian wars his estate greatly depreciated in value, what is now worth millions of dollars was sold by his administrator, on representation of insolvency, to the Pejepscot Company, bringing only 140*l*." For more on Richard Wharton's many business dealings, see Viola F. Barnes, "Richard Wharton, A Seventeenth Century New England Colonial," *Publications of the Colonial Society of Massachusetts* 26 [1927]: 238–70. She noted that his estate was in such shambles at his death that "two of his daughters, Sarah and Bethia, were later forced to support themselves by keeping a little shop in Boston" (269, citing *Collections of the Massachusetts Historical Society*, 3rd series, 7 [1838]: 198–99).

ix. ANNE WINTHROP, perhaps b. before 23 Feb. 1650/51[598] and d. at
Boston 27 June 1704.[599] She m., as his second wife, 1 Sept. 1692,[600]
JOHN RICHARDS, who was bp. at Pitminster, Somerset 13 Feb. 1625,
son of Thomas and Wealthian (Loring?) Richards.[601] John emigrated
with his parents when about five years old to Dorchester, Mass.
about 1630; in 1644, he bought from the sachem Robin Hood an
island called Arrowsie or Richards' Island, where he lived for about
ten years until selling it in 1654.[602] In July 1675, Capt. Richards

---

[598] Lucy Downing to John Winthrop, Jr., 23 February 1650[/51], *Winthrop Papers*, 6:
96. "I did by some body hear God has given you another littel, which I wish you
comfort in."

[599] *Boston News-Letter*, [Monday], 3 July 1704, 2. "Boston, July 2. On Tuesday morning
[27 June] Dyed Madam Anne Richards: was Buryed on Thursday last [29 June]." Also,
"Diary of Samuel Sewall, Vol. 2" *Collections of Massachusetts Historical Society*, 5th series,
6 [1879]: 107–8. "June 27th. *Feria tertia*. Madam Richards dies about 3 hours after
midnight. Heard not of it till at Mr. Stoddard's noble Treat in the evening."

[600] "Diary of Samuel Sewall, Vol. 1," *Collections of the Massachusetts Historical Society*,
5th series, 5 [1878]: 364. "Thursday, Sept. 1, 1692. Major John Richards marries
Mistress Anne Winthrop before Wm. Stoughton Esqr., the Lieut. Governour, at the
House of Madam Usher. Sept. 4th. Major Richards accompanies his Bride to our
Meeting, morning and evening." William Stoughton at the time was the lead judge
at the Salem witch trials, and Anne's brother Wait Winthrop was one of the seven
other jurists who had been convened in May.

[601] "The Ancestry of Thomas Richards," *The Utah Genealogical and Historical Magazine*
24 [1933]: 92. See also Anderson, *The Great Migration Begins*, 3: 1575–76. In the will
of Thomas Richards, dated 17 December 1650, he refers to his "brother" Thomas
Loring, leading to speculation Loring may have been a brother of "our dear mother
Welthian Richards," as named in administration on 28 January 1650[/51]. In 1652/53
John's mother considered matching him with William Tyng's eldest daughter
(*Winthrop Papers*, 6: 268); he instead married on 3rd of 3rd mo. [May] 1654, Elizabeth
(Hawkins) (Long) Winthrop, the widow of Adam[2] Winthrop (*A Report of the Record
Commissioners Containing Boston Births, Baptism, Marriages and Deaths, 1630–1699*, 9:
48). Elizabeth died 1 November 1691, per Savage, *A Genealogical Dictionary of the First
Settlers of New England*, 3: 533. In 1640 Joseph Hollway testified he had overheard the
wife of Thomas Richards call Henry and William Waltham "cozeners & cheaters"
(Edward Everett Hale, Jr., ed., *Note-book kept by Thomas Lechford, esq., lawyer, in Boston,
Massachusetts Bay, from June 27, 1638, to July 29, 1641* [Cambridge, Mass.: J. Wilson
& Son, 1885], 321). Although Henry Waltham defended himself in a letter to John
Winthrop dated 25th of the 11th mo. [January] 1640/41, indicating that Mrs. Richards
behaved in a way "unbeseeming a modest woman's carriage" (*Winthrop Papers*, 4:
310), Hale cited other court records to suggest Mrs. Richards' opinion of Henry "was
in some measure justifiable." In the second month [April] of 1640 Mrs. Richards
brought her maid to John Winthrop for judgment, charging that the servant was
"discovering the secrets of the family, one thing she confessed about a maid that drank
too much there" (4: 232). In 1653/54 Welthian Richards was threatened with the
charge of witchcraft after she allegedly threatened harm to those who angered her.
After Thomas Thacher testified that she had raised her children to be good Christians
(6: 362), the case apparently was not pursued.

[602] Noyes, Libby and Davis, *Genealogical Dictionary of Maine and New Hampshire*, 585.

was appointed to lead an infantry company to march in aid in the defense of Swansea, after an attack during King Philip's War; he supposedly "shamefully refused the employment."[603] However, John "does not seem to have lost in public estimation by this refusal," noted historian Edward Hale. "He was chosen an Assistant from 1680 to 1686; in [Gov.] Andros's time he was a 'high friend of liberty,' in Mr. Savage's phrase[604]; was a judge of the Supreme Court; and when he died was buried with all the honors. The 'shameful refusal' to take command of the foot may be the testy memorandum of an excited day."[605] John d. suddenly at Boston after an argument with a servant 2 April 1694 and was bur. at the North Burying Ground.[606] There were no children by either of his wives.[607]

    x.   UNNAMED CHILD, d. in infancy in 1654.[608]

[603] Edward E. Hale, "Boston in Philip's War," in Winsor, *The Memorial History of Boston,* 1: 312.

[604] Savage, *A Genealogical Dictionary of the First Settlers of New England,* 3: 533.

[605] Hale, "Boston in Philip's War," in Winsor, *The Memorial History of Boston,* 1: 316. Hale noted in a footnote at 312 that a comparison of the minutes of the meeting preserved in the *Massachusetts Archives Collection* 67: 204, and the original reproduced at 313 make it appear "this reproach seems to have been interlined later."

[606] "Diary of Samuel Sewall, Vol. 1," *Collections of the Massachusetts Historical Society,* 5th series, 5: 389–90. "April 2, 1694. Monday. . . . In the Afternoon, all the Town is filled with the discourse of Major Richard's Death, which was very extraordinarily suddain; was abroad on the Sabbath, din'd very well on Monday, and after that falling into an angry passion with his Servant Richard Frame, presently after, fell probably into a Fit of Apoplexy, and died. On Tuesday was opened and no cause found of his death; noble Parts being fair and sound. Friday, April 6. Major Richards is buried in his Tomb in the North Burying Place." Egan, *Register* 121 [1967]: 281, quotes the Hobart journal for 3 April 1694: "Major John Richards of Boston died suddenly."

[607] Savage, *A Genealogical Dictionary of the First Settlers of New England,* 3: 533.

[608] Mayo, *The Winthrop Family in America,* 57, calling the child a son, offers as evidence a letter by Samuel Symonds to John Winthrop, Jr., 11 June 1654, *Collections of the Massachusetts Historical Society,* 4th series, 7 [1865]: 129–30, in which Symonds says he is sorry that he must write on "such an occasion" and reminds John "you have many children still; count that you have none, give them all to the Lord; & then you shall be sure to have them againe with advantage." Further, in a letter dated 12 July 1654, Roger Williams references John's "branches, although some sad mixtures we have had from the sad tidings (if true) of youre late losse and the cutting off of one of them" (*Ibid.,* 3rd series, 10 [1849]: 1). See also, per Mayo, Winthrop Manuscripts 17: 95.

THE THIRD GENERATION

6. **WAITSTILL**[3] **WINTHROP** (*John*[2-1]) was born at Boston, Massachusetts 27th of the 12th month [February],[609] and baptized at First Church on 6 March 1641/42.[610] He died at Boston 7 November 1717[611] and was buried with his father and grandfather in a tomb at King's Chapel Burying Ground.[612] He married, first, before 18 February 1678,[613] **MARY BROWNE**, who was baptized at Salem, Massachusetts on the 25th day of the 11th month [January] 1656/57,[614] the daughter of William

609   *Collections of the Massachuetts Historical Society*, 5th series, 7 [1882]: 147. The editors at 356 note that two sermons delivered at Wait's funeral in November 1717 both said he was in his 77th year. They also noted "the recent discovery" [about 1882] of a memo in the hand of his son, John, that read: "Febr ye 27th 1710[–11], My good father blessed me and mine, it being his birth day & ye 70th year of his age compleat. He was borne at Boston in New England on the Sabbath Day, ye 27th of ye 12th month Febr, anno 1641, & was baptized by Mr. John Cotton. He has at this day ye vigor & vivacity of 30."

610   *A Report of the Record Commissioners Containing Boston Births, Baptism, Marriages and Deaths, 1630–1699*, 9: 13. "Waitstill of John Winthropp, the younger aged about 8 days, [on] 6 day of 1 month [6 March]." Mayo, *The Winthrop Family in America*, 97, gives Wait Still.

611   "Diary of Samuel Sewall," *Collections of the Massachusetts Historical Society*, 5th series, 7 [1882]: 146. "Novʳ. 7. 5. Last night died the Excellent Waitstill Winthrop, esqr." See also *Boston News-Letter*, 18 November 1717, 2: "Boston, on Thursday the 7th Currant died here the Honourable Major General Wait Winthrop Esq.; Aged 76 Years, Justly Dear to his Country for his Honourable Descent (being the son of the Honourable John Winthrop Esq; first Governour of Connecticut, and Grand-Son of the Honourable John Winthrop Esq.; the first Governour of New-England; in their Day the Glory and Support of Their Country) but dearer yet for her Person Character and Vertues. . . . And on Thursday last the 14th Currant he was Honourably Interr'd in the Tomb with his Ancestors."

612   Dunkle and Lainhart, *Inscriptions and Records of the Old Cemeteries of Boston*, 797. "Major General / Wait Still Winthrop / died Sepᵗ 7th [sic] 1717, Aged 76 Years." Bridgman, *Memorials of the Dead in Boston*, 27, gives same. See also "Diary of Samuel Sewall," *Collections of the Massachusetts Historical Society*, 5th series, 7 [1882]: 147.

613   Mayo, *The Winthrop Family in America*, 100.

614   Richard D. Pierce, ed., *The Records of the First Church in Salem, Massachusetts 1629–1736* (Salem, Mass.: Essex Institute, 1974), 25. "25:11 [1656] Mary, daughter of Mr.

and Sarah (Smith) Browne.[615] She died at Boston 14 June 1690.[616] Waitstill married, second, at Boston 13 November 1707,[617] **KATHARINE BRATTLE**, who was born at Boston 26 September 1664,[618] the daughter of Captain Thomas and Elizabeth (Tyng) Brattle. She married, first, John Eyre, by whom she had twelve children over a period of eighteen years; ten of the twelve died young.[619] Katharine died 2 August 1725, age 61, and was buried on 5 August in the South ("Granary") Burying Ground "in a tomb near the northeast corner."[620]

William Browne." Sidney Perley, *The History of Salem, Massachusetts*, 2 vols. (Salem: the author, 1924), 1: 366, gives 28 January 1656/57.

[615]   Will of William Brown, 12 March 1686/87, excerpted in Eugene Tappan, ed., "Essex County Estates Administered in Suffolk County, Prior to 1701," *The Essex Institute Historical Collections* 41 [1905]: 180, citing Docket 1616. Browne mentions his daughter Winthrop, who receives the largest balcer, the largest silver tankard, and six of the silver spoons. Savage, *A Genealogical Dictionary of the First Settlers of New England*, 1: 277, gives Sarah Smith. For more on the Browne family, see Sidney Perley, ed., "Descendants of William Browne of Salem," *The Essex Antiquarian* 13 [1909]: 159–62.

[616]   *A Report of the Record Commissioners Containing Boston Births, Baptism, Marriages and Deaths, 1630–1699*, 9: 194. "Mrs. Mary Winthrop wife of Waite Winthrop Esqr. Dyed June 14." Dunn, *Puritans and Yankees*, 259, attributes her death to smallpox.

[617]   *A Report of the Record Commissioners of the City of Boston, Containing the Boston Marriages from 1700 to 1751*, Vol. 28 (Boston: Municipal Printing Office, 1898), 17. "Wait Winthrop Esq. & Mdm. Katherine Eyre," married by Ebenezer Pemberton.

[618]   Edward Doubleday Harris, *An Account of Some of the Descendants of Capt. Thomas Brattle* (Boston: D. Clapp and Son, 1867), 5. See also note 620.

[619]   Harris, *An Account of Some of the Descendants of Capt. Thomas Brattle*, 25–26. Although Wait and Katharine had no children, Robert J. Dunkle and Ann S. Lainhart, eds., *Deaths in Boston 1700 to 1799*, 2 vols. (Boston: New England Historic Genealogical Society, 1999), 2: 1010, citing Old Sexton's Bills at Boston City Hall Archives, note curious records for the burials of two unnamed infant children of "Wait Winthrop, Esq." (no mother given) on 26 October 1713 and in April 1716. Wait may have been the father, but it seems far less likely that Katharine, who would have been 49 and 51 at the time of the births, was the mother. The draft of Wait's will, prepared in September 1713, makes no mention of a forthcoming child, nor do his letters of either period make reference to what would have been a somewhat astounding event. See *Collections of the Massachusetts Historical Society*, 6th series, 5 [1892]: 271–73, in which on 7th of 7th mo. [September] 1713, Wait tells his son John, "Your mother is better, and was at meting yesterday in the afternoon, but has som smale remembrance of her fit every other night." If the birth records are accurate, perhaps they were illegitimate, although Wait complains in the letters of the time of his poor health.

[620]   "Diary of Samuel Sewall," *Collections of the Massachusetts Historical Society*, 5th series, 7 [1882]: 363–64. "Monday, Aug.t 2. Mrs Katherine Winthrop, Relict of the hon.ble Waitstill Winthrop, esqr., died *Ætatis* 61. She was born in September 1664. The Escutcheons on the Hearse bore the Arms of Winthrop and Brattle, The Lion Sable. Aug.t 5. 1725. Bearers, His Hon.r L.t Gov.r Dummer, Sam.l Sewall; Col. Byfield; Edw. Bromfield esqr; Simeon Stoddard esqr. Adam Winthrop esqr. Was buried in the

Wait Winthrop was born seven months after his father had sailed for England to secure money and equipment for an ironworks. There are several thoughts about the origin of his unusual name. He may have been named for family friends, the Wait family of Essex and the Still family, who were connected by marriage to the Winthrops; "more probably," wrote the historian Richard Dunn, "his name was a characteristically Puritan invocation to wait still for the Lord, with the poignant added plea (in an era of terrible infant mortality) to wait still for the mortal father to come home from across the sea and see this child."[621]

Dunn provided an insightful, if brutally honest, take on Wait and his brother Fitz. He noted that the brothers, like many of their generation, felt resentment that they could not enjoy the wealth and power of the English aristocracy, adding:[622]

> [They] were men of ordinary talent, lacking their grandfather's driving moral purpose and their father's breadth and creative intelligence. Both brothers were humorous, easy-going and self-indulgent, half-aware of their many absurd quirks of character. Fitz's and Wait's conduct betrayed a fundamental moral confusion. Both men made enemies for trivial reasons and nourished longstanding grudges; they were susceptible to flattery and manipulation by cleverer and stronger persons. The accumulation of real estate was their main object, and the conduct of lawsuits over disputed land claims was among

South-burying place, in a Tomb near the North-east Corner. Will be much miss'd." See also 440. "Aug. 5. At the funeral of Mad^m K. Winthrop, ætat. 61." Also *Boston News-Letter*, 5 August 1725, 2. "On Monday last about 10 a Clock, Forenoon, died here Mrs. Katharine Winthrop, Relict of the late Honourable Wait Winthrop, Esq., *Ætatis* 61."

621 Dunn, *Puritans and Yankees*, 193. On 27 Sept. 1642, John Winthrop's sister-in-law wrote to him in England, saying his wife was lonely and "therefore I pray hastin to us and let not watestill wat any longer, you know I soppose your sones name is so" (*Winthrop Papers*, 4: 355). Mayo, *The Winthrop Family in America*, 97, goes with the family connection explanation, saying the boy was probably named by his grandfather, since his father was 3,000 miles away. But he acknowledges in a footnote at 98 that those who prefer the name as a "Puritan invention like Hopestill ... have much on their side of the argument: (1) the use of middle names was rare in New England prior to 1730, (2) the Psalms contain many exortations to 'wait on the Lord'; (3) Roger Clap, of Dorchester, Massaachusetts, named one of his sons Waitsill, and this son was born within a few months of Wait Still Winthrop, and (4) the record of his baptism gives his name as Waitstill, not Wait Still."

622 Dunn, *Puritans and Yankees*, 191–92.

their main occupations. The brothers also displayed an acute awareness of their status as gentlemen and the necessity of living in style. They were always exceedingly anxious to hear about the latest London fashions in waistcoats and wigs. The Winthrop dynasty was definitely on the wane.

Yet Fitz and Wait Winthrop, in their selfish, petty and confused behavior, accurately mirrored the social temper of late seventeenth-century New England. It was a time of rapid expansion in population, wealth, ease and comfort, in which the colonists were nevertheless sorely buffeted by strange new external pressures, dubious about their inherited values, ashamed of their parochialism and utterly bereft of first-class leadership. . . . . Due to their family pedigree, Fitz and Wait were called upon to perform greater public services than their talents warranted. . . . Actually, the brothers accomplished a great deal in their long and eventful public careers. Despite their preoccupation with private interest, they proved to be better guardians of New England's chartered liberties than of their own family fortune. . . . [They] epitomize the final secularization of the New England conscience, the completed evolution from Puritan to Yankee.

The men were close their entire lives and similar in many ways, Dunn noted:[623]

Both were homely men, indeed almost comic looking. Both were full-faced, with weak mouths, big eyes and (chief family trait), the wonderfully long, wide-flanged Winthrop nose. . . . The brothers were to quarrel with many people, not least with members of their own family, but all through their lives they maintained a close relationship with each other.

Fitz appeared to be more the outdoor type, and Wait the scholar. In 1652, both boys were sent to a school in Hartford run by Samuel Fitch. After eighteen months they transferred to Cambridge. Wait, 12, attended grammar school, while John Winthrop, Jr., tried to get his son Fitz,

---

[623] Dunn, *Puritans and Yankees*, 192–93.

then 16, admitted to Harvard, without success.[624] (Fitz returned home a year later.) After four years of grammar school, Wait was admitted in 1658 to Harvard,[625] where he studied medicine.[626] He dropped out two years later; that same year, he sailed to England with his father, who had been assigned to secure from the king an airtight charter for the Connecticut colony. Wait and his father returned in April 1663. Wait lived in New London and Hartford until about 1670, when he began spending most of his days in Boston. "Wait did not take the covenant; he did not join the Boston church; he was a second-class citizen," Dunn wrote, although "occasionally he was called on to act as Connecticut's representative" in dealings with Massachusetts.[627]

On 2 September 1685, Edward Randolph, the royal customs collector in London, submitted the names of twenty-one men to the Lords of Trade and Plantations. He had worked up the list with Joseph Dudley, an agent for the Massachusetts Bay Colony. The two men anticipated that the colonial charter granted to Massachusetts would be revoked and recommended the men on the list, including Wait Winthrop and his brother-in-law, Richard Wharton, as potential members of a Crown-friendly council to oversee New England.[628] The historian Theodore Lewis noted that he and other scholars "wondered why these men, several of whom belonged to the first families of Massachusetts, were willing to serve in a royal government." The answer, Lewis concluded, was profit. The Dudley Council of 1686, formed on the authority of a commission from James II, was stacked with land speculators, including Wait and Wharton, who had been in the business

---

[624] Dunn, *Puritans and Yankees*, 194.

[625] Mayo, *The Winthrop Family in America*, 99, citing Winthrop Manuscripts 9A: 32. His father paid a higher tuition so that he could be enrolled as a "fellow commoner," which allowed him to be recorded as Mr. and dine at the Fellow's table. He also had to give the college a piece of plate valued at £3 or more, which was a silver beaker "that holds a pint" and has since disappeared. See also William C. Lane, "Early Silver Belonging to Harvard College," *Publications of the Colonial Society of Massachusetts* 24 [1923]: 165–66, 31 [1935]: 264–65.

[626] Dunn, *Puritans and Yankees*, 195.

[627] Dunn, *Puritans and Yankees*, 200.

[628] Theodore B. Lewis, "Land Speculation and the Dudley Council of 1686," *The William and Mary Quarterly* 31 [1974]: 255. See J.W. Fortescue, ed., *Calendar of State Papers, Colonial Series, America and West Indies*, 44 vols. (London: 1899), 12: 87. Richard Wharton appeared on both the list of "well-disposed persons for the Council of Massachusetts Bay" and "fitting persons to be on the Council of the Colony of Charlestown Bay, New England," while Waite Winthrop appeared only on the latter.

for a quarter century already.[629] Fitz-John Winthrop was appointed to
the council, as well.[630] The proprietors began to "buy" large tracts of
Indian land at bargain prices so they could, after taking their seats on
the new council, approve their own patents. For example, on 7 May
1686, Wait and two other proprietors purchased the Connecticut
Nipmug and Wabbaquassett lands for £120 from Owaneco, "who, for
good measure, threw in his claims to Massachusetts lands," Lewis noted.
By one accounting, the council members claimed more than 400,000
acres. Wait (3,314 acres) and his brother Fitz-John (6,563) were relatively
small players, but Wharton was in for 208,814 acres, including 200,000
in Maine.[631] For him, especially, "the success or failure of the schemes
meant the difference being lords of great estates or going bankrupt,"
Lewis observed.[632]

The new royal governor, Edmund Andros, who arrived in December
1686 to succeed Dudley, disappointed them all. He "soon saw through
the speculators' scheme," Lewis wrote. "Undoubtedly he agreed with
Randolph's estimate of the situation. The customs commissioner wrote
in March 1687: 'It is no small unhappines to find in our whole Councill
not one man but either by private Interest or faction is touch'd, the
Generallity are possessed of Great Tracts of Land by Indian purchase
(at best, or not so well) and these will stickle hard when their titles of
Land are questioned.'"[633] So Andros simply decreed that all lands in
Massachusetts had reverted to the King when the charter was revoked.
Incensed, Wharton traveled to London in summer of 1687, where he
joined Increase Mather in trying to get Andros removed. Most of the
speculators, including Wait, joined the Boston rebellion of 18 April
1689 that overthrew Andros.[634]

It wasn't until that event that Wait became a first-class citizen, Dunn
wrote. He was admitted to South Church on 25 August 1689[635] and

---

[629] Lewis, *The William and Mary Quarterly* 31 [1974]: 255. Lewis defined speculator was
"an individual who was a member of a land company or an absentee proprietor of
a town, or who claimed over 1,000 acres, most of which was unimproved."

[630] Lewis, *The William and Mary Quarterly* 31 [1974]: 263.

[631] Lewis, *The William and Mary Quarterly* 31 [1974]: 271.

[632] Lewis, *The William and Mary Quarterly* 31 [1974]: 265.

[633] Lewis, *The William and Mary Quarterly* 31 [1974]: 266, citing Randolph to William
Blathwayt, 31 March 1687, reprinted in Robert N. Toppan and Alfred Goodrick,
eds., *Edward Randolph, Including His Letters and Official Papers from the New England,
Middle and Southern Colonies in America*, 7 vols. (Boston: The Prince Society, 1909),
6: 218.

[634] Lewis, *The William and Mary Quarterly* 31 [1974]: 269.

[635] Dunn, *Puritans and Yankees*, 257.

would consistently be reelected to the Massachusetts council until his death in 1717. Further, Dunn pointed out:[636]

> He became increasingly a champion of Massachusett's "antient liberty," the religious orthodoxy and chartered priveleges established by his grandfather. Having at last joined the church, Wait became the protégé of Cotton Mather, a zealous judge in witchcraft trials, a pious critic of his colleagues' self-seeking greed in office, and a stern defender of the old-time New England virtues. . . . [But] in politics, he proved to be a pawn of Cotton Mather. Undercutting his talk of preserving Massachusetts' "pure order of the Gospell," his chief motivating impulse was really hurt family pride. . . . Faced with greater obstacles than the Founder [John Winthrop] had ever encountered, Wait dissolved (in Edward Randolph's contemptuous phrase) into "a small practioner in physick."[637]

Wait only attended about 60 percent of the Massachusetts council meetings; he was also riding circuit as a judge and traveling to New London to visit his brother and check on the family estates.[638] (He had four small children to care for, as well, after Mary Winthrop died in 1690.) By the 1690s, Wait also was well known as a doctor; his secret was rubila, which his father had taught him to make. Another was horehound shredded into warm milk from a red cow.[639]

---

[636] Dunn, *Puritans and Yankees*, 258.

[637] Edward Randolph, "Crimes and Misdemeanors Charged Upon the Governors of the Propreitary Governments in America," 24 March 1700, reprinted in Toppan and Goodrick, *Edward Randolph*, 5: 268. "They have likewise Turn'd out Mr. Byfield, a man zealous for having the Acts of Trade duly executed [from the Court of Admiralty] . . . and [appointed] Mr. Waite Winthrop (a small practioner in Physick) to be Judge of That Court Tho' in no Sort qualified for ye Office instead of Mr. Byfield against whom they had nothing to Object."

[638] Dunn, *Puritans and Yankees*, 259.

[639] Wait Winthrop to Fitz-John Winthrop, 1 November 1694, *Collections of the Massachusetts Historical Society*, 5th series, 8 [1882]: 502–3. "If Wait Newman drink the decoction of lignum vitae two or thre times a day, it might help him; also the herb horehown, shred very small, and warmed a litle in a cup, and then m[i]lk from a red cow milked into it and drunk warm, the herb with the m[i]lk, morning and evening; which two medicines God was pleased to bless to me the last summer." Cotton Mather eulogized him, "Wherever he came, the diseased flock'd about him, as if the Angel of Bethesda had come among them" [*Hades Look'd Into: Sermon at the Funeral of the Honourable Wait Winthrop Esq.* (Boston: T. Crump, 1717), 40], although his cures were certainly suspect, such as when he wrote his brother Fitz in 1682, "I

In 1692, a new royal governor, William Phips, appointed Wait Winthrop to a special commission of seven judges to consider the cases of accused witches in Salem who would not confess. Wait and another judge were considered the old "moderates" of the group. The court opened at Salem on 2 June 1692. Within about a week the court had convicted and hung its first witch, Bridget Bishop. By 22 September 1692, the judges had tried twenty-seven suspects, all of whom denied being witches and all whom were condemned to death. (Nineteen were hanged and one pressed to death when he refused to stand trial.) Ironically, none of the fifty *confessed* witches had been executed, or even tried.[640] "The judges, as though bewitched themselves, could only drive on and on," wrote Dunn, until the governor finally stepped in and put a stop to the madness. "According to contemporary acocunts of the Salem proceedings, Wait played a relatively inconspicuous part," Dunn wrote. "He did not resign from the court in disgust, like Nathaniel Saltonstall, nor did he exhibit the conspicuously vengeful zeal of magistrates John Hathorne and Jonathan Corwin, who arraigned most of the suspects.... Nor did he have the courage or conviction to admit publicly that he had done wrong at Salem, like Judge Sewall, who stood up in South Meetinghouse in 1697 and asked to take the shame and blame."[641]

In his last years, Wait's overriding concern was preserving the Winthrop family estate, Dunn noted. His marriage to the wealthy widow Katharine Eyre in 1707 had "entailed neither profit nor loss," since they each renounced claim to the other's estate. But when Fitz died in 1707, the estate came to Wait, "[saddling] him with large debts and a violent family feud."[642] Fitz had left the New London house and adjoining property to his daughter Mary (Winthrop) Livingston, but

---

know no better antidote in fevers than the black powder, niter, snakeweed, lignum vitae, white cordial powder, unicorn's horn, all which [you?] know the use of" (*Collections of the Massachusetts Historical Society*, 5th series, 8 [1882]: 429).

[640] Dunn, *Puritans and Yankees*, 264–67, citing George Lincoln Burr, ed., *Narratives of the Witchcraft Cases* (New York: Charles Scribner's Sons, 1914), 355–67.

[641] Dunn, *Puritans and Yankees*, 267. Wait was next appointed to the Superior Court, which took up the witch trials again in January 1693. However, the judges were instructed not to consider spectral evidence (that the accused witch appeared to a witness in a dream), as the Salem panel had. The panel dismissed half of about fifty cases for lack of evidence, tried twenty-six, and gave death sentences to three women, which the governor then commuted. A few years later Winthrop became a judge of the "Vice-Admiralty of northern New England and New York" (Mayo, *The Winthrop Family in America*, 105, citing *Calendar of State Papes, Colonial Series, America and West Indies, 1699*, 457, *1700*, 392).

[642] Dunn, *Puritans and Yankees*, 283.

Wait said he held the estate in joint tenancy with his brother, which invalidated that bequest, and Governor Dudley agreed. In Dunn's view, Wait "procrastinated hopelessly in his old age," ignoring Dudley's advice to sell wilderness property to pay his debts, to settle persistant disputes with his tenants, and to make a will.[643] (Wait had one drafted on 28 September 1713 but never signed it.[644]) On the day after Wait's death in November 1717, his old friend Judge Sewall remembered him for his "Parentage, Piety, Prudence, Philosophy, Love to New England Ways and people very Eminent." He added, pointedly, that "his Son, not come, though sent for," although John[4] Winthrop did arrive within the week to arrange a lavish funeral. Judge Sewall, a pallbearer with the current and former governors of the colony and two colonels, wrote that "the corps[e] were carried to the Townhouse the night before [the funeral service], now buried from the Council Chamber." At the service, "the Regiment attended in arms. Mr. John Winthrop led the widow. Twas past five before we went. The streets were crowded with people; was laid in Govr Winthrop's Tomb in Old Burial Place. When returned I consoled Mr. Winthrop, Madam Lechmere, the Province, on the Loss of so excellent a Father."[645]

---

[643] Joseph Dudley to Wait Winthrop, 8 June 1713, *Collections of the Massachusetts Historical Society*, 6th series, 5 [1892]: 267. "It would be much better, in my opinion, that you would sell some wild lands that are of no benefit or income, which would now sell in peace, & leave no incumbrance upon your children. The English saying is, No wise man dyes without a will. I am sure it is much more true in our country, where courts please themselves often to destroy intestate estates by tearing them to pieces." See also Dudley's letter to John Winthrop, 5 February 1713/14 (283).

[644] "Will of Wait Winthrop, Not Executed," *Collections of the Massachusetts Historical Society*, 6th series, 5 [1892]: 367–70. For the inventory of his estate, see "Estate of Wait Winthrop," Boston, 1724, New London Probate District, No. 5794, scan at *ancestry.com* > Connecticut, Wills and Probate Records, 1609–1999, Hartford, Probate Packets, Wiley, I.-Wood, Erastus, 1675–1850 > images 1153–64.

[645] "Diary of Samuel Sewall," *Collections of the Massachusetts Historical Society*, 5th series, 7 [1882]: 146–47. Dunn notes that Sewall's (unsuccessful) courtship in 1720 of Wait's widow, Madam Winthrop, has become "the most celebrated passage" of his diary. See, for example, at 262: "I went to Madam Winthrop's just at 3. Spake to her, saying, my loving wife died so soon and suddenly, 'twas hardly convenient for me to think of Marrying again; however I came to this Resolution, that I would not make my Court to any person without first Consulting with her." See Mayo, *The Winthrop Family in America*, 400–1, for a discussion of a response in 1885 by Robert Charles[7] Winthrop, Jr., to George Ellis, a fellow member of the Massachusetts Historical Society, who had delivered a paper about the life of Judge Sewall in which he alleged that Katharine Winthrop had been a "worldly-minded woman" who encouraged Sewall to propose to her and then refused him. When the society refused to publish Winthrop's reply in its *Collections*, deeming it unseemly, he published it himself as *A Few Words in Defence of an Elderly Lady: A Difference of Opinion Concerning the Reasons Why Katharine Winthrop Refused to Marry Chief Justice Sewall.*

Children of Waitstill[3] and Mary (Browne) Winthrop:

     i.   JOHN[4] WINTHROP, b. at Boston 12 Sept. 1679[646] and died at about three months of age.[647]

7   ii. JOHN WINTHROP, b. at Boston 26 Aug. 1681; m. 16 Dec. 1707, ANNE DUDLEY.

     iii. ELIZABETH/BETTY WINTHROP, b. at Boston 11 May[648] and d. 20 Sept. 1683.[649]

     iv. WILLIAM WINTHROP, b. at Boston 4 Jan. 1684[650] and d. there 25 Sept. 1693 of the "bloody flux" (dysentery).[651]

     v. ANNE WINTHROP, b. 28 Nov. 1686[652] and d. at Boston 22 Nov. 1746.[653] She m. at the Old South Church, Boston 17 Nov. 1709,[654] THOMAS LECHMERE, the surveyor general of His Majesty's Customs

---

[646] *A Report of the Record Commissioners Containing Boston Births, Baptism, Marriages and Deaths, 1630–1699*, 9: 150. "John of Wait & Mary Winthrop born Sept. 12." Savage, *A Genealogical Dictionary of the First Settlers of New England*, 4: 52, gives a baptism of 12 October 1679.

[647] Wait Winthrop to Fitz-John Winthrop, January 1679[/80], *Collections of the Massachusetts Historical Society*, 5th series, 8 [1882]: 419. "Soone after you went from us I lost my hope, and the greatest part of my comfort; but Gods will is don, and he is just in all his dealings with us."

[648] *A Report of the Record Commissioners Containing Boston Births, Baptism, Marriages and Deaths, 1630–1699*, 9: 161. "Elizabeth of Wait & Mary Winthrop, born May 11." Wait Winthrop to Fitz-John Winthrop, 18 May 1683, *Collections of the Massachusetts Historical Society*, 5th series, 8 [1882]: 435. "My wife was brought to bed of a girle on Friday morning last, the 11th instant. She and the child are prety well, and little John is almost able to giue you a visit."

[649] Wait Winthrop to Fitz-John Winthrop, 27 September 1683, *Collections of the Massachusetts Historical Society*, 5th series, 8 [1882]: 437. "Gods hand has bin out against us, and I haue had two or thre ill fits since I saw you, but I thank God am just geting up againe, and it has pleased the all-wise God to take from us our little Bette Winthrop, who departed the last Munday, to our grate greife; but his will must be done, and I desire to submit."

[650] *A Report of the Record Commissioners Containing Boston Births, Baptism, Marriages and Deaths, 1630–1699*, 9: 164. "William of Waitstil & Mary Winthrop born Jan. 4." Mayo, *The Winthrop Family in America*, 110, gives 4 December 1684. Savage, *A Genealogical Dictionary of the First Settlers of New England*, 4: 52, gives 7 December.

[651] "Diary of Samuel Sewall," *Collections of the Massachusetts Historical Society*, 5th series, 5 [1878]: 384. "Sept. 25 [1693] Mr. Wm Winthrop dies of the bloody flux. Sept. 27. Mr. Joseph Winthrop dies of the same disease. Two children of Major Winthrop."

[652] Savage, *A Genealogical Dictionary of the First Settlers of New England*, 4: 52. Mayo, *The Winthrop Family in America*, 110, gives this as the baptism date.

[653] *Boston News-Letter*, 28 November 1746, 2. "Saturday Night last died Madam Ann Lechmere, Wife to the Honourable Thomas Lechmere, Esq., Surveyor-General of his Majesty's Customs in the Northern District of North America."

[654] *A Report of the Record Commissioners of the City of Boston, Containing the Boston Marriages from 1700 to 1751*, 28: 24. "Thomas Leechmere & Ann Winthrop," by Rev. Ebenezer Pemberton.

for the Northern District of America, a position he almost certainly procured through the influence of his elder brother, Nicholas Lechmere, first and last Lord Lechmere of Eversham.[655] Thomas was b. 18 June, bp. at St. Mary's Church, Hanley Castle, Worcestershire 6 July 1683,[656] son of Edmund and Lucy (Hungerford) Lechmere of Severn End, Hanley,[657] and d. at Boston 30 May 1765.[658]

After reading Thomas' correspondence with the Winthrops, one biographer characterized him as a "spoiled English aristocrat" and "embittered third son," who, despite marrying well, never seem satisfied with his lot.[659] Although from a wealthy family, he struggled to make a living as a merchant in Boston and "lived perpetually beyond his means, so that his wife . . . was in constant fear of ruin." The biographer Allegra di Bonaventura, a professor

---

[655] Allegra di Bonaventura, *For Adam's Sake: A Family Saga in Colonial New England* (New York: Liveright Publishing Corp., 2013), 211–12. Thomas used his influence to get his son, named Nicholas after his uncle, a job as customs collector of New London. Nicholas would gain notoriety in 1751 for beating a 9-year-old slave to death with a horsewhip, although a grand jury refused to indict (126–28).

[656] *Parish Registers for Hanley-Castle, 1538–1966*, indexed at *familysearch.org/ark:/61903/1:1:NGN5-34R*.

[657] Evelyn Philip Shirley, *Hanley and the House of Lechmere* (London: Pickering and Co., 1883), 47. Thomas Lechmere's grandfather, Sir Nicholas Lechmere, recorded in his diary on 18 June 1663, "My daughter Lechmere was delivered of a soñe named Thomas. *Benedict Deus Amen.*" A note appended to the entry reported that Thomas Lechmere was the "ancestor of the American branch of the family, still, I believe, existing. There is a piece of land in Hanley called New England, planted with oaks, the seeds of which were sent from America by Thomas Lechmere in January, 1733–34." The marriage of Edmund Lechmere and Lucy Hungerford on 7 August 1673 is recorded by Shirley at 44, and Lucy's 1703 obituary for her husband Edmund is at 53. A note in *Register* 46 [1892]: 180 on the family reported that "in [her great-grandson] Colonel Lechmere Russell's possession is Ann Winthrop's bible, with, in her son Richard Lechmere's writing, the statement it was his mother's bible." The family Bible of Nicholas Winthrop[5] Lechmere, son of Thomas and Ann, is held by the New England Historic Genealogical Society.

[658] *The Boston Gazette and Country Journal*, 3 June 1765, 3. "Last Thursday Evening, died very suddenly, in the 82d year of his Age, Thomas Lechmere, Esq., formerly Surveyor and Searcher of the Northern District of America. His Funeral is to be attended this Afternoon." Another contemporary source, John Boyle's "Journal of Occurrences in Boston, 1759–1778," *Register* 84 [1930]:168, gives the same date, with Boyle observing, "Tis conjectured by those who knew him, that a quantity of Maderia Wine equal to what he has drank, would be Sufficient to float a 74 Gun Ship." Samuel G. Drake, *The History and Antiquities of Boston* (Boston: Luther Stevens, 1856), 691, errs with "Tuesday the evening of the fourth of June" 1765," as does a note appended to the diary of Thomas' grandfather Nicholas Lechmere, transcribed in Shirley, *Hanley and the House of Lechmere*, 47, which states, "Mr Thos Lechmere died at Boston in New England, the 4th day of June 1765."

[659] Di Bonaventura, *For Adam's Sake*, 126, 207.

at Yale, noted that in 1716 Lechmere had returned to England to ask his widowed mother and elder brother Nicholas for money. His mother, Lucy Lechmere, remonstrated with him for being a spendthrift, then wrote a letter to her son's father-in-law, Wait Winthrop, scolding him for not providing sufficient funding for the couple.[660]

Thomas Lechmere had maintained a warm relationship with his brother-in-law, John Winthrop, and during the trip sent him English grape seeds and fruit stones. But Wait Winthrop's death in Nov. 1717 changed all that. Wait left no will, and so John informally took charge of the estate. Under the laws of Connecticut and Massachusetts, John, as the only surviving son, was entitled to a double share, and his sister, Anne, to one-third. (This division was the plan Wait had given, as well, in the 1713 unsigned draft of his will.) Di Bonaventura writes:[661]

> John [Winthrop] IV had no desire to sell assets to make a proper division, so he simply passed along funds according to his inclination, with the Lechmeres, buried in debt, becoming increasingly exasperated[662]. . . . Under threat of arrest for nonpayment of debts and complaining to John IV about selling household goods to buy bread for his children, Thomas Lechmere slipped away to England and his wealthy family again in 1721.

In the meantime, in Boston, Anne expressed outrage to her brother John that he was not moved to "afford me some of the sweepings of the mill your swine fed on to keep me and my poor children from perishing." To counter his sister's accusation of his "hoggish disposition," John hoggishly sent her a token £10 and reminded her of a £30 gift he had provided eight months before.[663] Soon after Thomas Lechmere returned to Boston in 1723, he and

---

[660] Di Bonaventura, *For Adam's Sake*, 209. The author noted that at the same time, "Nicholas Lechmere had continued to rise to dizzying heights of fortune and position in England, becoming solicitor general of the nation in 1714 and attorney general in 1718." For Lucy's letter, dated 24 May 1716, see *Collections of the Massachusetts Historical Society,* 6th series, 5 [1892]: 316.

[661] Di Bonaventura, *For Adam's Sake*, 210–11.

[662] Di Bonaventura, *For Adam's Sake*, 210, citing Thomas Lechmere to John Winthrop IV, 31 August 1719, *Winthrop Papers* microfilm, reel 19.

[663] Di Bonaventura, *For Adam's Sake*, 211, citing Ann Lechmere to John Winthrop IV, 8 May 1721, and his response of 11 May 1721, both in *Winthrop Papers*, microfilm 19.

his wife sued John Winthrop in Massachusetts and Connecticut probate courts for allegedly mishandling Wait's estate.[664] The case dragged on until March 1726, when Thomas and Anne prevailed in Connecticut and were given control of the estate.[665] (For John's reaction, see below.)

vi. JOSEPH WINTHROP, b. at Boston 10[666] and d. there 27 Sept. 1693, two days after his older brother William, "of the same disease." The boys were buried together on 28 Sept.[667]

[664] Di Bonaventura, *For Adam's Sake*, 211. For a detailed account of the Winthrop-Lechmere dispute, see Arthur M. Schlesinger, "Colonial Appeals to the Privy Council, II," *Political Science Quarterly* 28 [1913]: 440–42.

[665] Di Bonaventura, *For Adam's Sake*, 230.

[666] *A Report of the Record Commissioners Containing Boston Births, Baptism, Marriages and Deaths, 1630–1699*, 9: 186. "[1693] Joseph of Waite & Mary Winthrop born Sept. 10." Savage, *A Genealogical Dictionary of the First Settlers of New England*, 4: 52, gives 13 September.

[667] "Diary of Samuel Sewall," *Collections of the Massachusetts Historical Society*, 5th series, 5 [1878]: 384. "Both are buried together, being a very affecting sight."

The Kinship Between Robert[8] Winthrop
and the novelist Louis Stanton Auchincloss

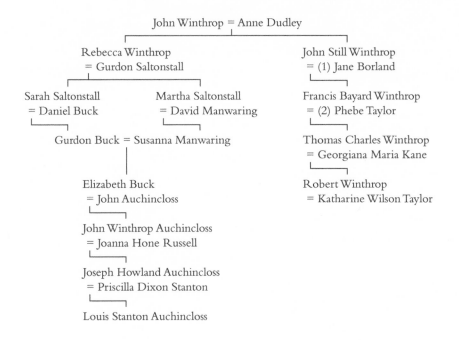

John Winthrop = Anne Dudley

Rebecca Winthrop
= Gurdon Saltonstall

John Still Winthrop
= (1) Jane Borland

Sarah Saltonstall
= Daniel Buck

Martha Saltonstall
= David Manwaring

Francis Bayard Winthrop
= (2) Phebe Taylor

Gurdon Buck = Susanna Manwaring

Thomas Charles Winthrop
= Georgiana Maria Kane

Elizabeth Buck
= John Auchincloss

Robert Winthrop
= Katharine Wilson Taylor

John Winthrop Auchincloss
= Joanna Hone Russell

Joseph Howland Auchincloss
= Priscilla Dixon Stanton

Louis Stanton Auchincloss

THE FOURTH GENERATION

7. **JOHN**[4] **WINTHROP** (*Waitstill*[3], *John*[2-1]) was born at Boston, Massachusetts 26 August 1681,[668] died at Sydenham, Kent 1 August 1747, and was buried at St. George's Church-yard in Beckenham, Kent.[669] (Both Sydenham and Beckenham are today part of Greater London.) He married at Roxbury, Massachusetts 16 December 1707,[670] **ANNE DUDLEY**, who was born at Roxbury 27 August 1684,[671] the daughter of Joseph Dudley, who later became Governor of Massachusetts, and Rebecca (Tyng) Dudley.[672] Anne married, second, at New London, Connecticut 30 September 1750, Jeremiah Miller.[673] She died at New London on 29 May 1776.[674]

John was the only one of the four sons of Waitstill and Mary (Browne) Winthrop to survive childhood, and so, by the judgment of

---

[668] *A Report of the Record Commissioners Containing Boston Births, Baptism, Marriages and Deaths, 1630–1699*, 9: 156. "John of Wait & Mary Winthrop born Aug. 26." Savage, *A Genealogical Dictionary of the First Settlers of New England*, 4: 52, gives 28 August. John is usually referred to by genealogists as John Winthrop, F.R.S., "not because he was the only John Winthrop ever elected a Fellow of the Royal Society," explained Mayo (118), "but because it was the highest distinction this one achieved."

[669] Commonplace book in the Winthrop Family Papers (reel 39, page 58). "John Winthrop the only Son of Wait Stll Winthrop, Died on the 1st August 1747 at Syndenham in the County of Kent in England, and was buried at Beckingham in the same County in the Church yard near the Road Side. This Mem[orial?] taken from a note in the hand writing of his Son John Still Winthrop, who was with his father in England at his Death."

[670] *Vital Records of Roxbury, Massachusetts, to the End of the Year 1849*, 2 vols. (Salem, Mass.: The Essex Institute, 1925), 2: 127. "Anne, Mrs., and John Winthrop, Dec. 16, 1707."

[671] *Vital Records of Roxbury, Massachusetts*, 1: 115. "Dudley, Ann, d. Joseph, Esq., and Rebeca, Aug. 27, 1684." John R. Totten, "Christophers Family," *Record* 51 [1920]: 220, gives her baptism date as 31 August 1684.

[672] *Register* 10 [1856]: 337–38.

[673] Mayo, *The Winthrop Family in America*, 136. See also *Collections of the New London County Historical Society*, 1 [1901]: 156. "Tuesd. 2d [Oct.] . . . I was at Court in the foren & to See madm Winthrop (that was). She was maried on Sunday morning by the Dept. Govr Woolcot to Mr. Miller."

[674] Mayo, *The Winthrop Family in America*, 136.

historian Lawrence Shaw Mayo, "his parents can hardly be blamed if they humored him until he became selfish if not actually spoiled. He was not a rugged boy."[675] When John was 14, his father wrote to his brother Fitz-John for help securing his son a chess board and also to ask that Fitz-John "advise with som of your acquaintance what is sutable and fashionable" for John and his sister Ann, then 9.[676] His father also offered John his own advice: "Pray to God earnestly. Loue your sister. Haue a care of eating green trash in the garden. Mind your studdye. I pray for Gods blessing upon you, and leaue you all under his divine protection."[677]

John entered Harvard in 1696, and "played the part of a young man of wealth and family, spending money lavishly, incurring frequent and heavy fines, and in one quarter paying more for broken windows than for study rent," observed one historian. At the same time:[678]

> He was gratified to have the use of a silver beaker given to the College by his father, and marked "W. W."[679] He was fascinated by family tales about his grandfather's alchemical experiments, signed his name with the Hermetic emblen, and copied into his commonplace book, "Hermetis Trismegisti Tabula Smaragdina" [the author and title of the *Emerald Tablet*, an ancient alchemist text], followed by the declaration: "Qualis a Majoribus nostris ad nos pervenit. . . . Secretae Alkymiae secrete servabo."[680] He noted that within a year of his birth there had been "Five very Notable Eclipses of the Sun and Moon" and that the anagram of "Iohannes Winthrope" was "I hope winns a throne."

---

[675] Mayo, *The Winthrop Family in America*, 118.

[676] Wait Winthrop to Fitz-John Winthrop, 11 November 1695, *Collections of the Massachusetts Historical Society*, 5th series, 8 [1882]: 512–13.

[677] Wait Winthrop to John Winthrop, 27 June 1695, *Collections of the Massachusetts Historical Society*, 5th series, 8 [1882]: 504.

[678] Clifford K. Shipton in Sibley, *Biographical Sketches of Graduates of Harvard University*, 4: 536.

[679] He mentions the beaker in a memoir copied into the Winthrop commonbook by his grandson Francis Bayard[6] Winthrop, saying "it holds a pint. . . . I had the use of it when I lived at the College" (Winthrop Family Papers, reel 39, Massachusetts Historical Society).

[680] "What manner of man has come to us from our ancestors. Keep secret the secrets of alchemy" (Shipton, in *Biographical Sketches of Those Who Attended Harvard College*, 4: 536, citing unnumbered volume, since disbound, in Winthrop Family Papers).

Despite the social and political prominence of John's family, Simon Bradstreet, a Dudley connection whose grandfather had recently been governor of the colony and whose father had graduated from Harvard in 1653, was placed at the top of the list of fourteen or fifteen freshmen, with John at number two. Waitstill had to pay extra to make his son a "fellow-commoner" and move him during his senior year to the head of the list of the Class of 1700.[681] To his credit, Mayo wrote, John was a good student and possessed a sense of humor and a decent, if florid, prose.[682] After graduation he hoped to see the world,[683] as he wrote to his uncle when his father had a chance to go to England, "I am in great hopes my father will accept of the offer of ye General Assembly have made him. It will be a very advantageious oppertunity for me to see the word."[684] (When the news arrived that Joseph Dudley has been appointed governor instead, the trip was cancelled.) A year later, apparently somewhat humbled, he wrote:[685]

> Since I came to years of understanding, I have taken a little notice of ye affairs of ye world, and have found it to be in a most distracted posture, full of confusion. Not a man of anything constant or true. I am now at present year 1702, twenty-one years old, and in all my life hitherto have never yet found at true friend, one ye I could trust. Even my very relations have proved false and betrayed me. When I reflect upon my mispent time and think how long I have lived, and what little I have done for ye servis of X^t I mourn and lye low in the dust before the Lord my creator.

In 1703, John attended the commencement at Harvard to receive his Master of Arts degree, holding forth in defense of the proposition

---

[681] Shipton, in *Biographical Sketches of Those Who Attended Harvard College*, 4: 536.

[682] Mayo, *The Winthrop Family in America*, 119.

[683] In a memoir copied into the Winthrop commonbook by his grandson Francis Bayard Winthrop, John wrote that upon leaving Harvard in 1700, he "traveled throughout New England to see learn all I could in my Native Country, before I visited any Strange Shoar. My curios[ity] having always been inflamed with a Most ardent desire of Travelling" (Winthrop Family Papers, reel 39, Massachusetts Historical Society).

[684] John Winthrop to Fitz-John Winthrop, 4 August 1701, *Collections of the Massachusetts Historical Society*, 5th series, 8 [1882]: 572.

[685] "Memorandums of Wait Winthrop's Son John, Relating to Naushon," in Daniel Ricketson, *The History of New Bedford, Bristol County, Massachusetts* (New Bedford, Mass.: the author, 1858), 351–52.

that a wound could be healed by treating an article stained with the patient's blood, rather than the patient.[686] John's father, Wait Winthrop, and Joseph Dudley, the newly appointed governor, had a longstanding political feud,[687] so it certainly caused alarm for both families when John announced in 1707 he planned to marry the governor's daughter. A few weeks before the wedding, John's uncle, Fitz-John Winthrop, died, leaving all his property to his brother Wait. In the summer of 1711, John moved to New London to take over management of the family estates there.[688]

By Mayo's assessment, John was not a particularly joyful companion. "People irritated him, and he irritated them," he wrote. "In his intercourse with them he seems to have been entirely devoid of either tact or diplomacy. One cannot help feeling sorry for him, because he had a likeable side which, unfortunately, he concealed from most of the world."[689] Except for his own family, "anyone who disagreed with him was wrong and probably crooked."[690] Another historian, Clifford Shipton, was no less harsh. "The trouble with John Winthrop was an unfortunate

---

[686] Mayo, *The Winthrop Family in America*, 120. Also known as "weapon salve," this notion was introduced in 1570 in a book called *Archidoxis Magica*; it was said the salve could cure a wound from a distance if applied to the weapon that had made the wound. John's grandfather, John[2] Winthrop, Jr., had been friendly with the alchemist Sir Kenelm Digby via the Royal Society, and Digby's 1658 treatise on "powder of sympathy" went through 29 editions.

[687] Mayo, *The Winthrop Family in America*, 121. "Winthrop did not trust Dudley," Mayo wrote, "and there was no reason why he should."

[688] Mayo, *The Winthrop Family in America*, 122. See the correspondence between Wait Winthrop and his son in *Collections of the Massachusetts Historical Society*, 6th series, 5 [1892]: 234–43, e.g. Wait to John, 19 July 1711 ("I did not think you could have been ready so soon; I shall now expect your coming, and shall send the coach-horses to the ferry at Boston Neck") and Wait to John, 1 August 1711 ("I am greatly distressed about your getting safe hither, and see almost an impossibility for a coach to get hither with children, or indeed without. . . . If your mother be with you, be careful of her and hear her advice").

[689] Mayo, *The Winthrop Family in America*, 122.

[690] Mayo, *The Winthrop Family in America*, 122. Mayo was not alone in his judgment of John Winthrop. The editors of the *Collections of the Massachusetts Historical Society*, in a footnote at 6th series, 5 [1892]: 350. "John Winthrop was a scholarly man, of scientific tastes, whose many good qualities were often neutralized by a hasty temper, a suspicious disposition, and an exaggerated sense of his own importance. Born and bred in Massachusetts, he did not begin to reside in Connecticut until he was past 30, and he did not conceal that he regarded his removal from Boston to New London in the light of an exile. . . . He became firmly persuaded that a conspiracy existed among his father's tenants to wipe off arrears of rent by fictitious pleas of produce furnished or labor performed. He persuaded himself that such proceedings were winked at, for political or selfish reasons, by some of the local authorities," including Governor Gurdon Saltonstall, who had been a cherished friend of his uncle Fitz-John Winthrop.

combination of ancestral pride and personal incompetence," he wrote. "He demanded at his due the respect that people had accorded to his ancestors, and which they naturally withheld from a pompous and somewhat ridiculous young man of mediocre talents."[691]

However, after his move to Connecticut, John was accepted at face value as a Winthrop, Mayo wrote, and appointed Justice of the Peace and Quorum in the County of New London. He also sat on the Governor's Council in 1713.[692] "But such demonstrations of regard soon became infrequent," Mayo recounted. "Much of his time was taken up with quarrels and lawsuits."[693] Cotton Mather wrote in 1718 suggesting he return to Boston because of "the uncivil and barbarous" treatment by the "Connecticotians," but in a draft of a letter of reply, John said that just as his grandfather had cited a duty to his family when it was suggested he return to England from the wilds of America, so John explained his duty to his children "enjoyns me to stay here and try to improve my estate" for their future benefit.[694]

John was convinced that the family estates, which included a remote wilderness lead mine called Tantiusques that his grandfather had acquired in 1644, contained great mineral wealth and apparently doctored maps to leave that impression, which lead to a legal morass that continued for his widow after his death. "His grandfather's lack of success [with the mine] could not dissuade him from entering upon the most ambitious schemes for the development of his properties," wrote historian George H. Haynes. "His optimism as a mining speculator was invincible," although he likely the first of the Winthrops who actually ever visited Tantiusques.[695] (John[2] Winthrop had tried but became lost

---

691 Shipton, in *Biographical Sketches of Those Who Attended Harvard College*, 4: 537.

692 Hoadly, *The Public Records of the Colony of Connecticut*, 5: 369, 390, 392.

693 Mayo, *The Winthrop Family in America*, 122. See *Collections of the Massachusetts Historical Society*, in a footnote at 6th series, 5 [1892]: 352–53, for Wait Winthrop's final letter to his son John, and, in a footnote, the last note sent by John to his father, which arrived after he had died. In it, John complained about the trouble he was having with a housemaid: "this Irish creature . . . lying & unfaithfull, w^d doe things on purpose in contradiction & vexation to her mistress; lye out of the house anights, and have contrivances wth fellows that have been stealing from o^r estate & gett drink out of ye cellar for them; saucy & impudent, as when we have taken her to task for her wickedness she has gon away to complain of cruell usage." He threatended to send her to Virginia if she didn't change her behavior.

694 John Winthrop to Cotton Mather (draft), September 1718, *Collections of the Massachusetts Historial Society*, 6th series, 5 [1892]: 384n.

695 George H. Haynes, "'The Tale of Tantiusques': An Early Mining Venture in Massachusetts," *Proceedings of the American Antiquarian Society*, new series, 14 [1902]: 485, which provides a full account of the family's misadventures with this mine.

in a snowstorm and, after spending the night in a deserted wigwam, turned back.[696])

John's pretentious view of his own abilities met public resistance in 1723 from a worthy adversary, the newspaper editor James Franklin, elder brother of Benjamin. While visiting Boston that summer, John attended a party to mark the anniversary of the ascension of George I. There, before the lieutenant governor of the colony and "other Gentlemen & Ladies and several of the Clergy," he uttered extemporaneously the following lines, which appeared in the 22 August issue of *Boston News-letter*:[697]

AD REGEM

To fix the *Laws*, and *Limits* of these *Colonies*;
My humble Muse to *Royal* GEORGE! now Flyes,
Live, *Mighty King!* all *Protestants* do Pray;
This *New World* too, Under Your *Feet* I Lay;
May *Peace* and *Plenty*, in *Your Kingdoms! Triumph Round*;
To Increase Your *Grandeur!* yet more *Worlds* be found;
And to Your *Glories!* Let there be *no Bound*.

Franklin, who published the rival *New-England Courant*, found this ridiculous and responded in print to the "Worshipful Author" with the verses:[698]

SILENCE!

With wrinkled Brow, and sevenfold Grin, he rose
And mumbled Rhime, more hobbling than his Nose.

This material was followed by two nonsensical parodies, the first of which referenced Winthrop's "snout." Mayo noted that while Franklin was busy making fun of Winthrop's appearance, he missed an easier target: that John felt he could present the colonies as a gift to the king.[699]

The latest reference to it in the Winthrop papers, Haynes notes at 495, was in the inventory of John Still Winthrop's estate in 1776. It was described then as "3184 acres of land, by estimation, being what still remains unsold of the Lead Mine Tract, so-called, appraised at £955.4." The mine is now a reserve in Sturbridge, Massachusetts. See *thetrustees.org/places-to-visit/central-ma/tantiusques.html*.

[696] Haynes, *Proceedings of the American Antiquarian Society*, new series, 14 [1902]: 476.
[697] *Boston News-letter*, 22 August 1723, 2.
[698] *The New-England Courant*, 26 August 1723, 1.
[699] Mayo, *The Winthrop Family in America*, 126.

Later that summer, while staying with his sister and brother-in-law, the Lechmeres,[700] John was issued a summons to appear before the Probate Court to account for the administration of his father's estate. He was arrested and required to post £4,000 bail.[701] John later said that although he had been staying with his sister and brother-in-law for three months, neither had mentioned any dissatisfaction with his management of his father's estate.[702] He had been dispensing money to his sister, but was probably reluctant to give her the full share with her husband's creditors waiting to pounce.[703] In fact, the creditors may have been behind the arrest and summons, figuring they would get their money more quickly this way. One larger creditor was the merchant James Bowdoin, who had loaned John Winthrop more than £2,000 until the estate could be settled and was still waiting for his money five years later. Bowdoin threatened to sue Lechmere, and when the couple got no response from Winthrop regarding this threat, they went to court themselves.[704]

When Winthrop *vs.* Lechmere got underway in the summer of 1724, the Massachusetts property in Wait Winthrop's estate was not at issue: the law clearly called for Anne (Winthrop) Lechmere to receive a third. But Thomas Lechmere also demanded a third of the Connecticut property. John argued that the Connecticut land had been given to him years before his father died and so was not part of the estate. For good measure, he noted, the Connecticut law at issue had never been formally approved by the king. That line of argument did not get him very far: the Lechmeres won every round, in June and September 1725 and March and April 1726. In May 1726, John demanded the right to appeal to the king, but the Connecticut Assembly instead said Thomas Lechmere could start selling off enough Winthrop land to pay Wait's remaining debts.[705]

Enraged, John wrote a protest that, when read to the Assembly, caused him to be arrested again, on 25 May, this time charged with

---

[700] John Winthrop to the Rev. Eliphalet Adams, September 1723, *Collections of the Massachusetts Historical Society*, 6th series, 5 [1892]: 406–7.

[701] Mayo, *The Winthrop Family in America*, 126.

[702] "Brief in Appeal to the Privy Council [1727]," *Collections of the Massachusetts Historical Society*, 6th series, 5 [1892]: 446–47.

[703] See *Collections of the Massachusetts Historical Society*, 6th series, 5 [1892]: 400n, for a discussion of John's distrust of Thomas Lechmere and his suspicion that the cash he sent to his sister did not always reach her.

[704] Mayo, *The Winthrop Family in America*, 128–29.

[705] Mayo, *The Winthrop Family in America*, 129–30. See also Hoadly, *The Public Records of the Colony of Connecticut*, 7: 576.

contempt.[706] According to the official record, Winthrop behaved "insolently, contemptuously and disorderly, not suffering the Hon[ble] Governour [Talcott] to speak to him without continual interruption, and declaring himself to stand upon a par with the whole Assembly, that he was *coram non judice*, and that they had nothing to do to call him to an account for any contempts, affronts and indignities he had put on that his Majestie's corporation." He spent at least one night in the custody of the sheriff but then slipped away to New London; the assembly fined him £20 and left it at that.[707]

John felt his only hope for justice was to appeal to the King's Council, so he sailed for London.[708] There, he hired two prominent lawyers and in January 1727 presented a brief to the Privy Council,[709] following that a few weeks later with an indictment of the Connecticut Assembly on twenty-nine counts. The Connecticut Assembly sent £100 to its agent in London to defend the colony, but Thomas Lechmere apparently never realized the peril.[710] The case was argued before the council in December 1727; on 15 February 1728 it ruled that the Connecticut court action was null and void, ordering that John Winthrop be "immediately restored" all the property taken from him, and that Thomas Lechmere hand over the rents and profits obtained during the period of Winthrop's "unjust detention."[711] A triumphant John Winthrop wrote to his wife from London on New Year's Day [25 March] 1728:[712]

---

[706] Hoadly, *The Public Records of the Colony of Connecticut*, 7: 576. See *Collections of the Connecticut Historical Society*, 31 vols. (Hartford, 1896), 5: 406, for the order to arrest John Winthrop.

[707] Hoadly, *The Public Records of the Colony of Connecticut*, 7: 43–44.

[708] *Collections of the New London County Historical Society*, 1 [1901]: 172. "Thursd 21 [July 1726] . . . I was taking my leave of Mr. Winthrop & visiting Mr. Adams &c. ye wind being Easterly Mr. Winthrop went home again to his house before night. Fryday 22 fair but Some Showers. In the foren[oon] I was at Mr. Winthrops taking leave of him again. he went on Bord Capt. Marks about 9. Clock was Set Sail with a N: West wind & fresh gail Bound for Bristol in great Brittain."

[709] "Brief in Appeal to the Privy Council," *Collections of the Massachusetts Historical Society*, 6th series, 5 [1892]: 440–96.

[710] Mayo, *The Winthrop Family in America*, 131.

[711] "Decree of the King in Council," 15 February 1727[/28], *Collections of the Massachusetts Historical Society*, 6th series, 5 [1892]: 496–509.

[712] John Winthrop to Ann Winthrop, New Year's Day 1727/28 [25 March 1728], *Collections of the Massachusetts Historical Society*, 6th series, 5 [1892]: 509–11. The editors note in a postscript that the letter was "unfinished and unsigned, as if the writer's exultant feelings had been too much for him. It was, however, a dear-bought victory, the fees of so many lawyers, and the incidental expenses of protracted litigation, on both sides of the Atlantic, having been, for that period, enormous. Aside from the

My dearest Heart, —Notwithstanding the many intollerable abuses, lyes & slanders that have been every way contriv'd to hurt me, yet yor injured husband is yet alive & safe. Blessed be God for it, who has kept me & preserved me from the innumerable evills that w^d have distrest me. Thrô the favo^r of Heaven, the envy, spight & malice of my enemyes has not prevailed against me; but God has given me favo^r in the sight of the King, and his Maj^{ty} has been gratiously pleased to decide the controversy in my favo^r, after two days long hearings before the Lords of the Councell. The Attorney Generall & the Sollicitor Generall pleaded for me; after wch I humbly beg'd leave wth great submission to speake a few words in my owne behalfe, wch I have inclosed, wth the other papers undr the seal of the Councell Office, for yor perusall and the perusall of some few friends. But lett none take a coppy of w^t is not und^r the seal. You must immediately see them recorded in the publick entry's of the Probate Court and the Superio^r Court, and the Secretary must recorde them in the Records of the Generall Assembly. It is the King's positive command, and you are not to pay for the entry.

There was present at the hearing of my case: the Lord President of the Councell, ye Duke of Devonshire, my Lord Trevor, Lord Privy Seal, the two Lord Chief Justices, the Lord Chancelor, Sr Robert Walpole, Lord Treasurer, the Master of the Rolls, my Lord Hay, my Lord Finlater, Chancelor of Scotland, Archbishop of York, Archbishop of Canterbury, my Lord Bishop of London, and a full Councell Board; and a very numerous auditory of knights & gentlemen, who wth one voice cryed, Shame on the New England Collony's! And I thank my God, who has kept my vertue and showed my innocence to the world. And as I was so openly insulted, & brought to the barr of the Connecticott Court, I am at length so honourably and publickly acquitted before the highest Court of the kingdom! And thô you were disregarded & obliged to dine alone on the Connecticott Thanksgiving Day, yet now rejoyce openly. And thô Mr Agent D. (who

gratification of triumphing against such odds, it is questionable whether it would not have been cheaper to have compromised with Lechmere at the outset."

> is reckned crazy & in a strange distemperd way) has given
> himselfe such aires as to write that I was so obscure & not
> knowne in England, and that my ancestors was forgotten,
> yet I must tell you y^t he never appear'd himselfe; but the
> Lords said, W^t a strange, madd sort of people are these,
> that are indeavoring to hurt a family that founded them!
> After wch I had the hono^r to kiss his Maj^{tyes} hand, being
> introduc't by the Right Honourable the Lord in waiting.

Although he had a wife and seven children ages 3 to 17 in
Connecticut awaiting his return, John would never again see New
England, instead remaining in England until his death nineteen years
later. While "Boston had never appreciated him" and "Connecticut
had persecuted him," Mayo explained, "in London he was called
'Governor Winthrop' and treated with great respect."[713] That regard was
demonstrated in January 1733/34 when John was recommended for
membership in the Royal Society as "a person well skill'd in Natural
Knowledge and particularly in Chemistry."[714] In June 1734 he presented
364 curiosities from New England to the society, which included a
moth, bark, pearls, shells, roots, berries, nuts, beans, petrified cedar, soil,
sandstone, slate, marble, pebbles, talc, crystals, sand, salts, sulphurs, tin,
lead, marcasite, and "a piece of pewter half melted by lightning, and a
piece of the shelf it stood on, half shattered but not burnt."[715]

John ignored many letters to him by family members pleading
with him to return home. In the spring of 1742, John's son John Still[5]
Winthrop, a recent graduate of Yale, came to London at the request
of his father, who said he had found an heiress for him to marry. That
match-making plan didn't work out, but John Still would stay for five
years, until his father's death in 1747, "after a Long and Tedious Illness,
the Palsie accompanied with a feaver." According to his son, "he was
very desirous of seeing his friends and dying in his native country, but
the Almighty had ordered it otherwise."[716]

---

[713] Mayo, *The Winthrop Family in America*, 132.

[714] "Recommendation of John Winthrop, Esq., to the Royal Society," *Collections of the Massachusetts Historical Society*, 3rd series, 10 [1849]: 121–22.

[715] Mayo, *The Winthrop Family in America*, 133. See "Ancient Catalogue of Objects of Natural History," *The American Journal of Science and Arts* 47 [1844]: 282–90, being an extract from the *Journal Book of the Royal Society*, Vol. 15, 27 June 1734, 451–87.

[716] Mayo, *The Winthrop Family in America*, 136, citing Winthrop Manuscripts 9: 146. A family Bible owned by John Winthrop is held by the Massachusetts Historical Society.

Children of John[4] and Anne (Dudley) Winthrop:

    i.   MARY[5] WINTHROP, b. at Boston 18 Sept. 1708[717] and d. at Newport, R.I. 25 Feb. 1767.[718] She m. at Newport 21 Aug. 1729,[719] JOSEPH WANTON, later governor of Rhode Island and Providence Plantations, who was b. at Portsmouth, R.I. 15 Aug. 1705,[720] son of William and Ruth (Bryant) Wanton.[721] He d. at Newport 19[722] and was bur. 22 July 1780,[723] having had issue.

        Joseph Wanton was admitted as a freeman in 1728 and appointed deputy collector of customs at Newport in 1738 (and sworn in by his father),[724] a position he held for ten years. He is among the prominent Rhode Island merchants depicted in the satirical 1750s painting by John Greenwood called *Sea Captains Carousing in Surinam*.[725] As a merchant, Wanton traded a variety of goods, and on 23 July 1758 he and his ship, the *King of Prussia*—with fifty-four slaves, twenty ounces of gold dust, and sixty-six hogsheads of rum—was captured off the coast of Africa by a French privateer.[726]

---

[717] *A Report of the Record Commissioners of the City of Boston Containing Boston Births from A.D. 1700 to A.D. 1800* (Boston: Rockwell and Churchill, 1894), 58. "Mary daughter of John Winthrop and Ann his Wife, 18 September 1708."

[718] James N. Arnold, *Vital Record of Rhode Island, 1636–1850, First Series,* 21 vols. (Providence: Narragansett Historical Publishing Co., 1891–1912), 14: 382. "Wanton, Mary, wife of Hon. Joseph, at Newport, in 49th year, Feb. 25, 1767."

[719] Mayo, *The Winthrop Family in America,* 137.

[720] Arnold, *Vital Record of Rhode Island, 1636–1850, First Series,* 4: 1: 104. "Wanton, Joseph, of William and Ruth, Aug. 15, 1705."

[721] John Osborne Austin, *The Genealogical Dictionary of Rhode Island* (Albany, N.Y.: Joel Mussell's Sons, 1887), 215.

[722] Arnold, *Vital Record of Rhode Island, 1636–1850, First Series,* 14: 382. "Wanton, Joseph, Esq., late Governor of the Colony, in 75th year, at Newport, July 19, 1780."

[723] Arnold, *Vital Record of Rhode Island, 1636–1850, First Series,* 10: 154.

[724] John Peagrum to Governor Wanton, 25 August 1738, reprinted in Gertrude Selywn Kimball, ed., *The Correspondence of the Colonial Governors of Rhode Island, 1723–1775,* 2 vols. (Boston: Houghton, Mifflin and Co., 1902), 1: 96.

[725] He is apparently the bald, portly figure shown passed out in his chair. H. Barbara Weinberg and Carrie Rebora Barratt, eds., *American Stories: Paintings of Everyday Life, 1765–1915* (New Haven: Yale University Press, 2009), 5. The original is at the Saint Louis Museum of Art.

[726] Statement by Joseph Wanton, reprinted in Kimball, *The Correspondence of the Colonial Governors of Rhode Island, 1723–1775,* 1: xxxvii–xxxviii. Joseph identified himself as "being one of the people called Quakers."

In 1769, he became the fourth and last member of his immediate family to become governor of the Rhode Island colony.[727] His first act was to write the British authorities that he could not obey the instructions of the Crown "without acting diametrically opposite to the constitution of the colony," expecially since the colonists had no representation in Parliament."[728] Nevertheless, when war seemed inevitable, he opposed a split, writing to the assembly on 2 May 1775, soon after he had been re-elected for a sixth time: "If once we are separated, where shall we find another Britain to supply our loss? Torn from the body to which we are united by religion, liberty, laws and commerce, we must bleed at every vein."[729] When he refused to raise a militia of fifteen hundred men or commission officers, and then skipped the session in which he was to take the oath of office, the assembly declined to seat him as governor.[730]

   ii.   ANNE WINTHROP, b. at Boston 13 Dec. 1709[731] and d. unm. at New London 19 June 1794.[732] Her will, dated 11 May 1793, left her estate to her "only sister (now living) Margaret Miller."[733]

   iii.   KATHERINE/CATHERINE WINTHROP, b. at Boston 9 March 1710/11,[734] d. at Salem, Mass. 11, and bur. 14 Jan. 1781.[735] She m.

---

[727] Austin, *The Genealogical Dictionary of Rhode Island*, 215–16. Besides his father, his uncle John and cousin Gideon also held the position.

[728] Thomas Williams Bicknell et al., *The History of the State of Rhode Island and Providence Plantations*, 5 vols. (New York: American Historical Society, 1920), 3: 1090–91.

[729] "Message of Governor Wanton to the General Assembly of Rhode Island," 2 May 1775, reprinted in John Russell Bartlett, ed., *Records of the Colony of Rhode Island and Providence Plantations*, 10 vols. (Providence: A. Crawford Greene, 1862), 7: 332–33.

[730] Bicknell, *The History of the State of Rhode Island and Providence Plantations*, 3: 1093–94. He was officially deposed in November 1775.

[731] *A Report of the Record Commissioners of the City of Boston Containing Boston Births from A.D. 1700 to A.D. 1800*, 65. "Ann daughter of John Winthrop and Ann his Wife, 13 December 1709."

[732] Mayo, *The Winthrop Family in America*, 137. See also *Connecticut Gazette*, New London, 3 July 1794, 3. "Died, in this city . . . Miss Ann Winthrop, age 86" [*sic*].

[733] "Estate of Ann Winthrop," 1794, No. 5788, New London Probate District, scan at *ancestry.com* > Connecticut, Wills and Probate Records, 1609–1999, Hartford, Probate Packets, Wiley, I.-Wood, Erastus, 1675–1850 > images 1000–1003. Proven 14 July 1794. In October 1805, three years after Margaret (Winthrop) Miller had died, her children petitioned the Connecticut Assembly to allow them to execute a copy of Ann's will, because the original had been lost (*Connecticut Gazette*, 12 March 1806, 4).

[734] *A Report of the Record Commissioners of the City of Boston Containing Boston Births from A.D. 1700 to A.D. 1800*, 79. "Katherine, a third daughter of John Winthrop and Ann his wife, 9 March 1710/11."

[735] Fitch Edward Oliver, *The Diary of William Pynchon of Salem* (Boston: Houghton, Mifflin and Co., 1890), 83. "11 [January] Thursday. A fine, warm day. Mrs. Sargent died to-day. . . . 14. Sunday. Snow. Mrs. Sargent was buried after church." Mayo, 137, gives 10 January.

(1) at New London 30 March 1731/32, her second cousin SAMUEL BROWNE, JR.[736] a 1727 graduate of Harvard College[737] who was b. at Salem 7 April 1708, son of Col. Samuel and Abigail (Keech) Browne.[738] He d. at Salem 26 Nov. 1742,[739] leaving an estate valued at more than £21,000, including 104,000 acres in Massachusetts, Connecticut, Maine, and New Hampshire.[740] His widow m. (2) at Salem 10 Aug. 1744, COLONEL EPES SARGENT,[741] Harvard class of 1712,[742] who was b. at Gloucester, Mass. 12 July 1690, son of William and Mary (Duncan) Sargent.[743] He d. at Salem 6 Dec. 1762.[744] Catherine had five children by each husband; her son, Col. Paul Dudley[6] Sargent, b. in 1745, according to one history, "commanded a regiment at the siege of Boston, was wounded at Bunker Hill, commanded a brigade in the summer of 1776, and fought at Harlem, White Plains, Trenton and Princeton."[745]

iv. REBECCA WINTHROP, bp. at the First Church, New London 11 Jan. 1712/13[746] and d. at New London 30 Oct. 1776.[747] She m. there

[736] Mayo, *Winthrop Family in America,* 137.

[737] Sibley, *Biographical Sketches of Graduates of Harvard University,* 13: 551.

[738] *Vital Records of Salem, Massachusetts to the End of the Year 1849,* 6 vols. (Salem: The Essex Institute, 1916), 1: 131. "Samuel, s. Col. Sam[ue]ll, Esq., and Abigail (Keech), Apr. 7, 1708." See also Perley, *The Essex Antiquarian* 13 [1909]: 160A. Samuel was a grandson of Major William Browne, a brother to Mary Browne, who married Waitstill[3] Winthrop.

[739] Fitch Edward Oliver, *The Diaries of Benjamin Lynde and of Benjamin Lynde, Jr.* (Boston, 1880), 163. "My [first] Coz. Sam[l] Browne, died, aged 34, leaving two sons and one daughter."

[740] Perley, *The Essex Antiquarian* 13 [1909]: 160A.

[741] *Vital Records of Salem, Massachusetts to the End of the Year 1849,* 4: 296. "Epes Sergent, Esq. of Gloucester and [Mrs.] Catharine Brown, Aug. 10, 1744."

[742] Sibley, *Biographical Sketches of Graduates of Harvard University,* 13: 551.

[743] *Vital Records of Gloucester, Massachusetts,* 3 vols. (Topsfield, Mass.: Topsfield Historical Society, 1917), 1: 625. "Eps, s. William and Mary, July 12, 1690." He married (1) at Roxbury in 1720, Esther MacCarty. See also John H. Sheppard, "Reminiscences of Lucius Manlius Sargent," *Register* 25 [1871]: 19–20.

[744] *The Boston-Gazette and Country Journal,* 13 December 1762, 3. "On Monday last [6 December] died at Salem, Epes Serjeant Esq.; aged 72 years. For many Years a noted Merchant in that Town." *Vital Records of Salem, Massachusetts,* 6: 207, gives 13 December, citing the diary of Zachariah Collins, now at the Peabody Essex Museum.

[745] James Grant Wilson and John Fiske, eds., *Appleton's Cyclopaedia of American Biography,* rev. ed., 7 vols. (New York: D. Appleton and Co., 1898), 5: 397.

[746] S. Leroy Blake, *The Later History of the First Church, New London* (New London, Conn.: Day Publishing, 1900), 475. "Baptisms, 1712. Jan. 11th (1713 N.S.) Mr. John Winthrop's child, Rebeckah."

[747] *Connecticut Journal* (New Haven), 6 November 1776, 1. "Wednesday Evening died here, very suddenly, Mrs. Rebecca Saltonstall, Consort to the Hon. Gurdon Saltonstall, Sq. of this Town."

15 March 1732/33,[748] General Gurdon Saltonstall, who was b. at New London 22 Dec. 1708,[749] son of Gurdon Saltonstall, who succeeded his friend Fitz-John[3] Winthrop that year as Governor of Connecticut, and Elizabeth (Rosewell) Saltonstall.[750] He d. at Norwich, Conn. 19 Sept. 1785,[751] and was interred at the burial ground in New London.[752] The couple had 14 children. After graduating from Yale in 1725, Gurdon became a prominent merchant and attained the rank of Brigadier General in the Revolutionary Army before 1776. He also was appointed in 1784 as the first collector of the Port of New London.[753]

   v. Elizabeth Winthrop, bp. at the First Church, New London 25 April[754] and bur. at Boston 14 Sept. 1714.[755]

  vi. John Winthrop, Jr., b. at New London 20[756] and bp. at the First Church, New London 22 April 1716.[757] He d. at New London

[748] Connecticut Vital Records (compiled under the direction of Lucius Barnes Barbour), "New London Births–Marriages–Deaths, 1646–1854" (Hartford, 1919), 325, citing 2: 89 of the original New London town records, accessed at *americanancestors.org.* "Rebeckah, d. John, of New London, m. Gurdon Saltonstall, s. Gurdon, the Gov. of Conn., March 15, 1732/3."

[749] Barbour, "New London Births–Marriages–Deaths, 1646–1854," 266, citing 1: 36 of original town records. "Gurdon, s. Gurdon, Esq. & Elizabeth, b. Dec. 22, 1708."

[750] Henry Bond, *Genealogies of the Families and Descendants of the Early Settlers of Watertown, Massachusetts,* 2nd ed. (Boston: New England Historic-Genealogical Society, 1860), 924–25.

[751] Bond, *Genealogies of the Families and Descendants of the Early Settlers of Watertown, Massachusetts,* 2nd ed., 925. See also *The Norwich Packet, or The Country Journal,* 22 September 1785, 3. "[Died] . . . . In this city, General Gurdon Saltonstall, of New-London, aged 76."

[752] Caulkins, *Register* 11 [1857]: 27.

[753] Bond, *Genealogies of the Families and Descendants of the Early Settlers of Watertown,* 2nd ed., 925–27.

[754] Blake, *The Later History of the First Church, New London,* 476. "Baptisms, 1714. April 25th. Mr. John Winthrop's child, Elizabeth."

[755] Dunkle and Lainhart, *Deaths in Boston 1700 to 1799,* accessed at *americanancestors. org,* citing Old Sexton's Bills transcribed by Elisha Copeland at Boston City Hall Archives. Record for unnamed child of John Winthrop. Mayo, *Winthrop Family in America,* 137, gives date of death as 12 September.

[756] Samuel Sewell, *Small Vial of Tears Brought from the Funeral of John Winthrop: A Very Goodly Child, the Only Son of John Winthrop Esq; and Anne His Wife; who was Born at New-London the 20th of April, 1716. and Died There the 15th of February Following; Being Three Hundred and Two Days Old* (1717). Text online at *quod.lib.umich.edu/e/ evans/N29833.0001.001.*

[757] Blake, *The Later History of the First Church, New London,* 478. "Baptisms, 1716. April 22d. Mr. John Winthrop's child, John." On 14 May 1716, Wait Winthrop wrote to his son John: "I rec'd our letters in the box, with the welcom news of your wife being delivered of a son, and I bless God for his mercy and goodness therin that he

15[758] and was bur. 17 Feb. 1716/17.[759] When John fell ill, his grandfather Wait sent advice for home remedies that included hanging iron ore at the pit of his stomach and placing the hair of an African lion under his arms.[760] After the infant's death, Samuel Sewall wrote a poem read at the funeral: "In loving, lovely, Darling John, / Winthrop, and Dudley Met in One: / Such Harmony of Charming Features / Rarely appears in Mortal Creatures. / But Oh—! What, meet to part so soon! / Must we Resign this Budding Boon? / We must: We will! Christ's Will is done; / Our wills shall make an Unison. / Jesus will call John from the Grave, / From Sin, Eternally to Save."[761]

---

has heard our prayers in that matter [after the birth of five daughters]. . . . The post will bring you a coat &c., for little John Winthrop" (*Collections of the Massachusetts Historical Society*, 6th series, 5 [1892]: 315–16).

[758] Samuel Sewall to John Winthrop, 8 April 1717, *Collections of the Massachusetts Historical Society*, 6th series, 2 [1888]: 69–70. "Thank you for your valuable Present, Mr. Adams's Sermon on the prodigious Storm. Am sorry that your estate was diminished thereby; Though that stroke was light, compared with the Death of your pleasant Son, whom you had waited for so long. I desire to sympathise with you and your Consort, in this painfull Bereavement. I buried my First-born, at 17 Monethes old, who died likewise of Convulsions. . . . 'Tis the Happiness of Christian Parents, more especially respecting their Infant-Children, that they sorrow not as those without Hope." Sewall attached a poem entitled "A little vial of Tears occasion'd by the death of John Winthrop at New-London, Febr. 15, aged Ten Moneths."

[759] John Winthrop to Wait Winthrop, 18 February 1716/17, *Collections of the Massachusetts Historical Society*, 6th series, 5 [1892]: 337fn: "We buried it yesterday, after the afternoon meeting, under the two broad stones where yo[r] father's children were inter'd. M[rs] Browne, who was its nurse, carried it to the grave. . . . A sensible, quiet, meek, yet cheerly-tempered child, strong-natured, hearty, fatt. How often have we pleasd o'selves with the thoughts of yo[r] seeing this yo[r] pretty grandson, who had so manly, beautifull & gracefull a look, but Providence has ordered otherwise. *Eheu, quam cito vanescunt gaudia vitae!*"

[760] Wait Winthrop to John Winthrop, 11 February 1717, *Collections of the Massachusetts Historical Society*, 6th series, 5 [1892]: 336. "Inclosed is the minera and a little of the lyons hair, what he would let his keeper get off at this time. The minera must be hung at the pit of the stomach, the lyons hair to be aplyed under the armes." Di Bonaventura, *For Adam's Sake*, 208, points out that this is undoubtedly a reference to a lion displayed by the sea captain Arthur Savage at his Boston home. Savage had returned from an overseas trip on 6 April 1716 (*Register* 67 [1913]: 213), and two years later, on 7 April 1718, an advertisement appeared in the *Boston News-Letter* that read: "All Persons having the Curiosity of seeing the Noble and Royal Beast the Lyon, never one before in America, may see him at the House of Capt. Arthur Savage near M[r] Colman's [Brattle Square] Church, Boston, before he is transported for London. But to prevent all disputes with the Negro at the Gate who constantly attends each Person (whether seen him before or not) is desired to pay to the said Negro six pence a piece."

[761] Sewall, *Small Vial of Tears Brought from the Funeral of John Winthrop*.

vii. MARGARET WINTHROP, bp. at the First Church, New London 26
Jan. 1717/18[762] and d. at New London in Feb. 1802.[763] She m. 16
May 1743,[764] JEREMIAH MILLER, who was b. at New London 19 and
bp. at the First Church 21 Aug. 1719,[765] son of Jeremiah Miller, a
Yale graduate who was then the schoolmaster of New London,[766]
and Mary (Saltonstall) Miller,[767] and had issue.[768] He d. at New
London 10 April 1797.[769]

During the decades before the Revolutionary War, Jeremiah
Miller served as a judge, naval officer, and postmaster in New
London, while his son Jeremiah[6] Miller (b. in 1749) was the deputy
at the customs office,[770] apparently the only local person to hold
such a position.[771] When their official duties ended in 1775 at the
onset of hostilities, the rebels offered to let Jeremiah III keep his
job but, he later testified, his father dismissed the idea.[772] When the

---

[762] Blake, *The Later History of the First Church, New London*, 479. "Baptisms, 1717. Jan.
26th (1718 N.S.) Mr. John Winthrop's child, Margaret."

[763] *Connecticut Gazette, and the Commercial Intelligencer*, 24 February 1802, 3, "Died in
this city [New London], Mrs. Margaret Miller, relict of the late Jeremiah Miller, Esq.
aged 84 years."

[764] George Adlard, *The Sutton-Dudleys of England and the Dudleys of Massachusetts in
New England* (London: John Russell Smith, 1862), 115.

[765] *Collections of the New London County Historial Society*, 1 [1901]: 519. "Sund 21 fair. . . .
A Son of Jer. Millers Baptized Jeremiah." Blake, *The Later History of the First Church,
New London*, 481, has "Baptisms, 1719. Aug. 23d. Mr. Jeremiah Miller his child,
Jeremiah." Hempstead mentioned Jeremiah Miller, Jr., again on 21 May 1752: "I
had £28 of Jer. Miller Junr. Old Tenr Rhd Island & left with him £28 Connecticut
new Tenr (vitz) 8 £3 10s 0d Bills to be Exchanged again when I See cause" (589).

[766] Caulkins, *History of New London*, 398–99.

[767] Barbour, "New London Births–Marriages–Deaths, 1646–1854," 210, citing 1: 65
and 2: 20 of original town records. "Jeremiah, s. Jeremiah and Mary, Aug. 19, 1719."
In 1750, Margaret and her husband became step-siblings when Margaret's widowed
mother, Anne (Dudley) Winthrop, married Jeremiah's widowed father.

[768] Watson, *Royal Families: Americans of Royal and Noble Descent*, 2nd ed., 102–3. "He
and Margaret apparently had nine children, but the birthdates of some of them
need further research."

[769] *Connecticut Gazette*, 13 April 1797, 3. "On Monday, 10th inst., departed this life,
Jeremiah Miller, Esq., who having attained the age of 77 years, in the practice of every social and private virtue that can adorn the character of man and the Christian,
exchanged this world for a better, amid the unceasing regrets of an affectionate
family and numerous acquaintance."

[770] Peter Wilson Coldham, *American Migrations, 1765–1799* (Baltimore: Genealogical
Publishing Co., 2000), 21, citing Public Records Office 12/74/773, 101/262 &
358, 102/21, 109/212, 13/42/92–106, 127–132, 146.

[771] Caulkins, *History of New London*, 477.

[772] Coldham, *American Migrations, 1765–1799*, 22, citing Public Records Office
12/74/223, 101/262, 102/21, 13/7/200–262.

turncoat Benedict Arnold, a native of New Haven, invaded New London on 6 Sept. 1781, Jeremiah III and his brother-in-law, James Tilley (who in 1771 had married Mary[6] Miller),[773] both known as "friends of government," hosted a dinner in his honor.[774] However, according to Arnold, hidden rebel gunpowder in the retail stores he had ordered his troops to burn exploded and set fire to the Tilley and Miller homes.[775] (By one account, the three men looked up from the meal to see the ceiling in flames.[776]) This left the Miller family impoverished, and they moved to a small farm outside town. Jeremiah III, by his own account, refused to take the rebel oath, moved his family to to Stratford, Conn., for their safety, and became a spy, conveying information to the Rev. Henry Vandyke of New York City, who passed it to British forces. After being arrested and detained for three weeks, he fled to London, arriving in Jan. 1784. On 5 March 1784, Jeremiah III testified on behalf of Benedict Arnold, who was seeking reimbursement for wartime losses.[777]

8   viii.   JOHN STILL WINTHROP, b. 15, bp. at the First Church, New London 24 Jan. 1719/20; m. (1) 4 Sept. 1750, JANE BORLAND; m. (2) 23 Nov. 1761, ELIZABETH (SHIRREFF) HAY.

      ix.   BASIL WINTHROP, b. 21,[778] bp. at the First Church, New London 26 Aug. 1722,[779] and d. at New London, apparently unm., on 21 Jan. 1771.[780]

---

773 Barbour, "New London Births–Marriages–Deaths, 1646–1854," 299, citing 3: 225 of original town records.

774 Charles Allyn, ed., *The Battle of Groton Heights*, rev. ed. (New London, the author, 1882), 100fn. Both men lived on Bank Street; some sources say Tilley hosted the meal, while others say it was Miller.

775 Coldham, *American Migrations, 1765–1799*, 22.

776 Allyn, *The Battle of Groton Heights*, 100fn.

777 Certificate of Jeremiah Miller, Jr., in "Correspondence of Benedict Arnold," *Register* 35 [1881]: 156. "I do certify that I was acquainted with Brig^r General Benedict Arnold for many years in America, and that He was for Several Years previous to the War considered as a Merchant of Property, and did a great deal of Business." Jeremiah Miller III had been "informed and believe[d]" the general's confiscated property in New Haven was worth more than £2,400.

778 Muskett, *Evidences of the Winthrops of Groton*, 27.

779 Blake, *The Later History of the First Church, New London*, 484. "Baptisms, 1722. Aug. 26th. Mr. John Winthrop's child, Bazil." Mayo noted at 137: "The name Basil derives from the Greek word meaning kingly, and therefore must have been especially attractive to John Winthrop. As far as the present writer knows, no other Winthrop was ever named Basil." See also *Collections of the New London County Historial Society*, 1 [1901]: 124. "[1722] Sund. 26 [August] fair. . . . Mr. Winthrop a Son Babtized Bayell."

780 *The Connecticut Journal, and New-Haven Post-Boy*, 1 February 1771, 3. "On Monday, the 21st ult. Died at New London, after a lingering indisposition, Mr. Basil Winthrop of that Town."

The Kinship Between Robert[8] Winthrop
and Henry White, U.S. Ambassador to Italy
1905–6 and France 1906–9

John Still Winthrop = (1) Jane Borland = (2) Elizabeth (Shirreff) Hay

Francis Bayard Winthrop
= (2) Phebe Taylor

Thomas Charles Winthrop
= Georgiana Maria Kane

Robert Winthrop
= Katharine Wilson Taylor

Benjamin Winthrop
= Judith Stuyvesant

Elizabeth Shirreff Winthrop
= John White Chanler

Margaret Stuyvesant Chanler
= Lewis Morris Rutherfurd

Margaret Stuyvesant Rutherfurd
= Henry White

THE FIFTH GENERATION

8. **JOHN STILL^5 WINTHROP** (*John^4, Waitstill^3, John$^{2-1}$*) was born "between 3 and 4 o'clock in the morning" 15[781] and baptized at the First Church of New London, Connecticut 24 January 1719/20.[782] He died at New London 6 June 1776,[783] a week after his 91-year-old mother, and was apparently buried at the Old Burying Ground.[784] He married, first, at Boston, Massachusetts 4 September 1750,[785] **JANE BORLAND**, who was born at Boston 24 April 1732,[786] daughter of Francis and

---

[781] Mayo, *The Winthrop Family in America*, 153, citing Winthrop Manuscripts, 1B: 42.

[782] Blake, *The Later History of the First Church, New London*, 481. "Baptisms, 1719. [January] 24th (1720 N.S.) Mr. John Winthrop's child, John Still."

[783] "Governor Thomas Dudley and His Descendants," *Register* 10 [1856]: 340. *The Connecticut Gazette; and the Universal Intelligencer*, 14 June 1776, 3: "Died here, John Still Winthrop, Esq.—Mrs. Elisabeth Sheriff, in an advanced Age, Widow of Maj.—Sheriff, late of Boston" – evidently John died in the same period as his mother and mother-in-law.

[784] Caulkins, *Register* 11 [1857]: 25. John Still Winthrop, his mother, and his brother Basil, "with probably the first wife of John Still Winthrop (Jane, daughter of Francis Borland), are supposed to be together in a cental portion of the ground, indicated by two heavy blocks of unhewn granite, oblong I form, and placed end to end, each covering two graves, but without any inscription. The name Winthrop appears to have been once rudely cut on these stones, but it has worn off by the gradual disintegration of the rough granite. These stones were evidently placed here as a temporary measure to prevent the remains from being disturbed until some more befitting family memorial could be procured." The war, Caulkins said, probably left the memorial "soon forgotten."

[785] *Report of the Record Commissioners of the City of Boston, Containing the Boston Marriages from 1700 to 1751*, 28: 268. "John Winthrop & Jane Borland by the Rev. Joseph Sewall, D.D., Sept. 4, 1750." He was 30 and she was 18. See also *Collections of the New London County Historial Society*, 1 [1901]: 557. "Sun 7 [October 1750] fair & pleasant. . . . Mr. Jno Still Winthrop and Bride at Meeting foren[oon] and [John's sister] Mrs. Wanton & Daughter came yesterday from R. Island by water."

[786] *A Report of the Record Commissioners of the City of Boston Containing Boston Births from A.D. 1700 to A.D. 1800*, 206. "Jane, daughter of Francis and Jane Borland, 24 April 1732."

Jane (Lindall) Borland.[787] She died at New London 5 April 1760.[788]
John married, second, at Trinity Church, Boston 23 November 1761,[789]
ELIZABETH SHIRREFF of Annapolis County in Nova Scotia, Canada.[790]
She was the daughter of William Shirreff, a longtime member of the
Governing Council of Nova Scotia who later moved to Boston,[791] and
widow of Alexander Hay of the 40th Regiment.[792] By one account,
Elizabeth died in England on 24 June 1793.[793]

---

[787] John A. Vinton, "Memoir of the Lindall Family," *Register* 7 [1853]: 23–24.

[788] Vinton, *Register* 7 [1853]: 24.

[789] *Records Relating to the Early History of Boston, Containing Boston Marriages from 1752
to 1809, Vol. 30* (Boston: Municipal Printing Office, 1903), 397. They declared their
intentions on 4 November: "John Winthrop Esq. of New London Ct. & Elizabeth
Hay, Nov. 4, 1761" (41). See also Andrew Oliver and James Bishop Peabody, eds.,
"The Records of Trinity Church, Boston, 1728–1830," vol. 56 in *Publications of the
Colonial Society of Massachusetts*, 179. "1761, November 23, John Still Winthrop &
Elizh. Hay."

[790] Watson, *Royal Families: Americans of Royal and Noble Descent*, 2nd ed., 1: 103, gives
her birthyear as 1724, without citation.

[791] "Governor Thomas Dudley and His Descendants," *Register* 10 [1856]: 340, calls
her "a daughter of Wm. Sheriff, a British field officer," although it was her brother
of the same name, not her father, who appears to have been a British officer. The
elder William Shirreff was probably born in Scotland, by one account, and appears
first in the Nova Scotia governor's Letter-Book in 1715 and last in its Commission
Book in 1739 (Arthur Eaton, "Chapters in the History of Halifax, Nova Scotia,"
Americana 11 [1916]: 209–10). William, Sr., came to Boston on at least one occasion, in 1737, as a member of the council to help settle boundary disputes between
Massachusetts and Rhode Island (Beamish Murdoch, *A History of Nova Scotia, or
Acadie*, 2 vols. [Halifax: John Barnes, 1866], 2: 8–9) and settled there after 12 January
1754, having written a will at Annapolis that was probated at Boston on 24 May
1768 following his death on 5 May. See *Boston Evening-Post*, 9 May 1768, 3: "Last
Thursday died here, in the 83d Year of his Age, William Sheriff, Esq; formerly an
Officer in Nova Scotia Government." His will appointed wife Elizabeth as execu-
trix and noted her great affection toward "our children," who were not named
(*ancestry.com* > Massachusetts, Wills and Probate Records, 1635–1991 > Suffolk >
Probate Records, Vol. 66–68, 1770–1772, images 269–70). She may be the elderly
Elisabeth Sheriff, widow of Major Sheriff, who died at Boston in 1776 [note 783].

[792] Although a number of sources identify Elizabeth as the widow of Captain John
Hay of the 40th Regiment, that name does not appear in R. H. Raymond Smythies,
Historical Records of the 40ᵗʰ (2ⁿᵈ Somersetshire) Regiment (Devonport, Devonshire:
A.H. Swiss, 1894). Instead, there is reference to Ensign Alexander Hay, who was
killed in New Brunswick on 21 June 1755 by friendly fire after he had been taken
prisoner by Indians (19). Further, the *Calendar of N.Y. Colonial Manuscripts Indorsed
Land Papers, 1643–1803* (Albany: Weed, Parsons & Co., 1864), 422, includes an
entry dated 11 November 1766 in which Captain William Shirreff testified that his
nephew, John Hay, son of the deceased Lieut. Alexander Hay of the 40th regiment,
hoped to receive a grant "on the same footing with the reduced officers." Alexander
Hay also was a witness to William Shirreff's 1754 will [note 791].

[793] Adlard, *The Sutton-Dudleys of England and the Dudleys of Massachusetts in New
England*, 13, gives place of death as England.

When John Still Winthrop was about six years old, his father left for England to petition the King in Council. He would not see his father again until he was 22 and a recent Yale College graduate. (He had enrolled at age 13 and graduated at the top of the class of 1737.[794]) In the summer of 1741 John received a letter from his father asking him to come to London:[795]

> I long to see you, and tho Mr. Salem [his rich son-in-law, Samuel Browne, of Salem, "whom he disliked intensely"[796]] would not Creditt me, perhaps he may be so friendly as to trust you with the Loan of a few Thousand pounds in order for yor coming over to me into England for I think now is yor time, whilst I am here and I have a very agreeable young lady of a Noble family in view for you; a fortune of Ten thousand pound; & a fine woman of sense & ingenuity, and an Heiress; and by the character [that] has been given of you, they approve of the match.... And as to the small Pox you need not be much afraid of it, being with me you will not goe into danger, it is as airy at this End of the Towne as it is in America. And it may be God will preserve you from it; tho my Father & Unckel had it in London, and did well.

John Still Winthrop sailed from Boston on 16 March 1742 aboard the *John Galley*, although the trip did not go smoothly. "Three Days after we Left Said Port our Ship Proved Leakey, to our great Surprise; and on the 7 day, near the banks of Newfound Land, we had a violent Storm and two foot Water in our Ships Hole; both our Pumps Constantly going, and being very weake Handed, we Began almost to dispare, thinking our Selves in Eminent Danger, but by the Good Providence of God the Storm abated and our Ship Ceased Leaking." They arrived at Dartmouth on 13 April; he found it "the most Romantick Place I Ever saw, but the People are not very Sevill to Strangers."[797] He wrote a quick

---

[794] *Catalogus Senatus Academici ... in Collegio Yalensis* (New Haven, Conn.: E. Hayes, 1859), 21.

[795] John Winthrop to John Still Winthrop, undated [1741], Winthrop Family Papers (reel 20, box 35), Massachusetts Historical Society. A subsequent letter from John Still Winthrop's brother-in-law, Joseph Wanton, described the unnamed heiress as being "as gental and beautifull as any in England" (Mayo, *The Winthrop Family in America*, 156).

[796] Mayo, *The Winthrop Family in America*, 156.

[797] "Mem. of a Voyage from Boston to London, by John Still Winthrop," *Proceedings of the Massachusetts Historical Society* 13 [1873]: 250.

letter to his father, saying he had arrived, and that he had two hundred ounces of gold dust with him, though not insured. He said he planned to remain on the ship to London (rather than going over land by coach), and his father replied that was by far the better sightseeing, with "many fine seats of nobility and gentry on both sides [of] the river."[798] John Still Winthrop sailed to Dover and then took a coach through Canterbury, arriving in London 27 April, taking a room at the Spread Eagle on Grations Street, "a most miserable Lodging Indeed."[799] The marriage did not materialize. John spent the next six years caring for a father Mayo characterized as "ailing, querulous, yet rather pathetic,"[800] which may have been the plan all along. When the two ran short of cash, John Still Winthrop's brother-in-law Gurdon Saltonstall would meet expenses.[801]

In the family historian Robert C. Winthrop's assessment of John Still Winthrop, "he had inherited neither the scientific tastes of his immediate ancestors, nor any ambition to distinguish himself in public life." His sole scientific effort was a "very brief paper on an unpleasant physiological subject," as Winthrop put it, read to the Royal Society on 14 March 1744/45.[802] "On the other hand," Winthrop continued, "he was an excellent man of business, and succeeded in disentangling his father's estate from the embarrassments resulting from the latter's imprudence."[803] After his father's death in 1747, John had to deal with large tracts of land in America and wasn't getting very generous offers, so he wrote a distant cousin in Cork, William Winthrop, offering his support to "honest, Industrious" Irish families who would emigrate and improve them with farming, linen manufacture, or fishing. "I will give them all the Incouragement I Possibly can when I know their Proposals," he said, noting he had already asked his brother-in-law Gurdon Saltonstall to send ships to Cork.[804] William Winthrop replied that he could gather weavers, tailors, masons, and farmers by the spring if a ship was sent from New London for them along with lumber such

---

[798]   Mayo, *The Winthrop Family in America*, 157.

[799]   *Proceedings of the Massachusetts Historical Society* 13 [1873]: 251.

[800]   Mayo, *The Winthrop Family in America*, 158.

[801]   Mayo, *The Winthrop Family in America*, 158–59, citing Winthrop Manuscripts 9: 142, 144, 145.

[802]   See *Philosophical Transactions* 43 [1 January 1744–45], 304-5.

[803]   Robert C. Winthrop, *A Short Account of the Winthrop Family* (Cambridge, Mass.: John Wilson and Son, 1887), 12. Winthrop noted that Fisher's Island, part of the original grant to John[2] Winthrop, Jr., in 1640, remained in the family until 1862.

[804]   Mayo, *The Winthrop Family in America,* 159, citing Winthrop Manuscripts 9: 146.

as staves and oak casks, but evidently the project was never developed any further.[805]

In the fall of 1748, after borrowing £100 for his passage, John and his second cousin Henrietta Hyde,[806] who had managed his father's affairs in London,[807] set sail for New London. They arrived on 25 November 1748; a neighbor recorded the homecoming: "I was att home all day. I mended one of Madm Winthrops wheels & in the Evening went up to Madm Winthrops & Met Mr. John Still Winthrop at Colln Saltonstalls who this night arived with Ms. Hide from London by way of Nantucket first & Rhoad Island Next & fishers Island Last. A great Joy to his mother & friends. He hath been gone Seven year Next feb."[808] Within three years, John Still Winthrop would be married to Jane Borland, whom he probably met while visiting his sister Kate, who lived in Salem. (The Borlands were a Boston family but her mother was originally a Lindall of Salem.)[809] When Jane died ten years later, she left her husband with eight young children, the youngest aged five weeks. He remarried eighteen months later and had six more children by Elizabeth (Shirreff) Hay.

John Still Winthrop preserved the family papers that eventually were given to the Massachusetts Historical Society, including his great-grandfather's journal, although he rather nonchalantly lent it out to historians and clergymen who showed interest.[810] On 2 March 1770, *The New-London Gazette* reported: "John Winthrop, Esq. of this Town, has found among a great Number of ancient Papers, left by his Predecessors," including a deed given by the Earl of Warwick to the first English settlers in Connecticut. "As the Lands included in this Deed

---

[805] Mayo, *The Winthrop Family in America*, 162, citing Winthrop Manuscripts 9: 161.

[806] Her grandmother's sister was Mary Browne, wife of Waitstill Winthrop (*Register* 27 [1873]: 420).

[807] In a letter to John Still Winthrop in the summer of 1741, his father had written, "Mrs. Hyde presents humble service to you all. Had it not been for her care, I might have dyed the last winter when I was so ill" (John Winthrop to John Still Winthrop, Winthrop Family Papers [reel 20, box 35], Massachusetts Historical Society).

[808] *Collections of the New London County Historical Society*, 1 [1901]: 509. See also Winthrop Manuscripts 9: 145.

[809] Mayo, *The Winthrop Family in America*, 160.

[810] "An early borrower was Thomas Prince, of Boston, when working on his *Annals of New England*; in 1760, Francis Borland wrote Winthrop, 'By Mr. Goreham I now send you the Books you lent the Reverend Mr. Prince, which I lately received from his widow.' This recovery was good as far as it went, but volume III of the manuscript of Winthrop's 'History' was found in Mr. Prince's library in the tower of the Old South Meeting House fifty-six years afterward, 'buried beneath a mass of pamphlets and papers'" (Mayo, *The Winthrop Family in America*, 162).

expressly extend to the South-Sea, and the Charter of this Colony is predicated upon this Deed, it may now be Difficult to assign any solid Reason why we should not own, protect, and improve so immensely Valuable an Inheritance, purchased and procured by our Ancestors, at a great Expence."[811]

The inventory of John Still Winthrop's estate amounted to almost £10,000. More than a quarter of that value resided in "The West Part of Poquonock Farm in Groton, now in the Occupation of Jesse Brownn, Containing by Estimation about 700 Acres, with the Buildings thereon and Appurtenances thereunto belonging" at £2,500.[812]

Children of John Still[5] and Jane (Borland) Winthrop:[813]

> i. JOHN[6] WINTHROP, b. at New London[814] 20 July 1751[815] and d. unm. at New York, N.Y. 15 Nov. 1780.[816]
>
>> At age 10, John Winthrop was sent to Boston Latin School, where he studied for five years.[817] He was admitted to Harvard in the summer of 1766, at age 15. In March 1767, during his freshman year, he was admonished during a faculty meeting after he lied to protect a student who had been among a group accused of associating with "one or more lewd women."[818] He graduated

---

[811] *The New-London Gazette*, 2 March 1770, 3.

[812] Mayo, *The Winthrop Family in America*, 162.

[813] Mayo, *The Winthrop Family in America*, 137, asserted that all members of the Winthrop family who bore the surname in 1948 descended from John Still Winthrop.

[814] Mayo, *The Winthrop Family in America*, 197.

[815] *Official Minutes, September 13, 1765 to January 3, 1775,* Harvard University Faculty of Arts and Sciences, Early Faculty Minutes, 1725–1806, Harvard University Archives, UAIII 5.5,Volume 14 (Box 10), 41 (image 60 of 296), at *nrs.harvard.edu/urn-3:HUL. ARCH:10957445?n=60.* "Winthrop, Johannes, N. London, Jul. 20, 1751."

[816] Adlard, *The Sutton-Dudleys of England and the Dudleys of Massachusetts in New England*, 126.

[817] Henry F. Jenks, *Catalogue of the Boston Public Latin School* (Boston: The Boston Latin School Association, 1886), 82 (appendix).

[818] *Official Minutes, September 13, 1765 to January 3, 1775,* Harvard University Faculty of Arts and Sciences, Early Faculty Minutes, 1725–1806, Harvard University Archives, UAIII 5.5,Volume 14 (Box 10), 39 (image 58 of 296), at *nrs.harvard.edu/urn-3:HUL.ARCH:10957445?n=58.* At a meeting on 23 March 1767, the faculty voted to demote three students who had been "found guilty of countenancing, encouraging & associating with one or more lewd women." At the same meeting "it was voted that Winthrop (John), Adams (Saml) & Cabot should be privately admonished before us for their misdemeanor in the Affair of the lewd woman as mentioned." John's crime, specifically, was "falsifying in the matter, endeavoring thereby to Skreen Sweett."

in 1770 with a bachelor's degree and a Master of Arts in 1774.[819]
After his father died in 1776, he inherited a large portion of
the family property, including Fisher's Island; he would struggle
for control of the latter. In 1775, British forces had carried off
eleven hundred sheep from the island; troops returned in March
1777 and during the summer of 1779, taking away anything they
could carry and burning the buildings. In Sept. 1779, John wrote
to one of his brothers, "At present I'm fully employed getting in
Corn, potatoes, etc.—or rather gleaning after the Military & civil,
or uncivil, Thieves."[820] The following spring John petitioned the
Council of Safety for the State of Connecticut for permission to
build a small brick house on the island so he could place a family
there for security. He also had been advised to go to Virginia "for
a change of air" to treat his failing health, and asked the council
for a pass to travel through British-occupied New York to first see
Dr. Middleton, the one man who had so far been able to provide
him relief.[821] He received permission for both requests on 11 April
1780.[822]

The plan was to travel to "the Jerseys," where his brother
Thomas, then a senior at Harvard, would accompany him south.
But John was too weak to travel beyond New York, where he died
in November at age 28.[823] John had been partly responsible for
the first publication of John[1] Winthrop's journal, Mayo pointed
out; after inheriting the manuscript from his father, he lent it to
Governor Jonathan Trumbull of Connecticut, who made a copy
that became the basis of the first printed edition in 1790.[824]

---

[819] *Quinquennial Catalogue of the Officers and Graduates of Harvard University, 1636–1915*
(Cambridge, Mass.: Harvard University Press, 1915), 146.

[820] John Winthrop to "Dear Brother," 28 September 1779, Winthrop Family Papers
(reel 20, box 37), Massachusetts Historical Society. The letter was not written to
William Winthrop, as John noted, "Last week Bro' Wm. Went to Hartford & bought
himself a House. . . . I hope he will not be disappointed in his expectations of the
Home's performance."

[821] "Petition[s] of John Winthrop," *Collections of the Massachusetts Historical Society*, 7th
series, 3 [1902]: 20, 21.

[822] Hoadly, *The Public Records of the Colony of Connecticut*, 2: 509.

[823] Mayo, *The Winthrop Family in America*, 199, citing Winthrop Manuscripts, 30A: 5.

[824] *Proceedings of the Massachusetts Historical Society*, 12 [1872]: 235. The journal manuscript
and a great trove of family letters and papers passed from John to his brother Francis
Bayard[6] Winthrop, and then in 1814 to the Massachusetts Historical Society (after
lobbying by their brother Thomas Lindall Winthrop, a society member), where they
still reside. The gift was described at the time as "a large trunk of books and pamphlets,
chiefly of ancient date, among which are many valuable tracts concerning the early

ii. JANE/JENNY WINTHROP, b. 1 Nov. 1752[825] and d. at Newport, R.I.
30 Nov. 1828.[826] She m. at New London 6 Dec. 1781,[827] WILLIAM
STEWART, who was b. at New London 14 June 1743, son of
Matthew and Abigail (Gardiner) Stewart.[828] They had a daughter,
Nancy[7] Stewart (1789–1859).[829] William d. "of the fever" outside
New London 10 Sept. 1798.[830]

9   iii. FRANCIS BAYARD WINTHROP, b. at New London 11 March 1754;
m. (1) 22 April 1779, ELSIE MARSTON; m. (2) 15 May 1790, PHEBE
TAYLOR.

10   iv. ANNE WINTHROP, b. 7 May 1755; m. 6 June 1786, DAVID SEARS.

v. WILLIAM WINTHROP, b. at New London[831] 5 June 1756[832] and d. unm.
at New York 27 April 1827.[833] William did not attend college.[834]
Instead, he used a small inheritance from his great-grandfather,
Timothy Lindall,[835] to establish a business in Norwich, Conn.[836] In

---

History of New England," per *Collections of the Massachusetts Historical Society*, 2nd
series, 2 [1846]: 285. See also 3rd series, 7 [1838]: 31.

825   Adlard, *The Sutton-Dudleys of England and the Dudleys of Massachusetts in New
England*, 126.

826   Adlard, *The Sutton-Dudleys of England and the Dudleys of Massachusetts in New
England*, 126. See also *Newport Mercury*, 6 December 1828, 3. "Died in this town on
Sunday morning last, Mrs. Jane Stewart, aged 76 years."

827   *The Connecticut Gazette; and the Universal Intelligencer*, 14 December 1781, 3:
"[Married.] Mr. William Stewart, Merchant, to the amiable and accomplish'd Miss
Jenny Winthrop, eldest Daughter of the late John-Still Winthrop, Esq."

828   Barbour, "New London Births–Marriages–Deaths, 1646–1854," 290, citing 2: 73 of
original town records.

829   Adlard, *The Sutton-Dudleys of England and the Dudleys of Massachusetts in New
England*, 126.

830   Adlard, *The Sutton-Dudleys of England and the Dudleys of Massachusetts in New England*,
126. See also *Springer's Weekly Oracle* (New London), 17 September 1798, 2. Died "in
the country, of the fever, Mr. William Stewart, aged 55, merchant, this city."

831   Mayo, *The Winthrop Family in America*, 205.

832   Adlard, *The Sutton-Dudleys of England and the Dudleys of Massachusetts in New
England*, 128.

833   *Evening Post*, New York, 28 April 1827, 2. "[Died] last evening, William Winthrop,
aged 71 years. His friends and acquaintances, and those of his deceased brother
Francis Bayard Winthrop, are requested to attend his funeral at 5 o'clock tomorrow
afternoon, from No. 14 Warren st., without further invitation." See also Adlard, *The
Sutton-Dudleys of England and the Dudleys of Massachusetts in New England*, 128.

834   Mayo, *The Winthrop Family in America*, 205.

835   Timothy Lindall of Salem left $2,000 in his 1760 will to his granddaughter Jane
(Borland) Winthrop's six older children, to be kept at interest until they came of age.
See *ancestry.com* > Massachusetts, Wills and Probate Records, 1635–1991 > Essex >
Probate Records, Vol. 337–338, Book 37–38, 1760–1762 > image 207 of 623.

836   Mayo, *The Winthrop Family in America*, 205. Mayo says he did this "as early as 1774,"
when he turned 18, but he would not have received the inheritance until 1777,
when he turned 21.

his letters, John[6] Winthrop occasionally reported on William's trips to Hartford to buy sugar or to conduct other business.[837] William also sometimes visited family in Salem, and on 16 April 1782 William Pynchon, a lawyer there, recorded encountering "Mr. W. Winthrop from N. London" who gave "an account of people at New York."[838]

Mayo noted that while this comment gives the impression that New Englanders "regarded New Yorkers as if they were a different species," Pynchon's interest was in fact piqued because William had gone behind the British lines.[839] Five months earlier, on 22 Nov. 1781, the governor and Council of Safety of Connecticut had given William permission "to go into [occupied] New York under the protection of a Flag, either by water or land, to transact business with Wm. Brown, Esq, from whom a large sum is due to his father's estate, and also settle some family matters with his brother Francis and respecting his brother John's affairs who has died there."[840] After the war William appears to have been merchant in or near New London until about 1794, when he first appears in a Manhattan directory with an office at 52 Wall Street.[841] He lived with Francis at Turtle Bay, on the east side near present-day Forty-Ninth Street.[842] Among his investments were some "Huron [Ohio] Lands" that he planned to visit although he was more than 60 years old. "It is a long tedious journey," wrote his brother Thomas, "and I hope he will get safe back again. He would do well to dispose of his lands there, and purchase nearer home."[843]

---

[837] Mayo, *The Winthrop Family in America*, 205, citing Winthrop Manuscripts 30A: 2, 3.

[838] Oliver, *The Diary of William Pynchon of Salem*, 119.

[839] Mayo, *The Winthrop Family in America*, 205. Mayo observed, "William Winthrop was much younger than Mr. Pynchon, but their attitudes toward the American Revolution seem to have been a good deal alike. Much might be said on either side of the controversy, but there was only one thing to do—mind your own business and await the outcome of the war. That was exactly what they did."

[840] Hoadly, *The Public Records of the State of Connecticut*, 3: 551.

[841] William Duncan, *The New-York Directory and Register for the Year 1794* (New York: T. and J. Swords, 1794), 206.

[842] Mayo, *The Winthrop Family in America*, 206, citing Winthrop Manuscripts 30A: 19.

[843] Mayo, *The Winthrop Family in America*, 206, citing Winthrop Manuscripts, 30A: 71.

vi. JOSEPH WINTHROP, b. at New London 19 June 1757, d. at Charleston,
     S.C. 26 July 1828,[844] and bur. there in St. Michael's Churchyard.[845]
     He m. at Charleston 6 Nov. 1788,[846] MARY FRASER, who was b. at
     Charleston 17 Aug. 1765, dau. of Alexander and Mary (Grimké)
     Fraser and a sister of Charles Fraser, the well-known painter of
     miniatures.[847] She d. at Charleston on 11 Sept. 1832, and was buried
     at St. Michael's.[848] The couple had twelve children.[849]

     According to Mayo, Joseph Winthrop, like his brother William,
     used the inheritance from his great-grandfather Timothy Lindall to
     start a business.[850] In about 1783 he moved to Charleston to become
     the senior member of Winthrop, Tod & Winthrop, merchants.[851]

---

[844] Clare Jervey, *Inscriptions on the Tablets and Gravestones in St. Michael's Church and Churchyard, Charleston, S.C.* (Columbia, S.C.: The State Company, 1906), 300. "Sacred to the Memory of Joseph Winthrop, who was born 19th, June 1757 in New London, Conn. and died 26th July 1828 in this City of which he had been for 45 years a worthy and respectable inhabitant." See also *Charleston Courier,* 29 July 1828, 3: "Died, on Saturday evening last, in the seventy-second year of his age, Joseph Winthrop, Esq., a native of New-England, but for the last forty-three years a resident of this city."

[845] Mayo, *The Winthrop Family in America,* 207

[846] Adlard, *The Sutton-Dudleys of England and the Dudleys of Massachusetts in New England,* 128.

[847] Charles Fraser, "Fraser Family Memoranda," *The South Carolina Historical and Genealogical Magazine* 5 [1904]: 56–58, citing family Bible for her birthdate.

[848] Jervey, *Inscriptions on the Tablets and Gravestones in St. Michael's Church and Churchyard, Charleston, S.C.,* 299. "Here Lie The Mortal remains of Mrs. Mary Winthrop, who died the 17th Septr. 1832, at Sixty Eight Years. In the midst of domestic retirement, to the duties of which her life was actively devoted. She exhibited a benevolent and affectionate disposition. To her maternal Offices was instrusted by Providence the Care of a numerous Offspring who survive to deplore her loss and to honor her memory." Adlard, *The Sutton-Dudleys of England and the Dudleys of Massachusetts in New England,* 128, gives 11 September 1832.

[849] Adlard, *The Sutton-Dudleys of England and the Dudleys of Massachusetts in New England,* 128.

[850] Mayo, *The Winthrop Family in America,* 207. See note 835.

[851] Winthrop, Tod and Winthrop to Christopher Champlin, 10 February 1784, reprinted in *Collections of the Massachusetts Historical Society,* 7th series, 10 [1915]: 192. "We should have ourselves the honor to have addressed you long before this day, but it not happened that altho' our J. Tod sail'd from Philadelphia on the 23rd October he did not reach us earlier than the 6th Inst. Owing to the extreme bad and tempestuous weather which the vessel he was aboard of, experienced upon this Coast, and by it compell'd to desist from the attempt of getting here, and to repair to the West Indies, during this time our J. Winthrop was much busied in the making of Shipments to Europe for account of our Friends." An advertisement for Winthrop, Tod, and Winthrop appeared in the *South-Carolina Gazette and General Advertiser* in Charleston as early as 1 January 1784, noting the *Providence* would sail for Amsterdam soon and those seeking passage with "good accommodations"

(The junior member was his brother, Thomas, who a few years later would return to New England.[852]) He appears to have struggled early, as in April 1789 he had to pay off a creditor, John Codman (II), with Boston real estate for a loan of more than £2,000.[853] "From the point of view of his younger brother Thomas, Joseph was too easy-going to be really successful," Mayo wrote. "His older brother Francis must have been somewhat of the same opinion, for in 1816 Joseph owed him about $15,000 and was behind in his interest payments."[854] In about 1797, Joseph built a house at 129 Tradd Street in Charleston that still stands.[855] About the same time, he appears to have been appointed vice-consul for Sweden to represent the interests of its ships at Charleston harbor, a position he would hold for about fifteen years before his son John Augustus[7] Winthrop took over.[856] In 1804 John was elected one of fifteen

---

should inquire with the firm at 89 Broad Street. By December, Winthrop, Tod & Winthrop had moved to 46 Bay.

[852] Mayo, *The Winthrop Family in America*, 207.

[853] *Codman vs. Winthrop*, 11 April 1789, scan of original at *familysearch.org* > Massachusetts Lands Records, 1620–1986 > Suffolk > Deeds 1789–1797, Vol. 165–66, images 37–38 of 613.

[854] Mayo 207, citing Winthrop Manuscripts 30A: 47, 69.

[855] "Tradd Street (78–196)," Charleston County Public Library, *ccpl.org/content. asp?id=15684 &catID=6025*. "About 1797, Joseph Winthrop, a Massachusetts man who became a Charleston merchant, built this typical single house on land belonging to his wife, the elder sister of Charles Fraser, the miniaturist and writer. It was built on an open 'green' backing on a salty creek leading to Ashley River. Interior details are in a simple but charming transitional style, keeping something from the late Georgian wood work of pre-Revolutionary days, but borrowing lightness from the Adamesque style which within a few years would conquer the town. In this house, the Winthrops shared six rooms with their 11 [*sic*] children."

[856] A 1794 Charleston directory lists Joseph Winthrop, merchant, in East Bay, and Joseph Winthrop, merchant, at 90 Tradd St. (James W. Hagy, *People and Professions of Charleston, South Carolina, 1782–1802* [Baltimore: Genealogical Publishing Co., 1999], 47). An 1806 edition has Joseph Winthrop, "His Swedish & Danish Majesty's Consul," with no address, followed by Joseph Merchant, 147 Bay, residence 57 Tradd St. (James W. Hagy, *City Directories for Charleston, South Carolina for the years 1803, 1806, 1807, and 1813* [Baltimore: Genealogical Publishing Company, 2000], 56). In 1813, the directory listed Joseph A. Winthrop, vice consul of Sweden, and Joseph Winthrop, vice consul of Denmark, both at 58 Tradd (162). According to one history, Joseph Winthrop on 3 May 1797 was appointed vice-consul for Sweden for South Carolina and Georgia, and "arrived" in Charleston on 26 May 1797 (Knute Emil Carlson, *Relations of the United States with Sweden* [Allentown, Pa.: H. Ray Haas & Co., 1921], 73). To add to the confusion, the subsequent 1800 Federal census for Charleston includes two Joseph Winthrop households: one in St. James parish with two males 26 to 44, one female 26 to 44, one male under 10, one male 16 to 25, and one female 10 to 15 (roll 48, 66); and the other with one male 26 to 44, one female 16 to 25, four males under 10, one female under 10, and eight slaves (roll 48, 113). Neither fits perfectly

directors of the South-Carolina Insurance Company,[857] and in 1817
its president.[858] When the New England Society of Charleston was
formed in 1819, Joseph became its first vice-president; the next
year he was elected president.[859]

vii. MARY WINTHROP, b. in Jan. 1759[860] and d. at New London 30
Aug. 1848, the last survivor of the fourteen children of John Still
Winthrop.[861] She m. at New London 9 July 1786,[862] RICHARD
WILLIAM PARKIN, who was bp. at Middleton Tyas in the North
Riding of Yorkshire 4 Sept. 1750,[863] son of William Parkin of

---

with the circumstances of Joseph[6] Winthrop, though he did then have four sons under 10. The 1810 census includes only one Joseph Winthrop, age 45 and over, living
alone (roll 60, 323), and the 1820 census again has only one Joseph Winthrop, leading
a household of twenty-eight people, including sixteen slaves (roll 119, 46). A letter
by the Swedish consul, Richard Söderström, dated 5 March 1814, noted that Joseph
Winthrop of Charleston had resigned his commission (*A Comprehensive Catalogue of
the Correspondence and Papers of James Monroe*, 2 vols. [Westport, Conn.: Greenwood
Press, 2001], 1: 386), but directories after that date continue to list Joseph Winthrop
as consul for Sweden, Denmark, and Norway, suggesting Joseph A. had taken over his
father's duties. On 21 November 1825, a notice in the *Charleston Courier* reported that
"Joseph A. Winthrop, Esq." had been appointed vice-consul for Sweden and Norway
for North and South Carolina, "to reside in this city."

857   *City Gazette* (Charleston), 23 June 1804, 3.

858   *City Gazette* (Charleston), 9 July 1817, 3.

859   William Way, *History of the New England Society of Charleston, South Carolina*
(Charleston: The Society, 1920), 3, 5, 6, 32.

860   Adlard, *The Sutton-Dudleys of England and the Dudleys of Massachusetts in New
England*, 128, gives 31 January. An obituary in *New London Daily Chronicle News*, 6
September 1848, 2, gave 3 January; see note 861.

861   *New London Daily Chronicle News*, 6 September 1848, 2. "Mrs. Mary Winthrop
Parkin—It is just 50 years since the yellow fever visited our town and swept a fear-
ful track of desolation through the midst of it. Young and old, rich and poor, with-
ered at its touch, and the hearse with its funeral pall was almost constantly moving
through the streets. Among those who were struck suddenly from the career and
life of usefulness was Richard William Parkin, esq., an intelligent, enterprising merchant. He died on the 10th of Sept. 1798, and was laid in the family tomb of his
brother-in-law, Francis B. Winthrop, esq. On Friday last the same tomb was opened
to receive the remains of his venerable relict, Mrs. Mary Parkin. How wide the
space of time separating these partners of youth! Mrs. Parkin had attained her 90th
year—having been born January 3rd, 1759, in the reign of George the Second. She
was the seventh child and the last survivor of the 14 children of John Still Winthrop,
esq. . . . In her 89th year, without apparent fatigue, she ascended to the summit of the
light-house at Harbor's Mouth, to enjoy once more the commanding prospect its
affords of the sound."

862   Barbour, "New London Births–Marriages–Deaths, 1646–1854," 228, citing 3: 87 of
original town records.

863   Middleton Tyas parish registers, North Yorkshire County Record Office, scan of
original at *findmypast.com* > Yorkshire Baptisms. "[1750] Richard the son of William
Parkin of Maulton, Sep. 4."

Malton, Yorkshire.[864] A merchant at New London, Richard d. there 10 Sept. 1798,[865] at age 49, when yellow fever swept through the town. He was buried in the Winthrop family tomb, as his widow would be fifty years later.[866] They had issue, including Thomas[7] Parkin, who m. Mary Jane[7] Winthrop, and Margaret Ann[7] Parkin, who m. William Henry[7] Winthrop.[867]

11 viii. THOMAS LINDALL WINTHROP, b. at New London 6 March 1760; m. 25 July 1786, ELIZABETH BOWDOIN TEMPLE.

Children of John Still[5] and Elizabeth (Shirreff) (Hay) Winthrop:

ix. BENJAMIN[6] WINTHROP, b. at New London 17 Sept. 1762, d. at New York 9 Jan. 1844, and bur. there with his wife at St. Mark's Church in the Bowery.[868] He m. at Trinity Church, New York 19 Jan. 1785,[869] JUDITH STUYVESANT, who was b. at New York 25 Dec. 1765 and d. 7 March 1844,[870] dau. of Peter and Margaret

---

[864] Franklin Bowditch Dexter, "John Still Winthrop Parkin," in *Biographical Sketches of the Graduates of Yale College,* 6 vols. (New York: Henry Holt & Co., 1911–12), 6: 274–75, citing a letter from William Parkin, March 1911. "He emigrated to this country as a young man [and] died in comparative youth, leaving a family of six children, and this son was educated by his uncle, Francis Bayard Winthrop." John Still Winthrop[7] Parkin (b. 25 March 1792) became a doctor and pharmacist and settled in Selma, Alabama, before returning to New York City in 1824.

[865] Barbour, "New London Births–Marriages–Deaths, 1646–1854," 228, citing 3: 87 of original town records. Adlard, *The Sutton-Dudleys of England and the Dudleys of Massachusetts in New England*, 128, gives 6 September.

[866] *New London Daily Chronicle News,* 6 September 1848, 2. See also *Weekly Oracle* (New London), 17 September 1798, 3. "Died In this city, since our last (two weeks) . . . Mr. Richard W. Parkin, merchant, aged 49." The *City Gazette* (Charleston, S.C.), 3 October 1798, 2, in reprinting a report dated 11 September, gave his age as 53.

[867] Adlard, *The Sutton-Dudleys of England and the Dudleys of Massachusetts in New England,* 128–29.

[868] "New York, New York City Municipal Deaths, 1795–1949," index of records at New York Municipal Archives, *familysearch.org/ark:/61903/1:1:FD16-GMR,* citing Family History Library film 0447,550. Benjamin Winthrop, d. 9 January 1844, res. 134 Second St., age 81, b. 1763 Conn. See also *Memorial of St. Mark's Church in the Bowery* (New York, 1899), 182: Memorial window: "In memory of Benjamin Winthrop, *Nat.,* New London, Connecticut, 17th September 1762. *Obt.* City of New York, 9th January 1844." The window is described as being the third from the front on the east end. Also, *Commercial Advertiser* (New York), 10 January 1844, 2: "On Tuesday morning, 9th inst., Benjamin Winthrop, Esq., in the 82d year of his age. His realatives and friends, and those of his son, Benjamin R. Winthrop, and of his sons-in-law, John W. Chanler and Geo. Folsom, are invited to attend his funeral to-morrow (Thursday) afternoon, at a quarter before 5 o'clock, from his late resident, No. 134 Second Avenue."

[869] Index to Trinity Church Parish Registers, online at *registers.trinitywallstreet.org.*

[870] "New York, New York City Municipal Deaths, 1795–1949," index of records at New York

(Livingston) Stuyvesant,[871] and had issue (including Elizabeth Shirreff[7] Winthrop, who m. Rev. John White Chanler; their daughter Margaret Stuyvesant[8] Chanler married the astronomer Lewis Morris Rutherfurd).[872]

Lawrence Shaw Mayo described the "peculiar political circumstances" under which Benjamin and his brother Robert grew up:[873]

> Their father died before Benjamin was 14 years old; their mother was, in all probability, a Loyalist, and should have been one. Her first husband had been an officer in the British Army; her brother, Major Shirreff, was in the British Army and was stationed in New York City, which the British captured in 1776. Quite understandably, Mrs. Winthrop leaned toward the Crown and preferred to have her boys become Englishmen instead of Yankees.
>
> Major Shirreff shared her views to such an extent that he offered to educate Benjamin and Robert in England and at his own expense if they could be got out of New London and into New York.[874] [In] the course of time Governor Trumbull and the Council of Safety gave their

---

Municipal Archives, *familysearch.org/ark:/61903/1:1:FD16-GXS*, citing FHL 447,550. Judith Winthrop, d. 7 March 1844, res. 134 Second Avenue, age 79, b. 1765, N.Y. See also *Memorial of St. Mark's Church in the Bowery*, 182: Memorial window: "In memory of Judith Winthrop, Wife of Benjamin Winthrop, Daughter of Petrus Stuyvesant, *Nat.* New York 25th December 1765. *Obt.*, 7th March 1844." Also, *Commercial Advertiser* (New York), 19 March 1844, 2: "On Thursday morning, 7th inst., in the 79th year of her age, Mrs. Judith Winthrop, widow of Benjamin Winthrop, and daughter of the late Petrus Stuyvesant. The friends of her son, Benjamin R. Winthrop, of her brother, Peter G. Stuyvesant, and of her sons-in-law, John W. Chanler and George Folsom, are invited to attend her funeral to-morrow (Sunday) at 5 o'clock P.M. from her late residence, No. 134 Second avenue."

[871] Mayo, *The Winthrop Family in America*, 221. "She was a direct descendant of Gov. Peter Stuyvesant who, in the summer of 1664, finally took the advice of Gov. John Winthrop of Connecticut and surrendered New Amsterdam to Britain [*sic*]."

[872] Cuyler Reynolds, ed., *Genealogical and Family History of Southern New York and the Hudson River Valley*, 3 vols. (New York: Lewis Historical Publishing Co., 1914), 3: 1231.

[873] Mayo, *The Winthrop Family in America*, 220–21.

[874] Joseph Webb to Jonathan Trumbull, 3 March 1778, *Collections of the Massachusetts Historical Society*, 7th series, 2 [1902]: 219–20. "I feel a little chagrind about the two young lads of M[rs] Winthrop. . . . Col. Sherriff was vastly civil in obtaining my permit for M[rs] Deane's son to go first into York, then in obtaining a pass for him to England, France, &c. Long after all this was completed, he was chatting with me about his sister, was anxious about her maintaining & taking care of so large a family & started a *scheem* of educating at his own expence the two lads; ask't me to obtain your leave, which civility he wou'd more return if ever in his power."

consent,[875] and toward the end of March 1778 Benjamin and Robert were on their way to Manhattan Island. . . . If the original plan was to send the boys to London together, something must have changed this after they reached New York. The younger one, Robert, was shipped off in the *Greyhound*, which "carried the news from Penobscot to England."[876] [But] for the time being Benjamin remained in New York. There are indications that he went to England before March 1781; but, as his mother knew to her sorrow, he was a poor correspondent and therefore we sometimes have to guess as to his whereabouts.

Benjamin was in England by the time his half-brother, Thomas Lindall Winthrop, arrived there in 1781,[877] but Mayo noted he apparently only stayed "long enough to decide that he preferred to be an American,"[878] for he was back in New York by 19 Jan. 1785, when he married at Trinity Church. "The Winthrops appear to have made their home about two miles out of town, in Bowery Village, which was a portion of the ancestral domain of the Stuyvesant family," Mayo wrote.[879] Benjamin's first office was at 2 Great Dock Street, then at 27 Pearl Street, and later in Wall Street. Seven of his eight children were baptized at St. Mark's Church in the Bowery.[880]

   x.   CHARLES WINTHROP, b. 17 Oct. 1763 and d.y.[881]

   xi.   ROBERT WINTHROP, b. at New London[882] 7 Dec. 1764[883] and d. of "paralysis"[884] at his home in Dover, Kent 10 May 1832.[885] He m. at

---

[875] Hoadly, *The Public Records of Connecticut*, 1: 572.

[876] Mayo, *The Winthrop Family in America*, 220, citing Winthrop Manuscripts 30A: 4. He noted that presumably this trip was in the summer of 1779, when the British seized Castine, Maine.

[877] Mayo, *The Winthrop Family in America*, 221, citing Winthrop Manuscripts 30A: 7.

[878] Mayo, *The Winthrop Family in America*, 220–21.

[879] Mayo, *The Winthrop Family in America*, 221, citing Winthrop Manuscripts 30A: 19. See also Benjamin Robert Winthrop, "Old New York," in D. T. Valentine, *Manual of the Corporation of the City of New York* (New York: Edmund Jones & Co., 1862), 689.

[880] "Records of St. Mark's Church in the Bowery, New York City," *The New York Genealogical and Biographical Record* 71 [1940]: 335–36.

[881] Adlard, *The Sutton-Dudleys of England and the Dudleys of Massachusetts in New England*, 130.

[882] Mayo, *The Winthrop Family in America*, 222.

[883] Adlard, *The Sutton-Dudleys of England and the Dudleys of Massachusetts in New England*, 130.

[884] "Obituary: Vice-Admiral Winthrop," *The Gentleman's Magazine and Historical Chronicle* 102 [1832]: 1: 641.

[885] *Findagrave.com* (memorial 40723241). From memorial plaque inside St. Mary the Virgin in Dover: "Robert Winthrop Vice Admiral of the Blue, Died at his resi-

Dover 23 Dec. 1804,[886] SARAH LAMBE FARBRACE, who was b. 4 and bp. at the Church of St. Mary the Virgin, Dover 23 April 1782,[887] dau. of George and Elizabeth Ann (Teale) Farbrace, and had issue.[888] She d. at Brussels, South Brabant [now Belgium] 27 April 1825.[889] A memorial to the couple placed by their son, George Teale Sebor[7] Winthrop, hangs inside St. Mary's Church in Dover.[890]

Robert was sent to England as an adolescent by his uncle William Shirreff for his education; he must have been an attractive boy, Mayo wrote, for two years later his uncle Charles Shirreff in England wrote of him: "Bob has been detain'd here [Old Alresford in Hampshire] from his Duty 5 days in hopes of meeting you [Thomas Lindall Winthrop] and leaves tomorrow for his ship, with a heavy heart at the disappointment. He is really a fine fellow and a credit to us all."[891] As a midshipman on the H.M.S. *Formidable*, Robert took part in the famous battle off Dominica on 12 April 1782 in which the British defeated a French fleet commanded by Admiral de Grasse. After peace he returned to America and went into business in New London with his half-brother, William, but

---

dence in Dover May 10 1832. Sarah Lambe his wife Died at Bruxelles April 27 1825. Elizabeth Ann, widow of George Farbrace Esq. and mother of Sarah Lambe Wintrhop, Died September 17 1856." He was buried on 15 May, age 68, a resident of Margate (*findmypast.com* > Kent, Canterbury Archdeaconry Burials 1538–1988 > Canterbury Cathedral Archives, U3/30/1/26, 375).

[886] Adlard, *The Sutton-Dudleys of England and the Dudleys of Massachusetts in New England*, 130.

[887] Adlard, *The Sutton-Dudleys of England and the Dudleys of Massachusetts in New England*, 130.

[888] "Extracts from Ashford Manor Court Rolls 1821 to 1830" (Kent Archaeological Society), transcript at *kentarchaeology.org.uk/Research/01/ASH/03/10.htm*, 15 January 1821, "One moiety to Elizabeth Ann Farbrace of Dover, widow, trustee appointed by indtres. 30/31 December 1806 (marriage settlement) (1) Isaac M. Teale (2) George Henry Teale Farbrace, son of George Farbrace, (3) Sarah Farbrace of Dover, widow, grandmother of Sarah Lambe Winthrop, (4) Robert Winthrop, commander of H.M. ship *Sybele* & wife Sarah Lambe, then Sarah Lambe Farbrace, only daughter of George, (5) Elizabeth Ann Farbrace & Edward Walsby, D.D., Prebendary of Canterbury, now deceased. Trust for Robert & Sarah Winthrop & their children." See also monument inscriptions recorded about 1795 posted by the Kent Archaeological Society (*kentarchaeology.org.uk/Research/Libr/MIs/MIsDoverStMarys/ 01.htm*), number 160, which transcribes a memorial created for George Farbrace by his widow, as well as for "James Teale, Esqr. (Father of the beforemention;d Elizabeth Ann Farbrace)."

[889] *Findagrave.com* (memorial 40723241). Adlard, *The Sutton-Dudleys of England and the Dudleys of Massachusetts in New England*, 130, gives 27 May.

[890] *Findagrave.com* (memorial 40723241).

[891] Mayo, *The Winthrop Family in America*, 222, citing Winthrop Manuscripts 30A: 7.

by 1790 had returned to England and re-entered the British Navy as a lieutenant.

An obituary that appeared in 1832 in the *Gentleman's Magazine* of London outlined the trajectory of his career: He commanded a battalion at the conquest of Martinique in 1794; commanded the sloop *Albicore* at the capture of St. Lucia in 1796; about the same time was captured near Barbados a French coverette of 14 guns; on 27 Aug. 1796, while aboard the frigate *Undaunted*, was wrecked in a gale in the Morant Keys; in 1798, was appointed to the *Circe*, with 28 guns, and sent in the expedition against the port of Ostend to disrupt French invasion plans; in the summer of 1799, destroyed or captured a number of Dutch vessels; in the autumn of 1800, in the expedition against the Spanish naval base at Ferrol, commanded the frigate *Stag*, which was stranded in Vigo Bay and had to be burned to avoid falling into enemy hands. After the peace of Amiens in 1802 (which lasted until Britain again declared war on France in 1803), Winthrop was placed in command of the *Ardent*, with 64 guns, on the coast of Spain, where he defeated a French frigate of 32 guns and two hundred men. In 1805, soon after he married, he took command of the frigate *Sybille*, and in 1807 captured the French schooner *l'Oiseau*. He was promoted to rear-admiral in 1809 and vice-admiral in 1830.[892] His sons George and Hay both also became commanders in the Royal Navy.[893] Robert's niece, Sarah Bowdoin[7] Winthrop, in a letter in the summer of 1805 to her father, Thomas Lindall Winthrop, offered a brief glimpse of the young couple. Sarah (Farbrace) Winthrop at the time would have been pregnant with their eldest son, Robert Shirreff Trevanion[7] Winthrop, who was born on 24 Sept. 1805:[894]

> I have the pleasure of informing you that I have been introduced to your brother, Capt. Winthrop. It is only ten days ago that he heard of our being in London, since when he has called on us twice and Mrs. W. once. Capt. W—has had a 50-gun ship built for him and is perfectly ready with the exception of wanting a few men to put to sea. He told me three or four days ago that he did

---

[892] *The Gentleman's Magazine and Historical Chronicle* 102 [1832]: 1: 641.

[893] "The Dudleys of Massachusetts," *The Herald and Genealogist* 2 [1865]: 411.

[894] Mayo, *The Winthrop Family in America*, 224, citing Winthrop Manuscripts 30A: 17. Robert lived only five months, and died on 18 February 1806.

not expect to sail in less than a fortnight or three weeks.
Mrs. Winthrop seems an uncommonly nice, fine woman;
from her appearance I should think her to be about
twenty-eight [actually, 23],—of rather larger stature and a
most interesting, lovely face. They are both in very good
health,—she a little out of spirits at the idea of his leaving
her so soon; this will be their first separation since their
marrage.

    xii.   Elizabeth Winthrop, b. 17 April 1766[895] and d. at Middletown,
Conn. 10 Feb. 1847.[896] She m. at New London 27 April 1786,[897]
Jacob Sebor, who was b. at Middletown 16 Jan. 1755[898] and d. there
5 May 1847,[899] son of Jacob and Jane (Woodbury) Sebor,[900] and had
issue.

    In Oct. 1779, when Elizabeth was 13, her half-brother John
Winthrop wrote to one of her brothers (unnamed) to say that
"my mother has concluded to put our two sisters Elizth & Marg^t
[then 12] to School in Newbury-port [Mass.], having from the
post heard from Mr. Wm Hubbard, who is now at Boston, that they
can be admitted. My mother therefore requests your assistance, and
mine, in conveying them to Newbury and begs you will, as soon
as possible, hire a good strong Horse & Chaise."[901] Following their
marriage, Elizabeth and Jacob seem to have lived in New London

---

[895] Adlard, *The Sutton-Dudleys of England and the Dudleys of Massachusetts in New England*, 131.

[896] *Constitution* (Middletown, Conn.), 17 February 1847, 3. "Died . . . in this city, on the 10th inst., Elizabeth Winthrop, wife of Jacob Sebor, Esq., in the 81st year of her age." See also Connecticut Vital Records (compiled under the direction of Lucius Barnes Barnour), "Middletown Births–Marriages–Deaths, 1651–1854," in 2 vols. (Hartford, 1923), 2: 400, citing 4: 8 of the original Middletown town records.

[897] Barbour, "New London Births–Marriages–Deaths, 1646–1854," 269, citing 3: 80 of original town records.

[898] Barbour, "Middletown Births–Marriages–Deaths, 1651–1854," 2: 400, citing 2: 90 of original town records. Son of Jacob & Jane.

[899] *Constitution* (Middletown, Conn.), 12 May 1847, 3. "Died in this city, on the 5th, inst., Jacob Sebor, Esq., in the 93d year of his age." See also Barbour, "Middletown Births–Marriages–Deaths, 1651–1854," 2: 400, citing 4: 8 of original town records, which gives his age at death as 92 years, 3 months and 29 days.

[900] See *Findagrave.com* (memorial 138882639) for a photo of their stone at Indian Hill Cemetery in Middletown.

[901] John Winthrop to "Dear Brother," 12 October 1779, Winthrop Family Papers (reel 20, box 37), Massachusetts Historical Society. In 1775, "a private school for the benefit of young Ladies" had opened in the town (John J. Currier, *History of Newburyport, Mass., 1764–1905* [Newburyport: the author, 1906], 311).

until the death of Jacob's older brother, James F. Sebor, in 1791, then moved to New York to take up his business at 9 Prince Street. In 1794, Jacob moved the business to 51 Beaver Street, and in 1801 to 13 Courtland Street. He apparently retired to Middletown around 1805, when Jacob's name no longer appears in New York directories. "He owned ships which traded to China and India and he sold the goods they brought back," wrote family historian Helen Beach. "Probably he did not go to sea himself, but his eldest son and his son-in-law were merchant captains for many years." In the 1790s he bought two shares at $200 each of the Tontine Coffee House at Wall and Water Streets in New York for his sons William and Charles, but the distribution of the property did not take place among the final seven shareholders until 1870, after both had died.[902]

xiii. MARGARET SHIRREFF WINTHROP, b. 17 July 1767,[903] d. at New York 7 Jan. 1822, and bur. at Trinity Church Cemetery.[904] She m. (1) at New London 1 Jan. 1788,[905] ADOLPHUS B. YATES, a New York merchant (after 1791, when he was operating from No. 12 Smith Street[906]) who was b. about 1763, d. at New York 7 Aug. 1799, and was bur. there in St. Paul's Churchyard.[907] She m. (2) at New

[902] Helen Beach, *The Descendants of Jacob Sebor, 170–91793, of Middletown, Connecticut* (1923), 8–10.

[903] Adlard, *The Sutton-Dudleys of England and the Dudleys of Massachusetts in New England*, 131.

[904] *American* (New York), 9 January 1822, 3. "Died . . . early on Monday morning, after a few days illness, Margaret S. wife of John Marston." See also "New York, New York City Municipal Deaths, 1795–1949," index of records at New York Municipal Archives, *familysearch.org/ark:/61903/1:1:FD15-VM9*, citing FHL 447,545. Margt. S. Marston, d. 8 [*sic*] January 1822, res. Courtland St., age 54, b. 1768 New London. Buried Trinity cemetery.

[905] Adlard, *The Sutton-Dudleys of England and the Dudleys of Massachusetts in New England*, 131.

[906] *New-York Daily Gazette*, 19 October 1791, 2 (advertisement).

[907] *Daily Advertiser* (New York), 9 August 1799, 3, "Died, on Wednesday, of a lingering illness, Mr. Adolphus Yates, aged 36 years. His remains were yesterday interred in St. Paul's Churchyard, accompanied by the New York Rifle Men, of which Corps he was a member. The procession, accompanied by solemn military music, and conducted with strict regularlity, was awfully interesting." Also, *New-York Gazette*, 9 August 1799, 3: "We have again to mention the Death of a *good* and *honest* Man!— Yesterday morning [*sic*], after a few weeks illness, departed this life, Mr. Adolphus B. Yates, Esq., Merchant, of this city. In the evening he was interred; on which occasion, the *Rifle Company*, Commanded by Lieut. Armstrong (of which Mr. Yates was an honorable Member), performed Funeral duties."

London 20 July 1801,[908] JOHN MARSTON, also a merchant, who was b. at New York 3 Sept. 1775, the son of John and Rachel (Lawrence) Marston.[909] He d. at New York 23 Nov. 1849 and was buried at Trinity Church Cemetery.[910] She had issue by both husbands,[911] including Richard Augustus[7] Yates, who rose to become a rear-admiral in the Royal Navy.[912]

    xiv.   HENRY WINTHROP, b. 19 Oct. 1768 and d.y.[913]

---

[908] Adlard, *The Sutton-Dudleys of England and the Dudleys of Massachusetts in New England*, 131.

[909] Charles P. Keith, *The Provincial Councillors of Pennsylvania Who Held Office Between 1733 and 1776* (Philadelphia, 1883), 442. See also Nathan Washington Marston, *The Marston Genealogy in Two Parts* (South Lubec, Me., 1888), 576–78.

[910] "New York, New York City Municipal Deaths, 1795–1949," index of records at New York Municipal Archives, *familysearch.org/ark:/61903/1:1:FD1N-3JM*, citing FHL 447,553. John Marston, d. 23 Nov. 1849, res. 43 20th St., age 74, b. 1775 N.Y., bur. Trinity Church. See also *Spectator* (New York), 26 November 1849, 2. "On Friday, the 23rd inst., Mr. John Marston, aged 74 years."

[911] Adlard, *The Sutton-Dudleys of England and the Dudleys of Massachusetts in New England*, 131.

[912] George Folsom, "Memoir of Hon. Thomas Lindall Winthrop, LL.D.," *Archaeologia Americana* 3 [1857]: 331.

[913] Adlard, *The Sutton-Dudleys of England and the Dudleys of Massachusetts in New England*, 131.

John[1] **Winthrop** (1588–1649). For twelve years the Governor of Massachusetts Bay Colony, John Winthrop's vision of a "city upon a hill" as a metaphor for New World values (and exceptionalism) has since been applied to America itself.

John[2] Winthrop (1606–1676). As Richard S. Dunn has noted, "Among second-generation New Englanders, there was no more attractive figure than John Winthrop, Jr."

Harvard University Portrait Collection, Gift of Robert Winthrop, representing the Winthrop family, to Harvard University, 1964, H601.

John ("Fitz John")[3] Winthrop (1638–1707). While he would come to be a distinguished Governor of Connecticut in middle age, Fitz Winthrop had first to understand "what his grandfather and father had never had to learn," as Dunn put it, "that in England he was an outsider."

Harvard University Portrait Collection, Gift of Robert Winthrop, representing the Winthrop family, to Harvard University, 1964, H609.

Waitstill[3] Winthrop (1642–1717). For Wait Winthrop, the Boston Rebellion of 1689 would prove transformative.

Harvard University Portrait Collection, Gift of Robert Winthrop, representing the Winthrop family, to Harvard University, 1964, H602.

Joseph Dudley (1647–1720). The son of John[1] Winthrop's colleague Thomas Dudley, Joseph Dudley was an inveterate rival of his daughter's father-in-law, Waitstill[3] Winthrop.

Collection of the Massachusetts Historical Society.

John Still[5] Winthrop (1720–1776). A Dudley as well as a Winthrop, John Still Winthrop would—by his two wives—father fourteen children; the descendants of three of these children are covered in this volume.

Harvard University Portrait Collection, Gift of Robert Winthrop, representing the Winthrop family, to Harvard University, 1964, H605.

Francis Bayard[6] Winthrop
(1754–1817) by John Trumbull.
In Lawrence Shaw Mayo's view,
"a vigorous, practical man of
affairs—determined but not
hard."

Harvard University Portrait Collection,
Gift of Robert Winthrop, representing
the Winthrop family, to Harvard
University, 1964, H607.

Thomas Lindall[6] Winthrop
(1760–1841) by Thomas Sully.
As he reminded his brother Francis,
"You promised me some time
since some old sermons and pamphlets printed in New England.
The older the better. Every piece
of paper that can throw light upon
the first settlement of this country
ought to go into the hands of those
who leisure, ability and inclination
to make them useful."

Collection of the Massachusetts
Historical Society.

David[7] Sears (1787–1871) by Bass Otis. The construction of his house at 42 Beacon Street in Boston was a prelude to Sears's "plans for doing his share in acts of public and private beneficence."

Private Collection.

Miriam Clarke Mason (1789?–1870) by Bass Otis. Senator Mason's daughter became the subject of an unhappy rivalry between Thomas Lindall[7] Winthrop, Jr. and his first cousin David[7] Sears; Sears was the victor, and their married life lasted for 61 years.

Private Collection.

Robert Charles[7] Winthrop
(1809–1894) by George Peter
Alexander Healy. As a family
connection noted, "Really
with all due respect for
Mr. W. one cannot but smile
at his persistent choice of
wealthy wives."

Collection of the Massachusetts
Historical Society.

Margaret Tyndal[9] Winthrop (1880–1970). "[A] strict woman who did
not hesitate to use a bamboo cane on her . . . children," Margaret Winthrop
Forbes was the mother of Mrs. Frederic[10] Winthrop and grandmother of
John Forbes[11] Kerry, most recently U.S. Secretary of State.

Heirs of Angela Winthrop, Groton House.

Major General Frederick[8] Winthrop (1839–1865), the last
Union general to die in battle.

Heirs of Angela Winthrop, Groton House.

Helen and Elizabeth Gardner, 1866. A year later, Libby Gardner married Charles Walter[9] Amory; their daughter Dorothy would marry her cousin Frederic[9] Winthrop in 1903.

Collection of Dorothy Bradford Wexler.

Frederic[10] **Winthrop** (1906– 1979) with his grandmother **Elizabeth Gardner Amory** (1843–1930).

Collection of Dorothy Bradford Wexler.

Robert[8] **Winthrop** (1833–1892). Three years after his death, his widow noted, "It is very difficult to be strong, when all the *meaning* is gone out of your life."

By permission of Grant F. Winthrop.

Kate Wilson Taylor (1839–1925). A *grande dame* and an intimate of
Edith Wharton, it amused Mrs. Robert Winthrop to affect ineffectuality:
"At the age of 35, she said she was too old to do anything any more.
They had lovely little coke fires in those days, and she'd sit by the fire-
place, next to the coke fire, lace cap on her head—and invest."

Collection of Dorothy Bradford Wexler.

38 East Thirty-seventh Street.
The Robert Winthrops' home
following a move from Fifth
Avenue; it was here that Tina
Winthrop and Herman van
Roijen were married in 1904.

Collection of Dorothy Bradford Wexler.

Robert Dudley[9] Winthrop
(1861–1912) by Daniel
Huntington. Dudley
Winthrop began buying
up the land that became
Groton Plantation in 1906.
Fourteen years later, his
niece Dorothy noted, "we
reached the place which is
too lovely in spite of the
awful roads. I think I like
bum roads. It makes the
place more wild."

By permission of Grant F. Winthrop.

Grenville Lindall[9] Winthrop
(1864–1943). "Quietly, unobtrusively,
[Grenville] had amassed some four
thousand works ranging from Near
Eastern and Asian jade and ritual
bronzes to English and American
painting and watercolors to the
decorative arts. . . . In its entirety
[the gift of his collection] represents
the most important such bequest ever
to an American university."

Collection of Dorothy Bradford Wexler.

Katharine Taylor[9] Winthrop
(1866–1943) with her son
John[10] **Kean** (1888–1949).

Collection of Dorothy Bradford Wexler.

Hamilton Fish Kean
(1862–1941), who married
Kitty Winthrop in 1888.

Collection of Dorothy Bradford Wexler.

Frederic[9] **Winthrop** (1868–1932) by Hermann Hanatschek.
"He did not like New York," Henry Adams wrote, because
his speech impediment "made it difficult for him to converse
freely with other people, and he felt he could never be
successful as a banker."

Heirs of Angela Winthrop, Groton House.

"Groton House Farm" in Hamilton, Massachusetts. Soon after their marriage,
Frederic and Dorothy Winthrop bought the shell of a house begun for
Robert and Nancy Shaw. More than a century later, Groton House remains in
the hands of the family of Frederic[10] Winthrop and Angela Elizabeth[10] Forbes.

Collection of Dorothy Bradford Wexler.

Dorothy[10] **Amory** (1878–1907). Her mother would write: "The early morning of Saturday, July 27th, 1907, Ned and I and George [Amory] watched the train out of sight, that bore her and the Winthrop family to N.Y. where our darling was placed in the family Tomb, in Greenwood Cemetery. *Just* 29 years old."

Collection of Dorothy Bradford Wexler.

Sarah Barroll Thayer (1885–1938) with her son **John**[10] **Winthrop** (1913–1915). "I am very poor at saying what I feel so please read between the lines and try to realize how much I care, both for her and for you. . . . Much love, Mamma," Sally Thayer Winthrop wrote on the death of her husband's former mother-in-law in 1930.

Collection of Dorothy Bradford Wexler.

Albertina Taylor[9] **Winthrop** (1871–1934) with her husband **Jan Herman van Roijen** (1871–1933) and their sons Robert and Herman. "During Dr. van Royen's seven years' residence in Washington [as Dutch Minister to the United States]," Cordell Hull would write, "we have all learned to respect and admire his high attributes and fine personality."

Collection of Dorothy Bradford Wexler.

Beekman[9] **Winthrop** (1874–1940) by Hermann Hanatschek. A classmate later recalled that, "deprived at the age of 40 of the profession he had originally chosen [as a member of the Roosevelt and Taft administrations], he adapted himself quickly to another of a very different type" by joining his father's banking firm, where he stayed for twenty-five years until his retirement in 1939.

Harvard University Portrait Collection, Gift of Robert Winthrop, 1986, H689.

THE SIXTH GENERATION

9. **FRANCIS BAYARD**[6] **WINTHROP** (*John Still*[5], *John*[4], *Waitstill*[3], *John*[2-1]) was born at New London, Connecticut[914] 11 March 1754[915] and died at New York, New York 16 May 1817.[916] He married, first, at Trinity Church, New York 22 April 1779,[917] **ELSIE MARSTON**, who was born at New York 11 December 1760, the daughter of Thomas and Cornelia (Lispenard) Marston.[918] She died at New London 27 April 1789, at age 29, and was buried there.[919] Francis married, second, at Trinity Church 15 May 1790,[920] **PHEBE TAYLOR**, who was born 2 April 1764[921] and

---

[914] Mayo, *The Winthrop Family in America*, 200.

[915] Adlard, *The Sutton-Dudleys of England and the Dudleys of Massachusetts in New England*, 126. As Mayo explained (200), Francis was named for his grandfather, Francis Borland, "a prominent Bostonian and a pillar of the Old South Church" and Colonel William Bayard, a merchant and Manhattan landowner who was a close friend of John Still Winthrop. It appears that Col. Bayard may have been staying with the Winthrops as a guest in New London about the time Francis was born. He wrote to John Still Winthrop in April 1754: "As I had not the pleasure of seeing Mrs. Winthrop before I cam away, I hope you have been so good as to make an excuse for disturbing her so much,—though hope ere this she is well recovered, and that my godson grows a fine boy" (Winthrop Manuscripts, 10: 144).

[916] *New-York Daily Advertiser*, 17 May 1817, 2. "Died, yesterday morning, in the 64th year of his age, Francis Bayard Winthrop, Esq. His funeral will take place from the house of his son, No. 34 Vesey-street, at 5 o'clock, on Sunday afternoon."

[917] "Records of Trinity Church Parish, New York City," *Record* 71 [1940]: 185, citing 42 of original. See also Robert H. Kelby, comp., "New York Marriage Licenses," *Record* 47 [1916]: 179, citing page 256 (insert) of original. "1779, April 22, Marston, Elsie, spinster, and Francis Bayard Winthrop (No place mentioned)."

[918] Lyman Horace Weeks, *Prominent Families of New York*, rev. ed. (New York: The Historical Company, 1898), 631.

[919] *Findagrave.com* (memorial 11368061). "Francis Bayard Winthrop Tomb – 1789. In Memory of Mrs. Elsie Winthrop, Wife of Francis Bayard Winthrop and Daughter of Mr. Thomas and Cornelia Marston of New York, who died the 27th of April 1789, in the 29th Year of her Age." See also *Connecticut Gazette*, 1 May 1789, 3: "Died. Mrs. Winthrop, consort of Mr. Francis B. Winthrop."

[920] "Records of Trinity Church Parish, New York City," *Record* 75 [1944]: 83.

[921] Charissa Taylor Bass, *Taylor-Snow Genealogy, In Memory of Oscar Taylor and Malvina Snow Taylor* (Freeport, Ill.: C.T. Bass, 1935), 35, apparently citing an 1877 record by Robert Charles[8] Winthrop.

died at New York 20 August 1841,[922] daughter of John and Mary
(Waddell) Taylor,[923] and sister of Charles Williams Taylor, who married
her stepdaughter Cornelia[7] Winthrop.[924]

As a young man Francis did not attend college but went straight
into business in New York. His godfather, Colonel William Bayard, was
a Loyalist who would lose most of his property, but Francis appeared
to have balanced his relationships with the British and Americans. In
the summer of 1777 he arrived at New London aboard the *Union* out
of New York, which was flying a flag of truce, and arranged visits with
his brother John at his home[925] and with his stepmother and sisters at
a house near the harbor.[926] Near the end of the war he donated £100
for rebel "prisoners lately taken from New London and Groton by the
enemy in their incursion there and carried to New York and confin'd
in the Sugar House there naked and in a suffering conditon."[927] Soon

---

[922]   *Commercial Advertiser* (New York), 21 August 1841, 2. "Died . . . on Friday morning,
        20th inst. Mrs. Phebe Winthrop, relict of the late Francis B. Winthrop, senior, aged
        76 years." "New York, New York City Municipal Deaths, 1795–1949," index of
        records at New York Municipal Archives, *familysearch.org/ ark:/61903/1:1:2WWG-
        JT9*, citing FHL 447,549, gives 22 August 1841, age 77. In Longworth's city direc-
        tory for 1840–41 she was said to be residing at 14 Warren Street (694).

[923]   John E. Stillwell, *Historical and Genealogical Miscellany: Early Settlers of New Jersey and
        Their Descendants,* 5 vols. (New York, 1932), 5: 58. "John Taylor was a member of the
        firm Taylor & Delancy, merchants, New York, about 1773." He m. (2) his late wife's
        sister, Ann (Waddell) Miller. See also John W. Jordan, ed., *Colonial and Revolutionary
        Families of Pennsylvania,* 3 vols. (New York: The Lewis Publishing Co., 1911), 2:
        804. Jordan noted a letter written by Captain Henry Waddell to his father, Lieut.
        Colonel William Waddell, dated 3 October 1803 referring to John's death from a
        fever then raging in New York City: "Uncle John Taylor died on the day of my
        arrival, unattended by any except Mrs. T. [Ann]: such is the fatality of this disorder
        that even his children did not come near him."

[924]   Stillwell, *Historical and Genealogical Miscellany,* 5: 58.

[925]   Hoadly, *The Public Records of the State of Connecticut,* 1: 333. 27 June 1777: "Voted
        and ordered, That Mr. Francis Bayard Winthrop, now on board the sloop Union in
        New London harbour, a flag from New York, be permitted to proceed from said
        sloop by water to the dwelling-house of Mr. John Winthrop and continue in said
        house and on Winthrop's Neck, so called, until said flag should return, and return
        by water from said Neck on board said flag."

[926]   Hoadly, *The Public Records of the State of Connecticut,* 1: 335. 30 June 1777: "A permit
        given to Francis Bayard Winthrop, now on board the sloop Union, a flag near the light-
        house in New London, to go on shore in the day time to the house of Thos. Harris
        near said light-house, to see his mother, brethren and sisters, under the direction of the
        commanding officer of the first, the civil authority and selectmen in New London."

[927]   Mayo, *The Winthrop Family in America,* 200–1, who noted that Francis's generosity
        was remembered when some goods he sent home were seized by a privateer, and
        the Connecticut Governor and Council of Safety ordered that the "pair of silver
        cans, silk for gowns for his five sisters, and a few other small articles" be delivered as
        addressed, citing Hoadly, *The Public Records of the State of Connecticut,* 3: 549.

after December 1781 he appears to have visited England. (His aunt Anne Winthrop at New London expressed hope in a letter he would see friends "on the other side of the water.")[928]

When his older brother John died unexpectedly in the fall of 1780, Francis found himself in charge of the family affairs and responsible for settling some ongoing disputes, such as the ownership division of a lead mine in Sturbridge, Massachusetts (he considered selling it in 1785 but could not sort out the many Winthrop heirs who claimed to have interest)[929] and a disagreement with the Saltonstalls over the estate of John Winthrop (which was settled in 1788, in the Saltonstalls' favor).[930] After 1790, he was "primarily a man of property in New York," wrote Mayo, with an office in Wall Street and membership in the British-loving Society of Saint George.[931] Although he sold the family homestead in New London, he never lost his affection for the town, Mayo noted. On 10 September 1803, he wrote to his younger brother Thomas:[932]

---

[928] Mayo, *The Winthrop Family in America*, 201, citing Winthrop Papers, 1B: 71. Mayo states that Anne's letter was entrusted to Francis's brother William, who had received permission to go into British-occupied New York to discuss family business with Francis (per Hoadly, *The Public Records of the State of Connecticut*, 3: 551). Mayo noted, "In some ways the American Revolution was a curiously friendly war."

[929] Silas Deane to Barnabas Deane, 9 May 1785, *Collections of the New-York Historical Society* 23 [1890]: 452–53. "I have this day wrote to Gurdon Saltonstall, Esq., on a subject for the particulars of which refer you to him, as he best knows them in detail. The substance, however, is this: There is an estate in Brimfield of about 3,000 acres, belonging to the Winthrop family, on which there is a black lead mine. Certain gentlemen here have proposed to join with me in the purchase of it, if to be had at the value of the lands without any consideration for the mine." Also, Barnabas Deane to Silas Deane, 14 October 1785, *Collections of the Connecticut Historial Society* 23 [1930]: 214–15. "I got Mʳ Sebor to Apply to the Mʳ Winthrops on the Affair of the Black Lead Mine, he writes me as follows. 'I Applied to Mʳ Francis Winthrop who wishes to have it Sold, but the Proprietors are So Numerous that nothing Can be done About it at Present. Mʳ Winthrop wishes to have Nothing Said about it, & will do his Endeavors to purchase them all out, at Some Rate or Other, which he Should be Able to Accomplish he will then Sell or Lease on good Terms. His Grandfather Lost About £10,000 by working this mine.'"

[930] Mayo, *The Winthrop Family in America*, 201.

[931] Mayo, *The Winthrop Family in America*, 201. He was listed in the 1796 edition of John Low's *The New-York Directory* (211) at 29 Wall Street. In 1792, he was a signatory to the Tontine Coffee House agreement, ultimate forebear of the New York Stock Exchange (Dorothy B. Wexler, *Reared in a Greenhouse: The Stories—and Story—of Dorothy Winthrop Bradford* [New York and London: Garland Publishing, 1998], 39, citing Joseph Alfred Scoville [Walter Barrett], *The Old Merchants of New York*, vol. 3 [New York: Greenwood Press], 1968).

[932] Francis Bayard Winthrop (New York) to Thomas L. Winthrop (Boston), 10 September 1803, Winthrop Manuscripts (reel 39), Massachusetts Historical Society. See also *American Journal of Science and Arts* 47 [1844]: 288, which notes that John⁴

Upon recollection there is a very remarkable Mineral
Spring under the Stables I built for the mansion house at
New London, now the property of John Coles. I remember
its being in great repute and much resorted to, when I
was a Boy. I think you must remember this spring. It is
about 3 Miles from the sea, which answers to the distance
in the Memor of Articles presented to the Royal Society.
I recollect at Doctor Smybet of Boston, who visited our
father, say about 33 or 34 years ago in Company with
Doct. Moffatt, say, this spring was the finest he ever exam^d.

Francis kept Fisher's Island in the family and in April 1793 leased it
to Thomas Allen, Jr., for $2,600 annually.[933] The Winthrop family might
have escaped there when yellow fever swept through New York in the
summer of 1798; instead they secluded themselves at Turtle Bay Farm
on the east side of Manhattan until, Mayo wrote, "a severe frost had
checked the epidemic."[934]

Mayo noted that a miniature of Francis Winthrop by William Dunlap
shows the face of "a vigorous, practical man of affairs,—determined but
not hard."[935] To his brothers, he may have seemed hard in 1816, when
he tried to call in $14,773.40 of principal and interest due from Joseph
and $13,281.55 owed him by Thomas; but he was nearing the end of
his life and wanted to put his house in order. Neither of the brothers
had paid the interest charges for a number of years."[936] As Francis wrote
Thomas:[937]

Winthrop had presented the Royal Society with sand "flung up by the waters of a
spring near Nanmeaug, three miles from the beach."

[933] Frances Mary Stoddard, *An Account of a Part of the Sufferings and Losses of Jolley Allen*
(Boston: Franklin Press, 1883), 46. Thomas Allen lived with his wife and seven children to the island, which was 9 miles in length and contained 5,000 acres, for the next
nineteen years. He had other families as tenants and employed five or six girls to spin
and weave as well as two dairy women (one at each end of the island) who made two
sixty-pound cheeses each day. Allen kept a hundred cows and two thousand sheep
and raised horses and mules. He also hired a man to act as teacher of the younger
children (the older children went to boarding school) and as chaplain for his own and
his tenants' families. He owned a sloop, *Betsey*, to travel New London and Stonington.

[934] Mayo, *The Winthrop Family in America*, 202, citing Winthrop Manuscripts, 30A: 13.
According to Charles H. Haswell, *Reminiscences of an Octagenarian of the City of New
York (1816 to 1860)* (New York: Harper & Brothers, 1896), 14, Turtle Bay was near
what is now East Forty-Sixth Street.

[935] Mayo, *The Winthrop Family in America*, 202, citing "Diary of William Dunlap (1766–
1839)" in *Collections of the New-York Historical Society* 62 [1930]: 294 (facing).

[936] Mayo, *The Winthrop Family in America*, 202–3.

[937] Mayo, *The Winthrop Family in America*, 203, citing Winthrop Manuscripts, 30A: 69.

If I am to be called upon to lend money and receive nothing for it, how am I to pay my own debts and to support my family? I have denied myself many indulgences because so much of my property has been locked up. My mode of living and the furniture of my house are not such as I should indulge myself with, if I received what I ought to do, to make it otherwise. And in addition to my family expenses I may add a great part of Sister Parkin's, for the small income she had does not support them, and without my aid they could not live.

Children of Francis Bayard[6] and Elsie (Marston) Winthrop:

    i.   Cornelia[7] Winthrop, b. at New York 1 Jan. 1780,[938] d. at Boston, Mass. 16 Nov. 1850,[939] and bur. at Mount Auburn Cemtery in Cambridge, Mass.[940] She m. at Trinity Church, New York 4 March 1801,[941] Charles Williams Taylor, who was b. 21 March 1779,[942] son of John and Mary (Waddell) Taylor,[943] and had issue.[944] He d. at Philadelphia, Pa. 17 Feb. 1842 and was buried at Mount Auburn.[945] Their son, John Winthrop[8] Taylor (1817–1886), was briefly surgeon general of the U.S. Navy.[946]

    ii. Anne Winthrop, b. at New York 26 May and d. 16 Aug. 1783.[947]

---

938 *Vital Records of Cambridge, Massachusetts to the Year 1850*, 2 vols. (Boston: New England Historic Genealogical Society, 1914), 1: 692, citing Mount Auburn Cemetery records.

939 *Evening Post* (New York), 22 November 1850, 3. "In Boston, on the 16th inst., Cornelia Winthrop, relict of the late Charles W. Taylor, and daughter of the late Francis B. Wintrop [*sic*], of this city."

940 *Findagrave.com* (memorial 157180972), which gives location as Buckthorn Path, Lot 3078. *Vital Records of Cambridge, Massachusetts*, 1: 692, includes her birthdate, citing cemetery records, but not her date of death.

941 "Records of Trinity Church Parish, New York City," *Record* 78 [1947]: 113.

942 *Vital Records of Cambridge, Massachusetts*, 1: 692, citing Mount Auburn Cemetery records.

943 Jordan, *Colonial and Revolutionary Families of Pennsylvania*, 2: 804.

944 Adlard, *The Sutton-Dudleys of England and the Dudleys of Massachusetts in New England*, 126.

945 *Vital Records of Cambridge, Massachusetts*, 2: 759, citing Mount Auburn Cemetery records for Charles W. Taylor. See also *Findagrave.com* (memorial 157180816), which gives location as Buckthorn Path, Lot 3078, and includes note: "Re-interred 16 Aug. 1861." It also says he d. at Philadelphia. The *Philadelphia Inquirer*, 18 February 1842, 2, gives, "Died . . . on the 17th inst., Charles W. Taylor, in the 63d year of his age."

946 Howard A. Kelly, *A Cyclopedia of American Medical Biography*, 2 vols. (Philadelphia: W.B. Saunders, 1912), 2: 434.

947 Adlard, *The Sutton-Dudleys of England and the Dudleys of Massachusetts in New England*, 126.

iii.   JOHN STILL WINTHROP, b. 14 Feb. 1785,[948] by one account at Lyme,
Conn.,[949] and d. the home of his son Charles Edward Rogers[8]
Winthrop in Tamaroa, Perry Co., Ill. 6 Sept. 1855.[950] He graduated
from Yale College in 1804, at age 19, and a received Master of Arts
degree three years later.[951] He m. at St. John's Church, Stamford,
Conn. 14 Aug. 1808,[952] HARRIET ROGERS, who was b. about 1787
and d. at Stamford 2 March 1835, age 48,[953] dau. of Fitch and
Hannah (Bell) Rogers, and had issue.[954] She was a first cousin to his
brother Francis's wife. (The two couples were married on the same
day and at the same church.)[955] Harriet was buried at St. Andrew's
and St. John's Cemetery in Stamford.[956]

In 1810, John Still Winthrop was living or working at 150
Greenwich Street in New York; by 1817 he had a residence at
109 Liberty Street and an office (J.S. Winthrop and F. Rogers) at
233 Pearl Street. Before 1820 he had retired to Stamford; Mayo

---

[948]   Adlard, *The Sutton-Dudleys of England and the Dudleys of Massachusetts in New England*, 126.

[949]   James Swift Rogers, *James Rogers of New London, Ct., and His Descendants* (Boston: the author, 1902), 239. Mayo, *The Winthrop Family in America,* 263, seemed skeptical, writing "How it happened that the child was born at Lyme instead of at the homestead in New London is a mystery."

[950]   Adlard, *The Sutton-Dudleys of England and the Dudleys of Massachusetts in New England*, 126. Mayo, *The Winthrop Family in America,* 264, gives location. Charles E.R. Winthrop (b. 1816) had emigrated to Perry Co. in the winter of 1839. "When a young man he was employed in a drug store, but not liking that work he engaged with an engineering corps in the state of Michigan, and also upon the route of the Erie Railroad" (*Portrait and Biographical Record of Randolph, Jackson, Perry and Monroe Counties, Illinois* [Chicago: Biographical Publishing Co., 1894], 575).

[951]   Mayo, *The Winthrop Family in America*, 262.

[952]   Adlard, *The Sutton-Dudleys of England and the Dudleys of Massachusetts in New England*, 126.

[953]   Adlard, *The Sutton-Dudleys of England and the Dudleys of Massachusetts in New England*, 126.

[954]   Mayo, *The Winthrop Family in America*, 264.

[955]   Dexter, *Biographical Sketches of the Graduates of Yale College,* 5: 731. See also Rogers, *James Rogers and His Descendants*, 158. Fitch Rogers was a Loyalist who traveled to New Brunswick during the war but returned to Connecticut and became a merchant in New York City. His will, dated 20 November 1826, named his son-in-law John S. Winthrop (Spencer P. Mead, "Abstract of Probate Records for the District of Stamford, County of Fairfield, and State of Connecticut, 1729–1848," 2 vols. [typescript, 1924], 2:214, citing Vol. 14 of original). Twelve years after this wedding, John Smyth Rogers, a first cousin of the brides, wed Augusta Temple[7] Winthrop, a first cousin of the grooms (Mayo, *The Winthrop Family in America,* 266).

[956]   Barbara Kaye, comp., Transcripts of stones at St. Andrew's & St. John's Cemetery, at *ctgenweb.org/ county/cofairfield/pages/cemetery/cm_stmfrd/stjohn-standrew.htm.* "Harriet Winthrop, wife of John Still Winthrop, died Mar. 2, 1835."

points out that his first five children were born in New York and his last five in Stamford. After his wife's death in 1835 he returned to the city; in 1841 he was a "resident" member of the New-York Historical Society and he appears in an 1845–46 directory residing on East Seventeenth Street near Fifth Avenue.[957] He left for Illinois sometime after 1850, when he was living in Elizabeth, N.J. with his children Catharine, 25; Emily, 24; Francis Bayard (a broker), 22; and Susan Remsen, 19, in the household of Susan T.E. Williamson (no occupation listed, but the owner of $12,000 in real estate).[958]

iv. FRANCIS BAYARD WINTHROP, JR., possibly b. at Boston[959] 20 March,[960] and bp. at Trinity Church, Boston 6 Sept. 1787.[961] He d. at New Haven, Conn. 21 March 1841[962] and was bur. at Grove Street Cemetery in New Haven.[963] He m. (1) at St. John's Church, Stamford[964] 14 Aug. 1808,[965] JULIA ANN ROGERS, who was b. in

957 Mayo, *The Winthrop Family in America*, 264, citing various city directories.

958 1850 U.S. Census, Elizabeth, Essex Co., N.J., roll M432_449, page 38A. In the 1855 New York state census, the four children were living in a boarding house in Brooklyn, with Francis working as a clerk and his three sisters indicating they had no occupation.

959 Benjamin W. Dwight, *The History of the Descendants of John Dwight of Dedham, Mass.*, 2 vols. (New York: John F. Trow & Son, 1874), 1: 253. There is no record of his birth in *A Report of the Record Commissioners of the City of Boston Containing Boston Births from A.D. 1700 to A.D. 1800*. Mayo, *The Winthrop Family in America*, 265, noted that Francis Bayard[6] Winthrop had returned from England shortly before his son's birth, "and during this period was occupied with the management of the Winthrops' sprawling territorial holdings. This work may account for Mrs. Winthrop's being in Boston at the time. As she was a dyed-in-the-wool New Yorker, there were no family reasons for her being in Boston or its vicinity." In 1790, Francis Bayard[6] Winthrop was living with his family in the North Ward of New York City (roll 6, 38); in 1800, in Ward 2 with a household of eleven people (roll 23, 677); and in 1810, in Ward 9 with a household of sixteen (roll 32, 779). However, the *New-England Palladium* (Boston), 20 May 1817, 2, in noting the death of Francis Bayard[6] in New York in 1817 called him "formerly of Boston."

960 Adlard, *The Sutton-Dudleys of England and the Dudleys of Massachusetts in New England*, 127.

961 Oliver and Peabody, *Publications of the Colonial Society of Massachusetts*, 56: 88. "Francis Bayard Son of Francis B. Winthrop by _____ his wife. Sponsors Mr. T.L. Winthrop, Mr. F.B. Winthrop & Wife."

962 *Vital Records of New Haven, 1649–1850*, 2 vols. (Hartford: The Connecticut Society, 1924), 2: 763. The record indicated he died at age 54 of erysipelas phlegmonoides (a skin infection). See also *Commercial Advertiser*, 24 March 1841, 2. "Died . . . at New Haven, on the 21st inst., Francis Bayard Winthrop, Esq. in the 55th year of this age."

963 Burial records comp. by Friends of the Grove Street Cemetery (*grovestreetcemetery. org*). Francis B. Winthrop, d. 21 March 1841, bur. 14 Cedar Ave.

964 Mayo, *The Winthrop Family in America*, 266.

965 Adlard, *The Sutton-Dudleys of England and the Dudleys of Massachusetts in New England*, 127.

1788, dau. of Moses and Sarah (Woolsey) Rogers.[966] She d. at New York 14 April 1814.[967] He m. (2) 29 Jan. 1816,[968] his late wife's first cousin, ELIZABETH WOOLSEY, who was b. 6 Oct. 1794, dau. of William Walton and Elizabeth (Dwight) Woolsey.[969] She d. at West New Brighton, Staten Island, N.Y. 28 Oct. 1863 and was bur. at Grove Street Cemetery.[970] Francis had issue by both wives.[971]

In 1800, when about 13 years old, Francis Bayard Winthrop enrolled at Yale with his older brother, John. He graduated in 1804 and three years later received his Master of Arts degree.[972] By 1815 he had an office at 229 Pearl Street and a house at 28 Vesey Street in New York.[973] Francis and Elizabeth Winthrop moved to New Haven in 1823, where Francis was a vestryman of Trinity Church[974] and a director at a bank owned by his father-in-law, W. W. Woolsey, but was said to have lost "a large sum" when it failed.[975]

---

966 Benjamin W. Dwight, "The Descendants of Rev. Benjamin Woolsey, of Dosoris (Glen Cove), L.I.," *Record* 4 [1873]: 151. The likenesses of Moses and Sarah (Woolsey) Rogers appear opposite 170 in Charles M. Selleck, *Norwalk* (Norwalk, Conn.: the author, 1896). Her earliest Connecticut ancestor, James Rogers, had "indulged in a long disagreement with his more aristocratic neighbor, Wait Still Winthrop. When this was settled by arbitration, about 1670, the two men signed an agreement 'as a final issue in all disputes, suits at law and controversies, from the beginning of the world to the date thereof.'... The relations between the two families appear to have been increasingly cordial" (Mayo, *The Winthrop Family in America*, 265–66).

967 Dwight, "The Descendants of Rev. Benjamin Woolsey," *Record* 4 [1873]: 151. See also *Connecticut Gazette*, 20 April 1814, 3, "At New-York, Mrs. Winthrop, the wife of Francis B. Winthrop, Esq., aged 25 years—youngest daughter of Moses Rogers, Esq." Adlard, *The Sutton-Dudleys of England and the Dudleys of Massachusetts in New England*, 127, errs with 21 April.

968 Adlard, *The Sutton-Dudleys of England and the Dudleys of Massachusetts in New England*, 127.

969 Dwight, "The Descendants of Rev. Benjamin Woolsey," *Record* 4 [1873]: 151. Sarah Woolsey (b. 1750) and William Walton Woolsey (b. 1766) were half-siblings (4: 149). Mayo, *The Winthrop Family in America*, 266, gives William Walter.

970 *New York Tribune*, 29 October 1863, 5. "Winthrop—At Castleton, Staten Island, on Wednesday, Oct. 28, Elizabeth Winthrop, widow of the late Francis B. Winthrop. Her remains will be taken to New Haven for interment." Burial records comp. by Friends of the Grove Street Cemetery (*grovestreetcemetery.org*). Elizabeth W. Winthrop, d. 28 October 1863, bur. 14 Cedar Ave.

971 Dwight, "The Descendants of Rev. Benjamin Woolsey," *Record* 4 [1873]: 151, 154.

972 Mayo, *The Winthrop Family in America*, 265.

973 David Longworth, *American Almanac, New-York Register and City Directory* (New York, 1815), 446.

974 Dexter, *Biographical Sketches of the Graduates of Yale College*, 5: 731.

975 Walter Barrett, *The Old Merchants of New York City*, 2nd series (New York: Carleton, Publisher, 1863), 383-84. The Eagle Bank was managed by William Walton Woolsey and his sons-in-law Francis Winthrop and George Hoadley. When Woolsey moved

Mayo noted that although Francis was not the eldest son, "a good many of the family papers seem to have been either in his possession or at his disposal, perhaps because he was known to be interested in colonial history." As early as 1821 he was a member of the New-York Historical Society,[976] and when James Savage was preparing his 1825 edition of Governor John Winthrop's journal, Francis allowed a first cousin who was working with Savage, James Bowdoin (originally James Bowdoin[7] Winthrop[977]), to copy from the family records for the appendix. Mayo wrote that he presumably also allowed Bowdoin to reprint about 130 Winthrop papers published in the Collections of the Massachusetts Historical Society.[978] In gratitude, the society in 1835 elected him a corresponding member.[979]

Francis's daughter, Laura, would recall her father as "a man of refined taste" who "owned what was called, 50 years ago, a fine library, of about 2,000 volumes selected by himself, besides a small collection of good pictures and engravings, in a time when such things were rare." Further:[980]

> He was an enthusiast in Art and Literature, and loved
> Music and the Theater. His children could see upon
> the walls Alston's *Angel* and Both's *Sunshine* [*sic*], and
> browsed freely in the library, till books became their
> familiar friends. Their father was one of the first persons
> to recognize the genius of Hawthorne, on reading his

---

back to New York, by this account, he appointed Hoadley as president, and he "broke the bank, I believe, by issuing post notes and used the funds in speculation," Barrett wrote. "Mr. Winthrop lost a large sum by that bank."

[976] *Collections of the New-York Historical Society* 3 [1821]: 13.

[977] A son of Thomas Lindall[6] Winthrop, he legally dropped his surname in 1813 to meet a condition in the will of a great-uncle who had bequeathed him a life interest in a large tract of land in Maine (Mayo, *The Winthrop Family in America*, 291).

[978] Mayo, *The Winthrop Family in America*, 266. See *Collections of the Massachusetts Historical Society*, 3rd series, vols. 9 and 10 (1846 and 1849). Mayo noted (266–67) that about forty-five years later, in 1880, his daughter Laura[8] (Winthrop) Johnson gave the society the originals of sixty-eight letters dated from 1620 to 1648 that her father had shared with Savage and Bowdoin "in the name of her sister, Elizabeth Winthrop, and her brother, Col. William Winthrop" (*Proceedings of the Massachusetts Historical Society* 18 [1880–81], 66–67).

[979] *Proceedings of the Massachusetts Historical Society* 2 [1880]: 19.

[980] Laura Winthrop Johnson, *The Life and Poems of Theodore Winthrop, Edited by His Sister* (New York: Henry Holt and Co., 1884), 6–8. Her brother had been killed in battle at Great Bethel, Va., in June 1861. She also wrote verse (*Poems of Twenty Years*, 1874) and prose (*Eight Hundred Miles in an Ambulance*, 1889).

Twice Told Tales in the winter of 1839–40. These pictures
and engravings from the old masters familiarized the
children with forms of beauty, and an old-fashioned
garden, with flowers and lilac bushes and pear-trees, gave
them a pleasant playground.

But their happiest recollections linger round their
woodland walks with their father. He was a man of delicate
health—(delicate and fond of reading when a boy, when
his brothers and sisters were romping and shooting arrows
at the eyes of the old Governor's portraits), a lawyer [*sic*]
who had retired from business in New York with reduced
fortune, to live quietly at New Haven, and educate his
children. Here he bought a roomy house on Wooster St.,
of the old-fashioned New England type, with four rooms
on a floor, and a hall through the middle, and a garret (not
an attic), with great oak beams overhead, cobwebs, dark
corners, and a mysterious cock-loft.

He was hospitable, and charming in his own family,
to whom he was a true father (one of the rarest things
in the world), and not a man whom they saw, sleepy and
harassed, once or twice a week. He had a wonderful
croon that always put the babies to sleep, he danced
quadrilles, sang songs, played games, told wonderful tales
in the twilight, and took them for long walks in the
woods. There were woods in those days not too far off.
His health required these walks, and the children were
usually his companions. . . .

A rarer pleasure was the long drive, taking their
mother with them, through the laurel lanes to some
lovely lake among the hills, where they dined "on dainty
chicken, snow-white bread," and spent a whole summer's
day of delight. . . . New Haven in those days was a quiet,
lovely little town, scholarly and demure, under the lofty
arch of whose elms strayed the college boy, studious
or otherwise, the professor, stern of exterior, and the
dreaming school girl. No sound of factories disturbed the
silence, the railroad was not dreamed of, the steamboat
had but lately begun to churn up the waters of the little
bay. The town seemed asleep, save when the buzzing boys
poured out chapel or recitation.

In his history of the Winthrop family, Lawrence Shaw Mayo shared another aspect of Francis that, admittedly, "does not redound entirely to [his] credit . . . as a patron of the art," but nevertheless is amusing. Francis had written the painter Washington Allston in 1816 to complain he had paid $500 for an Allston landscape, sight unseen, on the recommendation of another, and been disappointed with it. He had tried to sell the work but eventually could only recover $200. He asked that Allston send him a "small picture of your production" to make it up to him. Allston replied a year later from London saying that he would have gladly purchased the painting back had Francis not waited seven years to raise the issue. He also waxed on about the difficulty of placing a monetary value on art. Nevertheless, claiming he took no offense at the request, he promised to send a small work. Four years later, Francis noted he was still waiting; Allston assured him he had started the painting, which he was calling "Belshazzar's Feast," but had been forced to set it aside to complete other (paying) projects. Although Allston lived another twenty years, he never managed to finish the piece[981] (if it had ever existed), which was likely the plan all along.

Children of Francis Bayard[6] and Phebe (Taylor) Winthrop:

  v. WILLIAM HENRY[7] WINTHROP, b. at New York[982] 25 Sept. 1791[983] and d. at New London 3 Sept. 1860.[984] He m. at New London 7 June 1818,[985] his first cousin MARGARET ANN[7] PARKIN, who was b. posthumously at New London 30 Dec. 1798, dau. of Richard

---

[981] Mayo, *The Winthrop Family in America*, 267–271. The originals are preserved in the Dana Family Papers at the Massachusetts Historical Society.

[982] Mayo, *The Winthrop Family in America*, 274. "The William in his name reflects his father's affection for a bachelor brother, William, who made his home with the Francis Bayard Winthrops on Manhattan Island. As Henry is an unusual name in the family, presumably it came from the distaff side."

[983] Adlard, *The Sutton-Dudleys of England and the Dudleys of Massachusetts in New England*, 127. Dexter, *Biographical Sketches of the Graduates of Yale College*, 6: 286, gives October 1792.

[984] Charles Hale, ed., *Connecticut Newspaper Notices,* 68 vols. (Hartford: Connecticut State Library, 1941), 55: 151, citing *Norwich Aurora*, 8 September 1860. William H. Winthrop d. at New London 3 September 1860, age 69.

[985] Barbour, "New London Births–Marriages–Deaths, 1646–1854," 325, citing 3: 248 of original town records. "William Henry Winthrop of New York m. Margarett Ann Parkin, of New London, June 7, 1818, by Rev. Solomon Blakesley, of East Haddam." See also *New York Post*, 9 June 1818.

William and Mary[6] (Winthrop) Parkin,[986] and had issue.[987] Margaret
Ann d. at New London 27 Feb. 1863.[988]

William Henry Winthrop entered Yale when he was about 14
years old, after preparing with a tutor, and graduated in 1809.[989]
Around 1816 his father felt "compelled" to set him up "in a small
way of business" by selling at auction two houses that, he lamented,
had brought in $1,000 in rent annually.[990] Apparently William did
not succeed, for when his father died in 1817 he moved to New
London. He and Margaret Ann lived there on the northeast corner
of Huntington and Federal Streets in a home built in 1787 and
first occupied by her mother. However, they also spent much time
on Fisher's Island,[991] which William owned outright after buying
out the interests of his three brothers. He kept a manager on the
island and a small stock; in 1838, he had a hundred cows, five yoke
of oxen, a driving horse, twenty-five horses and colts, and twelve
hundred sheep.[992] In 1826, he also had inherited from his uncle

---

[986]   Adlard, *The Sutton-Dudleys of England and the Dudleys of Massachusetts in New England*,
        127, 129. See also Dexter, *Biographical Sketches of the Graduates of Yale College*, 6: 274.
        Margaret Ann was born nearly four months after her father died on 10 September
        1798.

[987]   Barbour, "New London Births–Marriages–Deaths, 1646–1854," 325, citing 3: 248
        of original town records. Their children included Francis Bayard[8] Winthrop, from
        whom Robert C. Winthrop noted in the prefatory note of his 1864 compilation,
        Life and Letters of John Winthrop, "many of the most interesting materials of the vol-
        ume were procured [purchased]; and who has since fallen a victim to disease con-
        tracted while he was serving as a volunteer in the army of the American Union."
        See also *Winthrop Papers*, 1: iv.

[988]   Hale, *Connecticut Newspaper Notices*, 57: 486, citing *Norwich Courier*, 5 March 1863.

[989]   Dexter, *Biographical Sketches of the Graduates of Yale College*, 6: 286.

[990]   Francis Bayard Winthrop (New York) to Thomas L. Winthrop (Boston), 4 May
        1816, Winthrop Family Papers (reel 21, box 37), Massachusetts Historical Society.

[991]   James Lawrence Chew, "The Houses of Old New London," *Records and Papers of
        the New London County Historical Society* 1: 4 [1893]: 91. "The house known as the
        Winthrop place, on the northeast corner of Huntington and Federal streets, last oc-
        cupied by Dr. Fuller, was built in 1787, and was, I think, first occupied by Mrs. Mary
        Parkin, the widow of Richard W. Parkin. It was the residence of William H. Winthrop,
        the son-in-law of Mr. Parkin, from the time of his marriage till his death, September
        3d, 1860; but it should be said that a portion of this time was spent on Fishers Island."

[992]   Henry L. Ferguson, *Fishers Island, N.Y. 1614–1925* (New York, privately printed,
        1925), 66. Mayo, *The Winthrop Family in America*, 275, commented: "Fisher's Island
        was—and, to a lesser degree, still is—a sort of Garden of Eden, a miniature, un-
        spoiled Bermuda. Cooled in summer by breezes from any direction whatever, kept
        at a moderate temperature in winter by the surrounding waters, it had a climate that
        was almost ideal. Its situation, too, left little to be desired: 10 miles southeast of New
        London but only two or three miles from the mainland, it was sufficiently remote
        to give one the feeling of living in another world, yet actually near enough to make

William[6] Winthrop a large part of the township of Huron, Ohio, bordering Lake Erie near Sandusky. He reduced the price and sold off the land.[993] At first glance of a photo of William Henry Winthrop, "one is inclined to exclaim, 'What a homely man!'" wrote Lawrence Mayo, who rarely missed a chance in his book to analyze a Winthrop visage. "He was indeed homely; there is not even a hint of good looks one is apt to expect in a Winthrop countenance. But it is an interesting face; the homeliness never wears off, but somehow familiarity changes the appearance of sourness into a look of determination, and the hard eye into a shrewd one."[994] The preface to the first volume of the six volumes of collected Winthrop Papers includes the assertion that William Henry Winthrop, "a recluse and valetudinarian," inherited a large part of the family papers from his father but "became annoyed by repeated requests for permission to examine the manuscripts, and at last refused access to them even to members of his own family."[995]

vi. CHARLOTTE ANN WINTHROP, b. 8 Jan. 1794,[996] d. at New York 16 April 1851,[997] and bur. at Prospect Cemetery in Jamaica, L.I.,

---

intercourse relatively easy." Ferguson noted that every Wednesday, William Winthrop sent his sloop, the *Arbella*, to New London or to Noank for mail and supplies; when a doctor was needed, a white flag was raised on a hill north of the Mansion House as a signal (66). When a shipwreck off the island on 28 November 1846 cost forty-two lives (per Caulkins, *History of New London*, 651), William agreed to sell the North Dumping to the U.S. government for a lighthouse (Ferguson, 89). The five Winthrop children sold the remainder to Robert Fox of New York after their widowed mother died in 1863, ending the family's ownership after 218 years (67).

[993] *The Fire Lands Pioneer* (Norwalk, Ohio) 4 [1863]: 66. William[6] Winthrop "never resided in the township, though making frequent visits to it. The first of these journeys he made on horseback; but this mode of travel was changed when steamboats began running on the lake. It is said that the high price at which he held the land operated against its early opening and improvement."

[994] Mayo, *The Winthrop Family in America*, 276. A photo is reproduced in Ferguson, *Fishers Island*, facing 66.

[995] *The Winthrop Papers*, 1: iv. Mayo, *The Winthrop Family in America*, 275–76, noted that he had been "unable either to confirm or to refute this somewhat uncomplimentary assertion. The important thing is that after his death the manuscripts were acquired by his cousin Robert C. Winthrop [from William's son, Francis Bayard[8] Winthrop], and in the course of time were given to the Massachusetts Historical Society."

[996] Adlard, *The Sutton-Dudleys of England and the Dudleys of Massachusetts in New England*, 127.

[997] *Spectator* (New York), 21 April 1851, 4. "Died . . . On Wednesday, 16th inst., Charlotte Ann, relict of John M. Aspinwall, and daughter of the late Francis B. Winthrop." See also "Manhattan Death Records, 1795–1865," index of records at New York Municipal Archives, *familysearch.org/ark:/61903/1:1:FD1D-NPV*, citing FHL 447,554, which gives d. 17 April 1851, age 56, Cemetery: "Remo. From City."

N.Y.[998] She m. at Trinity Church, New York in Nov. 1816,[999] JOHN MYER ASPINWALL, who was born at New York 31 March 1792, son of Gilbert and Ann (Sowers) Aspinwall, and had issue.[1000] He died at Brooklyn, N.Y. 19 July 1844 after ingesting laudanum (an alcoholic tincture of opium) "during a fit of insanity,"[1001] and was bur. at Prospect Cemetery.[1002] John went into business with his father as a young man in the firm G. Aspinwall & Son at 98 Pearl Street in New York. The couple resided at 20 Whitehall Street.[1003]

12   vii.   THOMAS CHARLES WINTHROP, b. at New York 9 June 1797; m. 23 Sept. 1823, GEORGIANA MARIA KANE.

        viii.   MARY JANE WINTHROP, b. 26 Jan. 1799,[1004] d. at New York 28 April 1867,[1005] and bur. at Green-Wood Cemetery in Brooklyn,

---

998   Charlotte Ann Winthrop stone at *Findagrave.com* (memorial 52746451). "In memory of Charlotte Ann, daughter of F.B. Winthrop and wife of John M. Aspinwall, Born Jan. 8 1794, Died Apr. 16 1851."

999   Timothy G. X. Salls, ed., "Record of the Gilbert Aspinwall family, 1708–1982," *New England Ancestors* 5: 1 [2004]: 50. "On the 19th November 1816 John M. Aspinwall was married to Charlotte Ann Winthrop in New York by the Right Reverand Bishop [John Henry] Hobart" of Trinity Church. "Records of Trinity Church Parish, New York City," *Record* 82 [1951]: 100, gives 16 November, while Adlard, *The Sutton-Dudleys of England and the Dudleys of Massachusetts in New England*, 127, gives 18 November.

1000   Salls, *New England Ancestors* 5: 1 [2004]: 50. "John Myer Aspinwall was born at New York the 31st day of March 1792 at half past seven o'clock in the morning and baptized by the Reverand Doctor Beach." His middle name is spelled Meyer in some records. John Myer Aspinwall's first cousin, Mary Rebecca (Aspinwall) Roosevelt, was the grandmother of President Franklin Delano Roosevelt.

1001   Salls, *New England Ancestors* 5: 2 [2004]: 48. "John Meyer Aspinwall eldest son of Gilbert Aspinwall died in Brooklyn N.Y. on the 19th July 1844 in consequence of taking labdanum [*sic*] during a fit of insanity." Adlard, *The Sutton-Dudleys of England and the Dudleys of Massachusetts in New England*, 127, errs with a death in July 1845. The *Centinel of Freedom* (Newark, N.J.), 23 July 1844, 3, gave an account that his body had been found "in a secluded coal yard at the foot of Joralemon street, on the East River, Brooklyn. In his pockets were three one-ounce, and one two-ounce vials, labelled laudenum, and all empty except one of the one-ounce vials which was full and from which he had in vain attempted to draw the cork with his teeth. His face was bruised, apparently by a fall. . . . He has appeared to be dull and low-spirited of late, and was missed by his family on Thursday evening."

1002   John Myer Aspinwall stone at *Findagrave.com* (memorial 52746405). "In memory of John Myer, son of Gilbert & Ann Aspinwall, Born 31 March 1792, Died 19 July 1844."

1003   Algernon Aikin Aspinwall, *The Aspinwall Genealogy* (Rutland, Vt.: The Tuttle Co., 1901), 107.

1004   Adlard, *The Sutton-Dudleys of England and the Dudleys of Massachusetts in New England*, 127.

1005   "Manhattan Death Records, 1795–1865," index of records at New York Municipal Archives, *familysearch.org/ ark:/61903/1:1:2WBS-7ZW,* citing FHL 1,324,517. Mary J. Parkin, d. 28 April 1867, age 68. See also *New York Tribune,* 30 April 1867, 5.

N.Y.[1006] She m. at Trinity Church, New York 28 Oct. 1822,[1007] her first cousin THOMAS[7] PARKIN, who was b. at New London 8 Nov. 1794, son of Richard William and Mary[6] (Winthrop) Parkin,[1008] and had issue.[1009] He d. at New York 2 Nov. 1861,[1010] and was bur. at Green-Wood Cemetery.[1011]

10. ANNE[6] WINTHROP (*John Still[5]*, *John[4]*, *Waitstill[3]*, *John[2-1]*) was born, probably at New London, Connecticut, on 7 May 1755.[1012] She died 2[1013] and was buried in King's Chapel Burying Ground in Boston, Massachusetts 5 October 1789.[1014] She married at Providence, Rhode Island 6 June 1786,[1015] DAVID SEARS, who was born at Chatham,

---

"Died . . . Parkin—Suddenly, on Sunday, April 28, Mary J., relict of Thomas Parkin and daughter of the late Francis B. Winthrop."

[1006] *Findagrave.com* (memorial 58394233). An index to Green-Wood Cemetery records at *green-wood.com* gives Mary J. Parkin bur. 2 May 1867, Lot 3609, Section 32.

[1007] "Records of Trinity Church Parish, New York City," *Record* 82 [1951]: 159. Adlard, *The Sutton-Dudleys of England and the Dudleys of Massachusetts in New England*, 127, gives 26 October.

[1008] Barbour, "New London Births–Marriages–Deaths, 1646–1854," 228, citing 3: 87 of original town records.

[1009] Adlard, *The Sutton-Dudleys of England and the Dudleys of Massachusetts in New England*, 127.

[1010] *Commercial Advertiser* (New York), 2 November 1861, 3, "Suddenly, on the 2[d] inst., Thomas Parkin, of New York city, in the 67th year of his age." Also, *New York Tribune*, 6 November 1861, 3. "Suddenly, on Saturday, Nov. 2, of disease of the heart, Thomas Parkin, aged 66 years." "Manhattan Death Records, 1795–1865," index of records at New York Municipal Archives, *familysearch.org/ark:/61903/1:1:2W4T-GGD*, citing FHL 447,564, errs with 2 October 1861, as he was bur. 6 November [note 1009].

[1011] *Findagrave.com* (memorial 58394243). An index to Green-Wood Cemetery records at *green-wood.com* gives Thomas Parkin bur. 6 November 1861, Lot 3609, Section 32.

[1012] Adlard, *The Sutton-Dudleys of England and the Dudleys of Massachusetts in New England*, 128. Mayo, in *The Winthrop Family in America*, gives New London as the birthplace of each of her male siblings.

[1013] Dunkle and Lainhart, *Inscriptions and Records of the Old Cemeteries of Boston*, 782. "Ann Winthrop Sears / the Wife of David Sears / died Oct[r] 2[d] 1789, Aged 33 Years." Adlard, *The Sutton-Dudleys of England and the Dudleys of Massachusetts in New England*, 128, gives the date of death as 4 October 1789.

[1014] Oliver and Peabody, *The Records of Trinity Church, Boston, 1728–1830*, 56: 247, gives bur. 5 October 1789. "Mrs. Anna Sears, wife of David Sears, 34y." See also *Findagrave.com* (memorial 11242895). Robert J. Dunkle and Ann S. Lainhart, *John Haven Dexter's Memoranda of the Town of Boston in the 18th & 19th Centuries* (Boston: New England Historic Genealogical Society, 1997), 455, gives the date as 8 October 1789, age 34, citing Vol. 1b.

[1015] Edwin M. Snow, comp., *Alphabetical Index of the Births, Marriages and Deaths, Recorded in Providence, Rhode Island*, 25 vols. (City of Providence, 1879–1945), 1: 379. Ann

Massachusetts 29 November 1752[1016] and died at Boston 23 October 1816,[1017] son of Daniel and Fear (Freeman) Sears.[1018]

After his father died in 1761, when David was about nine, his mother relocated the family from Chatham to Boston, where David would later become a successful merchant with a counting room on Central Wharf. In 1775, when about 23, he sailed for London, traveled through Europe for a few years, then narrowly escaped capture by an English frigate upon his return. "He engaged to some extent in privateering," wrote family historian Samuel May, "and in the summer of 1779 fitted out the *Mars*, of 22 guns, under command of Capt. Ash." During the presidency of John Adams he was chairman of a Committee of the Citizens of Boston for building a frigate, the *Boston*, at their own expense, to give to the federal government. David contributed $3,000.[1019] His death in 1816 came after "a too copious indulgence in that favorite repast of the olden time, a 'Saturday salt-fish dinner,' brought on serious indigestion, followed by a congestion which proved fatal," wrote Robert C. Winthrop, Jr.,The rector of Trinity Church, Boston, wrote a funeral sermon that cited "that well-known passage from the first book of Samuel, 'There is but a *step* between me and death,' in allusion to the fact that Mr. Sears had fallen on the step of his carriage in a fit of apoplexy."[1020]

Child of David and Anne[6] (Winthrop) Sears:

13   i.   DAVID[7] SEARS, b. at Boston 8 Oct. 1787; m. 13 June 1809, MIRIAM CLARKE MASON.

Winthrop and David Spear [*sic*], 6 June 1786, citing 5: 152 of city records. See also *Providence Gazette*, 10 June 1786, which gives "[Married.] By the Rev. Mr. Oliver, Mr. David Sears, of Boston, Merchant, to Miss Ann Winthrop, Daughter of the late John Stille Winthrop, Esq., of New-London."

[1016] Samuel B. May, *The Descendants of Richard Sares (Sears) of Yarmouth, Mass. 1638–1888* (Albany, N.Y.: Joel Munsell's Sons, 1890), 167, noting that another account gives 12 August 1752.

[1017] May, *The Descendants of Richard Sares (Sears)*, 167. Age 64.

[1018] May, *The Descendants of Richard Sares (Sears)*, 95. David Sears was a great-great-great-great-grandson of John Howland of the *Mayflower*.

[1019] May, *The Descendants of Richard Sares (Sears)*, 168.

[1020] Robert C. Winthrop, Jr., "Memoir of the Hon. David Sears, A.M.," *Proceedings of the Massachusetts Historical Society*, 2nd series, 2 [1886]: 408. May, *The Descendants of Richard Sares (Sears)*, 169, said Sears died getting into his carriage in front of his residence at the corner of Beacon and Somerset Streets.

11. **Thomas Lindall⁶ Winthrop** (*John Still⁵, John⁴, Waitstill³, John²⁻¹*) was born at New London, Connecticut 6 March 1760[1021] and died at his home on Walnut Street in Boston, Massachusetts 22 February 1841.[1022] He was buried in the Winthrop tomb in King's Chapel Burying Ground.[1023] He married at Brattle Square Church, Boston 25 July 1786,[1024] **Elizabeth Bowdoin "Betsy" Temple**, who was born at Boston 22 October 1769 and baptized at Trinity Church,[1025] daughter of Sir John Temple, 8th Baronet, and Elizabeth (Bowdoin), Lady Temple.[1026] She died at Boston 23 July 1825 and was buried at King's Chapel.[1027]

[1021] Folsom, *Archaeologia Americana* 3 [1857]: 331.

[1022] Thomas L. Winthrop death record, *Ancestry.com* > Massachusetts, Town and Vital Records, 1620–1988 > Boston > Birth, Marriages and Death (Provo, Utah: Holbrook Research Institute). Age 81, "old age," bur. Trinity Church. See also Hale, *Connecticut Newspaper Notices,* 14: 568, citing *Connecticut Herald,* 24 February 1841.

[1023] Folsom, *Archaeologia Americana* 3 [1857]: 341. His Boston burial record gives "Trinity Church." A memorial window given by his son there reads: "In memory of Thomas Lindall Winthrop, who died in 1841, aged 80 years, and Elizabeth Bowdoin Temple, his wife, who died 1825, aged 55. The Hon. Robert C. Winthrop, for fifth-three years a Vestryman, has given this window as a memorial to his father and mother. The Hon. Thomas L. Winthrop was Lieutenant-Governor of Massachusetts from A.D. 1826 to A.D. 1833" (Arthur H. Chester, *Trinity Church in the City of Boston* [Cambridge, Mass.: John Wilson and Son, 1888], 56–57).

[1024] *The Manifesto Church: Records of the Church in Brattle Square, Boston* (Boston: The Benevolent Fraternity of Churches, 1902), 257. 25 July 1786: "Thomas Lindell Winthrop Esqʳ and Miss Elizabeth Bowdoin Temple both of Boston" by Pastor Peter Thacher, with notation of "£4.16.0" (apparently the donation made for his service). See also Temple Prime, *Some Account of the Temple Family: Appendix* (New York, 1899), 136, citing "Memoranda from the Family Bible of Sir John Temple, 8ᵗʰ Bart.," communicated by Robert C. Winthrop, Jr., Esq. "Elizabeth Bowdoin their second child was married to Thomas Lindall Winthrop Esq. on the 25ᵗʰ day of July 1786." *Records Relating to the Early History of Boston, Containing Boston Marriages from 1752 to 1809, Vol. 30*, 111, gives 26 July.

[1025] Prime, *Some Account of the Temple Family: Appendix*, 135, citing "Memoranda from the Family Bible of Sir John Temple": "Elizabeth Bowdoin their second child was born on Sunday the 22ⁿᵈ of October 1769, at 7 oc. in the morning and was baptized at Trinity Church, John Irving Esq'r Mrs. Maria Irving and Miss Anne Hubbard were sponsors." Oliver and Peabody, *The Records of Trinity Church, Boston, 1728–1830, Vol.* 56, does not contain a record of the baptism, but then there are only two records in the three months after her birth. W.H. Whitmore, "An Account of the Temple Family," *Register* 10 [1856]: 76, gives birth on 23 October.

[1026] Prime, *Some Account of the Temple Family: Appendix*, 135, citing "Memoranda from the Family Bible of Sir John Temple": "John Temple and Elizabeth Bowdoin were married by the Rev. Samuel Cooper in Boston on the 20ᵗʰ day of January 1767 and went to housekeeping the 22ⁿᵈ of February following." Dunkle and Lainhart, *John Haven Dexter's Memoranda*, 571, gives parents' names, citing Vol. 1b.

[1027] Elizabeth Bowdoin Winthrop death record, *Ancestry.com* > Massachusetts, Town and Vital Records, 1620-1988 > Boston > Birth, Marriages and Death (Provo, Utah:

About four months before Thomas was born, his great-grandfather Timothy Lindall—who had only daughters who survived to adulthood and thus no direct descendants who shared his surname[1028]—proposed to his granddaughter Jane (Borland) Winthrop and her husband that Thomas Lindall Winthrop or Samuel Lindall Winthrop would be good names if she had a son. When on 6 March 1760 the couple followed his advice, Timothy Lindall wrote John Still[5] Winthrop to let him know the boy would be remembered in his will.[1029] He kept his vow on 7 July 1760 (he died on 25 October): while he left the six elder Winthrop great-grandchildren $2,000 to share once they came of age, his namesake received his land, warehouse, wharf, and flats in Salem and, after the death of Mrs. Timothy Lindall (the child's great-grandmother), the family mansion in Salem and farm in Danvers.[1030] John Still Winthrop administered the estate of his infant son,[1031] who was called "Tommy."[1032]

When his father John Still Winthrop died in 1776, Thomas was 16 and about to enter Yale College.[1033] During his junior year he transferred to Harvard, where his oldest brother John[6] Winthrop and cousin Gilbert Saltonstall had graduated in 1770. He enrolled at Cambridge in the spring of 1779[1034] and earned the nickname "English Tom," apparently because of his precise and upright demeanor.[1035] (Thomas L. Winthrop

---

Holbrook Research Institute). Age 56, of "organic disease of abdominal area." See also *Boston Traveler*, 26 July 1825, 3. "In this city, on Saturday last, Mrs. Elizabeth Bowdoin Winthrop, wife of the Hon. Thomas L. Winthrop."

[1028] Mayo, *The Winthrop Family in America*, 209: "Two great-grandchildren had already been named John Lindall Borland and Francis Lindall Borland" [see Vinton, *Register* 7 [1853]: 20], "but from the old gentleman's point of view, that was not enough."

[1029] Mayo, *The Winthrop Family in America*, 160–61, citing Winthrop Manuscripts 1B: 53. 58, 61. Sadly, Jane would die a month after her son's birth.

[1030] Vinton, *Register* 7 [1853]: 20.

[1031] Mayo, *The Winthrop Family in America*, 209, citing Winthrop Manuscripts 1B: 64–65.

[1032] Mayo, *The Winthrop Family in America*, 209.

[1033] Dunkle and Lainhart, *John Haven Dexter's Memoranda*, 490, citing Vol. 3, say Thomas was adopted by his uncle James Bowdoin, Jr., who lived on Milk Street at Hawley ("Bowdoin's Block").

[1034] "Early Faculty Minutes, 1725–1806," Harvard University Archives, UAIII 5.5, Vol. 15 (Box 11), image 118 of 322, scan at *nrs.harvard.edu/urn-3:HUL.ARCH:10954023*. "April 30th At a Meetg of the Presdt Profs & Tutors, Thos Lindall Winthrop, late a Student in Yale College, in the Junr Sophistser Class, applying for admission into this College, & producing a recommendatory Dismission from the Revd President Stiles Voted ~ That he be admitted to examination. N.B. Winthrop belongs to New London ~ Aged 19 ~ March 6, 1779. Examination being had of Thos Lendall Winthrop."

[1035] Mayo, *The Winthrop Family in America*, 210. Still, he may have had moments of

was "so conspicuous an example of the dignified and ceremonious demeanor of the old school," according to a grandson, that even after being elected to Congress his son Robert "did not venture to sit down in his father's presence uninvited."[1036]) Thomas received his bachelor's degree in July 1780, and afterward, "owing to the delicacy of his health," took a horseback tour of the west and south with a servant. His son, Robert Charles[7] Winthrop, would many years later recount the story as he heard it from his father:[1037]

> He had ridden along through our own State [Massachusetts], and had crossed over into New York. He had breakfasted at the Fishkill Inn, or, it may have been, the Inn at Fishkill Landing, and was just ready to mount his horse again, when a party of officers rode up and alighted, and sat down to the same table from which he had risen. They were Washington and his Staff. After a brief interval, my father rode on, and, in the course of the day, met a negro soldier coming through the wood. "What news, Sambo?" said my father. "Great news!" exclaimed the negro. "General Arnold, he gone off!" "Why, if you dare to tell such a story, you will be hung on the next tree." "My Captain, he close behind, and he will you tell you it is true." And the Captain and his company soon appeared, and confirmed the tidings. Of course all was confusion along the line of the Hudson. But my father always spoke of the calm composure of Washington that morning. He was still, however, to be informed of startling tidings of André's capture and Arnold's treason.

In February 1781, at age 21, Thomas wrote his family in New London to say he intended to visit England and Europe, despite the

---

inattention; during his sophomore year, he was chosen by the faculty to deliver "an English oration" at the semi-annual meeting of the Committee of Overseers; a postscript in the minutes noted "it was not deliver'd" ("Early Faculty Minutes, 1725–1806," Harvard University Archives, UAIII 5.5, Vol. 15 [Box 11], image 144 of 322, scan at *nrs.harvard.edu/urn-3:HUL.ARCH:10954023*).

[1036] Winthrop, *A Memoir of Robert C. Winthrop*, 328–29. In a footnote, the author, Robert C. Winthrop, Jr., wrote: "*Autres temps, autres moeurs* [Other times, other customs]. Not only did the son's children sit down in their father's presence when they felt like it, but they were even tempted, I am ashamed to say, upon more than one occasion to sit, figuratively speaking, upon him."

[1037] *Proceedings of the Massachusetts Historical Society* 16 [1878]: 367.

animosity between Britain and its rebellious colonies. His future brother-in-law, William Stewart, reported back that his letter had greatly upset his sisters Jenny, Nancy, and Polly. "Their tender bosoms are greatly moved, whilst the trembling tear sits drooping on their eye and filial affection excites a variety of fears from the dangers you may be subjected to," he reported. Jenny wrote separately: "It seems as if our Family was breaking all to pieces."[1038] Thomas sailed from Nantucket for Amsterdam but the vessel was captured by the British and taken to England. As an American, he might easily have been detained, but as a Winthrop he was allowed to visit London and some interior counties with his traveling companion, "Mr. Russell" (presumably a Harvard classmate, Thomas Walley Russell).[1039] The trip also included visits to Holland, Belgium, and France.[1040] Thomas returned from France in the winter of 1782 aboard the privateer *St. James*, which made the crossing to Philadelphia in less than thirty days.[1041]

Thomas had returned to Massachusetts by the end of the year, "where—in Salem, at least—there seems to have been a good deal of talk about a courtship he had been conducting," Mayo noted.[1042] Thomas didn't marry that particular paramour but instead became a partner in the mercantile house of Winthrop, Tod and Winthrop with his older brother Joseph. It was headquartered in Charleston, South Carolina, so Thomas traveled south in the spring of 1783 and stayed about two

---

[1038] Mayo, *The Winthrop Family in America*, 211, citing Winthrop Manuscripts 30A: 6, 7.

[1039] Mayo, *The Winthrop Family in America*, 212, citing a footnote by translator George Grieve in Marquis de Chastellux, *Travels in North-America in the Years 1780, 1781 and 1782*, 2nd ed., 2 vols. (London: G.G.J. and J. Robinson, 1787), 2: 284–85. "The Translator had the pleasure of begin acquainted with the son of Mr. Russell and his friend Winthrop in France and Holland. He had the good fortune likewise to meet with the latter at Boston. He takes pride in mentioning these amiable young men, as they cannot fail of becoming valuable members of a rising country which attracts the attention of the world."

[1040] "Memoir of the Late Thomas L. Winthrop," *Collections of the Massachusetts Historical Society*, 4th series, 2 [1854]: 210.

[1041] Mayo, *The Winthrop Family in America*, 212, citing Winthrop Manuscripts 30A: 8. See also Isaac J. Greenwood, *Captain John Manley, Second in Rank in the United States Navy, 1776–1783* (Boston: C.E. Goodspeed & Co., 1915), 121. Also aboard was "a very rich cargo," Count Benyowski, who hoped to submit to Congress his plan for a legionary corps, and number of privateer captains released from captivity, some who had been imprisoned since 1777.

[1042] Mayo, *The Winthrop Family in America*, 212, citing Oliver, *The Diary of William Pynchon of Salem*, 137. In an entry dated 25 November 1782, Pynchon wrote, "Cloudy morning; rains allday. Thos. Winthrop, Esq., dines here. See the poet. lampoon on his courtship."

years.[1043] On 15 September 1785, William Pynchon of Salem noted in his diary that Thomas had returned to Massachussetts when he wrote that "Mr. Winthrop, Misses Temple and Mr. Waldo came to town."[1044] One of those misses was no doubt Elizabeth Bowdoin Temple, a daughter of John Temple, who had recently been appointed Consul General of Great Britain in the United States, and soon would become Sir John Temple.[1045] Elizabeth's maternal grandfather, who raised her, was James Bowdoin, Governor of Massachusetts, president of the American Academy of Arts and Sciences, and one of the wealthiest merchants in New England.[1046]

In November 1785, Governor Bowdoin wrote his son-in-law John Temple:[1047]

> It is probable you have heard—and it is the design of this letter to inform you—that Mr. Winthrop has for some time paid his addresses to your daughter Betsy. When he asked our consent, he was given to understand that we had nothing to object to the connection, but as the disposal of her rested with her father and mother he must apply to them for their consent. Accordingly, as you have been expected for several months, he has been earnestly wishing your arrival, that might have an opportunity for that purpose. With this view he intends to proceed

---

[1043] See signed statement by principals in Winthrop, Tod and Winthrop dated at Charleston, 1 July 1783, reprinted in *Collections of the Massachusetts Historical Society*, 7th series, 10 [1915]: 193. "We take the Liberty to inform you, that we have established a House in this City, with intent to execute the Commands which our Friends may be pleased to honour us with, whether in the Sales of Consignment; Purchase of Cargoes; or the procuring Freights for Vessels." He may have been the "Mr. Winthrop" who arrived in Charleston from London aboard the *Eleanor* in January 1785 (*South Carolina Gazette*, 19 January 1785, 2) and perhaps the passenger Winthrop who "cleared outwards" on the *Barbados* bound for Boston on 14 February 1785 (*Columbia Herald*, 14 February 1785, 3), but it seems more likely that was a visit by his brother Robert.

[1044] Oliver, *The Diary of William Pynchon of Salem*, 222.

[1045] A few years earlier, a visiting French officer had commented that the 12-year-old Betsy was "formed to attract attention" and that she was "an angel in the disguise of a young girl." (Chastellux, *Travels in North-America*, 2: 287). Thomas also had his admirers. In 1824, Charles Fraser, the painter of miniatures, remarked of the couple: "I still think him one of the handsomest men of his age I ever saw; and Mrs. W. looks as young as one of her daughters" (Alice R. Huger Smith and D.E. Huger Smith, *Charles Fraser* [Charleston, S.C.: Garnier, 1967], 21).

[1046] Mayo, *The Winthrop Family in America*, 213. Folsom, *Archaeologia Americana* 3 [1857]: 332, calls Betsy Temple her grandparents' "adopted daughter."

[1047] Mayo, *The Winthrop Family in America*, 213, citing Winthrop Manuscripts 25: 35.

for New York immediately and it is with pleasure I take
the present occasion of introducing him to you and of
expressing my opinion concerning him, which is, that he
is a gentleman of good character, good family and good
circumstances: and I believe that your daughter and her
friends will be happy in the connection.

The couple married the following July (Thomas was 26 and
Elizabeth 16) and moved to a large house at the corner of Sudbury
Street and Alden Court.[1048] Thomas spent about eighteen months
in Charleston after the spring of 1789, winding up his interest in
Winthrop, Tod and Winthrop.[1049] He returned to Boston in the fall of
1790 and the *Boston Directory* of 1798 lists him as merchant who lived
on Beacon Street.[1050] About 1803 he moved his family moved to the
Bowdoin house on Milk Street and stayed there until about 1812,[1051]
when they relocated to 2 Hamilton Place, with a view of the Common.
About 1824 Thomas bought a brick mansion on the westerly corner of
Beacon and Walnut Streets and lived there until his death.[1052]

After he retired from business, Thomas kept his connection with
two banks, the Union and the Provident Institution for Savings in the
Town of Boston. With Union he was a director for about fifteen years
and became its president about 1820 to 1834.[1053] With Provident, the
first savings bank in New England, he was trustee when it formed in
1817 and remained on board until 1837.[1054] He also engaged in politics,
if not always willingly. In 1822, with the Federalists split and quarreling
over a candidate for the first Mayor of Boston, the Democrats on the
night before the election gathered on the North End and nominated
Mr. Winthrop "without the knowledge of that gentleman, and to his
great displeasure," as one historian put it.[1055] The plan was to keep either

---

[1048] Robert C. Winthrop, Jr., *A Memoir of Robert C. Winthrop Prepared for the Massachusetts Historical Society* (Boston: Little, Brown and Co., 1897), 5n.

[1049] Mayo, *The Winthrop Family in America*, 213, citing Winthrop Manuscripts, 30A: 9.

[1050] *The Boston Directory* (Boston: John West, 1798), 126.

[1051] Mayo, *The Winthrop Family in America*, 213, citing Winthrop, *A Memoir of Robert C. Winthrop*, 5n, and Winthrop Manuscripts, 29B.

[1052] Winthrop, *A Memoir of Robert C. Winthrop*, 5n. A view of the Hamilton Place house and the Common can be found in Winsor, *The Memorial History of Boston*, 4: facing 64.

[1053] Charles Stimpson, Jr., *Stimpson's Boston Directory* (Boston: Stimpson & Clapp, 1834), 21. In Stimpson's 1835 directory, Samuel Fales is listed as president of Union Bank.

[1054] Mayo, *The Winthrop Family in America*, 214.

[1055] Edmund Quincy, *Life of Josiah Quincy*, 6th ed. (Boston: Little, Brown and Co., 1874), 393.

Federalist candidate from being elected, and Winthrop did that by pulling 361 votes. Both candidates withdrew, and John Phillips a week later was chosen as the mayor.[1056]

That same year, as a Democrat, Thomas represented Boston in General Court, and in 1823 was promoted to the Senate. In 1826, he became Lieutenant Governor of the Commonwealth, but in 1832 asked not to be re-nominated[1057]; his age (73) may have been a factor, Mayo noted, or it may have been that Governor Lincoln had started court martial proceedings against his son, Grenville Temple[7] Winthrop (*see below*).[1058] Nevertheless, Thomas had left enough of an impression on his colleagues in the legislature that when he died nine years later, both houses adjourned to attend the funeral.[1059] He had another passion that kept him busy—American history. He was a member of the Massachusetts Historical Society as early as 1800 and elected its president in 1835, serving until his death. At the time he was already president of the American Antiquarian Society, having been voted into that post in 1831 after being a member since 1813. He was interested in the topic as early as 1803, when he wrote his brother Francis: "You promised me some time since some old sermons and pamphlets printed in New England. The older the better. Every piece of paper that can throw light upon the first settlement of this country ought to go into the hands of those who leisure, ability and inclination to make them useful."[1060]

[1056] James Mascarene Hubbard, "Boston's Last Town Meetings and First City Election," *The Bostonian Society Publications* 6 [1910]: 111–15.

[1057] Mayo, *The Winthrop Family in America*, 215, citing Winthrop Manuscripts, 30A: 101.

[1058] Mayo, *The Winthrop Family in America*, 215, 309–10.

[1059] Folsom, *Archaeologia Americana* 3 [1857]: 340.

[1060] *Proceedings of the Massachusetts Historical Society* 12 [1872]: 234. In the same letter he reported, "The manuscript Journals of Governor Winthrop are in the library of the Historical Society." They had been earlier lent to Jeremy Belknap, founder of the Massachutts Historial Society, but not returned at the time of his death in 1798. Thomas tracked them down, reclaimed them from Belknap's heirs, and persuaded Francis to donate them to the society. Thomas also gave the society a copy of Audubon's *The Birds of America*, which was sold in 1905 for $2,000 to create the Thomas Lindall Winthrop Fund. (In 2012, a copy sold at auction for $11.5 million.) To the AAS Thomas gave 128 books "selected by a learned antiquarian, at the cost of $350" that focused on the topography, heraldry, and genealogy of England and Wales. In 1830, he gave Trinity Church in Boston, where he was on the vestry from 1815 to 1833, a silver ewer adorned on the reverse with the Winthrop Arms (*Trinity Church in the City of Boston, Massachusetts* [Boston: Merrymount Press, 1933], 182, 205).

Children of Thomas Lindall[6] and Elizabeth Bowdoin (Temple) Winthrop:

   i. ELIZABETH BOWDOIN TEMPLE[7] WINTHROP, b. 14 May,[1061] bp. at
Trinity Church, Boston 25 July 1787,[1062] and d. at Augusta, Me.
9 March 1860.[1063] She m. at Boston 2 May 1814,[1064] the REV.
BENJAMIN TAPPAN, who was b. in Nov. 1788 and d. at Augusta 23
Dec. 1863,[1065] son of the Rev. David Tappan, a professor of divinity
at Harvard, and Mary (Sawyer) Tappan. Benjamin Tappan graduated
from Harvard in 1805 and was ordained in Augusta on 16 Oct.
1811.[1066] He was the pastor of the Congregational (Orthodox)
Church there and for many years secretary of the Maine Missionary
Society. The couple had seven children.[1067]

  ii. SARAH BOWDOIN WINTHROP, b. 3 June 1788,[1068] bp. at Trinity Church
13 Aug. 1789,[1069] and d. at Pau (Béarn), France 13 Feb. 1864.[1070] She
m. at Brattle Square Church 26 Jan. 1809, GEORGE SULLIVAN,[1071]
who was b. at Boston 22 Feb. 1783 and d. at Pau 14 Dec. 1866, son

---

[1061] "Marriages and Deaths: Elizabeth Bowdoin Temple Tappan," *Register* 14 [1860]:
293. Whitmore, *Register* 10 [1856]: 76, gives 16 May.

[1062] Oliver and Peabody, *The Records of Trinity Church, Boston, 1728–1830*, 56: 87–88.
"Elisabeth Bowdoin Temple Daughter of Thomas Winthrop by Elisabeth Bowdoin
Temple his wife. Sponsors: Mr. Winthrop & Wife, Mrs. Sears."

[1063] "Marriages and Deaths: Elizabeth Bowdoin Temple Tappan," *Register* 14 [1860]: 293.

[1064] Jay Mack Holbrook, ed., *Boston Marriage Publications, 1807–1817, Vol. 8*, 290, scan
of original at *Ancestry.com* > Massachusetts, Town and Vital Records, 1620–1988 >
image 148 of 233. Ethel Colby Conant, ed., *Vital Records of Augusta, Maine, to the Year
1892*, 2 vols. (Auburn, Me.: Maine Historical Society, 1934), 2: 151, has intentions
there on 7 May 1814. *Independent Chronicle* (Boston), 9 June 1814, 3, "In this town
[no date given], by the Right Rev. Bishop Dehone, the Rev. Benjamin Tappan,
of Augusta (Me.) to Miss Eliza T.B. Winthrop, daughter of the Hon. Thomas L.
Winthrop, Esq., of this town."

[1065] Dunkle and Lainhart, *John Haven Dexter's Memoranda*, 570, citing Vol. 3.

[1066] David Langdon Tappan, *Tappan-Toppan Genealogy: Ancestors and Descendants of
Abraham Toppan of Newbury, Massachusetts, 1606–1672* (Arlington, Mass: the author,
1915), 42–43.

[1067] John Adams Vinton, *The Giles Memorial* (Boston: Henry W. Dutton & Son, 1864), 337.

[1068] Whitmore, *Register* 10 [1856]: 77.

[1069] Oliver and Peabody, *The Records of Trinity Church, Boston, 1728–1830*, 56: 94. "Sarah
Bowdoin of Thoms. Lindall Winthrop by Elisabeth Temple his wife. Sponsors: Mr.
Sears, Mrs. Bowdoin, Mrs. Steward."

[1070] Dunkle and Lainhart, *John Haven Dexter's Memoranda*, 490, citing Vol. 3.

[1071] *The Manifesto Church: Records of the Church in Brattle Square, Boston*, 271. George
Sullivan and Sarah B. Winthrop. He was a member of the Porcellian Club in Harvard's
Class of 1801 (*Porcellian Club 1791–2016* [Cambridge, Mass.: the Club, 2016], 68).

of James Sullivan, Governor of Massachusetts in 1807 and 1808,[1072] and Mehitabel (Odiorne) Sullivan, and had issue.[1073]

iii. THOMAS LINDALL WINTHROP, JR., b. 23 July,[1074] and bp. Trinity Church, Boston 13 Aug. 1789.[1075] He d. unm. at Philadelphia, Pa. 12[1076] and was bur. there at Christ Church Cemetery 13 Jan. 1812.[1077]

When about 11 years old, he was sent to the Boston Public Latin School,[1078] and three years later admitted to Harvard. "His general behavior appears to have been fairly good until the final quarter of his Senior year," wrote Mayo. "Then he not only cut more classes than any other student in the College but was fined as well for absence from prayers ($1.62), for neglect of English composition (66 cents) and for not copying a theme (33 cents)."[1079] Apparently, Thomas became "deranged" over Miriam Mason, a daughter of Senator Jonathan Mason. During a performance before the Board of Overseers, his cousin and roommate David Sears invited her as his guest. "There was an exhibition at Cambridge & Sears was waiting upon Miss Mason down the steps of Harvard Hall where the chapel was, to the carriage [that his father sent for him every Saturday morning] which was at the door waiting for

---

[1072] James Winthrop, "Memoir of James Sullivan," in Thomas C. Amory, *Life of James Sullivan, with Selections from His Writings*, 2 vols. (Boston: Phillips, Sampson and Co., 1859), 2: 367.

[1073] Charles H. Browning, *Americans of Royal Descent*, 2nd ed. (Philadelphia: Porter & Coates, 1891), 38.

[1074] Whitmore, *Register* 10 [1856]: 77. Mayo, 284, notes that while he was presumably born in Boston, his father was a merchant in Charleston at the time and he may have been born there.

[1075] Oliver and Peabody, *The Records of Trinity Church, Boston, 1728–1830*, 56: 94. "Thoms. Lindall of Thoms. Lindall Winthrop by Elisabeth Temple his wife. Sponsors: Mr. Hutchinson for Sr. Jno. Temple, Mr. Sears, Lady Temple."

[1076] Adlard, *The Sutton-Dudleys of England and the Dudleys of Massachusetts in New England*, 129. Dunkle and Lainhart, *John Haven Dexter's Memoranda*, 571, citing Vol. 3, gives his death at Philadelphia 12 January 1812, aged 22.

[1077] *Poulson's American Daily Advertiser* (Philadelphia), 14 January 1812, 3. "Died on Sunday 12th instant, in this City, Thomas Lindall Winthrop, junr., Esq., aged 22, eldest son of Thomas Lindall Winthrop, Esq., of Boston. The deceased had lately returned from Denmark – his remains were yesterday deposited in the cemetery of Christ Church." See also index to Christ Church Register, 3690, at *philageohistory. org/rdic-images/ChristChurch*.

[1078] Jenks, *Catalogue of the Boston Public Latin School*, 136 (appendix).

[1079] Mayo, *The Winthrop Family in America*, 284, citing *Harvard College Faculty Official Minutes, 1725–1890*, 24 vols. (Harvard Archives; *nrs.harvard.edu/urn-3:HUL. ARCH:hua21010*), 7: 289, 8: 88.

her," recalled one contemporary. "Winthrop, while she had Sears's arm, drew a short whip & plied it hastily over Sears's shoulders. Sears took no notice of it. The attacks were very violent till the bystanders interfered & took away Winthrop. It caused tremendous excitement. Sears succeeded in marrying the girl & Mr. Winthrop was deranged as along as he lived."[1080]

Thomas earned his bachelor's degree in 1807 and his Master of Arts in 1810. According to his nephew Robert Charles[8] Winthrop, Jr., he and David Sears "entered upon the study of law together, becoming marked favorites in society."[1081] Two years later, perhaps in response to the marriage of Sears and Miriam in June 1809, Thomas had a breakdown of some kind, and his father "sent him off on horseback. . . ostensibly to look over the family's holdings of land and timber in the District of Maine.[1082] In the fall he set out on another trip, riding through Hartford and Rye to New York City, where he found lodging at the corner of Broadway and Cedar Streets. "I am much pleased with the city; it's to me a perfect London," he wrote his father. He then rode to Philadelphia and Pittsburgh and on to Ohio and Kentucky and New Orleans, arriving in Feb. 1810.[1083] By the following June he was in Saratoga, N.Y., "for the benefit of the waters," his father said. He was back in Boston by Feb. 1811, where he was admitted an attorney of the Court of Common Pleas.[1084] That same month he sailed from Newport, R.I., for Paris, then to Copenhagen.

By Dec. 1811, he had returned to Philadelphia and was very ill. His father arrived at his bedside on the morning of 12 Jan. 1812, about two hours before his son died at the age of 21, "perfectly easy, with his eyes fixed on his Father's."[1085] An obituary attributed his poor health to his intense study habits and "exclusive attachment to books" at Harvard, which "precluded all opportunities of convalescence."[1086] Mayo observed:[1087]

[1080] John Langdon Sibley, *Sibley's Manuscript Collections*, 2 vols., Harvard University Archives (HUG 1791.53), 2: 599.

[1081] Winthrop, *Proceedings of the Massachusetts Historical Society*, 2nd series, 2 [1886]: 409.

[1082] Mayo, *The Winthrop Family in America*, 285, citing Winthrop Manuscripts, 30A: 41.

[1083] Mayo, *The Winthrop Family in America*, 285, citing Winthrop Manuscripts, 30A: 43–47.

[1084] *Independent Chronicle* (Boston), 25 February 1811, 2.

[1085] Mayo, *The Winthrop Family in America*, 286–87, citing Winthrop Manuscripts 30A: 61.

[1086] *Columbian Centinel* (Boston), 22 January 1812, 2.

[1087] Mayo, *The Winthrop Family in America*, 287–88.

Few can read Tom Winthrop's letters to his father without emotion. He adored his parents, and they loved him dearly. He seems to have been handicapped not only by ill health but also by poor eyesight, which may have been a phase of his malady. This accounts, perhaps, for his proclivity for losing various articles while on this travels—a pen-knife here, a bundle there. . . . Underlying everything he did or tried to do was a deep-seated lack of self-confidence. . . . Today he might be called a perfectionist; as the present writer sees it, he was the victim of an exaggerated New England conscience.

    iv. AUGUSTA TEMPLE WINTHROP, b. 3,[1088] bp. 6 Nov. 1791[1089] and d. at Dorchester, Mass. 18 Sept. 1792.[1090] She was bur. at Trinity Church, Boston 20 Sept. 1792.[1091]

    v. AUGUSTA TEMPLE WINTHROP, b. 23 April,[1092] bp. at Trinity Church 25 July 1793,[1093] and d. at Hartford, Conn. 7 Dec. 1828.[1094] She m. at Trinity Church 3 Oct. 1820,[1095] DR. JOHN SMYTH ROGERS, who was b. about 1795, son of Henry and Frances (Moore) Rogers.[1096]

[1088] Whitmore, *Register* 10 [1857]: 77.

[1089] Oliver and Peabody, *The Records of Trinity Church, Boston, 1728–1830*, 56: 101. "Augusta Temple of Thomas L. Winthrop by Elizabeth B. Temple his wife. Greenville, Lady & Augusta Temple."

[1090] Whitmore, *Register* 10 [1857]: 77, gives date. *American Apollo* (Boston), 5 October 1792, 408, gives "At Dorchester, Miss Augusta Temple Winthrop, youngest daughter of Thomas Lindall Winthrop, of this town."

[1091] Oliver and Peabody, *The Records of Trinity Church, Boston, 1728–1830*, 56: 250. "Augusta Temple of Thoms. L. Winthrop, 10 mo."

[1092] Whitmore, *Register* 10 [1857]: 77.

[1093] Oliver and Peabody, *The Records of Trinity Church, Boston, 1728–1830*, 56: 105. "Augusta Temple of Thoms. Lindall Winthrop by Elisabeth B. Temple his wife. Mr. Winthrop & Wife, Augusta Temple."

[1094] *Sentinel and Witness* (Middletown, Conn.), 17 December 1828, 3. "At Hartford, on the 7th inst., Mrs. Augusta Temple Rogers, aged 34, wife of Dr. John Smyth Rogers, Professor of Chemistry in Washington College, and daughter of the Hon. Thomas L. Winthrop, of Boston, Lieut. Governor of Massachusetts."

[1095] Oliver and Peabody, *The Records of Trinity Church, Boston, 1728–1830*, 56: 210. "John Smyth Rogers of N. York to Augusta Temple Winthrop." However, "Boston Marriage Publications, 1817–1823, Vol. 9," in *Massachusetts Vital and Town Records* (Provo, Utah: Holbrook Research Institute), accessed at *ancestry.com* > Massachusetts, Town and Vital Records, 1620–1988 > Boston, has "John Smyth Rogers of N. York, Augusta Temple Winthrop of Boston, 20 Sept. 1820."

[1096] Benjamin W. Dwight, "Rogers Lineage," *Record* 16 [1885]: 78. On a passport application dated 6 July 1839, John Rogers stated he was 44 years old. The examiner noted he was 5' 10¾" tall, had grey eyes, a "large" nose, dark hair and light complex-

He d. at New York 30 March 1851.[1097] Augusta, who was an active supporter of and volunteer at the Orphan Asylum,[1098] died in Hartford after Dr. Rogers, in an effort to improve his own poor health, moved his family there to begin a job on 9 Aug. 1828 as a professor of mineralogy and chemistry at Washington (later Trinity) College.[1099] A history of the college recounted:[1100]

> The resignation of Professor Hall was a great loss to the College, for with him went his large mineral collection. Hall's successor, however, John Smyth Rogers, M.D., not only replenished the depleted mineral collection, but he also made valuable additions to the philosophical apparatus and, presumably at his own expense, set up an elegant chemical laboratory. After two years of service as Professor of Chemistry and Mineralogy, Dr. Rogers submitted his resignation. Rogers was prevailed upon to reconsider, and his resignation was withdrawn. The Trustees, by way of encouragement to the Professor of the Natural Sciences, appropriated another $300 for the purchase of additional philosophical apparatus. Dr. Rogers fully lived up to early expectations, and his laboratory and cabinet were always well-kept.

---

ion (*ancestry.com* > U.S. Passport Applications, 1795–1925 > Registers and Indexes for Passport Applications, 1810–1906 > 1834–1843 > Roll 1–Register of Passport Applications, 14 Nov. 1834—8 May 1843).

[1097] *Evening Post* (New York), 31 March 1851, 3. "Died . . . on Sunday morning, March 30th, Dr. J. Smyth Rogers, in the 57th year of his age." Dwight, "Rogers Lineage," *Record* 16 [1885]: 78, gives his death as 29 March 1851, aged 56. *College of Physicians and Surgeons in the City of New York, Medical Department of Columbia College: Catalogue of the Alumni, Officers and Fellows, 1807–1891* (New York: Bradstreet Press, 1891), 52, gives his death 29 March 1851, aged 57, of bladder cancer.

[1098] *American* (New York), 10 December 1828, 2.

[1099] *Episcopal Watchman* (Hartford, Conn.), August 1828, 166. Dwight, "Rogers Lineage," *Record* 16 [1885]: 78, errs saying the move to Hartford was in 1829. Rogers resided in West Hartford at the time of the 1830 census with a household of 12 people that included one free black servant (roll 7, 61).

[1100] Glenn Weaver, *The History of Trinity College* (Hartford: Trinity College Press, 1967), 75, citing Trustees' Minutes, 11 August 1830, 4 August 1831. See also *Connecticut Courant* (Hartford), 12 August 1828, 3.

Dr. Rogers taught at Trinity until 1839,[1101] but apparently returned briefly to New York in 1831, as his eldest son, John Smyth[8] Rogers, died there in December at age 7.[1102] In Dr. Rogers's will, dated at New York on 10 Jan. 1849 and proved 7 April 1851, he left his alma mater, the College of Physicians & Surgeons in New York,[1103] his "cabinet of Materia Medica now being in possession of said College"; gave his siblings $100 to $150 each to purchase "a piece of plate or some other memento of me"; bequeathed his daughter Frances Moore Rogers a hundred volumes from his library and half his engravings, and his son Henry Rogers the rest of his library and engravings as well as his "chemical and philosophical aparatus, specimens of natural history and all my plate and plated ware."[1104]

vi. JAMES BOWDOIN WINTHROP, b. at Boston[1105] 23 July,[1106] bp. at Trinity Church, Boston 19 Oct. 1794,[1107] and d. unm. of pulmonary tuberculosis at Havana, Cuba just after midnight on 6 March 1833.[1108] He was buried at the Granary Burying Ground in Boston.[1109]

[1101] *Quinquennial Catalogue of the Officers and Graduates of Harvard University, 1636–1915,* 819–20. Rogers graduated from Columbia College in 1812, Bowdoin College in 1825, received an honorary degree from Harvard in 1827, and later taught at the New York College of Pharmacy. In 1830, he donated a box of minerals to the Massachusetts Historical Society (*Collections of the Massachusetts Historical Society,* 3rd series, 2 [1830]: 368) and in 1832 was secretary of the African Missionary School Society. His father-in-law, Thomas Lindall[6] Winthrop, was a vice president (*Sword's Pocket Almanack* [New York: T. and J. Swords, 1832], 84).

[1102] *Evening Post* (New York), 26 December 1831, 2.

[1103] *College of Physicians and Surgeons in the City of New York, Medical Department of Columbia College: Catalogue of the Alumni, Officers and Fellows, 1807–1891,* 52. He was a trustee of the college for the last two years of his life.

[1104] A copy of John Smyth Rogers's will is included among the Probate Records of Vermilion Co., Illinois. (ancestry.com > Illinois, Wills and Probate Records, 1772–1999 > Vermilion > Will Records, Book C–E, 1848–1864 > images 384–86), perhaps because one or more of his siblings lived there. The will was also probated in New York (New York, Wills and Probate Records, 1659–1999 > New York > Proceedings, 1851 > Images 1353–60) and both of his children testified they resided in New York.

[1105] Mayo, *The Winthrop Family in America,* 289.

[1106] Whitmore, *Register* 10 [1857]: 77.

[1107] Oliver and Peabody, *The Records of Trinity Church, Boston, 1728–1830,* 56: 109. "James Bowdoin of Thoms. L. Winthrop by Elizabeth Temple his wife. Mr. Jas. B. Temple, Mr. Winthrop & Wife."

[1108] Whitmore, *Register* 10 [1857]: 77. See also Dunkle and Lainhart, *John Haven Dexter's Memoranda,* 570, citing Vol. 2b, and Mayo, 298, citing Winthrop Manuscripts 30A: 102.

[1109] *Gravestone Inscriptions and Records of Tomb Burials in the Granary Burying Ground, Boston, Mass.* (Salem, Mass.: The Essex Institute, 1918), 42. "James Bowdoin, at

James Bowdoin Winthrop legally dropped his surname in June 1813, becoming James Bowdoin, after his maternal great-uncle, James Bowdoin (III), "the last male of his race in New England."[1110] The elder Bowdoin in 1811 had left James a life interest in a large tract of land, with buildings, in Bowdoinham in the District of Maine, on the condition he drop his surname.[1111] The two had a long, close relationship; on 2 Dec. 1806, when James was 12, he wrote to his great-uncle, then the American minister to Spain but in Paris with his wife and James' older sister Sarah, to thank him for a gift of books:[1112]

> I am now studying *Selectae e profanis*, and the Greek Testament, at the Latin School, and I also attend a private School for Arithmetic, Writing, and Geography; I long very much to see you, my dear Aunt, and Sister, and when I pass the house in Beacon Street the good Apple pudding, pears, cake, etc., etc. together with the many marks of kindness and happy hours I have passed thre, makes me sigh and think of the great Atlantic ocean which separates us; this Sir, is my first attempt at letter writing. You will therefore be so good as to excuse all defects.

In 1807, James was admitted to Phillips Academy in Andover (where he was joined by his brother John in 1809). In 1810, he was among a class of about fifteen boys who enrolled at Bowdoin College in Brunswick, Maine, which had been named for Massachusetts governor James Bowdoin, his great-grandfather, and funded with contributions from his great-uncle.[1113] After graduating from Bowdoin, James read law, although apparently not with enthusiasm.

Havana, March 6, 1833, ae. 37 y. Tomb 6." His great-uncle, James Bowdoin (III), is also buried in the tomb.

[1110] Temple Prime, *Some Account of the Bowdoin Family, with a notice of the Erving family*, 3rd ed. (New York: DeVinne Press, 1900), 8. See also *Private and Special Statutes of the Commonwealth of Massachusetts*, 21 vols. (Boston: Wells and Lilly, 1805–1912), 4: 504. He received his degree from Bowdoin College in 1814 under that name (*General Catalogue of Bowdoin College and the Medical School of Maine, 1794–1916* [Brunswick, Me., 1912], 59).

[1111] Temple Prime, *Some Account of the Bowdoin Family*, 2nd ed. (New York, 1894), 23. His will was dated 4 June and proved 21 October 1811.

[1112] Mayo, *The Winthrop Family in America*, 289, citing Winthrop Manuscripts 30A: 25.

[1113] Mayo, *The Winthrop Family in America*, 290. See also *General Catalogue of Bowdoin College*, 59.

In 1819, he wrote a college friend, "How goes the law with you? To me it is not worth much. But I do not feel at all disheartened, firmly persuaded as I am that it is far better to lay a solid foundation before entering actively into practice."[1114] A memoir published after James's death would note that "having received a competent fortune" from James Bowdoin, "he soon relinquished the practice of the law, and devoted himself to pursuits of literature and science. He was particularly inclined to historical studies."[1115] That life of scholarship likely suited him better, as Mayo wrote:[1116]

> He was a very quiet young man,—so quiet, apparently, that he escaped the notice of the compilers of the *Boston Directory* until he was more than 30 years old! Perhaps they were bewildered by his change of name and decided that it was safer to lave him out altogether. Yet all this time—some 10 or 12 years—he seems to have been living at his father's house on Hamilton Place and later at the corner of Beacon and Walnut streets, going in and out, minding his own business, and succeeding in keeping out of the public eye.

James traveled quite a bit in his youth, including trips to Montreal and Washington, D.C., and a number of his letters along the way have been preserved.[1117] As a young man, he assisted James Savage with gathering family letters and articles for the appendix of Savage's edition of Gov. John[1] Winthrop's journals,[1118] and that work and Savage's endorsement appears to have put him in the good graces of the historical societies. In 1821, at age 27, he was elected as a member of the Massachusetts Historical Society, in 1822 to the American Antiquarian Society, and in 1825 to the American

---

[1114] Mayo, *The Winthrop Family in America*, 291, citing Winthrop Manuscripts 30A: 73.

[1115] "Memoir of James Bowdoin," *Collections of the Massachusetts Historical Society*, 3rd series, 9 [1846]: 225.

[1116] Mayo, *The Winthrop Family in America,* 291.

[1117] Mayo, *The Winthrop Family in America,* 292–93, citing Winthrop Manuscripts, 30A: 78, 82–84.

[1118] Savage thanked James Bowdoin in the preface of Volume 1, published in 1825, and when Bowdoin died in 1833, Savage wrote: "I am too far advanced in life to anticipate the opportunity of ever forming so close an intimacy with any other man, in view of our constant daily intercourse for so many years, and the congeniality of our studies and pursuits, some of which may now have to be abandoned" (*Proceedings of the Massachusetts Historical Society*, 2nd series, 12 [1898]: 298).

Academy of Arts and Sciences (of which his great-grandfather Bowdoin was the first president).[1119] In 1825, he succeeded Savage as secretary of the Provident Institution for Savings and in 1827 became a member of the School Committee formed as part of Savage's drive to establish public primary education in Boston. That led, in 1829, to James's election to the legislature. He also served as a director of the Boston Asylum for Indigent Boys. He pursued these and other good works, but, Mayo wrote, "if James Bowdoin had a weakness, it was for collecting academic degrees." He and his brother George "seem to have enjoyed picking up" courtesy (i.e., honorary, or what Mayo termed "unearned") master's degrees. He was awarded one in 1818 by Harvard and another in 1826 by Yale.[1120]

James's final descent from tuberculosis began in the fall of 1832, although he had likely suffered for quite a while. Rather than spend that winter in Boston, he was advised to travel to Cuba. After his arrival with two attendants on 3 Jan. 1833, he wrote a long letter home recounting his unfortunate passage and care. He managed to get himself dressed each day and ride for 2 or 3 miles despite "a severe and almost constant cough and a sort [of] horrid feeling over my whole system that I cannot describe." He added a postscript eleven days later:[1121]

> Should I die here, my remains will be forwarded for the Bowdoin Tomb [at Granary Burying Ground in Boston]. My feelings, for some days back, has been those of regret that I did [not] end life in my bed. It is a serious matter to die,—but to die without a friend at hand— . . . and without any friend to direct one's thoughts at such a moment—makes death most formidable. May it never be your fate.

[1119] Mayo, *The Winthrop Family in America,* 294.

[1120] Mayo, *The Winthrop Family in America,* 296. See also *General Catalogue of Bowdoin College,* 59.

[1121] Mayo, *The Winthrop Family in America,* 297–98, citing Winthrop Manuscripts, 30A: 102.

vii. JOHN TEMPLE WINTHROP, b. at Boston[1122] 14 May 1796,[1123] bp. at Trinity Church, Boston 18 June 1798,[1124] and d. unm. of pulmonary disease at Valparaiso, Chile 5 May 1843.[1125]

He entered Harvard in 1811, at age 15, but by the end of his freshman year had been suspended. "His father's reaction was interesting, and perhaps unique," wrote Mayo. "If anything was to be done to the boy, why make it a suspension? Why not dismissal? ... Apparently Mr. Winthrop believed in discipline and liked not this academic pussyfooting." Despite another suspension during his sophomore year for "inattention,"[1126] John managed to graduate with his class in 1815. By early 1820, he was an attorney in Boston with an office at 92 Court Street[1127] and in Feb. 1825 was admitted to the Federal bar.[1128] In 1821, he joined the Ancient and Honorable Artillery Company[1129] and the Boston Light Infantry[1130]; in 1828 he became commander of the Suffolk Brigade ("the Boston Brigade") of Militia with the rank of brigadier-general.[1131] This civic involvement led to politics; in 1826 and 1828 he was elected to the General Court as one of the Boston representatives.

[1122] Oliver Ayer Roberts, *History of the Military Company of the Massachusetts, now called The Ancient and Honorable Artillery Company of Massachusetts, 1637–1888*, 4 vols. (Boston: Alfred Mudge & Son, 1895–1901), 2: 452.

[1123] Whitmore, *Register* 10 [1857]: 77. He was named for his maternal grandfather, Sir John Temple, 8th Baronet, first of Boston, then of England and New York, who, Mayo wrote, "may have been a little too English for the Americans, and a little too American for the British taste, but he was a warm-hearted man and much beloved in the family circle" (300, citing *Collections of the Massachusetts Historical Society*, 6th series, 9 [1897]: xvii, which noted Sir John had an "impulsive temper" that "sometimes involved him in bitter controversies").

[1124] Oliver and Peabody, *The Records of Trinity Church, Boston, 1728–1830*, 56: 119. "John Temple, Francis William, Children of Thoms. L. Winthrop by Elisabeth Bowdoin Temple his wife. Mr. Winthrop & Wife."

[1125] Whitmore, *Register* 10 [1857]: 77 (date only). See *Daily National Intelligencer* (Washington, D.C.), 9 September 1843, 3. "At Valparaiso, whither he had gone for his health, being troubled with pulmonary complaints, John Temple Bowdoin Winthrop, of Boston, at the age of 47."

[1126] Mayo, *The Winthrop Family in America*, 300, citing *Harvard College Faculty Official Minutes, 1725–1890*, 8: 325, 356, 379.

[1127] *Columbian Centinel* (Boston), 12 January 1820, 4.

[1128] *Evening Post* (New York), 15 February 1825, 2.

[1129] Roberts, *History of the Military Company of the Massachusetts*, 2: 453.

[1130] *Weekly Messenger* (Boston), 16 August 1821, 2.

[1131] Roberts, *History of the Military Company of the Massachusetts*, 2: 453.

Until 1832, he lived at his father's home at Beacon and Walnut Streets,[1132] when he moved about two blocks away to Walnut and Sumner (now Mount Vernon) Streets.[1133] A year after his brother James Bowdoin died without issue in March 1833, John Temple Winthrop, "for reasons best known to himself," Mayo wrote,[1134] legally changed his name to John Temple James Bowdoin.[1135] By 1833, he had gone to Chile for his health; he may have visited or moved in Sept. 1830, when a Boston newspaper reported that "Brigadier General John Temple Winthrop had sailed from this port for Valparaiso."[1136]

viii. FRANCIS WILLIAM WINTHROP, b. 1 Dec. 1797,[1137] and bp. at Trinity Church, Boston 18 June 1798,[1138] He d. 23[1139] and was bur. at Trinity Church 25 June 1798.[1140] He presumably was named for his two uncles, Francis Bayard Winthrop and William Winthrop.

ix. (FRANCIS) WILLIAM WINTHROP, b. at Boston[1141] 31 May 1799,[1142] bp. at Trinity Church 2 Jan. 1800,[1143] and d. at Savannah, Ga. 7 March 1819.[1144] His remains were returned to Boston, where he was interred in the King's Chapel Burying Ground.[1145]

[1132] *Stimpson's Boston Directory* (Boston: Stimpson & Clapp, 1831), 339.

[1133] *Stimpson's Boston Directory* (Boston: Stimpson & Clapp, 1832), 341.

[1134] Mayo, *The Winthrop Family in America*, 301.

[1135] *Laws of the Commonwealth of Massachusetts*, Vol. 13 (Boston: Dutton & Wentworth, 1836), 121. Mayo noted that John does not appear under either name in Boston directories after 1832. See *Stimpson's Boston Directory* (Boston: Stimpson & Clapp, 1833), 88, 348.

[1136] *Boston Commercial Gazette*, 23 September 1830, 4.

[1137] Whitmore, *Register* 10 [1857]: 77.

[1138] Oliver and Peabody, *The Records of Trinity Church, Boston, 1728–1830*, 56: 119.

[1139] Whitmore, *Register* 10 [1857]: 77.

[1140] Oliver and Peabody, *The Records of Trinity Church, Boston, 1728–1830*, 56: 256. "Francis William Infant Son of Tho. L. Winthrop, 10 m."

[1141] Mayo, *The Winthrop Family in America*, 302. Mayo noted that his father, when writing, usually referred to him as Francis William, but among the family he was known as William, perhaps to avoid confusion with his cousin, Francis Bayard[7] Winthrop, Jr., who was 12 years older but of the same generation.

[1142] Whitmore, *Register* 10 [1857]: 77.

[1143] Oliver and Peabody, *The Records of Trinity Church, Boston, 1728–1830*, 56: 123. "Francis William Son of Thomas L. Winthrop by Eliza Bowdoin Temple his wife. Mr. Winthrop, Mr. Palmer, Lady Temple."

[1144] *Boston Daily Advertiser*, 22 March 1819, 2. "Died, on Sunday, the 7th inst., at Savannah, to which place he went a few months since for the benefit of his health, Mr. Francis William Winthrop, age 19; late a student in Divinity at Harvard University, and son of Thomas L. Winthrop, Esq."

[1145] *Findagrave.com* (memorial 11242899).

William Winthrop began to prepare for college at age 12 at Phillips Academy and two years later was admitted to Harvard. There he would graduate as valedictorian of his class in 1817,[1146] despite having led a minor rebellion as a sophomore against having to attend classes on the morning of Valedictory Day. On that occasion, William and five classmates skipped class and as a result were rusticated in July 1815. Six months later he was allowed to return to campus and, after an examination to make sure he was still on pace, was readmitted to Harvard in Feb. 1816.[1147] At graduation in Aug. 1817 he presented a twelve-minute English Oration, "in which the names of the benefactors of the University are to be respectfully mentioned."[1148] After graduating, he briefly read law, then returned to Harvard to study divinity.[1149] However, he suffered from tuberculosis and so, after only a few weeks in Cambridge, he retreated to Maine with his brother James to recover. His doctors next recommended he travel to Havana; instead, he set out for Darien, Georgia, about 50 miles south of Savannah, with his brother John. They sailed from Boston in Nov. 1818, but Francis got no further than Savannah,[1150] as a doctor there recounted to his father:[1151]

> After resting in comfortable lodgings, he so far recruited as to be able to ride out and even in some sort to enjoy the change. But his disease, though somewhat retarded

---

[1146] *Biographical Catalogue of the Trustees, Teachers and Students of Phillips Academy, Andover, 1778–1830* (Andover, Mass.: The Andover Press, 1903), 65. While at Harvard, he was a member of the Porcellian Club and the Deputy Master and Grand Master of the Knights of the Square Table (*Porcellian Club 1791–2016*, 79).

[1147] Mayo, *The Winthrop Family in America*, 302–3, citing *Harvard College Faculty Official Minutes, 1725–1890*, 9: 25, 49.

[1148] Mayo, *The Winthrop Family in America*, 303, citing *Harvard College Faculty Official Minutes, 1725–1890*, 9: 94, 109. Mayo notes that Francis was scheduled as the twenty-third speaker of the day, which meant he sat on the platform for three hours or more, "trying to remember his lines and hoping that he would not forget the name of a single important friend of the University. For a boy who had just turned 18 this must have been a tremendous ordeal." One pastor in attendance that day would comment, "The concluding oration of the Bachelors, by Winthrop, was well written but delivered so feebly as to be heard by a small part of the audience only" (John Pierce, "Some Notes on the Commencements at Harvard University, 1803–1848," *Proceedings of the Massachusetts Historical Society*, 2nd series, 5 [1890]: 183). The subject was "The Aspect of Revolutions on the Advancement of the Mind."

[1149] Mayo, *The Winthrop Family in America*, 304, citing Winthrop Manuscripts, 30A: 71.

[1150] Mayo, *The Winthrop Family in America*, 304.

[1151] Mayo, *The Winthrop Family in America*, 304, citing Winthrop Manuscripts, 30A: 71–75.

in its progress, advanced in the formation and discharge of ulcers in his lungs, bringing in their train the usual exhausting concomitants—till the evening of the 7 inst. the vital powers yielded and his soul rested with his God.

A few weeks before William's death, James had described his brother with admiration in a letter to a friend:[1152]

[He] graduated the year before last at Harvard University, and tho' only 17 years old, and deprived of his eyes, except for two or three hours daily, he had the first honour of the University in a class highly respectable for its talents. You may have seen a piece on the article in the *Enc. Brittanica* [*sic*] on Beauty, published in the *North American Review* in 1818,[1153] which, tho' written in great haste, and sadly mangled by the printer, does great honor to the pen of so young a man. His attack upon the opinions of Mr. Allison and Mr. Jeffries was, to say the least, unexpected. For most people received their opinions as law.[1154]

x.   JANE WINTHROP, b. 15 March,[1155] bp. at Trinity Church, Boston 20 April 1801,[1156] d. of consumption 21 Feb. 1819, age 17,[1157] and bur. at Trinity Church.[1158]

[1152] Mayo, *The Winthrop Family in America*, 305, citing Winthrop Manuscripts, 30A: 73.

[1153] *The North American Review and Miscellaneous Journal* 7 [1818]: 1–25. The author is not identified.

[1154] Archibald Alison was the author of *Essays on the Nature and Principles of Taste* (Edinburgh, 1790), cited by Francis Jeffrey in his *Britannica* entry for beauty. The latter appears in *Supplement to the Fourth, Fifth and Sixth Editions of the Encyclopædia Britannica*, 6 vols. (Edinburgh, 1824), 2: 172–97.

[1155] Whitmore, *Register* 10 [1857]: 77.

[1156] Oliver and Peabody, *The Records of Trinity Church, Boston, 1728–1830*, 56: 126. "Jane Daughter of Thomas L. Winthrop by Elisabeth B. Temple his wife. Mr. Winthrop & Wife. Lady Temple." Whitmore, *Register* 10 [1857]: 77, gives her death on 22 February.

[1157] Jane Winthrop death record, *Ancestry.com* > Massachusetts, Town and Vital Records, 1620–1988 > Boston > Birth, Marriages and Death (Provo, Utah: Holbrook Research Institute). Adlard, *The Sutton-Dudleys of England and the Dudleys of Massachusetts in New England*, 129, gives 22 February.

[1158] Oliver and Peabody, *The Records of Trinity Church, Boston, 1728–1830*, 56: 267.

xi. ANNE WINTHROP, b. 14 April,[1159] bp. at Trinity Church 19 May 1803,[1160] and d. at Boston 15 Dec. 1850.[1161] She was buried in the Warren tomb at St. Paul's Church and reinterred on 8 Aug. 1856 at Forest Hills Cemetery in Jamaica Plain (Boston).[1162] She m. 17 Oct. 1843,[1163] JOHN COLLINS WARREN, who was b. at Boston 1 Aug. 1778,[1164] the eldest of the sixteen children of Dr. John Warren, a surgeon with the Continental Army during the Revolutionary War and in 1783 the first professor of anatomy and surgery at Harvard, and Abigail (Collins) Warren.[1165] He d. at his home at 2 Park Street in Boston at about 3 a.m. on 4 May 1856, was bur. at St. Paul's,[1166] and reinterred 8 Aug. 1856 at Forest Hills.[1167]

Dr. John Collins Warren graduated from Harvard in 1797; in 1806, soon after he completed his medical studies, he was named an adjunct professor of anatomy and surgery. When his father died in 1815, he succeeded him as the Hersey Professor of Anatomy

---

[1159] Whitmore, *Register* 10 [1857]: 77. Some records give Ann.

[1160] Oliver and Peabody, *The Records of Trinity Church, Boston, 1728–1830*, 56: 131. "Ann Daughter of Thomas L. Winthrop by Elisa B. Temple his wife. Mr. Sears. Eliza & Sarah Winthrop."

[1161] Edward Warren, *The Life of John Collins Warren, M.D., Compiled Chiefly from His Autobiography and Journals*, 2 vols. (Boston: Ticknor & Fields, 1860), 2: 57. From his journal: "On the 15th of December died Mrs. Anne Warren, the daughter of Governor Winthrop [*sic*]. Her health had always been feeble, anhd she was for many years under the professional charge of the subject of his Memoir before their marriage took place (in October 1843, as mentioned in the Journal). Dr. Warren's house was again left desolate." Whitmore, *Register* 10 [1857]: 77, gives 16 December.

[1162] Samuel A. Forman, *Dr. Joseph Warren: The Boston Tea Party, Bunker Hill and the Birth of American Liberty* (Gretna, La.: Pelican Publishing, 2011), 362, citing the journal of Dr. John Collins Warren.

[1163] Journal of John Collins Warren, John Collins Warren Papers, Vol. 81, Massachusetts Historical Society. "Oct. 18—Last evening took place the celebration of my union with Miss Anne Winthrop. The ceremony was at a quarter before 9 and we left a quarter after 10. The entertainment by Mr. Winthrop was magnificent and the company most happy. To describe the anticipations that arise in my mind on this event would pass the power of my expression." A transcription gives, in error, "October 18—Married Miss Anne Winthrop."

[1164] Warren, *The Life of John Collins Warren*, 1: 1.

[1165] John Collins Warren, *Genealogy of Warren and Some Historical Sketches* (Boston: John Wilson and Son, 1854), 49–50. See also Thomas Warren, *A History and Genealogy of the Warren Family* (London: the author, 1902), 365–66.

[1166] *Daily Atlas* (Boston), 5 May 1856, 2. See also Deaths in Boston, in Massachusetts Vital and Town Records (Provo, Utah: Holbrook Research Institute), at *ancestry.com* > Massachusetts, Town and Vital Records, 1620–1988 > Boston > Deaths, 1856. "John C. Warren, age 77 years 9 months, d. at 2 Park St., physician, b. Boston, son of John and Abigail Warren, bur. St. Paul's, removed to Forest Hills 8 Aug. 1856."

[1167] *Findagrave.com* (memorial 56332914).

and Surgery, a position he held for the next thirty-two years, until his retirement in 1847. He was involved in the first surgical use of ether as an anesthesia when, on 16 Oct. 1846, he gave permission to a dentist to apply it to a patient while Warren performed surgery on a tumor on a patient's neck.[1168] He also co-founded in Jan. 1812 what is today the prestigious *New England Journal of Medicine*, served as president of the American Medical Association, was the first dean of the Harvard Medical School, and a founding member of the Massachusetts General Hospital.[1169] His medical interest was such that, in 1855 he had the remains of his father and his uncle, General Joseph Warren, who had been killed at the battle of Bunker Hill in 1775, disinterred from the family crypt and the skulls taken to his house on Park Street, where he studied and photographed them.[1170] After his retirement, he focused on his interest in natural history, serving as the president of the Boston Society of Natural History and writing a book on the American Mastadon, a skeleton of which he owned.[1171] Warren had six children who survived him by his first wife, Susan Powell Mason (who d. in 1841),[1172] but no issue by Anne Winthrop, who was 40 when they married.[1173]

[1168] Warren, *The Life of John Collins Warren*, 1: 381, 384–86. There was controversy surrounding the procedure, chiefly because the dentist, William Morton, wanted to keep the nature of his discovery secret so he could profit. But for Dr. Warren, using a secret or unknown patent medicine in an operation (in this case applied by holding a sponge to the patient's nose) was unethical. Warren refused to do more operations until Morton revealed the nature of the substance; three weeks later, he invited Morton to attend a more serious operation, a low-thigh amputation, and the pressure of wanting to take part apparently compelled him to reveal that it was pure unadulterated sulfuric ether and not a miracle drug he had been calling Letheon. See Francis D. Moore, "John Collins Warren and His Act of Conscience," *Annals of Surgery* 229 [1999]: 187–96.

[1169] *John Collins Warren Papers, 1738–1926, Guide to the Collection*, Massachusetts Historical Society, *masshist.org/collection-guides/view/fa0183*.

[1170] Forman, *Dr. Joseph Warren*, 361–63. Three months after John's death in May 1856, his son Dr. Jonathan Mason Warren had his father's remains moved in a heavy rain from the St. Paul crypt to one at Forest Hills, along with the bodies (and skulls) of his grandfather, great-uncle, mother, and stepmother Anne (Winthrop) Warren.

[1171] John C. Warren, *The Mastodon Giganteus of North America*, 2nd ed. (Boston: John Wilson and Son, 1855), 5–8. The skeleton had been unearthed in Newburgh, N.Y., in the summer of 1845, exhibited for three or four months, and then purchased by Warren. He had it assembled and displayed "in a fire-proof structure, erected January 1849, for its reception in Chestnut Street, Boston." A Boston newspaper noted "his museum of specimens in comparative anatomy, osteology and paleontology, including probably the most perfect specimen in existence of the *mastadon giganteus*, is undoubtedly one of the richest private collections in the world" (*Daily Atlas*, 5 May 1856, 2).

[1172] Her younger sister Miriam Clarke Mason married David[7] Sears [No. 13] in 1809.

[1173] *Daily Atlas* (Boston), 5 May 1856, 2.

xii. GEORGE EDWARD WINTHROP, b. at Boston[1174] 15 June 1805[1175] and d. unm. at Somerville, Mass., presumably at the McLean Asylum, on 30 Aug. 1875.[1176]

When he was 12, his father sent George to Phillips Academy, where three of his older brothers had studied,[1177] although none were there when he arrived in 1817. He left Andover after a year and probably had a tutor, because by 1822 he was a sophomore at Harvard.[1178] He graduated in 1825, studied law in the office of Daniel Webster[1179] (then serving in Congress), and added a Master of Arts from Harvard in 1828.[1180] Although the *Boston Directory* of 1835 lists him as a "counsellor" with an office at 17 Court Street,[1181] his brother Robert wrote in a letter in June 1836, to Massachusetts Gov. Edward Everett, that George "never took means to be admitted to any higher degree" in the legal profession, such as justice of the peace: "As he is now the only son permanently residing at home, it would be a convenience to my Father if it were in his power to take acknowledgements of deeds, etc. & were there now any regular steps of admission as Attorney & Counsellor of the Supreme Court, he would gladly go through them to this end."[1182]

Some two years later, probably around Oct. 1838, Robert wrote the governor again, labeling the letter "private" and reporting that "about four years ago, my brother George was taken down with typhus fever—from which he did not recover until after one or two relapses—and throughout his illness, as is not unusual in such cases,

---

[1174] Mayo, *The Winthrop Family in America*, 306.

[1175] Whitmore, *Register* 10 [1857]: 77.

[1176] *Boston Evening Transcript*, 31 August 1875, 5. "Winthrop—At Somerville, 30th inst., after many years' illness, George Edward Winthrop, 70 yrs."

[1177] *Biographical Catalogue of Trustees, Teachers and Students of Phillips Academy*, 92.

[1178] Mayo, *The Winthrop Family in America*, 306. He noted that George may have been a freshman the previous year but enrolled too late to be included in the catalog printed in October. He was a member of the Knights of the Square Table with his class (*Porcellian Club 1791–2016*, 85).

[1179] Mayo, *The Winthrop Family in America*, 307, citing Robert C. Winthrop to Edward Everett, 22 June 1836, Edward Everett Papers (reel 6), Massachusetts Historical Society.

[1180] Mayo, *The Winthrop Family in America*, 307, notes that "this could be done without further residence at the University and without any effort on his part except going to the exercises on Commencement Day," which he did when his younger brother, Robert Charles Winthrop, graduated.

[1181] *Stimpson's Boston Directory* (Boston: Stimpson & Clapp, 1835), 385.

[1182] Robert C. Winthrop to Edward Everett, 22 June 1836, Edward Everett Papers, Massachusetts Historical Society.

his brain was considerably affected. Dr. Warren prophecied at the
time no very speedy or sure recovery from this part of the malady."
After extended trips to Europe and within the United States, he
seemed better, Robert wrote, but "now again, this very autumn
and within a month past the malady has returned again, and with
his own consent he has become an inmate in the Institution in
question," which was McLean Asylum.[1183]

xiii.   GRENVILLE TEMPLE WINTHROP, b. at Boston[1184] 23 March,[1185] bp.
        at Trinity Church, Boston 25 July 1807,[1186] and d. at his home in
        Cambridge or Watertown, Mass. 14 Sept. 1852.[1187] He m. at King's
        Chapel, Boston 27 March 1831, FRANCES MARIA HEARD,[1188] who
        was b. ca. 1808,[1189] dau. of John and Susan (Oliver) Heard,[1190]

[1183] Mayo, *The Winthrop Family in America*, 307–8, citing Robert C. Winthrop to Edward
Everett, about October 1838, Edward Everett Papers, Massachusetts Historical
Society.

[1184] Mayo, *The Winthrop Family in America*, 309.

[1185] Whitmore, *Register* 10 [1857]: 77. Mayo noted he was presumably named for his
maternal uncle, Sir Greenville Temple, 9th Baronet (76).

[1186] Oliver and Peabody, *The Records of Trinity Church, Boston, 1728–1830*, 56: 140.
"Grenville Temple, son of Thomas Winthrop & wife. Sp. Eliza Winthrop. Thomas
Winthrop, Jr. & David Sears, Jr."

[1187] *Boston Evening Transcript*, 17 September 1852, 2. "At his residence in Cambridge,
14th inst., in the 46th year of his age, Grenville Temple Winthrop, Esq., son of the late
Lieut. Governor Winthrop." Other obituaries give the place of death as Watertown,
Massachusetts, and in the 1840 (roll 189, 63) and 1850 (roll M432_326, 356B)
censuses he lived there with his wife and children.

[1188] Arnold, *Vital Record of Rhode Island, 1636–1850, First Series*, 20: 490. "Grenville
Temple Winthrop, son of Lieutenant-Governor Winthrop, and Frances Maria
Heard, youngest daughter of John, Jr., at Boston, by Rev. Mr. Greenwood, March
27, 1831." See also Dunkle and Lainhart, "The Records of Baptisms, Marriages
and Deaths, The King's Chapel, Boston," in *Records of the Churches of Boston*, 390. In
July 1866, Mrs. Francis Henry Gray entertained the Winthrops' daughter Elizabeth
Winthrop Hooker at her house on Beacon Hill: "Another hot day. Mrs. J. C. Hooker
. . . came here yest'y for 3 days. A brisk, lively, entertaining woman unaffected and
sincere in manner, who has seen a good deal of life & the world. . . . She is the eldest
child of the Grenville Winthrops—the circumstances of whose marriage made such
a talk years & years ago" (entry for 13 July 1866: Hedwiga Regina Shober Gray
diary, R. Stanton Avery Special Collections, New England Historic Genealogical
Society).

[1189] England and Wales Civil Registration Indexes (London: General Register Office),
at *ancestry.com*, citing Isle of Wight Registration District, Volume 2B, 377, says she
d. 1878 at age 70. The 1850 U.S. Census, Watertown, Mass. (roll M432_326, 356B),
gives her age as 39 (born about 1811).

[1190] Andrew Johonnot, "The Johonnot Family," *Register* 7 [1853]: 144.

and had issue. She d. at Ryde on the Isle of Wight, Hampshire, England[1191] 10 Sept. 1878,[1192] and was bur. in Ryde Cemetery.[1193]

Grenville Temple Winthrop attended the Boston Latin School,[1194] but instead of enrolling at Harvard or Bowdoin chose Columbia in New York City, the first of the Boston family to do so, although who or what influenced his decision is not clear.[1195] He graduated in 1827 and returned to Boston in 1828 where, like his brother John, he read law and joined military organizations[1196] such as the Independent Company of Cadets. Around the New Year in 1832, he was ordered to parade his company on Election Day (4 Jan.) to the State House at noon and escort the governor and the two houses of legislators to the Old South Church. When he arrived with his men, he was told to return in a half hour.[1197] They did, but he would later write that after waiting an additional 15 or 20 minutes, he was "compelled by the intensity of the cold to march the company about town for exercise. . . . I continued to wait until the members of the company informed me 'that they could not handle their muskets,' that 'their fingers had lost all feeling.'" He left a man in the church to alert him when the service ended, then took his men to the basement of the Exchange Coffee House.[1198] "The net result of all this was that when the sermon was finally over and the governor and the rest of the notables emerged from the auditorium, Colonel Winthrop and his Cadets were nowhere to be seen," Mayo wrote. They ended up marching behind the

---

[1191] *Proceedings of the Massachusetts Historical Society* 17 [1879], 102.

[1192] Memorial plaque, St. John's Church, Ryde, Isle of Wight. See *isle-of-wight-fhs. co.uk/mis_bis/mis_ ryde_st_john_church.html*. Photo and transcript by Geoff Allan. It reads: "To the glory of God and in memory of Frances Maria Winthrop (widow of Grenville Temple Winthrop and daughter of the late John Heard, Chief Judge of the Courts of Probate and Divorce of Massachusetts) who died Sept. 10ᵗʰ 1878. The north aisle of this church was erected by her children 1879."

[1193] F.M. Winthrop stone, Ryde Cemetery, photo by Janette Gregson at *rshg.org.uk/ graves/mrs-frances-maria-winthrop*. "FM Winthrop, died 27ᵗʰ Sept. 1878." Her daughter Charlotte Anne⁸ Winthrop was buried under the same stone.

[1194] Jenks, *Catalogue of the Boston Public Latin School*, 163 (appendix).

[1195] Mayo, *The Winthrop Family in America*, 309.

[1196] Roberts, *History of the Ancient and Honorable Artillery Company*, 3: 108–9.

[1197] *Trial by a Court Martial of Lieut. Col. Grenville Temple Winthrop on Charges Preferred Against Him by Adjutant Gen. William H. Sumner in Pursuance of Orders from His Excellency Levi Lincoln, Governor of the Commonwealth of Massachusetts* (Boston: Carter, Hendee & Co., 1832), 16, 123–24.

[1198] *Trial by a Court Martial of Lieut. Col. Grenville Temple Winthrop*, 141–42.

governor, who had angrily set out on foot and waved off his escort when it caught up with him.[1199] By the end of the day, Grenville Winthrop had been arrested on charges of "disobedience of orders, neglect of duty and unmilitary and unofficer-like conduct" in the performance of escort duties to the governor.[1200] His trial began on 5 March 1832 and continued for about six weeks.[1201] He was found guilty on all counts and sentenced to be reprimanded.[1202] In response, Grenville paid to have a transcript of the proceedings printed as a book of 456 pages with his own "cogent, albeit sarcastic" preface, per Mayo.[1203]

The public response was supportive; voters elected him to the Common Council of Boston that year and re-elected him twice thereafter. In 1833, he was elected to the Ancient and Honorable Artillery Company, in 1835 he commanded the Independent Boston Fusiliers and he also served as brigadier general of the Suffolk Brigade.[1204] He moved to Watertown before the 1840 U.S. census,[1205] and after 1844 his name no longer appears in the *Boston Directory*, suggesting he had retired. But Mayo noted in the summer of 1845 Grenville wrote his friend George Bancroft, then Secretary of the Navy, to see if he might mention his name to the President for an Army commission for the impending fight against Mexico. During his sixteen years in the militia, Grenville noted, "I have not been content to be acquainted with the unimportant ceremonies pertaining to parade occasions; but have devoted a considerable part of my time to the study of the standard treatises on Artillery, Fortifications, etc., etc."[1206]

Following Grenville's death in 1852, his widow moved to the Isle of Wight with her son, where she collected autographs,

---

[1199] Mayo, *The Winthrop Family in America*, 310–11. In 1835, John Holloway dedicated a march to Grenville he called "Winthrop's Quick Step"; Mayo noted the apparently unintentional irony (312).

[1200] *Trial by a Court Martial of Lieut. Col. Grenville Temple Winthrop*, 1.

[1201] Mayo, *The Winthrop Family in America*, 311–12.

[1202] *Trial by a Court Martial of Lieut. Col. Grenville Temple Winthrop*, 443.

[1203] Mayo, *The Winthrop Family in America*, 312. He noted that an anonymous "farcical variant of the episode" appeared as "Reminiscences of a Retired Militia Officer," in *New-England Magazine* 3 [1832]: 53–57.

[1204] Roberts, *History of the Ancient and Honorable Artillery Company*, 3: 108–9.

[1205] 1840 U.S. Census, Watertown, Mass., roll 189, 63.

[1206] Grenville Winthrop to George Bancroft, 16 August 1845, George Bancroft Papers 1816–1890 (Massachusetts Historical Society).

and her collection expanded to include many royal and imperial signatures because she happened to share the same doctor with Queen Victoria's youngest son, Prince Leopold, a fellow collector. After her death, the collection was given by her request to the Massachusetts Historial Society and is now part of the Winthrop Family Papers.[1207]

14 xiv. ROBERT CHARLES WINTHROP, b. at Boston 12 May 1809; m. (1) 12 March 1832, ELIZABETH CABOT BLANCHARD; m. (2) 6 Nov. 1849, ELIZABETH LAURA (DERBY) WELLES; m. (3) 15 Nov. 1865, CORNELIA ADELINE (GRANGER) THAYER.

[1207] See Reel 39 and bound volumes 48–52 in Winthrop Family Papers, Massachusetts Historical Society, as well as *Proceedings of the Massachusetts Historical Society* 17 [1879], 101–2. Robert C. Winthrop: "On our table this morning, Gentlemen, there are five large volumes, and two or three smaller parcels, of interesting and valuable autographs. They are a collection made by Mrs. Frances Maria Winthrop, the widow of my elder brother, Grenville Temple Winthrop, and a daughter of the late Hon. John Heard, for many years Judge of Probate for Suffolk County. Mrs. Winthrop died during the past year at Ryde, in the Isle of Wight, where she resided, as an invalid, with her only son, Thomas Lindall Winthrop, for many years past. She had occupied and amused herself, while she was able to do so, in procuring and arranging these autographs, and had enjoyed some peculiar opportunities of obtaining not a few which were out of the common road or reach of collectors. It happened that during the earlier part of her residence in the Isle of Wight, at Cowes, not far from Osborne, she had the same physician who was in attendance on the young Prince Leopold. The prince being desirous to obtain some American autographs for his own collection, many exchanges were made between him and Mrs. Winthrop through the intervention of their common physician. . . . A large part of them are not mere signatures, but letters and documents of literary and historical interest, and in most cases there is a portrait, engraved or photographed, of the writer." A transcript of a chatty letter written to Mrs. Winthrop on 13 December 1867 by Henry Wadsworth Longfellow, after she wrote two weeks earlier to request his autograph on behalf of Prince Leopold, can be found in Andrew Hilen, ed., *The Letters of Henry Wadsworth Longfellow*, 6 vols. (Cambridge, Mass.: Harvard University Press, 1982), 5: 193.

The Seventh Generation

12. Thomas Charles[7] **Winthrop** (*Francis Bayard*[6], *John Still*[5], *John*[4], *Waitstill*[3], *John*[2-1]) was born at New York, New York 13 June 1797[1208] and died there 31 May 1873.[1209] He was buried with his wife at Green-Wood Cemetery in Brooklyn, New York.[1210] He married at the Reformed Dutch Church, New York 27 September 1823,[1211] **Georgiana Maria Kane**, who was born in New York ca. 1806,[1212] the daughter of John and Maria (Codwise) Kane.[1213] She died at New York 1 August 1863.[1214]

Thomas Charles Winthrop did not attend college. In the spring of 1817, when he was nearly 20, he sailed from New York to Liverpool

---

[1208] Adlard, *The Sutton-Dudleys of England and the Dudleys of Massachusetts in New England*, 127.

[1209] *The New York Times*, 4 June 1873, 5. "Died . . . on Saturday, May 31, Thomas Charles Winthrop, agd 76 years. The relatives and friends of the family are respectfully invited to attend the funeral, from the Church of the Annunciation, West Fourteenth street, on Thursday morning, June 5, at 9:30 o'clock."

[1210] Thomas C. Winthrop burial record, per database at *green-wood.com*. Buried 5 June 1873, lot 15764, section 99; Georgianna M. Winthrop burial record, per database at *green-wood.com*. Buried 7 May 1866, lot 15674, section 169.

[1211] Dutch Reformed Church, New York City, Marriages, Book 32, Holland Society of New York, accessed at *ancestry.com*, image 92 of 152. 27 September 1823. Thomas Charles Winthrop & Georgiana Maria Kane. See also *Evening Post* (New York), 27 September 1823. "Married this morning, by [the bride's brother-in-law] the Rev. Paschal N. Strong, Thomas Charles Winthrop, Esq., to Miss Georgianna Maria Kane, daughter of the late John Kane, Esquire."

[1212] J. Walter Wood, *William Wood (Born 1656) of Earlsferry, Scotland, and Some of His Descendants and Their Connections* (New Haven, Conn.: Tuttle, Morehouse & Taylor Co., 1916), 11. The 1850 U.S. Census, Ward 16, District 1, roll M432_553, 182A, gives her age as 44 and birthplace in New York.

[1213] Wood, *William Wood (Born 1656) of Earlsferry, Scotland*, 11. Georgiana's first cousin Cornelia Rutsen Van Rensselaer was the mother of Cornelia Adeline (Granger) Thayer, who married Robert Charles[7] Winthrop [No. 14] in 1865.

[1214] *The New York Times*, 3 August 1863, 5. "Winthrop.—In this City, on Saturday, Aug. 1, after a short, but painful illness, Georgiana, wife of Thomas Charles Winthrop, and daughter of the late John Kane. The relatives and friends of the family are requested to attend the funeral, at Trinity Church, on Tuesday afternoon, the 4th inst., at 3½ o'clock."

for what was apparently a coming-of-age tour of Europe.[1215] "His uncle
Thomas, up in Boston, expressed the hope that Charles [as his family
called him] would keep a journal of his travels, but whether he did so is
a question," Mayo wrote. "The fact is, we know little about the young
man until the autumn of 1823," when he married.[1216] A decade later
Thomas was established as a commission merchant at 220 Pearl Street
and living at 29 Bond Street in New York. By 1836 the couple lived
at 25 Hubert Street, but by 1845 they had moved to West Fourteenth
Street, where they resided for about twenty-five years at No. 119, before
Charles moved a final time, in 1868, as a widower, to No. 153. His office,
meanwhile, moved at least five times until he retired about 1859.[1217]

In 1850, the family was living in Ward 16, District 1; Thomas C.
was a "gentleman"; son Charles F. Winthrop, 23, a lawyer; and son
Robert Winthrop, 16, a bank clerk.[1218] In 1855, Charles F. Winthrop
was the head of household with his brothers Robert, 22, Grenville, 18,
and Frederick, 16, all brokers.[1219] The family seems to have not been
recorded in New York City in the 1860 census, although Thomas C.
Winthrop, 64, born in New York, gentleman, was residing alone on
a farm at Oyster Bay, Long Island, overseeing an Irish farmer and his
family and ten farmhands.[1220] By 1870, at age 73, widower Thomas C.
Winthrop was back in Ward 16 as a retired merchant of dry goods,
with Charles F., 42, and Clarence, 21 (both clerks); Gertrude, 28; Maria
A. (Winthrop) Robinson, 40, and her three daughters (Georgiana, 14,
Harriet, 12, and Gertrude, 9); and three servants.[1221]

Children of Thomas Charles[7] and Georgiana Maria (Kane) Winthrop:

    i.   CHARLES FRANCIS[8] WINTHROP, b. at New York[1222] 20 March
        1827,[1223] d. at Paris, France 16 Feb. 1898,[1224] and bur. at Green-Wood

---

[1215] Mayo, *The Winthrop Family in America*, 278, citing Winthrop Manuscripts, 30A: 71.

[1216] Mayo, *The Winthrop Family in America*, 278.

[1217] Mayo, *The Winthrop Family in America*, 278.

[1218] 1850 U.S. Census, Ward 16, District 1, roll M432_553, 182A.

[1219] 1855 New York State census, New York City, Ward 16, E.D.5

[1220] 1860 U.S. Census, Oyster Bay, Queens Co., N.Y., roll M653_844, 17. He was there
in 1850 as well, but only on the agricultural census (archive 6, roll 6, 53).

[1221] 1870 U.S. Census, New York, N.Y., Ward 16, District 1, roll M595_995, 78B.

[1222] Mayo, *The Winthrop Family in America*, 279.

[1223] Adlard, *The Sutton-Dudleys of England and the Dudleys of Massachusetts in New
England*, 127.

[1224] *The New York Times*, 17 February 1898, 7. "Winthrop.–At Paris, France, on
Wednesday, Feb. 16, Charles Francis Winthrop, in his 71st year."

Cemetery in Brooklyn.[1225] He m. at St. James's Church, London, England 5 Nov. 1887,[1226] GERTRUDE CLEVELAND WATERBURY, who was b. at Williamsburg, N.Y. (now part of Brooklyn) 21 Dec. 1845, dau. of Lawrence and Caroline Antoinette (Cleveland) Waterbury, and widow of Elliott Johnston.[1227] She d. at Menton (Provence), France 8 Dec. 1926.[1228] Charles attended Yale College from 1841 to 1843 and was a lawyer in New York City.[1229]

    ii.   MARIA ANTOINETTE WINTHROP, b. 29 May 1830[1230] and named for her maternal aunt, Maria Antoinette (Kane) (Hone) de Peyster.[1231] She d. at New York 20 Aug. 1873.[1232] Maria m. 3 Jan. 1855,[1233] HENRY BARCLAY ROBINSON, who was b. 12 April 1816, son of Morris and Henrietta Elizabeth (Duer) Robinson, and had issue.[1234] He d. at New York 26 Dec. 1863.[1235]

[1225] Charles F. Winthrop burial record, per database at *green-wood.com*. Buried 8 March 1898, lot 15674, section 99.

[1226] Marriage Record, No. 49, scan of original from Westminster Archives accessed at *findmypast.com*. Charles Francis Winthrop ("single") and Gertrude Cleveland Johnston ("unmarried"), dau. Laurence Waterbury. Charles resided in New York at time of the marriage, and Gertrude lived in St. James' parish.

[1227] George B. Kinkead, "Gilbert² Livingston and Some of his Descendants," *Record* 87 [1956]: 239. Lawrence Waterbury was the head of Lawrence Waterbury & Co., makers of cordage. Gertrude and Elliott Johnston had three children, 1871–73, all born abroad. Elliott died after 1881, when the couple moved to New York City. Kinkead does not mention her marriage to Charles Winthrop.

[1228] *The New York Times*, 11 December 1926, 17. "Winthrop—On Dec. 8, 1926, at Menton, France, Gertrude C. Waterbury, wife of the late Charles Francis Winthrop."

[1229] Mayo, *The Winthrop Family in America*, 279.

[1230] R. Burnham Moffat, *The Barclays of New York: Who They Are and Who They Are Not—and Some Other Barclays* (New York: Robert Grier Cooke, 1904), citing Records of St. James Church, New York. Also, Mayo, *The Winthrop Family in America*, 279.

[1231] Dutch Reformed Church Records, New York City, Vol. 2, Book 34, *ancestry.com*, image 372 of 436. Maria Antoinette Kane, dau. John Kane and Maria Codwise, b. 22 May, bp. 30 Sept. 1798.

[1232] *New York Herald*, 21 August 1873. "Died . . . on Wednesday afternoon, August 20, Maria A., widow of Henry Barclay Robinson and daughter of the late Thomas Charles Winthrop. The relatives and friends of the family are respectfully invited to attend her funeral, from the Church of the Annunciation, West Fourteenth street, on Saturday morning, at ten o'clock." Moffat, *The Barclays of New York*, 131, errs with 20 August 1875.

[1233] Mayo, *The Winthrop Family in America*, 279.

[1234] Moffat, *The Barclays of New York*, 117, 131. Henry m. (1) in 1845, Catherine Elisabeth Hudson.

[1235] Registers of Deaths, Vols. 39–41 (1863–64), in Manhattan Death Registers, 1795–1865, indexed at *familysearch.org/ark:/61903/1:1:2WHW-3LG*. Henry B. Robinson died 26 December 1863.

15   iii.   ROBERT WINTHROP, b. at New York 18 Aug. 1833; m. 23 June 1859,
               KATHARINE WILSON TAYLOR.

        iv.   GRENVILLE WINTHROP, b. 19 Feb. 1837[1236] and named for both his
               father's first cousin, Grenville Temple Winthrop of Boston,[1237] and
               his mother's brother Oliver Grenville Kane of New York. He d. at
               Pau (Béarn), France 6 March 1869.[1238] He m. at 82 Fifth Avenue,
               New York 11 June 1861, ELIZABETH VAN SCHAICK ODDIE,[1239] who
               was b. ca. 1841, dau. of William B. and Mary (Van Schaick) Oddie,
               and had issue.[1240] She d. at New York 25 Feb. 1916.[1241]

               Grenville Winthrop did not attend college but went into
               business; when the Civil War broke out, he was a broker at 49
               Exchange Place and living at the family home on West Fourteenth
               Street. He and his wife lived at 26 East Thirty-third Street; after the
               war, his firm became Grenville Winthrop & Co.[1242]

        v.   FREDERICK WINTHROP, b. at New York[1243] 3 Aug. 1839.[1244] He was
               killed at the Battle of Five Forks, Dinwiddie Co., Va. on 1 April
               1865, unm., and interred a year later at Green-Wood Cemetery.[1245]

[1236] Adlard, *The Sutton-Dudleys of England and the Dudleys of Massachusetts in New England*, 127.

[1237] Mayo, *The Winthrop Family in America*, 383.

[1238] *New York Herald*, 9 March 1869, 8. "At Pau, France, on Saturday, March 6, Grenville Winthrop, of this city, in the 33d year of his age."

[1239] *The New York Times*, 13 June 1861, 5. "Married . . . on Tuesday, June 11, at the residence of Myndert Van Schaick, by Rev. Dr. Hutton, Grenville Winthrop to Elizabeth Van Schaick Oddie." According to H. Wilson, comp., *Trow's New York (City) Directory* (New York: John F. Trow, 1860), 875, Myndert Vanschaick lived at 82 Fifth Avenue; he was the bride's grandfather (Reynolds, *Genealogical and Family History of Southern New York*, 3: 1440). Lily (Oddie) Winthrop was also the great-niece of Georgiana Maria (Kane) Winthrop's brother-in-law John Hone.

[1240] Mayo, *The Winthrop Family in America*, 384. See also Reynolds, *Genealogical and Family History of Southern New York*, 3: 1440.

[1241] *The New York Times*, 27 February 1916, 17. "On Feb. 25, 1916, of pneumonia, at her residence, Elizabeth Van Schaick Oddie, widow of the late Granville Winthrop. Funeral services at the West Park Presbyterian Church, 86th St., and Amsterdam Av. on Monday, Feb. 28, at 2:30 p.m. Interment private." See also *Index to New York City Deaths 1862–1948* (*ancestry.com*), Certificate Number 6580, age 75.

[1242] Mayo, *The Winthrop Family in America*, 383–84.

[1243] Mayo, *The Winthrop Family in America*, 384.

[1244] Adlard, *The Sutton-Dudleys of England and the Dudleys of Massachusetts in New England*, 127. Perhaps he was named for his mother's brother-in-law, Frederic de Peyster, who married Maria Antoinette (Kane) Hone in November 1839.

[1245] Gen. Frederick Winthrop burial record, per database at *green-wood.com*. Interred 7 May 1866, lot 15674, section 169. See also *Findagrave.com* (memorial 28079177). He was buried initially in the de Peyster family vault at Trinity Church (Wexler, *Reared in a Greenhouse*, 43).

When the Civil War broke out, Frederick Winthrop was a 21-year-old private in the 71st Regiment of the New York State Militia, "a somewhat elite organization that made a point of keeping itself 'exclusively American'—that is to say, free from the foreign-born element in New York City," Mayo wrote. "It called itself 'The American Guard.'"[1246] On 20 April 1861, the regiment assembled at its armory, then left for Washington, D.C., where it spent three months training before taking part in July 1861 in northern Virginia in the first battle of Bull Run, in which the Union was routed by a smaller Confederate force. The regiment was released from duty on 30 July 1861,[1247] but Frederick enrolled in the regular Army and on 26 Oct. 1861 was commissioned a captain in the 12th Regiment of the U.S. Infantry.[1248] He took part in a number of important battles, including the Seven Days' battle, the second battle of Bull Run, Antietam, and Fredericksburg (all in 1862), Gettysburg (1863), and White Oak Road and Five Forks (1865). He was promoted after his gallantry during fighting near Petersburg, Va., on 19 Aug. 1864, when the responsibility to lead the First Brigade fell to him after his commanding officer was captured,[1249] and by 1 Nov. 1864 he had been appointed Brevet Briadier General, U.S. Volunteers.[1250]

On 1 April 1865, Winthrop and his brigade moved from a point 2 miles north of Dinwiddie Courthouse to support Major General Philip Sheridan, as the latter attacked the far right of the Confederate line. As the men pressed down a hill to the edge of a swamp they discovered the enemy hidden in the undergrowth; the Union brigade charged and took some thousand prisoners with only four casualties: one officer and three men. Sadly, the officer was Frederick Winthrop,[1251] who became the last Union general

---

[1246] Mayo, *The Winthrop Family in America*, 385.

[1247] Augustus Theodore Francis, comp., *History of the 71st Regiment, N.G., N.Y.* (New York: The Veterans Association, 1919), 203.

[1248] Thomas H.S. Hamersly, comp., "Registers of the Army, 1815–1879," 871, in *Complete Regular Army Register of the United States for One Hundred Years (1779–1879)* (Washington, D.C.: T.H.S. Hamersly, 1881).

[1249] "Report[s] of Bvt. Brig. Gen. Frederick Winthrop," in *Official Records of the Union and Confederate Armies*, First Series (Washington, D.C.: National Archives, 1959), 42 (Part 1): 472–77. On 31 October 1864, Frederick was recommended to a board to give names to past battles and determine if they were important enough to inscribe on regiment battle flags (42 [Part 3]: 449).

[1250] Hamersly, *Complete Regular Army Register*, 925.

[1251] *Official Records*, First Series, 46 (Part 1): 840, 869–72. In his memoir *The Passing of the Armies* (New York: G.P. Putnam's Sons, 1915), Brevet Major-General Joshua

to die in battle. (General Lee surrendered to General Grant at Appomattox Court House eight days later.)

The *New York World* reported:[1252]

> He was riding along the breastworks, and in the act as I am assured of saving a friend's life, was shot through the left lung. He fell at once, and his men who loved him, gathered around and took him tenderly to the rear, where he died before the stretcher on which he lay could be deposited before the meeting-house door. On the way from the field to the hospital he wandered in his mind at times, crying out, "Captain Weaver how is that line? Has the attack succeeded, etc." When he had been resuscitated for a pause, he said: "Doctor, am I done for?" His last words were: "Straighten the line." And he died peacefully.

In 1867, Frederick Winthrop was posthumously promoted to Major General, retroactive to the day of his death.[1253]

  vi.   GERTRUDE WINTHROP, b. 7 April 1842,[1254] d. unm. at New York 20 March 1907,[1255] and bur. at Green-Wood Cemetery.[1256]

 vii.   EUGENE WINTHROP, b. 7 June 1844,[1257] d. unm. at New York 27 Jan. 1893,[1258] and bur. at Green-Wood Cemetery.[1259] He was a longtime

---

Lawrence Chamberlain recalled sharing a quick meal with Gen. Winthrop about a half hour before his colleague was shot dead. "We sat there on a log, close behind the lines, and acted host and guest, while he opened his heart to me as men sometimes will quite differently from their common custom, under the shadow of a forecasting presence" (123–24).

[1252] Wexler, *Reared in a Greenhouse*, 42, citing the *World*, 5 April 1865. Winthrop's aide-de-camp added details in a letter of 15 April: "He was in pain all the time. He would call out to me in his pain and ask if any cared for him now, and he seemed grateful to me for remaining with him. He would seize my hand, squeeze it, and press it to his lips. . . . He died [about two hours later] easily and as a soldier dies" (Wexler, *Reared in a Greenhouse*, 42–43).

[1253] James Grant Wilson and John Fiske, eds., *Appleton's Cyclopædia of American Biography*, 6 vols. (New York: D. Appleton and Co., 1889), 6: 578.

[1254] Mayo, *The Winthrop Family in America*, 279.

[1255] *Index to New York City Deaths 1862–1948* (*ancestry.com*), Certificate Number 9862, age 61.

[1256] Gertrude Winthrop burial record, per database at *green-wood.com*. Buried 22 March 1907, lot 15674, section 99.

[1257] Mayo, *The Winthrop Family in America*, 279.

[1258] *New York Times*, 28 January 1893, 5. "Died . . . on Friday, Jan. 27, 1893, of pneumonia, Eugene, son of the late Thomas Charles Winthrop, in the 49th year of his age. Funeral services will be held at Grace Church at 2:30 o'clock, Sunday, the 29th inst."

[1259] Eugene Winthrop burial record, per database at *green-wood.com*. Buried 29 January 1893, lot 15674, section 99.

member of the banking firm of Drexel, Harjes and Co. in Paris,[1260] in effect holding the position that the Morgan firm had once offered to his brother Robert (*see below*).

viii. CLARENCE WINTHROP, b. 9 Aug. 1848,[1261] d. unm. at New York 28 April 1873[1262] (about a month before his father), and bur. at Green-Wood Cemetery.[1263]

13. **DAVID**[7] **SEARS** (*Anne*[6] *Winthrop, John Still*[5]*, John*[4]*, Waitstill*[3]*, John*[2-1]) was born at Boston, Massachusetts 8 October 1787 and died at 42 Beacon Street, Boston 14 January 1871.[1264] He married at Trinity Church, Boston 13 June 1809,[1265] **MIRIAM CLARKE MASON**, who died at 42 Beacon Street 1 September 1870 aged 81, daughter of Jonathan Mason, U.S. Senator from Massachusetts, and Susan (Powell) Mason.[1266]

The second David Sears prepared for college at the Boston Latin School; he entered Harvard in 1803 and graduated in 1807. (At the time of his death, he was one of only three survivors of the class.)[1267] In 1809,

---

[1260] Mayo, *The Winthrop Family in America*, 279. See also *New York Times*, 23 December 1888, 5, in which he was identified as "Mr. Eugene Winthrop of the Paris house of Drexel, Harjes & Co" and among the friends who greeted the First Lady, Frances (Folsom) Cleveland, during a visit she made to Philadelphia, and 1 July 1893, 1, where the Paris firm's date of creation is given as 1867.

[1261] Mayo, *The Winthrop Family in America*, 279.

[1262] *Evening Post* (New York), 28 April 1873, 4. "Died . . . on Monday morning, Clarence Winthrop, son of Thomas Charles Winthrop, in the 25th year of his age. The relatives and friends of the family are respectfully invited to attend the funeral, from the Church of the Annunciation, West 14th st., on Thursday morning, May 1, at half-past 9 o'clock." "Deaths," *Register* 27 [1873]: 454, gives 27 April 1873, aged 24.

[1263] Clarence Winthrop burial record, per database at *green-wood.com*. Buried 1 May 1873, lot 15674, section 99.

[1264] May, *The Descendants of Richard Sears*, 167, 260 (birth); Massachusetts Vital Records, 1871, Boston, 240: 8, and *The New York Times*, 15 January 1871, 1 (death). On 15 January 1871, Regina Shober Gray noted that "Old Mr. David Sears died at last on Friday; he has been lingering so long. His wife died last summer. He has been much respected" (Hedwiga Regina Shober Gray diary, R. Stanton Avery Special Collections).

[1265] *American* (Providence), 20 June 1809: "Married . . . On Tuesday evening by the Reverend Mr. Gardner, Mr. David Sears, jun. to Miss Meriam Clark Mason, daughter of the Honourable Jonathan Mason."

[1266] May, *The Descendants of Richard Sears*, 167, 260, 263; Massachusetts Vital Records, 1870, Boston, 231: 149; Watson, *Governor Thomas Dudley and Descendants Through Five Generations*, 1: 347.

[1267] "Hon. David Sears," *Register* 26 [1872]: 207–8. While at Harvard, he was—like several of his Winthrop cousins—a member of the Porcellian Club (*Porcellian Club 1791–2016*, 71). He also studied law in the office of Harrison Gray Otis, but never followed the profession.

as already mentioned, he married Miriam Clarke Mason, the object of a one-sided rivalry with his cousin Thomas Lindall[7] Winthrop, Jr. Following the birth of their son David Mason[8] Sears, the young couple went abroad for several years of "foreign travel, at a most interesting period in Continental history."[1268] The Searses were evidently back in Boston for the birth of their daughter Anna in March 1813,[1269] although their son David's burial is recorded in Falmouth, Cornwall,[1270] during the following September: perhaps he remained behind when his mother returned home to Boston. Records are lacking for the births of Harriet and Ellen Sears, although their death records indicate that, like Anna, both were born in Boston.[1271]

The death of the elder David Sears, in October 1816, brought David, Jr., "the largest estate which had descended to any young man in Boston, amounting to some eight-hundred thousand dollars, which his father had accumulated in the China trade." With his inheritance Sears built a house on Beacon Street "said to have been the first dwelling-house of hewn granite ever erected in this city, and [which] at the time of its erection was regarded as the finest residence in Boston."[1272]

A Sears family genealogist regarded the construction of 42 Beacon Street as a prelude to David Sears's "plans for doing his share in acts of public and private beneficence." An early effort in this line was his support for St. Paul's Church on Tremont Street, across the Common from the Beacon Street house, "and he subsequently gave that parish a fund which now exceeds forty thousand dollars in value; this was followed in succeeding years by various provisions for other religious, literary and charitable objects, which, while accomplishing valuable purposes at once, may not exhibit their full fruit for a long time to come."[1273] A memorial minute in *The New England Historical and Genealogical Register* put it more tartly: "Mr. Sears was benevolent. His

---

[1268] May, *The Descendants of Richard Sears*, 261. An affinity for Napoleon I, suggested by the name of Longwood—for the Emperor's estate in exile on the island of Saint Helena—might be traced to this period.

[1269] John William Linzee, *The Linzee Family of Great Britain and the United States . . . ,* 2 vols. (Boston: Privately printed, 1917), 2: 765.

[1270] *England, Cornwall and Devon Parish Registers, 1538–2010,* online database at FamilySearch.org.

[1271] Massachusetts Vital Records, 1872, Boston, 249: 265; Massachusetts Vital Records, 1862, Boston, 158: 163.

[1272] *Register* 26 [1872]: 207, 208.

[1273] May, *The Descendants of Richard Sears*, 261. The Sears genealogy was published in 1890. The author notes that the amalgamation of all of David Sears's charitable funds in 1886 amounted to almost $280,000 (262).

benefactions for the relief of the destitute and for public purposes were numerous, and bestowed with much discrimination; but considering his vast wealth, which had long been accumulating by his judicious investments, his benevolence has perhaps been exceeded by others of comparatively less pecuniary means."[1274]

Soon after the Beacon Street house was completed, Sears bought 200 acres in Brookline which he developed into the village of Longwood. Toward the end of his life, his involvement in Christ's Church there extended to the form of service: it was later described as "'the Book of Common Prayer, with anything of the nature of Calvinism carefully weeded out, mildly tinctured with the writings of Channing,[1275] but more strongly flavored with Romanism,' and [this] stated service was maintained during the last eight years of his life." Also in Longwood, he built a block of houses—known as "The Seearstan Charter House" — for "such as had seen better days . . . [and for] the comfort and support of a large number of poor women, [bearing] testimony to his thoughtful and well-considered benevolence."[1276]

David Sears took his inheritance and multiplied it: he "was enterprising, though he rarely engaged in any undertaking, unless he was quite sure it would be pecuniarily successful. He was one of the corporators who built India Wharf[1277] in this city, and the State street block [in 1857], and was one of the largest proprietors of the Fifty Associates."[1278] He served in the Massachusetts Legislature as a representative 1816–18, 1824–25, and in 1828, and as a state senator in 1826 and again in 1851. In 1868, he entertained the President-elect, General Ulysses S. Grant, at 42 Beacon Street.[1279]

An enthusiastic amateur historian, his experience with the genealogical history of his family was an unhappy one. Sears "employed the late Mr. H. G. Somerby to make researches in England to trace his

---

[1274] *Register* 26 [1872]: 208.

[1275] Presumably the Rev. William Ellery Channing, the Unitarian rector of Boston's Federal Street Church.

[1276] May, *The Descendants of Richard Sears*, 262.

[1277] Actually, the corporator must be David Sears, Sr., as India Wharf was developed while David Sears, Jr., was in college.

[1278] *Register* 26 [1872]: 208. The Fifty Associates was the vehicle for many of David Sears's benefactions; a listing of its records can be found at masshist.org/collection-guides/view/fa0092.

[1279] May, *The Descendants of Richard Sears*, 262. The house—and its neighbor, also built by David and Miriam Sears—was acquired in 1871 by the Somerset Club, which still [in 2017] occupies the buildings.

ancestry, and expended a large sum on these researches. His kinsman, Rev. Edmund H. Sears, undertook to edit the material collected, but he had no practical acquaintance with genealogy, and allowed himself to become responsible for a series of romantic legends under the title of 'Pictures of the Olden Time.'" After Somerby and Edmund Sears's notes were deposited at the New England Historic Genealogical Society, "Subsequent investigation [indicated] that Mr. [David] Sears was grossly deceived in regard to many particulars of the pedigree and early history of his family, so that the monuments erected by him, and the genealogies he printed, now for the most part only serve to perpetuate unfortunate delusions."[1280]

The diarist Regina Shober Gray recorded the following story in December 1862, demonstrating the social fluidity of nineteenth-century Boston:[1281]

> We heard an interesting fact in the career of Gen. Banks[1282]—it seems, he was sent, when a poor little errand boy, with a bundle to the house of Mr. David Sears in Beacon St. and ordered round from the front to the back door, to deliver his message. He never went to the house again till the other day, when he was received as an honoured guest by the grandparents of his young aide de camp Fred. Hauteville; himself, a highly distinguished General, Ex-Governor, and <u>man</u>, about to lead an important expedition, no one has yet found out where— but we shall have news of great things ere long from it.

Sears was among the first Bostonians to summer at Nahant, "but finding it too bleak for his own taste, and tempted by the softer atmosphere of the Gulf Stream, he built, in 1845, a marine villa at Newport, to which he gave the name of 'Red Cross.' Its extensive grounds are [in 1890] built over, but the immediate neighborhood is still pleasantly associated in many minds with the remembrance of his refined, graceful and unostentatious hospitality."[1283]

[1280] May, *The Descendants of Richard Sears*, 262–63.

[1281] Entry for 14 December 1862: Hedwiga Regina Shober Gray diary, R. Stanton Avery Special Collections.

[1282] Major General Nathaniel Prentiss Banks (1816–1894), Governor of Massachusetts 1858–61, newly appointed commander of the Army of the Gulf.

[1283] May, *The Descendants of Richard Sears*, 263.

Children of David[7] and Miriam Clarke (Mason) Sears, ii–vii born at Boston:[1284]

  i. DAVID MASON[8] SEARS, bp. at Trinity Church, Boston 20 May 1810[1285] and bur. at Falmouth, Cornwall, England 14 Sept. 1813.[1286]

16 ii. ANNA POWELL GRANT SEARS, b. 16 March 1813; m. 17 Jan. 1833, WILLIAM AMORY.

  iii. HARRIET ELIZABETH DICKASON SEARS, d. at 89 Beacon Street, Boston 31 Dec. 1872.[1287] She m. at Paris, France 2 Feb. 1837,[1288] GEORGE CASPAR CROWNINSHIELD,[1289] who was bp. at Salem, Mass. 2 Feb. 1812[1290] and d. at Boston 18 Jan. 1857,[1291] son of Benjamin Williams and Mary (Boardman) Crowninshield, and had issue.[1292]

  iv. ELLEN SEARS, d. at Boston 30 Nov. 1862.[1293] She m. at Montreux (Vaud), Switzerland 22 Aug. 1837, PAUL DANIEL GONSALVE BARON GRAND D'HAUTEVILLE, who was b. at Geneva, Switzerland 14 Aug. 1812 and d. at Hauteville (Fribourg), Switzerland 23 March

---

[1284] May, *The Descendants of Richard Sears*, 262–63.

[1285] *Boston, MA: Church Records*, online database at AmericanAncestors.org.

[1286] *England, Cornwall and Devon Parish Registers, 1538–2010*, online database at FamilySearch.org.

[1287] Massachusetts Vital Records, 1872, Boston, 249: 265. As the financial crisis of 1872–73 gathered speed, on 1 January 1873 Regina Shober Gray noted that "there is nothing going on—naturally enough—we have neither spirits nor funds for much gaiety in Boston just now. [Her niece] Ellen Gray's ball is to be Jan. 15th; [invitation] cards sent out yesterday. I am glad [Ellen's parents] have decided to give it—they are among the few who can afford to this season—and it is really very dull for the young people. The Fred. Sears ball must be given up, his sister Mrs. George Crowninshield having just died of pneumonia." Writing of Ellen Gray's ball, the diarist added: "There was a great crowd of young dancers exquisitely dressed—but very few of the young married or elderly people who are generally met at a big ball here, and whose splendid jewels & laces, brocades & velvets, add so much effective style to the crowd. In fact they are all in mourning—the Sears, Crowninshield, Warren, Mason, Dexter, Amory, Dehon, and other large connexions are all out of society" (entry for 18 January 1873: Hedwiga Regina Shober Gray diary, R. Stanton Avery Special Collections).

[1288] "Index of Marriages in Massachusetts Centinel and Columbia Centinel 1784–1840," 8 vols. (bound typescript at NEHGS), 7: Sears, Harriet Elizabeth, to George Caspar Crowninshield.

[1289] He was a member of the Porcellian Club in Harvard's Class of 1832 (*Porcellian Club 1791–2016*, 90).

[1290] *Vital Records of Salem, Massachusetts*, 1: 220.

[1291] Massachusetts Vital Records, 1857, Boston, 113: 5.

[1292] *Harvard College. Report of the Class of 1860, 1860–1880* (New York: S. Angell, Printer and Stationer), 28.

[1293] Massachusetts Vital Records, 1862, Boston, 158: 163.

1889,[1294] son of Eric Magnus Louis Baron Grand d'Hauteville and (his cousin) Aimée Philippine Marie Grand d'Hauteville.[1295]

On 25 Nov. 1862, Regina Shober Gray wrote, "Mrs. Hauteville is very ill I hear—her son[1296] telegraphed for, could get only such leave of absence as allowed him to reach Boston at midnight, and leave at noon next day."[1297] A few days later, she noted:

> A week ago to-day [on 30 Nov.] died sweet Mrs. Hauteville—her son reached home the night before, but too late for her to be conscious of his arrival—poor young fellow, it is a lonely lot for him.
>
> For her, one feels that to have laid down forever her clouded sorrowful life, must be great gain. Blighted from early youth in all a woman's fondest, dearest hopes, and in a way too, most mortifying by its publicity,[1298] to every sensitive feeling of pride delicacy and reserve; cut off too by her extreme deafness from all satisfactory social intercourse, she yet maintained in daily life a constant sweetness, cheerfulness, and tender consideration for others, beautiful to see. The trials must have been truly sanctified to her, which instead of embittering her heart

---

[1294] Sven Stelling-Michaud, ed., *Le Livre du Recteur de l'Académie de Genève*, 6 vols. (Geneva, Switzerland: Librairie Droz, 1972–80), 3: 518.

[1295] *Report of the d'Hauteville Case: The Commonwealth of Pennsylvania, at the suggestion of Paul Daniel Gonsalve Grand d'Hauteville, versus David Sears, Miriam C. Sears, and Ellen Sears Grand d'Hauteville* (Philadelphia: Printed by William S. Martien, 1840), 200–2.

[1296] Frederic Sears Grand d'Hauteville (1838–1918). In March 1863, Mrs. Gray noted that "Fred. Hauteville's engagement to Miss Bessie Fish, daughter of Hamilton Fish of New York, gains general sympathy—his position seemed so sad since his sweet mother's death, so isolated from the near ties of life" (entry for 8 March 1863: Hedwiga Regina Shober Gray diary, R. Stanton Avery Special Collections). Almost a decade later, Mrs. Gray noted "So at Fred Hauteville's marriage to Miss Macomb of New York last week, the New Yorkers say: 'Oh, the Boston family who came to the wedding were all very nice proper people, unexceptionable in manners & dress—but they don't know how to mingle with the rest of the world. Boston is a mere provincial town & its society has all the small provincial exclusiveness and formality; it cannot unbend & is afraid to be genial for fear it may offend the proprieties! So there were two distinct factions, so to speak, at the wedding, who kept as aloof as oil & water!!' —and there is too much truth in the criticism, as respects Boston society in general. In this particular case, I do suppose that [the] Amory, Sears, & Crowninshield connection might bear off the palm from the rest of Boston for unbending formality & hauteur to all outsiders to their own special 'set'" (entry for 14 April 1872).

[1297] Hedwiga Regina Shober Gray diary, R. Stanton Avery Special Collections.

[1298] She was divorced from her husband in a flurry of international press coverage.

and character, filled them with the light of a better hope than this world's best.[1299]

v. MIRIAM CORDELIA MASON SEARS, b. 1 Nov. 1819 and d. unm. at Boston 10 March 1850.[1300]

vi. DAVID SEARS,[1301] b. in June 1822 and d. at 86 Beacon Street, Boston 14 March 1873.[1302] He m. at New York, N.Y. 29 May 1849,[1303] EMILY ESTHER HOYT, who d. at New York 27 March 1888, dau. of Goold Hoyt,[1304] and had issue (including Dr. Henry Francis[9] Sears, who m. Jean Irvine Struthers; their daughter Emily Esther[10] Sears m. Senator Henry Cabot Lodge of Massachusetts).[1305]

vii. FREDERICK RICHARD SEARS, b. 20 March 1824 and d. at 51 Beacon Street, Boston 27 June 1907.[1306] He m. (1) at Boston 31 March 1852,[1307] MARIAN SHAW, who was b. at Boston 21 Dec. 1828 and d. there 9 March 1855,[1308] dau. of Robert Gould and Elizabeth Willard (Parkman) Shaw; m. (2) at Boston 18 June 1857,[1309] ALBERTINA HOMER SHELTON, who was b. at Boston 21 March 1834 and d. at 51 Beacon Street 31 March 1915,[1310] dau. of Philo Strong and Georgianna Albertina (Homer) Shelton, and had issue by both wives.

Marian Shaw's great-nephew Quincy Adams Shaw McKean married Katharine[10] Winthrop [No. 33]. By his first wife, Sears was the father of Frederick Richard[9] Sears, who married Eleonora Randolph Coolidge;[1311] their daughter was the athlete Eleonora

---

[1299] Entry for 7 December 1862: Hedwiga Regina Shober Gray diary, R. Stanton Avery Special Collections.

[1300] Massachusetts Vital Records, 1850, Boston, 50: 17.

[1301] He was a member of the Porcellian Club in Harvard's Class of 1842 (*Porcellian Club 1791–2016*, 95).

[1302] Massachusetts Vital Records, 1873, Boston, 258: 58.

[1303] "Marriages and Deaths," *Register* 3 [1849]: 286.

[1304] May, *The Descendants of Richard Sares (Sears)*, 405.

[1305] Of this latter marriage, Emily's cousin Dorothy Winthrop Bradford wrote, Lodge "got where he got partly because he had the most wonderful wife that anybody ever had. She was really charming, really and truly charming, and delightful. And so good with him" (Wexler, *Reared in a Greenhouse*, 196).

[1306] Massachusetts Vital Records, 1907, Boston, 14: 233. He was a member of the Porcellian Club in Harvard's Class of 1843 (*Porcellian Club 1791–2016*, 96).

[1307] Massachusetts Vital Records, 1852, Boston, 62: 30.

[1308] Massachusetts Vital Records, 1855, Boston, 95: 17.

[1309] Massachusetts Vital Records, 1857, Boston, 110: 57.

[1310] Massachusetts Vital Records, 1915, Boston, 54: 120.

[1311] Sister of Thomas Jefferson Coolidge, Jr.—see entry for Charles Walter[9] Amory [No. 23].

Randolph "Eleo"[10] Sears. By his second wife, Sears was the father of Richard Dudley[9] Sears, U.S. national champion in lawn tennis 1881–87.

viii. WINTHROP SEARS, b. in May 1826 and d. at Boston 12 Sept. 1827.[1312]

  ix. GRACE WINTHROP SEARS, b. 23 Aug. 1828 and d. at 1723 I Street, N.W., Washington, D.C. 3 May 1919.[1313] She m. at Boston 15 May 1849,[1314] WILLIAM CABELL RIVES,[1315] who was b. at Cobham, Albemarle Co., Va. 18 Jan. 1826 and d. at Washington, D.C. 7 April 1889,[1316] son of William Cabell Rives, U.S. Senator from Virginia, and Judith Page (Walker) Rives, and had issue.[1317]

  x. KNYVET WINTHROP SEARS,[1318] b. Winthrop Sears at Boston 9 April 1832 and d. at Nahant 17 June 1891. He m. at 29 Washington Square, Salem 10 June 1858, MARY CROWNINSHIELD PEABODY, who was b. at Salem 26 July 1836 and d. at Harvard, Mass. 28 Aug. 1929, dau. of George and Clarissa (Endicott) Peabody, and had issue.[1319]

Regina Shober Gray's story of a Leap Year ball in Boston features Isabella Stewart Gardner in a starring role:[1320]

> The last "Snapping Turtle" of the Season was a leap year party, carried out with much spirit. The ladies sent bouquets to their partners—having invited them—[and] led them to supper &c. Mrs. Jack Gardner led the

---

[1312] "Deaths and Interments in Boston" and "Record of the Deaths and Burials in the Middle District for the Year 1827" in *Massachusetts Town and Vital Records, 1620–1988*, online database at *ancestry.com*. See also *Columbian Centinel*, 15 September 1827.

[1313] *District of Columbia Deaths, 1874–1961*, online database at FamilySearch.org. See also *Washington Times*, 5 May 1919, 19.

[1314] Massachusetts Vital Records, 1849, Boston, 38: 239.

[1315] A graduate of Harvard Law School, he was an honorary member of the Porcellian Club in 1847 (*Porcellian Club 1791–2016*, 97).

[1316] Massachusetts Vital Records, 1889, Brookline, 401: 283.

[1317] George Lockhart Rives, comp., *Genealogical Notes* (New York, 1914), 11–12.

[1318] He was a member of the Porcellian Club in Harvard's Class of 1852 (*Porcellian Club 17912016*, 99).

[1319] Whitehill, *Captain Joseph Peabody, East Indian Merchant of Salem (1757–1844)*, 171, 172, 180–81.

[1320] Entry for 25 February 1872: Hedwiga Regina Shober Gray diary, R. Stanton Avery Special Collections. Several years later Mrs. Gray encountered the Searses at a hotel in Ragaz while traveling with her invalid husband: "The Knyvett Searses are the only people we know here; and they keep to themselves, and do not come to the table d'hôte—so we see nothing of them. I know them but slightly, and it is as fit they should call on us as we on them— beside we have little heart for visiting any one" (entry for 10 July 1878).

German,[1321] and seeing Dr. Frank Greenough and Willie Stackpole were without partners, she remonstrated with Mrs. Powell Mason & Mrs. Knyvet Sears, who were also looking on, and begged they would ask the gentlemen at once—it seemed awkward for them to be left while any ladies who could dance were also unsupplied with partners!! & in that style the whole thing was well carried out, and pretty keen lessons given in a lady like way to many a selfish, conceited *beau*![1322]

14. **ROBERT CHARLES**[7] **WINTHROP** (*Thomas Lindall*[6], *John Still*[5], *John*[4], *Waitstill*[3], *John*[2-1]) was born at the Milk Street home of his great-uncle James Bowdoin in Boston, Massachusetts, the youngest of fourteen children, on 12 May 1809.[1323] He died at 90 Marlborough Street, Boston 16 November 1894,[1324] and was buried at Mount Auburn Cemetery in Cambridge, Massachusetts.[1325] He married, first, at Boston 12 March 1832,[1326] **ELIZABETH CABOT "ELIZA" BLANCHARD**, who was born at Boston 27 May 1809,[1327] the only child of Francis and Mary Ann

---

[1321] A waltz.

[1322] A commentary on the way ball organizers might leave wallflowers to sit out the dance.

[1323] Winthrop, *Memoir of Robert C. Winthrop*, 5. Mayo, *The Winthrop Family in America*, 315, presumes he was named for his father's half-brother Robert Winthrop and for Charles Fraser of Charleston, S.C., the highly esteemed brother-in-law of Thomas Lindall Winthrop's brother Joseph Winthrop, who had visited the family in Boston in the summer of 1806 (Huger Smith and Huger Smith, *Charles Fraser*, 17, 21).

[1324] Winthrop, *Memoir of Robert C. Winthrop*, v.

[1325] Winthrop, *Memoir of Robert C. Winthrop*, 346–47. He had intended to be buried with his ancestors at King's Chapel, but "when the growth of Boston rendered interments undesirable in the heart of a business community, he built a similar tomb at Mount Auburn, over the doorway to which was placed a slab intended for an inscription to himself. Not long before his death, [his son] sounded him as to how this should be worded. 'I leave that to you,' he answered, 'but make it short and comprehensive.'" Robert, Jr., decided on, "Eminent as a scholar, an orator, a statesman, and a philanthropist—above all, a Christian." The son commented: "This does not seem to me excessive, and I doubt whether he could be better described in 15 words."

[1326] Adlard, *The Sutton-Dudleys of England and the Dudleys of Massachusetts in New England*, 129 (date only). Mayo, *The Winthrop Family in America*, 319, citing Robert C. Winthrop to Anna Winthrop, 29 March 1832, in the Winthrop Manuscripts, 36A, noted that the couple visited Maryland and Virginia on their honeymoon and then Washington, D.C., where they were presented to President Andrew Jackson at the "President's Palace." They also visited with former President James Madison and Charles Carroll, 95, the last survivor of the signers of the Declaration of Independence (Winthrop, *Memoir of Robert C. Winthrop*, 10–11).

[1327] Henry Herbert Edes, "Robert Charles Winthrop, Jr., A.M.," *Register* 60 [1906]: 224.

(Cabot) (Lee) Blanchard.[1328] She died of consumption at Boston 14 June 1842, and was buried at Trinity Church.[1329] He married second, at King's Chapel, Boston 6 November 1849,[1330] **ELIZABETH LAURA DERBY**, who was born at Salem, Massachusetts 9 February 1811, the daughter of Captain John and Eleanor (Coffin) Derby, and widow of Arnold Francis Welles. She died at Boston 26 April 1861.[1331] Regina Shober Gray—a family connection of Eliza Blanchard Winthrop's—noted in her diary: "Mrs. R. C. Winthrop died last night after a long & terribly suffering illness. She is a real loss to Boston society."[1332] Robert Charles Winthrop married, third, at Brookline, Massachusetts 15 November

---

See also L. Vernon Briggs, *History and Genealogy of the Cabot Family, 1475–1927*, 2 vols. (Boston: Charles E. Goodspeed & Co., 1927), 1: 155.

[1328] Winthrop, *Memoir of Robert C. Winthrop*, 10. Both her parents died before she was five years old, and she was raised by her great-uncle Samuel Pickering Gardner, who lived on Summer Street in Boston.

[1329] Eliza Cabot Blanchard death record, *Ancestry.com* > Massachusetts, Town and Vital Records, 1620–1988 > Boston > Birth, Marriages and Death (Provo, Utah: Holbrook Research Institute).

[1330] Marriage record, *Ancestry.com* > Massachusetts, Town and Vital Records, 1620–1988 > Boston > Marriages, 1849 (Provo, Utah: Holbrook Research Institute). "Robert C. Winthrop and Laura Derby ~~Welles~~," second marriage for both, age 40 and 35 years, 6 November 1849. It was registered on 31 December 1849. Robert recorded their first meeting in a letter dated 7 September 1849: "Have pity on me. I went to Newport about four weeks ago free and unshackled. I met there a widow with one little boy. I had known her when she was a girl, and had been intimate with her husband, so it was not unnatural we should sympathize. Suffice it to say, I returned ten days ago a bondman, and to-day it is publicly announced that I am going to be married. The worst of it is that I am unable to deny it. My only consolation is that the lady—to one eye at least in the world—is a very charming person, not too young for a man who was made a Doctor of Laws day before yesterday, and one of the most thoroughly amiable women under the sun" (Winthrop, *Memoir of Robert C. Winthrop*, 95). The author gives the date of the marriage as 15 October 1849; he may have transposed his own marriage date, which was 15 October 1857 (Winthrop, *Memoir of Robert C. Winthrop*, 96).

[1331] Winthrop, *Memoir of Robert C. Winthrop*, 216. While the couple was traveling in Europe in 1859–60, she developed "a troublesome affection of the eye" and soon after their return to the U.S. showed symptoms of "an internal malady which in the following spring proved fatal" (214).

[1332] Entry for 27 April 1861: Hedwiga Regina Shober Gray diary, R. Stanton Avery Special Collections. Mrs. Gray was amused by Robert C. Winthrop's marital history, noting (on 22 October 1865) that "Mr. R. C. Winthrop's engagement is 'out' to Mrs. John E. Thayer. Really with all due respect for Mr. W. one cannot but smile at his persistent choice of wealthy wives—this third one being the superlative, to which the former play positive & comparative. He turns to gold as instinctively as the witch-hazel to water!"

1865,[1333] **Cornelia Adeline "Adele" Granger,** who was born at Canandaigua, New York 15 September 1819, the daughter of Francis and Cornelia Rutsen (Van Rensselaer) Granger,[1334] and widow of John Eliot Thayer.[1335] She died at Brookline 16 June 1892.[1336]

Robert C. Winthrop, as he was commonly known, was educated by his mother until he was about 7, when he was sent to a succession of tutors.[1337] He later recalled meeting James Monroe when he was about eight years old during a visit by the fifth U.S. president to Boston. "I remember well sitting on his knees or haply standing between them at the house of my sister, Mrs. George Sullivan, where he spent part of an evening," Robert wrote.[1338] At age twelve he began attending the Boston Public Latin School with his brother Grenville; at the end of his final year the master, greatly impressed, presented him with a copy of John Murray's edition of the works of Washington Irving. He entered Harvard in 1824 (waiting a year to take the entrance exam "by his father's desire not to precede an older brother less studious than himself," recalled his son), staying in private homes until his senior year, when he roomed on campus with Charles Chauncy Emerson, a younger brother of Ralph Waldo Emerson, who in 1828 finished first in the class (Robert was third). Robert was president of his class, orator of the Hasty Pudding Club, sang bass in the Chapel choir, and commanded the military company of the college. He probably would have finished first in his class, but, as a professor told him, he "did too many things."[1339]

[1333] Massachusetts Vital Records, 1865, Brookline, 181: 195; Winthrop, *Memoir of Robert C. Winthrop*, 268. In the latter, the author refers to her as "Adele." As with his second wife, Robert was a friend of her father's and so had known her since she was a girl. "Fortunately they were not alike in temperament," his son recalled, "as Mr. Winthrop's uncertain health often made him despondent, while his wife's native buoyancy of disposition supplied the precise tonic he needed" (268–69).

[1334] Florence Van Rensselaer, *The Livingston Family in America and Its Scottish Origins* (New York, 1949), 318, 329; Massachusetts Vital Records, 1865, Brookline, 181: 195 (place of birth).

[1335] Hedwiga Regina Shober Gray diary, R. Stanton Avery Special Collections. Mrs. Gray encountered the Winthrops on holiday during the summer of 1872: "The elder Mr. & Mrs. Robt. C. Winthrop were a pleasant addition to our circle last week, for a few days. Mrs. W's paralyzed daughter Adele Thayer is a very interesting girl of 15—but it is very sad to see her so helpless and shut out from all the gladness of youth and the possible happiness of mature life" (entry for 8 September 1872).

[1336] Massachusetts Vital Records, 1892, Brookline, 428: 451.

[1337] Winthrop, *Memoir of Robert C. Winthrop*, 5–6.

[1338] Mayo, *The Winthrop Family in America*, 316, citing Winthrop Manuscripts 33, Part III, 7.

[1339] Winthrop, *Memoir of Robert C. Winthrop*, 6–7. He was also Deputy Master of the Knights of the Square Table and Deputy Marshal of the Porcellian Club (*Porcellian Club 1791–2016*, 87).

His graduation reception at Porter's Tavern was attended by President John Quincy Adams.[1340]

Robert read law with Daniel Webster's firm (although Webster spent most of his time in Washington) and in 1831 was admitted to the bar in Suffolk County.[1341] He soon after opened an office on Court Street,[1342] occasionally writing magazine articles, such as one "Temperance Pledges" for *New England Magazine,* and another on "American Annuals" (for which he was paid $8) for the *North American Review.*[1343] In the fall of 1833, he was appointed chairman of a committee to greet Henry Clay when the statesman and recent presidential candidate visited Boston.[1344] Winthrop gave two speeches for the visitor that greatly impressed Clay and others; he was then invited to speak at the caucus of the National Republican (i.e., anti-Jackson) party, which also earned rave reviews. (An audience member would judge it "not merely a good speech for a first effort, but one which any practised man might have been proud to make."[1345]) Soon after, Robert was appointed to the staff of the Massachusetts governor[1346] and in 1834 elected to the state legislature, where he served six years, including the last three as speaker.[1347] He kept the occasional diary, and his son, in a memoir, transcribed a passage from 1836:[1348]

> July 28. Dined at my father's in company with J.Q. Adams, Chief Justice Shaw, and others. President Adams did all the talking and was, as usual, very interesting. He said that he despaired of the Union. He believed that the population of the United States was destined soon to be overrun not only [by] Texas, but Mexico, and that the inevitable result would be two or more confederacies. The soil of Mexico was inviting, the climate alluring, and

[1340] Winthrop, *Memoir of Robert C. Winthrop,* 7–8. The speaker in the Senate, a Virginian, was invited but did not appear, apparently because he had misinterpreated a Bible passage ("neither from the East, nor from the West, nor yet from the South") that Winthrop read during a commencement speech as an endorsement of the North.

[1341] Winthrop, *Memoir of Robert C. Winthrop,* 8–9.

[1342] *Stimpson's Boston Directory* (1832), 341.

[1343] Winthrop, *Memoir of Robert C. Winthrop,* 10.

[1344] Winthrop, *Memoir of Robert C. Winthrop,* 12.

[1345] Winthrop, *Memoir of Robert C. Winthrop,* 12, citing a letter by William Sullivan. For examples of Robert's rhetoric, transcribed from his notes by his son, see 14–19.

[1346] Winthrop, *Memoir of Robert C. Winthrop,* 13.

[1347] Winthrop, *Memoir of Robert C. Winthrop,* 19.

[1348] Winthrop, *Memoir of Robert C. Winthrop,* 21.

he believed the country would fall an easy prey to our hardy adventurers. He prophesied that a century hence would find the whole North American continent, from Labrador to Panama, and from the Atlantic to the Pacific, controlled by the Anglo-Saxon race, which would then number 100 millions. He thought the Canadians were rapidly nearing a separation from British rule, though it might be difficult to unite them with us.

When Boston merchant Abbott Lawrence resigned his seat in Congress for health reasons in 1839, Winthrop was easily elected to succeed him.[1349] Daniel Webster, who had endorsed Robert, wrote him:[1350]

> You have gone fast in Massachusetts politics, and you may go far in National ones. You are thoroughly equipped for public affairs. You have in addition the advantages of not having to work for your living, and of an acquired readiness in debate, which is a precious thing in the hour of need. But, with all of this, I question whether to a man of your scholarly instincts and fastidious tastes, the atmosphere of self-seeking and misrepresentation which is so apt to surround a public man of the first rank at the Capital, will not prove grievous and disheartening,—whether you will not one day weary of it all, and wish yourself back in your study at home.

Years later, Robert Charles[8] Winthrop, Jr., would make a similar assessment of his father, whom he wrote had the "dignified and ceremonious demeanor of the old school" from an early age, noting he had been nicknamed "English Winthrop" during his time at Harvard. Like his father, "he had a good deal of what is traditionally known as 'the English manner,'" the younger Winthrop wrote. "I doubt if he ever saw a race, or a ball-match, in his life."[1351] Furthermore:[1352]

> He held many old-fashioned views upon a variety of subjects, some of which were of a character to excite disgust or derision in the breast of any self-respecting "advanced-thinker." For instance . . . although a tender-

---

[1349] Winthrop, *Memoir of Robert C. Winthrop*, 24.

[1350] Winthrop, *Memoir of Robert C. Winthrop*, 23.

[1351] Winthrop, *Memoir of Robert C. Winthrop*, 329.

[1352] Winthrop, *Memoir of Robert C. Winthrop*, 326, 328, 330–31.

hearted man, he not merely approved of the death-penalty, but considered flogging an admirable corrective to certain classes of offenses. . . .

He had a very high opinion of the average ability of American public men of all parties, and a still higher opinion of the capacity and ingenuity of that composite race, the American people; but he sometimes wished they would not be so boastful, so credulous, so sensitive to the slightest foreign criticism, and so absorbingly agog about the doings—or alleged misdoings—of persons of title on the other side of the Atlantic. . . .

A more than indifferent horseman, he was so deplorable a whist-player that it was fortunate for his family that he was principled against any kind of stakes, so bad a shot that, at an annual battue on Naushon Island, he barely escaped the ignominy of bringing down a tame doe which had approached him in a confiding spirit. One additional trait would stamp him in the opinion of many as thoroughly "un-American": he never put himself in the way of receiving railway-passes, declined to make use of the complimentary ones which were often sent him, and insisted on traveling at his own expense. Worse remains behind. The lip of an "up to date" Harvard graduate would curl with passing pity for a bigoted old man who actually attached more importance to Greek and Latin than to athletic sports. . . . He even upheld that system of committing to memory strings of names, facts and dates, now lightly esteemed as "memorizing," and he largely attributed his early success as a public speaker to his having been continually drilled, both at the Boston Latin School and in college, in learning by heart and reciting in public long extracts from ancient and modern speakers and authors.

In the spring of 1842, Robert resigned his seat in Congress and returned to Boston with his wife, who had fallen mortally ill. Following her death in June, he was promptly re-elected and returned to Washington[1353]; in December 1847, representing what had become

---

[1353] Winthrop, *Memoir of Robert C. Winthrop*, 32.

known as the Whig Party, he was elected Speaker.[1354] (One of his first acts was to close the saloon under the House chamber.[1355]) His son would recall that his father disliked the task of keeping tabs on the rules and orders, as well as the clerks, but loved the opportunity the position gave him for "increased hospitality."[1356]

> He had hardly been elected before he took a house, engaged a French cook, and began to give two large dinners a week, with smaller ones as occasion served. From boyhood he had been accustomed to meet at his father's table the principal persons in New England, together with all the distinguished strangers who passed through Boston, and it was a genuine pleasure to him—a pleasure which never palled—to assemble those around his own board not merely the celebrities of Washington society, but his associates in Congress of all shades of opinion.

On 4 July 1848 Robert spoke at the laying of the cornerstone of the Washington monument[1357]; John Quincy Adams was scheduled to do it but had died the previous February. Robert was not re-elected

---

[1354] Mayo, *The Winthrop Family in America*, 323, noted that not all of his party colleagues voted for him; the Northerners had disliked his earlier vote to go to war with Mexico and the Southerners thought him anti-slavery. A political biographer noted that "with those who know him well, on both sides of the House, he is a great favorite, but the criticism has been made that he is a little too refined and dignified for some of his surroundings. A man of rougher temperament, even if less intellectual, is often better suited for a party captain" (*Sketches of the Twenty-Eighth Congress*, printed in a "Pennsylvania newspaper about 1845," quoted in Winthrop, *Memoir of Robert C. Winthrop*, 43). On the first vote on 6 December, he received 108 of 220 votes, but needed 111 to be chosen. After convincing two Whigs who had not voted for him, and a Democrat who nullified his vote by walking out in protest, Winthrop had the 110 votes he needed (70–71).

[1355] Winthrop, *Memoir of Robert C. Winthrop*, 77. The saloon, like one in the Senate basement, was open to the public and "not infrequently the scene of disgusting inebriety." His son wrote, "Mr. Winthrop was by no means a rigid Puritan. He habitually drank wine at dinner. He was no stranger to the occasional use of whiskey for the stomach's sake, and he thoroughly enjoyed tobacco in the form of cigars until he was 85 years old. But he detested the convivial habit of gathering around a public counter to partake of spirits between meals."

[1356] Winthrop, *Memoir of Robert C. Winthrop*, 80–81. His guest lists included one instance of the name of Abraham Lincoln, the freshman Congressman from Illinois who had been elected as a Whig in August 1846.

[1357] Winthrop, *Memoir of Robert C. Winthrop*, 84. His speech was reprinted in Robert C. Winthrop, *Addresses and Speeches on Various Occasions* (Boston: Little, Brown and Co., 1852), 70–89.

as Speaker in December 1849 after a contentious battle that took 63 votes over three weeks.[1358] In 1850, after Robert suggested to President Millard Fillmore that he appoint Daniel Webster as Secretary of State, a grateful Webster wrote to the Governor of Massachusetts and suggested he in turn appoint Winthrop to complete Webster's term in the U.S. Senate.[1359]

Robert took that seat on 30 July 1850[1360] but lost it the following year, a defeat Mayo attributes to Robert not being as passionately anti-slavery as his opponent, the firebrand Charles Sumner.[1361] Winthrop returned to Boston, where the local Whigs recruited him to run for governor. When Daniel Webster did not offer a full-throated endorsement, Winthrop felt betrayed.[1362] In his memoirs, Henry Cabot Lodge would recall his surprise at mentioning Webster's name to

---

[1358] Winthrop, *Memoir of Robert C. Winthrop*, 96. Joshua R. Giddings, in *History of the Rebellion: Its Authors and Causes* (New York: Follett, Foster & Co., 1864), attributed Winthrop's defeat to "his devotion to the interests of slavery." Winthrop himself noted that an abolitionist newspaper dismissed him as a "lickspittle of slavery . . . a doughface of showy but mediocre ability, the self-satisfied and self-sufficient agent of the wealth of Boston—[who] has fallen under the wheels of the bright car of Liberty." The House elected, on 22 December 1849, Howell Cobb of Georgia, a pro-slavery Democrat, who received 102 votes to Winthrop's 99 (97, 99). Robert gave a speech called "Personal Vindication" on 21 February 1850 to answer his critics, saying that "I have no expectation that my political career will excite the smallest interest in the distant future, but I should be glad if anyone curious in such matters would turn to this particular speech and read it from beginning to end" (102).

[1359] Winthrop, *Memoir of Robert C. Winthrop*, 130–33. In his journal, Robert recalls meeting with the new president alone at Willard's Hotel. Fillmore had been considering Webster or Winthrop for Secretary of State, but Robert argued that Webster was the better choice because "I was obnoxious to men of extreme opinions at both ends of the Union."

[1360] Winthrop, *Memoir of Robert C. Winthrop*, 134.

[1361] Winthrop, *Memoir of Robert C. Winthrop*, 38, 146. See also Mayo, *The Winthrop Family in America*, 327–28. While a Congressman, Robert did not go so far as some of his colleagues who suggested in 1845 that New England secede from the Union if Texas were annexed with slavery intact. He felt it more important to maintain the Union, "however otherwise bounded or described," which earned him criticism from abolitionists as supporting the doctrine of "our country, right or wrong" (44–45).

[1362] Winthrop, *Memoir of Robert C. Winthrop*, 148–49. June 14. "Our Boston men keep the incense burning under Webster's nose with more than the assiduity of vestal virgins. . . . I would give much for a long talk with Webster, to know precisely how he feels, if he chose to tell me." On 11 August, Robert heard from an intermediary that "Webster has asked him to say to me that he was as much my friend as ever, but that he doubted the expediency of running me for Governor for a couple of years, for the reason that [it] *might have a bad effect on the South, particularly in Georgia. . . .* I think I shall hold my tongue and let things take their course."

Winthrop: "The real man came to the surface through the gracious, formal manner, and I was interested to see what very strong, human feelings the real man possessed."[1363] Although Robert won the most votes in a three-way gubernatorial race, it was not a plurality and the legislature appointed the incumbent (who had finished second).[1364]

In defeat, Robert would consider that while he would have enjoyed being governor, especially some 220 years after John[1] Winthrop had held the position, he would not have enjoyed "being tethered to a little round of petty duties, daily drudgery in the council-chamber, riding on big horses, sitting in big chairs, and making big and little speeches all over the Commonwealth."[1365] So, at age 43, he retired from politics and returned to being, as Mayo wrote, "a gifted and distinguished Bostonian."[1366] Although he could not deny that "after an absence of eleven winters, Boston occasionally seems a trifle narrow and a trifle humdrum," and that local gatherings are "perhaps a little tame to one who has passed so many years at work on the affairs of the Nation,"[1367] he saw "many ways in which I can be useful." To that end, he accepted a number of volunteer positions over subsequent years, such as president of the Harvard Alumni Association and chair of the boards of the Boston Public Library, Overseers of the Poor of Boston, the Peabody Museum of Archaeology and Ethnology,[1368] and the Peabody Trust for Southern Education.[1369] He also served for fifty-nine years on the vestry at

---

[1363] Henry Cabot Lodge, *Early Memories* (New York: Charles Scribner's Sons, 1913), 301–2. "I had gathered the vague idea that he was little better than a pro-slavery Democrat [who] . . . had abandoned the cause of freedom and of the country. When I came to know him I changed my conception of him very materially, although I never thought he was right in the political course which he adopted. . . . He was nearly 70 when I first knew him, and seemed so much older, for he appeared to cultivate an appearance of age, although he was really strong and active and lived to be over 80."

[1364] Mayo, *The Winthrop Family in America*, 329–30. See also Winthrop, *Memoir of Robert C. Winthrop*, 151.

[1365] Winthrop, *Memoir of Robert C. Winthrop*, 147. Dorothy Bradford Wexler notes that his nickname in some circles was Robert "Chloroform" Winthrop (Wexler, *Reared in a Greenhouse*, 6).

[1366] Mayo, *The Winthrop Family in America*, 330. In November 1855, Robert wrote: "Did you hear that I was unanimously nominated for Mayor of Boston by the 'Citizens' Union,' and that I unanimously declined? It would have been more distasteful to me than the presidency of Harvard, for which some well-meaning friends continue to suggest my name" (Winthrop, *Memoir of Robert C. Winthrop*, 181.)

[1367] Winthrop, *Memoir of Robert C. Winthrop*, 162.

[1368] Mayo, *The Winthrop Family in America*, 340.

[1369] Winthrop, *Memoir of Robert C. Winthrop*, 201.

Trinity Church[1370] and for thirty years as president of the Massachusetts Historical Society.[1371] In June 1858, he judged a newly erected statue of Governor John[1] Winthrop by Richard Saltonstall Greenough, at the chapel of Mount Auburn Cemetery, as "perhaps a little too youthful and saint-like in its general effect, but on the whole a successful work," although he noted he had sat as the artist's model for its hands.[1372]

As secession clouds gathered in the 1850s, Robert wrote that while he was for "resisting the aggressions of slavery," he could not support "taking the first great step for rending the Union by the formation of a sectional party" such as the new Republican Party, which was hostile to the Southern states.[1373] In the election of 1860 he endorsed the candidates from the conservative Constitutional Party instead, writing that "intemperate antislavery agitation" was "the source of a very large part of the troubles with which the country has been disturbed."[1374] Robert wrote in a letter on 1 October:[1375]

> If Lincoln be chosen, which seems not unlikely, you and I must do what we can to prevent mischief, but I fear there will be more than we or anybody else can manage. I believe him to be at heart a moderate man; and if Southern Senators and Representatives would only keep their tempers, things might not go along as badly as they fear. The danger is that, in the first flush of such an election, madness will rule the hour.

In January 1861, Robert traveled to Washington armed with a petitition signed by fifteen thousand Boston voters seeking a compromise between North and South, but he returned home certain that war was on the horizon.[1376] It arrived in April. Later that year, he returned to Washington,

---

[1370] Winthrop, *Memoir of Robert C. Winthrop*, 338–39, excepting a few months after he had been kicked out of office by what he called a "Puseyite cabal" (338–39fn).

[1371] Winthrop, *Memoir of Robert C. Winthrop*, 315–16.

[1372] Winthrop, *Memoir of Robert C. Winthrop*, 274.

[1373] Winthrop, *Memoir of Robert C. Winthrop*, 181. "It might better be called the semi-Republican party, for its organization embraces only about half the Republic," he wrote (191), adding "A semi-republican party is only the first step to a semi-republic" (194).

[1374] David Savile Muzzey, *The United States of America: Through the Civil War*, 2 vols. (Boston: Ginn and Co., 1922), 1: 531.

[1375] Transcribed in Winthrop, *A Memoir of Robert C. Winthrop*, 211–12.

[1376] Winthrop, *Memoir of Robert C. Winthrop*, 214–15. Charles Sumner dismissed the petition as "a penny-whistle in a tempest."

where he met with Secretary of State William Seward and President Lincoln about the prospect of moving to London and Paris to counteract the Confederates who had sailed to Europe to plead for support. He visited with Lincoln again in the spring of 1863, although he was growing more hostile to the president's policies, believing that Lincoln was prolonging the war by insisting the South give up slavery rather than simply come back into the fold.[1377] He began to feel that Lincoln was committed to keeping the war going "until the whole social structure of the South has been reorganized."[1378] In the 1864 elections, Robert endorsed the Democratic candidate, General George B. McClellan, and made speeches on his behalf, which did not endear him to his pro-Lincoln neighbors.[1379]

On 4 April 1865, he spoke at the invitation of the Boston City Council to celebrate the fall of Richmond, noting that "no Conservative spoke but myself. Frederick Douglass (whom I never saw before) did well, and other colored men took part. It was odd company for me, but I can rejoice at the success of the Union arms in any company."[1380] He was invited six days later, on 10 April, to speak in celebration of Lee's surrender but declined, as he was leaving for New York to attend the funeral of his first cousin's son, Frederick Winthrop, who had been killed in action in Virginia.[1381] Two days after he returned to Boston came the news that President Lincoln had been

---

[1377] Winthrop, *Memoir of Robert C. Winthrop*, 228. "I do not believe that blacks or whites are to be benefited by sudden and sweeping Acts of Emancipation," wrote Robert, who also felt Lincoln's order violated the Constitution. "We must pursue constitutional ends by constitutional means" (248). He noted on 7 November that "yesterday's mail brought me a *New York Times* of the 5th, containing a tirade against myself a column long, as well as a notification that I had just been elected in the same city a Vice-President of the American Bible Society. Thus the bane and the antidote may be said to have come together" (258).

[1378] Winthrop, *Memoir of Robert C. Winthrop*, 247. In 1881, he would say of Reconstruction: "Slavery is but half abolished, emancipation is but half completed, while millions of freemen with votes in their hands are without education" (319). Robert's concern over the effect of the war on the southern economy led to his being referred to as a "cotton Whig" (Muzzey, *The United States of America: Through the Civil War*, 1: 531).

[1379] Winthrop, *Memoir of Robert C. Winthrop*, 38, 249.

[1380] Winthrop, *Memoir of Robert C. Winthrop*, 263. Douglass would later chastize Winthrop in an 1881 memoir, *The Life & Times of Frederick Douglass*, for waiting too long in the battle against slavery. "The time when the Union needed him, and all others, was when the slaveholding rebellion raised its defiant head, not when as now that head was in the dust and ashes of defeat and destruction" (323). In defense of his father, Robert C. Winthrop, Jr., suggested Douglass visit the Library of Congress to read the content of his father's volumes dealing with the Civil War, after which Robert, Jr., said he received an apology and a promise to revise the passage in any further editions.

[1381] Winthrop, *Memoir of Robert C. Winthrop*, 264.

assassinated on 15 April. Winthrop delivered a eulogy during a meeting of the Massachusetts Historical Society, noting that although he had opposed Lincoln's re-election in 1864, "during the last six months of his life, his whole policy was modified, if not absolutely reversed," and he, for instance, "abandoned all interference with his generals."[1382]

About this time, in 1863 and 1866, after being inspired by a visit to the Winthrop ancestral home in Groton two decades earlier, Robert completed a two-volume biography of John[1] Winthrop in the form of collected letters and journal entries.[1383] He also published, between 1852 and 1886, four volumes of his addresses and speeches, including those given to groups such as the American Sunday School Union, the Union Ratification Meeting, the Boston City Council, the Bristol County Agricultural Society, and the Massachusetts Charitable Mechanic Association. The topics included the Pilgrims, the imprisonment of free colored seamen, the annexation of Texas,[1384] river and harbor improvements, horticulture, the Ottoman Empire,[1385] Benjamin Frankin,[1386] how to increase the circulation of religious books, music in schools, Christianity as a remedy for social and political evils, luxury and the fine arts, Dante, African colonization, Irish military recruits, Shakespeare, and the officers of the Russian fleet.[1387]

About 1872, Robert and his third wife moved to a new home at 90 Marlborough Street, where they resided for the winter. In the summer and early fall they retreated to Brookline.[1388] Robert spoke in Boston on 4 July 1876 at the centennial celebration of the Declaration of Independence.[1389] In 1879, he wrote a biography of Henry Clay for

---

[1382] Winthrop, *Memoir of Robert C. Winthrop*, 266.

[1383] Mayo, *The Winthrop Family in America*, 338.

[1384] Winthrop, *Memoir of Robert C. Winthrop*, 38. He opposed it, he said, "now and always ... above all, because I am uncompromisingly opposed to the extension of domestic slavery, or to the addition of another inch of slaveholding territory to this nation."

[1385] Winthrop, *Addresses and Speeches on Various Occasions* (1852), vii–xi.

[1386] At the end of a speech on "Archimedes and Franklin" delivered on 29 September 1853, he called for a statute of Franklin to be erected in front of Boston City Hall, and he spoke at its unveiling on 17 September 1856. Sculpted by Richard Saltonstall Greenough, it still stands.

[1387] Robert C. Winthrop, *Addresses and Speeches on Various Occasions, from 1852 to 1867* (Boston: Little, Brown and Co., 1867), vii–xiii. His son would explain that "before making a political speech he thought over what he wished to say, relied much on the inspiration of the moment, writing it out afterward for publication, if he had time. In his commemorative addresses he pursued an opposite course, preparing his material carefully in advance, using in delivery as much as seemed desierable, but printing the whole" (Winthrop, *Memoir of Robert C. Winthrop*, 306fn).

[1388] Mayo, *The Winthrop Family in America*, 339.

[1389] Winthrop, *Memoir of Robert C. Winthrop*, 288.

the first volume of *Memorial Biographies*, published by the New England Historic Genealogical Society.[1390] In 1885, at age 75, Robert was meant to deliver a speech at the completion of the Washington Monument, having given one thirty-seven years earlier at the laying of the cornerstone. But he fell ill with pneumonia that nearly killed him, and Representative John D. Long, the former Governor of Massachusetts, stepped in to deliver the address Robert had written.[1391] In 1886, a school for teachers in Columbia, South Carolina, today known as Winthrop College, was named for him; on his birthday in 1894, the cornerstones of its new buildings in Rock Hill were laid.[1392] After his wife Adele died in 1892, he spent the summers of 1893 and 1894 at Nahant, but "the interest in life had gone out of him—mental depression and physical suffering remained," his son would recall.[1393] Robert wrote on 23 August 1893, "I am told that my miserable condition is due, for the most part, to my being in my 86th year.... I am not afraid to die, but I am weary, weary of the life I lead."[1394] On the last afternoon before he lost consciousness, Robert sat in his study at 90 Marlborough, where he lived the last twenty years of his life, "turning over the leaves of his favorite hymn book, unable to collect his thoughts," his son recalled. He died two days later.[1395]

Children of Robert Charles[7] and Elizabeth Cabot (Blanchard) Winthrop, the last three born at Boston:

  i. INFANT SON[8], d. 12 Feb. 1833, aged two months, and bur. at Trinity Church, Boston.[1396]

17 ii. ROBERT CHARLES WINTHROP, JR., b. 7 Dec. 1834; m. (1) 15 Oct. 1857, FRANCES PICKERING ADAMS; m. (2) 1 June 1869, ELIZABETH MASON.

[1390] Winthrop, *Memoir of Robert C. Winthrop*, 298.

[1391] Winthrop, *Memoir of Robert C. Winthrop*, 311, 314.

[1392] Winthrop, *Memoir of Robert C. Winthrop*, 319–20. See also Mayo, *The Winthrop Family in America*, 341.

[1393] Winthrop, *Memoir of Robert C. Winthrop*, 344. Mayo, *The Winthrop Family in America*, 342–43, notes there are at least three oil portraits of an older Robert by Daniel Huntington (from 1871, 1882, and 1885), three busts, and a medallion. The medallion, showing him at age 32, is reproduced facing 26 in Winthrop, *Memoir of Robert C. Winthrop*; at the time, two busts were at the Massachusetts Historical Society and one at Harvard library.

[1394] Winthrop, *Memoir of Robert C. Winthrop*, 345.

[1395] Winthrop, *Memoir of Robert C. Winthrop*, 346.

[1396] Child Winthrop death record, *Ancestry.com* > Massachusetts, Town and Vital Records, 1620–1988 > Boston > Birth, Marriages and Death (Provo, Utah: Holbrook Research Institute), age 2 months, "son of Robert C. Winthrop," of "affection of brain." See also Winthrop, *Memoir of Robert C. Winthrop*, 346.

iii.   ELIZABETH CABOT "ELIZA" WINTHROP, b. 13 May 1838,[1397] d. unm.
of "senile decay" at the Hotel Metropolitain, Paris, France 28 Sept.
1921, and bur. at the cemetery at St.-Germain en Laye (Île de
France).[1398] She had been living in Paris since about the turn of the
century.[1399]

Regina Shober Gray recorded the following in her diary for 11
Dec. 1864:[1400]

> Eliza Winthrop has had a narrow escape of burning to death.
> About a week ago, her window draperies caught fire in
> the gas jet—it was midnight, she was locked in the room,
> fortunately had on her flannel dressing gown, and no hoop.
> She tore down the curtain, threw it on the floor, dragged
> upon the bed clothes, extinguished the flames which had
> caught in the chintz sofa covers &c, and then turned to see
> that the sheets &c were on fire—she dragged the mattress
> upon them, and succeeded at last in smothering the flames,
> at the cost of several bad burns on her hands & neck. She
> had no time to call for help, or to unlock her doors, till all
> danger was over. It was a frightful situation to be in, and she
> certainly showed great presence of mind, and resolution.

iv.   JOHN WINTHROP, b. 20 June 1841[1401] and d. at Stockbridge, Mass.
18 Sept. 1895 after returning from a fishing trip in Maine.[1402] He
m. at St. Paul's Church, Stockbridge 30 March 1864, ISABELLA
COWPLAND WEYMAN,[1403] who was b. at New Rochelle, N.Y.

[1397] Elizabeth Cabot Winthrop passport application, scan at *Familysearch.org* > United
States Passport Applications, 1795–1925 > (M1490) Passport Applications January
2, 1906–March 31, 1925 > Roll 396, 1917 Aug., certificate 63475 (Aug. 1917). The
examiner wrote her father's name down as "Robert Childs Winthrop." Elizabeth
said she planned to return to the U.S. "when my health permits." See also *Report
of the Secretary of the Class of 1863 of Harvard College, June, 1893, to June, 1903*
(Cambridge, Mass.: John Wilson and Son, 1903), 122.

[1398] "Report of the Death of an American Citizen: Elisa [*sic*] Cabot Winthrop," at
ancestry.com > Reports of Deaths of American Citizens Abroad, 1835–1974 >
NARA Inventory 15, Entry 205, 1910–1962 > Box 4182, 1910–1929. Her effects
were handled by her nephew, Robert M. Winthrop of Paris.

[1399] Mayo, *The Winthrop Family in America*, 344.

[1400] Hedwiga Regina Shober Gray diary, R. Stanton Avery Special Collections.

[1401] Mayo, *The Winthrop Family in America*, 406.

[1402] *Report of the Secretary of the Class of 1863 of Harvard College, June, 1893, to June, 1903*, 123.

[1403] "News from the Classes," *The Harvard Graduates' Magazine* 4 [1895]: 295. Their
engagement lasted for some time, as on 14 December 1862 Regina Shober Gray
noted that she had called "on Miss Wayman [*sic*], John Winthrop's fiancée. A
wee little body, easy, chatty, but not graceful or finished in manner, and with no

21 June 1840, dau. of John and Henrietta B. (Gassner) Weyman. She m. (2) 5 Oct. 1899, Dr. Henry Cecil Haven, and d. at Stockbridge 25 Nov. 1905.[1404]

John Winthrop's mother died when he was a year old, and from the age of two he lived with his kinsman John C. Gray.[1405] He entered Harvard in 1858 but later recalled that "at the end of my freshman year Prex. Walker said he was 'sorry to inform' me that I hadn't passed my examinations satisfactorily, that I hadn't got my matriculation, and that my time of probation was over; I was therefore dismissed from my class for the space of one year." He traveled to the village of Stockbridge, in Berkshire County, and "had a good time" until April, when he sailed for Europe. He returned in September but again did not pass the exams and so had to join the Class of 1863.[1406] "I have a particular fondness for horses and dogs," he would write when a senior at Harvard. "I have kept more or less dogs since I first came to College; at present I have three. My plans of life are still in embryo."[1407] After he graduated, John oversaw 200 acres in Stockbridge[1408] as a "gentleman farmer," which he defined as "one who has a farm, does not labor, and loses money at steadily."[1409] He spent the winter months in Boston.[1410] A classmate would recall that "he was never fond of books. He was fond of nature and animals, and understood them. He was bluff, honest, outspoken, straightforward in his manners and conversation—'without any nonsense.'"[1411] His brother Robert

---

beauty—but less plain than I expected to see" (Hedwiga Regina Shober Gray diary, R. Stanton Avery Special Collections).

[1404] Isabella Cowpland Haven Death Certificate, *Americanancestors.org* > Massachusetts Vital Records, 1841–1910, > 190587 (deaths) > image 69 of 550. See also "Obituary Record 1914," *Amherst College Bulletin* 3 [1914]: 214.

[1405] John Chipman Gray married Elizabeth Pickering Gardner in 1820; they were childless. Mrs. Gray was the daughter of Eliza Blanchard Winthrop's foster father (and great-uncle), Samuel Pickering Gardner (Scott C. Steward and Christopher C. Child, *The Descendants of Judge John Lowell of Newburyport, Massachusetts* [Boston: Newbury Street Press, 2011], 18).

[1406] He was a member of the Porcellian Club with that class (*Porcellian Club 1791–2016*, 103).

[1407] Mayo, *The Winthrop Family in America*, 406–7, citing manuscript of Records of the Class of 1863, 943, in Harvard Archives.

[1408] *The Harvard Graduates' Magazine* 4 [1895]: 294.

[1409] *Report of the Secretary of the Class of 1863 of Harvard College, June, 1893, to June, 1903*, 122.

[1410] *The Harvard Graduates' Magazine* 4 [1895]: 294.

[1411] *Report of the Secretary of the Class of 1863 of Harvard College, June, 1893, to June, 1903*, 123.

would add: "With much native intelligence, he had no love of literature or disposition to mix in general society. A single trip to Europe satiated him with art, and a single term of office as respresentative of the Fifth Berkshire District in the Massachusetts Legislature tired him of politics."[1412] Elsewhere Robert wrote that John's death was "a great grief to me, for tho' we had few tastes in common, we were very fond of one another and everyone was fond of him."[1413]

[1412] *The Harvard Graduates' Magazine* 4 [1895]: 294–95. *Report of the Secretary of the Class of 1863 of Harvard College, June, 1893, to June, 1903*, 124, identifies the author as Robert C. Winthrop, Jr.

[1413] Charles Francis Adams, "Memoir of Robert C. Winthrop, Jr.," *Proceedings of the Massachusetts Historical Society*, 2nd series, 20 [1906]: 197.

The Eighth Generation

15. **Robert**[8] **Winthrop** (*Thomas Charles*[7], *Francis Bayard*[6], *John Still*[5], *John*[4], *Waitstill*[3], *John*[2-1]) was born at New York, New York 18 August 1833[1414] and known for a time as an adult as Robert B. Winthrop.[1415] He died at New York 18 November 1892.[1416] He married at St. George's Church, New York 23 June 1859,[1417] **Katharine Wilson "Kate" Taylor**, who was born at New York 4 February 1839,[1418] the youngest daughter of Moses and Catherine Ann (Wilson) Taylor.[1419] She died at home at 38 East Thirty-seventh Street in New York 7 June 1925.[1420]

[1414] "Memoirs: Frederic Winthrop," *Register* 86 [1932]: 444.

[1415] Mayo, *The Winthrop Family in America*, 381, citing editions of *Trow's New York City Directory* between 1856 and 1860, which lists him as "Robert B. Winthrop," suggests his given name may have been Robert Bayard Winthrop (honoring his grandfather and great-uncle) or Robert Benjamin Winthrop (honoring two of his grandfather's half-brothers). Robert was also the given name of his mother's first cousin Robert Kane Morris, who died in Baton Rouge 6 June 1833 (Elizabeth Dennistoun Kane, *Story of John Kane of Dutchess County, New York* [Philadelphia: J. B. Lippincott Co., 1921], 115).

[1416] "Memoirs: Frederic Winthrop," *Register* 86 [1932]: 444. Mayo, *The Winthrop Family in America*, 382, gives the place.

[1417] Mayo, *The Winthrop Family in America*, 382.

[1418] *The New York Times*, 25 June 1859, 5. "Married . . . in this city, on Thursday, June 23, at St. George's Church, by the Rev. Dr. Tyng, Robert Winthrop to Kate W., daughter of Moses Taylor."

[1419] "Moses Taylor," *The National Cyclopaedia of American Biography* (New York: James T. White & Co., 1897), 7: 255–56. "The island of Cuba was Mr. Taylor's main field of foreign commerce, but his ships were also well known in India, China, the West Indies and South America. . . . He became president of the City Bank in 1855, holding that office until his death. . . . As chairman of the loan committee of the Associated Banks it was chiefly owing to his efforts that the loan of $200 million was raised and the government found itself in funds, in 1861, to carry on the war. Mr. Taylor held intimate personal relations with Pres. Lincoln, the secretary of the treasury, and the finance committees of both branches of Congress. He refused the secretaryship of the treasury which was offered him by Pres. Lincoln in 1866 [*sic*]. . . . He was one of the five associates who laid the first Atlantic cable. The last act of his life was the gift of $270,000 for the construction and maintenance of a hospital at Scranton, Pa." for injured and disabled railroad workers. See also Daniel Hodas, *The Business Career of Moses Taylor: Merchant, Finance Capitalist, and Industrialist* (New York: New York University Press, 1975). Moses' grandfather, Moses Taylor, who emigrated from England to New York in 1736, had been a brass and copper kettle dealer, but his son, Jacob Bloom Taylor, became a trusted business agent for John Jacob Astor (2, 5).

[1420] *The New York Times*, 8 June 1925, 15. "Mrs. Kate Taylor Winthrop, widow of Robert Winthrop, head of the banking firm of his name, died yesterday at her residence, 39

Robert began his career with the New York branch of the Glasgow banking firm of J. & A. Dennistoun Wood, a principal financier of the cotton and sugar trade.[1421] By 1856, Robert Winthrop was at work at 10 Wall Street and residing with his kinsman Benjamin Winthrop at 134 Second Avenue.[1422] In 1859, he became a partner in the banking firm of Read, Drexel.[1423] In 1860, he was described for the first time as a "banker," and in 1862 he was admitted to the New York Stock Exchange.[1424] In 1863, when W.G. Read retired, he and Anthony J. Drexel became the sole partners of Drexel, Winthrop, with offices at the City Bank Building on Wall Street.[1425] Toward the end of the Civil War, he moved his family to 118 Fifth Avenue.[1426]

In this period, the financier Junius S. Morgan intervened in the affairs of Drexel, Winthrop, with the result that Anthony Drexel became Morgan's son's partner (creating Drexel, Morgan, later J. P. Morgan & Co. and successor firms) and Robert Winthrop established his own namesake company in 1871.

> One family story is that J.P. Morgan [Junius Morgan's son] invited both Drexel and Robert Winthrop to join the new firm. The plan, however, was that Winthrop would go to Paris to set up a branch there—a move he didn't want to make. Another version holds that he dropped out because he didn't want to get involved in the speculative European markets in which the Morgan money was heavily invested. The Morgan side of the story, however, is that Drexel wasn't particularly interested in keeping Winthrop in the new partnership. . . . 'A proud and wealthy man, with many

---

East Thirty-seventh Street, at the age of 86. . . . Mrs. Winthrop was married in 1859, and ever since had lived in this city, except for the Summers at her house in Lenox, Mass."

[1421] Hodas, *The Business Career of Moses Taylor*, 130. William Wood (1808–1894), husband of his aunt Harriet Amelia Kane and then his cousin Margaret Van Horne Lawrence, was connected with this firm.

[1422] H. Wilson, comp., *Trow's New York City Directory for the Year Ending May 1, 1857* (New York: John F. Trow, 1856), 896.

[1423] Wexler, *Reared in a Greenhouse*, 34, 396.

[1424] Wexler, *Reared in a Greenhouse*, 34. "Family lore has it that [Kate Winthrop] set Robert Winthrop up in business, and it may have been she who provided the $3,000 that enabled him to buy his seat on the Stock Exchange in 1862" (36).

[1425] Wexler, *Reared in a Greenhouse*, 34–35, citing Wood, Struthers & Winthrop company brochure, 1968.

[1426] Mayo, *The Winthrop Family in America*, 382.

outside interests,'[1427] Winthrop resigned to take care of his personal and family affairs and help out his sixty-five year-old father-in-law, Moses Taylor.[1428]

He died in November 1892—following the family move from 118 Fifth Avenue to 38 East Thirty-Seventh Street—and, in his great-granddaughter's view, his obituary recorded the life "of a worthy gentleman, one who had brought new professional credibility to an old family and had done so in a modest and unassuming way."[1429]

His marriage was a happy one. Almost three years after his death, his grieving widow recorded the following observation in her memory book: "It is very difficult to be strong, when all the *meaning* is gone out of your life."[1430] Near the outset of their union, Captain Frederick Winthrop (with the Army of the Potomac) had written his brother: "You must be settled very pleasantly by this time in your new home. You are a damned lucky dog to get such as a woman as Kate and that enormous baby of yours [Dudley], how is it! It's evidently a big thing. Kiss them both for me and in particular remember me to Kate."[1431]

As Dorothy Bradford Wexler observed, "It's hard to know whether by, 'such a woman,' brother Frederic was referring to Kate or her purse." Mayo, in his earlier genealogy of the Winthrop family, explained the circumstances:[1432]

> When her father died in 1882, she fell heir to about $8 million. This money she determined to put to work in such a manner that she might leave that amount to *each* of her four sons; in other words, she proposed to quadruple her own patrimony in the 30 years that presumably lay ahead of her. It was a very interesting resolve; and more than interesting than the resolve itself is the fact that she carried it out with complete success. Whatever views others

---

[1427] Wexler, *Reared in a Greenhouse*, 44, citing Vincent P. Carosso, *The Morgans: Private International Bankers, 1854–1913* (Cambridge: Harvard University Press, 1987), 138.

[1428] Wexler, *Reared in a Greenhouse*, 43–44, citing Robert Winthrop, "Draft history of Robert Winthrop & Co.," 1973, and Robert Winthrop Kean, *Fourscore Years: My First Twenty-four* (privately printed, 1974), 43.

[1429] Wexler, *Reared in a Greenhouse*, 45. Another comment noted "the charmed circle broken / A dear face missed day by day from its accustomed place . . . ." (45).

[1430] Wexler, *Reared in a Greenhouse*, 45.

[1431] Frederick Winthrop to Robert Winthrop, 15 August 1862 (Wexler, *Reared in a Greenhouse*, 35).

[1432] Mayo, *The Winthrop Family in America*, 382.

might hold, Mrs. Winthrop knew that her father—who bought a controlling interest in the Delaware, Lackawanna and Western Railroad when the stock had fallen to $5 a share and still had it seven years later when it was selling for $240—would have applauded her magnificant achievement.[1433]

In *Reared in a Greenhouse*, Dorothy Bradford Wexler gives a further account of Kate Wilson (Taylor) Winthrop:[1434]

During Robert's lifetime, neither he nor Kate had sought the social spotlight. Both were "nobs," the term coined by society's self-appointed arbiter Ward McAllister to separate the conservative old families from the "swells," rich and often vulgar newcomers like the Vanderbilts, who had outdone everyone by building an entire block of mansions along Fifth Avenue shortly after the Civil War.[1435] Nobs could dress shabbily, squirrel away their money, and look down on swells, but swells never looked down on nobs. Robert particularly, despite his lineage, had no sense of entitlement. . . . "There but for the grace of God go I," he would say, when he encountered a beggar or a drunk in the street.[1436]

Kate, though she had a swell's credentials (plenty of new money), was more outspokenly nobbish than Robert. She filled her "inspirational" notebooks with poems poking fun at society figures. . . . Kate counted among her close friends two women who looked as grandly down upon social climbers as she did. Her grandson Robert Winthrop Kean remembered that the pair, Edith Wharton and Sara Delano Roosevelt, would often drop by at teatime.[1437] No fool would have been gladly suffered at these "power" teas. The well-born Wharton . . . made her name primarily by

---

[1433] Mayo, perhaps concerned the Winthrop men would take offense, added a disclaimer: "In the attainment of her objective, Mrs. Winthrop was, of course, ably assisted by her banker husband" (until his death in 1892).

[1434] Wexler, *Reared in a Greenhouse*, 46–47.

[1435] Wexler, *Reared in a Greenhouse*, 46, citing Cleveland Amory, *Who Killed Society?* (New York: Harper & Brothers, 1960), 119.

[1436] Wexler, *Reared in a Greenhouse*, 46, citing Kean, *Fourscore Years*, 43.

[1437] Wexler, *Reared in a Greenhouse*, 46, citing Kean, *Fourscore Years*, 46.

drawing devastating word portraits of New York society. As for Sara Delano Roosevelt, mother of Franklin, [one biographer] wrote: "She hated, with considerable verve and in no particular order, ostentation, vulgarity, shabby politicians, the new resorts of the new rich, and virtually all races, nationalities, and families other than her own."[1438]

Kate Winthrop could be just as scathing as her two women friends. Her grandson remembered her grumbling about Mrs. E. H. Harriman's having been given the seat of honor at a dinner party one evening. Mrs. Harriman, she sniffed, had probably earned her place at the right hand of the host "just because her husband has made so much money."[1439] Unlike her husband, however, Mrs. Winthrop was lordly not only toward the common rich but also toward the common man. "Please be quiet. My children are trying to sleep," she reportedly once chided a noisy garbageman clattering outside her Fifth Avenue window. When the garbage collector shot back a rude comment, she promptly lodged a complaint with the Sanitation Department. "I am Mrs. Robert Winthrop," she is said to have announced, "and my garbage man is not a gentleman." "I'm sorry, Mrs. Winthrop," the official is said to have replied, "but it's very hard to get a gentleman to pick up your garbage."[1440]

After the inheritance from her father, after the move to Murray Hill, and after her husband's death, Kate Winthrop began to shuck some of her modest ways and assume the proportions of a grand dowager. The interior of the Murray Hill house was, at least in my mother's recollections, quite awe-inspiring. "Everything was enormous and heavy . . . the dark brown woodwork, the furniture, the ornamentation. The rugs were so thick you couldn't hear a thing when people walked along. That was stylish—and very practical. It never got dirty. . . .

[1438] Wexler, *Reared in a Greenhouse*, 46, citing Blanche Wiesen Cook, *Eleanor Roosevelt, Vol. 1: 1884–1933* (New York: Penguin Books, 1992), 144.

[1439] Wexler, *Reared in a Greenhouse*, 46, citing Kean, *Fourscore Years: My First Twenty-four*, 46.

[1440] Wexler, *Reared in a Greenhouse*, 46–47. The author noted the story, "perhaps apocryphal," was shared by her cousin, John[11] Winthrop (399).

In the dining room, somebody was standing behind each
chair at the table . . . a first butler, a second butler, and a
couple of maids flourishing around."[1441]

But "Grandma Winthrop was smart," her granddaughter Dorothy
Winthrop Bradford would recall. "When she was about 35 years old,
she retired, put on a little lace cap and sat by the fire. That's what my
father [Frederic Winthrop] said. At the age of 35, she said she was too
old to do anything any more. They had lovely little coke fires in those
days, and she'd sit by the fireplace, next to the coke fire, lace cap on her
head—and invest."[1442]

Children of Robert[8] and Katharine Wilson (Taylor) Winthrop, ii–vii born
at New York:

    i.   Kate Taylor[9] Winthrop, b. and d. at New York 3 June 1860. She
        was bur. at Green-Wood Cemetery in Brooklyn, N.Y.[1443]

    ii. Robert Dudley Winthrop, b. 22 July 1861[1444] and d. unm. of
        heart disease at his mother's home at 38 East Thirty-Seventh Street
        16 April 1912.[1445]

        R. Dudley Winthrop prepared for college at Duane S. Everson's
        School in New York, and was admitted to Harvard College in June
        1879[1446]; in 1882, he was runner-up for a heavyweight wrestling
        championship. He roomed all four years at Mrs. Brown's, on the
        corner of Brattle and Story Streets, "that famous oasis of Club

---

[1441] Wexler, *Reared in a Greenhouse*, 47.

[1442] Wexler, *Reared in a Greenhouse*, 68. Robert Winthrop Kean observes that while "my
grandmother lived very comfortably, it was impossible in those days of no income
tax for her to spend all her income, and her property increased greatly over the
forty years between her father's death and hers" (Kean, *Fourscore Years*, 46).

[1443] Register of Births, Borough of Manhattan, 1847–1873 (New York Municipal
Archives), 7: 215 (Family History Library film 1,315,313), indexed at *familysearch.
org/ark:/61903/1:1:27Y2-GK2*. The child is identified as female but not named.
Wexler, *Reared in a Greenhouse*, 34, gives Kate T. Winthrop, citing a record provided
by Green-Wood Cemetery, where she was interred on 11 April 1894, which gives
her birthdate and says she died aged "2 hours" (396). She does not appear in an
index to Green-Wood Cemetery records at *green-wood.com*.

[1444] *Class of 1883. Harvard College. Thirtieth Anniversary, 1883–1913. Sixth Report*
(Boston: E.O. Cockayne, 1913), 203. Mayo, *The Winthrop Family in America*, 421,
noted: "Although most of the Winthrops born after 1720 were descended from
both Thomas Dudley and his unpopular son Joseph, this is, as far as we know, the
first instance where that fact was given prominence by using Dudley as part of a
Winthrop's name."

[1445] *Class of 1883. Harvard College. Thirtieth Anniversary, 1883–1913. Sixth Report*, 203–4.

[1446] *Class of 1883. Harvard College. Thirtieth Anniversary, 1883–1913. Sixth Report*, 203.

Tables."[1447] In the summer after his graduation in 1883, he went abroad for a few months and then returned to work at his father's bank. On 1 Jan. 1884, at age 22, he was admitted to the firm.[1448] During the war with Spain in 1898, he served as aide-de-camp (with the rank of captain) on the staff of Major Gen. J.J. Coppinger, who commanded the 4th Army Corps. He was discharged on 1 Nov. 1898, when Coppinger retired.[1449] During the 1890s and early part of the century he traveled extensively in the United States,[1450] Europe, and Mexico, and nearly every year went to Ireland for the hunting season. (He also had a great interest in horse breeding.[1451])

He had a country house at Westbury, L.I.,[1452] and a farm in Allendale County, S.C.: "In 1906, when Dudley started buying up the place, land in that part of South Carolina had been dirt cheap, as low as $4.50 an acre. Over a four-year period, he purchased nearly ten thousand acres." His niece Dorothy, visiting Groton Plantation in Dec. 1920, wrote, "we reached the place which is too lovely in spite of the awful roads. I think I like bum roads. It makes the place more wild."[1453]

    iii.   GRENVILLE M. WINTHROP, b. and d. at New York in 1863. He was bur. in the family vault at Green-Wood Cemetery.[1454]

18   iv.   GRENVILLE LINDALL WINTHROP, b. 11 Feb. 1864; m. 2 June 1892, MARY TALLMADGE TREVOR.

19   v.   KATHARINE TAYLOR WINTHROP, b. 8 Feb. 1866; m. 12 Jan. 1888, HAMILTON FISH KEAN.

20   vi.   FREDERIC BAYARD WINTHROP, b. 15 Nov. 1868; m. (1) 20 Jan. 1903, DOROTHY[10] AMORY; m. (2) 12 July 1911, SARAH BARROLL THAYER.

[1447] *The Harvard Graduates' Magazine* 20 [1911–12]: 711.

[1448] *Class of 1883. Harvard College. Thirtieth Anniversary, 1883–1913. Sixth Report*, 203; also *Secretary's Report, No. 2* (1886), 78.

[1449] *The Harvard Graduates' Magazine* 20 [1911–12]: 711.

[1450] A letter to his mother of 2 September 1896 reports: "I was not arrested for scrapping [in Wyoming] but for trying to smuggle a Chinaman into the United States from Canada. I found an officer jumping on Noon on the train and wanting $10 to let him through. Of course I jumped in [to the dispute] and as I looked pretty hard (I have my head shaved and a beard) and as he did not know Noon was my servant he said he would arrest me too" (Kean, *Fourscore Years*, 50).

[1451] *The Harvard Graduates' Magazine* 20 [1911–12]: 711.

[1452] *The Harvard Graduates' Magazine* 20 [1911–12]: 711.

[1453] Wexler, *Reared in a Greenhouse*, 151.

[1454] Wexler, *Reared in a Greenhouse*, 34. The Municipal Archives have no record of his birth or death, and his name does not appear in an index to Green-Wood Cemetery records at *green-wood.com*.

21   vii.   ALBERTINA TAYLOR WINTHROP, b. 9 Nov. 1871; m. 17 May 1904,
             JAN HERMAN VAN ROIJEN.
22   viii. BEEKMAN WINTHROP, b. at Orange, N.J. 18 Sept. 1874; m. 7 Oct.
             1903, MELZA RIGGS WOOD.

16. **ANNA POWELL GRANT**[8] **SEARS** (*David*[7] *Sears, Anne*[6] *Winthrop, John
Still*[5]*, John*[4]*, Waitstill*[3]*, John*[2-1]) was born at Boston, Massachusetts 16
March 1813[1455] and died at Brookline, Massachusetts 29 November
1895.[1456] She married at 42 Beacon Street, Boston 17 January 1833,
WILLIAM AMORY, who was born 15 June and baptized at Trinity
Church, Boston 8 July 1804, son of Thomas Coffin and Hannah Rowe
(Linzee) Amory.[1457] He died at home at 41 Beacon Street 9 December
1888[1458] and was buried with his wife at the Sears Chapel in Longwood
(Brookline).[1459]

William Amory prepared for Harvard at Jacob Newman Knapp's
school in Brighton and Jamaica Plain, near Boston, and entered college
in 1819:

> On account of the Rebellion, in which his class took
> part, he with many others was expelled, but received the
> degree of Master of Arts in 1845.[1460] In 1823, he entered
> the law office of Luther Lawrence[1461] in Groton, where
> he remained five months, then going to Europe and
> remaining five years. On his return he studied in the
> offices of Franklin Dexter and William H. Gardiner, and
> was admitted to the Suffolk bar in October, 1830. He
> abandoned law and became one of the most eminent and
> respected merchants of Boston.[1462]

"William Amory," according to one biographer, "was a gentleman
of the old school, tall, graceful, exceedingly courteous and polite,

---

[1455] Linzee, *The Linzee Family of Great Britain and the United States*, 2: 765.

[1456] Massachusetts Vital Records, 1895, Brookline, 455: 478.

[1457] Linzee, *The Linzee Family of Great Britain and the United States*, 2: 764–65.

[1458] Massachusetts Vital Records, 1888, Boston, 393: 415.

[1459] Linzee, *The Linzee Family of Great Britain and the United States*, 2: 764–65.

[1460] He was a member of the Porcellian Club in the Class of 1823 (*Porcellian Club 1791–2016*, 82).

[1461] Later the first mayor of the city of Lowell.

[1462] William T. Davis, *Bench and Bar of the Commonwealth of Massachusetts*, 2 vols. (Boston: The Boston History Company, 1895), 1: 261.

dignified yet always approachable by his neighbors [in Brookline]."[1463] His daughter-in-law Elizabeth Gardner Amory thought him "the sweetest tempered and eas[iest] going man . . . intellectual, reading all the time, and [with] a wonderful memory . . . very handsome." Her mother-in-law she found more challenging: while she "had an air of great elegance and refinement [she was] morbid and quite melancholy in temperament" (perhaps because of her deafness).[1464] In a memorial published after her death, Anna Sears Amory was remembered as having been "imbued with the spirit of benevolence and possessing many beautiful qualities of mind and heart."[1465]

Children of William and Anna Powell Grant[8] (Sears) Amory, born at Boston:[1466]

> i. WILLIAM[9] AMORY,[1467] b. 4 Oct. 1833 and d. at Dublin, N.H. 16 June 1907. He m. (1) at King's Chapel, Boston 8 Feb. 1860, ELLEN BREWER, who was b. at Boston 8 Feb. 1836[1468] and d. at 140 Beacon Street, Boston 16 Jan. 1873,[1469] dau. of Gardner and Mary (Weld) Brewer; m. (2) at the Church of the Holy Communion, New York, N.Y. 1 Sept. 1874,[1470] JEANNE PHILOMENE GUICHARD,[1471] who was b. at Buffières (Saône et Loire), France 5 March 1832 and d. at New York 21 April 1894; m. (3) at 163 Commonwealth Avenue, Boston 18 July 1896, LOUISE ANNETTE GAUDELET, who was b. at Thetford, Vt. 29 Dec. 1856[1472] and d. at Belmont, Mass. 15 Dec. 1944,[1473] dau.

[1463] "The William Amory House," *Proceedings of the Brookline Historical Society at the Annual Meeting, January 28, 1902* (Brookline: Published by the society, 1902), 11.

[1464] Wexler, *Reared in a Greenhouse*, 18.

[1465] *Sixty-fifth Annual Report of the Trustees of the Perkins Institution and Massachusetts School for the Blind for the year ending August 31, 1896* (Boston: Press of George H. Ellis, 1897), 32.

[1466] May, *The Descendants of Richard Sears*, 260; Linzee, *The Linzee Family of Great Britain and the United States*, 2: 765, 772–76, 777.

[1467] He was a member of the Porcellian Club in Harvard's Class of 1855 (*Porcellian Club 1791–2016*, 100).

[1468] Linzee, *The Linzee Family of Great Britain and the United States*, 2: 772.

[1469] Massachusetts Vital Records, 1873, Boston, 258: 15. On 18 January 1873, Regina Shober Gray noted that "Young Mrs. Wm. Amory, Jr. (Brewer) died of ship fever—has been a bed-ridden invalid for years" (Hedwiga Regina Shober Gray diary, R. Stanton Avery Special Collections).

[1470] Linzee, *The Linzee Family of Great Britain and the United States*, 2: 772.

[1471] Mrs. Gray remarked: "Mr. William Amory, jr.'s engagement to his children's governess, Miss Guichard, is out. She is a niece of Lamartiné, and a very charming woman, I hear" (entry for 18 July 1874).

[1472] Linzee, *The Linzee Family of Great Britain and the United States*, 2: 772.

[1473] Massachusetts Vital Records, 1944, Belmont, 5: 53; *Boston Social Register 1945 Dilatory Domiciles January 1945*, 2.

of Alfred and Harriet Hooper (Chase) Gaudelet, and had issue by his first wife (Caroline[10] Amory, who married George Hinckley Lyman, and Anna Sears Amory, who married George Francis Weld) and his third wife (Harriet Sears[10] Amory, who married Warwick Potter).[1474]

  ii. Harriet Sears Amory, b. 27 Sept. 1835 and d. at 147 Beacon Street, Boston 26 Nov. 1865.[1475] She m. at 41 Beacon Street 14 Nov. 1860,[1476] Joseph Peabody Gardner,[1477] who was b. at Boston 2 Aug. 1828 and d. at Beverly, Mass. 11 June 1875, son of John Lowell and Catherine Elizabeth (Peabody) Gardner,[1478] and had issue.

      The elder brother of John Lowell Gardner (Jr.), and thus brother-in-law of Isabella Stewart Gardner, Joe Gardner brought up his three motherless sons after his wife's death.[1479] Like his father, the eldest—a second Joseph Peabody[10] Gardner—died young. The middle son was William Amory Gardner, the exuberant co-founder (with Endicott Peabody and Sherrard Billings) of the Groton School west of Boston. The last was Augustus Peabody Gardner, who married Constance Lodge, daughter of Senator Henry Cabot Lodge; he would later be a member of Congress. Their daughter Constance[11] Gardner married Grafton Winthrop[10] Minot, a son of Joseph Grafton Minot and Honora Elizabeth Temple[9] Winthrop, in turn the daughter of Thomas Lindall[8] Winthrop and granddaughter of Grenville Temple[7] Winthrop.[1480]

  iii. Ellen Sears Amory, b. 6 Sept. 1837 and d. at 391 Commonwealth Avenue, Boston 28 May 1908.[1481] She m. at 41 Beacon Street 21 Dec. 1865, Brevet Brig. General John Francis Anderson, who

---

[1474] Linzee, *The Linzee Family of Great Britain and the United States*, 2: 772, 773; "Miss Amory Engaged," *The New York Times*, 10 November 1921, 19.

[1475] Massachusetts Vital Records, 1865, Boston, 185: 152.

[1476] Linzee, *The Linzee Family of Great Britain and the United States*, 2: 773.

[1477] He was a member of the Porcellian Club in Harvard's Class of 1847 (*Porcellian Club 1791–2016*, 97). Mrs. Gray noted: "Mr. Joe P. Gardner—son of John L.G.—was found dead on Friday near his house at Beverly with a bullet in his head and a pistol in his hand. He leaves 3 sons, the eldest about 14. His wife Harriet Amory died at the birth of the youngest some 8 or 10 years since. No one can account for the deed, if intentional—but it may have been caused by an accidental stumble in the woods" (entry for 13 June 1875).

[1478] Steward and Child, *The Descendants of Judge John Lowell of Newburyport, Massachusetts*, 33.

[1479] Whitehill, *Captain Joseph Peabody*, 182, 183, 194.

[1480] Linzee, *The Linzee Family of Great Britain and the United States*, 2: 773, 791, 801; Mayo, *The Winthrop Family in America*, 309–14.

[1481] Masachusetts Vital Records, 1908, Boston, 11: 695.

was b. at Belfast, Me. 4 Dec. 1832 and d. at Portland, Me. 19 April 1902,[1482] son of Hugh Johnston Anderson, Governor of Maine, and Martha Jane (Dummer) Anderson,[1483] and had issue (Harriet Amory[10] Anderson, who married Francis Stanley Parker; Ellen Amory Anderson, who married Charles Pelham Curtis; and Anna Dummer Anderson, who married Francis Reginald Bangs).[1484]

23   iv.   CHARLES WALTER AMORY, b. 16 Oct. 1842; m. 23 Oct. 1867, ELIZABETH GARDNER.

       v.   FRANCIS INMAN AMORY,[1485] b. 5 June 1850 and d. at New York 7 Jan. 1921.[1486] He m. at the Church of the Advent, Boston 12 May 1886, GRACE JOSEPHINE MINOT, who was b. at New York 19 Sept. 1859 and d. at Boston 15 April 1911, dau. of Charles Henry and Maria Josephine (Grafton) Minot,[1487] and had issue (Mary Josephine[10] Amory, who married Fulton Cutting; Charles Minot Amory, who married Gladys Mildred Munn and Margaret Emerson McKim Vanderbilt Baker; Grace Sears Amory; and Francis Inman Amory, who married Margaret Perin).[1488]

17. **ROBERT CHARLES**[8] **WINTHROP, JR.** (*Robert Charles*[7], *Thomas Lindall*[6], *John Still*[5], *John*[4], *Waitstill*[3], *John*[2-1]) was born at home at 7 Tremont Street in Boston, Massachusetts 7 December 1834[1489] and died at 10 Walnut Street, Boston 5 June 1905.[1490] He married, first, at Boston 15 October 1857,[1491] **FRANCES PICKERING ADAMS**, who was born at Boston 10 May

[1482] Linzee, *The Linzee Family of Great Britain and the United States*, 2: 773.

[1483] *Obituary Record of the Graduates of Bowdoin College and the Medical School of Maine* (Lewiston, Me.: Journal Printshop, 1911), 488.

[1484] Linzee, *The Linzee Family of Great Britain and the United States*, 2: 773, 776, 792–93.

[1485] He was a member of the Porcellian Club in Harvard's Class of 1871 (*Porcellian Club 1791–2016*, 106).

[1486] *Boston Social Register 1921 Dilatory Domiciles February 1921*, 1.

[1487] Linzee, *The Linzee Family of Great Britain and the United States*, 2: 777.

[1488] Linzee, *The Linzee Family of Great Britain and the United States*, 2: 777, 795; "Amory-Perin," *The New York Times*, 9 January 1921, 23; "Mrs. Raymond T. Baker Married to C. M. Amory by Archbishop Francis at F. Cutting Home," *The New York Times*, 25 October 1928, 25; "Charles M. Amory Dies of Pneumonia," *The New York Times*, 9 October 1936, 25.

[1489] Adams, *Proceedings of the Massachusetts Historical Society*, 2nd series, 20 [1906]: 179. He was known as "the younger Robert C. Winthrop" and kept the "Jr." after his name during the decade he survived his father. Mayo, *The Winthrop Family in America*, 390, noted that "Tremont Place was, and still is, a by-way running from Beacon Street to the Granary Burying-ground on the eastern slope of Beacon Hill."

[1490] Massachusetts Vital Records, 1905, Boston, 13: 501.

[1491] Massachusetts Vital Records, 1857, Boston, 110: 107.

1835, the youngest daughter of Benjamin and Louisa Ann (Walter) Adams.[1492] She died while the couple was traveling in Rome, Italy 23 April 1860.[1493] Regina Shober Gray, a close friend of Fanny Winthrop's Walter cousins, remarked that, "like his father, [Robert C. Winthrop, Jr.,] has the luck to seek & win rich wives! He did not get much however from his first wife Fanny Adams—her father left them each only $15,000 at their own disposal [while] the rest reverted, in default, to [Fanny's] sisters."[1494] Robert married, second, at Boston 1 June 1869,[1495] **ELIZABETH "BESSIE" MASON**, who was born there 1 October 1844, the daughter of Robert Means and Sarah Ellen (Francis) Mason. She died at Boston 22 April 1924.[1496] Mrs. Gray noted the Winthrop–Mason engagement in January 1869: "He has waited almost as long for her as Jacob for Rachel. It must be 5 or 6 years since we first find their engagement rumored—when she was very young, during her mother's life—and he has been very persistent since. He is a highly cultivated man, talks well, and is a gentleman by birth & breeding. . . . Miss Mason holds her $2 or 300,000, in her own right!"[1497]

[1492] Andrew N. Adams, comp., *A Genealogical History of Robert Adams of Newbury, Mass., and His Descendants, 1635–1900* (Rutland, Vt.: The Tuttle Co., Printers, 1900), 130.

[1493] Mayo, *The Winthrop Family in America*, 395.

[1494] Entry for 18 January 1869: Hedwiga Regina Shober Gray diary, R. Stanton Avery Special Collections.

[1495] Massachusetts Vital Records, 1869, Boston, 219: 64.

[1496] Scott C. Steward and John Bradley Arthaud, eds., *A Thorndike Family History: Descendants of John and Elizabeth (Stratton) Thorndike* (Boston: Newbury Street Press, 2000), 115.

[1497] Entry for 18 January 1869: Hedwiga Regina Shober Gray diary, R. Stanton Avery Special Collections. There was a sequel to this story that sheds another light on the match: "Boston has had two great sensations lately, in social life. One the disastrous marriage of George Welles, Mr. R. C. Winthrop's stepson, to a Parisian lorette, [the] divorced wife of a New Yorker named De Courcy, and kept mistress of a dozen other men. She is about 40 years old—he just 25 & enters into absolute possession of his million of money this month—his grandfather's will having placed his majority at 25 or 26 years! The horror of the story is that the woman has been for years kept by Robt. C. W. jr., who ~~after his engagement to Bessie Mason~~ introduced George Welles to her—made her over to him, came home and offered himself for the 4th or 5th time to Bessie Mason, who accepted at last, perhaps for his 'importunity's sake'— married in June, and took his bride to Paris, to arrive just as all the world rings with this *escalandre*—that George Welles had married her husband's cast-off mistress whom her husband, 10 years older than George & occupying the position of elder brother to him, had specially introduced him to. Think of the mortification to her—a proud, fastidious, pure-minded girl—of the shock to her moral sense, to all her trust, love, & pride. It is enough to <u>crush</u> her. I don't see how either he or George can ever hold their heads up again at home" (entry for 8 August 1869).

Before Robert turned seven, his father had been elected to Congress. "Mr. Winthrop was a Whig and the outgoing President of the United States, Martin Van Buren, was a Democrat," Mayo wrote. "Nevertheless, when young Robert was taken to the White House [in early 1841] he was allowed to sit upon the presidential knee while Mr. Van Buren showed him his watch and seals."[1498] After his mother died in the summer of 1842, Robert's "home life and school were somewhat disorganized," Mayo wrote.[1499] His father moved the family to 21 Summer Street, and a neighbor, "Grandfather" Gardner, became a mentor: "I often sat with him in his study, almost a separate building, adjoining the garden, when he showed me many curious and interesting books or talked about early days in Wenham and elsewhere," Robert would recall.[1500] At age 9 Robert was sent to boarding school in Roxbury; during vacations he visited his mother's relatives in Salem, where a cousin recalled that he "devoured" books in his uncle's library, "utterly oblivious to all that was passing around him."[1501] In April 1847 his father, who would soon be elected Speaker of the U.S. House of Representatives, took Robert on a six-month tour of Europe where they had audiences with the Duke of Wellington and King Louis Philippe of France, among other prominent men.[1502]

Upon their return, Robert enrolled at Phillips Academy at Andover; he entered Harvard College in the fall of 1850, when he was about to turn 16. However, in Cambridge he discovered that "going to the theatre was much more fun than going to lectures and classes, and he developed a habit of seeing almost all the plays in town," Mayo wrote.[1503] Robert would later recall that his grandfather had been nicknamed "English Tom" and his father "English Winthrop," because of their "native reserve and ceremonious manners," so he was a bit cautious when, as a sophomore, a professor took him to task good-naturedly for his "English hauteur." "There was no affectation about it," Robert recalled. "I was by nature reserved except with intimates, combining a

---

[1498] Mayo, *The Winthrop Family in America*, 390, citing Adams, *Proceedings of the Massachusetts Historical Society*, 2nd series, 20 [1906]: 179–80.

[1499] Mayo, *The Winthrop Family in America*, 390.

[1500] Mayo, *The Winthrop Family in America*, 391. Gardner was Robert's great-great-uncle and had been his mother's guardian.

[1501] Edes, *Register* 60 [1906]: 224.

[1502] Winthrop, *Memoir of Robert C. Winthrop*, 64. See also Robert C. Winthrop, *Reminiscences of Foreign Travel: A Fragment of Autobiography* (Privately printed, 1894).

[1503] Mayo, *The Winthrop Family in America*, 391.

sort of youthful bashfulness with extreme shortness of vision, and my inability to recognize people at a little distance often made me seem cold or indifferent."

From the start of his second year to his last, "he was almost continuously a source of irritation and exasperation to the powers that make academic rules and regulations and try to enforce them," Mayo wrote.[1504] He was briefly suspended as a sophomore and during his junior year had to spend part of his vacation making up his Latin and astronomy studies. He missed classes, lectures, and prayers, and the faculty sent warning to his parents early in his senior year that if he returned for the second term it was "at their own risk," for they had no expectation he would graduate with his class.[1505] He was admonished in May for shelling and eating peanuts at the annual Dudleian Lecture.[1506] He also threw a party on Friday, 23 June 1854—"at which spirituous liquors were provided and great disturbances were made and continued to a late hour of the night" —that prompted the faculty on 26 June to vote to withhold his degree. (It would be another year before he received it.)[1507] In 1854, Robert entered Harvard Law School, where he spent a year before joining the firm of Hodges & Saltonstall.[1508] He was admitted to the Suffolk Bar in 1857 but developed what he called "a distaste for the profession which was perhaps unreasonable," and never practiced.[1509]

In 1857, when he was nearly 23, Robert married Fanny Adams.

[1504] Mayo, *The Winthrop Family in America*, 392. The author noted that the faculty faced special challenges with Robert, namely (1) he was a Winthrop, (2) he was extremely capable, and (3) his father was a U.S. senator and member of the college's Board of Overseers.

[1505] Mayo, *The Winthrop Family in America*, 393.

[1506] Mayo, *The Winthrop Family in America*, 393–94, citing faculty records (he recounted it happening during junior year, but faculty records show it was senior year). During a private session with the college president, Robert would recall, he could not deny the charge, given that a professor had seen the pile of shells under his seat. So he argued that part of the lecture "had been devoted to undermining certain [Episcopalian] religious tenets which I had been taught from childhood to reverence." Robert reported seeing a "shadow" of a smile from the president.

[1507] Mayo, *The Winthrop Family in America*, 394, citing faculty records. He was a member of the Porcellian Club in the Class of 1854 (*Porcellian Club 1791–2016*, 99).

[1508] Adams, *Proceedings of the Massachusetts Historical Society*, 2nd series, 20 [1906]: 184. "In the summer of 1856, Winthrop entered the law office of our late associate Leverett Saltonstall, whose marriage to a cousin of his had led to an intimacy": this was Rose Smith Lee, daughter of John Clarke Lee, the elder half-brother of Robert's mother Elizabeth Cabot (Blanchard) Winthrop (Scott C. Steward, *The Descendants of Dr. Nathaniel Saltonstall of Haverhill, Massachusetts* [Boston: Newbury Street Press, 2013], 112).

[1509] Mayo, *The Winthrop Family in America*, 395.

"She was very fond of music," Mayo wrote, "and being an exceptionally good dancer and having a good soprano voice, she was much in demand for social occasions." At the time of the marriage she had a cough that led to the suggestion she spend a few winters in the south of Europe, so the couple sailed for Europe a week after their wedding. "Although Mrs. Winthrop was not really well, she had a sunny disposition" during their travels by carriage through England, France, and Italy. While they were in Rome in the spring of 1860, her health grew rapidly worse and she died there at age 24. Robert went back to Boston but between 1862 and 1865 he returned repeatedly to Europe. Forty years later, he would recall that he had few options—he disliked the law, didn't want to go into politics after hearing the attacks on his father, and could not fight in the war "owing to my liability to water on the knee"; even if he could, "service would be distasteful to me as I had friends and relatives at the South and believed the Republican party [of Lincoln] to be largely responsible for the conflict." He considered moving to San Francisco to pursue a career in newspaper journalism but was discouraged by a friend of his father's, who said he would find the city too coarse for his tastes. "I was always more of a dreamer than a worker," Robert wrote, "capable of much energy by fits and starts, alternating with periods of more or less indulgence and indolence. I wrote verses and short stories which failed to satisfy me,—a novel which I turned when half finished, it fell so short of my ideal,—but it was a pleasure to me to assist my father in his various historical and commemorative undertakings."

In 1866 and 1867, he again traveled to Europe and did not return until the fall of 1868, when he had been away for more than two years. He spent the winter in Boston and in June 1869 was married a second time, this time to Elizabeth Mason, who was ten years his junior and the daughter of a successful merchant. They had met at the French resort of Pau about seven years earlier. She also loved Europe, and so about a month after their marriage they sailed and remained overseas for the next two years, spending most of their time in Italy, Switzerland, and Germany as the Franco-Prussian War had made Paris difficult. They returned to Paris in June 1871 for about five weeks, visited England and Wales, and sailed home. Robert would never return after that visit. He said later that he had not gone back for a variety of reasons, including "the birth of children, my father's dependence upon me, my father-in-law's indisposition to part with his daughter, etc."[1510] By his own

---

[1510] Mayo, *The Winthrop Family in America*, 397.

recollection, after 1871 he led "for the most part a quiet domestic life, the one best suited to my mature tastes, but a great contrast to my early ones." Fading to the background suited him well, he said. "I have felt flattered to find it sometimes said that 'he might have been distinguished had he chosen to exert himself,' but I should have been stung by any insinuation that I tried to make a figure in the world and failed."[1511]

He noted that he had been a member of the Massachusetts Historical Society for some twenty years and had published some hundred communications in its Collections, including a 360-page memoir of his father that he printed and distributed to libraries around the world. He paid for most of the cost of the first volume of J.J. Muskett's *Suffolk Manorial Families*, and reprinted fifty copies of the first four parts that dealt with the Winthrop family. He wrote in 1897 a *Memoir of Robert C. Winthrop*,[1512] as well as memoirs of his father-in-law, Robert M. Mason, and his father's cousin, David Sears, and a sketch of John Winthrop the Younger. Finally, he spent many hours arranging and transcribing the Winthrop Papers from the close of the fifteenth to the middle of the eighteenth century, distributing them among various libraries. He also wrote an outline of the family genealogy in 1874, *A Pedigree of the Family of Winthrop*, and in 1887, *A Short Account of the Winthrop Family*.[1513] He was a trustee at the Boston Athenaeum but "preferred to retire on account of dissatisfaction with the management," and for many years was a member of the Wednesday Evening Club of 1777, "until an increasing deafness, combined with less and less inclination to go out of an evening, decided me to retire."[1514]

[1511] Mayo, *The Winthrop Family in America*, 397.

[1512] Mayo, *The Winthrop Family in America*, 402. Mayo noted that rather than a hagiography, the son included many of the criticisms leveled at his father by his contemporaries. Robert would write of the value he placed on a well-rounded portrait in a letter found pasted inside his copy of the book, now at the Harvard College Library: "I have always contended that the weakness of much political biography lies in the suppression or glossing over of the charges of opponents, but I am not sanguine enough to believe that my example will be generally followed" (402–3).

[1513] Mayo, *The Winthrop Family in America*, 401–2. Mayo commented: "The first is the more comprehensive; the second is the more accurate," and his annotated copy now at the Massachusetts Historical Society is "especially valuable." Robert also wrote *Some of Account of the Early Generations of the Winthrop Family in Ireland* (Cambridge: John Wilson and Son, 1883).

[1514] Adams, *Proceedings of the Massachusetts Historical Society*, 2nd series, 20 [1906]: 196. Mayo commented: "To Philistine ears a good deal of this may sound like a page or two from *The Late George Apley* [a satirical novel about Boston's upper class published in 1937] but anyone who has worked on his own family papers and has any conception of the extent of the Winthrop Papers understands that what Robert

After returning from Europe in 1872, the Winthrops moved to 37½ Beacon Street, and in 1884 to a mansion at 10 Walnut Street. They spent summers in the country in rented homes, and in 1894 he bought an unfinished house at Manchester-by-the-Sea on about 40 acres. He finished the house and named the estate Lanthorne Hill, after a Connecticut estate owned by Governor John Winthrop, Jr.[1515] He became more reclusive as he grew older and frequented only the Somerset Club, where he might be seen alone, reading a magazine or a newspaper. He had surgery in the spring of 1905 and died at home on 5 June at age 70 due to heart failure, which was attributed to the operation. The funeral services were held at St. John's Memorial Chapel of the Episcopal Theological School at Cambridge, which had been given to the school thirty years earlier as a gift by his father-in-law, Robert Mason.[1516] He left more than $30,000 in bequests to historical societies, as well as to Bowdoin College and Phillips Academy, Andover, "for the encouragement of the study of Greek and Latin authors."[1517]

Children of Robert Charles[8] and Elizabeth (Mason) Winthrop:

    i.   ROBERT MASON[9] WINTHROP, b. at 37½ Beacon Street 7 March 1873[1518] and d. unm. at Nice (Alpes Maritimes), France 6 May 1938.[1519]

C. Winthrop, Jr., attempted in this field alone was no easy task, however congenial the work may have been. And anyone who has used any of the many cumbersome volumes in which the letters and documents were mounted and labeled by him appreciates the time and labor the process required in addition to the arduous preliminary work of identifying, sorting and organizing. . . . He was better equipped than any paid worker could have been." At his death, his widow gave the Massachusetts Historical Society 43 folio volumes of Winthrop material (*The Winthrop Family in America*, 398–99).

[1515] Mayo, *The Winthrop Family in America*, 403.

[1516] Mayo, *The Winthrop Family in America*, 404–5.

[1517] Edes, *Register* 60 [1906]: 236.

[1518] Massachusetts Vital Records, 1873, Boston, 252: 49.

[1519] Mayo, *The Winthrop Family in America*, 440. His funeral was held at St. Germain, near Paris, on 11 May (*Boston Evening Transcript*, 7 May 1938).

Mrs. Gray noted the birth of Robert Mason Winthrop: "Mrs. R. C. Winthrop, Jr., has a baby son over whom there are great rejoicings, as the name threatened to become extinct in this branch."[1520] Bertie Winthrop graduated from the Groton School, Groton, Mass., and then from Harvard in 1895.[1521] He returned the next year to study law, but remained only a year. About five years later, in 1902, he entered the diplomatic service and for fifteen months was First Secretary of the Legation at Brussels; in 1903, he transferred to Madrid.[1522] He was later stationed in Rome and Athens. In 1910, he resigned and lived mainly in the family home at 10 Walnut Street in Boston,[1523] as well as in Paris.[1524]

ii.   CLARA BOWDOIN WINTHROP, b. at 37½ Beacon Street 12 March 1876[1525] and d. unm. at Manchester 15 March 1969.[1526]

Lawrence Shaw Mayo reported that Clara Winthrop "continued the family tradition of giving to the Massachusetts Historical Society valuable memorabilia of the Winthrop, Temple and Bowdoin families."[1527] Later in life Miss Winthrop would play a role in the development of her great-nephew, John Forbes[11] Kerry, her sister Margaret's grandson: "Among the array of relatives who looked after John, none was more important to his education than great-aunt Clara Winthrop, who had no children of her own. . . . [She] offered to pay for much of John's prep school education, an expensive proposition far beyond the means of Kerry's parents. 'It was a great and sweet and nice thing from an aunt who had no place to put [her money],'" Kerry would recall.[1528]

[1520] Entry for 10 March 1873: Hedwiga Regina Shober Gray diary, R. Stanton Avery Special Collections.

[1521] *Harvard College, Class of 1895, Fifth Report* (Cambridge: Crimson Printing, 1915), 360.

[1522] *Harvard College, Class of 1895, Third Report* (Cambridge: The University Press, 1905), 153.

[1523] *Harvard College, Class of 1895, Fourth Report*, 216–17.

[1524] *Harvard College, Class of 1895, Fifth Report*, 360. He listed his current occupation as "unemployed."

[1525] Massachusetts Vital Records, 1876, Boston, 279: 179; Mayo, *The Winthrop Family in America*, 405.

[1526] *The New York Times*, 18 March 1969, 45.

[1527] Mayo, *The Winthrop Family in America*, 405.

[1528] Michael Kranish, "A privileged youth, a taste for risk," *The Boston Globe*, 15 June 2003.

24   iii.   MARGARET TYNDAL WINTHROP, b. at 1 Walnut Street 27 Feb. 1880; m. 28 Nov. 1906, JAMES GRANT FORBES.

Kinships Between Frederic[9] Winthrop and Dorothy[10] Amory, and Frederic[10] Winthrop and Angela Elizabeth[10] Forbes

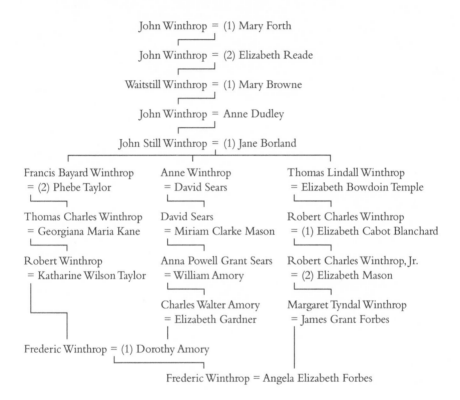

John Winthrop = (1) Mary Forth

John Winthrop = (2) Elizabeth Reade

Waitstill Winthrop = (1) Mary Browne

John Winthrop = Anne Dudley

John Still Winthrop = (1) Jane Borland

Francis Bayard Winthrop
= (2) Phebe Taylor

Anne Winthrop
= David Sears

Thomas Lindall Winthrop
= Elizabeth Bowdoin Temple

Thomas Charles Winthrop
= Georgiana Maria Kane

David Sears
= Miriam Clarke Mason

Robert Charles Winthrop
= (1) Elizabeth Cabot Blanchard

Robert Winthrop
= Katharine Wilson Taylor

Anna Powell Grant Sears
= William Amory

Robert Charles Winthrop, Jr.
= (2) Elizabeth Mason

Charles Walter Amory
= Elizabeth Gardner

Margaret Tyndal Winthrop
= James Grant Forbes

Frederic Winthrop = (1) Dorothy Amory

Frederic Winthrop = Angela Elizabeth Forbes

THE NINTH GENERATION

18. **GRENVILLE LINDALL**[9] **WINTHROP** (*Robert*[8], *Thomas Charles*[7], *Francis Bayard*[6], *John Still*[5], *John*[4], *Waitstill*[3], *John*[2-1]) was born at New York, New York 11 February 1864[1529] and died at home at 15 East Eighty-first Street, New York 19 January 1943.[1530] He married at St. John's Episcopal Church, Yonkers, New York 2 June 1892,[1531] **MARY TALLMADGE TREVOR**, who was born at Yonkers 21 July 1871, daughter of John Bond and Emily (Norwood) Trevor. She died at "Glenview" in Yonkers 1 December 1900.[1532]

Grenville Lindall Winthrop graduated from Duane S. Everson's School, New York, and Harvard University. During his freshman year at Harvard he roomed at 48 Brattle Street in Cambridge with his brother Dudley, then a senior. He graduated *cum laude* in 1886 with "honorable mention" in natural history.[1533] He studied law for two years at Harvard Law School and received his degree in 1889. He first worked at the office of John E. Parsons[1534] and in April 1892 formed a partnership with James B. Ludlow and Frederic D. Phillips at 45 Cedar Street. This partnership continued until 1896, and by 1898 he had joined the banking house of Robert Winthrop and Co. at 40 Wall Street.[1535]

He had a country place in Lenox, Massachusetts, where in 1903 he became a member of the Town Library Association and in 1915 its president. He restored the one-time courthouse in town, "the present library building," built in 1816, as well as the Congregational

---

[1529] Mayo, *The Winthrop Family in America*, 422.

[1530] Mayo, *The Winthrop Family in America*, 427. See also *The New York Times*, 20 January 1943, 19.

[1531] "Winthrop-Trevor," *The New York Times*, 3 June 1892, 8.

[1532] *The New York Times*, 3 December 1900, 7, which noted "a special car will leave 42d St. Station at 9:10" on 4 December for the funeral service at the Glenview.

[1533] He was a member of the Porcellian Club with this class (*Porcellian Club 1791–2016*, 111).

[1534] *Harvard College. Class of 1886, Secretary's Report, No. 2* (1889) 59.

[1535] *Harvard College. Class of 1886, Secretary's Report, No. 4* (1898), 71.

meeting-house and the Lenox Academy building.[1536] He served as president
of the Woman's Hospital, his principal charity, from 1915 to 1941.

He also was a dedicated art collector, inspired in part by his study
of Fine Arts at Harvard. His extensive collection, which he donated
to the Fogg Museum at Harvard in 1943, was stored at his homes in
New York City and Lenox.[1537] Said one friend: "Mr. Winthrop was the
particular bright exemplar in our country of the true connoisseur, the
knowing amateur. . . . He shared my conviction that for the beginner it
is the training of the eye which counts and that the eye is best trained
through an intimate knowledge of the best."[1538]

> Quietly, unobtrusively, he had amassed some four
> thousand works ranging from Near Eastern and Asian
> jade and ritual bronzes to English and American painting
> and watercolors to the decorative arts. The collection was
> planned specifically so that Harvard students could have
> an overview of the world's greatest art. In its entirety it
> represents the most important such bequest ever to an
> American university.[1539]

Children of Grenville Lindall[9] and Mary Tallmadge (Trevor) Winthrop,
born at New York:[1540]

25   i.   EMILY LINDALL[10] WINTHROP, b. 10 March 1893; m. 6 Sept. 1924,
             COREY LUCIEN MILES.

[1536] Mayo, *The Winthrop Family in America*, 423. Edith Wharton found him impenetrable:
"I never was intimate with Grenville—that very word is a contradiction!" (Wexler,
Reared in a Greenhouse, 222, citing Marjorie B. Cohn, "Turner ★ Ruskin ★ Norton
★ Winthrop," *Harvard University Art Museums Bulletin* 2: 1 [Fall 1993]: 36.)

[1537] See "Winthrop Art Left to Fogg Museum," *The New York Times*, 17 October 1943, 50.
This bequest gave the Fogg "the best collection in this country of archaic Chinese
jades, nineteenth-century European drawing and pre-raphaelite art." According to
Mayo, *The Winthrop Family in America*, 426, citing "after-dinner gossip," the collection
had been earmarked for the Metropolitan Museum in New York but Grenville had a
disagreement with the trustees because, by one account, he wanted the art to remain
in the Eighty-first Street house as a separate museum run by the Met.

[1538] Mayo, *The Winthrop Family in America*, 424–25, citing *Art News* 42, No. 16 [1–14
January 1944].

[1539] Wexler, *Reared in a Greenhouse*, 230–31, citing the author's interview with Marjorie
B. Cohn during the summer of 1994. Edgar Peters Bowron, in 1989 the director
of the Harvard University Art Museums, ranked "the collection among the finest
in the country, along with those of John D. Rockefeller, Henry Clay Frick, Isabella
Stewart Gardner, William and Henry Walters, and J. Pierpont Morgan" (231).

[1540] Mayo, *The Winthrop Family in America*, 427 (dates of birth).

26   ii. KATE WINTHROP, b. 9 Dec. 1899; m. 6 Sept. 1924, DARWIN SPURR
         MORSE.

19. **KATHARINE TAYLOR**[9] **WINTHROP** (*Robert*[8], *Thomas Charles*[7], *Francis
Bayard*[6], *John Still*[5], *John*[4], *Waitstill*[3], *John*[2-1]) was born at New York, New
York 8 February 1866[1541] and died at "Green Lane Farm," her summer
home in Deal, New Jersey, on 24 August 1943.[1542] She was buried in the
Winthrop family vault at Green-Wood Cemetery in Brooklyn, New
York.[1543] She married at Grace Church, New York 12 January 1888,
HAMILTON FISH KEAN,[1544] who was born at "Ursino," near Elizabeth,
Union County, New Jersey 27 February 1862, son of John and Lucy
(Halstead) Kean. He died at New York 27 December 1941,[1545] and was
buried in the Winthrop vault at Green-Wood Cemetery.[1546]

Katharine Winthrop Kean's reflections on her garden at Deal
suggest something of her resolute character:

> My wind-swept garden—250 feet from the sea—is a
> 'lovesome spot' to no one but myself. 'Why does anyone
> attempt a garden so close to the sea?' is, I fear, the question
> uppermost in the minds of most people who descend the
> steps that lead to the garden, and gaze at the signs of
> devastation—which alas, may be seen at every season of
> the year—by the salt wind, the wind which we call a 'sea
> breeze' when it lures us humans to pitch our tents close
> to the ocean. . . .
>
> In spite of our many, very many failures, I advise all
> dwellers by the sea to persevere with their planting, for in
> spite of all the discouragements, success will sometimes

[1541] Mayo, *The Winthrop Family in America*, 383. She was baptized at St. George's Church
in New York 12 April 1866; it seems likely that she was born at her parents' house,
118 Fifth Avenue (Kean, *Fourscore Years*, 89).

[1542] *The New York Times*, 25 August 1943, 19, calls the Deal house "Green Lake Farm";
see Kean, *Fourscore Years*, illustration between 68–69 ("Greenlane Farm"), 74
("Green Lane Farm").

[1543] Index to Green-Wood Cemetery records at *green-wood.com*. Interred 24 August
1943, Lot 15764, section 99.

[1544] Mayo, *The Winthrop Family in America*, 383. The wedding was "a blue-blooded affair throughout [attended by] everybody of any consequence in the social world."
(Wexler, *Reared in a Greenhouse*, 66, citing a contemporary article in *Town Topics*).

[1545] "Hamilton Fish Kean, 1862–1941," *Biographical Dictionary of the United States Congress,
1774 to Present*, online at *bioguide.congress.gov/scripts/biodisplay.pl?index=K000026*.

[1546] Index to Green-Wood Cemetery records at *green-wood.com*. Interred 30 December
1941, Lot 15764, section 99.

crown their efforts, when least expected, and then the joy
of the find will make up for many disappointments.

Each one of our successful plants is to us a triumph
as well as a flower and is a delight indeed.[1547]

Following her brother Grenville's death, Mrs. Kean reflected that
"I don't think any girl or woman ever had such brothers as mine. All
four, so different, and so adorable, and each one so wonderful to me. I
have had great happiness and I *try* to think of this instead of the lonely
present, without so many of 'dearest and my best.' It is dreadful to be the
last of one's generation."[1548]

Hamilton Fish Kean was educated at St. Paul's School, Concord, New
Hampshire, and Stevens Institute;[1549] following an apprenticeship in the
investment house of John S. Kennedy & Co., he formed the investment
firm of Kean & Van Cortlandt with Robert V. Van Cortlandt in 1893.[1550]

A lifelong Republican, Mr. Kean took an interest in
politics from his youth. When he was little more than
21 years old he became a member of the Republican
Committee of Union County and between 1884 and
1906 was successively chairman, secretary and treasurer
of the group. . . .[1551]

In 1905, Mr. Kean became a member of the
Republican State Committee. In 1916, he was a delegate
to the Republican National Convention in Chicago
which nominated Charles Evans Hughes to oppose the
re-election of Woodrow Wilson, a former Governor of
New Jersey.[1552]

[1547] Kean, *Fourscore Years*, 98.

[1548] Wexler, *Reared in a Greenhouse*, 324. Her funeral, like her husband's in 1941, was held at
Grace Church: it was "well attended, for that time of year" (Kean, *Fourscore Years*, 104).

[1549] Kean, *Fourscore Years*, 66.

[1550] "Ex-Senator Kean of New Jersey Dies," *The New York Times*, 28 December 1941,
29. This firm later became Kean, Taylor & Company; his partner was Moses Taylor,
his wife's first cousin ("Associates Mourn Hamilton F. Kean," *The New York Times*,
31 December 1941, 17).

[1551] "Ex-Senator Kean of New Jersey Dies," *The New York Times*, 28 December 1941,
29. His older brother John Kean (1852–1914) served as a congressman from New
Jersey 1882–84 and 1886–88: "In 1889 he was unanimously chosen for U.S. senator from New Jersey, receiving the solid votes of both houses of the legislature, and
in 1905 he was again elected, his term expiring in 1911" (*National Cyclopaedia of
American Biography*, 18: 153).

[1552] "Ex-Senator Kean of New Jersey Dies," *The New York Times*, 28 December 1941,
29.

His biographer in the *National Cyclopaedia of American Biography* noted that Kean's "direction of the presidential campaign of Warren G. Harding in New Jersey in 1920 was largely credited with giving the Republican candidate the largest majority in the political history of the state to that time. He also directed the pre-convention campaign in New Jersey for Calvin Coolidge [in 1924]."[1553]

> [Kean] remained a national committeeman until his nomination for the United States Senate, in 1928. . . . In the November election, in which Herbert Clark Hoover was elected President, carrying New Jersey, Mr. Kean defeated the incumbent, Senator Edward I. Edwards.[1554]
>
> Mr. Kean sought re-election in 1934, but was defeated by former Governor A. Harry Moore. After his term as Senator he returned to banking and was elected to several new directorates.[1555]

His son noted, "My father was never a good speaker. . . . Though he could campaign with vigor, covering the State well, his speeches were always short. In 1934, at the age of 73, he amazed me by his endurance during his campaign for reelection."[1556] Senator Kean's funeral was held at Grace Church on 30 December 1941. His cousins Mrs. Hamilton Fish, Miss Janet Fish, Mr. and Mrs. John W. Cutler, and Mr. and Mrs. Henry Forster were among the mourners, along with his nephew Robert[10] Winthrop.[1557]

Children of Hamilton Fish and Katharine Taylor[9] (Winthrop) Kean:[1558]

27   i.   JOHN[10] KEAN, b. at New York 22 Nov. 1888; m. 20 Jan. 1925, MARY ALICE BARNEY.

[1553] *National Cyclopaedia of American Biography,* 46: 596. See also his interim biography in Volume C: 173–74 (to 1930).

[1554] At one point during their time in Washington, the Keans rented 2300 S Street from President Hoover (Kean, *Fourscore Years*, 102).

[1555] "Ex-Senator Kean of New Jersey Dies," *The New York Times*, 28 December 1941, 29. "As senator, he was a member of the civil service, District of Columbia, interstate commerce, and naval affairs committees" (*National Cyclopaedia of American Biography*, 46: 596).

[1556] Kean, *Fourscore Years*, 82. He adds: "I have some of his speeches. They seem to me dull and very conservative."

[1557] "Associates Mourn Hamilton F. Kean," *The New York Times*, 31 December 1941, 17.

[1558] Kean, *Fourscore Years*, 94 (John), 106 (Robert).

28   ii. ROBERT WINTHROP KEAN, b. at Elberon, N.J. 28 Sept. 1893; m. 18
          Oct. 1920, ELIZABETH STUYVESANT HOWARD.

20. **FREDERIC**[9] **WINTHROP** (*Robert*[8], *Thomas Charles*[7], *Francis Bayard*[6], *John
Still*[5], *John*[4], *Waitstill*[3], *John*[2-1]) was born Frederic Bayard Winthrop[1559] at
New York, New York 15 November 1868[1560] and died at home at 299
Berkeley Street[1561] in Boston, Massachusetts 6 May 1932.[1562] He married,
first, at Emmanuel Church, Boston 20 January 1903,[1563] **DOROTHY**[10]
AMORY, who was born at Beverly, Massachusetts 16 July 1878,[1564]
daughter of Charles Walter[9] Amory (*Anna Powell Grant*[8] *Sears, David*[7]
Sears, Anne[6] *Winthrop, John Still*[5]) and Elizabeth (Gardner) Amory.[1565]
She died at "Groton House Farm," Hamilton, Massachusetts 23 July
1907, five days after being injured in a riding accident.[1566] Frederic

---

[1559] *Register* 86 [1932]: 443. He dropped his middle name when he was in his twenties
    to avoid confusion with his relative Frederic Bronson Winthrop, who by agreement
    dropped the Frederic from his name and became Bronson Winthrop (Mayo, *The
    Winthrop Family in America*, 429).

[1560] Massachusetts Vital Records, 1911, Lancaster, 604: 363 (place); *Register* 86 [1932]:
    443 (date).

[1561] Mayo, *The Winthrop Family in America*, 433.

[1562] *Register* 86 [1932]: 444.

[1563] *Register* 86 [1932]: 444. See also "Winthrop-Amory," *The New York Times*, 21 January
    1903, 7. "I think," Frederic Winthrop would write, "I must have loved her from the
    time that I first knew her" (Wexler, *Reared in a Greenhouse*, 51).

[1564] Massachusetts Vital Records, 1878, Brookline, 296: 240: "_____ Amory," born at
    Beverly 16 July. Wexler, *Reared in a Greenhouse*, 55, and Steward and Child, *The
    Descendants of Judge John Lowell of Newburyport, Massachusetts*, 37, 61, give 17 July.

[1565] *Register* 86 [1932]: 444.

[1566] *Register* 86 [1932]: 444. Mayo, *The Winthrop Family in America*, 431, gives one ver-
    sion, citing *Boston Evening Transcript*, 20 July 1907, 1: "The accident occurred [on 18
    July] shortly after mounting a new horse she was trying at her own place. As she
    turned from her driveway into the fields her horse began to buck. Mr. Winthrop,
    who accompanied her, immediately jumped from his mount and rushed to his
    wife's assistance, but Mrs. Winthrop was pitched from her saddle face-downward
    just as he reached her horse's bridle." Robert Winthrop and Dorothy Winthrop
    Bradford had an identical version of the incident, one that differed from the news-
    paper account: "We were all out in front of the house when it happened," Mrs.
    Bradford would write. "It was a riding accident. . . . [The Winthrop children] were
    all out there, outside what we called the den, and my mother and father started off
    riding. They didn't get any farther than half way to what is now the swimming pool
    [when] my mother's horse began to buck most terribly, and my father leapt from his
    horse to assist her. He grabbed her horse by the bridle and then helped her down,
    off the horse. But the pommel had upset her insides. That's what had happened.
    The pommel. She was riding sidesaddle and the horse had bucked most awfully"
    (Wexler, *Reared in a Greenhouse*, 100). Dorothy Bradford Wexler adds: "Robert, then
    just three and a half, remembered running into the house to get a glass of water
    for his mother . . . but, poor, frightened little boy, spilling it all before he reached

married, second, at Lancaster, Massachusetts 12 July 1911,[1567] **SARAH BARROLL THAYER**,[1568] who was born at Lancaster 18 February 1885, daughter of Nathaniel and Cornelia Street (Barroll) Thayer.[1569] She died in an automobile accident at Portsmouth, New Hampshire 5 August 1938.[1570]

Frederic Winthrop, known as "Freddie,"[1571] struggled in his studies and in making friends because of his stammer.[1572] He enrolled at Harvard in 1887 and as a junior made the varsity rowing team. But "the strain and tension of training . . . had been too much for his growing strength," according to one account, and a doctor advised him not to row during his senior year. (In the spring of 1892, while at law school, he returned to the team for one final year.)[1573] Frederic had a larger reputation as a boxer, which some attributed in part to his "highly strung nervous energy."[1574] In his junior year he was college champion in middleweight and heavyweight sparring.[1575] According to a classmate, "His hardhitting

---

her" (100). Mrs. Winthrop's mother preserved a "white rosebud taken from off my darling's coffin, when waiting at Hamilton station. The early morning of Saturday, July 27th, 1907, Ned and I and George watched the train out of sight, that bore her and the Winthrop family to N.Y. where our darling was placed in the family Tomb, in Greenwood Cemetery. *Just* 29 years old" (103).

[1567] Massachusetts Vital Records, 1911, Lancaster, 604: 363.

[1568] Dorothy Bradford Wexler sheds an attractive light on the second Mrs. Frederic Winthrop, quoting from a letter sent her stepdaughter Dorothy following Elizabeth Gardner Amory's death in 1930: "I think Grandma [Amory] is the most wonderful character I have ever known. I shall never be able to express how much I appreciate what she has done for me since I became engaged to Father [Frederic Winthrop]. . . . I am so glad I saw her last week. She called me in and said she wanted to tell me that she was perfectly happy about you and that her mind was at rest. They are very few really perfect people in this world but she is one of them. I am very poor at saying what I feel so please read between the lines and try to realize how much I care, both for her and for you. . . . Much love, Mamma" (Wexler, *Reared in a Greenhouse*, 263).

[1569] *Register* 86 [1932]: 444.

[1570] Wexler, *Reared in a Greenhouse*, 321.

[1571] Mayo, *The Winthrop Family in America*, 428.

[1572] Henry Adams, "Frederic Winthrop: A Memoir," *Proceedings of the Massachusetts Historical Society* 65 [1934]: 361. In 1888, he wrote his father about his affliction: "If you knew what a trial and misfortune it was to stutter, you would see that it was not such a small thing after all. Because if I am not cured, by the time I go into business, I will never be able to accomplish anything, and besides my life would be a great deal happier if I could behave as other people do" (Wexler, *Reared in a Greenhouse*, 61).

[1573] Adams, *Proceedings of the Massachusetts Historical Society* 65 [1934]: 362. "By the irony of fate, the sole victory of Yale in those years came in his senior year, 1891."

[1574] Adams, *Proceedings of the Massachusetts Historical Society* 65 [1934]: 362.

[1575] *Harvard College Class of 1891 Secretary's Report No. 1* (Cambridge, Mass.: W. H.

ability was so unusual that his name became a byword at Harvard for some years after he had left college. . . . His modest, unassuming manner was deceptive, and there are many tales of occasions when those who attempted to impose on him found they had picked on the wrong man."[1576] He left Harvard Law School after a year to travel; during the summer of 1892 he went big-game hunting in the Rockies and explored the western U.S. and Canada. In 1894, he visited Europe, and upon his return was admitted as a partner in his father's firm, Robert Winthrop & Company, on 1 October 1894. After a bout of typhoid fever, he left New York on 21 February 1895 for Vancouver and then Japan.[1577]

He had tired of banking by 1898 and resigned from the family firm. In 1900, he moved to Boston. "He did not like New York," wrote a biographer, Henry Adams, because his speech impediment "made it difficult for him to converse freely with other people, and he felt he could never be successful as a banker."[1578] He found Boston's social scene more to his liking: "Always a reader and of thoughtful mind, he preferred literary pursuits and the society of literary men," Adams wrote. In 1902, he went back for another tour of Europe with a college classmate, William Amory, and after his return he married, in January 1903, Amory's sister Dorothy.[1579] He purchased a farm in Hamilton and called it Groton House[1580]; it had formerly been part of Ipswich, founded by John[2] Winthrop, Jr., some 250 years earlier. (Frederic later

---

Wheeler, 1892), 62, 64, 65, 83, 91; *The Harvard Portfolio 1889–90: An Annual Illustrated Record of Men and Events of permanent interest to Harvard Students, vol. 1* (Cambridge: Published by Students of Harvard University, 1890), facing 16.

[1576] Adams, *Proceedings of the Massachusetts Historical Society* 65 [1934]: 362. He was a member of the Porcellian Club in Harvard's Class of 1891 (*Porcellian Club 1791–2016*, 112).

[1577] Mayo, *The Winthrop Family in America*, 429.

[1578] Adams, *Proceedings of the Massachusetts Historical Society* 65 [1934]: 363.

[1579] Frederic Winthrop courted Dorothy Amory for the better part of a decade, receiving little encouragement along the way. On 30 November 1901, for example, he wrote her: "I have made up my mind to win you if I can, because I know it means my happiness or the reverse. I have staked everything on this and it is win all or lose all. I am going to wait and hope. I can do nothing else. . . . It may be as you say that if I had an absorbing occupation I might be better off, although I doubt if in my state of mind I could have an absorbing occupation." (Wexler, *Reared in a Greenhouse*, 75–76).

[1580] The house—designed by Guy Lowell—had been begun for Robert Gould Shaw II and his wife, Nancy Langhorne Shaw (later Lady Astor), who separated before it was finished (Wexler, *Reared in a Greenhouse*, 84, 85). A barn across Highland Street, called Nancy's Corner, used to mark a meeting place for the Myopia Hunt.

also owned a farm in Allendale County, South Carolina, inherited in 1912 from his brother Dudley.[1581]) After his first wife died in 1907, he lived for a few years at 280 Beacon Street,[1582] then moved to 299 Berkeley Street in Boston.[1583]

Frederic was a captain in the Red Cross during the first World War, serving as a volunteer with the U.S. Signal Corps (supervising the instruction of cadets) as well as the Flying Branch and the Air Service at Washington, D.C.[1584] In 1930, at the tercentenary of the arrival of Governor Winthrop in Massachusetts Bay, the governor appointed Winthrop to the commission planning the program. The pageant reenacted the arrival of the *Arbella* in Salem Harbor, and despite his known shyness, Frederic was persuaded to portray his ancestor aboard a replica ship.[1585] Beginning in 1920, Frederic and his surviving brothers and sisters donated a total of $40,000 to the Massachusetts Historical Society for the publication of the first five volumes of *The Winthrop Papers*.[1586]

Mayo concludes his account of Frederic Winthrop with the comment that, as he aged, Winthrop "lost neither his good looks nor his kindly eye, but gradually there were added to these the lines that indicate what a man is made of and how he has met the various problems that have made his journey through life less easy, if not actually difficult. . . . He was magnificent to look upon, and many who saw him but did not know his name must have wondered who he was. Without the slightest effort on his part he gave the impression of being somebody one *ought* to know, at least by sight."[1587]

[1581] Adams, *Proceedings of the Massachusetts Historical Society* 65 [1934]: 365. See also *Harvard College Class of 1891, Secretary's Report, No. 4*, 138.

[1582] His mother bought the house, which was next door to Ned and Libby Amory at 278 Beacon Street, so that the Winthrop grandchildren could grow up with their Amory grandparents (Wexler, *Reared in a Greenhouse*, 112). See also http://backbay-houses.org/280-beacon/, citing *The Boston Globe*, 5 January 1908.

[1583] Mayo, *The Winthrop Family in America*, 432. In April 1930, the American Antiquarian Society hosted a luncheon at the house, with the society's president, Calvin Coolidge, "in excellent form," according to Mayo.

[1584] *Register* 86 [1932]: 444.

[1585] Adams, *Proceedings of the Massachusetts Historical Society* 65 [1934]: 365–66.

[1586] Adams, *Proceedings of the Massachusetts Historical Society* 65 [1934]: 366–67. See also *Proceedings of the Massachusetts Historical Society* 53 [1919]: 188.

[1587] Mayo, *The Winthrop Family in America*, 433.

Children of Frederic[9] and Dorothy[10] (Amory) Winthrop, last two born at Hamilton:[1588]

29   i.   ROBERT[10] WINTHROP, b. at Boston 21 Jan. 1904; m. (1) 9 April 1928, THEODORA AYER; m. (2) 25 April 1942, MARGARET (STONE) MANN; m. (3) 20 April 1988, FLOREINE JUNE (NELSON) (HAAS) (HAILPARN) WILKES.

30   ii. DOROTHY WINTHROP, b. 21 May 1905; m. 29 Aug. 1931, STANDISH BRADFORD.

31   iii. FREDERIC WINTHROP, b. 30 June 1906; m. 4 July 1933, ANGELA ELIZABETH[10] FORBES.

Children of Frederic[9] and Sarah Barroll (Thayer) Winthrop:[1589]

32   iv. NATHANIEL THAYER[10] WINTHROP, b. at Hamilton 20 May 1912; m. (1) 3 July 1935, SERITA BARTLETT; m. (2) 17 June 1950, ELEANOR ROSEMOND BEANE.

      v.   JOHN WINTHROP, b. at Lancaster 4 June 1913[1590] and d. at 299 Berkeley Street 12 March 1915.[1591]

33   vi. KATHARINE WINTHROP, b. at Hamilton 17 July 1914; m. 21 Nov. 1947, QUINCY ADAMS SHAW MCKEAN.

21. ALBERTINA TAYLOR[9] WINTHROP (*Robert[8]*, *Thomas Charles[7]*, *Francis Bayard[6]*, *John Still[5]*, *John[4]*, *Waitstill[3]*, *John[2-1]*) was born at New York, New York 9 November 1871[1592] and died at The Hague (South Holland), the Netherlands 19 April 1934.[1593] She married at 38 East Thirty-Seventh Street, New York 17 May 1904,[1594] **JAN HERMAN VAN ROIJEN**, who was born Jan Herman van Royen at Zwolle (Overijssel), the Netherlands

---

[1588] Scott C. Steward, *The Sarsaparilla Kings: A Biography of Dr. James Cook Ayer and Frederick Ayer, with a record of their family* (Cambridge, Mass.: Privately printed, 1993), 92; Steward and Child, *The Descendants of Judge John Lowell of Newburyport, Massachusetts*, 115–17.

[1589] Mayo, *The Winthrop Family in America*, 434 (dates only); Massachusetts Vital Records, 1912, Hamilton, 606: 521 (Nathaniel); 1914, Hamilton, 622: 525 (Katherine [*sic*]).

[1590] Massachusetts Vital Records, 1913, Lancaster, 616: 351.

[1591] Massachusetts Vital Records, 1915, Boston, 1: 380.

[1592] Mayo, *The Winthrop Family in America*, 383 (date only).

[1593] *The New York Times*, 21 April 1934, 15; Mayo, *The Winthrop Family in America*, 383.

[1594] "Van Roijen–Winthrop," *The New York Times*, 18 May 1904, 9.

28 November 1871, son of Jan Hermannus and Anna Aleida (van Engelen) van Royen.[1595] He died at The Hague 31 August 1933.[1596]

A graduate of the University of Groningen,[1597] in August 1902 J. H. van Roijen of the Netherlands Legation was among the guests at a dinner at the Newport Casino; one of his dinner partners was Alice Roosevelt, the President's daughter.[1598] His engagement to Albertina Winthrop was announced during Lent in 1904.[1599] On 3 May, *The New York Times* was correct in forecasting that the wedding would take place at the Winthrops' house on East Thirty-Seventh Street in two weeks' time;[1600] this venue marked a move from Grace Church, where the bride's older sister had been married in 1888. The wedding itself was celebrated in the drawing room, overlooking Park Avenue and limited to family and close friends; a reception for three hundred followed.[1601]

After Washington, D.C., the van Roijens were stationed in Istanbul, where their son Jan Herman[10] van Roijen was born in 1905. Robert Dudley van Roijen followed in 1907; he was born in London.[1602] In the next two decades, the elder Jan Herman van Roijen would serve as Dutch minister to Japan, Spain, and Italy.[1603] In July 1923, J. Herman van Roijen—by then Queen Wilhelmina's envoy in Rome—and his wife arrived in Lenox to visit Mrs. Van Roijen's mother, Mrs. Robert Winthrop; they planned a short visit to Newport.[1604]

Three years later, Jan Herman van Roijen was named the Dutch minister to the United States. As noted by the *New York Times*, he "was mentioned for the Washington Post [*sic*] as early as 1917, when he was

---

[1595] "van Royen," *Nederland's Patriciaat*, 46 vols. (The Hague: Centraal Bureau voor Genealogie en Heraldiek, 1910–60), 3: 345–46.

[1596] "Mourned in Washington," *The New York Times*, 1 September 1933, 17. "Washington, Aug. 31—The State Department was notified today of the death this morning at The Hague of Dr. J.H. van Royen, Minister of the Netherlands to the United States. He had been accredited to this government since March 15, 1927, and had been on leave of absence in Europe this summer."

[1597] Alberta Lawrence, ed., *Who's Who among North American Authors*, vol. 4 (Los Angeles: Golden Syndicate Publishing Company, 1929), 1055.

[1598] "The News of Newport," *The New York Times*, 8 August 1902, 7.

[1599] "Society, at Home and Abroad," *The New York Times*, 13 March 1904, 29.

[1600] "What is Doing in Society," *The New York Times*, 3 May 1904, 9.

[1601] At the time he was the Legation's Chargé d'Affaires; the Minister, Jonkheer Reneke de Marees van Swinderen, was the best man. "Weddings of a Day: Van Roijen–Winthrop," *The New York Times*, 18 May 1904, 9.

[1602] *Nederland's Patriciaat*, 3: 346.

[1603] "Mourned in Washington," *The New York Times*, 1 September 1933, 17.

[1604] "Social Notes," *The New York Times*, 17 July 1923, 19.

Minister to Spain and again in 1921 [when he had moved to Rome]."[1605]
He was still the Dutch ambassador to the United States in August 1933
and died while on leave of absence in Europe. The Secretary of State,
Cordell Hull, stated: "During Dr. van Royen's seven years' residence in
Washington we have all learned to respect and admire his high attributes
and fine personality. His death will be sincerely felt by every official
of the department who had dealings with him. We greatly sympathize
with Mrs. Van Royen in her affliction."

When Rutgers University granted Minister van Roijen an honorary
doctorate in 1931, the citation read:

> Scholar, author and diplomat; worthy representative
> of that great country whose culture and leadership in
> education contributed so much to the building of this
> institution established to carry on the high scholastic
> ideals of the Dutch Fatherland. In recognition of your
> ability, character and accomplishments and of the high
> office you now occupy, the trustees of Rutgers University
> confer upon you the degree of Doctor of Laws.[1606]

Children of Jan Herman and Albertina Taylor[9] (Winthrop) van Roijen:[1607]

34   i.   JAN HERMAN[10] VAN ROIJEN, b. Jan Herman van Royen at
             Constantinople, Turkey 10 April 1905; m. 13 Dec. 1934,
             JONKVROUWE ANNE SNOUCK HURGRONJE.

35   ii. ROBERT DUDLEY VAN ROIJEN, b. Robert Dudley van Royen at
             London, England 13 March 1907; m. 21 June 1938, HILDEGARDE
             PORTNER GRAHAM.

22. BEEKMAN[9] WINTHROP (*Robert*[8], *Thomas Charles*[7], *Francis Bayard*[6],
John Still[5], *John*[4], *Waitstill*[3], *John*[2-1]) was born at Orange, New Jersey 18
September 1874[1608] and died at St. Luke's Hospital in New York, New
York 10 November 1940.[1609] He married at St. Bartholomew's Church,

---

[1605] "To Be New Dutch Envoy," *The New York Times*, 13 September 1926, 22.

[1606] "Mourned in Washington," *The New York Times*, 1 September 1933, 17.

[1607] *Nederland's Patriciaat*, 3: 346; *Nederland's Adelsboek 1937* (The Hague: W. P. Van
Stockum & Zoon), 309; "Miss Hildegarde Graham, Debutante of '34, Married
Here to Robert Dudley van Roijen," *The New York Times*, 22 June 1938, 20.

[1608] *Ancestry.com* > California, Passenger and Crew Lists, 1882–1959 > M1764 – Los
Angeles, Selected Suburbs, 1907–1948 > 058, image 220 of 1038. Aboard S.S. *Santa
Rosa*, New York to Los Angeles, February 1935.

[1609] "Ex-Gov. Winthrop, Puerto Rico, Dies," *The New York Times,* 11 November 1940, 19.

New York 7 October 1903, **MELZA RIGGS WOOD**,[1610] who was born at New York 27 March 1875, daughter of John Dunn and Alice Riggs (Colgate) Wood.[1611] She died at home at 38 East Thirty-Seventh Street in New York 10 December 1928.[1612]

Beekman Winthrop graduated from Cutler's School, New York, and Harvard University (1897 and 1900). In his senior year at Harvard he received one of the newly created John Harvard Scholarships;[1613] he was elected a member of the Phi Beta Kappa honor society and received his degree *magna cum laude*.[1614] Known as "Beek," he returned to Harvard in the fall of 1897 for law school. He was a member of the *Harvard Law Review* and finished second in his class.[1615]

After passing his examinations for the New York Bar, in 1900 he became the private secretary in the Philippines to William Howard Taft, then president of the Philippine Commission; a year later he was appointed assistant executive secretary for the Philippines.[1616] In December 1903 he was appointed as Judge of the Court of First Instance there, holding court in Malolos and Manila until he left to assume the office of Governor of "Porto Rico" on 4 July 1904.[1617] He served in

---

[1610] *Harvard College Class of 1897, Third Report* (Cambridge, Mass.: Crimson Printing Co., 1907), 235. "On October 7, 1903, I was married in New York City to Melza Riggs Wood." See also "Winthrop-Wood Wedding," *The New York Times*, 8 October 1903, 9. Mayo errs with 3 October 1903 (*The Winthrop Family in America*, 436).

[1611] Truman Abbe and Hubert Abbe Howson, *Robert Colgate the Immigrant: A Genealogy of the New York Colgates. . . .* (New Haven, Conn.: The Tuttle, Morehouse and Taylor Company, 1941), 197.

[1612] *The New York Times*, 11 December 1928, 30.

[1613] *The Harvard University Catalogue, 1896–97* (Cambridge, Mass.: Published by the University, 1896), 619–20.

[1614] He was a member of the Porcellian Club in Harvard's Class of 1897 (*Porcellian Club 1791–2016*, 114).

[1615] Mayo, *The Winthrop Family in America*, 435.

[1616] *Harvard College Class of 1897, Twenty-fifth Anniversary Report, No. 6* (Cambridge, Mass.: The Riverside Press, 1922), 615.

[1617] *Harvard College Class of 1897, Third Report*, 235. Melza Wood Winthrop made a good impression while serving in Puerto Rico: the press "praised Melza's Spanish and her hospitality, writing that she 'knew the Latin heart' and through her charm was able to '[persuade] the women to trust her, and come to her teas and receptions. . . . Soon she had the governor's old palace filled with native officials and their families.'" Writing from Cuba following a visit to San Juan, Dorothy Amory Winthrop noted, "Everyone is so enthusiastic about Melza. And they ought to be. Her tact and never failing interest in everyone are wonderful'" (Wexler, *Reared in a Greenhouse*, 95, 96). In Robert Winthrop Kean's view, Melza Winthrop "was noted as a good conversationalist, but studying why[,] I found it was because she was a good listener. Gay and friendly[,] her successful method was to ask questions about what her dinner partner was doing and was thinking. Most politicians and government officials loved that, and decided she was a very intelligent woman" (Kean, *Fourscore Years*, 59).

that position until 1907, resigning to become Assistant Secretary of the Treasury.[1618]

When Taft became president in 1909, Beekman was appointed Assistant Secretary of the Navy. In March 1913, when the Democrats under Woodrow Wilson came into power, he resigned and in February 1914 became a partner in Robert Winthrop & Co. A classmate later recalled that, "deprived at the age of 40 of the profession he had originally chosen, he adapted himself quickly to another of a very different type" by joining his father's banking firm, where he stayed for twenty-five years until his retirement in 1939.[1619]

At the end of his chapter on Beekman Winthrop's generation of the Winthrop family, Robert Winthrop Kean noted:

> The Winthrop brothers were attractive people. They were very proud of being Winthrops. They kidded about it among themselves and with their sisters. They used to speak of themselves as "The Holy Family." But though they were kidding, I think in their hearts they really believed in their superiority. In fact, they were so proud of the Winthrop name that with their approval my grandmother left the share of her estate which would have gone to her deceased son, Dudley, to "male descendants with the surname Winthrop." And Beekman, who had no children, left, I believe, his money also to his Winthrop nephews. The strange thing about it is that most of it was not Winthrop money, but money made by [their maternal grandfather] Moses Taylor that they were leaving to "males with the surname of Winthrop."[1620]

23. **CHARLES WALTER**[9] **AMORY** (*Anna Powell Grant*[8] *Sears, David*[7] *Sears, Anne*[6] *Winthrop, John Still*[5]*, John*[4]*, Waitstill*[3]*, John*[2-1]) was born at 43 Beacon Street, Boston, Massachusetts[1621] 16 October 1842 and died at 278 Beacon Street 5 November 1913.[1622] He married at 67 Beacon Street 23 October 1867, **ELIZABETH GARDNER**, who was born at

[1618] Mayo, *The Winthrop Family in America*, 436.
[1619] Mayo, *The Winthrop Family in America*, 436, citing Joseph Warren.
[1620] Kean, *Fourscore Years*, 61–62. Both Mayo and Wexler ascribe greater financial agency to Kate Wilson (Taylor) Winthrop than does Winthrop Kean.
[1621] Wexler, *Reared in a Greenhouse*, 18.
[1622] Massachusetts Vital Records, 1913, Boston, 19: 359.

Boston 28 June 1843 and died at Manchester, Massachusetts 31 January 1930, daughter of George and Helen Maria (Read) Gardner.[1623]

Handsome, with a "clear brain, sweet nature, easy and a firm character,"[1624] Charles Walter Amory was a member of the Class of 1863 at Harvard College.[1625] He joined the Second Massachusetts Cavalry as a second lieutenant in April 1864; by July of that year he had been in combat thrice, the third time against Colonel Mosby's Partisan Raiders in a short set-to that ended with his capture. His time as a prisoner in Lynchburg and then Charleston was grim: "He was very ill all the hot weeks in Charleston prison—and *never* well afterwards."[1626] On his release from prison in October, his family "didn't recognize the gaunt figure who emerged from the train [in Boston]. He looked like 'someone in the last stages of consumption, having a weak hacking cough and almost skeleton-like emaciation.'"[1627]

His time at home effected recovery of a sort, and in January 1865 "Ned" Amory returned to the front: "When he wrote Libby, he transformed [a] homemade hut into his 'spacious mansion of mud and logs.'" Wexler wrote. "His letters to Libby centered not on his discomforts, but . . . on her, and on his ardent hopes for their future together. He had a charming way with words, a knack for making poetry out of the simple comings and goings of their friends."[1628]

He was at City Point during President Lincoln's visit in March, then at Petersburg. Following Lee's surrender, he wrote Libby, "I almost fear sometimes that I shall wake up and find I've been dreaming, it is too good to be true." After the war's end, he did not come home until July, surprising his family in Longwood: his mother wrote "To think of our old Ned walking in so quietly, and looking through the window . . . without our having an idea of his coming."[1629] But his return did not mark the recovery of his health, so he went abroad for the better part

---

[1623] "Libbie Gardner was married to Mr. Ned Amory on Wednesday" (entry for 27 October 1867: Hedwiga Regina Shober Gray diary, R. Stanton Avery Special Collections); Steward and Child, *The Descendants of Judge John Lowell of Newburyport, Massachusetts*, 24, 37.

[1624] Wexler, *Reared in a Greenhouse*, 11, citing Elizabeth (Gardner) Amory.

[1625] He was a member of the Porcellian Club with that class (*Porcellian Club 1791–2016*, 103).

[1626] Wexler, *Reared in a Greenhouse*, 27.

[1627] Wexler, *Reared in a Greenhouse*, 29, quoting J. C. Warren, *Class of 1863 of Harvard College. Memoir of Charles Walter Amory* (Cambridge, Mass.: The University Press, 1914), 2, 3.

[1628] Wexler, *Reared in a Greenhouse*, 29.

[1629] Wexler, *Reared in a Greenhouse*, 30–31.

of a year, until—in the winter of 1867—he was well enough to propose to Libby Gardner.[1630]

In 1868, Ned Amory and Henry Chapman Wainwright formed a partnership as Wainwright and Amory, but in 1875, the Amorys moved to Ned's mother's house in Longwood and for two years he did no work at all. His health was frail—warm weather was debilitating—and during the summers he would seek cool climes while Libby took the growing family to Nahant (with the Amorys) or Beverly (with the Gardners).[1631] At last, in his late thirties, Ned Amory's health markedly improved: "In his prime, with directorships in most of Boston's leading businesses, Amory had gained a reputation as one of two or three of the highest business authorities on [Boston's] State Street."[1632]

After his death, his widow wrote the following observations: "Charles Walter Amory was very shy, retiring and modest—he was inclined to be melancholy at times, a little morbid, but as he grew older he was less so. . . . He was active minded and needed to be occupied to take his mind from himself for he was never feeling well. . . . He never spoke of his torments and spoke cheerfully when other mentioned his poor health."[1633] When the indomitable Libby Amory was on her own deathbed, her granddaughter Dorothy Winthrop Bradford recalled, "Uncle George [Amory] and the rest of the family were gathered around Grandma's bed and Grandma noticed that George was looking very gloomy. 'George,' she scolded him, 'why do you look so glum? Why don't you cheer up and dance a jig?'"[1634]

Children of Charles Walter[9] and Elizabeth (Gardner) Amory, first two born at Boston:[1635]

    i.   WILLIAM[10] AMORY,[1636] b. 19 Sept. 1869 and d. at Boston 16 Jan. 1954. He m. at St. Paul's Church, Boston 14 Oct. 1903, MARY

[1630] Wexler, *Reared in a Greenhouse*, 32.

[1631] Wexler, *Reared in a Greenhouse*, 54–55.

[1632] Wexler, *Reared in a Greenhouse*, 55.

[1633] Wexler, *Reared in a Greenhouse*, 115.

[1634] Wexler, *Reared in a Greenhouse*, 262. Mrs. Bradford's short-hand notes of this event read, in part, "Don't look like that George . . . or Dorothy, Billy [Amory]. . . . You're forlorn George . . . [go dance] a jig with Clara [Coolidge]" (262).

[1635] *Boston Social Register 1904* (1903), 124; Robert Means Lawrence, *The Descendants of Major Samuel Lawrence of Groton, Massachusetts, with some mention of allied families* (Cambridge, Mass.: Printed at the Riverside Press, 1904), 132; Steward and Child, *The Descendants of Judge John Lowell of Newburyport, Massachusetts*, 37, 60, 61.

[1636] Like his kinsman (and brother-in-law) Frederic[9] Winthrop, he was a member of the Porcellian Club with his class (*Porcellian Club 1791–2016*, 112).

REMINGTON STOCKTON, who was b. at Brookline, Mass. 10 May 1872 and d. at Wareham, Mass. 25 Aug. 1964, dau. of Howard and Mary (Mason) Stockton.

William Amory graduated from the Hopkinson School, Boston, and Harvard (1891). In 1911, he reported to his Harvard classmates that he had "neither written any books nor been honored with any degrees since graduation."[1637]

ii. CLARA AMORY, b. 3 Jan. 1872 and d. at Manchester 4 Aug. 1957. She m. at the First Unitarian Church, Longwood (Brookline) 30 Sept. 1891, THOMAS JEFFERSON COOLIDGE, JR., who was b. at Boston 6 March 1863 and d. at Manchester 14 April 1912,[1638] son of Thomas Jefferson Coolidge, U.S. Minister to France, and Hetty Sullivan (Appleton) Coolidge, and had issue (Thomas Jefferson[11] Coolidge, who married Catherine Hill Kuhn; Amory Coolidge; William Appleton Coolidge, the art collector; and John Linzee Coolidge).[1639]

T. Jefferson Coolidge graduated from the G. W. C. Noble School, Boston, and Harvard (1884). According to his 1899 class report, "[In] May, 1890, on the charter being obtained for the incorporation of the Old Colony Trust Company, Coolidge became president of that Company, and has continued since to fill that position. In addition he has been connected with a number of corporations as a director, amongst others, the Bay State Trust Company, of Boston; Boston Elevated Railway Company, National Bank of Commerce of Boston, General Electric Company, the Kansas City, Fort Scott and Memphis Railroad, Oregon Short Line Railroad, Pacific Coast Company, Union Pacific Railroad Company, and The American Bell Telegraph Company. He has been identified so prominently with large financial interests that it is likely that the Secretary has omitted a number of boards in which Coolidge is of the directorate. In the fall of 1885 he had a very narrow escape from becoming a member of the Massachusetts Legislature."[1640]

[1637] *Harvard College Class of 1891 Secretary's Report Number V* (Printed for the use of the class, 1911), 3.

[1638] "Thomas Jefferson Coolidge," *The New York Times*, 16 April 1912, 13. Steward and Child, *The Descendants of Judge John Lowell of Newburyport, Massachusetts*, 60, give his death as 4 April 1912.

[1639] Steward and Child, *The Descendants of Judge John Lowell of Newburyport, Massachusetts*, 60.

[1640] *Harvard College. Report of the Secretary No. V June 1899* (New York: Evening Post Job Printing House, 1899), 23.

iii. GEORGE GARDNER AMORY,[1641] b. at Nahant 22 June 1874 and d.
      unm. at Manchester 11 July 1933.

      George Gardner Amory was educated at the Hopkinson School
      and Harvard (1896 and 1899x).

iv.   DOROTHY AMORY, b. at Beverly 16 July 1878;[1642] m. 20 Jan. 1903,
      FREDERIC[9] WINTHROP [No. 20].

24. MARGARET TYNDAL[9] WINTHROP (*Robert Charles[8-7]*, *Thomas Lindall[6]*, *John Still[5]*, *John[4]*, *Waitstill[3]*, *John[2-1]*) was born at 1 Walnut Street, Boston, Massachusetts 27 February 1880[1643] and died at Saint-Briac-sur-Mer (Bretagne), France 7 July 1970.[1644] She married at 10 Walnut Street 28 November 1906,[1645] **JAMES GRANT FORBES,** who was born at Shanghai, China 22 October 1879,[1646] son of Francis Blackwell and Isabel (Clarke) Forbes.[1647] He died at Paris, France 24 April 1955.[1648]

J. Grant Forbes prepared for Harvard at the Uppingham School in Rutlandshire, England, and at Hopkinson's School in Boston. He entered with his class in 1897 and received an A.B. in 1901, an A.M. in 1902, and an LL.B. from the Law School in 1904. After positions with two Boston law firms, he wrote this account:

> In 1910 I became a partner of Stimson, Stockton, Livermore
> and Forbes, successor to the firm in which President
> Lowell of Harvard had at one time been associated. I found
> myself . . . drawn into foreign work,[1649] and in 1911 was

---

[1641] He was a member of the Porcellian Club with his class (*Porcellian Club 1791–2016*, 114).

[1642] Massachusetts Vital Records, 1878, Brookline, 296: 240, listing a Beverly birth.

[1643] Massachusetts Vital Records, 1880, Boston, 315: 79. Mayo, *The Winthrop Family in America*, 405, gives her date of birth as 23 February.

[1644] *The New York Times*, 9 July 1970, 37. Her son Alastair's obituary includes the detail that Mrs. Forbes was "a strict woman who did not hesitate to use a bamboo cane on her ten children [*sic*]" ("Alastair Forbes," *The Times*, 21 May 2005).

[1645] Massachusetts Vital Records, 1906, Boston, 565: 295 (date). One press account indicated that their engagement "will unite two noted Boston families" ("Miss Winthrop to Wed," *The New York Times*, 17 August 1906, 7).

[1646] *Harvard College Class of 1901 Twenty-fifth Anniversary Report* (Cambridge, Mass.: The Riverside Press, 1926), 238.

[1647] Ralph E. Forbes, *The Forbes Family* (Milton, Mass.: the author, 1934), 23, 61. See also "Mrs. Francis B. Forbes," *The New York Times*, 2 September 1931, 21.

[1648] "J. Grant Forbes, 75, Lawyer and Banker," *The New York Times*, 26 April 1955, 27: "Surviving are his widow, Mrs. Winthrop Forbes, eleven children, a brother and two sisters. A son, John W. Forbes[,] and a daughter, Mrs. Frederic Winthrop, live in Ipswich, Mass. The other children reside in Europe."

[1649] Because of "my fairly extensive knowledge of French" (*Harvard College Class of 1901 Twenty-fifth Anniversary Report*, 239).

appointed special counsel to the Brazil Railway Company, an important group of companies operating in South America, but controlled by French, British and Belgian capital, with its head office in Paris. During 1913 I made an extensive tour of South America, visiting Brazil, the Argentine and Paraguay.

When the war broke out in 1914, I was in Paris, and witnessed events there until the battle of the Marne. Soon after that, I went to New York, to arrange for the appointment as receiver of the Brazil Railway Company of the Honorable W. Cameron Forbes,[1650] who had just ended his term as Governor General of the Philippines. I then returned to France, and for the rest of the War acted as counsel for the receiver and for the various bondholders' committees. In this capacity, I made several trips to America, and constantly crossed between France and England throughout the War, fortunately without a single misadventure. . . .

[During these years] I acted as councillor in London for the Rockefeller War Relief Administration, and as a member of the executive committees in London of the American Red Cross, and of the American Y.M.C.A. [In 1916, he became associated with the American International Corporation.] I gave up the law for good after the armistice, and became the regular representative in London for this company and of its various affiliated interests. . . . In 1922 I became a managing partner of Blair and Company (London), Ltd., in which capacity I have, up to the present time [1925–26], been acting as European representative of the New York investment house of Blair and Company, Inc.[1651]

Forbes ended his relationship with Blair and Company in 1932, spending the next decade[1652] as a freelance legal and financial negotiator

---

[1650] Forbes's third cousin.

[1651] *Harvard College Class of 1901 Twenty-fifth Anniversary Report*, 239–40. Facing page 240, the class report's editors placed a photograph of the eleven Forbes children; on page 239, referring to this image, they wrote: "The prize exhibit of the Report goes to Jimmie Forbes. No one will dispute his claim to having the most fascinating family in the Class, after examining the proof he submits. Our only regret is that the group does not include Mrs. Forbes, whom we understand to be the most charming of all." Two photographs of James Grant Forbes are included facing page 238.

[1652] In March 1934, *The New York Times* reported that (with Clarence Graff) he would have the management of Shearson, Hammill & Co.'s London office ("Financial Notes," 29 March 1934, 36).

in Europe, the Far East, and South America. In this period, the family relocated to Saint-Briac-sur-Mer in Brittany, where their house—as Forbes noted laconically in his fiftieth college reunion report—was "destroyed by Germans in June, 1944."[1653]

In that same year, he was a member of the Navy Price Adjustment Board in Washington, D.C., and in 1945–46 he served in the office of the Foreign Liquidation Commissioner in Paris, for which he was later named a Chevalier of the French Legion of Honor. Forbes finished his career with the Export–Import Bank in Washington and as the special representative of the President of the International Bank for Reconstruction and Development;[1654] he retired 1 January 1950. In 1951, he reported, "My wife and eleven children are alive and well. I have, at this date, 11 American, 6 British and 4 French grandchildren."[1655]

Fittingly, after a married life as expatriates, Grant and Margaret Forbes's sons- and daughters-in-law included Americans (their cousin Frederic[10] Winthrop and diplomat Richard Kerry), Frenchmen (Francis Tailleux, the painter, and Alain Lalonde), Englishmen (the civil servant Dunstan Curtis, writer John Pudney, and explorer Terence Armstrong), Danes (Charlotte Bergsøe), and the English actress Georgina Ward.

Children of James Grant and Margaret Tyndal[9] (Winthrop) Forbes:[1656]

> i. JAMES GRANT[10] FORBES, b. at 10 Walnut Street 14 Feb. 1908[1657] and d. unm. at Rowley, Mass. 25 July 1993.[1658] He graduated from Cambridge University in 1930.[1659]

[1653] *Harvard Class of 1901 Fiftieth Anniversary . . . Report* (Boston: C. A. Peters, 1951), 50.

[1654] "Formerly with the Export–Import Bank, Mr. Forbes has served with several international financial concerns. He also served as field commissioner for France under the foreign liquidation commissioner" ("Grant Forbes named as World Bank Aide," *The New York Times*, 27 July 1948, 30).

[1655] *Harvard Class of 1901 Fiftieth Anniversary Report*, 51. In 2004, Brice Lalonde recalled summer visits from his cousin John Kerry at Saint-Briac in the 1950s: "He was the big American, the leader of our gang" (William Echikson, "Candidate's Cousin Roots in a Low Key; Why? He's French," *The Wall Street Journal*, 30 July 2004).

[1656] *Harvard College Class of 1901 Twenty-fifth Anniversary Report*, 238, which lists John Winthrop Forbes's date of birth as 3 March 1909; Massachusetts Vital Records, 1908, Boston, 577: 216; 1909, Dover, 584: 37; 1910, Dover, 592: 35; Steward and Arthaud, *A Thorndike Family History*, 115–17.

[1657] Massachusetts Vital Records, 1908, Boston, 577: 216.

[1658] Massachusetts Death Index, 1970–2003; notes by Jonathan Winthrop 2016.

[1659] *Boston Social Register 1958* (1957), 97.

ii. JOHN WINTHROP FORBES, b. at Boston 3 May 1909[1660] and d. at
Rowley 5 Jan. 1998.[1661] He m. at Kensington Register Office,
Kensington (London) 6 May 1939,[1662] VIOLET GILMORE,[1663] who
was b. at Enfield (London) 18 Nov. 1910,[1664] formerly wife of
Frederick Lepard,[1665] and dau. of John and Emily Harrison (Smith)
Gilmore,[1666] and had issue (Nicholas Winthrop[11] Forbes and David
Winthrop Forbes). She d. 19 June 1996.[1667]

J. Winthrop Forbes graduated from Cambridge in 1931.[1668]

iii. GRISELDA MARGARET FORBES, b. at Dover, Mass. 19 Dec. 1910[1669]
and d. at Terrasson (Dordogne), France 30 July 2000.[1670] She m.
at St. Mary's Church, Westerham, Kent 9 July 1931,[1671] WARREN
DELANO MARTINEAU, who was b. at 3 Oxford Square, Paddington
(London) 22 June 1909[1672] and d. at 155 Kingsway, Hove (Brighton),
Sussex 15 Feb. 1983,[1673] son of Cyril and Muriel Delano (Robbins)
Martineau, from whom she was divorced.[1674]

iv. ANGELA ELIZABETH FORBES, b. at Paris 5 April 1912; m. 4 July 1933,
FREDERIC[10] WINTHROP [No. 31].

[1660] Massachusetts Vital Records, 1909, Dover, 584: 37.

[1661] Massachusetts Death Index, 1970–2003; Social Security Death Index.

[1662] Kensington district (London) civil registration indices, 1939, 01a: 450, no. 240.

[1663] Edmonton district (Middlesex), 1931, 03a: 1533, no. 27: marriage of Frederick
Lepard, 28, bachelor, son of Alfred Lepard (deceased), and Violet Gilmore, 21,
daughter of John Gilmore.

[1664] *England & Wales, Civil Registration Birth Index, 1837-1915* [database on-line] (place);
Social Security Death Index (date).

[1665] Kensington district (London), 1939, 01a: 450, no. 240.

[1666] *London, England, Church of England Marriages and Banns, 1754–1921* [database on-
line]; *1911 England Census* [database on-line] for household at 43 Cecil Avenue,
Enfield, in 1911.

[1667] Social Security Death Index, listed as Violet Barton of Hampstead, Rockingham
Co., N.H.

[1668] *Boston Social Register 1958* (1957), 97.

[1669] Massachusetts Vital Records, 1910, Dover, 592: 35.

[1670] *U.S., Social Security Applications and Claims Index, 1936–2007* [database on-line].

[1671] Sevenoaks district (Kent), 1931, 02a: 2769, no. 409. *Boston Social Register 1932*
(1931), 77, and *New York Social Register 1932* (1931), 531, give London as the place.

[1672] Paddington district (London), 1909, 01a: 73, no. 30.

[1673] Hove district (Sussex), 1983, 18: 1343, no. 122.

[1674] *Boston Social Register 1932* (1931), 77; New York Passenger Lists, 1820–1957; Social
Security Death Index; England & Wales Death Index, 1916–2007. *Surrey, England,
Church of England Baptisms, 1813–1912*, scan of original at *ancestry.com*, bp. Elstead,
St. James, 16 Aug. 1909, son of Cyril Edgar and Muriel Delano Martineau, who
resided at 3 Oxford Square, London; notes by Jonathan Winthrop 2016.

    v. ROSEMARY ISABEL FORBES, b. at Paris 27 Oct. 1913 and d. at Manchester, Mass. 14 Nov. 2002.[1675] She m. at Montgomery, Ala. 8 Feb. 1941,[1676] RICHARD JOHN KERRY, who was b. at 10 Downing Road, Brookline, Mass. 28 July 1915[1677] and d. at Boston 29 July 2000, son of Frederick A. and Ida (Löwe) Kerry,[1678] and had issue (Margaret Anne[11] Kerry, who married George Henry Kaler; John Forbes Kerry, U.S. Senator from Massachusetts, Democratic candidate for the U.S. presidency in 2004, and [in 2013–17] U.S. Secretary of State, who married Julia Stimson Thorne and Maria Teresa Thierstein Simões-Ferreira Heinz; Cameron Forbes Kerry, briefly Acting Secretary of Commerce in 2013 and General Counsel at the U.S. Department of Commerce in 2017, who married Kathy Weinman; and Diana Frances Kerry).[1679]

    Richard John Kerry graduated from Phillips Academy, Andover, Mass.; Yale College (1937); and Harvard (1940). Like his father-in-law, he would make a career in international law, although his focus tended toward foreign service:

> As a law student at Harvard in the late '30s, he read continental philosophers like Kierkegaard and histories about Bismarck and Metternich; he traveled to France, where he took sculpture classes and met his wife. . . . After World War II, which he spent in the Army Air Corps testing new airplanes at high altitudes, he moved his family to Washington to take a spot in the Department of the Navy's Office of General Counsel, hoping that his proximity to the State Department might help him land a job there. . . .
>
> In 1954, Kerry received an assignment that put him at ground zero of the cold war. He moved to Berlin to advise former Harvard President James B. Conant, whom Dwight D. Eisenhower had charged with overseeing the rehabilitation of West Germany. . . . During his tenure in Europe, he attended conferences in Paris, London, and The Hague, where he discussed with other mid-level diplomats the future of the transatlantic alliance and the possibilities of a new continental order.

[1675] *The Washington Post,* 20 November 2002, B6.

[1676] "Troth is Announced of Rosemary Forbes," *The New York Times,* 24 November 1940, 46; *Summer Social Register 1941,* 668.

[1677] Massachusetts Vital Records, 1915, Brookline, 630: 22.

[1678] *The Boston Globe,* 31 July 2000, C9; Massachusetts Death Index, 1970–2003; wargs.com/political/kerry.html.

[1679] Notes by Sarah Fields Getchell and George Henry Kaler 2016.

Richard Kerry disagreed with much of America's post-war foreign policy, and he was not shy about voicing his opinions, but "For all his impolitic instincts, Kerry's undeniable competence kept propelling his career forward. Following his posting in Berlin, he served as top aide to Georgia Democrat Walter George, the chairman of the Senate Foreign Relations Committee." In 1958, he became chief political officer in Oslo, serving into the years of the Kennedy administration. "They seem not to listen to what I have to say," Kerry told his family, "so I'm going to quit." Douglas Brinkley noted that "He saw his role as becoming a protester, criticizing the government from the outside in lectures and [in] his book"[1680]— *The Star-Spangled Mirror,* a critique of American foreign policy at the end of the Cold War-era, published in 1990.

vi. EILEEN MASON FORBES, b. at Paris 3 Feb. 1915[1681] and d. at "Le Bertrane," Le Tholonet (Bouches-du-Rhône), France 17 Feb. 2007.[1682] She m. at Paris in March 1940,[1683] the painter FRANCIS TAILLEUX, who was b. at Paris 18 March 1913 and d. 6 July 1981, and had issue (Vanessa[11] Tailleux and Carlo Tailleux).[1684]

"In 1926, he exhibited at the Salon de la Nationale [e.g., one of the annual salons of the Société Nationale des Beaux Arts]—without revealing his age. [He was no more than 13.] At Jacques Emile Blanche's suggestion, he studied at the Académie Scandinave in Paris under Othon-Friesz, [Henry] Waroquier and [Charles] Dufresne." In 1948, he was awarded the Prix National des Arts.[1685]

[1680] Franklin Foer, "Kerry's World: Father Knows Best," *The New Republic,* 4 March 2004. It was during Richard Kerry's posting in Berlin that the family spent summers with the Forbeses at Saint-Briac (Echikson, *The Wall Street Journal,* 30 July 2004).

[1681] *Harvard College Class of 1901 Twenty-fifth Anniversary Report,* 238.

[1682] Notes by Pierre Tailleux 2016.

[1683] *Summer Social Register 1942,* 648.

[1684] Notes by Sarah Fields Getchell 2016.

[1685] "En 1926 il est reçu au Salon de la Nationale (n'ayant pas révélé son âge). Sur les conseils de Jacques Emile Blanche, il suivit les cours de l'Académie Scandinave à Paris où il eut pour Maîtres: Othon-Friez, Waroquet [*sic*] et Dufresne" (*Les personnages célèbres de Dieppe et de sa région depuis l'Antiquité jusqu'à nos jours,* http://dieppe76.pagesperso-orange.fr/t-personnages.html). He also studied at the Royal College of Art 1941–44, and was the focus of a retrospective exhibition at Dieppe in 1971 (http://www.ledelarge.fr/6071_artiste_tailleux__francis). Christopher Long's blog (http://www.christopherlong.co.uk/pub/fourcade.html) gives some details on the Tailleuxes' war-time experiences in Aix-en-Provence.

vii. MONICA ETHEL FORBES, b. at "The Grove," Princes Road,
Wandsworth (London) 11 Nov. 1916[1686] and d. at London 13 May
2014. She m. (1) at Lewes Register Office, Lewes, Sussex 26 Aug.
1939,[1687] DUNSTAN MICHAEL CARR CURTIS, C.B.E. (1963), D.S.C.
(1942), who was b. at 68 Elm Park Road, Chelsea (London) 26 Aug.
1910[1688] and d. at Brynawel, Montgomeryshire 9 Sept. 1983,[1689] son
of Arthur Cecil and Elizabeth (Carr) Curtis, from whom she was
divorced;[1690] m. (2) at St. Pancras Register Office, London 7 July
1955,[1691] JOHN SLEIGH PUDNEY, who was b. at Homewood Farm,
Langley, Buckinghamshire 19 Jan. 1909[1692] and d. at 4 Macartney
House, Chesterfield Walk, Greenwich (London) 10 Nov. 1977,[1693]
son of Henry William and Mabel Elizabeth (Sleigh) Pudney,[1694]
and had issue by her first husband (Lucinda[11] Curtis and Dunstan
Christopher Curtis).[1695]

Dunstan Curtis was educated at Eton College, Windsor, Berkshire,
and received his B.A. from Trinity College, Oxford, in 1933.[1696] After
qualifying as a barrister, he worked for the theatrical director of the
Old Vic drama school.[1697] In March 1942, he commanded "the lead
ship in the famous St. Nazaire raid . . . , which came to be known
as the Greatest Raid of All. He was subsequently the senior naval
officer in the fabled 30th Assault Unit which was commanded by
Ian Fleming under Lord Mountbatten, and he is considered amongst
three or four other officers as forming the basis of the James Bond
character."[1698]

[1686] Wandsworth district (London), 1916, 01d: 1140, no. 255.

[1687] Lewes district (Sussex), 1939, 02b: 722, no. 7; *Summer Social Register 1942*, 648.

[1688] Chelsea district (London), 1910, 01a: 357, no. 436.

[1689] Welshpool and Llanfyllin district (Powys), 1983, 26: 0254, no. 36, indexed as West
Hartlepool, Durham.

[1690] *Oxford Dictionary of National Biography*, 14: 764–65.

[1691] St. Pancras district (London), 1955, 05d: 1030, no. 190.

[1692] Eton district (Buckinghamshire), 1909, 03a: 910, no. 139.

[1693] Greenwich district (Greater London), 1977, 12: 1223, no. 216.

[1694] *Oxford Dictionary of National Biography*, 45: 506–7.

[1695] *Oxford Dictionary of National Biography*, 14: 765; notes by Sarah Fields Getchell 2016.

[1696] During the summer of 1932, he was part of a group of friends studying at
Wimereux, near Boulogne, which included Terence Rattigan, who would use this
episode as the basis for his play *French without Tears* (1936) (*Oxford Dictionary of
National Biography*, 14: 764).

[1697] *Oxford Dictionary of National Biography*, 14: 765.

[1698] Notes by Christopher Curtis 2016. "[His] knowledge of German helped him receive the surrender of Kiel, after a spirited telephone conversation with Admiral

When the war was over he was a tireless advocate for peace. In 1947, he became deputy secretary-general of the European Movement. When the consultative assembly of the Council of Europe met in August 1949 at Strabourg University, he helped in drafting their proposals, including the European convention on human rights, the council's outstanding achievement. . . . In 1954 the assembly elected him deputy secretary-general. . . . Curtis should have been appointed secretary-general in 1960 but the assembly decided in favour of a politician.

"Curtis was good-looking—his fair hair was an oriflamme. His personality radiated fun, his courage, especially in final ill health, was profound, and he had a great sense of humour."[1699]

John Pudney was educated at Gresham's School in Holt, Norfolk, where his friends included W. H. Auden, Benjamin Britten, and Humphrey Spender. He did not go to university and got an early start as a poet, publishing *Spring Encounter* in 1933. A biographer observes a "distinctive note . . . in all Pudney's verse—incisive rhythm, simple diction, and a courageous, if occasionally mawkish, effort to celebrate man's place in nature."[1700] Pudney's first novel, *Jacobson's Ladder*, was published in 1938; in 1940, he joined the Air Ministry's Creative Writers Unit.

His most famous verse was *For Johnny*: "First published over initials by the *News Chronicle* in 1941, it was broadcast on radio by Laurence Olivier, and spoken by Michael Redgrave in *The Way to the Stars* (1945), a film directed by Anthony Asquith. After that it almost attained the status of a ballad, and was often quoted without permission of attribution." It begins:

> *Do not despair*
> *For Johnny-head-in-air;*
> *He sleeps as sound*
> *As Johnny underground.*[1701]

Later in the war, "After flying over the beaches during the invasion of France, Pudney accompanied General Leclerc's victorious troops

---

Dönitz, the German naval commander-in-chief" (*Oxford Dictionary of National Biography*, 14: 765).

[1699] *Oxford Dictionary of National Biography*, 14: 765.

[1700] Roger Lubbock, in *Oxford Dictionary of National Biography*, 45: 506.

[1701] Roger Lubbock, "Pudney, John Sleigh (1909–1977)," rev. *Oxford Dictionary of National Biography*, Oxford University Press, 2004; online edn, May 2009.

into Paris, [where he] was the first member of Allied forces to visit Pablo Picasso in his studio."

He unsuccessfully contested Sevenoaks for the Labour Party in the 1945 General Election, then served as a literary advisor for Evans Bros. and Putnam & Company while publishing novels and children's books each year: "This versatile energy, and his talent for turning out effective prose to order, may have tended to discourage critical appreciation of his more serious work." Following his second marriage and concerned about his drinking, "he made up his own mind to tackle his problem by therapy, and then described his successful cure in periodicals and a later book. This public confession was deliberately made, for Pudney believed that medical efforts to treat alcoholism were handicapped by the general reluctance to discuss it as a normal medical problem." His last book, published posthumously by Michael Joseph in 1978, was entitled *Thank Goodness for Cake*.[1702]

viii.   ALASTAIR CAMERON FORBES, b. at "The Grange," Limpsfield, Surrey 2 May 1918[1703] and d. at Cromwell Hospital, Kensington 19 May 2005.[1704] He m. (1) in 1957, CHARLOTTE BERGSØE, who was b. at Copenhagen (Zealand), Denmark 21 March 1930, dau. of Flemming Vilhelm and Grethe (Utzon-Frank) Bergsøe,[1705] from whom he was divorced in 1960;[1706] m. (2) at Kensington Register Office 7 Dec. 1966,[1707] HON. GEORGINA ANNE WARD, who was b. at Chipping Sodbury, Gloucestershire 12 March 1941,[1708] dau. of George Reginald Ward, 1st Viscount Ward of Witley, and Anne Diana France Aysham (Capel) Ward, from whom he was divorced

---

[1702] Lubbock, "Pudney, John Sleigh (1909–1977)," rev. *Oxford Dictionary of National Biography*; online edn, May 2009. Pudney's papers are on deposit at the Harry Ransom Humanities Research Center at the University of Texas at Austin; they include his correspondence with Kingsley Amis, Sir John Betjeman, Britten, Sir Winston Churchill, C. Day-Lewis, T. S. Eliot, Dame Margot Fonteyn, Sir Compton Mackenzie, Lady Ottoline Morrell, Olivier, Redgrave, V. Sackville-West, Dame Edith Sitwell, and Evelyn Waugh, among others (see http://norman.hrc.utexas.edu/fasearch/findingAid.cfm?eadid=00112).

[1703] Godstone district (Surrey), 1918, 02b: 363, no. 181.

[1704] Kensington and Chelsea district (London), 2005, 1a: 239, no. 178.

[1705] http://noblecircles.com/genealogy/getperson.php?personID=I28256&tree=tree1. Her daughter Camilla Simonsen is named as Alastair Forbes's stepdaughter on his death certificate.

[1706] A.N. Wilson, "Alastair Forbes," *The Independent*, 20 May 2005, *independent.co.uk/news/obituaries/alastair-forbes-491556.html*.

[1707] Kensington district (Middlesex), 1966, 05c: 1547, no. 75. Their engagement was announced in *The New York Times*, 9 September 1966, 50.

[1708] Sodbury district (Gloucestershire), 1941, 06a: 527, no. 76.

in 1971,[1709] and had issue by his first wife (Peter Christopher[11] Forbes).[1710]

Alastair Forbes graduated from Winchester College in Hampshire and from King's College, Cambridge, in 1938. Geoffrey Wheatcroft begins his obituary of "Ali" Forbes in *The Guardian* as follows: "In the novels of Henry James and one or two less illustrious writers, the American expatriate in Europe is a standard figure, and some American plutocrats, like the Astors, were so badly afflicted by Anglophilia that they settled here and were completely assimilated. Alastair Forbes, who has died aged 87, was one of the last of a line, a curious product of Anglo-American culture, who became a journalist in London and enjoyed two brief seasons of fame, but who was, in the end, better known as a boulevardier and courtier."[1711]

Forbes was already moving in exalted circles as a boy, when he befriended Queen Victoria's granddaughter Grand Duchess Kirill of Russia: she was, he recalled, "a most affectionate and un-puritan surrogate mother during many of the long summers of my boyhood."[1712] Invalided out of the Royal Marines during the Second World War, "he became one of the best known 'spare men' in London, found at every dinner table. Evelyn Waugh knew and greatly disliked 'pretty little Ali Forbes,'[1713] and there might have been a touch of him in the character of 'the Loot,' who appears in Waigh's great war novel *Unconditional Surrender*,[1714] the man who knows everyone and goes everywhere."[1715]

His career progressed in fits and starts: "He was usually appointed to a paper thanks to his friendship with the proprietor, never the way for a journalist to endear himself to colleagues."[1716] At various

[1709] Wilson, *The Independent*, 20 May 2005.

[1710] Mosley, *Burke's Peerage and Baronetage*, 1: 1191.

[1711] Geoffrey Wheatcroft, "Alastair Forbes," *The Guardian*, 27 May 2005.

[1712] "Alastair Forbes," *The Telegraph*, 21 May 2005. She was born Princess Victoria Melita of Edinburgh (and Saxe-Coburg and Gotha).

[1713] In 1943, for instance, James Lees-Milne described him as "a deb's delight of classic beauty, with fair, unblemished skin . . . witty, mischievous, censorious and bright" ("Alastair Forbes," *The Times*, 21 May 2005).

[1714] Only published in 1961.

[1715] Wheatcroft, *The Guardian*, 27 May 2005.

[1716] Wheatcroft, *The Guardian*, 27 May 2005. Like his future brother-in-law J. S. Pudney, he stood (as a Liberal) for Hendon South in the 1945 General Election (*The Telegraph*, 21 May 2005); he was also unsuccessful in the 1959 election (Wilson, *The Independent*, 20 May 2005).

times Forbes was associated with the *Observer*, the *Sunday Times*, the *Daily Mail*, the *Sunday Dispatch*, the *Times Literary Supplement*, the *Listener*, and the *Daily Sketch*, among other publications. More than once, as his *Telegraph* obituary noted (of the *Daily Mail*), "he eventually left after a dispute with the editor."[1717]

Of Forbes's later book reviews, Wheatcroft noted, they were "unique, immensely long, written in a convoluted style which was more 'European' than English, scurrilous, allusive and abusive. . . ."[1718]

"All the same, and unlike the columns in the tabloids, it was authentic gossip—the tittle-tattle of clubland, palaces and drawing rooms, not to say bedrooms, by someone who really did know half the European royal families, the English aristocracy and the international rich."[1719]

"He was frequently dismissed from lunch tables," his *Telegraph* obituary concluded, "and viewed the early train home on a Sunday morning after upsetting his hostess as an occupational hazard."[1720] In A. N. Wilson's judgment, "He was essentially kind. . . . He used to say, after he had lost his faith,[1721] that remembering one's friends was the performance of a requiem for them inside one's head or in conversation. For as long as his many friends remember Ali Forbes, with amusement, affection, and bewilderment, the requiem will be chanted, or drawled, in their heads."[1722]

ix. IAN ARCHIBALD FORBES, b. at "Barrow Green Court," Oxted, Surrey 29 Nov. 1919[1723] and d. near Avignon (Provence), France 21 May 2016.[1724] He m. (1) in 1941, PHOEBE VIOLA THOMAS, who d. 27 June 1954,[1725] and had issue (Veronica[11] Forbes and Griselda Forbes); m. (2) in 1957, JACQUELINE N. R. (SHAW) NASH, and had further issue (Felicity[11] Forbes and Alexander Forbes).

Ian Forbes graduated from Cambridge in 1939.

[1717] *The Telegraph*, 21 May 2005.

[1718] His jokes could be merciless: he called the Temple de la Gloire, the French home of Sir Oswald and Lady Mosley—jailed for their leadership of the British Union of Fascists before World War II—the Concentration of Camp (Wilson, *The Independent*, 20 May 2005).

[1719] Wheatcroft, *The Guardian*, 27 May 2005.

[1720] *The Telegraph*, 21 May 2005. Princess Margaret called him "That awful Ali Forbes," but Noel Coward "used to say that there was almost no one whose company he enjoyed more" (Wilson, *The Independent*, 20 May 2005).

[1721] He had briefly converted to Catholicism.

[1722] Wilson, *The Independent*, 20 May 2005.

[1723] Godstone district (Surrey), 1919, 02a: 419, no. 370.

[1724] Notes by Jonathan Winthrop 2016.

[1725] https://www.thegazette.co.uk/London/issue/40316/page/6244/data.pdf.

     x. IRIS DECIMA FORBES, b. at Barrow Green Court 27 March 1921[1726] and d. at 38 Royston Road, Harston, Cambridgeshire 17 June 1999.[1727] She m. at St. Peter's Church, Tandridge, Surrey 20 Dec. 1943,[1728] TERENCE EDWARD ARMSTRONG, who was b. at "Lunchwood," Oxted 7 April 1920[1729] and d. at 38 Royston Road 21 Feb. 1996,[1730] son of Thomas Mandeville Emerson and Jane Crawford (Young) Amstrong, and had issue (Kevin Patrick[11] Armstrong, Benedict Graham Armstrong, Deirdre Margaret Armstrong, and Damaris Rose Armstrong).[1731]

     Like his father-in-law an excellent linguist, Terence Armstrong was educated at Winchester and then Magdalene College, Cambridge, where "he was persuaded by the legendary Russian scholar Elizabeth Hill, who was recruiting for her new small department of Slavonic studies, to drop [the study of] German in favour of Russian." He studied French and Russian and received "the B.A. with a first-class degree in 1941."[1732]

     Following the war,[1733] at Dame Elizabeth's suggestion, and lacking any experience in polar studies, he applied to be a research fellow at the Scott Polar Research Institute (SPRI): "Thus began a professional life of thirty-six years during which time he established for himself and for SPRI an international reputation for research in the polar north, and particularly the Russian Arctic." Successively research fellow (1947–56), assistant director of research (1956–77), reader in Arctic studies, and acting director in 1982–83, he retired from the Institute in 1983.[1734]

     He wrote and traveled extensively—for instance, on HMCS *Labrador*'s maiden voyage through the North-west Passage in 1954, which led to his 1958 ice atlas, *Sea Ice North of the U.S.S.R.*;[1735]

[1726] Godstone district (Surrey), 1921, 02a: 422, no. 276.

[1727] Cambridge district (Cambridgeshire), 1999, 1c: 331, no. 51.

[1728] Surrey South-Eastern district, 1943, 02a: 1073, no. 38.

[1729] Godstone district (Surrey), 1920, 02a: 499, no. 185.

[1730] Cambridge district (Cambridgeshire), 1996, 1d: 331, no. 128.

[1731] *Oxford Dictionary of National Biography*, 2: 441–42; notes by Kevin Patrick Armstrong 2016.

[1732] He had already joined the Army intelligence corps (in 1940), and would be "one of the first [allied troops] in the liberation of Oslo" (*Oxford Dictionary of National Biography*, 2: 441).

[1733] Armstrong served in North Africa, Italy, Holland, Germany, and Norway (Harry King, "Terence Armstrong," *The Guardian*, 29 February 1996).

[1734] *Oxford Dictionary of National Biography*, 2: 441–42.

[1735] "Through his writings his reputation as a polar scholar went ahead of him: using information gleaned from his daily reading of *Pravda* he published in the SPRI house

spent a sabbatical at the University of Alaska; and, following his retirement, served as a visiting professor at Trent University.[1736] He was elected a fellow of the Royal Geographical Society, and received both its Cuthbert Peck Award (1954) and the Victoria Medal in 1978. Armstrong was also a foundation fellow of Clare Hall at Cambridge in 1964, serving as senior tutor in 1966 and later as the college's vice president. His colleague Sir Michael Stoker would recall, "I never heard him speak ill of any-one—I suspect that during nearly three decades Terence was the most popular member of Clare Hall. Everyone loved him."[1737]

xi.   FIONA DEIRDRE FORBES, b. at Barrow Green Court 9 Jan. 1924[1738] and d. at Sartilly (La Manche), France 25 Dec. 2010. She m. at Neuilly-sur-Seine (Hauts de Seine), France 24 Oct. 1946, ALAIN-GAUTHIER LÉVY [from 1950 LALONDE], who was b. at Jouy-en-Josas (Seine-et-Oise), France 26 June 1913 and d. at Paris 21 Aug. 1974, son of Roger Raphaël and Elise (Séligmann) Lévy, and had issue (Caroline Angela[11] Lalonde, who married Claude Roger Léon Ballot-Lena; Olivier *Brice* Achille Lalonde, a candidate for the French presidency in 1981 and France's Minister of the Environment 1991–92, who married Patricia Marie Raynaud; and Valérie Marianne Lalonde, who married James Lyttleton Fox).[1739]

---

journal *Polar Record* his analysis of shipping movements and mineral developments that were otherwise largely unknown to northern commentators within Russia itself" (*Oxford Dictionary of National Biography*, 2: 442).

[1736] King, *The Guardian*, 29 February 1996.

[1737] *Oxford Dictionary of National Biography*, 2: 442.

[1738] Godstone district (Surrey), 1924, 02a: 380, no. 313.

[1739] Notes by Brice and Valérie Lalonde 2016.

THE TENTH GENERATION

25. EMILY LINDALL[10] WINTHROP (*Grenville Lindall[9], Robert[8], Thomas Charles[7], Francis Bayard[6], John Still[5], John[4], Waitstill[3], John[2-1]*) was born at New York, New York 10 March 1893,[1740] died in New York 25 December 1962, and was buried at Sharon, Connecticut.[1741] She married at Interlaken (Stockbridge), Massachusetts 6 September 1924,[1742] COREY LUCIEN MILES, who was born Corey Lucius Miles at Milton, Vermont 7 August 1891 and died at Wickenburg, Arizona 27 February 1960, son of John J. and Viola H. (Caswell) Miles.[1743] The marriage had ended by 1930.[1744]

Her cousin Dorothy Bradford Wexler notes that Emily Winthrop Miles "became a collector of some note, bringing together several unique collections including six hundred pieces of American glass, now owned by the Metropolitan Museum of Art, and an extensive collection of Wedgwood, Meissen, and Staffordshire china, much of which is at the Brooklyn Museum along with some of her Audubon, Gould, and Elliott prints. More creative than her father, Emily also received recognition as a sculptor, artist, and poet, with shows in many New York Galleries."[1745]

[1740] Certificate 10031, Manhattan Birth Certificates, 1866–1897 (Municipal Archives), FHL 1,322,276, indexed at *familysearch.org/ark:/61903/1:1:2WD3-QDX*.

[1741] *Connecticut Death Index, 1949–2012* [database on-line]; http://www.findagrave.com/cgi-bin/fg.cgi?page=gr&GRid=105427767&ref=acom.

[1742] "Winthrop Sisters in Dual Elopement," *The New York Times*, 7 September 1924, 1, 18; "News of Elopement Unnerves Winthrop," *The New York Times*, 8 September 1924, 1, 7; Mayo, *The Winthrop Family in America*, 427.

[1743] *World War II Draft Registration Cards, 1942* [database on-line]; Arizona State Department of Health Division of Vital Statistics Certificate of Death 1922; Social Security Death Index.

[1744] Wexler, *Reared in a Greenhouse*, 227. See also "In the Berkshires," *The New York Times*, 3 August 1930.

[1745] Wexler, *Reared in a Greenhouse*, 227, citing a clipping found in Dorothy Winthrop Bradford's scrapbooks entitled "Memorial Exhibition Emily Winthrop Miles (1893–1962) September 12–September 27." This exhibition was held at the Southern

26. **KATE**[10] **WINTHROP** (*Grenville Lindall*[9], *Robert*[8], *Thomas Charles*[7], *Francis Bayard*[6], *John Still*[5], *John*[4], *Waitstill*[3], *John*[2-1]) was born at New York, New York 9 December 1899[1746] and died at Richmond, Massachusetts 30 August 1972.[1747] She married at Interlaken (Stockbridge), Massachusetts 6 September 1924,[1748] **DARWIN SPURR MORSE**, who was born 12 May 1901,[1749] son of Thomas Spurr and Jessie M. (Cooper) Morse.[1750] He died at Richmond 5 November 1984.[1751]

The twin elopement of Emily and Kate Winthrop in September 1924 diverted the East Coast press for a season, but it had long-term repercussions for the family. Brought up by their father in relative seclusion in New York and Lenox, by the early 1920s the Winthrop sisters had come to understand that their chances of leaving home were slight. While his intentions were doubtless caring, Grenville Winthrop's effect on his daughters was stifling, and whatever the private reservations of other family members, no one dared intervene to allow them to seek out romantic attachments. The result was a carefully planned escape, with the sisters pairing off with men working at the Winthrops' country estate in Lenox. Dorothy Bradford Wexler suggests that Emily and Corey Miles's marriage was the after-thought, and that it was Kate and Darwin Morse—whose marriage would last until her death in 1972—who precipitated the events of 6 September 1924.[1752]

Vermont Art Center's Festival of the Arts in 1964 (see Stephen Wolohojian, ed., and Anna Tahinci, *A Private Passion: 19th-Century Paintings and Drawings from the Grenville L. Winthrop Collection, Harvard University* [New York and New Haven: Metropolitan Museum of Art and Yale University Press, 2003], 503). See, for example, "A Reviewer's Notebook," *The New York Times*, 23 November 1941 ("A large provocative bronze called 'Hymn to the Sun,' by Emily Winthrop Miles, is on view at MacBeth's") and "In the Galleries: Shows One by One," *The New York Times*, 11 January 1948 ("Emily Winthrop Miles shows monumental nudes in the Maillol tradition along with competent, realistic portrait sculpture at French & Co.").

[1746] Certificate 46655, State of New York Certificate and Record of Birth (Borough of Manhattan) 1898–1909 (Municipal Archives), Family History Library film 1953,619, indexed at *familysearch.org/ark:/61903/1:1:2WW6-WDY*; Mayo, *The Winthrop Family in America*, 427.

[1747] Massachusetts Death Index, 1970–2003; Social Security Death Index.

[1748] "Winthrop Sisters in Dual Elopement," *The New York Times*, 7 September 1924, 1, 18; "News of Elopement Unnerves Winthrop," *The New York Times*, 8 September 1924, 1, 7; Mayo, *The Winthrop Family in America*, 427.

[1749] Social Security Death Index.

[1750] Massachusetts Vital Records, 1891, Lenox, 415: 67.

[1751] Massachusetts Death Index, 1970–2003; Social Security Death Index.

[1752] Wexler, *Reared in a Greenhouse*, 216, 227. "[One] story, from an unidentified clipping in my mother's scrapbook, seemed to hit on the real reason for their secret affairs. 'Seldom if ever,' the report read, 'did the daughters assume the hostess role for cote-

The *New York Times*' initial headline read "Winthrop Sisters in Dual Elopement," and, in smaller type, added "Event Causes a Sensation in Social Circles":

> Miss Emily Winthrop, who is 31 years old and a sculptress of considerable attainment, married her father's chauffeur, Corey Lucian Miles. Miss Kate, who is 24, married a young electrician, Darwin Spurr Morse, who had done work on the Winthrop estate, Groton Place. . . . More than ordinary astonishment was occasioned by the secret marriages because the Winthrop girls had been known here as ultraexclusive. . . . [Their] father had brought them up in unusually strict seclusion, so much so that they mingled but little even in the fashionable society of Lenox. . . .
>
> Little is known here about Mr. Miles except that he is 34 years old, a widower, without children, who came from Milton, Vt., and had been driving for Mr. Winthrop for some time. . . .
>
> Mr. Morse was born in Lenox 23 years ago, and is just a year younger than his bride. He was graduated from the Lenox High School and went to work about three years ago for Ben H. Rogers, a consulting electrician of Lenox.[1753]

The next day's paper provided further breathless details about the family reaction: "So unnerved was Grenville Lindall Winthrop by the elopement of his two daughters on Saturday that, it became known today, a physician was called to attend him soon after he learned that Miss Emily Lindall Winthrop had married the family chauffeur and Miss Kate Winthrop an electrician formerly employed about the family estate." He had evidently learned of the marriages on his return from New York; the sisters' governess, Miss Holmes, met him at the front door, "and she told him the news. . . . Her friends say she knew nothing about the love affairs of the sisters."[1754]

---

ries of youthful guests; indeed young people were taboo, evidently, and hospitalities were confined almost entirely, so it is said, to gatherings of the older circles'" (216).

[1753] "Winthrop Sisters in Dual Elopement," *The New York Times*, 7 September 1924, 1, 18.

[1754] "News of Elopement Unnerves Winthrop," *The New York Times*, 8 September 1924, 1.

There was evidently a complete break between father and daughters, even after the birth of Kate's son Thomas in May 1925.[1755] The following August, the *Times* reported that, while visiting her mother-in-law in Lenox, Mrs. Morse "refuses to go near [her father's] home until he extends his invitation to her husband, who was the poultryman on the Winthrop estate until a year ago."[1756] A month later, the Corey Mileses came from Santa Barbara, California, to stay with the Morses at their rented house in Lenox: "This is the first visit of Mr. and Mrs. Miles to Lenox since their elopement. They were accompanied by Miss Helen Holmes, who has been with the Winthrop girls as governess and secretary for twenty-four years. Mr. Winthrop never has become reconciled to the elopement and only his daughters are welcome to his villa."[1757]

While in time relations between the sisters and their father gradually improved, Grenville Winthrop's attitude to their elopement seems to have expressed itself most tellingly in his estate planning, when he left his collections to Harvard's Fogg Museum, including portraits of his daughters by John Singer Sargent. He also left his residuary estate to his nephew, Robert[10] Winthrop.[1758]

The Morses settled at "Green Meads Farm" in Richmond, where they sponsored prizes at the Lenox Dog Show[1759] and won them at the Springfield Horse Show.[1760] In July 1972, their house was the setting for Darwin Morse's niece Rosemary Hall Colgate's marriage to James Hulbert Evans.[1761]

[1755] "Morses of Lenox Have Son," *The New York Times*, 29 May 1925, 17.

[1756] "Avoids Her Father's Home," *The New York Times*, 16 August 1925.

[1757] "Winthrop Sisters Reunite," *The New York Times*, 14 September 1925, 21.

[1758] "G. L. Winthrop Will Bequeaths $4,500,000," *The New York Times*, 29 January 1943, 26. "On the face of it," Dorothy B. Wexler notes, "his daughters were included in his will. The second clause [covers a trust for Emily and Kate and then Kate's children, but] according to grandson Thomas S. Morse, though Grenville had set up this trust for his daughters, he had never funded it. Rather, his will explicitly states that he made 'no further provision for my daughters as they have been otherwise adequately provided for' (referring to money left to them by their mother)" (Wexler, *Reared in a Greenhouse*, 228, citing a letter dated 12 May 1996 from Thomas S. Morse).

[1759] "In the Berkshires," *The New York Times*, 3 August 1930.

[1760] "Horse Show Honors Annexed by [the Morses'] Tide Gate," *The New York Times*, 22 September 1932, 30.

[1761] "Mrs. Colgate Bride of J. H. Evans," *The New York Times*, 2 July 1972, 36.

Children of Darwin Spurr and Kate[10] (Winthrop) Morse:[1762]

36   i.   THOMAS SPURR[11] MORSE, b. at Santa Barbara, Calif. 25 May 1925;[1763] m. 26 June 1948, PATRICIA ANN BIRT.

      ii.   ROBERT FLOYD MORSE, b. at Richmond 31 March 1927 and d. at Pompano Beach, Fla. 17 May 2009. He m. IRENE FLORENCE CLEATOR, formerly wife of Roy Nash; at his death, he was survived by a stepson, David Carl Nash.[1764]

27. JOHN[10] KEAN (*Katharine Taylor*[9] *Winthrop, Robert*[8]*, Thomas Charles*[7]*, Francis Bayard*[6]*, John Still*[5]*, John*[4]*, Waitstill*[3]*, John*[2-1]) was born at New York, New York 22 November 1888[1765] and died there at Roosevelt Hospital 23 October 1949.[1766] He married at the Church of the Incarnation, New York 20 January 1925,[1767] **MARY ALICE BARNEY**, who was born Mary Alice Priscilla Barney at New York 12 April 1902, daughter of John Stewart Walker and Mary Alice (Van Nest) Barney.[1768] She died at "Liberty Hall," Union, New Jersey 4 September 1995.[1769]

John Kean graduated from St. Mark's School, Southborough, Massachusetts, and Harvard University (1911 and 1913). A lawyer in Newark before the First World War, he was wounded in the Meuse-Argonne and spent time recovering in France. He entered business on his return to New Jersey, becoming "treasurer of the Elizabethtown Gas Company, a vice president of the Elizabethtown Water Company and a vice president of the National State Bank." He was president of the National State Bank at the time of his death.[1770]

His widow survived him by forty-five years. The first female trustee of the New-York Historical Society (from 1967 until 1984), she was also the president general of the Colonial Dames of America 1956–60.

[1762] Taylor, *The Lion and the Hare*, Chart H; [John Winthrop], *Descendants of Robert Winthrop & Kate Wilson Taylor, 1833–2000* (Privately printed, 2006), 13; questionnaire from Amy Bradford Morse 2013.

[1763] "Morses of Lenox Have Son," *The New York Times*, 29 May 1925, 17, gives date of birth as 27 May.

[1764] http://www.fhnfuneralhome.com/obituaries/DavidCarl-Nash-28526/#!/Obituary.

[1765] *Harvard College Class of 1911 Twenty-fifth Anniversary Report* (1936), 383.

[1766] "John Kean, Banker in New Jersey, 60," *The New York Times*, 25 October 1949, 27.

[1767] "Miss Alice Barney Wed to John Kean," *The New York Times*, 21 January 1925, 21.

[1768] Thomas Townsend Sherman, *Sherman Genealogy: Including Families of Essex, Suffolk, and Norfolk, England* . . . (New York: T. A. Wright, 1920), 356.

[1769] "Mary Alice Barney Kean, 93, a Leader in Historical Preservation," *The New York Times*, 7 September 1995.

[1770] "John Kean, Banker in New Jersey, 60," *The New York Times*, 25 October 1949, 27.

"[Long] prominent in the historical preservation field," she was president of the Elizabethtown Historical Foundation at her death.[1771]

Children of John[10] and Mary Alice (Barney) Kean, born at New York:[1772]

37   i.   MARY ALICE[11] KEAN, b. 14 Oct. 1927; m. 12 May 1951, DAVID
          ROBERT WALLACE RAYNOLDS.

38   ii.   JOHN KEAN, b. at New York 28 Oct. 1929; m. (1) 25 June 1952,
          JOAN EMILY JESSUP; m. (2) 10 Sept. 1983, PAMELA ANN (SUMMERS)
          WOJCICKI.

    iii.   STEWART BARNEY KEAN, b. 10 May 1934 and d. unm. at Elizabeth,
          N.J. 6 June 2002.

          The founder and president of the Liberty Hall Foundation,
          organized to preserve the Kean family homestead, Stewart Barney
          Kean graduated from the Brooks School, North Andover, Mass.,
          and the University of Virginia (1957).

28. **ROBERT WINTHROP**[10] **KEAN** (*Katharine Taylor*[9] *Winthrop, Robert*[8], *Thomas Charles*[7], *Francis Bayard*[6], *John Still*[5], *John*[4], *Waitstill*[3], *John*[2-1]) was born at Elberon, New Jersey 28 September 1893[1773] and died at Livingston, New Jersey 21 September 1980.[1774] He married at the Church of St. Mark-in-the-Bouwerie, New York, New York 18 October 1920, **ELIZABETH STUYVESANT HOWARD**, who was born at New York 31 January 1897, daughter of Thomas Howard and Rose Anthony (Post) Howard.[1775] She died at Livingston 28 January 1988.[1776]

Robert Winthrop Kean graduated from St. Mark's School, Southborough, Massachusetts, and Harvard College (1915). During World War I, he served as a first lieutenant with the Second Division of the American Expeditionary Force in France and was awarded the Distinguished Service Cross and the Silver Star for gallantry. After the

---

[1771] "Mary Alice Barney Kean, 93, a Leader in Historical Preservation," *The New York Times*, 7 September 1995.

[1772] Taylor, *The Lion and the Hare*, Chart H; *The New York Times*, 11 September 1983; *Summer Social Register 2003*, 205; questionnaire from John Kean 2014.

[1773] *Harvard College Class of 1915 Twenty-fifth Anniversary Report* (Cambridge, Mass.: The Cosmos Press, 1940), 397.

[1774] Joan Cook, "Robert W. Kean, 86; Formerly in House," *The New York Times*, 24 September 1980, D23.

[1775] "Miss Howard Wed in Old St. Mark's," *The New York Times*, 19 October 1920, 11; New York Passenger Lists, 1820–1957; *Summer Social Register 1988*, Deaths, 19; Social Security Death Index.

[1776] "Elizabeth S. Kean, 90, Mother of Governor," *The New York Times*, 29 January 1988, B5.

war, he became a partner in the New York investment firm of Kean, Taylor & Co.; Kean was also the founder of the Livingston National Bank, where he served as chairman.

He was first elected to Congress in 1938, where he served on the Banking and Currency Committee and later became the ranking Republican on the powerful Ways and Means Committee.[1777] In 1940, he described the casual way in which he entered elective politics: having been involved with the New Jersey Republican Party since 1931 (and as the son of former Senator Hamilton Kean), "the leaders in my Congressional District . . . asked me to run for Congress. The investment business not being what it had been, I decided to do so. (The fact that it was about time for this [Harvard Class of 1915 reunion] Report in which I would have to relate to my classmates of what use I had been in the world may have had some influence upon my decision.)"[1778]

He was known for his expertise on Social Security and taxation; during the Truman adminstration he led an investigation into the Internal Revenue Service that resulted in the convictions of several top officials there.[1779] In 1958, he had served ten terms in the House of Representatives, and, he recalled, when "New Jersey's senior Senator decided to retire, I took a gamble and ran for his job. I won the Primary by 24,000 votes; but it was a Democratic year, and I lost in November. However, campaigning state-wide as the Republican senatorial candidate was an experience I would not have missed. After my defeat I was appointed chairman of the Advisory Committee for the White House Conference on Aging, and had an interesting two years serving in that capacity."[1780]

[1777] Cook, *The New York Times*, 24 September 1980, D23.

[1778] *Harvard College Class of 1915 Twenty-fifth Anniversary Report* (Cambridge, Mass.: The Cosmos Press, 1940), 398.

[1779] Cook, *The New York Times*, 24 September 1980, D23. "Am chairman of the subcommittee on Administration of the Internal Revenue Laws, which investigated and brought out the scandals in administration of our tax laws in the Internal Revenue Bureau" (*Harvard College Class of 1915 Fortieth Anniversary Report* (Cambridge: The Cosmos Press, 1955]. 91). "He was one of the first Republicans to speak out against McCarthy," [his son Thomas H.] Kean recalled in a recent interview. "Because of his position, we used to get these awful letters in the mail.

"His integrity always impressed me," he said. "I was very aware he never took the easy way out on issues. Someone would tell him to take a particular position because it would be helpful in the district. He'd never take it. I know that had an impression on me" (Michael Norman, "Man in the News: A Reluctant Politician, Thomas Howard Kean," *The New York Times*, 20 January 1982).

[1780] *Harvard Class of 1915 Fiftieth Anniversary Report* (Cambridge, Mass.: Printed at the University, 1965), 281.

In retirement, he continued his involvement with local banks and utilities, serving on several boards; he also wrote books: *Dear Marraine (1917–1919)* (1969), about his service in the First World War, and *Fourscore Years: My First Twenty-four* (1974), covering his Kean and Winthrop relatives and his own early life.

Children of Robert Winthrop[10] and Elizabeth Stuyvesant (Howard) Kean, last four born at New York:[1781]

39   i.   ELIZABETH STUYVESANT[11] KEAN, b. at New York 13 Sept. 1921; m. 29 Oct. 1942, EDWARD LIVINGSTON HICKS, 3RD.

40   ii.   ROBERT WINTHROP KEAN, JR., b. at Hewlett, L.I., N.Y. 18 Aug. 1922; m. (1) 19 April 1947, LUZ MARIA SILVERIO; m. (2) 4 Nov. 1982, KATHERINE (TCHOUKALEFF) TOBEASON.

41   iii. HAMILTON FISH KEAN, b. 1 March 1925; m. (1) 25 March 1950, ELLEN SHAW GARRISON; m. (2) 6 July 1981, ALICE (NEWCOMER) BAKER; m. (3) 23 Sept. 1989, EDITH MORGAN (WILLIAMSON) BACON.

42   iv.   ROSE ANTHONY KEAN, b. 1 Feb. 1931; m. 12 Aug. 1955, EDGAR GEORGE LANSBURY.

43   v.   THOMAS HOWARD KEAN, b. 21 April 1935; m. 3 June 1967, DEBORAH ELIZABETH BYE.

        vi.   KATHARINE WINTHROP KEAN, b. 28 March 1939.

29. ROBERT[10] **WINTHROP** (*Frederic*[9], *Robert*[8], *Thomas Charles*[7], *Francis Bayard*[6], *John Still*[5], *John*[4], *Waitstill*[3], *John*[2-1]. Also *Dorothy*[10] *Amory, Charles Walter*[9] *Amory, Anna Powell Grant*[8] *Sears, David*[7] *Sears, Anne*[6] *Winthrop, John Still*[5]) was born at 439 Marlborough Street, Boston, Massachusetts 21 January 1904[1782] and died at Upper Brookville, Long Island, New York 25 September 1999.[1783] He married, first, at the Cathedral Church of St. Paul, Boston 9 April 1928,[1784] **THEODORA AYER**, who was born at Beverly Farms, Massachusetts 27 September 1905[1785]

[1781] *The New York Times*, 30 March 1939, 27; Winthrop, *Descendants of Robert Winthrop & Kate Wilson Taylor, 1833–2000*, 14; questionnaires from Thomas Howard Kean and James Edgar Lansbury 2014; notes by Christopher Kean 2014.

[1782] Massachusetts Vital Records, 1904, Boston, 545: 3; Mayo, *The Winthrop Family in America*, 434.

[1783] William H. Honan, "Robert Winthrop, 95, a Banker, Philanthropist and Sportsman," *The New York Times*, 30 September 1999, B15.

[1784] "Theodora Ayer Wed in Boston," *The New York Times*, 10 April 1928, 23.

[1785] Massachusetts Vital Records, 1905, Beverly, 440: 396.

and died at "Oakley," Upperville, Virginia 11 June 1996,[1786] daughter of Charles Fanning and Sara Theodora (Ilsley) Ayer, from whom he was divorced at Reno, Nevada 5 March 1942. She married, second, 3 September 1942, Dr. Archibald Cary Randolph.[1787] Robert Winthrop married, second, at the Riverside Church, New York, New York 25 April 1942,[1788] **MARGARET STONE**,[1789] who was born at Boston 8 January 1904[1790] and died at Old Westbury, Long Island 4 November 1985, formerly wife of Robert Colgate Vernon Mann, and daughter of Charles Augustus and Mary Adams (Leonard) Stone;[1791] and, third, 20 April 1988, **FLOREINE JUNE NELSON**, who was born at San Francisco, California 14 June 1918[1792] and died at Glen Cove, Long Island 27 August 2014,[1793] formerly wife of i) Milton Haas and widow of ii) Albert Hailparn and iii) Franklin John Wilkes, and daughter of Thomas E. and Mary R. (Parkins) Nelson.[1794]

Robert Winthrop, a member of the tenth generation of the Winthrop family to attend Harvard University,[1795] was educated at St. Mark's School, Southborough, Massachusetts; Harvard (1926 and 1928x);[1796] and Trinity College at Cambridge University. He married Theo Ayer, a neighbor on Boston's North Shore, at the end of his year at Harvard Business School, and in 1928–29 clerked at the National City Bank in New York. In 1929, he joined the family firm (Robert Winthrop & Co.) as a clerk, becoming a partner in 1931 and senior partner in 1940.[1797] When Robert Winthrop & Co. merged with Wood,

---

[1786] Robert McG. Thomas, Jr., "Theodora Ayer Randolph, Fox Hunting's First Lady, Dies at 90," *The New York Times*, 15 June 1996, 11.

[1787] Steward, *The Sarsaparilla Kings*, 86 (parents), 92 (divorce, remarriage).

[1788] "Mrs. M.S. Mann Married," *The New York Times*, 26 April 1942, 37.

[1789] Mayo, *The Winthrop Family in America*, 434.

[1790] Massachusetts Vital Records, 1904, Boston, 545: 3.

[1791] Steward and Child, *The Descendants of Judge John Lowell of Newburyport, Massachusetts*, 115–16.

[1792] *California Birth Index, 1905–1995*.

[1793] *The New York Times*, 31 August 2014, 21.

[1794] Steward and Child, *The Descendants of Judge John Lowell of Newburyport, Massachusetts*, 61, 115–16.

[1795] Honan, *The New York Times*, 30 September 1999, B15.

[1796] In 1983, Harvard bestowed an honorary Doctorate of Laws upon him (*Porcellian Club 1791–2016*, 128). The citation on his honorary degree read, "A grateful university pays honor to a devoted and generous son whose vision and conviction have enlarged the scope of Harvard's usefulness to the world of scholarship" (Wexler, *Reared in a Greenhouse*, 328).

[1797] *National Cyclopaedia of American Biography*, L: 353. "The weeks following the crash [in 1929] were a frenzy of activity for the company. A tremendous volume of odd-

Struthers & Co.,[1798] Bob Winthrop became senior partner of that firm as well. He retired as honorary chairman of Wood, Struthers & Winthrop in 1969.[1799]

At the time of his graduation from Harvard College, Robert Winthrop was a member of the U.S. Army Reserve Corps, serving (ultimately as a lieutenant) until 1937. During the Second World War, he was commissioned a lieutenant in the U.S. Naval Reserve; he was discharged in 1945 with the rank of commander.[1800]

In addition to his business interests[1801] and war service, Winthrop would become president (and a trustee) of the North American Wildlife Foundation and trustee of the New York Zoological Society. For more than a decade (1946–57), he served as president of Nassau Hospital in Mineola, Long Island;[1802] after fifty years' service on the board, in 1985 the hospital changed its name to Winthrop-University Hospital in his honor.[1803] From 1955 until 1957, he was president of Ducks Unlimited;[1804] a few years later, he took part in an unusual exercise (for the time) in public relations meant to highlight:

---

lot buying had come its way. Back office clerks worked feverishly, dealing with these small clusters of stocks and snatching a few hours of sleep on office tables or the floor. Even Robert—who always seemed unflappable—would remember it as 'a traumatic experience'" (Wexler, *Reared in a Greenhouse*, 273, citing Winthrop, draft history of Robert Winthrop & Co.).

[1798] A related company, originally established by members of Georgiana Maria (Kane) Winthrop's extended family.

[1799] *National Cyclopaedia of American Biography*, L: 353. At the time this article was published, in 1972, the firm had offices in New York, Chicago, Los Angeles, Boston, New Haven (Conn.), Rochester (N.Y.), Dallas, and San Francisco.

[1800] *National Cyclopaedia of American Biography*, L: 353–54. At one point, he ran the post office in Trinidad (Wexler, *Reared in a Greenhouse*, 299, citing a letter from her uncle of 22 September 1995).

[1801] His entry in the *National Cyclopaedia of American Biography* lists his service as a trustee of the Seaman's Bank for Savings; a director of the Austral Oil Co. and the National Reinsurance Co.; and a member of the trust board of the First National City Bank (L: 353).

[1802] *National Cyclopaedia of American Biography*, L: 353. He was also a trustee of Presbyterian Hospital and New York Hospital in Manhattan; a trustee of the Village of Old Westbury 1946–67; a member of the executive council of C.W. Post College of Long Island University 1965–67 (and a trustee of L.I.U. in 1968); onetime treasurer of Cooper Union; and a member of the visiting committee of Harvard Medical School.

[1803] He established a chair at Harvard Medical School as well as the Robert Winthrop Scholarship Fund for Harvard students (Honan, *The New York Times*, 30 September 1999, B15).

[1804] *National Cyclopaedia of American Biography*, L: 353.

[the] decline of the mallard [duck] along its migration route, the Mississippi flyway. The cause of the ducks' decline appeared to be the unrestricted draining of wetlands in several states along the route, so Mr. Winthrop believed that Federal action was necessary.

To get the attention of the Government, he and a former state duck-calling champion from Tennessee, J. C. Boals, Jr., agreed to ask duck hunters to send President Lyndon B. Johnson postcards with only one word on them: "Ducks."

Mr. Boals was to write a letter of explanation to President Johnson, a duck hunter himself, but instead gave his letter to a Congressman, who misunderstood his instructions and delivered it to the Interior Department.

The White House received 5,460 postcards but no explanation. The immediate result was confusion in the White House mail room, but the eventual discovery of the letter magnified the effect of the lobbying and turned it into a public relations success.

It has also contributed to a series of laws that has held the annual average loss of wetlands acreage to only a third of what it was in the 1960s.[1805]

In 1942, following his divorce from Theo Ayer, Robert Winthrop married Margaret Stone Mann, the former wife of his Harvard contemporary Colgate Mann.[1806] Meg Winthrop died in 1985, and three years later he married Floreine Nelson Wilkes, who outlived him by fourteen years and died (at the age of 96) in August 2014, 110 years after Bob Winthrop's birth.

His first wife would, during and after her second marriage, become a public figure in her own right. When she died in 1996,

> It had been years since Mrs. Randolph had donned her dark-blue, gold-collared coat, tucked her auburn hair under her helmet and galloped off over the vast expanse of farmland that makes up the grounds of the 150-year-old landowners' association known as the Piedmont Hunt. [Among other responsibilities as Master,] it would

---

[1805] Honan, *The New York Times*, 30 September 1999, B15.
[1806] *Porcellian Club 1791–2016*, 127.

be Mrs. Randolph's duty to pay . . . newcomers a call.
Over a cup of tea, perhaps, she would acquaint them with
the customs and traditions of the neighborhood, assuring
them that the members of the Piedmont Hunt were
always careful to close gates they might have opened and
not to trample any flower beds near the house. . . .

But she was something of a newcomer herself. In an
area where the first families of Virginia can be downright
condescending to those who trace their ancestry to only
the second wave of settlers, Mrs. Randolph achieved
social prominence and fox-hunting distinction despite
the fact that she was an actual Yankee.[1807]

A member of a hunting family in Massachusetts, "she readily
acknowledged that she received some of her most vivid training in
advanced fence-jumping during Virginia visits to her daredevil uncle,
General George S. Patton."[1808]

After her second marriage,

She became active in every aspect of equestrian affairs,
breeding show and steeplechase champions, leading a
drive to ban the use of performance-enhancing drugs
and receiving numerous honors for her work, including
an honorary degree from the University of Pennsylvania
School of Veterinary Medicine.[1809]

But it was as a highly accomplished horsewoman,
one who could take the lead in an organization that
prides itself on being the nation's fastest hunt ("Keep up
or go home" is one of its official rules), that she won
greatest acclaim.

It was a tribute to her standing, and her reputation
for social observation, that in her later years newcomers
tended to come to her.[1810]

[1807] She did have the advantage of having attended the Foxcroft School in Middleburg,
Virginia, before her first marriage.

[1808] Thomas, *The New York Times*, 15 June 1996, 11. Her father, Charles Fanning Ayer,
was the older half-brother of Beatrice Banning Ayer, who married Lieut. George
Smith Patton, Jr., in 1910. During the year between the First and Second World
Wars, the Pattons were stationed more than once in the area around Washington,
D.C., not far from Upperville. (Steward, *The Sarsaparilla Kings*, 86, 87)

[1809] Mrs. Randolph later established the Theodora Ayer Randolph Professorship of
Equine Surgery at Virginia Polytechnic Institute and State University in Blacksburg.

[1810] Thomas, *The New York Times*, 15 June 1996, 11. With regard to her tart appreciation

Children of Robert[10] and Theodora (Ayer) Winthrop, born at New York:[1811]

44 i. THEODORA[11] WINTHROP, b. 16 July 1929; m. (1) 11 Sept. 1948, THOMAS LEE HIGGINSON; m. (2) 10 June 1984, BRUCE DUFF HOOTON.

45 ii. ELIZABETH AMORY WINTHROP, b. 14 Dec. 1931; m. (1) 16 June 1951, FRANCIS ELLSWORTH BAKER; m. (2) 21 Sept. 1957, HERBERT SCOTT SNEAD; m. (3) 21 April 1958, MALCOLM PENNINGTON RIPLEY; m. (4) 4 July 1979, PHILLIP IRWIN SHATZ.

46 iii. CORNELIA BEEKMAN WINTHROP, b. 31 Dec. 1934; m. 27 Feb. 1960, EDWARD SHELBY BONNIE.

30. **DOROTHY**[10] **WINTHROP** (*Frederic*[9], *Robert*[8], *Thomas Charles*[7], *Francis Bayard*[6], *John Still*[5], *John*[4], *Waitstill*[3], *John*[2-1]. Also *Dorothy*[10] *Amory, Charles Walter*[9] *Amory, Anna Powell Grant*[8] *Sears, David*[7] *Sears, Anne*[6] *Winthrop, John Still*[5]) was born at "Groton House Farm," Hamilton, Massachusetts 2 May 1905[1812] and died at Beverly Hospital in Beverly, Massachusetts 29 November 1987.[1813] She married at Groton House 29 August 1931,[1814] **STANDISH BRADFORD**, who was born at Orange, New Jersey 23 September 1900, son of Harold Standish and Mary Frances (McCullagh) Bradford. He died at "Black Brook Farm," Hamilton 19 June 1983.[1815]

Dorothy B. Wexler's *Reared in a Greenhouse* has been an important resource for this book, and it is really a book-length account of Dorothy[10] Winthrop and her "Stories—and Story." After a rather bleak childhood—influenced by her mother's early death, her remote father's

---

of the milieu in which she made herself "The Kingfisher," her step-granddaughter told a story highlighting Mrs. Randolph's "wry delight in the extravagant idiosyncrasies of the very wealthy." A near neighbor of Paul and Bunny Mellon, whenever "she would see the Mellons' private plane land and then take off again 10 minutes later . . . , Mrs. Randolph would take a sip of her tea and nod knowingly: It was only Mrs. Mellon, she would say, come home to fetch a scarf."

[1811] Steward, *The Sarsaparilla Kings*, 92, 104–5; Steward and Child, *The Descendants of Judge John Lowell of Newburyport, Massachusetts*, 116.

[1812] Massachusetts Vital Records, 1905, Hamilton, 550: 423; Wexler, *Reared in a Greenhouse*, 87.

[1813] Wexler, *Reared in a Greenhouse*, 360; Steward and Child, *The Descendants of Judge John Lowell of Newburyport, Massachusetts*, 116.

[1814] Mayo, *The Winthrop Family in America*, 434; Wexler, *Reared in a Greenhouse*, 279.

[1815] *Harvard Class of 1924 Twenty-fifth Anniversary Report* (Cambridge, Mass.: Printed for the Class, 1949), 83; Steward and Child, *The Descendants of Judge John Lowell of Newburyport, Massachusetts*, 61, 116.

remarriage to an (initially) uncongenial stepmother, and a pervading lack of self-esteem[1816]—Dorothy blossomed into a poised young woman. Her romance with Standish Bradford had some of the elements of her parents' years-long courtship, but where her mother had been reluctant to accept Frederic Winthrop's hand, in this case it was Mr. Winthrop's objection to his daughter's choice that kept the two apart.

While waiting for this long trial period to end, Dorothy went abroad during the spring of 1931 with her father and her uncle Beekman Winthrop. While in Madrid, on 12 April, she wrote in her diary that there had been a "riot at midnight before Post Office only one block from [the] hotel and firing on the street. [There were] 9 wounded" in what proved to be the outbreak of the Spanish Revolution. The next day the Queen of Spain and the royal children left for Paris: "Huge mob before Palace. . . . Uproar has increased. Red banners everywhere." Although the hotel staff warned the Winthrop party about going out in the streets, Dorothy would recall, in the capital the revolution was marked by the crowds snake-dancing, "all night, all day, and all the next night, through the streets, and all the policemen turned their little capes inside out, because the insides were red. And all the donkeys had red ribbons in their hair."[1817]

Two months before, also in her diary, Dorothy Winthrop had written the following about Standish Bradford:

> There is something precious and old-fashioned about him which I love, something chivalrous, seldom met with now. . . . In my mind's eye I shall always see him standing in the fast gathering darkness by the snow-covered back street, tall and fair with head bared, his hands hanging by his side, and his clear clear eyes looking into mine as I moved away. I love him, I love him. The more I learn about other people, the more do I appreciate Standish and the more I see I have underestimated him in the

---

[1816] These features were countered by her maternal grandmother, the other great character in *Reared in a Greenhouse*. Perhaps Frederic Winthrop was also influenced by the unhappy effects of his brother Grenville's approach to choosing suitors for his daughters.

[1817] Wexler, *Reared in a Greenhouse*, 271. "[After] a decent interval . . . , the men even 'interviewed' some of the new government officials. For Uncle Beek, it was a bit of déjà vu. 'I shall have seen four rulers in England, two in Spain, two in Portugal, three in Germany, and two in Russia,' he wrote Dorothy later. 'Of these, one abdicated, two were overthrown by a revolution, one fled, two were murdered. This is a dreadful record'" (272).

ignorance of my youth and the blindness of my point of view. . . . He was once a wonderful part of my life, now he's my whole life.[1818]

When, in July 1931, Dorothy told her father she planned to marry Bradford with, or without, his permission, and Frederic acquiesced, Standish wrote her: "How did you ever bring your Father around? He was so set against this and being a man of very strong purposes anyway, I thought only a miracle would do the trick. But you are a miracle to me, so that explains it." As their daughter adds, "maybe it does."[1819]

Following her marriage, Dorothy Bradford played a role in the ongoing debate on family planning in Massachusetts. In 1936, Massachusetts was one of two states still banning contraceptives, and the Masachusetts Birth Control League, with one (illegal) clinic in Brookline, decided to mark the American Medical Association's general approval of birth control by opening new clinics. One was the North Shore Mothers' Health Office in Beverly, with Dorothy W. Bradford as executive committee chairman.

Her daughter noted that:

> She developed her position on birth control methodically, studying all sides of the question and filing information she gathered under topics ranging from "population" to "crime," from "patients" to "R.C." (Roman Catholics). Though she was a member of the American Eugenics Society (perhaps it was her sly way of getting their mail!), my mother realized this group was extreme. A news story in her files warned that their rhetoric could all "too easily ... be made a cloak for class snobbery, ancestor worship and race prejudice."[1820]

On 3 June 1937, the North Shore Mothers' Health Office on Essex Street was raided. Her daughter wrote, "We children always liked to

---

[1818] Wexler, *Reared in a Greenhouse*, 276. Years later, Mrs. Bradford remembered their courtship in this way: "No 'acceptable' boy ever cared for me, no matter how many my brothers brought home and no matter how many danced with me at parties. . . . Daddy [Standish Bradford] was quite different from the other boys—very quiet, no smoothness, no polish, no *savoir faire*, so to me he was full of charm. He was in many ways, as you [Dotty Wexler] express it, 'screwed-up' but so was I. Perhaps we were both in revolt against the superficial and artificial aspects of life" (341).

[1819] Wexler, *Reared in a Greenhouse*, 277.

[1820] Wexler, *Reared in a Greenhouse*, 287–89 at 289.

imagine our mother, primly attired in a white, button-down dress with the obligatory broad-brimmed hat, being hauled off to jail. Alas, that didn't happen. She wasn't even at the clinic when the police burst in, seized confidential medical records and birth control 'paraphernalia,' and lodged complaints against the attending doctor, nurse, and social workers." Mrs. Bradford later testified "that the clinic was nonprofit and set up to help the underprivileged." The Boston *Daily Record* summed the court case up with headlines like "Ovation at Trial" and "Society Folk Back Birth Control!"[1821]

In February 1938, the Commonwealth's Supreme Court confirmed a ban on birth control in Massachusetts. Mrs. Bradford's statement read, in part: "Common sense is outraged by a decision so out of touch with the realities of the world today. It means that a law is construed to interfere with a medical practice approved by the American Medical Association. It means that a safeguard to the health of women and children is considered illegal. It means the continued prevalence of abortion, an evil which has been reduced to a minimum in communities with medically directed birth control clinics," and she warned of an "underground bootleg trade in contraceptives." It took another twenty-eight years for her position to become Massachusetts law.[1822]

Judge Standish Bradford graduated from the Groton School, Groton, Massachusetts, and Harvard University (1924 and 1927).[1823] At the time of his fiftieth reunion at Harvard College, Bradford wrote, "I think it is correct to say that my life has been principally governed by a wonderful person whom I was lucky enough to marry back in 1931.

"We have lived in only one place during our married life. This place used to be a farm and we reconstituted it as such after the Second World War—a way of life that appealed to both of us."[1824]

During the Second World War, Lieutenant Colonel Bradford commanded the 71st Replacement Battalion of the Third Army. His daughter summarized his service:

[1821] Wexler, *Reared in a Greenhouse*, 291, 292.

[1822] Wexler, *Reared in a Greenhouse*, 293, 294.

[1823] He was a member of the Porcellian Club with his Harvard College class (*Porcellian Club 1791–2016*, 127).

[1824] In 1974, he reported that a change to the Massachusetts constitution and a new retirement policy at Ropes & Gray "forced my retirement after seven years on the bench"; he had also "to leave the firm with which I had been associated since 1927, after reaching the age of seventy-two. I have now become counsel for H. C. Wainwright & Company, a firm for which I have done legal work for a number of years" (*Harvard Class of 1924 Fiftieth Anniversary Report* [Cambridge, Mass.: Printed at the University, 1974], 68).

It was a glorious assignment. Their work was critical, for resistance [from the retreating Germans in 1944] was fierce and casualties high. Reinforcements were needed constantly, fresh troops who could step in where others had been mowed down. The Allies seemed to have almost unlimited reserve manpower. The Germans had virtually exhausted theirs. His assignment placed my father hard by some of the heaviest fighting in France.[1825]

His friend Harrison Gardner had a slightly different, comic interpretation of Standish Bradford's war service. At "tea and strumpets" (perhaps imagined) with General Douglas MacArthur, the general told him:

Standish was personally, alone, responsible for stopping the Germans in France in the recent unpleasantness. Mac told me that, with complete disregard for his own safety, Standish stood up in his jeep and coolly shouted "Ils ne passeront pas." But his French was so bad that the Germans thought he said, "Hitler has married Eleanor Roosevelt" so that was too much and they all quit, every damn one of them.[1826]

Children of Standish and Dorothy[10] (Winthrop) Bradford, born at Boston, Massachusetts:[1827]

47   i.   DOROTHY AMORY[11] BRADFORD, b. 18 May 1932; m. 2 Dec. 1967, ARTHUR IRVIN WEXLER.

48   ii.   STANDISH BRADFORD, JR., b. 2 Dec. 1933; m. 1 May 1971, BRIGITTE HILDEGARD PULLERDT.

      iii.   KATHARINE BRADFORD, b. 10 Oct. 1938; she graduated from Smith College in 1960.

49   iv.   ELIZABETH GARDNER BRADFORD, b. 6 Feb. 1940; m. 21 Aug. 1965, GAVIN GAIL BORDEN.

[1825] Wexler, *Reared in a Greenhouse*, 301.

[1826] Wexler, *Reared in a Greenhouse*, 303–4. He came home from Europe in late 1945 with a "theater ribbon with four stars, a Bronze Star, and a promotion to full colonel to attest to a job well done" (313).

[1827] *Harvard Class of 1924 Twenty-fifth Anniversary Report*, 83; Steward and Child, *The Descendants of Judge John Lowell of Newburyport, Massachusetts*, 116; questionnaires from Elizabeth Bradford Borden and Dorothy Bradford Wexler 2013.

31. **FREDERIC**[10] **WINTHROP** (*Frederic*[9], *Robert*[8], *Thomas Charles*[7], *Francis Bayard*[6], *John Still*[5], *John*[4], *Waitstill*[3], *John*[2-1]. Also *Dorothy*[10] *Amory, Charles Walter*[9] *Amory, Anna Powell Grant*[8] *Sears, David*[7] *Sears, Anne*[6] *Winthrop, John Still*[5]) was born at "Groton House Farm," Hamilton, Massachusetts 30 June 1906[1828] and died there 16 February 1979.[1829] He married at St. Peter's Church, Tandridge, Surrey, England 4 July 1933,[1830] **ANGELA ELIZABETH**[10] **FORBES**,[1831] who was born at Paris, France 5 April 1912 and died at Groton House 5 August 2011, daughter of James Grant Forbes and Margaret Tyndal[9] Winthrop (*Robert Charles*[8-7], *Thomas Lindall*[6], *John Still*[5]).[1832]

Frederic Winthrop graduated from St. Mark's School, Southborough, Massachusetts, and Harvard College (1928).[1833] After college, "I tried living in New York for nearly a year," he later wrote, "but I decided, even in those days, that Boston was more liveable than the Big Apple. So when G. M. P. Murphy & Company opened its Boston office, I came back here. I did not stay long in the brokerage business."

> The year 1931 was pretty depressing in the world of securities; so shortly after having had a prospective investor say to me—"If you're trying to sell bonds, God have mercy on your soul, but don't bother me!"—I left the world of finance and entered zoology. Including a collection trip to Mexico, I spent two years in the Agassiz Museum, which was then guided by that remarkable naturalist, Tom Barbour.
>
> In 1933 I married Angela Forbes and settled down in the family homestead in Hamilton, Massachusetts, to busy myself in agriculture and dairying. . . . When the

---

[1828] Massachusetts Vital Records, 1906, Hamilton, 558: 441; Mayo, *The Winthrop Family in America*, 434.

[1829] Steward and Child, *The Descendants of Judge John Lowell of Newburyport, Massachusetts*, 117.

[1830] Godstone district (Surrey), 1933, 02a: 805, no. 22.

[1831] Mayo, *The Winthrop Family in America*, 434. Her niece wrote, "Angela proved to be an effervescent addition to the family, attracting the world to Groton House with her irrepressible wit and infectious laugh. Her only drawback, it seemed, was that one could never expect her at the appointed hour. Winthrops prize punctuality—so compulsively that, like their thriftiness, it could be considered as much a vice as a virtue" (Wexler, *Reared in a Greenhouse*, 191–92).

[1832] Steward and Child, *The Descendants of Judge John Lowell of Newburyport, Massachusetts*, 117.

[1833] He was a member of the Porcellian Club with his college class (*Porcellian Club 1791–2016*, 129).

war came my old ROTC commission was reactivated and I became an aide to General Sherman Miles of the First Service Command in Boston. In early 1944 I went to Hawaii where I became Chief of the Information and Education Section of the Central Pacific Command. Only once did I hear shots fired in anger. That was when I was watching the movie of *Dorian Gray* [1945] just below Mount Suribachi on Iwo Jima, and two unfortunate Japanese planes flew over and were promptly shot down. I had a quiet war. In later 1945 I was retired as a Lieutenant Colonel.[1834]

At the time of his twenty-fifth reunion at Harvard, Winthrop wrote:

My life since leaving Cambridge has on the whole been happy, even though not studded with great accomplishments. My friends have been fine, my health good, and my worries few. On top of this, I am fortunate in having seven splendid children, two girls and five boys....

My sports are golf, shooting, and riding. Since the war I have been Master of the Myopia Hounds. These, together with my farm, keep me in the open air a great deal.... As a farmer, I believe that soil conservation and proper use is vital to the future of the country.[1835]

Ten years later, he reported that in the interim "I have not been hungry or thirsty. On the contrary, while my weight is the same, I have eaten many good meals and quaffed many good cups. I have awkwardly slid down hills from Colorado to Switzerland, and have shot birds in South Carolina, Canada and Scotland. I have played many cheery rounds of golf.... I have also ridden some good horses—and even read some good books."[1836]

His widow outlived him by more than thirty years; in all, Angela Forbes Winthrop spent the better part of seventy-eight years at Groton House, and she was Hamilton's oldest resident when she died there in

---

[1834] *Harvard Class of 1928 Fiftieth Anniversary Report* (Cambridge: Printed for the University, 1978), 712–13.

[1835] *Harvard Class of 1928 Twenty-fifth Anniversary Report* (Cambridge: Printed for the Class, 1953), 1183.

[1836] *Harvard College Class of 1928 Thirty-fifth Anniversary Report* (Cambridge: Printed for the Class, 1963), 321.

August 2011. As her obituary related, she long "presided over Groton House Farm, her countless dogs, horses, and other animals, an endless parade of international guests, as well as her own seven children." It continued:

> After her marriage in 1933, Mrs. Winthrop made annual visits to her parents and brothers and sisters, who were then living abroad. On one such trip in 1939, to the coast of Brittany where her parents had a summer house, Mrs. Winthrop learned that the Nazis had invaded Poland and thus both France and England were on the brink of war with Germany. A quick departure was clearly advisable but escape to England was blocked. Accompanied by her husband and her three eldest children with their Scottish nanny, Mrs. Winthrop fled south to Bordeaux where they were among the last to sail on an American flagged vessel.
>
> During the later years of World War II, Mrs. Winthrop opened her Hamilton home to refugee children from Britain and the Netherlands. She also made Groton House a welcome retreat for numerous officers of the Royal Navy whose ships were refitting in Boston.
>
> Shortly after the end of the war in Europe, and while her husband, a colonel in the U.S. Army, was still in the Pacific Theatre, Mrs. Winthrop arranged a posting with the Save the Children Federation to assess the needs of school children in the war zone. In uniform, with a U.S. Army jeep and driver arranged by General George Patton,[1837] a friend and neighbor from Hamilton, she travelled throughout France. In the course of this mission she was able to reconnect with two of her younger sisters who had been active with the French Resistance. . . .
>
> Mrs. Winthrop held a great interest in civic and international issues. In the Cold War years, she was actively involved with the Word Federalist Organization and was a staunch supporter of the United Nations. Mrs. Winthrop was chairman of the board of The Boston Center for Adult Education and for many years served on the board of The Animal Rescue League of Boston. She was especially loyal to the English Speaking Union

---

[1837] Patton's wife, Beatrice, was Theo Winthrop's aunt.

in Boston. In the 1930s, Mrs. Winthrop, with her sister-in-law Theodora Ayer Winthrop, established a women's reproductive health clinic in rural South Carolina. . . .

Even into the last years of her life, Mrs. Winthrop remained intrigued by world affairs. She unfailingly read three daily newspapers, and ended her day with the 11 o'clock television news. Intelligent, aware and well informed, she considered herself a moderate Republican. She was proud to say that the only times she voted Democratic were for her nephew U.S. Senator John Kerry.[1838]

Children of Frederic[10] and Angela Elizabeth[10] (Forbes) Winthrop, first six born at Boston:[1839]

50   i.   IRIS[11] WINTHROP, b. 18 April 1935; m. 29 June 1968, WILLARD CLARK FREEMAN.

51   ii. ANGELA WINTHROP, b. 8 Sept. 1936; m. 16 Sept. 1961, CHARLES WILLARD GETCHELL, JR.

52   iii. ADAM WINTHROP, b. 20 Sept. 1938; m. 29 Jan. 1977, MIRANDA TOWNSEND MCCAGG.

53   iv. FREDERIC WINTHROP, b. 11 June 1940; m. 27 July 1968, SUSAN BAILEY SHAW.

54   v. ROBERT WINTHROP, 2ND, b. 14 Dec. 1946; m. 1 April 1978, CAROL ANN VEATCH.

55   vi. GRANT FORBES WINTHROP, b. 22 Feb. 1949; m. 10 Aug. 1975, HOPE HARTLEY BROCK.

56   vii. JONATHAN WINTHROP, b. at Ipswich, Mass. 1 Jan. 1953; m. 1 Oct. 1988, SYDNEY CHESTON.

32. NATHANIEL THAYER[10] WINTHROP (*Frederic[9], Robert[8], Thomas Charles[7], Francis Bayard[6], John Still[5], John[4], Waitstill[3], John[2-1]*) was born at "Groton House Farm," Hamilton, Massachusetts 20 May 1912[1840] and died at New York, New York 3 June 1980.[1841] He married, first, at St. John's Church,

---

[1838] "Angela Forbes Winthrop," *The Salem News*, 10 August 2011.

[1839] Steward and Child, *The Descendants of Judge John Lowell of Newburyport, Massachusetts*, 117; questionnaires from Frederic and Robert Winthrop, 2nd, 2013; questionnaire from Miranda McCagg Ellis 2014.

[1840] Mayo, *The Winthrop Family in America*, 434.

[1841] Peter Kihss, "N.T. Winthrop, 68; An Estate Lawyer," *The New York Times*, 6 June 1980, 87.

Beverly Farms, Massachusetts 3 July 1935,[1842] **SERITA BARTLETT**, who was born at 10 Monmouth Street, Brookline, Massachusetts 9 December 1912[1843] and died at Beverly 23 July 1983,[1844] daughter of Matthew and Serita (Lincoln) Bartlett, from whom he was divorced 25 November 1947. She married, second, 24 September 1948, Bartlett Harwood, and, third, 15 October 1977, Francis Murray Forbes.[1845] Nathaniel Thayer Winthrop married, second, at Appleton Chapel, Harvard University, Cambridge, Massachusetts 17 June 1950,[1846] **ELEANOR ROSEMOND BEANE**, who was born at Woonsocket, Rhode Island 16 January 1919 and died at New York 25 March 2008, daughter of Arthur and Ruth Bergman (Richards) Beane.[1847]

Nathaniel Thayer Winthrop graduated from St. Mark's School, Southborough, Massachusetts; Harvard (1934); and the University of Virginia (1938). While he was still an undergraduate he made a private vow that, in professional life (and "if I could afford it"), he would take a sabbatical every ten years "to assess where I stood and where I wanted to go. The [Second World War] took care of the first 'Sabbatical.' My naval service . . . consisted of much more inactivity than action and there was plenty of time for assessing goals and aspirations."[1848]

After the war he moved from Boston to New York: "The reasons for the move were various, but, being somewhat of a New Dealer in philosophy, I had found the then business pessimism of Boston distasteful, and, for myself, had confidence that the world was not going to hell in a hack. I wanted to settle in a community where some of the excitement of business enterprises and enthusiasms for public improvement might brush off on me."[1849] In 1950, he remarried, and with two more children by 1954 Nat and Eleanor Winthrop "paused a little before deciding that the time had come for a 'Second Sabbatical.'" For the winter of 1954–55, "we made Beirut, Lebanon, our headquarters for several months

---

[1842] "Nathaniel Winthrop Weds Miss Bartlett," *The New York Times*, 4 July 1935, 19.

[1843] Massachusetts Vital Records, 1912, Brookline, 608: 25. "Serila Bartlett"; corrected to Serita, 1074: 431. Her mother's name is given as Serafina Lincoln (608: 25).

[1844] Massachusetts Death Index, 1970–2003.

[1845] *Boston Social Register 1949* (1948), 108; *Social Register 1979* (1978), 330; Massachusetts Death Index, 1970–2003; Social Security Death Index.

[1846] *Harvard Class of 1934 Twenty-fifth Anniversary Report* (Cambridge, Mass.: Printed for the Class, 1959), 1539;

[1847] *Harvard College Class of 1911 Decennial Report* (Boston: The Four Seas Company, 1921), 34; "Descendants of Cornelia P. Van Rensselaer Thayer and Nathaniel Thayer" (1975), Chart 3-C-I.

[1848] *Harvard Class of 1934 Twenty-fifth Anniversary Report*, 1539.

[1849] *Harvard Class of 1934 Twenty-fifth Anniversary Report,* 1538–39.

and managed to visit such exotic spots as Aleppo, Babylon, Bagdad, Damascus and Palmyra, to name a few. My wife and I studied people and history, sociological and political, of an area about which we knew next to nothing."[1850]

On their return to New York, he joined the law firm of Shearman & Sterling, where he remained until his retirement in 1977. For ten years, beginning in 1962, he was a trustee of the Experiment in International Living, based in Brattleboro, Vermont; he served as chairman of its national advisory council in 1976–77. As the *New York Times* mentioned, "Four of his children took part in its exchanges, Beekman going to Japan, Serita to Sweden, Nathaniel, Jr., to Ghana and Katharine to France." Late in life, he became interested in the Center for the Study of World Religions at Harvard Divinity School.[1851]

Children of Nathaniel Thayer[10] and Serita (Bartlett) Winthrop, born at Boston:[1852]

57   i.   JOHN[11] WINTHROP, b. 22 June 1936[1853]; m. (1) 22 Feb. 1963, DEBORAH HOLBROOK; m. (2) 31 Aug. 1983, ELIZABETH GOLTRA.

     ii.   MATTHEW BARTLETT WINTHROP, b. 8 May 1938[1854] and d. unm. at Boston 1 Jan. 2013.[1855]

           His older brother wrote of Matthew, "When he was a small child, he survived a brain operation which left him with paralysis in his left arm and left leg. He never graduated from high school, he never went to college, and he never married. Matthew gave to charity and worked with and for a number of charitable causes, including Toastmasters International and a number of Boston-based charities.

           "He loved classical music, and had a rich sense of humor and an excellent long-term memory. The bond between us prevailed from childhood to old age."[1856]

[1850] *Harvard Class of 1934 Twenty-fifth Anniversary Report,* 1539.

[1851] Kihss, *The New York Times,* 6 June 1980, 87.

[1852] "Descendants of Cornelia P. Van Rensselaer Thayer and Nathaniel Thayer," Charts 3-C-I and 3-C-1-b; Frederick Wallace Pyne, *Descendants of the Signers of the Declaration of Independence,* 7 vols. (Camden, Me.: Picton Press, 1997–2002), 2: 221; Steward and Child, *The Descendants of Judge John Lowell of Newburyport, Massachusetts,* 184; questionnaire from Serita Winthrop 2013.

[1853] Mayo, *The Winthrop Family in America,* 434.

[1854] Mayo, *The Winthrop Family in America,* 434.

[1855] *Summer Social Register 2013 Dilatory Domiciles,* 63.

[1856] Notes by John Winthrop 2015.

58   iii.   BEEKMAN WINTHROP, b. 6 April 1941; m. 27 Aug. 1969, PHOEBE
               JANE WOOD.
59   iv.   SERITA WINTHROP, b. 22 Dec. 1943; m. (1) 10 Sept. 1966, ROGER
               MARTIN BARZUN; m. (2) 22 Aug. 1996, JONATHAN JAMES GRAHAM
               ALEXANDER; m. (3) 28 June 2006, THOMAS MCCANCE, JR.

        Children of Nathaniel Thayer[10] and Eleanor Rosemond (Beane) Winthrop,
born at New York:[1857]

60   v.   NATHANIEL THAYER[11] WINTHROP, JR., b. 30 Nov. 1951; m. 17 June
               1974, MARTHA DUNN.
        vi.   KATHARINE WINTHROP, b. 20 April 1954. She m. at the First
               Congregational Church, Blue Hill, Me. 30 July 1994, ROBERT
               PETER HAGEN, JR., from whom she is divorced, and has issue
               (Taylor Bonnet[12] Hagen and Robert Christopher Powell Hagen).
                   Kate Winthrop graduated from Abbot Academy, Andover, Mass.;
               Wheelock College (1978); and Lesley College (1984). R. Peter
               Hagen, Jr., was educated at the United States Military Academy
               (1967) and Stanford University (1974).
        vii.   CORNELIA THAYER WINTHROP, b. 5 July 1956.
        viii. STEPHEN VAN RENSSELAER WINTHROP, b. 18 Aug. 1958. He m. at
               the First Parish Church, Wayland, Mass. 20 July 1991, MARTHA
               JANE WILLIAMSON, who was b. at Syracuse, N.Y. 18 Oct. 1958, dau.
               of J. Claude and Hazel M. Williamson, and has issue (Katharine
               Christine[12] Winthrop and Hannah Winthrop).
                   Stephen Van Rensselaer Winthrop was educated at Milton
               Academy, Milton, Mass.; Phillips Academy, Andover; Harvard
               (1980); the University of Pennsylvania (1988); and Johns Hopkins
               University (1988). M. Jane Williamson graduated from Wayland
               High School, Radcliffe College (1980), and Duke University
               (1984).

33. KATHARINE[10] **WINTHROP** (*Frederic[9]*, *Robert[8]*, *Thomas Charles[7]*, *Francis
Bayard[6]*, *John Still[5]*, *John[4]*, *Waitstill[3]*, *John[2-1]*) was born at "Groton House
Farm," Hamilton, Massachusetts 17 July 1914[1858] and died at Hamilton
12 February 1997.[1859] She married at 770 Park Avenue, New York,

---

[1857] "Descendants of Cornelia P. Van Rensselaer Thayer and Nathaniel Thayer," Chart
       3-C-I; *The New York Times*, 17 March 1991, 66; 21 July 1991, 39; 31 July 1994, 45;
       Pyne, *Descendants of the Signers of the Declaration of Independence*, 2: 221.
[1858] Massachusetts Vital Records, 1914, Hamilton, 622: 525.
[1859] "Katharine McKean, Tennis Player, 82," *The New York Times*, 22 February 1997;
       Summer Social Register 1997 Dilatory Domiciles May 1997, 46.

New York 21 November 1947,[1860] **QUINCY ADAMS SHAW McKEAN,** who was born at Philadelphia, Pennsylvania 1 November 1891, son of Henry Pratt McKean and Marian (Shaw) (McKean) Haughton. He died at Hamilton 27 July 1971.[1861]

As early as August 1925, when she was eleven, Kay Winthrop was regarded as a possible "'Helen Wills' in the making"; by 1928, she was Massachusetts state girls' tennis champion. Her niece Dorothy B. Wexler noted that "Katharine was as full of bubbling assurance in her studies as she was in tennis, writing to [her older half-sister in 1927]: 'We are going to have exams. . . . I find I am a little behind but as I am so bright it is easy for me to catch up. I am still at the head of my class, *of course*.'"[1862] Her niece added that Kay was somehow able to escape "the family strains," perhaps because of her position as the youngest daughter.

> For her, everything came easily. As she grew from a teenager to a woman in her early thirties, she moved on from four junior national tennis titles to five national women's titles (indoors in both singles and doubles) and thirteen national rankings in women's singles, including twice in ninth place (1936 and 1939). In 1936 she played in Centre Court at Wimbledon where her partner was the great Alice Marble and her costume, according to my mother [Dorothy Winthrop Bradford], was shorts— making her the first woman to play before the queen so clad.[1863]

Kay Winthrop was women's national indoor singles champion in 1944. In 1938, 1942, and 1944, she and her partner won the women's national championships in indoor doubles.[1864] Her obituary noted that she "toured South America in the years before World War II with Sarah Palfrey, Jack Kramer and Bobby Riggs."[1865] After her marriage, she won

---

[1860] "Miss K. Winthrop Becomes a Bride," *The New York Times*, 22 November 1947, 12.

[1861] *Harvard College Class of 1913 Twenty-fifth Anniversary Report* (Cambridge, Mass.: The Cosmos Press, 1938), 567; *The New York Times*, 22 November 1947, 12; "Descendants of Cornelia P. Van Rensselaer Thayer and Nathaniel Thayer," Chart 3-C-I; Pyne, *Descendants of the Signers of the Declaration of Independence*, 5: 81.

[1862] Wexler, *Reared in a Greenhouse*, 209.

[1863] That is, Queen Mary (Wexler, *Reared in a Greenhouse*, 332).

[1864] Mayo, *The Winthrop Family in America*, 434. She was the top-ranked women's singles player in the United States Lawn Tennis Associations rankings in 1941 ("Katharine Winthrop to Wed," *The New York Times*, 13 November 1947, 36).

[1865] *The New York Times*, 22 February 1997.

"four senior national titles and [ranked] between first and ninth in senior doubles almost every year between 1955 and 1970, when she finally retired at the age of fifty-six."[1866]

Q. A. Shaw McKean graduated from Chestnut Hill Academy, Philadelphia, and Harvard College (1913). Before the First World War, he worked for the Calumet & Hecla Mining Company, a Michigan firm with strong ties to Boston and to the Shaw family. An artillery officer during the war, he had "received orders to join an English outfit as [a] liaison officer" when the armistice was declared. He then spent about a decade in a Boston brokerage firm before entering "private banking, being chiefly interested in the placing of going businesses which wish to expand. In this occupation I am still engaged. . . .

"Business has occasionally taken me to Europe. Three months in Berlin, several years ago [i.e., ca. 1935], were particularly interesting. Two years ago I took my family abroad for ten months spent in England, France and Germany. It was a worth-while experience for both young and old."[1867]

During the Second World War, Shaw McKean succeeded Christian A. Herter as chairman of the 'Citizens' Committee for the Army and Navy' in Boston: "We built up rather a large volunteer organization which in time was financed by the National U.S.O. . . . Our committee furnished and equipped a great many 'Day Rooms' in Army camps in New England. As an example, we collected and distributed over eight hundred pianos, many thousand books and countless games. . . . All of this was on a 'non-paid' basis and the cooperation of various theatrical groups was quite wonderful."[1868]

His first marriage, to the artist Margarett Sargent, ended in 1947, and in November of that year he married Kay Winthrop. He wrote, "My wife and I now spend our winters in Pinehurst, North Carolina, and the rest of our time in Hamilton. . . . We breed a few thoroughbred horses and I have a small racing stable which has been quite successful. Mrs. McKean rides a lot and keeps up her tennis. For the sixth time she is National Senior Doubles Champion. I no longer ride as I have some back trouble due to rather ancient polo injuries. . . .

"I'm a very staunch and probably 'old hat' Republican and I can see no reason to change. I am sure that at times I bore my elder children

---

[1866] Wexler, *Reared in a Greenhouse*, 333.

[1867] *Harvard College Class of 1913 Twenty-fifth Anniversary Report*, 567–68.

[1868] *Harvard Class of 1913 Fiftieth Anniversary Report* (Cambridge: Printed at the University, 1963), 424.

with my ideas, but after all they are mine!"[1869]

Children of Quincy Adams Shaw and Katharine[10] (Winthrop) McKean, born at Beverly, Massachusetts:[1870]

> i. JOHN WINTHROP[11] MCKEAN, b. 7 Aug. 1948; he graduated from St. Mark's School, Southborough, Mass.; Harvard (1971); and Suffolk University (1975).
>
> In 1996, he reported that, "Since leaving the rarefied atmosphere of Cambridge almost twenty-five years ago, I have led a varied, interesting life. Unlike many classmates I have not married, have no children, have never gone bankrupt, never made a fortune, never published a book or fought in a war. I went to law school, worked on a presidential campaign, ran for and was elected to public office, spent two years in every prison in Massachusetts listening to people tell me that 'they were in the wrong place at the wrong time' as a member of the Massachusetts Parole Board [in 1984–86], helped found the Robert Kennedy Action Corps, an agency that helps troubled children[,] and for the last five years practiced law with my brother Tom ('72)."[1871]
>
> At the time of his fortieth Harvard reunion, he noted that he was retired and living in North Carolina: "Very excited to have a Harvard nephew in the Class of 2013 (son of my brother, David '79). . . . Travel remains a great passion. Going to Iceland and Greenland this summer before they melt and fall into the sea."[1872]

61   ii. THOMAS MCKEAN, b. 10 Aug. 1949; m. 22 March 1980, SYLVIA CHENEY WYMAN.

62   iii. ROBERT WINTHROP MCKEAN, b. 2 Nov. 1951; m. 6 May 1995, SANDRA NAOMI (KANENAKA) RAINS.

> iv. SALLY THAYER MCKEAN, b. 26 April 1953 and d. at Groveland, Mass. 23 Nov. 1972.[1873]

[1869] *Harvard Class of 1913 Fiftieth Anniversary Report*, 423, 424.

[1870] "Descendants of Cornelia P. Van Rensselaer Thayer and Nathaniel Thayer," Chart 3-C-III; *The New York Times*, 23 March 1980, 58; 16 October 1988, 52; *Social Register 1998* (1997), 472; Winthrop, *Descendants of Robert Winthrop & Kate Wilson Taylor, 1833–2000*, 16; questionnaire from Robert Winthrop McKean 2013; questionnaires from John Winthrop McKean and Thomas McKean 2014.

[1871] *Harvard and Radcliffe Class of 1971 Twenty-fifth Anniversary Report* (Cambridge, Mass.: Printed for the Class, 1996), 773.

[1872] *Harvard and Radcliffe Class of 1971 Fortieth Anniversary Report* (Cambridge, Mass.: Printed for the Class, 2011), 341, 342.

[1873] Massachusetts Death Index 1970–2003; Wexler, *Reared in a Greenhouse*, 417; notes by Thomas McKean 2016.

63   v. DAVID MCKEAN, b. 20 Sept. 1956; m. 15 Oct. 1988, KATHLEEN
      MARY KAYE.

34. JAN HERMAN[10] VAN ROIJEN (*Albertina Taylor*[9] *Winthrop, Robert*[8],
Thomas Charles[7], *Francis Bayard*[6], *John Still*[5], *John*[4], *Waitstill*[3], *John*[2-1])
was born Jan Herman van Royen at Constantinople [now Istanbul],
Turkey 10 April 1905[1874] and died at Wassenaar (South Holland), the
Netherlands 16 March 1991.[1875] He married at The Hague (South
Holland) 13 December 1934,[1876] JONKVROUWE ANNE SNOUCK
HURGRONJE, who was born at The Hague 22 November 1913[1877] and
died at Wassenaaer 11 February 2009,[1878] daughter of Jonkheer Aarnout
Marinus Snouck Hurgronje and Jonkvrouwe Henriette Arnoldine van
Tets van Goudriaan.[1879]

"[A] diplomat by predestination," according to the *New York Times*,
Dr. Jan Herman van Roijen was born "in Constantinople, where his
father was Dutch attaché and his American mother ministered without
portfolio[;] he was cradled in the diplomatic pouch."[1880] After graduating
from the University of Utrecht in 1929, he served as an attaché in his
father's embassy in Washington, D.C. (1930–33), before returning to the
Foreign Office in The Hague for three years' service.[1881] During that period
he married Anne Snouck Hurgronje; their daughter Tina was born in The
Hague in 1935.

In 1936, the van Roijens went to Tokyo, where two more children
were born: Jan Herman (in 1936) and Digna (in 1939). In 1939, Dr.
van Roijen was again assigned to the Foreign Ministry in The Hague,
where he joined the Political Division: "When the Germans overran
the Netherlands at the start of World War II, he became active in the
Resistance and was jailed three times by the Nazis before he made his
escape to England in 1944." For a brief period in 1946, he entered the
Dutch cabinet as Foreign Minister. In 1947, Dr. van Roijen was named
Holland's Ambassador to Canada. Three years later, in a recapitulation of
his father's career, he became Ambassador to the United States.[1882]

[1874] *Nederland's Patriciaat*, 3: 346.

[1875] "Jan H. van Roijen, 85, Former Envoy to U.S.," *The New York Times*, 20 March
1991, B9.

[1876] *Nederland's Adelsboek 1937*, 309.

[1877] *Nederland's Adelsboek 1914* (The Hague: W. P. van Stockum & Zoon), 387.

[1878] https://www.genealogieonline.nl/west-europese-adel/I1073989394.php.

[1879] *Nederland's Adelsboek 1914*, 387.

[1880] "15,000 at N.Y.U. See 7,237 Get Degrees," *The New York Times*, 11 June 1953, 26.

[1881] "Negotiator for Dutch: Dr. Jan Herman van Roijen," *The New York Times*, 16
August 1962, 6.

[1882] In 1948–49, he was also Dutch representative to the United Nations Security

American universities were quick to recognize him with honorary degrees:

> He is one of the most youthful career statesmen ever assigned to top diplomatic status, has been knighted by his Queen, and enjoys superlative repute abroad as at home. (New York University citation, 1953)[1883]

> Nearly two centuries ago, in this building, the Continental Congress welcomed from the Netherlands the first Foreign Minister accredited to the American Republic. Now another Congress welcomes another Netherlander: skilled diplomat, resistance leader during the war-time occupation of his country and champion of that freedom without which church and state alike would languish (Princeton University citation, 1956).[1884]

As one American diplomat put it, "he's the kind of ambassador I'd like to have pleading my case." A particular focus of his career was Indonesia. At a particularly fraught moment during negotiations in 1946, the *New York Times* wrote, "Dr. Jan Herman van Roijen, then the Dutch Foreign Minister, added one sentence that has stuck in the memories of several of the participants. 'Let us not forget that there is more that unites us than divides us,' he said."

> Those who have watched Dr. van Roijen continue as one of his country's chief negotiators on Indonesian matters say this thought has been one of his guiding principles. The result, they say, is the exceptional rapport that exists between him and Indonesian officials.

> This rapport eased the painful negotiations on the transfer of Netherlands New Guinea to Indonesia that were concluded at the United Nations today [15 August 1962]. Dr. van Roijen, now the Dutch Ambassador in Washington, headed his country's negotiating team in the delicate discussions that have been going on for almost six months.

> For more than one reason Dr. van Roijen was a

Council "as it debated the Indonesian question" (*The New York Times*, 16 August 1962, 6).

[1883] "15,000 at N.Y.U. See 7,237 Get Degrees," *The New York Times*, 11 June 1953, 26.

[1884] "The List of the Citations at Princeton," *The New York Times*, 24 September 1956, 29.

logical selection for the arduous and unpleasant task of presiding over the liquidation of the Netherlands' last colonial possession in Southeast Asia.

The first, of course, is his long association with the Indonesia question. . . . Moreover, in the twelve years that he has served as Ambassador to the United States, the 57-year-old Dr. van Roijen has gained a reputation as one of the most effective diplomats in Washington. . . . He has been described as "a diplomat's diplomat" and as "the ultimate in ambassadors." Now the third senior ambassador in Washington, he occasionally functions as dean of the diplomatic corps here when his two predecessors, the Nicaraguan and Peruvian envoys, are out of town. . . .

There is a British sort of reserve about him that contrasts with the more genial hand-pumping style of some of the new-school ambassadors. He is correct, precise, polite, punctual and always meticulously dressed, shod and combed. . . .

Although Dr. van Roijen is not exactly a "hail fellow well met," his friends say that he genuinely enjoys meeting people. Certainly he knows a lot of them. Perhaps no Ambassador is Washington has such a wide acquaintanceship among United States officials.

"And he knows the right ones, too," one official notes. . . .

Dr. van Roijen makes a sharp break between his official life during the week, when he drives himself unusually hard, and his private life on week-ends at his 300-acre farm in Warrenton, Va. An active entertainer in Washington, he refuses to take official guests with him to the farm. . . .

He is dedicated to his family, which consists of his attractive and articulate wife, Anne, and four children: Henriette Albertina, who is married to a lawyer in the Netherlands; Digna, a student there; Jan Herman, now a Dutch soldier in New Guinea; and Willem, a student at Groton.[1885]

On Dr. Jan Herman van Roijen's retirement in 1964, Max Frankel wrote that the Ambassador "says he will take with him a great confidence

---

[1885] "Negotiator for Dutch: Dr. Jan Herman van Roijen," *The New York Times*, 16 August 1962, 6.

in United States diplomacy. He does not subscribe to the view that Americans are only slowly maturing and learning their responsibilities in the world. In constitutional and other respects, he points out, the United States is not so young and its performance since World War II has been wise and moderate and usually generous."

In Frankel's view, the "diplomatically dressed but often undiplomatically frank" Dr. van Roijen had been "among the most admired foreign officials here and one of the most respected Washington analysts of any nationality."

> His admirers believe they pay him the highest compliment by saying that he is a superb diplomat and still an honest man.
>
> Intellectual honesty, more than gregariousness or other cocktail-party talents, is the Ambassador's own standard of excellence. He believes that the diplomat, like any advocate, must recognize and contain the prejudices of his position.[1886]

His next post, announced on 12 March 1964, was the dual role of Dutch Ambassador concurrently to Britain and Iceland.[1887] Dr. van Roijen retired in 1971, having "received numerous awards and honors from the countries in which he served."[1888]

Children of Jan Herman[10] van Roijen and Jonkvrouwe Anne Snouck Hurgronje:[1889]

64   i.   HENRIETTE ALBERTINE[11] VAN ROIJEN, b. at The Hague 5 Dec. 1935; m. 11 July 1959, MARINUS MICHIEL VAN NOTTEN.

65   ii. JAN HERMAN ROBERT DUDLEY VAN ROIJEN, b. at Tokyo, Japan 17 Dec. 1936; m. 13 Dec. 1963, JONKVROUWE CAROLINA HELENA WILHELMINA REUCHLIN.

66   iii. DIGNA ANNE VAN ROIJEN, b. at Tokyo 24 Feb. 1939; m. 13 March 1965, JONKHEER JAN DERCK CORNELIS VAN KARNEBEEK.

[1886] Max Frankel, "Dutch Envoy Gets Warm Goodbye after 13 Years in Post in U.S.," *The New York Times*, 2 March 1964.

[1887] "Van Roijen Gets Two Posts," *The New York Times*, 13 March 1964, 2.

[1888] *The New York Times*, 20 March 1991, B9.

[1889] Taylor, *The Lion and the Hare*, Chart H; Winthrop, *Descendants of Robert Winthrop & Kate Wilson Taylor, 1833–2000*, 17; questionnaires from Henriette Albertina van Roÿen van Notten, Digna Anne van Roÿen van Karnebeek, and Willem Joris Winthrop John van Roijen 2013; questionnaire from Carolina Reuchlin van Roijen 2014; notes by Willem Joris Winthrop John van Roijen 2014.

67   iv.   WILLEM JORIS WINTHROP JOHN VAN ROIJEN,[1890] b. at The Hague 21
              April 1945; m. 10 Nov. 1973, JONKVROUWE EMILIE SOLANGE (VAN
              NISPEN) SWELHEIM.

35. **ROBERT DUDLEY**[10] **VAN ROIJEN** (*Albertina Taylor*[9] *Winthrop, Robert*[8],
Thomas Charles[7], *Francis Bayard*[6], *John Still*[5], *John*[4], *Waitstill*[3], *John*[2-1]) was
born Robert Dudley van Royen at London, England 13 March 1907[1891]
and died at 3033 N Street, Washington, D.C. 14 January 1981.[1892] He
married at 960 Fifth Avenue, New York, New York 21 June 1938,[1893]
HILDEGARDE PORTNER GRAHAM, who was born at Washington, D.C. 1
November 1915[1894] and died at 3033 N Street 1 June 1993,[1895] daughter
of Commander Lorimer Clement Graham and Elsa Eugenia (Portner)
(Graham) Humes.[1896]

Robert Dudley van Roijen graduated from the University of
Utrecht in 1936. During the Second World War, "he served as an
intelligence officer in the Army Air Corps [and] rose to the rank of
lieutenant colonel before his retirement in 1950. He then joined the
C.I.A. as a covert operations officer and retired in 1962." He later owned
the Robert B. Luce publishing house, based in Washington, D.C.,[1897]
and served as chairman of the board of both the Fauquier Hospital and
the Highland School in Warrenton, Virginia.

A printmaker and sculptor, Hildegarde Portner Graham was
educated at the Fermata School, Aiken, South Carolina; Chateau
Brillantmont, Lausanne, Switzerland; and the Corcoran School of
Art. An obituary noted that "Mrs. van Roijen, whose studio was in
Georgetown, was on the board of directors of Artists' Equity gallery

---

[1890] Dr. van Roijen sent his cousin Dorothy a telegram asking him to be godmother
to his son Willem using a different order of names: Willlem Joris John Winthrop
(Wexler, *Reared in a Greenhouse*, 317).

[1891] *Nederland's Patriciaat*, 3: 346.

[1892] "Robert van Roijen, Ex-Official of CIA," *The Washington Post*, 17 January 1981.
"Robert D. van Roijen," *The New York Times*, 17 January 1981, gives 13 January.

[1893] "Troth Announced of Miss Graham," *The New York Times*, 1 June 1938, 20; "Miss
Hildegarde Graham, Debutante of '34, Married Here to Robert Dudley van
Roijen," *The New York Times*, 22 June 1938, 20.

[1894] Helen Graham Carpenter, *The Reverend John Graham of Woodbury, Connecticut, and
His Descendants* (Chicago: Monastery Hill Press, 1942), 468.

[1895] "Hildegarde Graham van Roijen," *The Washington Post*, 5 June 1993.

[1896] *The New York Times*, 22 June 1938, 20.

[1897] *The New York Times*, 17 January 1981. See also Monica Potts, "Robert Luce, 83,
Former Editor and Publisher of New Republic, Is Dead," *The New York Times*, 18
December 2005.

in Washington and also exhibited at Gallery 10 in Washington. One of her welded bronze pieces and two prints are owned by the Phillips Collection and other work was exhibited in galleries elsewhere on the East Coast and in Europe."[1898]

Children of Robert Dudley[10] and Hildegarde Portner (Graham) van Roijen, first three born at New York, last four born at Washington, D.C.:[1899]

68   i. Robert Dudley[11] van Roijen, b. 25 July 1939; m. 31 Jan. 1981, Susan Emily Frelinghuysen.

      ii. Melza Montrose van Roijen, b. 2 March 1941 and d. at Warrenton 20 Sept. 1960.[1900]

69   iii. Peter Portner van Roijen, b. 26 Nov. 1944; m. 27 June 1970, Beatrice Sterling Frelinghuysen.

      iv. Hildegarde Roberta Valaer van Roijen, b. 19 June 1950. She m. at Washington, D.C. 2 June 1979, John Alden Goodrich, who was b. 16 June 1938, son of John Wallace Goodrich and Priscilla Alden (Dennett) (Goodrich) Ramsey, and has issue (Lauren Valaer[12] Goodrich; John Alden Goodrich, Jr.; and Winthrop Pullen Graham Goodrich).

          H. R. Valaer van Roijen graduated from Miss Porter's School, Farmington, Conn., and Briarcliff College (1970). John Alden Goodrich was educated at St. Mark's School, Southborough, Mass., and the University of Pennsylvania (1961).

      v. Laura Winthrop van Roijen, b. 15 March 1952. She m. at Warrenton, Va. 28 July 1979, Willem F. P. de Vogel, from whom she was divorced.

          Laura Winthrop van Roijen graduated from the University of Virginia (1974), Yale University (1976), and Columbia University (1982).

70   vi. David Montrose van Roijen, b. 17 Aug. 1954; m. 25 July 1981, Mary Amie Johnson.

    vii. Christopher Taylor van Roijen, b. 5 April 1956.

[1898] *The Washington Post*, 5 June 1993. Mrs. Van Roijen's half-brother, John Portner Humes, served as U.S. Ambassador to Austria 1969–75 ("Susan E. Frelinghuysenn Maried in Capital," *The New York Times*, 1 February 1981, and "John P. Humes Dies; Former Envoy Was 64," *The New York Times*, 3 October 1985).

[1899] Winthrop, *Descendants of Robert Winthrop & Kate Wilson Taylor, 1833–2000*, 17; questionnaire from Robert Dudley van Roijen 2013; questionnaire from Christopher Taylor van Roijen 2014; questionnaire from and notes by David Montrose van Roijen 2014.

[1900] "Envoy's Niece Dead," *The New York Times*, 22 September 1960, 20; Findagrave. com (28431473).

The Eleventh Generation

36. **Thomas Spurr**[11] **Morse** (*Kate*[10] *Winthrop, Grenville Lindall*[9], *Robert*[8], *Thomas Charles*[7], *Francis Bayard*[6], *John Still*[5], *John*[4], *Waitstill*[3], *John*[2-1]) was born at Santa Barbara, California 25 May 1925[1901] and died at Lenox, Massachusetts 26 August 2012.[1902] He married at St. Stephen's Church, Pittsfield, Massachusetts 26 June 1948,[1903] **Patricia Ann Birt**, who was born at Racine, Wisconsin 26 April 1927 and died at Lenox 25 January 2010, daughter of Harry Robert and Cathryn (Carpenter) Birt.[1904]

Dr. Thomas Spurr Morse graduated from Deerfield Academy, Deerfield, Massachusetts, and Cornell University (1950 and 1953). Patricia Ann Birt was educated at the Mary A. Burnham School, Northampton, Massachusetts; Vassar College (1949x); and Cornell (1949). An obituary noted that Dr. Morse joined the Marines during the Second World War "planning to return [home after the war] and study agriculture. His experiences in the Marines set him on a different course, and he went on to medical school at Cornell University. He maintained that the best decision he ever made was to marry Patty, his tender comrade of 62 years. . . . He knew that neither he nor the family would ever go wrong if Patty was setting the course. He adored her and that was, perhaps, the greatest gift he gave his children."

Dr. Morse spent much of his career at Children's Hospital in Columbus, Ohio:[1905]

[1901] *California Birth Index, 1905–1995* [database online].

[1902] "Thomas S. Morse, M.D.," *The Berkshire Eagle*, 31 August 2012; Social Security Death Index.

[1903] "Miss Patricia A. Birt Becomes Affianced," *The New York Times*, 31 August 1947, 35; "T. S. Morse Weds Patricia A. Birt," *The New York Times*, 27 June 1948, 49.

[1904] Taylor, *The Lion and the Hare*, Chart H; *Cornell Alumni Magazine*, July/August 2010; notes by Amy Bradford Morse 2014.

[1905] *The Berkshire Eagle*, 31 August 2012.

He was very interested in trauma, running the Emergency Room, training pediatricians in emergency care and working on the delivery of emergent care both at the hospital and with the City of Columbus. He was the author of over 60 articles on various topics in pediatric medicine and surgery, and was a founding member and President of the American Trauma Society. He was a member of numerous other medical and surgical societies as well.

No physician ever enjoyed going to work to meet with his young patients as much as Tom did. He was entranced by his young charges and had a great deal of fun helping them. Tom never passed a little child with whom he did not engage, or a baby he didn't enjoy. . . .

Tom served as a beacon of nobleness, grace and courage, and was certainly made better by the "lamps" of others shining on him. A testament to this is his book *A Gift of Courage* (Doubleday, 1982).

Tom was an extremely kind and generous man who gave his all to his patients and their families, his family and the communities in which he lived.

Children of Thomas Spurr[11] and Patricia Ann (Birt) Morse, first three born at New York, New York:[1906]

71   i.   JEFFREY BIRT[12] MORSE, b. 13 March 1950; m. (1) 27 July 1974, CAROL LYNN GINGLES; m. (2) 29 Sept. 2009, JENNIFER (BRUGGEMAN) HAMILTON.

72   ii. KATE WINTHROP MORSE, b. 18 Sept. 1951; m. (1) 13 March 1982, JOHN DAVID ERWIN; m. (2) 7 Aug. 1999, THOMAS LANDES HORN.

73   iii. AMY BRADFORD MORSE, b. 14 May 1953; m. (1) 15 Jan. 1977, PHILLIP ANTHONY HARDING; m. (2) 10 Sept. 2011, LISA MARIE KANE.

74   iv. PETER DARWIN MORSE, b. at Boston, Mass. 17 July 1957; m. 15 March 1980, KAREN MICHELLE FOYCIK.

[1906] Notes by Jeffrey Birt Morse and Kate Morse Erwin 2013; questionnaire from Amy Bradford Morse 2013; notes by Amy Bradford Morse 2014.

37. **Mary Alice**[11] **Kean** (*John*[10] *Kean, Katharine Taylor*[9] *Winthrop, Robert*[8], *Thomas Charles*[7], *Francis Bayard*[6], *John Still*[5], *John*[4], *Waitstill*[3], *John*[2-1]) was born at New York, New York 14 October 1927. She married at Grace Church, New York 12 May 1951, **David Robert Wallace Raynolds**, who was born at Newtown, Connecticut 15 February 1928 and died at Denver, Colorado 19 June 2015, son of Robert Frederick and Marguerite Evelyn (Gerdau) Raynolds.[1907]

Mary Alice Kean graduated from the Chapin School, New York, and Smith College (1949). David Robert Wallace Raynolds was educated at the Putney School, Putney, Vermont; Dartmouth College (1949); Wesleyan University (1956); Johns Hopkins University; and the National War College (1973). His obituary noted, "Joining the Foreign Service in 1956, he served in the Diplomatic Corps in El Salvador, France, Haiti, Pakistan, and Washington, D.C. He was the recipient of the Meritorious Service Award by the Department of State in 1966."[1908]

> Following the trail of his great-uncle William Franklin Raynolds, who explored the Yellowstone region, Dave and May discovered Lander [in Wyoming], and became familiar with the character and sinews of the west. In 1964, the family spent a year in Lander while Dave wrote a book on El Salvador's economy. The couple settled permanently in the Lander area in 1975, and developed a bison herd at Table Mountain Ranch, perched above the Popo Agie River west of town.
>
> Here Dave spent almost forty years becoming deeply involved in the community. He was especially proud of his 26-year membership on the steering committee of the Wyoming Business Alliance, with its Leadership Wyoming program. . . . Dave and May shared their buffalo meat with the community through the Farmers Market, and at the annual Fourth of July Buffalo Barbecue. Dave, in his cowboy hat and shaggy buffalo coat, shared his taste and enthusiasm for the west with all he encountered. . . .

[1907] Taylor, *The Lion and the Hare*, Chart H; "Mary Kean Married to David R. Raynolds in Grace Episcopal Church," *The New York Times*, 13 May 1951, 86; questionnaire from John Kean 2014; notes by Robert Gregory Honshu Raynolds 2015.

[1908] http://www.obitsforlife.com/obituary/1122719/Raynolds-David.php.

His encyclopedic knowledge and his generous and gregarious nature made him a valued member of the community and of the organizations he joined. An entertaining storyteller, he delighted in recounting tales from his travels and encounters that would surprise and inform his audience. He loved books and the printed word, and had an astounding memory and ability to comprehend and communicate the larger contexts of history, society and economics. . . .

Dave's love of adventure took him and his family from the Serengeti to the Sweetwater. His last trip . . . was to the South of France within the walled city of Carcassonne, where he and May introduced their granddaughters to the subtleties of croissants and siege strategies of European armies.

Children of David Robert Wallace and Mary Alice[11] (Kean) Raynolds:[1909]

75   i.   ROBERT GREGORY HONSHU[12] RAYNOLDS, b. at Tokyo, Japan 27 Jan. 1952; m. 24 June 1980, MARY VERA BARTHOLOMAY.

        ii. LINDA SHIKOKU RAYNOLDS, b. at Tokyo 1 Jan. 1953. She m. ELIJAH COBB.

        iii. MARTHA KEAN RAYNOLDS, b. at Washington, D.C. 27 March 1957. She m. SAMUEL SOLOMON DASHEVSKY, and has had issue (Marguerite Nularvik[13] Dashevsky, Daniel Sithylemenkat Dashevsky, and Sophia Kanuti Dashevsky).

             Dr. Martha Kean Raynolds was educated at Putney; Dartmouth (1979); Virginia Polytechnic Institute; and the University of Alaska, Fairbanks.

        iv. LAURA TERESA RAYNOLDS, b. at San Salvador, El Salvador 21 Jan. 1959. She m. ALEXANDER BLACKMER, and has issue (Courtney Kean[13] Blackmer Raynolds and Lisa Dexter Blackmer Raynolds).

             Dr. Laura Teresa Raynolds was educated at Putney and Cornell University.

        v.   DAVID ALAN FERNANDO RAYNOLDS, b. at San Salvador 3 Aug. 1960. He m. SHARON ELISABETH BOLLES, and has issue (Jasper Forest[13] Bolles Raynolds and Kyrianna Rose Raynolds-Bolles).

             David Alan Fernando Raynolds was educated at Putney and Hampshire College.

[1909] Winthrop, *Descendants of Robert Winthrop & Kate Wilson Taylor, 1833–2000*, 20; notes by Robert Gregory Honshu Raynolds 2014.

38. JOHN[11] KEAN (*John*[10] *Kean, Katharine Taylor*[9] *Winthrop, Robert*[8], *Thomas Charles*[7], *Francis Bayard*[6], *John Still*[5], *John*[4], *Waitstill*[3], *John*[2-1]) was born at New York, New York 28 October 1929. He married, first, at Trinity Church, Roslyn, Long Island, New York 25 June 1952, JOAN EMILY JESSUP, who was born at Glen Cove, Long Island 9 May 1928, daughter of Dr. Everett Colgate and Helen Batho (Castle) Jessup, from whom he was divorced in October 1980. She married, second, 12 October 1984, Morris Riley Eddy, 2nd. John Kean married, second, at Bedminster, New Jersey 10 September 1983, PAMELA ANN (SUMMERS) WOJCICKI, who was born at Glen Cove 9 October 1946, daughter of Oscar Davis and Miriam (Greene) Summers.[1910]

John Kean graduated from St. Mark's School, Southborough, Massachusetts, and Harvard College (1953). Joan Emily Jessup was educated at Miss Porter's School, Farmington, Connecticut, and Sarah Lawrence College (1951). Pamela Ann Summers graduated from Oyster Bay High School, Oyster Bay, Long Island, and La Salle College (1967). In 1978, John Kean wrote of his "part-time political career" in Bedminster Township, where he served as Mayor from 1962 until 1970: "I also had the good fortune to be elected president of the New Jersey State League of Municipalities and served as delegate to my party's national convention. Having done my civic duty, and somewhat influenced by the comment of my then twelve-year-old daughter Kitty, 'Daddy, did you know you have never been home on a Monday night since I was born,' I retired from elective office." At the time of his reunion report, he was president of the National Utilities & Industries Corporation and the incoming president of the American Gas Association.[1911] Thirty years later, he had retired from the utilities field, but, not "content with doing nothing, I have ventured into the real estate market, and am currently [2008] building some townhouses in Florida. In light of the market, this does not seem like a very smart move, but we will see." He added that he was enjoying "twelve grandchildren ranging in age from twenty-one to six."[1912]

[1910] Taylor, *The Lion and the Hare*, Chart H; "Miss Joan Jessup Married in Roslyn," *The New York Times*, 26 June 1952, 22; 11 September 1983; *Social Register 1984* (1983), 527; *Social Register 1986* (1985), 458; notes by John Kean 2013; questionnaire from John Kean 2014.

[1911] *Harvard Class of 1953 Twenty-fifth Anniversary Report* (Cambridge, Mass.: Printed for the Class, 1978), 479–81 at 480.

[1912] *Harvard Class of 1953 55th Anniversary Report* (Cambridge: Printed for the Class, 2008), 107.

Children of John[11] and Joan Emily (Jessup) Kean, born at Morristown, New Jersey:[1913]

76   i.   MARY LITA[12] KEAN, b. 4 March 1955; m. 15 Oct. 1983, FREDERICK
             LEOPOLD HAACK, 3RD.

77   ii. JOHN KEAN, JR., b. 22 April 1957; m. 6 Aug. 1983, ABIGAIL
             MARGARET MURPHY.

78   iii. KATHARINE JESSUP KEAN, b. 24 March 1959; m. 7 Sept. 1985, DAVID
             WILLIAM CZARNECKI.

79   iv. SUSAN LIVINGSTON KEAN, b. 29 Oct. 1964; m. 15 May 1993, DINO
             GUIDO CATTANEO.

39. ELIZABETH STUYVESANT[11] KEAN (*Robert Winthrop[10] Kean, Katharine Taylor[9] Winthrop, Robert[8], Thomas Charles[7], Francis Bayard[6], John Still[5], John[4], Waitstill[3], John[2-1]*) was born at New York, New York 13 September 1921. She married at St. Mark's Church, West Orange, New Jersey 29 October 1942, **EDWARD LIVINGSTON HICKS, 3RD**, who was born at Sioux City, Iowa 8 January 1920 and died at Greenwich, Connecticut 3 July 1997, son of Edward Livingston and Mary (Flournoy) Hicks.[1914]

Edward Livingston Hicks, 3rd, graduated from Phillips Exeter Academy, Exeter, New Hampshire, and Yale College (1942). Following the Second World War, he worked for New Jersey Zinc Company and Guantanamo Sugar Company before entering Columbia University's Teachers' College, from which he received a master's degree in 1961. He then joined the faculty at Greenwich Country Day School. A prominent civic leader in Greenwich, he served as chairman of the American Red Cross annual campaign and as a director and president of the Greenwich Land Trust, among other offices.[1915]

[1913] *The New York Times*, 12 March 1955, 10; 7 August 1983, 51; 16 October 1983, 63; 8 September 1985, 73; 21 February 1993, V12; *Social Register 1984* (1983), 527; *Social Register 1994* (1993), Marriages, 13; notes by Susan Kean Cattaneo 2013; questionnaire from John Kean 2014.

[1914] Taylor, *The Lion and the Hare*, Chart H; *The New York Times*, 30 October 1942, 16; 6 July 1997, 19; John Frederick Dorman III, "Descendants of Ann Clark[,] Wife of Owen Gwathmey," *The Filson Club History Quarterly* 27 [1953]: 139–51 at 146; *Social Register 1997* (1996), 345; Social Security Death Index.

[1915] *The New York Times*, 6 July 1997, 19.

Children of Edward Livingston and Elizabeth Stuyvesant[11] (Kean) Hicks:[1916]

80   i.   EDWARD LIVINGSTON[12] HICKS, b. at New York 27 July 1943; m. 14 Aug. 1976, KATHY MAXWELL.

        ii. ELIZABETH STUYVESANT HICKS, b. 13 March 1947. She m. at 390 East Mount Pleasant Avenue, Livingston, N.J. 20 March 1982, PETER MATTHIESSEN WHEELWRIGHT, who was b. 15 Nov. 1949, son of Dr. Henry Jefferds and Mary Seymour (Matthiessen) Wheelwright, and has issue (Elizabeth Hicks[13] Wheelwright; Josephine Kean Wheelwright; and Peter Matthiessen Wheelwright, Jr.).[1917]

            Elizabeth Stuyvesant Hicks graduated from the Ethel Walker School, Simsbury, Conn., and Smith College (1969). Peter Matthiessen Wheelwright was educated at St. Paul's School, Concord, N.H.; Trinity College (1972); Cornell University; and Princeton University (1975).

81   iii. CYNTHIA MONTGOMERY HICKS, b. 13 Dec. 1951; m. (1) 3 Jan. 1976, PETER WALTER NILES; m. (2) ROY WESTBYE CUTTING.

82   iv. STEPHEN WINTHROP HICKS, b. at Stamford, Conn. 16 Sept. 1954; m. 13 Sept. 1992, ELIZABETH HAZAN.

40. **ROBERT WINTHROP**[11] **KEAN, JR.** (*Robert Winthrop*[10] *Kean, Katharine Taylor*[9] *Winthrop, Robert*[8], *Thomas Charles*[7], *Francis Bayard*[6], *John Still*[5], *John*[4], *Waitstill*[3], *John*[2-1]) was born at Hewlett, Long Island, New York 18 August 1922. He married, first, at the Chapel of Santo Tomas de Villanueva, Havana, Cuba 19 April 1947, **LUZ MARIA SILVERIO**, who was born at Marianao, Cuba 12 April 1924 and died at New York, New York 3 April 2012,[1918] daughter of Dr. Nicasio Silverio y Sainz, Cuban Ambassador to the Pan-American Union, and Luz Maria Ferrer y Lage, from whom he was divorced; and, second, at the Madison Avenue Presbyterian Church, New York 4 November 1982, **KATHERINE TCHOUKALEFF**, who was born at Alton, Illinois 13 January 1934, widow of Hans Fredrik Tobeason, and daughter of Peter and Nedelka (Stoyanov) Tchoukaleff.[1919]

[1916] *The New York Times*, 31 July 1943, 14; 4 January 1976, 54; 15 August 1976, 57; 21 March 1982, 56; *Social Register 1977* (1976), 519; Dorman, *The Filson Club History Quarterly* 27 [1953]: 146; notes by Robert Gregory Honshu Raynolds 2013; questionnaire from Stephen Winthrop Hicks 2013.

[1917] Dorman, *The Filson Club History Quarterly* 27 [1953]: 146; *The New York Times*, 21 March 1982, 56; *Social Register 1977* (1976), 519.

[1918] She died "after a full, adventurous, loving life at the core of her family. She made an indelible impression on all she met, and we will never forget her generous spirit and incandescent charm" (*The New York Times*, 29 April 2012).

[1919] Taylor, *The Lion and the Hare*, Chart H; "Luz Silverio Plans Marriage in Havana," *The New York Times*, 9 April 1947, 29; *Social Register 1984* (1983), 527; Winthrop,

Robert Winthrop Kean graduated from St. Mark's School, Southborough, Massachusetts, and Princeton University (1944). During the Second World War, he served as a pilot with the Army's Field Artillery; he was discharged in 1946 as a captain, with the Distinguished Flying Cross, two Air Medals, and three Campaign Stars. An executive with New Jersey banking and utilities corporations, he served as chairman and CEO of the Elizabethtown Water Company; at one time he was president of the New Jersey Utilities Association. In 1965, the New Jersey Society of Professional Engineers named him its Citizen of the Year.[1920]

Children of Robert Winthrop[11] and Luz Maria (Silverio) Kean, last four born at Glen Ridge (Montclair), New Jersey:[1921]

83   i.   ROBERT WINTHROP[12] KEAN, 3RD, b. at New York 30 Jan. 1948; m. (1) 12 Sept. 1970, PATRICIA COXE PATTERSON; m. (2) 18 Aug. 1999, MALLORY GIBBS (BLIMM) (HARRINGTON) CROSBY.

84   ii. PETER STUYVESANT KEAN, b. at New York 3 May 1949; m. 17 Sept. 1977, SUSAN KATHLEEN CAROW.

85   iii. ALEXANDER LIVINGSTON KEAN, b. 11 May 1952; m. (1) in Aug. 1972, LAUREL JEAN HOPE; m. (2) 14 April 2000, INA EICHHOF.

        iv. ANA MARIA KEAN, b. 27 May 1955 and d. 9 Nov. 1958.

86   v.   NICHOLAS KEAN, b. 3 June 1957; m. 21 Sept. 1992, MARY-MARGARET KIRK GROOME.

        vi. CHRISTOPHER KEAN, b. 22 Sept. 1965; he graduated from St. George's School, Newport, R.I.; Georgetown University (1988); and Columbia University (2000).

41. HAMILTON FISH[11] KEAN (*Robert Winthrop[10] Kean, Katharine Taylor[9] Winthrop, Robert[8], Thomas Charles[7], Francis Bayard[6], John Still[5], John[4], Waitstill[3], John[2-1]*) was born at New York, New York 1 March 1925 and died at 130 East End Avenue, New York 7 April 2016.[1922] He married,

---

Descendants of Robert Winthrop & Kate Wilson Taylor, 1833–2000, 14; *The Miami Herald*, 1 May 2012; Social Security Death Index.

[1920] Notes by Robert Winthrop Kean and Christopher Kean 2016.

[1921] *The New York Times*, 22 February 1949, 26; 5 May 1949, 32; 23 May 1952, 18; 18 November 1958, 37; 13 September 1970, 88; 10 October 1982, 94; *Summer Social Register 1973*, 107; *Social Register 1994* (1993), Marriages, 12; *Social Register 2000* (1999), 381; Winthrop, *Descendants of Robert Winthrop & Kate Wilson Taylor, 1833–2000*, 22; questionnaire from and notes by Christopher Kean 2014 and 2015; questionnaire from Robert Winthrop Kean, 3rd, 2014.

[1922] *Social Register 2016* (2015), 404; *The New York Times*, 12 April 2016.

first, at the Church of the Epiphany, New York 25 March 1950, ELLEN SHAW GARRISON, who was born 14 February 1926,[1923] daughter of Lloyd Kirkham and Ellen (Jay) Garrison, from whom he was divorced; second, at the Nevelson Chapel, St. Peter's Lutheran Church, New York 6 July 1981, ALICE NEWCOMER, who died at New York 27 February 1986, widow of Edgar Robey Baker, and daughter of Vincent Kay Newcomer; and, third, at St. Peter's Church, Lithgow, New York 23 September 1989, EDITH MORGAN WILLIAMSON, who was born 24 May 1937, formerly wife of James Edmund Bacon.[1924]

Hamilton Fish Kean graduated from St. Mark's School, Southborough, Massachusetts; Princeton University (1947); and Columbia University (1954). Ellen Shaw Garrison was educated at the North Shore Country Day School, Winnetka, Illinois, and Sarah Lawrence College (1949). Edith Morgan Williamson graduated from Abbot Academy, Andover, Massachusetts, and Vassar College (1958).

His *New York Times* obituary noted that "Ham, as all his friends called him, was a lifelong New Yorker who led a rich and varied life that centered around his passions for learning, music, the environment, and his family."[1925]

> While Ham practiced law for several years, the majority of his professional life was dedicated to the causes he cared deeply about. Most prominent among these was the preservation of the environment. One of the earliest members of the board of Natural Resources Defense Council (NRDC), Ham taught environmental law courses at both the New York University School of Law and the State University of New York. He was an honorary trustee of NRDC at his death. . . . A state leader for mental health advocates, he was a member of New York's Advisory Council on Mental Health and the Mental Health Services Council. . . .

[1923] *Harvard Class of 1919 Twenty-fifth Anniversary Report* (Cambridge, Mass.: Printed for the Class, 1944), 317 (date).

[1924] Taylor, *The Lion and the Hare*, Chart H; "H.F. Kean Marries Ellen S. Garrison," *The New York Times*, 26 March 1950, 88; 12 June 1969; 13 June 1969; 7 July 1981, A13; 1 March 1986, 32; "H.F. Kean Wed to Edith Bacon," 24 September 1989, 70; *Social Register 1982* (1981), 530; *Summer Social Register 1986 Dilatory Domiciles May 1986*, 21; *Social Register 1987* (1986), Deaths, 35; *Summer Social Register 1990* (1989), Marriages, 11.

[1925] *The New York Times*, 12 April 2016.

At his death, he was an honorary director of Action for Children. Even past 90, he was still active in civic life. He served on the board of Citizens for Global Solutions, eventually becoming its Chairman. At his death, he was the Chairman of a think tank called Center for War/Peace Studies. In addition to his dedication to the causes about which he was most passionate, his friends and family will remember his wonderful enthusiasm for musical theater and opera, his delight in history and poetry, his gentle humor and his deep generosity to all in need.

Children of Hamilton Fish[11] and Ellen Shaw (Garrison) Kean:[1926]

i. LESLIE BARLOW[12] KEAN, b. 12 Feb. 1951. She m. (1) at Mount Kisco, N.Y. 16 Dec. 1972, JOHN CHALMERS; m. (2) JOHN McKIM, and has issue; m. (3) JERRY ROSSER.[1927]

Leslie Barlow Kean was educated at Bard College and Union College.

ii. ELIZABETH STUYVESANT KEAN, b. 7 June 1952. She m. at St. Matthew's Church, Bedford, N.Y. 18 June 1983, PHILIP LE BRETON DOUGLAS, who was b. 18 April 1950, son of Paul Wolff and Colette Marie-Louise (Smith) Douglas, and has issue (Elizabeth Shaw[13] Douglas, Samuel Garrison Douglas, and Henry Hamilton Douglas).[1928]

Elizabeth Stuyvesant Kean was educated at the Spence School, New York; New York University; and the University of Wisconsin. Philip Le Breton Douglas graduated from Deerfield Academy, Deerfield, Mass.; Princeton University (1972); and N.Y.U.

iii. LLOYD GARRISON KEAN, b. 23 April 1955 and d. 24 Jan. 2013.[1929]

L. Garrison Kean was educated at the Browning School, New York; Ripon College; and Antioch College.

[1926] *Harvard Class of 1919 Thirty-fifth Anniversary Report* (Cambridge, Mass.: Printed for the Class, 1954), 69; *The New York Times*, 19 June 1983, 51; Winthrop, *Descendants of Robert Winthrop & Kate Wilson Taylor, 1833–2000*, 22, 35.

[1927] *New York Social Register 1974* (1973), 447; Winthrop, *Descendants of Robert Winthrop & Kate Wilson Taylor, 1833–2000*, 35.

[1928] "Miss Kean is Married," *The New York Times*, 19 June 1983, 51; 24 September 2011; Winthrop, *Descendants of Robert Winthrop & Kate Wilson Taylor, 1833–2000*, 35.

[1929] *The New York Times*, 31 January 2013.

iv.	LEWIS MORRIS KEAN, b. 15 March 1957. He m. ANNE SQUIRE and has issue (Nicholas Squire[13] Kean and Simon Garrison Kean).

Lewis Morris Kean was educated at Browning, Syracuse University, and Connecticut College.

42. **ROSE ANTHONY**[11] **KEAN** (*Robert Winthrop*[10] *Kean, Katharine Taylor*[9] *Winthrop, Robert*[8], *Thomas Charles*[7], *Francis Bayard*[6], *John Still*[5], *John*[4], *Waitstill*[3], *John*[2-1]) was born at New York, New York 1 February 1931. She married at St. James' Church, New York 12 August 1955, **EDGAR GEORGE LANSBURY**, who was born Edgar George McIldowie Lansbury at Paddington (London), England 12 January 1930, twin son of Edgar Isaac and Charlotte Lilian (McIldowie) (Denham) Lansbury, from whom she was divorced.[1930]

Rose Anthony Kean graduated from St. Timothy's School, Catonsville, Maryland, and Vassar College (1953). Edgar George Lansbury was educated at the Choate School, Wallingford, Connecticut, and the University of California at Los Angeles (1952x); a movie producer, his films include *Godspell* (1973). Edgar Lansbury is a younger brother of Dame Angela Lansbury; their elder half-sister was at one time married to Sir Peter Ustinov.

Children of Edgar George and Rose Anthony[11] (Kean) Lansbury:[1931]

87	i.	JAMES EDGAR[12] LANSBURY, b. at Hollywood, Calif. 30 Oct. 1956; m. 27 Nov. 1981, SUSAN ALICE SNORF.

ii.	MICHAEL BRUCE LANSBURY, b. in Los Angeles Co., Calif. 18 April 1958. He m. at Venice, Calif. 6 May 1990, JANET LOUISE JOHNSON, who was b. at Evanston, Ill. 10 July 1959, and has issue (Charlotte Rose[13] Lansbury, Madeline Virginia Lansbury, and Benjamin George Lansbury).[1932]

Michael Bruce Lansbury graduated from the Hotchkiss School, Lakeville, Conn., and Trinity College (1980). Janet Louise Johnson was

---

[1930] Paddington district (London), 1930, 01a: 12, no. 246; Taylor, *The Lion and the Hare*, Chart H; "Edgar Lansbury Weds Rose Kean," *The New York Times*, 13 August 1955, 14; The Internet Movie Database (IMDb) entries for Edgar Lansbury and Moyna MacGill (Charlotte Lillian McIldowie); questionnaire from James Edgar Lansbury 2014.

[1931] *The New York Times*, 24 November 1956, 15; 28 November 1981, 47; 18 June 1989, 48; 7 February 1993, V15; 23 May 1993, V15; 10 August 1997, 44; *California Birth Index, 1905–1995*; IMDB entries for David Lansbury and Ally Sheedy; notes by Katharine Rose Lansbury 2013; questionnaire from James Edgar Lansbury 2014.

[1932] *California Birth Index, 1905–1995*; *The New York Times*, 7 May 1990, B16; IMDb entry for Janet Julian [Janet Louise Johnson].

educated at North Hollywood High School, North Hollywood, and the University of California at Los Angeles.

88   iii.   DAVID ANTHONY LANSBURY, b. in Los Angeles Co. 25 Feb. 1961; m. (1) 10 Oct. 1992, ALEXANDRA ELIZABETH SHEEDY; m. (2) 6 June 2013, KRISTINA ANNE MIKKELSEN.

89   iv.   GEORGE WINTHROP LANSBURY, b. at New York 7 Oct. 1963; m. (1) 17 June 1989, MARIANNA CAROLINE MORGAN; m. (2) 22 May 1993, EMILY ALLEN BICKFORD.

90   v.   BRIAN McILDOWIE LANSBURY, b. at New York 16 April 1965; m. 9 Aug. 1997, TASHA HILL CORNELL.

Adopted child of Edgar George and Rose Anthony[11] (Kean) Lansbury:[1933]

vi.   KATHARINE ROSE LANSBURY, b. at New York 14 Aug. 1968; m. at the Cosmopolitan Club, New York 30 Oct. 1999, JONATHAN GREENWALD, who was b. Jonathan Forrest Independence Greenwald at Oxford, England 4 July 1968, son of Dr. A. Seth and Evelyn (Leff) Greenwald.[1934]

Katharine Rose Lansbury graduated from the Emma Willard School, Troy, N.Y.; Skidmore College (1991); and Rutgers University (2005). Jonathan Greenwald was educated at the University School, Hunting Valley, Ohio; Skidmore (1990); King's College, London; and Columbia University (2005).

Child of Jonathan Greenwald and Katharine Rose Lansbury:[1935]

a.   *Griffin Lansbury Greenwald*, b. at Cleveland, Ohio 6 March 2008.

43.   **THOMAS HOWARD**[11] **KEAN** (*Robert Winthrop*[10] *Kean, Katharine Taylor*[9] *Winthrop, Robert*[8], *Thomas Charles*[7], *Francis Bayard*[6], *John Still*[5], *John*[4], *Waitstill*[3], *John*[2-1]) was born at New York, New York 21 April 1935. He married at Old Drawyers Presbyterian Church, Odessa, Delaware 3 June 1967, **DEBORAH ELIZABETH BYE**, who was born 15 May 1943, daughter of Robert Coleman and Elizabeth (Griffenberg) Bye.[1936]

[1933] Notes by Katharine Rose Lansbury 2013; questionnaire from James Edgar Lansbury 2014.

[1934] *The New York Times*, 31 October 1999, ST8; notes by Katharine Rose Lansbury 2013; notes by Jonathan Greenwald 2015.

[1935] Notes by Jonathan Greenwald 2015.

[1936] "Delaware Nuptials for Deborah E. Bye," *The New York Times*, 4 June 1967, 94; questionnaire from Thomas Howard Kean 2014; http://en.wikipedia.org/wiki/Thomas_Kean.

Thomas Howard Kean graduated from St. Mark's School, Southborough, Massachusetts; Princeton University (1957); and Columbia University (1964). Deborah Elizabeth Bye was educated at the Tower Hill School, Wilmington, Delaware, and Bennett College. After Princeton, Thomas H. Kean taught at St. Mark's, and his original career path seemed destined to pass through Columbia to a Ph.D. An earlier compliment proved pivotal, however:[1937]

> In 1958, at the age of 23, fresh from four years at Princeton University and a stint on active duty for training with the Army National Guard, he was drafted by his family— dragged, really—to help his father with what turned out to be a losing campaign for the Senate.
>
> "I was pulled in," Mr. Kean recalled. "One day the people at campaign headquarters said I had to go out and say a few words. I said, 'Get somebody else—I'm not gonna do it.' They said, 'You have to do it.' I went with some fear and trepidation."
>
> "I gave a short discourse on why my father should be elected," he continued, "and afterwards the Mayor of the town came up to me and said that was one of the best talks he'd ever heard. Well, the next day, I told the campaign people, 'Any time you want me to speak, that's fine, that's easy.' But if the Mayor hadn't thought I was good, I wouldn't have done it again—ever. That was the beginning."

Elected to the New Jersey State Assembly in 1967, he served there for the next decade. After an unsuccessful campaign for a congressional seat, and one previous try for Governor, "at 46 years old, he won the Governor's office, but by the narrowest of margins—1,677 votes of 2.28 million cast."

> Unlike other politicians, he appears not to have left a trail of animosity in his wake. "I'll tell you something," says Roger Stone, the Republican political consultant who helped engineer Mr. Kean's victory. "He's the only politican I've worked for who has no enemies, and that's rare in politics.

[1937] Michael Norman, "Man in the News: A Reluctant Politician, Thomas Howard Kean," *The New York Times.* 20 January 1982.

> "You also can't get Tom to say something he doesn't
> mean," Mr. Stone said. "He's absolutely rigid in his beliefs,
> and that makes it hard to win an election."

The state responded to these qualities, and in November 1985 he
won reelection by a convincing margin:

> New Jersey voters did more than re-elect a Governor
> Tuesday. They transformed Tom Kean from an accidental
> leader into one with a powerful mandate. In the process,
> they gave the nation a lesson about new political possibilities.
>
> Mr. Kean, a Republican, won the governorship four
> years ago by fewer than 1,800 votes, the smallest margin in
> New Jersey history. This year he outpolled his Democratic
> opponent, Peter Shapiro, by 2 to 1. The voters also heeded
> Mr. Kean's call for a Republican majority in the State
> Assembly, ending the Democrats' 12-year reign in that house.
>
> Mr. Kean won virtually every major voting bloc,
> including 60 percent of the black vote. He thereby shattered
> what he termed "an article of faith in the Republican
> Party"—that blacks won't vote for a Republican so it is
> pointless to woo them. Mr. Kean succeeded in wooing
> them with intelligence and sensitivity, with no sacrifice
> of support among white voters. Therein lies a lesson of
> transcendent importance.
>
> Republican moderates, like Senators Bob Dole and
> Bob Packwood and Secretary of Labor Bill Brock, have
> been challenging that "article of faith" for some time, but
> with little success among their more right-wing brethren.
> The Kean victory hands them powerful evidence.[1938]

In February 1989, months before the end of his second term,
Governor Kean was named President of Drew University in Madison,
New Jersey. (He had already declined a cabinet position in President
George H. W. Bush's administration.) In his book *The Politics of Inclusion*
(1988), "Mr. Kean briefly compared his work as government official
and teacher," wrote Robert Hanley for *The New York Times*: "'You feel
good knowing that your infant nutrition program is keeping babies
healthy or your transportation program is putting people back to work,'

[1938] "Local Landslides, National Lessons; Governor Kean Shatters an 'Article of Faith,'"
The New York Times, 7 November 1985.

he wrote. 'But it still doesn't beat getting a letter from a former student telling you that something you did made a difference in his life.'"[1939] He served as Drew's president for fifteen years, retiring in 2005.

Following the attacks of 11 September 2001, former Secretary of State Henry Kissinger was named the head of a commission to review the U.S. Government's handling of terrorist threats in the years before 2001. Kissinger resigned in December 2002, citing professional conflicts, and former Governor Thomas Kean succeeded him as chairman. Reporting on this change, the *New York Times* wrote,

> Mr. Kean, the president of Drew University, is a moderate Republican known for his integrity and independence. These traits help offset his lack of experience on national security matters. Other commission members, and their staff, will be more familiar than Mr. Kean with the ins and outs of America's intelligence-gathering agencies. But if this commission, which can exercise its subpoena power only when six members vote to do so, is to engage in credible fact-finding of its own on behalf of the American people, its chairman must quickly set a tone of unyielding independence, despite the fact that half its members are appointed by each party.[1940]

The 9/11 Commission Report, released on 22 July 2004, found that the "Clinton and Bush administrations failed to grasp the gravity of the threat from Al Qaeda before the September 11, 2001, attacks[,] and left counterterrorism efforts to a disparate collection of uncoordinated, underfinanced and dysfunctional government agencies. . . .

"'Across the government, there were failures of imagination, policy, capabilities and management,' the panel said in its report, which was harshly critical of how the intelligence, law enforcement and military branches performed before the attacks." In an article for the *New York Times*, reporters Johnson and Jehl conveyed Mr. Kean's remarks on this important subject: "'Our failures took place over many years and many administrations,'" the panel chairman, Thomas H. Kean, said at a news conference. 'There's no single individual who is responsible for our failures. Yet individuals and institutions cannot be absolved of responsibility. Any

---

[1939] Robert Hanley, "Kean Named New President of Drew U.," *The New York Times*, 11 February 1989.

[1940] "A New Chairman for 9/11 Review," *The New York Times*, 17 December 2002.

person in a senior position within our government during this time bears some element of responsibility for our government's actions.'"[1941]

In 2006, Governor Kean and Commission vice chairman Lee H. Hamilton published *Without Precedent: The Inside Story of the 9/11 Commission.*

Children of Thomas Howard[11] and Deborah Elizabeth (Bye) Kean:[1942]

91   i.   THOMAS HOWARD[12] KEAN, JR., twin, b. at Livingston, N.J. 5 Sept. 1968; m. 12 Nov. 1994, RHONDA LEE NORTON.

92   ii.   REED STUYVESANT KEAN, twin, b. at Livingston 5 Sept. 1968; m. (1) 9 Dec. 2000, DORIAN DREES; m. (2) 9 May 2009, MICHELLE TERESA PETILLO.

93   iii. ALEXANDRA DICKINSON KEAN, b. 11 Oct. 1974; m. 9 Sept. 2000, BENJAMIN BREWSTER STRONG.

44. THEODORA[11] **WINTHROP** (*Robert*[10], *Frederic*[9], *Robert*[8], *Thomas Charles*[7], *Francis Bayard*[6], *John Still*[5], *John*[4], *Waitstill*[3], *John*[2-1]. Also *Robert*[11] *Winthrop*, *Dorothy*[10] *Amory, Charles Walter*[9] *Amory, Anna Powell Grant*[8] *Sears, David*[7] *Sears, Anne*[6] *Winthrop, John Still*[5]) was born at New York, New York 16 July 1929.[1943] She married, first, at the Church of the Advent, Westbury, Long Island, New York 11 September 1948,[1944] **THOMAS LEE HIGGINSON**, who was born at New York 2 January 1920 and died at Cold Spring Harbor, Long Island 13 April 1990, son of James Jackson Higginson and Lucy Virginia (Mitchell) (Higginson) Prince, from whom she was divorced in 1984;[1945] and, second, at the Orthodox Church of Our Lady of Kazan, Sea Cliff, Long Island 10 June 1984,[1946] **BRUCE DUFF HOOTON**, who was born at Waukegan, Illinois 11 December 1928 and died at Brookville, Long Island 17 May 1995, son of Bruce Duff and Elizabeth Romine (Garrison) Hooton.[1947]

[1941] David Johnston and Douglas Jehl, "Threats and Responses: Findings: Report Cites Lapses across Government And 2 Presidencies," *The New York Times*, 23 July 2004.

[1942] *The New York Times*, 13 November 1994; *Summer Social Register 1995 Dilatory Domiciles May 1995*, 37; *The New York Times*, 10 September 2000, ST13; 10 December 2000, ST15; 10 May 2009, ST15; questionnaire from Thomas Howard Kean 2014; http://www.nndb.com/people/363/000109036/.

[1943] Steward, *The Sarsaparilla Kings*, 104; Steward and Child, *The Descendants of Judge John Lowell of Newburyport, Massachusetts*, 227.

[1944] "Nuptials are Held for Miss Winthrop," *The New York Times*, 12 September 1948, 68.

[1945] Steward, *The Sarsaparilla Kings*, 104; Steward and Child, *The Descendants of Judge John Lowell of Newburyport, Massachusetts*, 227.

[1946] "Theodora Higginson Weds," *The New York Times*, 11 June 1984.

[1947] Steward, *The Sarsaparilla Kings*, 104; Steward and Child, *The Descendants of Judge John Lowell of Newburyport, Massachusetts*, 227.

Theodora Winthrop was educated at the Foxcroft School, Middleburg, Virginia, and Radcliffe College (1951x). Thomas Lee Higginson graduated from the Groton School, Groton, Massachusetts, and Harvard University (1942 and 1949);[1948] he became a partner at Shearman & Sterling, specializing in corporation and securities law, in 1957. Like his father-in-law, he was a trustee of the Green Vale School and a director of the Winthrop-University Hospital on Long Island. Bruce Duff Hooton had an eclectic career in the arts, with stints as general manager of the Living Theater in New York, as a reviewer for *Arts Magazine*, and as editor of *Drawing* magazine and founder of the Drawing Society. He was also a critic and editor at *The New York Herald Tribune* 1962–65:

> During those years, he wrote extensively on Jackson Pollock and Willem de Kooning, recognizing the increasing influence of the American abstract art movement of the 1960s and 1970s. . . .
>
> Mr. Hooton was the editor and publisher of *Art/World* from its inception in 1975 until it folded in 1991. The journal shunned the look of many monthly arts publications and was printed on newsprint in a tabloid format. The diverse roster of writers included the psychologist Julian Jaynes, the theater critic Brendan Gill, and the artists Paul Jenkins and Robert De Niro, Sr. . . .
>
> He also headed the New York office of the American Archives of Art and was executive director of the Sculptors' Guild, a nonprofit educational organization of professional sculptors.[1949]

Children of Thomas Lee and Theodora[11] (Winthrop) Higginson, born at New York:[1950]

94   i. THOMAS LEE[12] HIGGINSON, JR., b. 16 Sept. 1949; m. 12 June 1982, FEROLINE PERKINS BURRAGE.

[1948] He was a member of the Porcellian Club with his college class (*Porcellian Club 1791–2016*, 134).

[1949] J. Michael Elliott, "Bruce Hooton, 66, Founder and Editor of Arts Newspaper," *The New York Times*, 19 May 1995. Duell, Sloan & Pierce published his *Mother and Child in Modern Art* in 1964.

[1950] Steward, *The Sarsaparilla Kings*, 104, 125–26; Steward and Child, *The Descendants of Judge John Lowell of Newburyport, Massachusetts*, 227.

95   ii.   ELIZABETH HIGGINSON, b. 29 Dec. 1951; m. 26 Feb. 1983, LARRY
           ALAN RIDEMAN.

96   iii. ROBERT WINTHROP HIGGINSON, b. 14 April 1956; m. 19 Aug. 1982,
           JUDY ANN JONES.

45. ELIZABETH AMORY[11] **WINTHROP** (*Robert*[10], *Frederic*[9], *Robert*[8], *Thomas
Charles*[7], *Francis Bayard*[6], *John Still*[5], *John*[4], *Waitstill*[3], *John*[2-1]. Also *Robert*[11]
Winthrop, Dorothy[10] *Amory, Charles Walter*[9] *Amory, Anna Powell Grant*[8]
Sears, David[7] *Sears, Anne*[6] *Winthrop, John Still*[5]) was born at New York,
New York 14 December 1931 and died at Poughkeepsie, New York
26 February 1998.[1951] She married, first, at the Church of the Advent,
Westbury, Long Island, New York 16 June 1951,[1952] **FRANCIS ELLSWORTH
BAKER**, who was born at New York 20 December 1929, son of Francis
Ellsworth and Viva Cynthia (Bushway) Baker, from whom she was
divorced in 1954;[1953] second, at the Church of the Advent 21 September
1957,[1954] **HERBERT SCOTT SNEAD**, who was born at Montclair, New
Jersey 22 November 1922 and died at Norwalk, Connecticut 4
November 1998, son of Herbert Scott and Lydia Benita (Post) Snead,
from whom she was divorced in 1958;[1955] third, at Carson City, Nevada
21 April 1958,[1956] **MALCOLM PENNINGTON RIPLEY**, who was born
at New York 12 November 1926 and died at La Quinta, California
12 August 2005, son of Henry Baldwin Hyde and Lesley Frederica
(Pearson) Ripley, from whom she was divorced in 1974;[1957] and, fourth,
at Katonah, New York 4 July 1979,[1958] **PHILLIP IRWIN SHATZ**, who was
born at White Plains, New York 1 September 1926, son of Hyman and
Ruth (Futoran) Shatz, from whom she was divorced in 1986.[1959]

[1951] Steward, *The Sarsaparilla Kings*, 104; Steward and Child, *The Descendants of Judge John
Lowell of Newburyport, Massachusetts*, 227.

[1952] "Miss E. Winthrop Married to Senior," *The New York Times*, 17 June 1951, 83.

[1953] Steward, *The Sarsaparilla Kings*, 104; Steward and Child, *The Descendants of Judge John
Lowell of Newburyport, Massachusetts*, 227.

[1954] "Mrs. Baker Remarried," *The New York Times*, 22 September 1957, 95.

[1955] Steward, *The Sarsaparilla Kings*, 104; Steward and Child, *The Descendants of Judge John
Lowell of Newburyport, Massachusetts*, 227.

[1956] "Mrs. Winthrop, Malcolm Ripley Wed in Nevada," *The New York Times*, 26 April
1958, 17.

[1957] Steward, *The Sarsaparilla Kings*, 100, 104; Steward and Child, *The Descendants of
Judge John Lowell of Newburyport, Massachusetts*, 227.

[1958] "Amory Winthrop, Philip Shatz," *The Brewster Standard*, 15 November 1979, 3.

[1959] *The Putnam County Courier*, 22 April 1966, 5; Steward, *The Sarsaparilla Kings*, 104;
St. Andrew's Magazine, Winter 1998, 46; Steward and Child, *The Descendants of Judge
John Lowell of Newburyport, Massachusetts*, 227–28, http://prabook.org/web/person-
view.html?profileId=335229.

E. Amory Winthrop graduated from the Foxcroft School, Middleburg, Virginia, and Bradford Junior College (1951). Francis Ellsworth Baker was educated at St. Paul's School, Garden City, Long Island, and Harvard University (1951 and 1955). H. Scott Snead graduated from St. Andrew's School, Middletown, Delaware, and Trinity College (1948). At the time of their marriage, Amory Winthrop was a director and Malcolm Ripley—a general partner in Henderson, Harrison & Struthers, stockbrokers—was president of the Judson Health Center in New York. Phillip Irwin Shatz, a lawyer, was educated at Syracuse University (1948) and Columbia University (1954); at the time of their marriage, Amory Winthrop was president of the New York State Humane Society and a special agent for the American Society for the Prevention of Cruelty to Animals.

46. **CORNELIA BEEKMAN**[11] **WINTHROP** (*Robert*[10], *Frederic*[9], *Robert*[8], *Thomas Charles*[7], *Francis Bayard*[6], *John Still*[5], *John*[4], *Waitstill*[3], *John*[2-1]. Also *Robert*[11] *Winthrop*, *Dorothy*[10] *Amory*, *Charles Walter*[9] *Amory*, *Anna Powell Grant*[8] *Sears*, *David*[7] *Sears*, *Anne*[6] *Winthrop*, *John Still*[5]) was born at New York, New York 31 December 1934.[1960] She married at St. James' Church, New York 27 February 1960,[1961] **EDWARD SHELBY BONNIE**, who was born at Louisville, Kentucky 29 October 1929, son of Sevier and Judith (Farrell) Bonnie.[1962]

Cornelia Beekman Winthrop was educated at the Foxcroft School, Middleburg, Virginia; Vassar College (1957x); and Columbia University. Edward Shelby Bonnie graduated from the Hotchkiss School, Lakeville, Connecticut, and Yale University (1952 and 1955). With his wife, Nina, Ned Bonnie owns a horse and cattle farm in Oldham County, Kentucky. In 2016, he was a partner in Frost, Brown, Todd LLC in Louisville, with a focus on equine law. Ned Bonnie has been honored for his contributions to "the horse business" by the University of Louisville and the United States Equestrian Federation.[1963]

[1960] Steward, *The Sarsaparilla Kings*, 105; Steward and Child, *The Descendants of Judge John Lowell of Newburyport, Massachusetts*, 228.

[1961] "Edward Bonnie Marries Miss Cornelia Winthrop," *The New York Times*, 28 February 1960, 87. While in college, Edward S. Bonnie was a member of Book and Snake and the Yale Whiffenpoofs.

[1962] Steward, *The Sarsaparilla Kings*, 105; Steward and Child, *The Descendants of Judge John Lowell of Newburyport, Massachusetts*, 228.

[1963] http://khrc.ky.gov/Documents/CommissionBonnie.pdf.

Children of Edward Shelby and Cornelia Beekman[11] (Winthrop) Bonnie, born at Louisville:[1964]

97   i.   SHELBY WINTHROP[12] BONNIE, b. 16 July 1964; m. 25 Oct. 1997, CAROL JEANNE NAVONE.
98   ii. ROBERT FARRELL BONNIE, b. 18 Dec. 1967; m. (1) 15 May 1993, CYNTHIA ANNE POLK; m. (2) 7 Sept. 2002, JULIE ANN GOMENA.

47. **DOROTHY AMORY**[11] **BRADFORD** (*Dorothy*[10] *Winthrop, Frederic*[9], *Robert*[8], *Thomas Charles*[7], *Francis Bayard*[6], *John Still*[5], *John*[4], *Waitstill*[3], *John*[2-1]. Also *Dorothy*[11] *Winthrop, Dorothy*[10] *Amory, Charles Walter*[9] *Amory, Anna Powell Grant*[8] *Sears, David*[7] *Sears, Anne*[6] *Winthrop, John Still*[5]) was born at Boston, Massachusetts 18 May 1932. She married at Hamilton, Massachusetts 2 December 1967, **ARTHUR IRVIN WEXLER**, who was born at Springfield, Illinois 23 September 1929, son of Jacob and Helen (Klein) Wexler. He died in Barbados 28 March 1979.[1965]

Dorothy Amory Bradford graduated from St. Timothy's School, Stevenson, Maryland, and Smith College (1954); she is the author of *Reared in a Greenhouse: The Stories—and Story—of Dorothy Winthrop Bradford*, published in 1998. Arthur Irvin Wexler was educated at Springfield High School, the University of Southern California (1951), and Loyola University (1961); he was a deputy director of VISTA at his death. His obituary in *The Washington Post* noted:[1966]

> He fought to preserve the mission of VISTA and its service to poor people during politically unfavorable and neglectful times and devoted his life during the last two years to rebuilding and rekindling VISTA's impact on poor communities throughout the United States," VISTA Director Margery Tabankin said in a tribute to him.
>
> As a deputy director, Mr. Wexler had been in charge of recruiting, training and directing more than 3,200 VISTA volunteers.

[1964] Steward, *The Sarsaparilla Kings*, 105, 126; *Social Register 2001* (2000), 68; Steward and Child, *The Descendants of Judge John Lowell of Newburyport, Massachusetts*, 228; questionnaire from Robert Farrell Bonnie 2013.

[1965] *Harvard Class of 1924 Twenty-fifth Anniversary Report*, 83; Steward and Child, *The Descendants of Judge John Lowell of Newburyport, Massachusetts*, 228; questionnaire from Dorothy Bradford Wexler 2013.

[1966] "Arthur Wexler, 49, Deputy Chief of VISTA, Former L.A. Lawyer," *The Washington Post*, 31 March 1979.

He began his career with VISTA in 1967, when its programs were part of the Office of Economic Opportunity. He became acting director of the division of plans and management in 1969 and the following year was named director of the plans administration and budget division. From 1972 to December 1975, when he was named deputy director, he was chief of the operations branch.

Children of Arthur Irvin and Dorothy Amory[11] (Bradford) Wexler, born at Washington, D.C.:[1967]

99   i.   DOROTHY AMORY[12] WEXLER, b. 13 April 1969; m. 16 Aug. 2004, LUKE ALI SADRIAN.

100   ii.   JACOB WINTHROP WEXLER, b. 14 Sept. 1970; m. 14 April 2001, SARI SALLY YOSHIOKA.

48. **STANDISH**[11] **BRADFORD, JR.** (*Dorothy*[10] *Winthrop, Frederic*[9]*, Robert*[8]*, Thomas Charles*[7]*, Francis Bayard*[6]*, John Still*[5]*, John*[4]*, Waitstill*[3]*, John*[2-1]. Also *Dorothy*[11] *Winthrop, Dorothy*[10] *Amory, Charles Walter*[9] *Amory, Anna Powell Grant*[8] *Sears, David*[7] *Sears, Anne*[6] *Winthrop, John Still*[5]) was born at Boston, Massachusetts 2 December 1933 and died at Magnolia (Gloucester), Massachusetts 15 September 2016. He married at the River Club, New York, New York 1 May 1971, **BRIGITTE HILDEGARD PULLERDT**, who was born at Toruń, Poland 4 April 1943, daughter of Gerhard Kurt and Hildegard Klara (Eglinski) Pullerdt.[1968]

Standish Bradford, Jr., graduated from the Groton School, Groton, Massachusetts; Williams College (1955); and Harvard University (1962). Brigitte Hildegard Pullerdt was educated at Helene Lange Gymnasium, Hamburg, [West] Germany, and Hamburg University (1965). For many years a staff lawyer for Arthur D. Little, Stanna Bradford served on the corporation of the Boston University Medical Center Hospital and as a director of Plimoth Plantation. His obituary noted that "Stanna was a loyal friend, a warm family patriarch, and a source of delight for all who knew and loved him, both friends and family. We will miss his wicked wit, his sometimes mediocre but always amusing jokes, his trove of

---

[1967] Steward and Child, *The Descendants of Judge John Lowell of Newburyport, Massachusetts*, 228; questionnaire from Dorothy Bradford Wexler 2013.

[1968] *Harvard Class of 1924 Twenty-fifth Anniversary Report*, 83; Steward and Child, *The Descendants of Judge John Lowell of Newburyport, Massachusetts*, 229; http://www.obittree.com/obituary/us/massachusetts/beverly/campbell-funeral-home/standish-bradford-jr/2710959/.

limericks and golf trivia, his wry intelligence, his exuberant and gleeful spirit, and his tremendous heart."[1969]

Children of Standish[11] and Brigitte Hildegard (Pullerdt) Bradford, born at Cambridge, Massachusetts:[1970]

101	i.	TATYANA AMORY[12] BRADFORD, b. 30 Sept. 1971; m. 27 June 1998, JAN TIMOTHY OUHRABKA.

ii.	AMANDA DOROTHY BRADFORD, b. 20 Dec. 1974; she graduated from St. Mark's School, Southborough, Mass., and the University of Vermont (1997).

102	iii.	STANDISH BRADFORD, 3RD, b. 12 Jan. 1977.

49. **ELIZABETH GARDNER**[11] **BRADFORD** (*Dorothy*[10] *Winthrop, Frederic*[9], *Robert*[8], *Thomas Charles*[7], *Francis Bayard*[6], *John Still*[5], *John*[4], *Waitstill*[3], *John*[2-1]. Also *Dorothy*[11] *Winthrop, Dorothy*[10] *Amory, Charles Walter*[9] *Amory, Anna Powell Grant*[8] *Sears, David*[7] *Sears, Anne*[6] *Winthrop, John Still*[5]) was born at Boston, Massachusetts 6 February 1940. She married at Hamilton, Massachusetts 21 August 1965, **GAVIN GAIL BORDEN**, who was born at Chicago, Illinois 1 May 1939 and died at New York, New York 20 December 1991, son of Gail and Elizabeth (Frey) Borden, from whom she was divorced.[1971]

Elizabeth Gardner Bradford graduated from St. Timothy's School, Stevenson, Maryland; Radcliffe College (1962); and Yale University (2004). Gavin Gail Borden was educated at Culver Military Academy, Culver, Indiana, and Harvard College (1962). The Bordens established Garland Publishing, Inc., and remained business partners after the end of their marriage.

> In 1984, the company published a three-volume, corrected edition of James Joyce's *Ulysses*. The company updated the original version of the seminal 20th-century novel, which was published in the United States in 1934 by Random House.

[1969] http://www.obittree.com/obituary/us/massachusetts/beverly/campbell-funeral-home/standish-bradford-jr/2710959/.

[1970] *Social Register 2000* (1999), 75; Steward and Child, *The Descendants of Judge John Lowell of Newburyport, Massachusetts*, 229; notes by Amanda Dorothy Bradford 2013.

[1971] *Harvard Class of 1962 15th Anniversary Report* (Cambridge, Mass.: Printed for the Class, 1977), 25; *The New York Times*, 25 December 1991, 38; *Harvard Class of 1962 Thirtieth Anniversary Report* (Cambridge, Mass.: Printed for the Class, 1992), 255; Steward and Child, *The Descendants of Judge John Lowell of Newburyport, Massachusetts*, 229; questionnaire from Elizabeth Bradford Borden 2013.

At the time of its publication, the Garland edition was thought to be the definitive version of *Ulysses*. Two years later, Random House reprinted the Garland version in paperback.[1972]

Children of Gavin Gail and Elizabeth Gardner[11] (Bradford) Borden, born at New York:[1973]

103   i.   SARAH GARDNER[12] BORDEN, b. 22 July 1971; m. 18 May 1996, JOHN COOLEY WARECK.

      ii.   GAVIN HAMILTON BORDEN, b. 16 April 1973; he graduated from the Berkshire School, Sheffield, Mass., and Rollins College (1996).

104   iii.   FREDERIC AMORY NALLE BORDEN, b. 15 Feb. 1978; m. 24 July 2012, KATHERINE LEONE HALL.

50. **IRIS**[11] **WINTHROP** (*Frederic*[10-9], *Robert*[8], *Thomas Charles*[7], *Francis Bayard*[6], *John Still*[5], *John*[4], *Waitstill*[3], *John*[2-1]. Also *Frederic*[11] *Winthrop, Dorothy*[10] *Amory, Charles Walter*[9] *Amory, Anna Powell Grant*[8] *Sears, David*[7] *Sears, Anne*[6] *Winthrop, John Still*[5] and *Angela Elizabeth*[10] *Forbes, Margaret Tyndal*[9] *Winthrop, Robert Charles*[8-7], *Thomas Lindall*[6], *John Still*[5]) was born at Boston, Massachusetts 18 April 1935.[1974] She married at Hamilton, Massachusetts 29 June 1968, **WILLARD CLARK FREEMAN**, who was born at Providence, Rhode Island 23 February 1929, son of Harry Boit and Theodora (Hollander) Freeman. He died at Saratoga Springs, New York 17 April 2013.[1975]

Iris Winthrop graduated from Chatham Hall, Chatham, Virginia, and Radcliffe College (1957). W. C. "Mike" Freeman was educated at St. Mark's School, Southborough, Massachusetts, and Rhode Island

---

[1972] The Garland *Ulysses* proved controversial: the director of Boston University's James Joyce Research Center found its revisions of the text contained "serious mistakes." A friend reported that Gavin Borden felt "that it was a scholarly enterprise and well worth doing. It was clearly an important edition because it did make an attempt to get closer to the text as Joyce actually wrote it" ("Gavin G. Borden, 52, Founder of Book Firm," *The New York Times*, 25 December 1991). The 1969–91 records of Garland Publishing are at Princeton University: http://findingaids.princeton.edu/collections/C0850.

[1973] Steward and Child, *The Descendants of Judge John Lowell of Newburyport, Massachusetts*, 229; questionnaire from and notes by Elizabeth Bradford Borden 2013; questionnaire from Sarah Gardner Borden 2014.

[1974] Mayo, *The Winthrop Family in America*, 434.

[1975] Mayo, *The Winthrop Family in America*, 434; Steward and Child, *The Descendants of Judge John Lowell of Newburyport, Massachusetts*, 230; Social Security Death Index; questionnaire from Frederic Winthrop 2013; http://burkefuneralhome.com/sitemaker/sites/BURKES1/obit.cgi?user=975813Freeman.

Agricultural College. Together the Freemans owned Chime Bell Farm in Aiken, South Carolina. At first a steeplechase rider (he won his first race at Narragansett Park in 1952), Mike Freeman spent more than fifty years as a thoroughbred trainer: his most successful horse was perhaps Shuvee,[1976] who raced at Aqueduct in October 1971.

> The 5-year-old mare owned by Mrs. Whitney Stone took the two-mile context by a smashing seven lengths over Sigmund Sommer's Paraje, with William Haggin Perry's Loud next in the field of seven. . . .
>
> In scoring, Shuvee brought about a second straight triumph in the Jockey Club Gold Cup. She won last year's race under Ron Turcotte, but in this renewal she had the services of Jorge Velasquez. . . .
>
> It is the intention of Mrs. Stone to retire the Virginia-bred Shuvee, a daughter of Nashua, to a career as a broodmare. And the mare will take with her the record of having earned more money than any other female thoroughbred. . . .
>
> Shuvee has been trained by W. C. (Mike) Freeman, who did not hesitate to send her against colts last year and this year. Of Shuvee's rivals yesterday, all except Our Cheri Amour, who finished last, were males.
>
> In the winner's circle, Freeman and Velasquez were among part of the group in which Ogden Phipps, chairman of the Jockey Club, presented the trophy to Mrs. Stone.[1977]

Child of Willard Clark and Iris[11] (Winthrop) Freeman:[1978]

    i. MICHAEL WINTHROP[12] FREEMAN, b. at Augusta, Ga. 27 Dec. 1975. He m. JESSIE ADAMS MILNE and has issue (Michael Winthrop[13] Freeman, Jr.).

51. **ANGELA**[11] **WINTHROP** (*Frederic*[10-9], *Robert*[8], *Thomas Charles*[7], *Francis Bayard*[6], *John Still*[5], *John*[4], *Waitstill*[3], *John*[2-1]. Also *Frederic*[11] *Winthrop, Dorothy*[10] *Amory, Charles Walter*[9] *Amory, Anna Powell Grant*[8] *Sears, David*[7]

[1976] http://www.burkefuneralhome.com/memsol.cgi?user_id=975813.

[1977] Joe Nichols, "Shuvee Captures 2-Mile Gold Cup," *The New York Times*, 31 October 1971, 5: 1, 9.

[1978] Winthrop, *Descendants of Robert Winthrop & Kate Wilson Taylor, 1833–2000*, 26, 43; notes by John Winthrop Sears 2012.

Sears, Anne[6] Winthrop, John Still[5] and *Angela Elizabeth[10] Forbes, Margaret Tyndal[9] Winthrop, Robert Charles[8-7], Thomas Lindall[6], John Still[5])* was born at Boston, Massachusetts 8 September 1936.[1979] She married at Ascension Memorial Church, Ipswich, Massachusetts 16 September 1961, CHARLES WILLARD GETCHELL, JR., who was born at Los Angeles, California 29 May 1929 and died at Danvers, Massachusetts 8 November 2010, son of Charles Willard and Katharine (Fitch) Getchell.[1980]

Angela Winthrop graduated from Chatham Hall, Chatham, Virginia, and Radcliffe College (1958). Charles Willard Getchell, Jr., was educated at South Pasadena High School, South Pasadena, California; Stanford University (1951 and 1954); and the Institut Universitaire des Hautes Études Internationales. Since 1978, Ann Getchell has been involved in all aspects of the management of the "Groton House Farm" three-day events, including a breeding program: "Ann raises horses for herself and other amateurs. She acknowledges that generally only pure thoroughbreds have the speed and stamina for three- and four-star competition, but stresses that top level three-day riders represent a tiny percentage of the eventing population. She believes the majority of competitors are much safer and happier on a mount that has naturally good movement, jumps safely and is levelheaded—the offspring that Groton House is breeding today."[1981]

The Getchells lived in Brussels for more than a decade, while Chuck Getchell worked for the First National Bank of New York in its Belgian branch; later, on their return to Massachusetts, he worked as a lawyer in Boston and then Ipswich. His *Boston Globe* obituary noted that he "was a writer and poet at heart. In 1980, he founded the Ipswich Press, and his commentary and light verse often appeared in local and regional publications."[1982]

[1979] Mayo, *The Winthrop Family in America*, 434.

[1980] Mayo, *The Winthrop Family in America*, 434; *The Boston Globe*, 14 November 2010; Steward and Child, *The Descendants of Judge John Lowell of Newburyport, Massachusetts*, 230; questionnaire from Frederic Winthrop 2013.

[1981] http://www.grotonhousefarm.com/html/horse_breeding.html.

[1982] *The Boston Globe*, 14 November 2010. See, for instance, his poem "Wainscott Hollow—Looking West," which appeared in *The New York Review of Books* in the 28 February 2002 issue (http://www.nybooks.com/articles/2002/02/28/wain-scott-hollowlooking-west/): "The lady, after all, / had been somebody: mother, even wife, / grandparent, trustee, loyal friend—a wall / of strength, of doing right."

Children of Charles Willard and Angela[11] (Winthrop) Getchell, born at Brussels, Belgium:[1983]

      i.   KATHARINE CHISHOLM[12] GETCHELL, b. 15 Dec. 1964; she was educated at Milton Academy, Milton, Mass., and Naropa Institute.

105   ii. EMILY ERSKINE GETCHELL, b. 24 Dec. 1966; m. 31 Oct. 1992, GABRIEL GRENOT-PORTUONDO.

106   iii. SARAH FIELDS GETCHELL, b. 18 Oct. 1970; m. 18 March 2011, JOSHUA LONGSTREET ELLSWORTH.

52. ADAM[11] **WINTHROP** (*Frederic*[10-9], *Robert*[8], *Thomas Charles*[7], *Francis Bayard*[6], *John Still*[5], *John*[4], *Waitstill*[3], *John*[2-1]. Also *Frederic*[11] *Winthrop, Dorothy*[10] *Amory, Charles Walter*[9] *Amory, Anna Powell Grant*[8] *Sears, David*[7] *Sears, Anne*[6] *Winthrop, John Still*[5] and *Angela Elizabeth*[10] *Forbes, Margaret Tyndal*[9] *Winthrop, Robert Charles*[8-7], *Thomas Lindall*[6], *John Still*[5]*) was born at Boston, Massachusetts 20 September 1938[1984] and died at Ipswich, Massachusetts 24 August 1982. He married at St. Nicholas' Church, Remenham (Henley-on-Thames), Oxfordshire, England 29 January 1977, **MIRANDA TOWNSEND MCCAGG,** who was born at Ruislip, Middlesex 21 October 1954, daughter of Louis Butler and Katharine Townsend (Jackson) McCagg. She married, second, 30 September 1983, William Albert Ellis.[1985]

Adam Winthrop graduated from St. Paul's School, Concord, New Hampshire, and Harvard College (1961).[1986] Miranda Townsend McCagg was educated at Friends' Seminary, New York, New York, and Sarah Lawrence College (1977x). A broker and then real estate developer, Adam Winthrop was majority owner of Northway Industrial Park in Peabody and the New England Telephone Company computer building in Burlington, both in Massachusetts. At Harvard and then as a member of the Myopia Hunt Club team, he excelled at the game of polo: "He played in and won a number of major national and

---

[1983] Winthrop, *Descendants of Robert Winthrop & Kate Wilson Taylor, 1833–2000,* 26; questionnaire from Sarah Fields Getchell 2016.

[1984] Mayo, *The Winthrop Family in America,* 434.

[1985] *Summer Social Register 1977,* 284; Scott Campbell Steward and Newbold Le Roy 3rd, *The Le Roy Family in America, 1753–2003* (Laconia, N.H.: Peter E. Randall, 2003), 373; Steward and Child, *The Descendants of Judge John Lowell of Newburyport, Massachusetts,* 230; questionnaire from Frederic Winthrop 2013; questionnaire from Miranda McCagg Ellis 2014.

[1986] He was a member of the Porcellian Club with his college class (*Porcellian Club 1791–2016,* 143).

international tournaments, and was a nationally ranked player with a solid 4-goal handicap."[1987]

Children of Adam[11] and Miranda Townsend (McCagg) Winthrop, born at Beverly, Massachusetts:[1988]

> i. ANGELA FREDERICA[12] WINTHROP, b. 23 Aug. 1977; she was educated at Wheaton College.
>
> 107 ii. MIRANDA ROSEMARY WINTHROP, b. 12 Sept. 1981; m. 22 Aug. 2008, DANIEL JOSEPH MARTIN KACYVENSKI.

53. FREDERIC[11] WINTHROP (*Frederic*[10-9], *Robert*[8], *Thomas Charles*[7], *Francis Bayard*[6], *John Still*[5], *John*[4], *Waitstill*[3], *John*[2-1]. Also *Frederic*[11] *Winthrop*, *Dorothy*[10] *Amory, Charles Walter*[9] *Amory, Anna Powell Grant*[8] *Sears, David*[7] *Sears, Anne*[6] *Winthrop, John Still*[5] and *Angela Elizabeth*[10] *Forbes, Margaret Tyndal*[9] *Winthrop, Robert Charles*[8-7], *Thomas Lindall*[6], *John Still*[5]) was born at Boston, Massachusetts 11 June 1940. He married at Trinity Church, Concord, Massachusetts 27 July 1968, **SUSAN BAILEY SHAW**, who was born at Concord 6 December 1944, daughter of Robert Hallowell and Cornelia Couch (Bailey) Shaw.[1989]

Frederic Winthrop graduated from St. Paul's School, Concord, New Hampshire, and Harvard College (1963).[1990] Susan Bailey Shaw was educated at Concord Academy, Concord, Massachusetts; the University of Wisconsin (1966); and Boston University. Fred Winthrop served as Massachusetts' Commissioner of Food and Agriculture 1975–85 and as executive director of The Trustees of Reservations from 1985 until 2000; he is also a former chairman of the American Farmland Trust and trustee of Hampshire College.

At the time of his twenty-fifth college reunion, he reflected: "I used to think man is master of his own destiny, particularly if he went to Harvard. But now I'm not so sure. Life is too unpredictable, too full of surprises, some bad, but in my case mostly good. Not I, not even Harvard,

---

[1987] *Harvard Class of 1961 Twenty-fifth Anniversary Report* (Cambridge, Mass.: Printed for the Class, 1986), 949, 950.

[1988] Steward and Le Roy, *The Le Roy Family in America, 1753–2003*, 502; Steward and Child, *The Descendants of Judge John Lowell of Newburyport, Massachusetts*, 230; questionnaire from Miranda McCagg Ellis 2014.

[1989] *Harvard and Radcliffe Class of 1963 Twenty-fifth Anniversary Report* (Cambridge, Mass.: Printed for the Class, 1988), 1265; Steward and Child, *The Descendants of Judge John Lowell of Newburyport, Massachusetts*, 231; questionnaire from Frederic Winthrop 2013, notes by Frederic Winthrop 2015.

[1990] He was a member of the Porcellian Club with his college class (*Porcellian Club 1791–2016*, 144).

can take credit for the fact that I have a wonderful wife, four bright and healthy children, some beautiful land and a little extra cash. . . .

"Land use has been an abiding interest. I am currently running The Trustees of Reservations, the largest private owner of conservation land in Massachusetts and said to be the oldest land trust in the world. . . .

"They say a good farmer tries to leave his place better off than he finds it. That seems to me a goal all of us should follow, whatever we do in life."[1991]

Children of Frederic[11] and Susan Bailey (Shaw) Winthrop, born at Beverly, Massachusetts:[1992]

108   i.   REBECCA[12] WINTHROP, b. 29 Dec. 1971; m. 29 June 1996, RONALD MONAHAN.
109   ii.   FREDERIC WINTHROP, 3RD, b. 4 June 1974; m. 14 May 2005, ALICE HELEN MACINNES.
110   iii. LAURA WINTHROP, b. 23 Jan. 1978; m. 28 May 2011, CHARLES SPENCER ABBOT.
111   iv.   ROBERT SHAW WINTHROP, b. 23 Feb. 1981; m. 26 May 2012, CARLA FELISA HOLLETT.

54. **ROBERT**[11] **WINTHROP, 2ND** (*Frederic*[10-9], *Robert*[8], *Thomas Charles*[7], *Francis Bayard*[6], *John Still*[5], *John*[4], *Waitstill*[3], *John*[2-1]. Also *Frederic*[11] *Winthrop, Dorothy*[10] *Amory, Charles Walter*[9] *Amory, Anna Powell Grant*[8] *Sears, David*[7] *Sears, Anne*[6] *Winthrop, John Still*[5] and *Angela Elizabeth*[10] *Forbes, Margaret Tyndal*[9] *Winthrop, Robert Charles*[8-7], *Thomas Lindall*[6], *John Still*[5]) was born at Boston, Massachusetts 14 December 1946.[1993] He married at Emmanuel Church, Athens, Georgia 1 April 1978, **CAROL ANN VEATCH**, who was born at Quincy, Illinois 31 October 1950, daughter of Earl Leonard and Margaret (Day) Veatch.[1994]

Robert Winthrop, 2nd, graduated from St. Mark's School, Southborough, Massachusetts; Stanford University (1969); and the University of Georgia (1974). Dr. Carol Ann Veatch was educated at Iowa Wesleyan University (1972), the University of Missouri (1974), and the University of Georgia (1983).

[1991] *Harvard and Radcliffe Class of 1963 Twenty-fifth Anniversary Report* (Cambridge, Mass.: Printed for the Class, 1988), 1265.

[1992] Steward and Child, *The Descendants of Judge John Lowell of Newburyport, Massachusetts*, 231; questionnaire from Frederic Winthrop 2013.

[1993] Mayo, *The Winthrop Family in America*, 434.

[1994] *Social Register 1980* (1979), 1079; Steward and Child, *The Descendants of Judge John Lowell of Newburyport, Massachusetts*, 231; questionnaire from Robert Winthrop, 2nd, 2013.

Child of Robert[11] and Carol Ann (Veatch) Winthrop:[1995]

    i.   MARGARET KATHERINE[12] WINTHROP, b. at Athens 7 Nov. 1989; she graduated from Athens Academy and Colby College (2012).

55. GRANT FORBES[11] WINTHROP (*Frederic*[10-9], *Robert*[8], *Thomas Charles*[7], *Francis Bayard*[6], *John Still*[5], *John*[4], *Waitstill*[3], *John*[2-1]. Also *Frederic*[11] *Winthrop, Dorothy*[10] *Amory, Charles Walter*[9] *Amory, Anna Powell Grant*[8] *Sears, David*[7] *Sears, Anne*[6] *Winthrop, John Still*[5] and *Angela Elizabeth*[10] *Forbes, Margaret Tyndal*[9] *Winthrop, Robert Charles*[8-7], *Thomas Lindall*[6], *John Still*[5]) was born at Boston, Massachusetts 22 February 1949. He married at Annisquam Church, Annisquam (Gloucester), Massachusetts 10 August 1975, **HOPE HARTLEY BROCK**, who was born at New York, New York 22 December 1949, daughter of Horace and Hope Hartley (Distler) Brock.[1996]

Grant Forbes Winthrop graduated from St. Mark's School, Southborough, Massachusetts; Harvard College (1971);[1997] and Stanford University (1975). Hope Hartley Brock was educated at the Garrison Forest School, Garrison, Maryland; Radcliffe College (1971); and Boston University (1975). "In the summer of 1970, between my junior and senior years," Grant Winthrop wrote in 1996, "I took a summer job working in a securities firm in New York City. I hated the experience, and vowed I'd never work on Wall Street or live in New York. But after living in Washington, Boston, and California, working in government, politics, fund-raising, and journalism, I wound up in New York in 1977 and have lived here ever since. I gravitated from financial journalism to finance, and have been a partner in an investment advisory firm for the past seven years. The moral: never say never. Life doesn't always unfold the way you expect or plan."[1998]

In her twenty-fifth reunion entry, Hope Brock Winthrop also noted ways in which her "youthful expectations" did and did not pan out: "I became a lawyer, married a college classmate, and moved to California. I had a typical young professional life working for the then nascent computer industry. We then made a career move to New York City. . . .

[1995] Steward and Child, *The Descendants of Judge John Lowell of Newburyport, Massachusetts*, 231; notes by Margaret Katherine Winthrop 2013; questionnaire from Robert Winthrop, 2nd, 2013.

[1996] *The New York Times*, 11 August 1975, 18; *Harvard and Radcliffe Class of 1971 Twenty-fifth Anniversary Report* (Cambridge, Mass.: Printed for the Class, 1996), 134, 1257; Steward and Child, *The Descendants of Judge John Lowell of Newburyport, Massachusetts*, 231–32; questionnaire from Frederic Winthrop 2013.

[1997] He was a member of the Porcellian Club with his college class (*Porcellian Club 1791–2016*, 149).

[1998] *Harvard and Radcliffe Class of 1971 Twenty-fifth Anniversary Report*, 1257, 1258.

"With the birth of my second daughter, Fernanda, I decided to take some time off. I felt guilty that I wasn't a superwoman of the '80s, but I realized I didn't have the strength, patience, and flexibility to do everything. I also worried about what kind of role model I was going to be for my daughters. Was there a better solution?

"The death of my parents precipitated the next turn in my life. . . . [Out] of the experience of being the executor of my mother's will, I discovered my next career. I felt that there had to be a better way to resolve conflicts in families than through lawyers and courts, and so became involved in the field of alternative conflict resolution. . . .

"So much for the linear life we expected in 1971. . . . I'm still no closer to knowing how to advise my daughters how to plan for a balance in their adult lives, except to say, live each part of your life to the fullest and don't be surprised where you end up."[1999]

Children of Grant Forbes[11] and Hope Hartley (Brock) Winthrop, born at New York:[2000]

112   i.   ELIZABETH HARTLEY[12] WINTHROP, b. 25 June 1979; m. 17 June
             2006, ADIN RYAN MURRAY.
113   ii. FERNANDA WOOD WINTHROP, b. 15 Jan. 1982; m. 23 Dec. 2013,
             JOHN ALEXANDER MICHAS.
114   iii. CHARLOTTE BROCK WINTHROP, b. 1 March 1986; m. 10 Aug. 2013,
             WELLINGTON WEST SCULLEY.

56. JONATHAN[11] **WINTHROP** (*Frederic*[10-9], *Robert*[8], *Thomas Charles*[7], *Francis Bayard*[6], *John Still*[5], *John*[4], *Waitstill*[3], *John*[2-1]. Also *Frederic*[11] *Winthrop, Dorothy*[10] *Amory, Charles Walter*[9] *Amory, Anna Powell Grant*[8] *Sears, David*[7] *Sears, Anne*[6] *Winthrop, John Still*[5] and *Angela Elizabeth*[10] *Forbes, Margaret Tyndal*[9] *Winthrop, Robert Charles*[8-7], *Thomas Lindall*[6], *John Still*[5]*) was born at Ipswich, Massachusetts 1 January 1953. He married at the Church of St. Mary-by-the-Sea, Northeast Harbor, Maine 1 October 1988, **SYDNEY CHESTON**, who was born at Philadelphia, Pennsylvania 26 July 1957, daughter of George Morris and Winifred Dodge (Seyburn) (McIlvain) (de Bragança) Cheston.[2001]

[1999] *Harvard and Radcliffe Class of 1971 Twenty-fifth Anniversary Report*, 134–35.

[2000] Winthrop, *Descendants of Robert Winthrop & Kate Wilson Taylor, 1833–2000*, 26; Steward and Child, *The Descendants of Judge John Lowell of Newburyport, Massachusetts*, 232; notes by Charlotte Brock Winthrop, Elizabeth Hartley Winthrop, and Fernanda Wood Winthrop 2013.

[2001] Hervé Douxchamps et Henry Hoff, "La Souche Stiers," *Le Parchemin* 35 [1985]: 413; *The New York Times*, 2 October 1988, 55; Steward and Child, *The Descendants*

Jonathan Winthrop graduated from St. Mark's School, Southborough, Massachusetts; Harvard University (1975);[2002] and the University of Pennsylvania (1982). Sydney Cheston was educated at the Shipley School, Bryn Mawr, Pennsylvania; Briarcliff College; and Harvard. In 2015, Jonathan Winthrop reported that, after "a quarter century in architecture, I closed my [Boston] office in 2008, and have since focused on the operations of a number of properties owned by my broader family. . . .

"Despite the convenience of the Red Line, I do not get back to Cambridge very often—rather like my undergraduate years when getting to Boston was a special excursion. . . . Harvard's own building projects continue to astound, especially the new Fogg [Museum]. As a history of art concentrator, I considered the Fogg very much my home. The new building and its program are staggering. While I miss the intimacy of the old, I am intrigued by the technical bravura of the new. I hope it works well for future generations of students.

"It did not work well, or even open in time, for my daughter, Georgina Cheston Winthrop '14. Like her dad, she was an art history concentrator. It is ironic that the Fogg, the Sackler, and the Busch [Museums] were closed and their collections stored away in a high-security warehouse in darkest Somerville, just as she declared her major. Despite that inconvenience and impediment to hands-on study, I am pleased to say that she loved her Harvard experience. . . .

"Our younger daughter, Augusta. . . , has just completed her sophomore year at George Washington University, where she is following the family pattern of design and art history studies. I am amazed at her ability to juggle the demands of academics while she rows . . . for GW's division one crew team. . . .

"Those forty years [since graduation] have seemingly evaporated, but the memories of people and places of our Harvard days remain indelible."[2003]

---

of Judge John Lowell of Newburyport, Massachusetts, 232; questionnaire from Frederic Winthrop 2013.

[2002] He was a member of the Porcellian Club with his college class (*Porcellian Club 1791–2016*, 150).

[2003] *Harvard and Radcliffe Class of 1975 Fortieth Anniversary Report* (Cambridge, Mass.: Printed for the Class, 2015), 429–30.

Children of Jonathan[11] and Sydney (Cheston) Winthrop, born at Boston:[2004]

115   i.   GEORGINA CHESTON[12] WINTHROP, b. 16 May 1991; m. 17 Sept.
            2016, ROBERT HOOPER STEVENSON.
       ii. AUGUSTA AMORY WINTHROP, b. 25 May 1994; she was educated at
            the Winsor School, Boston; the London College of Fashion; and
            George Washington University.

57. JOHN[11] WINTHROP (*Nathaniel Thayer*[10], *Frederic*[9], *Robert*[8], *Thomas
Charles*[7], *Francis Bayard*[6], *John Still*[5], *John*[4], *Waitstill*[3], *John*[2-1]) was born at
Boston, Massachusetts 22 June 1936. He married, first, at Sewickley,
Pennsylvania 22 February 1963, **DEBORAH HOLBROOK**, who was
born at Worcester, Massachusetts 8 February 1938, daughter of Luther
Gardner and Ruth (Price) Holbrook, from whom he was divorced 22
December 1976; and, second, at Greenwich, Connecticut 31 August
1983, **ELIZABETH GOLTRA**, who was born at St. Louis, Missouri 26
August 1945, daughter of Edward Field and Elizabeth (Hoff) Goltra.[2005]

John Winthrop graduated from St. Mark's School, Southborough,
Massachusetts; Harvard College (1958);[2006] and Columbia University
(1962). Deborah Holbrook was educated at Abbot Academy, Andover,
Massachusetts, and Wheaton College (1960). A tree farmer, businessman,
and trustee based in Charleston, South Carolina, John Winthrop has
served on more than fifteen for-profit and non-profit boards, among
them the Fresh Air Fund, the National Audubon Society, and the
American Farmland Trust. He received an honorable discharge from
the U.S. Navy and reached the level of Knight of Grace through the
Order of St John of Jerusalem with the blessing of Queen Elizabeth II.
In 2000, the Governor of South Carolina awarded him the Order of the
Palmetto, the state's highest honor.

John also noted: "Gren established two successful tree service
companies in South Carolina. In addition to having a growing list
of satisfied customers, he also is known for his work in real estate
renovation, gutter installation, and wine importing. He has been an

---

[2004] *Social Register 1992* (1991), Births, 6; Steward and Child, *The Descendants of Judge John
Lowell of Newburyport, Massachusetts*, 232; "Georgina Winthrop, Robert Stevenson,"
The New York Times, 18 September 2016, Sunday Styles, 26.

[2005] "Descendants of Cornelia P. Van Rensselaer Thayer and Nathaniel Thayer,"
Charts 3-C-I and 3-C-1-a; *Harvard Class of 1958 Twenty-fifth Anniversary Report*
(Cambridge, Mass.: Printed for the Class, 1983), 923; *Harvard Class of 1958 Thirty-
fifth Anniversary Report* (Cambridge, Mass.: Printed for the Class, 1993), 274; notes
by Elizabeth Goltra Winthrop and John Winthrop 2015.

[2006] He was a member of the Porcellian Club with his college class (*Porcellian Club
1791–2016*, 142).

overseer of Groton Plantation as well. His wife, Mary, is both creative and thoughtful.

"Bayard Winthrop grew up in Connecticut and began his career in investment banking with Donaldson Lufkin Jenrette in New York City, which he left to pursue a career as an entrepreneur. He resides in San Francisco, California, with his wife, the former Alice Roche, and their three children.

"Teddy's creative ability was established in boarding school, where he received recognition. Moving to California, he created his own company to manufacture and sell the Edward Field wallet for cell phones and credit cards, with a growing list of U.S. and international customers."[2007]

Children of John[11] and Deborah (Holbrook) Winthrop, first two born at New York, New York:[2008]

116   i.   JOHN[12] WINTHROP, JR., b. 27 June 1964; m. 10 Sept. 1994, LOUISA LEWIS DALEY.

117   ii.   HENRY GRENVILLE WINTHROP, b. 5 March 1966; m. 16 May 2007, MARY ANNE (TETANICH) HUTSON.

       iii.   BAYARD WINTHROP, b. at Greenwich 19 April 1969. He m. ALICE ROCHE and has issue (Agnes Roche[13] Winthrop, Kevin Luther Winthrop, and Rose Holbrook Winthrop).

           Bayard Winthrop graduated from Deerfield Academy, Deerfield, Mass., and the University of Vermont (1991); he is the founder and president of American Giant, a San Francisco apparel maker.

Child of John[11] and Elizabeth (Goltra) Winthrop:[2009]

       iv.   EDWARD FIELD[12] WINTHROP, b. at New York 28 June 1986; he graduated from the Salisbury School, Salisbury, Conn., and the College of Charleston (2009).

58. **BEEKMAN**[11] **WINTHROP** (*Nathaniel Thayer*[10], *Frederic*[9], *Robert*[8], *Thomas Charles*[7], *Francis Bayard*[6], *John Still*[5], *John*[4], *Waitstill*[3], *John*[2-1]) was born at Boston, Massachusetts 6 April 1941 and died at Washington, D.C. 6 May 2014. He married at New York, New York 27 August 1969, **PHOEBE JANE WOOD**, who was born at Lafayette, Indiana 30 June 1941.[2010]

[2007] Notes by John Winthrop 2016.

[2008] "Descendants of Cornelia P. Van Rensselaer Thayer and Nathaniel Thayer," Chart 3-C-I-a; *The New York Times*, 11 September 1994, 68; notes by Bayard Winthrop 2013; questionnaire from John Winthrop, Jr., 2013; notes by John Winthrop, Jr., 2015.

[2009] *Harvard Class of 1958 Thirty-fifth Anniversary Report* (1993), 274; notes by Edward Field Winthrop 2013; questionnaire from John Winthrop, Jr., 2013.

[2010] "Descendants of Cornelia P. Van Rensselaer Thayer and Nathaniel Thayer," Chart 3-C-I; *The Washington Post*, 21 May 2014.

Beekman Winthrop was educated at the Hill School, Pottstown, Pennsylvania; Institut Le Rosey, Gstaad, Switzerland; and Columbia University (1963 and 1965): "After a brief enrollment in the Harvard Divinity School, he left to pursue writing, inspired by the work of Robert Coles on race relations in the south. In 1971, he won the Robert F. Kennedy Journalism Award for Outstanding Coverage of the Problems of Poverty and Discrimination for a *New South* magazine article on intestinal parasites in poor black children on the developing resort island of Hilton Head."

> In 1972, concerned community members brought to his attention the murder of an 18-year-old black youth in a town near his family's South Carolina property. Beekman's persistence and partnership with the press to expose the injustice ultimately led to the indictment of two white men. His involvement was later highly fictionalized in a reporter's book and movie. Beekman went on to form a small investment advisory firm where he worked as a manager and trustee until his retirement, after which he continued work as a private investor.[2011]

Child of Beekman[11] and Phoebe Jane (Wood) Winthrop:

118   i.   DUDLEY[12] WINTHROP, b. 18 Feb. 1972; m. in Oct. 2005, JENNIFER LOUISE SNEE.

59. SERITA[11] WINTHROP (*Nathaniel Thayer*[10], *Frederic*[9], *Robert*[8], *Thomas Charles*[7], *Francis Bayard*[6], *John Still*[5], *John*[4], *Waitstill*[3], *John*[2-1]) was born at Boston, Massachusetts 22 December 1943. She married, first, at Christ Church Chapel, Hamilton, Massachusetts 10 September 1966, ROGER MARTIN BARZUN, who was born at Boston 11 November 1941, son of Jacques Martin and Mariana (Lowell) Barzun, from whom she was divorced 10 March 1983;[2012] second, at New York, New York 22 August 1996, JONATHAN JAMES GRAHAM ALEXANDER, who was born Jonathan James Graham Brown at London, England 20 August 1935, son of Arthur Ronald Brown and Frederica Emma (Graham) (Brown) Alexander, from whom she was divorced in 2001; and, third, at New York 28 June 2006, THOMAS McCANCE, JR., who was born 16 November 1933, son

---

[2011] Death notice for Beekman Winthrop, *The New York Times*, 18 May 2014.
[2012] *Harvard and Radcliffe College Class of 1963 Thirtieth Anniversary Report* (Cambridge, Mass.: Printed for the Class, 1993), 16.

of Thomas and Elizabeth Day (Ferguson) McCance,[2013] from whom she was divorced.[2014]

Serita Winthrop graduated from Chatham Hall, Chatham, Virginia; Briarcliff Junior College (1963); Columbia University (1966); and Simmons College (1990). Roger Martin Barzun was educated at Phillips Academy, Andover, Massachusetts; Harvard College (1963); and Columbia (1967). Dr. Jonathan James Graham Alexander graduated from Magdalen College, Oxford University (1960, 1963, and 1964); in 2016, he was the Sherman Fairchild Professor Emeritus at New York University's Institute of Fine Arts. Thomas McCance, Jr., was educated at the Brooks School, North Andover; Yale College (1955); and Columbia University (1958).

Children of Roger Martin and Serita[11] (Winthrop) Barzun, first two born at New York, last two born at Boston:[2015]

119   i.   Mariana Lowell[12] Barzun, b. 5 March 1969; m. 1 May 1999, Jonathan Lee Mensch.

120   ii. Matthew Winthrop Barzun, b. 23 Oct. 1970; m. 18 Sept. 1999, Brooke Lee Brown.

121 iii. Lucretia Mott Barzun, b. 14 May 1973; m. 30 Sept. 2006, Robert Donnelly.

122 iv. Charles Lowell Barzun, b. 19 March 1975; m. 14 July 2012, Emily Bradford Little.

60. **Nathaniel Thayer[11] Winthrop, Jr.** (*Nathaniel Thayer[10], Frederic[9], Robert[8], Thomas Charles[7], Francis Bayard[6], John Still[5], John[4], Waitstill[3], John[2-1]*) was born at New York, New York 30 November 1951. He married

---

[2013] "Miss Francine Jaques is Married Here," *The New York Times*, 25 January 1959, 82; "Thomas McCance Dead; Partner in Brown Brothers Harriman Co.," *The New York Times*, 30 March 1979, 22.

[2014] "Bay State Nuptials for Serita Winthrop," *The New York Times*, 11 September 1966, 93; "Descendants of Cornelia P. Van Rensselaer Thayer and Nathaniel Thayer," Chart 3-C-I-b; *Harvard and Radcliffe Class of 1963 Twenty-fifth Anniversary Report* (Cambridge, Mass.: Printed for the Class, 1988), 69; *Summer Social Register 1997 Dilatory Domiciles May 1997*, 78; *The International Who's Who* (Abingdon-on-Thames, Oxfordshire: Routledge, 2004), 29; *Social Register 2008* (2007), 886; Steward and Child, *The Descendants of Judge John Lowell of Newburyport, Massachusetts*, 94–95, 184; questionnaire from Serita Winthrop 2013.

[2015] "Descendants of Cornelia P. Van Rensselaer Thayer and Nathaniel Thayer," Chart 3-C-I-b; *The New York Times*, 2 May 1999, ST9; *Summer Social Register 2000 Dilatory Domiciles May 2000*, 6; Steward and Child, *The Descendants of Judge John Lowell of Newburyport, Massachusetts*, 184; questionnaires from Charles Lowell Barzun, Mariana Barzun Mensch, and Serita Winthrop 2013.

at Randolph Center, Vermont 17 June 1974, **MARTHA DUNN**, who was born at Brockton, Massachusetts 1 December 1951, daughter of Edward Joseph and Jeannette (Belanger) Dunn.[2016]

Nathaniel Thayer Winthrop graduated from Harvard College (1974) and Goddard College (1977). An independent filmmaker, he wrote, "I studied documentary film-making at MIT and Goddard College under the late Ricky Leacock and Ed Pincus in the 1970s. I have coproduced two documentaries, *Rookies at the Road* [2004] and *Act of Faith: The Making of Disappearances* [2006], which aired on Vermont Public Television.

"For the past seven years [2007–14], I have been executive producer of *Freedom and Unity: The Vermont Movie*, a collaborative, six-part historical and cultural documentary all about my home state. It premiered in September 2013."[2017]

Children of Nathaniel Thayer[11] and Martha (Dunn) Winthrop, last two born at Duxbury, Vermont:[2018]

123   i.   ELIAS DUNN[12] WINTHROP, b. at Randolph 12 Aug. 1975.
124   ii.   EMMA O'MEARA WINTHROP, b. 12 May 1978; m. 28 Aug. 2004, PETTER MORITZ BAY-HANSEN.
125   iii. DANIEL WINTHROP, b. 3 May 1980; m. 15 Feb. 2014, MICHELE LYNN CRONAN.

61. **THOMAS**[11] **McKEAN** (*Katharine*[10] *Winthrop, Frederic*[9], *Robert*[8], *Thomas Charles*[7], *Francis Bayard*[6], *John Still*[5], *John*[4], *Waitstill*[3], *John*[2-1]) was born at Beverly, Massachusetts 10 August 1949. He married at the Church of the Redeemer, Chestnut Hill (Newton), Massachusetts 22 March 1980, **SYLVIA CHENEY WYMAN**, who was born at Boston, Massachusetts 27 November 1950, daughter of Franklin and Ruth (Cheney) Wyman.[2019]

[2016] Vermont Department of Health Copy of Certificate of Marriage 01869; "Descendants of Cornelia P. Van Rensselaer Thayer and Nathaniel Thayer," Chart 3-C-I; *Harvard and Radcliffe Class of 1974 Thirtieth Anniversary Report* (Cambridge, Mass.: Printed for the Class, 2004), 344; notes by Martha Dunn Winthrop 2013 and 2015.

[2017] *Harvard and Radcliffe Class of 1974 Fortieth Anniversary Report* (Cambridge, Mass.: Printed for the Class, 2014), 459. See Nat Winthrop's entry at The Internet Movie Database (IMDb): http://www.imdb.com/name/nm2008302/?ref_=tt_ov_dr.

[2018] Vermont Birth Records, 1909–2008; *Harvard and Radcliffe Class of 1974 Thirtieth Anniversary Report*, 344; notes by Daniel Winthrop 2013; notes by Martha Dunn Winthrop 2015.

[2019] *Harvard Class of 1913 Fiftieth Anniversary Report* (Cambridge, Mass.: Printed at the University, 1963), 424; *The New York Times*, 23 March 1980, 58; "Descendants of

Thomas McKean graduated from St. Mark's School, Southborough, Massachusetts; Harvard College (1972); and American University (1975). Dr. Sylvia Cheney Wyman was educated at the Winsor School, Boston; Yale College (1972); and Dartmouth College (1977). In 1997, Thomas McKean wrote, "To reflect on the past twenty-five years adequately requires more ability or time than I have, but here goes. Most importantly, I married my date to the Harvard–Yale game of 1968, although not until 1980, and we have three sons, Adam, Matt, and Ben.... Career involves being an attorney with an office in Boston, which is shared with my brother, John.... I remain active in local Democratic politics and various educational institutions, most particularly Fay School where I have been a trustee for over fifteen years."[2020]

Children of Thomas[11] and Sylvia Cheney (Wyman) McKean, born at Boston:[2021]

    i. ADAM SHAW[12] McKEAN, b. 22 Sept. 1981; he graduated from Phillips Exeter Academy, Exeter, N.H.; Georgetown University (2004); and Columbia University (2011).

    ii. MATTHEW THORNTON McKEAN, b. 7 June 1983; he graduated from St. Paul's School, Concord, N.H.; Georgetown (2005); and Columbia (2012).

    iii. BENJAMIN PIERCE McKEAN, b. 7 Feb. 1986; he graduated from St. Mark's and Georgetown (2008).

62. **ROBERT WINTHROP**[11] **McKEAN** (*Katharine*[10] *Winthrop, Frederic*[9], *Robert*[8], *Thomas Charles*[7], *Francis Bayard*[6], *John Still*[5], *John*[4], *Waitstill*[3], *John*[2-1]) was born at Beverly, Massachusetts 2 November 1951. He married at Honolulu, Hawaii 6 May 1995, **SANDRA NAOMI (KANENAKA) RAINS**, who was born at Honolulu 9 November 1959, daughter of Edwin N. and Janet F. Kanenaka.[2022]

Cornelia P. Van Rensselaer Thayer and Nathaniel Thayer," Chart 3-C-I; questionnaire from Thomas McKean 2014.

[2020] *Harvard and Radcliffe Class of 1972 Twenty-fifth Anniversary Report* (Cambridge, Mass.: Printed for the Class, 1997), 708.

[2021] *Harvard and Radcliffe Class of 1972 Twenty-fifth Anniversary Report*, 708; questionnaires from Benjamin Pierce McKean, Matthew Thornton McKean, and Thomas McKean 2014.

[2022] "Descendants of Cornelia P. Van Rensselaer Thayer and Nathaniel Thayer," Chart 3-C-I; Winthrop, *Descendants of Robert Winthrop & Kate Wilson Taylor, 1833–2000*, 16; questionnaire from Robert Winthrop McKean 2013.

Robert Winthrop McKean graduated from the Brooks School, North Andover, Massachusetts; the Rhode Island School of Design (1975); and the University of California, Los Angeles (1985). Sandra Naomi Kanenaka was educated at UCLA (1981) and the University of Southern California (1985).

Children of Robert Winthrop[11] and Sandra Naomi (Kanenaka) (Rains) McKean, born at Boston, Massachusetts:[2023]

    i.   ROBERT WINTHROP[12] MCKEAN, JR., b. 9 Oct. 1996; he was educated at Concord Academy in Concord, Mass.

    ii. SARAH NAOMI MCKEAN, b. 12 Jan. 1999; she was educated at St. Paul's School in Concord, N.H.

    iii. JOHN PRATT MCKEAN, b. 23 Aug. 2000.

63. **DAVID**[11] **MCKEAN** (*Katharine*[10] *Winthrop, Frederic*[9]*, Robert*[8]*, Thomas Charles*[7]*, Francis Bayard*[6]*, John Still*[5]*, John*[4]*, Waitstill*[3]*, John*[2-1]) was born at Beverly, Massachusetts 20 September 1956. He married at St. Paul's Chapel, Cambridge, Massachusetts 15 October 1988, **KATHLEEN MARY KAYE**, who was born 29 May 1953, daughter of Charles Forbes and Donna Mary (Kallin) Kaye.[2024]

David McKean graduated from Phillips Exeter Academy, Exeter, New Hampshire; Harvard College (1980); Duke University (1986); and Tufts University (1986). Kathleen Mary Kaye was educated at Boston College and the University of Pennsylvania. After graduating from Harvard, David McKean worked on a farm, for an economic development agency, and then at a boarding school in Swaziland: "My nine months at the Waterford Kamhlaba School. . . , located on a hilltop in Mbabane, were among the most interesting in my life. Swaziland borders South Africa, and I lived there during the height of apartheid's ugliness. Many of the students at Waterford had parents and older brothers and sisters involved in the struggle in their country. As a result, the school had a political conscience and a vibrancy that was immensely stimulating."

After receiving a law degree from Duke and a master's degree in international relations from Tufts, McKean worked for his kinsman John Kerry, then a freshman Senator from Massachusetts, "mostly on foreign

---

[2023] *Social Register 1998* (1997), 472; *Summer Social Register 2000 Dilatory Domiciles May 2000*, 52; Winthrop, *Descendants of Robert Winthrop & Kate Wilson Taylor, 1833–2000*, 28; questionnaire from Robert Winthrop McKean 2013.

[2024] *Minnesota, Birth Index, 1900–1934* [database on-line]; "Descendants of Cornelia P. Van Rensselaer Thayer and Nathaniel Thayer," Chart 3-C-I; *The New York Times*, 16 October 1988, 52.

policy and banking issues. The highlight of my time in the Senate came when I served as chief investigator into the scandal surrounding the Bank of Credit and Commerce International, a Byzantine and fascinating case involving Arab sheiks, corrupt bankers, drug lords, and the CIA."

In 1994, after leaving Kerry's office to write a book, McKean became chief of staff for Congressman Joseph P. Kennedy. He had short stints in the Clinton administration, on the 1996 campaign finance investigation, and then the permanent subcommittee on investigations. Then, he wrote, "In 1999, Senator Kerry asked me to come back to his office and to be his chief-of-staff, and I have been in that position for the last five years [1999–2004]. Early in the Bush presidency, it became evident that the president was taking the country in the wrong direction; I joined with others in encouraging Senator Kerry to become a candidate for president in 2004 and in helping to lay the groundwork for his candidacy."[2025]

After leaving Senator Kerry's office in 2008 to become Staff Director for the Senate Foreign Relations Committee, McKean served as CEO of the John F. Kennedy Library Foundation in Boston.[2026] In 2011, he was a Public Policy Scholar at the Woodrow Wilson International Center for Scholars; the following year he joined the State Department as a senior advisor to then Secretary of State Hillary R. Clinton. After a stint as Director of Policy Planning, he was named U.S. Ambassador to Luxembourg; he was sworn in in March 2016,[2027] joining his cousin Matthew Winthrop[12] Barzun as an American envoy until January 2017.

Children of David[11] and Kathleen Mary (Kaye) McKean:[2028]

    i.   SHAW FORBES[12] MCKEAN, b. 28 Sept. 1989; he graduated from the Sidwell Friends School, Washington, D.C., and Harvard (2013).

    ii. CHRISTIAN KALLIN MCKEAN, b. 25 Feb. 1991; he graduated from Sidwell Friends and Boston College (2014).

    iii. KAYE THAYER MCKEAN, b. in 1994; she was educated at Sidwell Friends and Boston College.

[2025] *Harvard and Radcliffe Class of 1979 Twenty-fifth Anniversary Report* (Cambridge, Mass.: Printed for the Class, 2004), 806–7.

[2026] http://www.jfklibrary.org/About-Us/News-and-Press/Press-Releases/David-McKean-Named-CEO-of-JFK-Library-Foundation.aspx.

[2027] http://www.state.gov/r/pa/ei/biog/191760.htm.

[2028] *Social Register 1992* (1991), Births, 3; *Harvard and Radcliffe Class of 1979 Twenty-fifth Anniversary Report* (Cambridge, Mass.: Printed for the Class, 2004), 807; Winthrop, *Descendants of Robert Winthrop & Kate Wilson Taylor, 1833–2000*, 28.

64. **HENRIETTE ALBERTINE**[11] **VAN ROIJEN** (*Jan Herman*[10] *van Roijen, Albertina Taylor*[9] *Winthrop, Robert*[8], *Thomas Charles*[7], *Francis Bayard*[6], *John Still*[5], *John*[4], *Waitstill*[3], *John*[2-1]) was born at The Hague (South Holland), the Netherlands 5 December 1935 and died at Wassenaar (South Holland) 25 March 2015. She married at The Hague 11 July 1959, **MARINUS MICHIEL VAN NOTTEN**, who was born at Zeist (Utrecht), the Netherlands 8 December 1933 and died at Nîmes (Languedoc), France 5 June 2002, son of Willem Ferdinand Jacob van Notten and Barones Cornelie Jeanne van Tuyll van Serooskerken, from whom she was divorced.[2029]

Tina van Roijen was educated at St. Timothy's School, Stevenson, Maryland; Bryn Mawr College (1957x); and the University of Utrecht. Michael van Notten graduated from the Vosius Gymnasium, Amsterdam (North Holland), and the University of Leiden (1958); he founded the Institutum Europaeum, a libertarian policy research center, and wrote *The Law of the Somalis: A Stable Foundation for Economic Development in the Horn of Africa*.[2030]

Children of Marinus Michiel and Henriette Albertine[11] (van Roijen) van Notten:[2031]

126   i.   ANNE MARINA[12] VAN NOTTEN, b. at Rotterdam (South Holland) 2 Aug. 1960; m. 31 Dec. 1987, JOHANNES PAULUS ALOYSIUS MARIE PETIT.

127   ii. HENRIETTE DIGNA ALBERTINA WINTHROP VAN NOTTEN, twin, b. at New York, N.Y. 10 Aug. 1962; m. 23 Sept. 1992, REINDERT CARL FRANS EDUARD HOUBEN.

128   iii. ARIANE SIGRID VAN NOTTEN, twin, b. at New York 10 Aug. 1962; m. 7 Sept. 1996, FREDERIK HAROLD FENTENER VAN VLISSINGEN.

129   iv. ISABELLE FERNANDE VAN NOTTEN, b. at Ixelles (Brussels), Belgium 28 June 1964; m. 5 Feb. 1992, DAVID MICHAEL ROSENBERG.

[2029] Taylor, *The Lion and the Hare*, Chart H; "Law Student Fiance of Miss van Roijen," *The New York Times*, 6 July 1958, 54; *Washington Social Register 1960* (1959), 147; notes by Henriette Digna van Notten 2013; questionnaire from Henriette Albertina van Roÿen van Notten 2013; notes by Jonathan Winthrop 2017; http://heirsofeurope.blogspot.com/2010/12/fentener-van-vlissingen.html.

[2030] https://en.wikipedia.org/wiki/Michael_van_Notten.

[2031] Winthrop, *Descendants of Robert Winthrop & Kate Wilson Taylor, 1833–2000*, 29; questionnaire from Henriette Albertina van Roÿen van Notten 2013; http://heirsofeurope.blogspot.com/2010/12/fentener-van-vlissingen.html; http://gw.geneanet.org/kooler?lang=en;pz=louise+elisabeth;nz=koole;ocz=1;alwsurn=yes;p=henriette+albertina;n=van+royen.

65. **Jan Herman Robert Dudley**[11] **van Roijen** (*Jan Herman*[10] *van Roijen, Albertina Taylor*[9] *Winthrop, Robert*[8], *Thomas Charles*[7], *Francis Bayard*[6], *John Still*[5], *John*[4], *Waitstill*[3], *John*[2-1]) was born at Tokyo, Japan 17 December 1936. He married at Rotterdam (South Holland), the Netherlands 14 Devember 1963, **Jonkvrouwe Carolina Helena Wilhelmina Reuchlin**, who was born at Utrecht, the Netherlands 30 January 1941, daughter of Jonkheer Henri Reuchlin and Johanna Helena Jacoba Lichtenbelt.[2032]

Jan Herman Robert Dudley van Roijen graduated from the Groton School, Groton, Massachusetts, and the University of Utrecht (1960).

Children of Jan Herbert Robert Dudley[11] van Roijen and Jonkvrouwe Carolina Helena Wilhelmina Reuchlin:[2033]

130   i.   Jan Herman[12] van Roijen, b. at The Hague (South Holland) 27 Dec. 1964; m. 5/13 July 1996, Sophie Charlotte Egbertine van der Kuip.

131   ii.   Anne van Roijen, b. at Jakarta, Indonesia 7 May 1966; partner Jan Pieter de Kok.

132   iii.   Theodora Helena Wilhelmina van Roijen, b. at Ukkel (Brussels), Belgium 16 Oct. 1968; m. 15 May 1999, Frank van den Merkenhof.

66. **Digna Anne**[11] **van Roijen** (*Jan Herman*[10] *van Roijen, Albertina Taylor*[9] *Winthrop, Robert*[8], *Thomas Charles*[7], *Francis Bayard*[6], *John Still*[5], *John*[4], *Waitstill*[3], *John*[2-1]) was born at Tokyo, Japan 24 February 1939. She married at The Hague (South Holland), the Netherlands 13 March 1965, **Jonkheer Jan Derck Cornelis van Karnebeek**, who was born at Jakarta, Indonesia 12 February 1939, son of Jonkheer Herman Adriaan van Karnebeek and Jonkvrouwe Adriana Johanna Thelma Pauw van Wieldrecht.[2034]

Digna Anne van Roijen graduated from Milton Academy, Milton, Massachusetts, and the University of Utrecht (1964). Jonkheer Jan Derck Cornelis van Karnebeek was also educated at the University of Utrecht (1963).

[2032] Taylor, *The Lion and the Hare*, Chart H; questionnaires from Digna Anne van Roÿen van Karnebeek 2013 and Carolina Reuchlin van Roijen 2014.

[2033] http://www.lichtenbelt.com/genealogie/lichtparenteel/tekst.htm; questionnaires from Carolina Reuchlin van Roijen and Sophie van der Kuip van Roijen 2014; notes by Anne van Roijen and Jan Pieter de Kok 2014.

[2034] Questionnaire from Digna Anne van Roÿen van Karnebeek 2013; http://www.kloek-genealogie.nl/Block3.htm.

Children of Jonkheer Jan Derck Cornelis van Karnebeek and Digna Anne[11] van Roijen:[2035]

133   i.   JONKHEER JAN DERCK[12] VAN KARNEBEEK, b. at The Hague 12 April 1967; m. 13 Dec. 1998, JACQUELINE THŸSSEN.

134   ii.   JONKVROUWE EMILIE THELMA VAN KARNEBEEK, b. at Rheden (Gelderland), the Netherlands 7 March 1969; m. 27 June 1998, JEROEN HENK LEONARD PIT.

135   iii.   JONKVROUWE CLARA DIGNA MALOUT VAN KARNEBEEK, b. at Zwolle (Overijssel), the Netherlands 26 Sept. 1972; m. 31 Dec. 2003, RODERICK FRANCIS ARTHUR HOUBEN.

67. **WILLEM JORIS WINTHROP JOHN**[11] **VAN ROIJEN** (*Jan Herman*[10] *van Roijen, Albertina Taylor*[9] *Winthrop, Robert*[8], *Thomas Charles*[7], *Francis Bayard*[6], *John Still*[5], *John*[4], *Waitstill*[3], *John*[2-1]) was born at The Hague (South Holland), the Netherlands 21 April 1945. He married at Rotterdam (South Holland) 10 November 1973, **JONKVROUWE EMILIE SOLANGE VAN NISPEN**, who was born at Middelburg (Zeeland), the Netherlands 26 April 1946, formerly wife of Hartog Swelheim, and daughter of Jonkheer Gneomar Adalbert Alfred van Nispen and Jonkvrouwe Geertruida Hermanna Elisabeth Laman Trip.[2036]

Willem Joris Winthrop John van Roijen graduated from the Groton School, Groton, Massachusetts, and the University of Utrecht (1966).

Children of Willem Joris Winthrop John[11] van Roijen and Jonkvrouwe Emilie Solange van Nispen, born at The Hague:[2037]

136   i.   JORIS WILLEM PETER[12] VAN ROIJEN, b. 10 June 1975; m. 28 Aug. 2005, MARIE-ANNE ODINK.

137   ii.   ROBERT DUDLEY VAN ROIJEN, b. 17 Sept. 1977; m. 31 Jan. 2009, EMILIE PLOEG.

[2035] Questionnaires from Digna Anne van Roÿen van Karnebeek 2013 and Emilie van Karnebeek Pit 2014; http://www.kloek-genealogie.nl/Block3.htm.

[2036] Winthrop, *Descendants of Robert Winthrop & Kate Wilson Taylor, 1833–2000*, 17; questionnaire from Willem Joris Winthrop John van Roijen 2013; notes by Willem Joris Winthrop John van Roijen 2014; http://gw.geneanet.org/kooler?lang=en&alwsurn=yes&m=D&p=willem&n=van+weede&oc=1&t=L&sosab=10&v=12.

[2037] Winthrop, *Descendants of Robert Winthrop & Kate Wilson Taylor, 1833–2000*, 29; notes by Joris Willem Peter van Roijen and Robert Dudley van Roijen 2013; questionnaires from Willem Joris Winthrop John van Roijen 2013 and Joris Willem Peter van Roijen 2015.

68. **Robert Dudley**[11] **van Roijen** (*Robert Dudley*[10] *van Roijen, Albertina Taylor*[9] *Winthrop, Robert*[8], *Thomas Charles*[7], *Francis Bayard*[6], *John Still*[5], *John*[4], *Waitstill*[3], *John*[2-1]) was born at New York, New York 25 July 1939. He married at 3033 N Street, Washington, D.C. 31 January 1981,[2038] **Susan Emily Frelinghuysen**, who was born at Fayetteville, North Carolina 15 October 1944, daughter of Joseph Sherman and Emily (Lawrance) Frelinghuysen.[2039]

Robert Dudley van Roijen, Jr., graduated from St. Paul's School, Concord, New Hampshire, and Harvard College (1961). Susan Emily Frelinghuysen was educated at the Masters School, Dobbs Ferry, New York, and Bennett College (1964); her grandfather, also Joseph Sherman Frelinghuysen, served as a Senator from New Jersey between the terms of John Kean and Hamilton Fish Kean. In 2011, Robert Dudley van Roijen reflected on his life since Harvard: "At college, I looked forward to a career in teaching. I ended up having a much more exciting and diversified life, first, as an officer in the marine corps in the Far East, followed by nine years with IBM as a computer salesman and then as a lobbyist. Tiring of the bureaucracy of a big company, I turned into a venture capitalist and then became the CEO of one of my investments, a laser manufacturing company. For the last twenty years I have been a money manager, a profession I plan to continue for the foreseeable future."[2040]

Children of Robert Dudley[11] and Susan Emily (Frelinghuysen) van Roijen, born at Orlando, Florida:[2041]

    i. **Victoria Frelinghuysen**[12] **van Roijen**, b. 19 Sept. 1981; she graduated from St. Paul's and Brown University (2004).

    ii. **Valaer Montrose van Roijen**, b. 23 April 1983; she graduated from St. Paul's, Dartmouth College (2005), and Bard Graduate Center (2010).

[2038] "Susan E. Frelinghuysen Married in Capital," *The New York Times*, 1 February 1981.

[2039] *The New York Times*, 1 February 1981, 52; *Social Register 1985* (1984), 934; *Harvard Class of 1961 Twenty-fifth Anniversary Report* (Cambridge, Mass.: Printed for the Class, 1986), 907; questionnaire from Robert Dudley van Roijen 2013.

[2040] *Harvard and Radcliffe Classes of 1961 Fiftieth Anniversary Report* (Cambridge, Mass.: Printed for the Class, 2011), 733–34.

[2041] *Harvard Class of 1961 Twenty-fifth Anniversary Report*, 907; questionnaires from Robert Dudley van Roijen 2013 and Valaer Montrose van Roijen 2014.

69. **PETER PORTNER**[11] **VAN ROIJEN** (*Robert Dudley*[10] *van Roijen, Albertina Taylor*[9] *Winthrop, Robert*[8], *Thomas Charles*[7], *Francis Bayard*[6], *John Still*[5], *John*[4], *Waitstill*[3], *John*[2-1]) was born at New York, New York 26 November 1944. He married at St. Peter's Church, Morristown, New Jersey 27 June 1970,[2042] **BEATRICE STERLING FRELINGHUYSEN**, who was born at Washington, D.C. 1 March 1944, daughter of Peter Hood Ballantine and Beatrice Sterling (Procter) Frelinghuysen.[2043]

Peter Portner van Roijen was educated at St. Paul's School, Concord, New Hampshire; McGill University (1967); and George Washington University. Beatrice Sterling Frelinghuysen graduated from the Westover School, Middlebury, Connecticut; Bradford Junior College (1964); and George Washington (1969).

Children of Peter Portner[11] and Beatrice Sterling (Frelinghuysen) van Roijen:[2044]

    i.   THEODORA ALBERTINA[12] VAN ROIJEN, b. at New York 25 May 1973; she was educated at the Landmark School, Beverly, Mass.; Lesley University (2005); and Cortiva Institute.

    ii. LINDEN FRELINGHUYSEN VAN ROIJEN, twin, b. at Washington, D.C. 10 April 1977; she was educated at the Oldfields School, Glencoe, Md., and Clark University.

    iii. PETER MATTHEW VAN ROIJEN, twin, b. at Washington, D.C. 10 April 1977; he graduated from the Eagle Hill School, Hardwick, Mass., and the University of Denver (2002).

70. **DAVID MONTROSE**[11] **VAN ROIJEN** (*Robert Dudley*[10] *van Roijen, Albertina Taylor*[9] *Winthrop, Robert*[8], *Thomas Charles*[7], *Francis Bayard*[6], *John Still*[5], *John*[4], *Waitstill*[3], *John*[2-1]) was born at Washington, D.C. 17 August 1954. He married at the Unitarian Church, Santa Monica, California 25 July 1981, **MARY AMIE JOHNSON**, who was born at Charlottesville, Virginia 20 June 1955, daughter of Lewis Benjamin and Alice Lewis (Tucker) Johnson.[2045]

[2042] "Peter van Roijen Fiance of Miss Frelinghuysen," *The New York Times*, 21 December 1969, 58; "Peter van Roijen Weds Beatrice Frelinghuysen," *The New York Times*, 28 June 1970, 58.

[2043] *The New York Times*, 4 March 1944, 16; questionnaire from Robert Dudley van Roijen 2013.

[2044] Winthrop, *Descendants of Robert Winthrop & Kate Wilson Taylor, 1833–2000*, 30; questionnaires from Peter Matthew van Roijen and Theodora Albertina van Roijen 2014.

[2045] *California Marriage Index, 1960–1985*; Winthrop, *Descendants of Robert Winthrop &*

Dr. David Montrose van Roijen graduated from the Landon School, Washington, D.C.; the University of Virginia (1976); and Oxford University. M. Amie Johnson was also educated at the University of Virginia.

Children of David Montrose[11] and Mary Amie (Johnson) van Roijen, born at Charlottesville:[2046]

    i. DAVID BEREND[12] VAN ROIJEN, b. 11 Aug. 1984; he graduated from Episcopal High School, Alexandria, Va., and Tulane University (2006 and 2008).

   ii. MELZA RIDING VAN ROIJEN, b. 12 March 1988; she graduated from St. Anne's-Belfield School, Charlottesville; the College of Charleston (2010); and Tulane (2014).

Kate Wilson Taylor, 1833–2000, 17; questionnaire from Robert Dudley van Roijen 2013; questionnaires from David Montrose van Roijen 2013 and 2014.

[2046] Winthrop, *Descendants of Robert Winthrop & Kate Wilson Taylor, 1833–2000,* 30; questionnaires from David Montrose van Roijen 2013 and 2014; questionnaire from Melza Riding van Roijen 2014.

The Twelfth Generation

71. **Jeffrey Birt**[12] **Morse** (*Thomas Spurr*[11] *Morse, Kate*[10] *Winthrop, Grenville Lindall*[9], *Robert*[8], *Thomas Charles*[7], *Francis Bayard*[6], *John Still*[5], *John*[4], *Waitstill*[3], *John*[2-1]) was born at New York, New York 13 March 1950. He married, first, at "Green Meads Farm," Richmond, Massachusetts 27 July 1974, **Carol Lynn Gingles,** who was born at Nashville, Tennessee 3 May 1950, daughter of Pat Morris and Linda Sue (Jones) Gingles; and, second, at South Dartmouth, Massachusetts 29 September 2009,[2047] **Jennifer (Bruggeman) Hamilton,** who was born at Pittsfield, Massachusetts 24 September 1961, daughter of Gunther Carl and Elizabeth Binless (Aitchison) Bruggeman.[2048]

Jeffrey Birt Morse graduated from Deerfield Academy, Deerfield, Massachusetts, and Washington University (1972). Jennifer Bruggeman was educated at Taconic High School, Pittsfield, and Smith College (1998).

Children of Jeffrey Birt[12] and Carol Lynn (Gingles) Morse, born at Richmond:[2049]

138   i.   Joshua Elias[13] Morse, b. 29 Nov. 1978.
       ii. Jason Cooper Morse, b. 9 Aug. 1983.

72. **Kate Winthrop**[12] **Morse** (*Thomas Spurr*[11] *Morse, Kate*[10] *Winthrop, Grenville Lindall*[9], *Robert*[8], *Thomas Charles*[7], *Francis Bayard*[6], *John Still*[5], *John*[4], *Waitstill*[3], *John*[2-1]) was born at New York, New York 18 September 1951. She married, first, at Columbus, Ohio 13 March 1982, **John**

[2047] Winthrop, *Descendants of Robert Winthrop & Kate Wilson Taylor, 1833–2000,* 31; http://www.imesmiller.com/obituaries/pat-gingles; notes by Jeffrey Birt Morse and Jennifer Bruggeman Morse 2013; questionnaire from Amy Bradford Morse 2013; notes by Amy Bradford Morse 2014 and Jeffrey Birt Morse 2015.

[2048] Massachusetts Vital Records, 1961, Pittsfield, 171: 188.

[2049] Winthrop, *Descendants of Robert Winthrop & Kate Wilson Taylor, 1833–2000,* 31; http://www.legacy.com/obituaries/tcpalm/obituary.aspx?page=notice&pid=1391 52304#fbLoggedOut; notes by Joshua Elias Morse 2013; notes by Amy Bradford Morse 2014.

DAVID ERWIN, who was born at Steubenville, Ohio 10 September 1949 and died 19 July 2000, from whom she was divorced; and, second, at St. Aidan's Chapel, South Dartmouth, Massachusetts 7 August 1999,[2050] **THOMAS LANDES HORN**, who was born at Philadelphia, Pennsylvania 12 August 1946, son of Robert Chisholm and Dorothy Louise (App) Horn, from whom she was divorced.[2051]

Dr. Kate Winthrop Morse graduated from Concord Academy, Concord, Massachusetts; Vassar College (1973); Boston University; and Ohio State University. John David Erwin was educated at Steubenville High School, Ohio State, and Bowling Green State University. Dr. Thomas Landes Horn graduated from Yale University in 1986.

Children of John David and Kate Winthrop[12] (Morse) Erwin, born at Columbus:[2052]

    i.   CATHRYN BIRT[13] ERWIN, b. 18 Oct. 1983.

    ii. ELLIOT WINTHROP ERWIN, b. 17 April 1988; he graduated from Suffolk University in 2011.

73. **AMY BRADFORD**[12] **MORSE** (*Thomas Spurr*[11] *Morse, Kate*[10] *Winthrop, Grenville Lindall*[9], *Robert*[8], *Thomas Charles*[7], *Francis Bayard*[6], *John Still*[5], *John*[4], *Waitstill*[3], *John*[2-1]) was born at New York, New York 14 May 1953. She married, first, at Gahanna, Ohio 15 January 1977, **PHILLIP ANTHONY HARDING**, who was born at Cleveland, Ohio 9 December 1952 and died at Belmont, Massachusetts 19 August 2003, son of James Gordon and Phyllis Mae (Meyer) Harding, from whom she was divorced in 1998; and, second, at South Dartmouth, Massachusetts 10 September 2011, **LISA MARIE KANE**, who was born at Fitchburg, Massachusetts 11 April 1961, daughter of George Bernard and Constance Ann (Cormier) Kane.[2053]

Amy Bradford Morse graduated from the Columbus School for Girls, Columbus, Ohio; Hamilton College (1975); Boston University

---

[2050] Massachusetts Vital Records, 1999, South Dartmouth, certificate #29201.

[2051] Winthrop, *Descendants of Robert Winthrop & Kate Wilson Taylor, 1833–2000*, 19, 31; Ohio Marriage Index, 1970, 1972–2007; questionnaire from Amy Bradford Morse 2013; notes by Amy Bradford Morse 2014; notes by Kate Winthrop Morse 2016.

[2052] Winthrop, *Descendants of Robert Winthrop & Kate Wilson Taylor, 1833–2000*, 31; notes by Amy Bradford Morse 2014; http://www.legacy.com/obituaries/tcpalm/obituary.aspx?page=notice&pid=139152304#fbLoggedOut.

[2053] Winthrop, *Descendants of Robert Winthrop & Kate Wilson Taylor, 1833–2000*, 19, 31; questionnaire from Amy Bradford Morse 2013; notes by Amy Bradford Morse and Chloe Callan Morse-Harding 2014.

(1984); and Smith College (2013). She is the author of *Cultivating a Math Coaching Practice* (2009). Phillip Anthony Harding was educated at Shaker Heights High School, Shaker Heights, Ohio; Ohio State University (1975x); and the Berklee College of Music. Lisa Marie Kane graduated from Fitchburg High School and the Katharine Gibbs School (1980).

Children of Phillip Anthony Harding and Amy Bradford[12] Morse, born at Boston, Massachusetts:[2054]

    i. CHLOE CALLAN[13] MORSE-HARDING, b. 4 March 1980; she graduated from Belmont High School, Emerson College (2002), Tufts University (2004), and Simmons College (2013).

    ii. LILA ELIZABETH MORSE-HARDING, b. 12 Feb. 1985; she graduated from Belmont High School and Bunker Hill Community College (2013).

74. **PETER DARWIN**[12] **MORSE** (*Thomas Spurr*[11] *Morse, Kate*[10] *Winthrop, Grenville Lindall*[9]*, Robert*[8]*, Thomas Charles*[7]*, Francis Bayard*[6]*, John Still*[5]*, John*[4]*, Waitstill*[3]*, John*[2-1]) was born at Boston, Massachusetts 17 July 1957 and died at Tucson, Arizona 26 June 2012. He married at Columbus, Ohio 15 March 1980, **KAREN MICHELLE FOYCIK**, who was born at Youngstown, Ohio 21 July 1957, daughter of Michael Joseph and Muriel Joy (Henning) Foycik, from whom he was divorced in 2010.[2055]

Peter Darwin Morse was educated at Columbus Academy and Ohio State University. Karen Michelle Foycik graduated from Ursuline High School, Youngstown, and Ohio State (1980).

Children of Peter Darwin[12] and Karen Michelle (Foycik) Morse, ii-iii born at Tucson:[2056]

139   i. LUCAS TYLER[13] MORSE, b. at Columbus 26 Aug. 1980; m. 26 Oct. 2013, AMANDA LOUISE JONES.

[2054] Winthrop, *Descendants of Robert Winthrop & Kate Wilson Taylor, 1833–2000*, 31; notes by Lila Elizabeth Morse-Harding 2013; questionnaire from Amy Bradford Morse 2013.

[2055] Winthrop, *Descendants of Robert Winthrop & Kate Wilson Taylor, 1833–2000*, 19; Ohio Marriage Index, 1970, 1972–2007; notes by Karen Foycik Morse 2013; questionnaires from Amy Bradford Morse 2013 and Lucas Tyler Morse 2014; notes by Amy Bradford Morse 2014.

[2056] Winthrop, *Descendants of Robert Winthrop & Kate Wilson Taylor, 1833–2000*, 31; http://www.legacy.com/obituaries/tcpalm/obituary.aspx?page=notice&pid=139152304#fbLoggedOut; notes by Gabrielle Alexis Morse and Lucas Tyler Morse 2013; notes by Amy Bradford Morse 2014; questionnaire from Lucas Tyler Morse 2014.

140   ii. JAMES THOMAS MORSE, b. 8 Feb. 1987; m. 9 March 2012, AMANDA
            ELIZABETH MOODY.
       iii. GABRIELLE ALEXIS MORSE, b. 22 Aug. 1990; she graduated from
            Sabino High School, Tucson, and Arizona State University (2012).

75. **ROBERT GREGORY HONSHU**[12] **RAYNOLDS** (*Mary Alice*[11] *Kean,
John*[10] *Kean, Katharine Taylor*[9] *Winthrop, Robert*[8], *Thomas Charles*[7], *Francis
Bayard*[6], *John Still*[5], *John*[4], *Waitstill*[3], *John*[2-1]) was born at Tokyo, Japan 27
January 1952. He married at Scottsdale, Arizona 24 June 1980, **MARY
VERA BARTHOLOMAY**, who was born at Chicago, Illinois 10 December
1952, daughter of Herman and Wilma (Swissler) Bartholomay.[2057]

Dr. Robert Gregory Honshu Raynolds graduated from the Putney
School, Putney, Vermont; Dartmouth College (1973 and 1981); and
Stanford University (1976).

Children of Robert Gregory Honshu[12] and Mary Vera (Bartholomay)
Raynolds:[2058]

       i.   WILLIAM FREMONT PETER[13] RAYNOLDS, b. at Lander, Wy. 16 July
            1982.
       ii. ROBERT KEAN LACKMAN RAYNOLDS, b. at Houston, Tex. 16 July
            1984.

76. **MARY LITA**[12] **KEAN** (*John*[11-10] *Kean, Katharine Taylor*[9] *Winthrop,
Robert*[8], *Thomas Charles*[7], *Francis Bayard*[6], *John Still*[5], *John*[4], *Waitstill*[3], *John*[2-1])
was born at Morristown, New Jersey 4 March 1955. She married at St.
Peter's Church, Morristown 15 October 1983, **FREDERICK LEOPOLD
HAACK, 3RD**, who was born at Wassenaar (South Holland), the
Netherlands 29 December 1955, son of Frederick Leopold Haack, Jr.,
and Janneke (Seton-Jansen) (Haack) Neilson.[2059]

Lita Kean graduated from St. Mark's School, Southborough,
Massachusetts, and Lake Forest College (1977). Frederick Leopold
Haack, 3rd, was educated at Avon Old Farms School, Avon, Connecticut,
and Lake Forest (1979).

[2057] Winthrop, *Descendants of Robert Winthrop & Kate Wilson Taylor, 1833–2000*, 32; notes by
        Robert Gregory Honshu Raynolds 2014; http://articles.chicagotribune.com/2006-
        04-13/news/0604130062_1_lake-forest-marshall-field-memorial-service.
[2058] Winthrop, *Descendants of Robert Winthrop & Kate Wilson Taylor, 1833–2000*, 32; notes
        by Robert Gregory Honshu Raynolds 2014.
[2059] *The New York Times*, 12 March 1955, 10; 16 October 1983, 63; *Summer Social Register
        1984 Dilatory Domiciles May 1984*, 15; notes by Lita Kean Haack 2013; question-
        naire from John Kean 2014.

Children of Frederick Leopold and Mary Lita[12] (Kean) Haack:[2060]

  i. ALEXANDRA KEAN[13] HAACK, b. at Morristown 12 July 1986; she graduated from St. Mark's and Hobart-William Smith College (2009).

  ii. BENJAMIN KEAN HAACK, b. at Bangor, Me. 17 July 1988; he graduated from St. George's School, Newport, R.I., and Franklin and Marshall College (2011).

  iii. CHRISTINA KEAN HAACK, b. at Pittsburgh, Pa. 28 Oct. 1990; she graduated from St. George's and the University of New Hampshire (2013).

77. JOHN[12] KEAN, JR. (*John[11-10] Kean, Katharine Taylor[9] Winthrop, Robert[8], Thomas Charles[7], Francis Bayard[6], John Still[5], John[4], Waitstill[3], John[2-1]*) was born at Morristown, New Jersey 22 April 1957. He married at the Church of St. George-by-the-River, Rumson, New Jersey 6 August 1983, **ABIGAIL MARGARET MURPHY**, who was born at Montclair, New Jersey 5 October 1959, daughter of Ray Bradford and Rachel Margaret (Giles) Murphy.[2061]

John Kean, Jr., graduated from St. Mark's School, Southborough, Massachusetts; Lake Forest College (1979); and Harvard University (1994). Abigail Margaret Murphy was educated at the Masters School, Dobbs Ferry, New York; Boston College (1982); and Columbia University (1983).

Children of John[12] and Abigail Margaret (Murphy) Kean, born at Morristown:[2062]

  i. JOHN[13] KEAN, 3RD, b. 26 June 1986; he graduated from the Morristown-Beard School, Morristown; Dickinson College (2008); and Roger Williams University (2015).

  ii. MARGARET EMILY KEAN, b. 18 April 1988; she graduated from Morristown-Beard and Elon University (2010).

  iii. ELIZABETH MURPHY KEAN, b. 3 May 1990; she graduated from Morristown-Beard and Colgate University (2012).

  iv. HENRY LIVINGSTON KEAN, b. 28 Feb. 1992; he graduated from Morristown-Beard and Elon (2014 and 2015).

[2060] Winthrop, *Descendants of Robert Winthrop & Kate Wilson Taylor, 1833–2000*, 33; notes by John Kean 2013; questionnaire from John Kean 2014.

[2061] *The New York Times*, 7 August 1983, 51; questionnaire from John Kean 2014.

[2062] *Social Register 1995* (1994), 407; Winthrop, *Descendants of Robert Winthrop & Kate Wilson Taylor, 1833–2000*, 33; notes by John Kean and John Kean, 3rd, 2013; questionnaire from John Kean 2014.

78. **KATHARINE JESSUP**[12] **KEAN** (*John*[11-10] *Kean, Katharine Taylor*[9] *Winthrop, Robert*[8], *Thomas Charles*[7], *Francis Bayard*[6], *John Still*[5], *John*[4], *Waitstill*[3], *John*[2-1]) was born at Morristown, New Jersey 24 March 1959. She married at Bedminster, New Jersey 7 September 1985, **DAVID WILLIAM CZARNECKI**, who was born at Wilmington, Delaware 29 August 1954, son of William Joseph and Dorothy T. (Williams) Czarnecki.[2063]

Kitty Kean graduated from Choate Rosemary Hall, Wallingford, Connecticut, and Harvard-Radcliffe College (1981). David William Czarnecki was educated at Alexis I. DuPont High School, Wilmington, and Ithaca College (1976). In 1996, Kitty Kean Czarnecki wrote: "After spending all of my life gearing up for a career in theater, it was a shock to my system when I realized that part of my life was over. Waiting around for countless hours to meet people who had no interest in hiring me in the first place . . . just wasn't very fulfilling. Despite this revelation, I did have the most exciting experience in 1992 when my husband, David, and I were invited to the White House to sing for President Bush at an intimate state dinner with notables Secretary [of State James Addison] Baker and [General] Colin Powell. . . . I continue to sing with a Big Band and returned to the theatrical stage this year for the first time in ten years to play the leading role in *Evita*."[2064]

Children of David William and Katharine Jessup[12] (Kean) Czarnecki:[2065]

  i.   SARAH ELIZABETH[13] CZARNECKI, b. at Allentown, Pa. 29 June 1989; she graduated from Oak Ridge High School, Oak Ridge, Tenn., and the University of California, San Diego (2011).

  ii. JOHANNA ERICKSON CZARNECKI, b. at Bethlehem, Pa. 26 Aug. 1992; she graduated from Oak Ridge High School and Loyola Marymount University (2015).

  iii. ISABEL WILLIAMS CZARNECKI, b. at Bethlehem 30 March 1994; she was educated at Oak Ridge High School and the University of California, Santa Barbara.

[2063] "Kitty Kean Becomes a Bride," *The New York Times*, 8 September 1985, 73; *Social Register 1986* (1985), 458; questionnaire from John Kean 2014.

[2064] *Harvard and Radcliffe College Class of 1981 Fifteenth Anniversary Report* (Cambridge, Mass.: Printed for the Class, 1996), 148.

[2065] Winthrop, *Descendants of Robert Winthrop & Kate Wilson Taylor, 1833–2000*, 33; notes by Johanna Erickson Czarnecki 2013; questionnaire from John Kean 2014.

79. **Susan Livingston**[12] **Kean** (*John*[11-10] *Kean, Katharine Taylor*[9] *Winthrop, Robert*[8], *Thomas Charles*[7], *Francis Bayard*[6], *John Still*[5], *John*[4], *Waitstill*[3], *John*[2-1]) was born at Morristown, New Jersey 29 October 1964. She married at Union, New Jersey 15 May 1993, **Dino Guido Cattaneo**, who was born at Torino (Piedmont), Italy 10 October 1965, son of Franco and Carla (Ucelli) Cattaneo.[2066]

Susan Livingston Kean graduated from Miss Porter's School, Farmington, Connecticut; Pomona College (1986); and Berklee College of Music (1998); in 2017, she was an associate professor of songwriting at Berklee. Dino Guido Cattaneo was educated at Luigi Bocconi University (1990) and Harvard University (1996).

Children of Dino Guido and Susan Livingston[12] (Kean) Cattaneo, born at Boston, Massachusetts:[2067]

  i. Nicholas Everett[13] Cattaneo, b. 16 June 1999; he was educated at Concord Academy in Concord, Mass.
  ii. Charlotte Kean Cattaneo, b. 19 Sept. 2001.

80. **Edward Livingston**[12] **Hicks** (*Elizabeth Stuyvesant*[11] *Kean, Robert Winthrop*[10] *Kean, Katharine Taylor*[9] *Winthrop, Robert*[8], *Thomas Charles*[7], *Francis Bayard*[6], *John Still*[5], *John*[4], *Waitstill*[3], *John*[2-1]) was born at New York, New York 27 July 1943. He married at Livingston, New Jersey 14 August 1976, **Kathy Maxwell**, who was born at Derry, New Hampshire 12 August 1949, daughter of Harold Lee and Alice (Nojunas) Maxwell, from whom he was divorced.[2068]

Dr. Edward Livingston Hicks graduated from Yale College and Georgetown University. Dr. Kathy Maxwell was educated at Hahnemann Medical College and Temple University.

[2066] "Susan L. Kean, Dino Cattaneo," *The New York Times*, 21 February 1993, V12; *Social Register 1994* (1993), Marriages, 12; notes by Susan Kean Cattaneo 2013; questionnaire from John Kean 2014.

[2067] Winthrop, *Descendants of Robert Winthrop & Kate Wilson Taylor, 1833–2000*, 33; notes by Nicholas Everett Cattaneo 2013; questionnaire from John Kean 2014; notes by Susan Kean Cattaneo 2014.

[2068] *The New York Times*, 31 July 1943, 14; 15 August 1976, 57; Dorman, *The Filson Club History Quarterly* 27 [1953]: 146; *Social Register 1977* (1976), 519; notes by Robert Gregory Honshu Raynolds 2013 and Sarah Hicks Dean 2014.

Children of Edward Livingston[12] and Kathy (Maxwell) Hicks, born at Philadelphia, Pennsylvania:[2069]

141   i. SARAH LIVINGSTON[13] HICKS, b. 22 Aug. 1982; m. 23 June 2012, JOSEPH WAYNE DEAN.

       ii. JESSICA MAXWELL HICKS, b. 22 Nov. 1985; she was educated at Sarah Lawrence College.

81. **CYNTHIA MONTGOMERY**[12] **HICKS** (*Elizabeth Stuyvesant*[11] *Kean, Robert Winthrop*[10] *Kean, Katharine Taylor*[9] *Winthrop, Robert*[8]*, Thomas Charles*[7]*, Francis Bayard*[6]*, John Still*[5]*, John*[4]*, Waitstill*[3]*, John*[2-1]) was born 13 December 1951. She married, first, at the Trinitarian Congregational Church, Concord, Massachusetts 3 January 1976, **PETER WALTER NILES**, who was born 13 June 1953, son of Seymour Mansfield Niles; and, second, **ROY WESTBYE CUTTING**, who was born at Peterborough, Ontario, Canada 23 November 1944, son of Roy Harlow and Olga Louise (Westbye) Cutting.[2070]

Cynthia Montgomery Hicks graduated from Concord Academy and Boston University (1976). Peter Walter Niles was educated at Winchester High School, Winchester, Massachusetts, and the University of Massachusetts.

Children of Peter Walter and Cynthia Montgomery[12] (Hicks) Niles:[2071]

       i. ORION MANSFIELD[13] NILES, b. 25 Aug. 1976.

142   ii. ELIZA JOY NILES, b. 15 June 1978; m. 2 Sept. 2007, CHAD HOSKINS.

143   iii. JULIA KEAN NILES, b. 31 March 1980; m. 15 July 2011, SEAN EASTON.

82. **STEPHEN WINTHROP**[12] **HICKS** (*Elizabeth Stuyvesant*[11] *Kean, Robert Winthrop*[10] *Kean, Katharine Taylor*[9] *Winthrop, Robert*[8]*, Thomas Charles*[7]*, Francis Bayard*[6]*, John Still*[5]*, John*[4]*, Waitstill*[3]*, John*[2-1]) was born at Stamford, Connecticut 16 September 1954. He married at the Church of St. Mark-in-the-Bouwerie, New York, New York 13 September 1992, **ELIZABETH HAZAN**, who was born at New York 19 January 1965, daughter of Joseph and Jane (Niederhoffer) (Freilicher) Hazan.[2072]

[2069] Winthrop, *Descendants of Robert Winthrop & Kate Wilson Taylor, 1833–2000*, 34; questionnaire from and notes by Sarah Hicks Dean 2014.

[2070] *The New York Times*, 4 January 1976, 54; http://familytreemaker.genealogy.com/users/c/u/t/Mikey-B-Cutting/GENE2-0012.html; http://familytreemaker.genealogy.com/users/c/u/t/Mikey-B-Cutting/GENE2-0011.html.

[2071] Winthrop, *Descendants of Robert Winthrop & Kate Wilson Taylor, 1833–2000*, 34; http://familytreemaker.genealogy.com/users/c/u/t/Mikey-B-Cutting/GENE2-0012.html; notes by Eliza Niles Hoskins and Julia Kean Niles 2013.

[2072] Questionnaire from Stephen Winthrop Hicks 2013; https://en.wikipedia.org/wiki/Jane_Freilicher.

Stephen Winthrop Hicks graduated from Greenwich High School, Greenwich, Connecticut; Colorado College (1977); Columbia University (1984); and Yale University (1995). Elizabeth Hazan was educated at the United Nations International School, New York, and Bryn Mawr College (1986); an artist, she is the daughter of the landscape painter Jane Freilicher.

Children of Stephen Winthrop[12] Hicks and Elizabeth Hazan, born at New York:[2073]

    i. BENJAMIN BAYARD[13] HICKS, b. 28 Feb. 1996; he was educated at St. Ann's School, Brooklyn, N.Y., and Wesleyan University.

    ii. KATHARINE TAYLOR HICKS, b. 26 Oct. 1998; she was educated at St. Ann's.

    iii. LUCIAN ELIAS HICKS, b. 29 Oct. 2002; he was educated at St. Ann's.

83. **ROBERT WINTHROP**[12] **KEAN, 3RD** (*Robert Winthrop*[11-10] *Kean, Katharine Taylor*[9] *Winthrop, Robert*[8], *Thomas Charles*[7], *Francis Bayard*[6], *John Still*[5], *John*[4], *Waitstill*[3], *John*[2-1]) was born at New York, New York 30 January 1948. He married, first, at St. Mary's Church, Roslyn, Long Island, New York 12 September 1970, **PATRICIA COXE PATTERSON**, who was born at New York 21 February 1949, daughter of Edward and Joan (Metzger) Patterson, from whom he was divorced 19 February 1997; and, second, at Far Hills, New Jersey 18 August 1999, **MALLORY GIBBS (BLIMM) (HARRINGTON) CROSBY**, who was born at Plainfield, New Jersey 28 November 1953 and died at Martinsville, New Jersey 27 January 2006, daughter of Robert William Blimm.[2074]

Roy Kean graduated from the Pingry School, Elizabeth, New Jersey, and the University of California, Santa Barbara (1970). Patricia Coxe Patterson was educated at the Oldfields School, Glencoe, Maryland, and Colby Junior College (1971x). Mallory Gibbs Blimm attended the Hartridge School, Plainfield, and Bard College.

[2073] *Social Register 1997* (1996), 345; *Summer Social Register 1999 Dilatory Domiciles May 1999*, 35; Winthrop, *Descendants of Robert Winthrop & Kate Wilson Taylor, 1833–2000*, 34; notes by Robert Gregory Honshu Raynolds 2013; questionnaire from Stephen Winthrop Hicks 2013; notes from Stephen Winthrop Hicks 2014.

[2074] *The New York Times*, 22 February 1949, 26; 13 September 1970, 88; 10 October 1982; 5 February 2006; Winthrop, *Descendants of Robert Winthrop & Kate Wilson Taylor, 1833–2000*, 35; *New York Social Register 1971* (1970), 451; *Social Register 2000* (1999), 281; http://www.newyorksocialdiary.com/list/im/120im.php; Social Security Death Index; notes by Christopher Kean 2014; questionnaire from and notes by Robert Winthrop Kean, 3rd, 2013 and 2014.

Children of Robert Winthrop[12] and Patricia Coxe (Patterson) Kean:[2075]

    i. ROBERT WINTHROP[13] KEAN, 4TH, b. at New York 26 Jan. 1979 and d. there unm. 6 Oct. 2011; he graduated from Pingry and the College of Charleston (2001).

144   ii. PHILIP EDWARD PATTERSON KEAN, b. at Morristown, N.J. 23 Aug. 1982; m. 30 March 2013, STEFANIE COLEMAN.

145   iii. CRISTINA DEAR KEAN, b. at New York 4 Sept. 1984.

84. PETER STUYVESANT[12] **KEAN** (*Robert Winthrop*[11-10] *Kean, Katharine Taylor*[9] *Winthrop, Robert*[8], *Thomas Charles*[7], *Francis Bayard*[6], *John Still*[5], *John*[4], *Waitstill*[3], *John*[2-1]) was born at New York, New York 3 May 1949. He married at Livingston, New Jersey 17 September 1977, **SUSAN KATHLEEN CAROW**, from whom he was divorced.[2076]

Children of Peter Stuyvesant[12] and Susan Kathleen (Carow) Kean:[2077]

146   i. JESSE CAROW[13] KEAN, b. at Belleville, N.J. 5 March 1978; m. 8 Sept. 2007, DAWN ALLISON STICKLOR.

147   ii. HALLIE ELIZABETH KEAN, b. at Livingston 2 May 1983; m. 10 Jan. 2004, JOSHUA COUNCIL.

85. ALEXANDER LIVINGSTON[12] **KEAN** (*Robert Winthrop*[11-10] *Kean, Katharine Taylor*[9] *Winthrop, Robert*[8], *Thomas Charles*[7], *Francis Bayard*[6], *John Still*[5], *John*[4], *Waitstill*[3], *John*[2-1]) was born at Glen Ridge (Montclair), New Jersey 11 May 1952. He married, first, in August 1972, **LAUREL JEAN HOPE**; and, second, 14 April 2000, **INA EICHHOF**.[2078]

Children of Alexander Livingston[12] and Laurel Jean (Hope) Kean:[2079]

148   i. ADAM[13] KEAN, b. at Pequannock, N.J. 22 June 1973; m. 29 April 2000, CAROLINA DA SILVA MONZA.

    ii. JEDIAH KEAN, b. at Boulder, Colo. 18 Feb. 1976.

[2075] Winthrop, *Descendants of Robert Winthrop & Kate Wilson Taylor, 1833–2000*, 35; http://law.onecle.com/tax/2003/kean.tcm.wpd03.html; Social Security Death Index; notes by Philip Edward Patterson Kean 2013; questionnaire from Robert Winthrop Kean, 3rd, 2014.

[2076] *The New York Times*, 5 May 1949, 32; Winthrop, *Descendants of Robert Winthrop & Kate Wilson Taylor, 1833–2000*, 35; notes by Jesse Carow Kean 2014.

[2077] Winthrop, *Descendants of Robert Winthrop & Kate Wilson Taylor, 1833–2000*, 35; notes by Christopher Kean and Jesse Carow Kean 2014.

[2078] *The New York Times*, 23 May 1952, 18; *Summer Social Register 1973*, 107; Winthrop, *Descendants of Robert Winthrop & Kate Wilson Taylor, 1833–2000*, 35; notes by Alexander Livingston Kean 2014.

[2079] Winthrop, *Descendants of Robert Winthrop & Kate Wilson Taylor, 1833–2000*, 35, 54; notes by Adam Kean 2013 and Alexander Livingston Kean 2014.

86. **Nicholas**[12] **Kean** (*Robert Winthrop*[11-10] *Kean, Katharine Taylor*[9] *Winthrop, Robert*[8], *Thomas Charles*[7], *Francis Bayard*[6], *John Still*[5], *John*[4], *Waitstill*[3], *John*[2-1]) was born at Glen Ridge (Montclair), New Jersey 3 June 1957. He married at New Orleans, Louisiana 21 September 1992, **Mary-Margaret Kirk Groome**, who was born at Mexico City, Mexico 11 November 1966, daughter of David Kirk and Myra Maude (Bourgeois) Groome.[2080]

Children of Nicholas[12] and Mary-Margaret Kirk (Groome) Kean, born at New York, New York:

    i.   Schuyler Livingston Kirk[13] Kean, b. 6 April 1999;[2081] he was educated at the Isidore Newman School in New Orleans.

    ii.   Nicholas Maximillian Winthrop Kean, b. 11 Jan. 2002.[2082]

87. **James Edgar**[12] **Lansbury** (*Rose Anthony*[11] *Kean, Robert Winthrop*[10] *Kean, Katharine Taylor*[9] *Winthrop, Robert*[8], *Thomas Charles*[7], *Francis Bayard*[6], *John Still*[5], *John*[4], *Waitstill*[3], *John*[2-1]) was born at Hollywood, California 30 October 1956. He married at the First Presbyterian Church, Carmel, California 27 November 1981, **Susan Alice Snorf**, who was born at Chicago, Illinois 23 June 1956, daughter of Dr. Charles Roberts and Roberta Frances (Buffett) Snorf.[2083]

James Edgar Lansbury graduated from the Salisbury School, Salisbury, Connecticut, and the University of Southern California (1978). Susan Alice Snorf was also educated at U.S.C.

Children of James Edgar[12] and Susan Alice (Snorf) Lansbury, born at Santa Monica, California:[2084]

    i.   Charles Edgar[13] Lansbury, b. 21 Sept. 1986; he graduated from the Harvard-Westlake School, North Hollywood, and Northwestern University (2009).

[2080] *Social Register 1994* (1993), Marriages, 12; questionnaire from Christopher Kean 2014; notes by Christpoher Kean 2015.

[2081] *Social Register 2000* (1999), 381.

[2082] *Social Register 2003* (2002), 937.

[2083] *The New York Times*, 24 November 1956, 15; 28 November 1981, 47; *California Birth Index, 1905–1995*; Doris Buffett, *An Obscure Family: The Buffetts in America* (Fredericksburg, Va., 2012), 237, 238–39; notes by James Edgar Lansbury 2013; questionnaire from James Edgar Lansbury 2014.

[2084] *California Birth Index, 1905–1995*; *Social Register 1989* (1988), Births, 3; *Summer Social Register 1996 Dilatory Domiciles May 1996*, 41; *Social Register 2000* (1999), 411; *Summer Social Register 2004*, 204; Winthrop, *Descendants of Robert Winthrop & Kate Wilson Taylor, 1833–2000*, 36; notes by Robert Bruce Lansbury 2013; questionnaire from James Edgar Lansbury 2014.

ii. ROBERT BUFFETT LANSBURY, b. 6 July 1989; he graduated from Salisbury and the University of San Diego (2013).

iii. GALEN KEAN LANSBURY, b. 31 Oct. 1994; he was educated at St. Paul's School, Concord, N.H., and Northwestern.

iv. WILLIAM JAMES LANSBURY, b. 21 Aug. 1998; he was educated at the Stevenson School in Pebble Beach, Calif., and Northwestern.

v. THOMAS HOWARD LANSBURY, b. 18 Feb. 2004.

88. DAVID ANTHONY[12] LANSBURY (*Rose Anthony*[11] *Kean, Robert Winthrop*[10] *Kean, Katharine Taylor*[9] *Winthrop, Robert*[8], *Thomas Charles*[7], *Francis Bayard*[6], *John Still*[5], *John*[4], *Waitstill*[3], *John*[2-1]) was born in Los Angeles County, California 25 February 1961. He married, first, 10 October 1992, ALEXANDRA ELIZABETH SHEEDY, who was born at New York, New York 13 June 1962, daughter of John J. and Charlotte (Baum) Sheedy, from whom he was divorced; and, second, at 141 Worth Street, New York 6 June 2013, KRISTINA ANNE MIKKELSEN, who was born in Santa Clara County, California 5 October 1978.[2085]

David Lansbury was educated at the North Country School, Lake Placid, New York; Connecticut College (1983); and the Central School of Speech and Drama. Ally Sheedy attended Columbia Grammar and Preparatory School, New York, and the University of Southern California. Both David Lansbury and Ally Sheedy have had lengthy acting careers, appearing in films and television series since the 1980s. David's first film was *Gorillas in the Mist* (1988), and he later appeared on Angela Lansbury's long-running television series *Murder, She Wrote*; for two guest appearances on *Oz* he was nominated for an OFTA Television Award in 1999.[2086]

First seen on *The Mike Douglas Show* in 1977, Ally Sheedy's early films included *WarGames* (1983), *Oxford Blues* (1984), and *The Breakfast Club* and *St. Elmo's Fire* (1985); she has appeared on television series (including *Oz*) and in television movies. In 1998–99, she won the Independent Spirit Award as Best Female Lead and was named the Los Angeles Film Critics' and National Society of Film Critics' Best Actress for her role as Lucy Berliner in *High Art* (1998); in 2005, she shared

---

[2085] *California Birth Index, 1905–1995*; IMDb entries for David Lansbury, Ally Sheedy, and Charlotte Sheedy; http://www.nndb.com/people/545/000023476/; http://en.wikipedia.org/wiki/Ally_Sheedy; notes by David Lansbury and Kristina Mikkelsen Lansbury 2013.

[2086] http://www.imdb.com/name/nm0487050/?ref_=nmbio_sp_1.

the MTV Movie Awards Silver Bucket of Excellence with Anthony Michael Hall, Judd Nelson, and Molly Ringwald for their work in *The Breakfast Club*.[2087]

Child of David Anthony[12] Lansbury and Alexandra Elizabeth Sheedy:[2088]

    i. BECKETT ALEXANDER[13] LANSBURY, b. Rebecca Elizabeth Lansbury at Santa Monica, Calif. 15 March 1994; he graduated from the Calhoun School, New York, and Bard College (2016).

Child of David Anthony[12] and Kristina Anne (Mikkelsen) Lansbury:[2089]

    ii. EMMET AUDEN CLAUS[13] LANSBURY, b. at New York 31 July 2013.

89. **GEORGE WINTHROP**[12] **LANSBURY** (*Rose Anthony*[11] *Kean, Robert Winthrop*[10] *Kean, Katharine Taylor*[9] *Winthrop, Robert*[8], *Thomas Charles*[7], *Francis Bayard*[6], *John Still*[5], *John*[4], *Waitstill*[3], *John*[2-1]) was born at New York, New York 7 October 1963. He married, first, at the First Congregational Church, Peru, Vermont 17 June 1989, **MARIANNA CAROLINE MORGAN**, who was born at New York 3 September 1963, daughter of Matthew and Rosetta (Chiabrera) Morgan, from whom he was divorced; and, second, at St. James' Church, New York 22 May 1993, **EMILY ALLEN BICKFORD**, who was born at New York 27 April 1965, daughter of Nathaniel Judson and Jewelle Ann (Wooten) Bickford.[2090]

George Winthrop Lansbury and Marianna Caroline Morgan graduated from Skidmore College in 1985. Emily Allen Bickford was educated at Friends Seminary, New York; Skidmore (1987); and Bank Street College of Education (1999).

[2087] http://www.imdb.com/name/nm0000639/?ref_=nmbio_sp_2. Three 1980s films garnered Razzie Award nominations: *Blue City* (1986), *Heart of Dixie* (1989), and *Betsy's Wedding* (1990).

[2088] *California Birth Index, 1905–1995*; Winthrop, *Descendants of Robert Winthrop & Kate Wilson Taylor, 1833–2000*, 36; questionnaire from James Edgar Lansbury 2014.

[2089] Notes by George Winthrop Lansbury and Kristina Mikkelsen Lansbury 2013; questionnaire from James Edgar Lansbury 2014.

[2090] Department of Health, Vermont License and Certificate of Marriage 89-002423; "George Lansbury, a Research Analyst, Weds Marianna Morgan in Vermont," *The New York Times*, 18 June 1989, 48; "Emily Bickford, George Lansbury," 7 February 1993, V15; 23 May 1993, V15; Steward and Le Roy, *The Le Roy Family in America, 1753–2003*, 402, 526; notes by Emily Bickford Lansbury 2013 and 2015; questionnaire from James Edgar Lansbury 2014.

Children of George Winthrop[12] and Emily Allen (Bickford) Lansbury, born at New York:[2091]

    i. ELIZABETH LAURA[13] LANSBURY, b. 24 Aug. 1994; she was educated at the Masters School, Dobbs Ferry, N.Y., and Skidmore.

   ii. NATALIE ROSE TABER LANSBURY, b. at New York 13 July 1999; she was educated at Masters.

90. **BRIAN MCILDOWIE**[12] **LANSBURY** (*Rose Anthony*[11] *Kean, Robert Winthrop*[10] *Kean, Katharine Taylor*[9] *Winthrop, Robert*[8], *Thomas Charles*[7], *Francis Bayard*[6], *John Still*[5], *John*[4], *Waitstill*[3], *John*[2-1]) was born at New York, New York 12 April 1965. He married at Peru, Vermont 9 August 1997, **TASHA HILL CORNELL**, who was born at Townshend, Vermont 30 August 1966, daughter of Peter McKown and Raylene Ann (Hill) Cornell.[2092]

Brian McIldowie Lansbury graduated from the Middlesex School, Concord, Massachusetts; the University of Vermont (1987); Yale University (1993); and New York University (1997). Tasha Hill Cornell was educated at Burr & Burton Academy, Manchester, Vermont; New York University (1991); and the Metropolitan Institute for Training in Psychoanalytic Psychology (1996).

Children of Brian McIldowie[12] and Tasha Hill (Cornell) Lansbury, born at Burlington, Vermont:[2093]

    i. MACKLIN PETER[13] LANSBURY, b. 22 Dec. 2000.

   ii. QUINN EDGAR LANSBURY, b. 28 Nov. 2003.

91. **THOMAS HOWARD**[12] **KEAN, JR.** (*Thomas Howard*[11] *Kean, Robert Winthrop*[10] *Kean, Katharine Taylor*[9] *Winthrop, Robert*[8], *Thomas Charles*[7], *Francis Bayard*[6], *John Still*[5], *John*[4], *Waitstill*[3], *John*[2-1]), twin, was born at Livingston, New Jersey 5 September 1968. He married at Holy Trinity Roman Catholic Church, Washington, D.C. 12 November 1994, **RHONDA LEE NORTON**, who was born 20 July 1968, daughter of Robert Lee and Barbara Ann (Yoder) Norton.[2094]

[2091] *Social Register 1996* (1995), 424; *Social Register 2002* (2001), 441; Winthrop, *Descendants of Robert Winthrop & Kate Wilson Taylor, 1833–2000*, 36; questionnaire from James Edgar Lansbury 2014; notes by Emily Bickford Lansbury 2015.

[2092] Department of Health, Vermont License and Certificate of Marriage 97-005905; notes by Brian McIldowie Lansbury and Tasha Cornell Lansbury 2013; questionnaire from James Edgar Lansbury 2014.

[2093] *Vermont Birth Records, 1909–2008.*

[2094] "Rhonda Norton, Thomas Kean Jr.," *The New York Times*, 13 November 1994; *Summer Social Register 1995 Dilatory Domiciles May 1995*, 37; questionnaire from

Thomas Howard Kean, Jr., was educated at the Pingry School, Elizabeth, New Jersey; Dartmouth College (1990); and Tufts University. Rhonda Lee Norton graduated from Allegheny College in 1990. Thomas H. Kean, Jr., has served in the New Jersey State Senate since 2003 and as Minority Leader in the State Senate since 2008. In 2006, he ran unsuccessfully for the U.S. Senate.

Children of Thomas Howard[12] and Rhonda Lee (Norton) Kean:[2095]

    i. ELIZABETH WINTHROP[13] KEAN, b. 18 Jan. 1999.

    ii. MEREDITH LEE KEAN, b. 13 July 2003.

92. REED STUYVESANT[12] **KEAN** (*Thomas Howard*[11] *Kean, Robert Winthrop*[10] *Kean, Katharine Taylor*[9] *Winthrop, Robert*[8], *Thomas Charles*[7], *Francis Bayard*[6], *John Still*[5], *John*[4], *Waitstill*[3], *John*[2-1]), twin, was born at Livingston, New Jersey 5 September 1968. He married, first, at the Chapel of the Convent of the Sacred Heart, New York, New York 9 December 2000, **DORIAN DREES**, who was born 26 August 1968, daughter of John M. Drees and Susan (Altman) (Drees) Sugarman, from whom he was divorced; and, second, at Christ Church, Short Hills, New Jersey 8 May 2009, **MICHELLE TERESA PETILLO**, who was born 29 December 1977, daughter of John J. and Sharyn P. Petillo.[2096]

Reed Stuyvesant Kean graduated from the Pingry School, Elizabeth, New Jersey, and Lehigh University (1990). Dorian Drees was educated at Boston University. Michelle Teresa Petillo graduated from Fordham University in 1999.

Children of Reed Stuyvesant[12] and Michelle Teresa (Petillo) Kean:[2097]

    i. WILLIAM STUYVESANT[13] KEAN, b. 12 May 2011.

    ii. MEGAN WINTHROP KEAN, b. 8 Aug. 2013.

Thomas Howard Kean 2014; http://en.wikipedia.org/wiki/Thomas_Kean,_Jr.; http://www.nndb.com/people/363/000109036/; http://www.angelfire.com/pa2/peppermusic/pafg182.htm.

[2095] Notes by Robert Gregory Honshu Raynolds 2013; questionnaire from Thomas Howard Kean 2014.

[2096] "Dorian Drees, Reed Kean," *The New York Times*, 10 December 2000, ST15; "Michelle Petillo, Reed Kean," 9 May 2009; http://www.nndb.com/people/363/000109036/.

[2097] Questionnaire from Thomas Howard Kean 2014.

93. **ALEXANDRA DICKINSON**[12] **KEAN** (*Thomas Howard*[11] *Kean, Robert Winthrop*[10] *Kean, Katharine Taylor*[9] *Winthrop, Robert*[8], *Thomas Charles*[7], *Francis Bayard*[6], *John Still*[5], *John*[4], *Waitstill*[3], *John*[2-1]) was born 11 October 1974. She married at St. John's Church, Fishers Island, New York 9 September 2000, **BENJAMIN BREWSTER STRONG**, who was born 1 July 1972, son of Raymond Brewster and Ann Barbara (Schroedel) Strong.[2098]

Alexandra Dickinson Kean graduated from Colby College (1996), Wheelock College, and Simmons College. Benjamin Brewster Strong was educated at Colby (1994) and the State University of New York at Stony Brook.

Children of Benjamin Brewster and Alexandra Dickinson[12] (Kean) Strong:[2099]

    i. KATHARINE KEAN[13] STRONG, b. at Boston, Mass. 1 Feb. 2003.
    ii. THOMAS BREWSTER STRONG, b. 5 March 2005.
    iii. CAMPBELL TAYLOR STRONG, b. 9 Nov. 2007.

94. **THOMAS LEE**[12] **HIGGINSON, JR.** (*Theodora*[11] *Winthrop, Robert*[10], *Frederic*[9], *Robert*[8], *Thomas Charles*[7], *Francis Bayard*[6], *John Still*[5], *John*[4], *Waitstill*[3], *John*[2-1]. Also *Theodora*[12] *Winthrop, Robert*[11] *Winthrop, Dorothy*[10] *Amory, Charles Walter*[9] *Amory, Anna Powell Grant*[8] *Sears, David*[7] *Sears, Anne*[6] *Winthrop, John Still*[5]) was born at New York, New York 16 September 1949. He married at St. James' Church, Warrenton, Virginia 12 June 1982, **FEROLINE PERKINS BURRAGE**, who was born at Washington, D.C. 15 September 1952, daughter of William Clarence Burrage and Hope (Wallach) (Burrage) Porter.[2100]

Thomas Lee Higginson, Jr., graduated from the Groton School, Groton, Massachusetts; Harvard College (1972); and the University of Virginia (1976). Feroline Perkins Burrage was educated at the Madeira School, Greenway, Virginia, and the University of Virginia (1974).

[2098] "Alexandra Kean, Benjamin Strong," *The New York Times*, 10 September 2000, ST13; questionnaire from Thomas Howard Kean 2014.
[2099] *Social Register 2004* (2003), 973; notes by Robert Gregory Honshu Raynolds 2013.
[2100] Steward, *The Sarsaparilla Kings*, 125–26; Steward and Child, *The Descendants of Judge John Lowell of Newburyport, Massachusetts*, 398.

Children of Thomas Lee[12] and Feroline Perkins (Burrage) Higginson, born at Washington, D.C.:[2101]

> i. HENRY LEE[13] HIGGINSON, b. 17 May 1984; he graduated from Groton and Drew University (2008).

149 ii. THEODORA WINTHROP HIGGINSON, b. 26 Jan. 1987; m. 3 Oct. 2015, BENJAMIN OSTLER HANNA.

95. ELIZABETH[12] **HIGGINSON** (*Theodora*[11] *Winthrop, Robert*[10]*, Frederic*[9]*, Robert*[8]*, Thomas Charles*[7]*, Francis Bayard*[6]*, John Still*[5]*, John*[4]*, Waitstill*[3]*, John*[2-1]. Also *Theodora*[12] *Winthrop, Robert*[11] *Winthrop, Dorothy*[10] *Amory, Charles Walter*[9] *Amory, Anna Powell Grant*[8] *Sears, David*[7] *Sears, Anne*[6] *Winthrop, John Still*[5]) was born at New York, New York 29 December 1951. She married at the Inn at Castle Hill, Newport, Rhode Island 26 February 1983, **LARRY ALAN RIDEMAN**, who was born at Boston, Massachusetts 17 February 1952, son of Robert and Marjorie (Willis) Rideman, from whom she was divorced.[2102]

Elizabeth Higginson graduated from St. Timothy's School, Stevenson, Maryland, and Radcliffe College (1975). Larry Alan Rideman was educated at Miami Norland Senior High School, Miami Gardens, Florida, and Northeastern University (1975).

Child of Larry Alan and Elizabeth[12] (Higginson) Rideman:[2103]

150 i. MIRANDA CLAIRE[13] RIDEMAN, b. at Boston 23 Aug. 1983; m. 20 June 2015, JONATHAN EVERETT TRAHAN.

96. ROBERT WINTHROP[12] **HIGGINSON** (*Theodora*[11] *Winthrop, Robert*[10]*, Frederic*[9]*, Robert*[8]*, Thomas Charles*[7]*, Francis Bayard*[6]*, John Still*[5]*, John*[4]*, Waitstill*[3]*, John*[2-1]. Also *Theodora*[12] *Winthrop, Robert*[11] *Winthrop, Dorothy*[10] *Amory, Charles Walter*[9] *Amory, Anna Powell Grant*[8] *Sears, David*[7] *Sears, Anne*[6] *Winthrop, John Still*[5]) was born at New York, New York 14 April 1956. He married at Santa Fe County Court House, Santa Fe, New Mexico 19 August 1982, **JUDY ANN JONES**, who was born at

---

[2101] Steward, *The Sarsaparilla Kings*, 126, 140–41; Steward and Child, *The Descendants of Judge John Lowell of Newburyport, Massachusetts*, 398; notes by Henry Lee Higginson 2013.

[2102] Steward, *The Sarsaparilla Kings*, 126; Steward and Child, *The Descendants of Judge John Lowell of Newburyport, Massachusetts*, 398.

[2103] Steward, *The Sarsaparilla Kings*, 126, 141; Steward and Child, *The Descendants of Judge John Lowell of Newburyport, Massachusetts*, 399; notes by Theodora Winthrop Hooton 2015.

Chambersburg, Pennsylvania 5 April 1942, daughter of Morris Edgar and Annabelle (Young) Jones, from whom he was divorced.[2104]

Robert Winthrop Higginson was educated at the Groton School, Groton, Massachusetts, and the University of Pennsylvania (1978x).

Children of Robert Winthrop[12] and Judy Ann (Jones) Higginson, born at Santa Fe:[2105]

> i.   JEREMY JOSEPH[13] HIGGINSON, b. 22 Aug. 1982; he was educated at Santa Fe Country Day School, Bates College (2005), Harvard University (2007), and Boston University.
>
> 151 ii. AURELIA ANNE HIGGINSON, b. 21 March 1985; m. 10 Aug. 2013, SPENCER LAUDER BEANE.

97. **SHELBY WINTHROP**[12] **BONNIE** (*Cornelia Beekman*[11] *Winthrop, Robert*[10], *Frederic*[9], *Robert*[8], *Thomas Charles*[7], *Francis Bayard*[6], *John Still*[5], *John*[4], *Waitstill*[3], *John*[2-1]. Also *Cornelia Beekman*[12] *Winthrop, Robert*[11] *Winthrop, Dorothy*[10] *Amory, Charles Walter*[9] *Amory, Anna Powell Grant*[8] *Sears, David*[7] *Sears, Anne*[6] *Winthrop, John Still*[5]) was born at Louisville, Kentucky 16 July 1964. He married at Carmel Valley, California 25 October 1997, **CAROL JEANNE NAVONE**, who was born at Seattle, Washington 27 April 1963, daughter of James Henry and Patricia Lee (Hogan) Navone.[2106]

Shelby Winthrop Bonnie graduated from the Hotchkiss School, Lakeville, Connecticut; the University of Virginia (1986); and Harvard University (1990). Carol Jeanne Navone was educated at the Seattle Preparatory School and the University of Washington (1985). Shelby Bonnie spent two years after graduating from college at Morgan Stanley, and the two-and-a-half years after business school at Tiger Management, both in New York. In 1993, he joined CNET, a media company based in San Francisco, as its second employee.[2107] His roles there included chief operating officer, chief financial officer, vice chairman, and (from 2000 until 2006) chairman and chief executive officer. As reported in

---

[2104] Steward, *The Sarsaparilla Kings*, 126; Steward and Child, *The Descendants of Judge John Lowell of Newburyport, Massachusetts*, 399.

[2105] Steward, *The Sarsaparilla Kings*, 126, 141; Steward and Child, *The Descendants of Judge John Lowell of Newburyport, Massachusetts*, 399; questionnaires from Aurelia Higginson Beane and Theodora Winthrop Hooton 2014.

[2106] Steward, *The Sarsaparilla Kings*, 126; Steward and Child, *The Descendants of Judge John Lowell of Newburyport, Massachusetts*, 399; questionnaire from Robert Farrell Bonnie 2013.

[2107] David B. Yoffie and Mary Kwak, *Judo Strategy: Turning Your Competitors' Strength to Your Advantage* (Boston: Harvard Business School Press, 2001), 148.

Judo Strategy: Turning Your Competitors' Strength to Your Advantage, in his view, "Any company that carries the baggage of their current business tends to think with respect to their old models. [CNET] had no legacy anything." In the rough and tumble world of internet startups in the early 1990s, "Bonnie was the yin to [CNET founder] Halsey [Minor]'s yang. 'I'm not as aggressive or as outspoken or as in-your-face as Halsey,' Bonnie acknowledged, 'so I'm a nice check.'"[2108]

Originally named C|NET, its mission was "to redefine television in the age of interactive media." After an initially bumpy start for the company, *c|net central*, a television show likened to *Entertainment Tonight* for technophiles, debuted in April 1995, and the website followed in June. David B. Yoffie and Mary Kwak observed that the startup's early use of the World Wide Web as "its main marketing channel was only one example of CNET's ability to make the most of the new medium." Another was the realization that "intuitively obvious domain names could be a critical asset, [so Bonnie's cousin—and the company's fourth employee—Matthew] Barzun made it his mission to hunt down and buy 'easy-to-understand, easy-to-spell domain names for what we thought users wanted,' including News.com, Search.com, and Computers.com. 'Download.com is a really cool name,' Barzun continued. 'Bought it for $20,000.'"[2109]

In March 2000, Shelby succeeded Halsey Minor as CEO at CNET, "a move that caused the stock to plunge. The two parted friends, complete with a lighthearted video of Bonnie giving Minor the boot."

> Bonnie soon proved his worth, taking the role of head evangelist and picking up the pieces after CNET's market cap and expectations popped with the tech bubble. He brainstormed the comeback strategy that helped lift the company from the dot-com dustbin, snapping up media properties to appeal to new audiences and pushing new types of advertising that went beyond the much-maligned banner ad.
>
> As a result, CNET was well-positioned for a resurgence in online advertising as tech companies again began to aggressively market their wares to everyone from gear-heads to soccer moms. In fact, Bonnie was so successful at the online advertising game that he took on

---

[2108] Yoffie and Kwak, *Judo Strategy*, 147, 149.
[2109] Yoffie and Kwak, *Judo Strategy*, 149, 152, 154 at 154.

another post as chairman of the Interactive Advertising Bureau, the nonprofit trade group that sets industry standards for online advertising. His rising profile also earned him other coveted positions, such as a seat on the board of Warner Music Group, where [in 2006] he sits on the audit committee.

In October 2006, following an internal report that found fault with the way stock options were handled at the company, Shelby resigned as CNET's chairman and chief executive officer. His peers deplored the situation: "'He was certainly the heart and soul of CNET,' said John Battelle, a serial entrepreneur who founded *Wired* magazine and the now-defunct magazine *Industry Standard.* 'He has been a leader in this space for a long time and he built CNET into an extraordinary set of properties.'"[2110]

Bonnie went on to co-found Whiskey Media, serving as CEO from 2007 until 2012. The company "built community-driven, wiki-like content including ComicVine, the gaming site GiantBomb, and the anime site AnimeVice," and was sold in February 2012. Later that year, he joined Allen & Company as a managing director in the San Francisco office.[2111]

Children of Shelby Winthrop[12] and Carol Jeanne (Navone) Bonnie, born at San Francisco:[2112]

    i.   Mason Winthrop[13] Bonnie, b. 11 Sept. 1998; he was educated at Deerfield Academy in Deerfield, Mass.

   ii.   Henry Sevier Bonnie, b. 5 Aug. 2000; he was educated at St. Ignatius High School in San Francisco.

  iii.   Virginia Ayer Bonnie, b. 9 Dec. 2003.

98. Robert Farrell[12] Bonnie (*Cornelia Beekman[11] Winthrop, Robert[10], Frederic[9], Robert[8], Thomas Charles[7], Francis Bayard[6], John Still[5], John[4], Waitstill[3], John[2-1]*. Also *Cornelia Beekman[12] Winthrop, Robert[11] Winthrop, Dorothy[10] Amory, Charles Walter[9] Amory, Anna Powell Grant[8] Sears, David[7] Sears, Anne[6] Winthrop, John Still[5]*) was born at Louisville, Kentucky

[2110] Jessica Guynn, "CNET loses its 'heart and soul' executive/Backdating sends popular Bonnie out the door," 12 October 2006, http://www.sfgate.com/business/article/ Cnet-loses-its-heart-and-soul-executive-2486902.php.

[2111] Connie Loizos, "Silicon Valley Exec Shelby Bonnie Joins Allen & Co.," 25 September 2012, https://www.pehub.com/2012/09/silicon-valley-exec-shelby-bonnie-joins-allen-co/.

[2112] Steward and Child, *The Descendants of Judge John Lowell of Newburyport, Massachusetts*, 399.

18 December 1967. He married, first, at Trinity Church, Upperville, Virginia 15 May 1993, CYNTHIA ANNE POLK, daughter of Robert H. and Blanche (Monzon) Polk, from whom he was divorced in July 1999; and, second, at Trinity Church 7 September 2002, JULIE ANN GOMENA, who was born at Nampa, Idaho 17 July 1962, daughter of John and Gayla (Bill) Gomena.[2113]

Robert Farrell Bonnie graduated from the Brooks School, North Andover, Massachusetts; Harvard College (1989); and Duke University (1994). Cynthia Anne Polk was educated at the Foxcroft School, Middleburg, Virginia, and the University of Virginia (1986). Julie Ann Gomena graduated from Lake Oswego High School, Portland, Oregon, and George Mason University (1997). After graduating from Duke with joint degrees in forestry and environmental management, Robert Bonnie joined the Environmental Defense Fund, where in 2009 he was vice president for land conservation.[2114] In that year, he wrote, "I took a job in the Obama administration as a senior advisor to Secretary of Agriculture Tom Vilsack, covering natural resource and climate issues. In August 2013, I became under secretary for natural resources and environment at USDA, where I oversee the work of the US Forest Service and Natural Resources Conservation Service. While there is considerable cynicism about politics and policy in Washington, I have the pleasure of working with two great agencies dedicated to the conservation of natural resources. Public service has been the hardest, but most rewarding, job I've had."[2115]

Child of Robert Farrell[12] and Cynthia Anne (Polk) Bonnie:[2116]

    i.   CAMILLA CLEMENTINE[13] BONNIE, b. at Washington, D.C. 30 Dec. 1995; she graduated from Foxcroft.

99. DOROTHY AMORY[12] WEXLER (*Dorothy Amory*[11] *Bradford, Dorothy*[10] *Winthrop, Frederic*[9]*, Robert*[8]*, Thomas Charles*[7]*, Francis Bayard*[6]*, John Still*[5]*, John*[4]*, Waitstill*[3]*, John*[2-1]. Also *Dorothy Amory*[11] *Bradford, Dorothy*[11]

[2113] Steward, *The Sarsaparilla Kings*, 126; Steward and Child, *The Descendants of Judge John Lowell of Newburyport, Massachusetts*, 400; *Harvard and Radcliffe Class of 1989 Twenty-fifth Anniversary Report* (Cambridge, Mass.: Printed for the Class, 2014), 83; questionnaire from Robert Farrell Bonnie 2013.

[2114] http://www.usda.gov/wps/portal/usda/usdahome?contentidonly=true&contentid=bio-bonnie.xml.

[2115] *Harvard and Radcliffe Class of 1989 Twenty-fifth Anniversary Report*, 83.

[2116] Steward and Child, *The Descendants of Judge John Lowell of Newburyport, Massachusetts*, 400; questionnaire from Robert Farrell Bonnie 2013.

Winthrop, Dorothy[10] *Amory, Charles Walter*[9] *Amory, Anna Powell Grant*[8] *Sears, David*[7] *Sears, Anne*[6] *Winthrop, John Still*[5]*)* was born at Washington, D.C. 13 April 1969. She married at "Les Essarts," Saint-Briac-sur-Mer (Bretagne), France 16 August 2004, **LUKE ALI SADRIAN**, who was born at London, England 28 August 1969, son of Bijan and Ann Christine (Byrne) Sadrian.[2117]

Dorothy Amory Wexler graduated from Sarah Lawrence College (1991) and Columbia University (1998). Luke Ali Sadrian was educated at the University of Pennsylvania (1991).

Children of Luke Ali Sadrian and Dorothy Amory[12] Wexler, born at London:[2118]

  i. ARTHUR IAN[13] SADRIAN, b. 28 April 2005.
  ii. NOAH WINTHROP PEPPER SADRIAN, b. 16 May 2007.
  iii. JACOB PHINEAS SADRIAN, b. 16 Sept. 2009.

100. **JACOB WINTHROP**[12] **WEXLER** (*Dorothy Amory*[11] *Bradford, Dorothy*[10] *Winthrop, Frederic*[9]*, Robert*[8]*, Thomas Charles*[7]*, Francis Bayard*[6]*, John Still*[5]*, John*[4]*, Waitstill*[3]*, John*[2-1]. Also *Dorothy Amory*[11] *Bradford, Dorothy*[11] *Winthrop, Dorothy*[10] *Amory, Charles Walter*[9] *Amory, Anna Powell Grant*[8] *Sears, David*[7] *Sears, Anne*[6] *Winthrop, John Still*[5]*)* was born at Washington, D.C. 14 September 1970. He married at Malibu, California 14 April 2001, **SARI SALLY YOSHIOKA**, who was born at Los Angeles, California 19 August 1970, daughter of Yu and Tomoko (Sasaki) Yoshioka.[2119]

Jacob Winthrop Wexler graduated from the Sidwell Friends School, Washington, D.C.; the University of California, Berkeley (1993); Columbia University (1996); and Harvard University (1998). Sari Sally Yoshioka was educated at Venice High School, Venice, California; Berkeley (1992); and the University of Washington (1999).

Children of Jacob Winthrop[12] Wexler and Sari Sally Yoshioka:[2120]

  i. YUJI ART YOSHIOKA[13] WEXLER, b. 7 July 2003.
  ii. HANAMI AMORY YOSHIOKA WEXLER, b. 27 March 2006.

[2117] Steward and Child, *The Descendants of Judge John Lowell of Newburyport, Massachusetts*, 400; notes by Luke Ali Sadrian 2013; questionnaire from Dorothy Bradford Wexler 2013.

[2118] Steward and Child, *The Descendants of Judge John Lowell of Newburyport, Massachusetts*, 400.

[2119] Steward and Child, *The Descendants of Judge John Lowell of Newburyport, Massachusetts*, 400; questionnaire from Dorothy Bradford Wexler 2013.

[2120] Steward and Child, *The Descendants of Judge John Lowell of Newburyport, Massachusetts*, 400.

101. **TATYANA AMORY**[12] **BRADFORD** (*Standish*[11] *Bradford, Jr., Dorothy*[10] *Winthrop, Frederic*[9], *Robert*[8], *Thomas Charles*[7], *Francis Bayard*[6], *John Still*[5], *John*[4], *Waitstill*[3], *John*[2-1]. Also *Standish*[11] *Bradford, Jr., Dorothy*[11] *Winthrop, Dorothy*[10] *Amory, Charles Walter*[9] *Amory, Anna Powell Grant*[8] *Sears, David*[7] *Sears, Anne*[6] *Winthrop, John Still*[5]) was born at Cambridge, Massachusetts 30 September 1971. She married at Brookline, Massachusetts 27 June 1998, **JAN TIMOTHY OUHRABKA**, who was born at Providence, Rhode Island 5 April 1970, son of Jan Michael and Niki (Burt) Ouhrabka.[2121]

Tanya Bradford graduated from the Ethel Walker School, Simsbury, Connecticut, and Lake Forest College (1994). J. Timothy Ouhrabka was educated at the Moses Brown School, Providence; Kimball Union Academy, Meriden, New Hampshire; and Lake Forest (1993).

Children of Jan Timothy and Tatyana Amory[12] (Bradford) Ouhrabka, born at Providence:[2122]

   i. JAN CHASE[13] OUHRABKA, b. 30 April 1999; he was educated at Kimball Union.

   ii. THACHER BRADFORD OUHRABKA, b. 24 Oct. 2001; he was educated at Barrington High School in Barrington, R.I.

   iii. ALEXIS AMORY OUHRABKA, b. 28 Feb. 2005.

102. **STANDISH**[12] **BRADFORD, 3RD** (*Standish*[11] *Bradford, Jr., Dorothy*[10] *Winthrop, Frederic*[9], *Robert*[8], *Thomas Charles*[7], *Francis Bayard*[6], *John Still*[5], *John*[4], *Waitstill*[3], *John*[2-1]. Also *Standish*[11] *Bradford, Jr., Dorothy*[11] *Winthrop, Dorothy*[10] *Amory, Charles Walter*[9] *Amory, Anna Powell Grant*[8] *Sears, David*[7] *Sears, Anne*[6] *Winthrop, John Still*[5]) was born at Cambridge, Massachusetts 12 January 1977.[2123]

Standish Bradford, 3rd, was educated at Brookline High School, Brookline, Massachusetts, and Northeastern University (2000x).

Child of Standish[12] Bradford, 3rd, and Elizabeth Dawn Miles:[2124]

   i. STANDISH CHRITZ[13] MILES-BRADFORD, b. 16 Jan. 2007.

[2121] Steward and Child, *The Descendants of Judge John Lowell of Newburyport, Massachusetts*, 401; notes by Tanya Bradford Ouhrabka and J. Timothy Ouhrabka 2013.

[2122] Steward and Child, *The Descendants of Judge John Lowell of Newburyport, Massachusetts*, 401.

[2123] Steward and Child, *The Descendants of Judge John Lowell of Newburyport, Massachusetts*, 401; notes by Standish Bradford, 3rd, 2013.

[2124] Steward and Child, *The Descendants of Judge John Lowell of Newburyport, Massachusetts*, 401.

103. **Sarah Gardner**[12] **Borden** (*Elizabeth Gardner*[11] *Bradford, Dorothy*[10] *Winthrop, Frederic*[9]*, Robert*[8]*, Thomas Charles*[7]*, Francis Bayard*[6]*, John Still*[5]*, John*[4]*, Waitstill*[3]*, John*[2-1]. Also *Elizabeth Gardner*[11] *Bradford, Dorothy*[11] *Winthrop, Dorothy*[10] *Amory, Charles Walter*[9] *Amory, Anna Powell Grant*[8] *Sears, David*[7] *Sears, Anne*[6] *Winthrop, John Still*[5]) was born at New York, New York 22 July 1971. She married at Norfolk, Connecticut 18 May 1996, **John Cooley Wareck**, who was born at New York 19 August 1969, son of Stephen A. and Barbara Joan (Cooley) Wareck, from whom she was divorced.[2125]

Sarah Gardner Borden graduated from the Chapin School, New York; the University of Virginia (1993); and Southern Connecticut State University (2003).

Children of John Cooley Wareck and Sarah Gardner[12] Borden, born at New Haven, Connecticut:[2126]

    i. Anya Gardner[13] Wareck, b. 25 Jan. 2001.

    ii. Stella Rose Wareck, b. 1 Nov. 2003.

104. **Frederic Amory Nalle**[12] **Borden** (*Elizabeth Gardner*[11] *Bradford, Dorothy*[10] *Winthrop, Frederic*[9]*, Robert*[8]*, Thomas Charles*[7]*, Francis Bayard*[6]*, John Still*[5]*, John*[4]*, Waitstill*[3]*, John*[2-1]. Also *Elizabeth Gardner*[11] *Bradford, Dorothy*[11] *Winthrop, Dorothy*[10] *Amory, Charles Walter*[9] *Amory, Anna Powell Grant*[8] *Sears, David*[7] *Sears, Anne*[6] *Winthrop, John Still*[5]) was born at New York, New York 15 February 1978. He married at Milton, New York 24 July 2012, **Katherine Leone Hall**, who was born 26 February 1990.[2127]

Frederic Amory Nalle Borden was educated at Columbia Grammar and Preparatory School, New York, and Occidental College.

Child of Frederic Amory Nalle[12] Borden and Katherine Leone Hall:[2128]

    i. Antonia Leone[13] Borden, b. at New York 4 Feb. 2013.

[2125] *The New York Times*, 13 March 1960, 115; 8 July 1992; Steward and Child, *The Descendants of Judge John Lowell of Newburyport, Massachusetts*, 401; questionnaire from and notes by Elizabeth Bradford Borden 2013; questionnaire from Sarah Gardner Borden 2014.

[2126] Steward and Child, *The Descendants of Judge John Lowell of Newburyport, Massachusetts*, 401; questionnaire from and notes by Elizabeth Bradford Borden 2013; questionnaire from Sarah Gardner Borden 2014.

[2127] Steward and Child, *The Descendants of Judge John Lowell of Newburyport, Massachusetts*, 229; questionnaire from and notes by Elizabeth Bradford Borden 2013; questionnaire from Sarah Gardner Borden 2014.

[2128] Questionnaire from Elizabeth Bradford Borden 2013.

105. **EMILY ERSKINE**[12] **GETCHELL** (*Angela*[11] *Winthrop, Frederic*[10-9]*, Robert*[8]*, Thomas Charles*[7]*, Francis Bayard*[6]*, John Still*[5]*, John*[4]*, Waitstill*[3]*, John*[2-1]. Also *Angela*[12] *Winthrop, Frederic*[11] *Winthrop, Dorothy*[10] *Amory, Charles Walter*[9] *Amory, Anna Powell Grant*[8] *Sears, David*[7] *Sears, Anne*[6] *Winthrop, John Still*[5] and *Angela*[11] *Winthrop, Angela Elizabeth*[10] *Forbes, Margaret Tyndal*[9] *Winthrop, Robert Charles*[8-7]*, Thomas Lindall*[6]*, John Still*[5]) was born at Brussels, Belgium 24 December 1966. She married at Havana, Cuba 31 October 1992, **GABRIEL GRENOT-PORTUONDO**, from whom she was divorced.[2129]

Children of Gabriel Grenot-Portuondo and Emily Erskine[12] Getchell, born at San Francisco, California:[2130]

    i. CASSIUS GABRIEL[13] GRENOT, b. 21 Feb. 1994.
    ii. ULYSSES CHARLES GRENOT, b. 3 Aug. 1997.

106. **SARAH FIELDS**[12] **GETCHELL** (*Angela*[11] *Winthrop, Frederic*[10-9]*, Robert*[8]*, Thomas Charles*[7]*, Francis Bayard*[6]*, John Still*[5]*, John*[4]*, Waitstill*[3]*, John*[2-1]. Also *Angela*[12] *Winthrop, Frederic*[11] *Winthrop, Dorothy*[10] *Amory, Charles Walter*[9] *Amory, Anna Powell Grant*[8] *Sears, David*[7] *Sears, Anne*[6] *Winthrop, John Still*[5] and *Angela*[11] *Winthrop, Angela Elizabeth*[10] *Forbes, Margaret Tyndal*[9] *Winthrop, Robert Charles*[8-7]*, Thomas Lindall*[6]*, John Still*[5]) was born at Brussels, Belgium 18 October 1970. She married at Wilmington, North Carolina 18 March 2011, **JOSHUA LONGSTREET ELLSWORTH**, who was born 16 January 1973, son of Thomas Alan and Jane (Longstreet) Ellsworth.[2131]

Sarah Fields Getchell graduated from Phillips Academy, Andover, Massachusetts, and Brown University.

107. **MIRANDA ROSEMARY**[12] **WINTHROP** (*Adam*[11]*, Frederic*[10-9]*, Robert*[8]*, Thomas Charles*[7]*, Francis Bayard*[6]*, John Still*[5]*, John*[4]*, Waitstill*[3]*, John*[2-1]. Also *Adam*[12] *Winthrop, Frederic*[11] *Winthrop, Dorothy*[10] *Amory, Charles Walter*[9] *Amory, Anna Powell Grant*[8] *Sears, David*[7] *Sears, Anne*[6] *Winthrop, John Still*[5] and *Adam*[11] *Winthrop, Angela Elizabeth*[10] *Forbes, Margaret Tyndal*[9] *Winthrop, Robert Charles*[8-7]*, Thomas Lindall*[6]*, John Still*[5]) was born at Beverly, Massachusetts 12 September 1981. She married at Ipswich, Massachusetts 22 August 2008, **DANIEL JOSEPH MARTIN KACYVENSKI**,

[2129] Questionnaire from Sarah Fields Getchell 2016.
[2130] Questionnaire from Sarah Fields Getchell 2016.
[2131] Questionnaire from Sarah Fields Getchell 2016.

who was born at Johnson City, New York 31 October 1971, son of David and Margaret Elizabeth (Kulakowski) Kacyvenski.[2132]

Children of Daniel Joseph Martin and Miranda Rosemary[12] (Winthrop) Kacyvesnki, born at Beverly:[2133]

> i. STORMY RIVER DANIEL ADAM WAITSTILL[13] KACYVENSKI, b. 16 Jan. 2009.
> ii. ROCCO DANIEL MOON KACYVENSKI, b. 25 March 2011.

108. **REBECCA**[12] **WINTHROP** (*Frederic*[11-9], *Robert*[8], *Thomas Charles*[7], *Francis Bayard*[6], *John Still*[5], *John*[4], *Waitstill*[3], *John*[2-1]. Also *Frederic*[12-11] *Winthrop, Dorothy*[10] *Amory, Charles Walter*[9] *Amory, Anna Powell Grant*[8] *Sears, David*[7] *Sears, Anne*[6] *Winthrop, John Still*[5] and *Frederic*[11] *Winthrop, Angela Elizabeth*[10] *Forbes, Margaret Tyndal*[9] *Winthrop, Robert Charles*[8-7], *Thomas Lindall*[6], *John Still*[5]) was born at Beverly, Massachusetts 29 December 1971. She married at Ipswich, Massachusetts 29 June 1996, **RONALD MONAHAN**, who was born at Warwick, Rhode Island 23 June 1955, son of Ronald and Kathleen (McMahon) Monahan.[2134]

Dr. Rebecca Winthrop graduated from the Pingree School, South Hamilton, Massachusetts; the University of Colorado (1994); and Colorado State University (2002).

Children of Ronald and Rebecca[12] (Winthrop) Monahan, born at Boulder, Colorado:[2135]

> i. FIONA WINTHROP[13] MONAHAN, twin, b. 19 Nov. 2003.
> ii. RILEY WINTHROP MONAHAN, twin, b. 19 Nov. 2003.

109. **FREDERIC**[12] **WINTHROP, 3RD** (*Frederic*[11-9], *Robert*[8], *Thomas Charles*[7], *Francis Bayard*[6], *John Still*[5], *John*[4], *Waitstill*[3], *John*[2-1]. Also *Frederic*[12-11] *Winthrop, Dorothy*[10] *Amory, Charles Walter*[9] *Amory, Anna Powell Grant*[8]

[2132] Steward and Le Roy, *The Le Roy Family in America, 1753–2003*, 502; Steward and Child, *The Descendants of Judge John Lowell of Newburyport, Massachusetts*, 230, 402; questionnaire from Miranda McCagg Ellis 2014.

[2133] Steward and Child, *The Descendants of Judge John Lowell of Newburyport, Massachusetts*, 402; questionnaire from Miranda McCagg Ellis 2014.

[2134] Steward and Child, *The Descendants of Judge John Lowell of Newburyport, Massachusetts*, 402; notes by Dr. Rebecca Winthrop Monahan 2013; questionnaire from Frederic Winthrop 2013.

[2135] Winthrop, *Descendants of Robert Winthrop & Kate Wilson Taylor, 1833–2000*, 45; Steward and Child, *The Descendants of Judge John Lowell of Newburyport, Massachusetts*, 402.

Sears, David[7] Sears, Anne[6] Winthrop, John Still[5] and Frederic[11] Winthrop, Angela Elizabeth[10] Forbes, Margaret Tyndal[9] Winthrop, Robert Charles[8-7], Thomas Lindall[6], John Still[5]) was born at Beverly, Massachusetts 4 June 1974. He married at Upham (Winchester), Hampshire, England 14 May 2005, **ALICE HELEN MACINNES**, who was born at London, England 14 November 1975, daughter of Colin David and Sarah Victoria (Cottrell) MacInnes.[2136]

Frederic Winthrop, 3rd, graduated from St. Paul's School, Concord, New Hampshire, and the University of Colorado (1996). Alice Helen MacInnes was educated at St. Swithun's School, Winchester, and the University of Durham (1998).

Children of Frederic[12] and Alice Helen (MacInnes) Winthrop:[2137]

- i. LUCINDA[13] WINTHROP, b. at Boston, Mass. 8 Aug. 2007.
- ii. CAROLINE WINTHROP, b. at Beverly 12 May 2010.
- iii. FREDERIC WINTHROP, 4TH, b. at Beverly 30 Nov. 2011.

110. **LAURA**[12] **WINTHROP** (*Frederic[11-9], Robert[8], Thomas Charles[7], Francis Bayard[6], John Still[5], John[4], Waitstill[3], John[2-1]*. Also *Frederic[12-11] Winthrop, Dorothy[10] Amory, Charles Walter[9] Amory, Anna Powell Grant[8] Sears, David[7] Sears, Anne[6] Winthrop, John Still[5] and Frederic[11] Winthrop, Angela Elizabeth[10] Forbes, Margaret Tyndal[9] Winthrop, Robert Charles[8-7], Thomas Lindall[6], John Still[5]*) was born at Boston, Massachusetts 23 January 1978. She married at Ascension Memorial Church, Ipswich, Massachusetts 28 May 2011, **CHARLES SPENCER ABBOT**, who was born at Cleveland, Ohio 18 April 1973, son of Admiral Charles Stevenson and Marjorie (Sellars) Abbot.[2138]

Laura Winthrop graduated from the Pingree School, South Hamilton, Massachusetts; Harvard College (2000); and Cambridge University (2002). Commander C. Spencer Abbot was educated at Hampton Roads Academy, Newport News, Virginia; the United States Naval Academy (1995); Tufts University (1997 and 2011); and the Instituto de Empresa in Madrid. After graduating from Harvard, Laura

---

[2136] Steward and Child, *The Descendants of Judge John Lowell of Newburyport, Massachusetts*, 402; questionnaire from Frederic Winthrop 2013.

[2137] Steward and Child, *The Descendants of Judge John Lowell of Newburyport, Massachusetts*, 402; questionnaire from Frederic Winthrop 2013.

[2138] "Laura Winthrop, Spencer Abbot," *The New York Times*, 29 May 2011, ST15; Steward and Child, *The Descendants of Judge John Lowell of Newburyport, Massachusetts*, 402, 403; questionnaire from Frederic Winthrop 2013.

Winthrop worked for the Council on Foreign Relations in New York, then moved to England to study international relations at Cambridge, after which she worked in London and then New York. She wrote, "In the summer of 2008 I packed my bags and moved to Denver to work on the Obama campaign. The 'change we can believe in' mantra sank in with me, and after a couple of fantastic post-elections months traveling around Asia, I am now based in Washington, D.C., trying to make the world a better place as a staff member of the Senate Foreign Relations Committee."[2139]

In 2015, she reported that she had been living in Japan for the last four years: "I am the executive director of the TOMODACHI Initiative, a public-private partnership between the U.S. Embassy in Tokyo and the U.S.–Japan Council. The TOMODACHI Initiative is a cross-cultural youth leadership development program that we started following the great eastern Japan earthquake and tsunami in 2011, initially focused on helping young people from the tsunami-hit region and now serving Japan more broadly. . . .

"My husband, Spencer, commands a squadron of FA-18s for the U.S. Navy, and periodically deploys aboard the aircraft carrier U.S.S. *George Washington*."[2140] In June 2015, Laura Winthrop Abbot became the Washington-based senior vice president of the U.S.–Japan Council; in 2016, Spencer Abbot was serving as a White House Fellow.

Children of Charles Spencer and Laura[12] (Winthrop) Abbot:[2141]

    i.   Eloise Arabella[13] Abbot, b. at Tokyo, Japan 12 Dec. 2012.

    ii. Elizabeth Winthrop Abbot, b. at Arlington, Va. 10 Oct. 2015.

111. **Robert Shaw**[12] **Winthrop** (*Frederic*[11-9], *Robert*[8], *Thomas Charles*[7], *Francis Bayard*[6], *John Still*[5], *John*[4], *Waitstill*[3], *John*[2-1]. Also *Frederic*[12-11] *Winthrop, Dorothy*[10] *Amory, Charles Walter*[9] *Amory, Anna Powell Grant*[8] *Sears, David*[7] *Sears, Anne*[6] *Winthrop, John Still*[5] and *Frederic*[11] *Winthrop, Angela Elizabeth*[10] *Forbes, Margaret Tyndal*[9] *Winthrop, Robert Charles*[8-7], *Thomas Lindall*[6], *John Still*[5]) was born at Beverly, Massachusetts 23 February 1981. He married at Hamilton, Massachusetts 26 May 2012, **Carla Felisa Hollett**, who was born at Beverly 24 October 1981,

---

[2139] *Harvard Class of 2000 Tenth Anniversary Report* (Cambridge, Mass.: Printed for the Class, 2010), 344.

[2140] *Harvard Class of 2000 Fifteenth Anniversary Report* (Cambridge: Printed for the Class, 2015), 339–40.

[2141] Questionnaire from Frederic Winthrop 2013; notes by C. Spencer Abbot 2015.

daughter of Claudio Miller Quiñones and Kathryn Joan Hollett.[2142]

Robert Shaw Winthrop graduated from the Pingree School, South Hamilton, Massachusetts, and Lewis & Clark College (2003). Carla Felisa Hollett was educated at Pingree and the University of Massachusetts, Amherst (2004).

Child of Robert Shaw[12] and Carla Felisa (Hollett) Winthrop:[2143]

    i.   ROBERT LINCOLN[13] WINTHROP, b. at Beverly 13 Sept. 2012.

112. **ELIZABETH HARTLEY**[12] **WINTHROP** (*Grant Forbes*[11], *Frederic*[10-9], *Robert*[8], *Thomas Charles*[7], *Francis Bayard*[6], *John Still*[5], *John*[4], *Waitstill*[3], *John*[2-1]. Also *Grant Forbes*[12] *Winthrop, Frederic*[11] *Winthrop, Dorothy*[10] *Amory, Charles Walter*[9] *Amory, Anna Powell Grant*[8] *Sears, David*[7] *Sears, Anne*[6] *Winthrop, John Still*[5] and *Grant Forbes*[11] *Winthrop, Angela Elizabeth*[10] *Forbes, Margaret Tyndal*[9] *Winthrop, Robert Charles*[8-7], *Thomas Lindall*[6], *John Still*[5]) was born at New York, New York 25 June 1979. She married at "Sheeprocks," Annisquam (Gloucester), Massachusetts 17 June 2006, **ADIN RYAN MURRAY**, who was born at Beverly, Massachusetts 25 August 1974, son of Mark Eldin and Katherine Maureen (Dermody) Murray.[2144]

A graduate of the Nightingale-Bamford School, New York; Harvard College (2001); and the University of California, Irvine (2004), Elizabeth Hartley Winthrop is the author of three novels, the most recent of which is *The Why of Things* (2013). Adin Ryan Murray was educated at Tulane University (1997) and the Savannah College of Art and Design (2009).

Child of Adin Ryan Murray and Elizabeth Hartley[12] Winthrop:[2145]

    i.   HAZEL HARRIETT WINTHROP[13] MURRAY, b. at Savannah 21 April 2012.

113. **FERNANDA WOOD**[12] **WINTHROP** (*Grant Forbes*[11], *Frederic*[10-9], *Robert*[8], *Thomas Charles*[7], *Francis Bayard*[6], *John Still*[5], *John*[4], *Waitstill*[3], *John*[2-1]. Also *Grant Forbes*[12] *Winthrop, Frederic*[11] *Winthrop, Dorothy*[10] *Amory, Charles Walter*[9] *Amory, Anna Powell Grant*[8] *Sears, David*[7] *Sears, Anne*[6] *Winthrop,*

[2142] Steward and Child, *The Descendants of Judge John Lowell of Newburyport, Massachusetts*, 231; notes by Carla Hollett Winthrop 2013; questionnaire from Frederic Winthrop 2013.

[2143] Questionnaire from Frederic Winthrop 2013.

[2144] Winthrop, *Descendants of Robert Winthrop & Kate Wilson Taylor, 1833–2000*, 26; Steward and Child, *The Descendants of Judge John Lowell of Newburyport, Massachusetts*, 232; notes by Charlotte Brock Winthrop 2013 and Elizabeth Hartley Winthrop 2015.

[2145] Notes by Jonathan Winthrop 2017.

John Still⁵ and *Grant Forbes*[11] *Winthrop, Angela Elizabeth*[10] *Forbes, Margaret Tyndal⁹ Winthrop, Robert Charles*[8-7]*, Thomas Lindall⁶, John Still⁵*) was born at New York, New York 15 January 1982. She married at New York 23 December 2013, **JOHN ALEXANDER MICHAS**,[2146] who was born at London, England 13 February 1979, son of George and Catherine (Dewatre) Michas.[2147]

Fernanda Wood Winthrop graduated from the Nightingale-Bamford School, New York, and Harvard College (2004). J. Alexander Michas was educated at Yale College (2001). In 2014, Fernanda Winthrop wrote, "After several years in the art world and then a few more in event planning around nonprofit fundraising, fashion, and film events, I reversed course and found education. I spent two years teaching kindergarten in New York City and am now in my third year as a third-grade teacher."[2148] In 2016, Alex Michas was senior vice president and chief operating officer of VINTUS.

Child of John Alexander Michas and Fernanda Wood[12] Winthrop:[2149]

    i.   EDITH WISE[13] MICHAS, b. at New York 7 Oct. 2015.

114. **CHARLOTTE BROCK**[12] **WINTHROP** (*Grant Forbes*[11], *Frederic*[10-9], *Robert⁸, Thomas Charles⁷, Francis Bayard⁶, John Still⁵, John⁴, Waitstill³, John*[2-1]. Also *Grant Forbes*[12] *Winthrop, Frederic*[11] *Winthrop, Dorothy*[10] *Amory, Charles Walter⁹ Amory, Anna Powell Grant⁸ Sears, David⁷ Sears, Anne⁶ Winthrop, John Still⁵* and *Grant Forbes*[11] *Winthrop, Angela Elizabeth*[10] *Forbes, Margaret Tyndal⁹ Winthrop, Robert Charles*[8-7]*, Thomas Lindall⁶, John Still⁵*) was born at New York, New York 1 March 1986. She married at "Twin Quarries," Lanesville (Gloucester), Massachusetts 10 August 2013, **WELLINGTON WEST SCULLEY**, who was born at New York 16 August 1985, son of Sean West and Rose Ann (Kvaraceus) Sculley.[2150]

Charlotte Brock Winthrop graduated from the Nightingale-Bamford School, New York, and Harvard College (2008). Wellington West Sculley was educated at the Kent School, Kent, Connecticut; Eton

---

[2146] Notes by Fernanda Wood Winthrop 2013.

[2147] *England & Wales, Civil Registration Birth Index, 1916-2005* [database on-line]; *England & Wales, Civil Registration Marriage Index, 1916-2005* [database on-line].

[2148] *Harvard Class of 2004 Tenth Anniversary Report* (Cambridge, Mass.: Printed for the Class, 2014), 315.

[2149] Notes by Wellington West Sculley 2015.

[2150] Steward and Child, *The Descendants of Judge John Lowell of Newburyport, Massachusetts*, 232; notes by Wellington West Sculley and Charlotte Brock Winthrop 2013; notes by Sean West Sculley 2014.

College, Windsor, Berkshire, England; and Harvard (2008).[2151] In 2013, Charlotte Winthrop wrote that, on her move from Cambridge to San Francisco, "the best way to experience such a beautiful part of the world was on foot, and I quickly developed a passion for distance running.... I now work for a social fitness start-up in San Francisco, and lucky for me, running is pretty much a job requirement. I can't get enough of the trails in the Marin Headlands and am looking forward to running my first fifty-miler in 2013."[2152]

Her then-fiancé, Welly Sculley, reported that, in 2008 he had driven "with my wonderful girlfriend, Charlotte Winthrop '08, to the edge of the continent to settle in San Francisco, which happens to be the most beautiful city in the country. I was lucky enough to find a job in a midsized tech company . . . , where I learned some ropes for a year before moving to a smaller tech start-up. In addition to having me spend too much time glued to a computer, work has taken me to great places I may have not been able to visit on my own: Toronto, London, Amsterdam, Stockholm, and Berlin."[2153]

115. **GEORGINA CHESTON**[12] **WINTHROP** (*Jonathan*[11], *Frederic*[10-9], *Robert*[8], *Thomas Charles*[7], *Francis Bayard*[6], *John Still*[5], *John*[4], *Waitstill*[3], *John*[2-1]. Also *Jonathan*[12] *Winthrop*, *Frederic*[11] *Winthrop*, *Dorothy*[10] *Amory*, *Charles Walter*[9] *Amory*, *Anna Powell Grant*[8] *Sears*, *David*[7] *Sears*, *Anne*[6] *Winthrop*, *John Still*[5] and *Jonathan*[11] *Winthrop*, *Angela Elizabeth*[10] *Forbes*, *Margaret Tyndal*[9] *Winthrop*, *Robert Charles*[8-7], *Thomas Lindall*[6], *John Still*[5]) was born at Boston, Massachusetts 16 May 1991. She married at the Church of St. Mary-by-the-Sea, Northeast Harbor, Maine 17 September 2016, **ROBERT HOOPER STEVENSON,** who was born at Boston 4 April 1984, son of Robert Hooper and Louisa Este (Jenkins) Stevenson.[2154]

Georgina Cheston Winthrop graduated from the Winsor School, Boston, and Harvard College (2014). Robert Hooper Stevenson was educated at St. George's School, Newport, Rhode Island, and Hobart–William Smith College (2006).

[2151] He was a member of the Porcellian Club with his college class (*Porcellian Club 1791–2016*, 164).

[2152] *Harvard Class of 2008 Fifth Anniversary Report* (Cambridge, Mass.: Printed for the Class, 2013), 355.

[2153] *Harvard Class of 2008 Fifth Anniversary Report*, 302.

[2154] *The Baltimore Sun*, 28 June 2011; "Georgina Winthrop, Robert Stevenson," *The New York Times*, 18 September 2016, Sunday Styles, 26; notes by Jonathan Winthrop 2016.

116. **JOHN**[12] **WINTHROP, JR.** (*John*[11], *Nathaniel Thayer*[10], *Frederic*[9], *Robert*[8], *Thomas Charles*[7], *Francis Bayard*[6], *John Still*[5], *John*[4], *Waitstill*[3], *John*[2-1]) was born at New York, New York 27 June 1964. He married at Trinity Church, Boston, Massachusetts 10 September 1994, **LOUISA LEWIS DALEY**, who was born at Boston 31 May 1965, daughter of Robert Lewis and Jennie Lee (Bradford) Daley.[2155]

John Winthrop, Jr., graduated from Deerfield Academy, Deerfield, Massachusetts, and Harvard University (1986 and 1992). Louisa Lewis Daley was educated at Milton Academy, Milton, Massachusetts; Duke University (1987); and Boston University (1989). In 2016, Jay Winthrop wrote:

> I am incredibly lucky to have found Louisa, the most graceful and kind person I know. My wife and our sons, Brad and Robbie, are the light of my life. To see Louisa achieve her potential as a clinical therapist, and Brad develop his academic interests, and to be with Robbie as he navigates the tricky path from childhood to being a young man—these are my happiest moments. Nothing is better than casting a dry fly or playing guitar or sharing happy news with them.
>
> Professionally, I am a co-founder of Douglass Winthrop Advisors LLC, an investment advisory firm with offices in New York and Washington, D.C. A unifying theme to my life's work is the belief that business models and private capital can be more effective than traditional aid or regulatory approaches in mitigating environmental challenges. The Conservation Fund, where I serve as vice chairman, is pioneering new approaches to conservation, grounded in the principles of finance and partnership with innovative companies such as Apple. Similarly, as a member of the State Department's Advisory Committee on International Economic Policy, I appreciate the opportunity to advise policy makers on trade and investment in developing countries, where environmental issues are critical.[2156]

[2155] "Descendants of Cornelia P. Van Rensselaer Thayer and Nathaniel Thayer" (1972), Chart 3-C-1-a; *The New York Times*, 11 September 1994, 68; questionnaire from John Winthrop, Jr., 2013.

[2156] Notes by John Winthrop, Jr., 2016. Jay Winthrop also served as chairman of the American Farmland Trust 2006–10.

Children of John[12] and Louisa Lewis (Daley) Winthrop, born at New York:[2157]

    i.   JOHN BRADFORD[13] WINTHROP, b. 2 Jan. 1997; he was educated at the Middlesex School, Concord, Mass., and St. Lawrence University.

    ii. ROBERT DALEY WINTHROP, b. 29 Jan. 2000; he was educated at Middlesex.

117. **GRENVILLE**[12] **WINTHROP** (*John*[11], *Nathaniel Thayer*[10], *Frederic*[9], *Robert*[8], *Thomas Charles*[7], *Francis Bayard*[6], *John Still*[5], *John*[4], *Waitstill*[3], *John*[2-1]) was born Henry Grenville Winthrop at New York, New York 5 March 1966. He married at Las Vegas, Nevada 16 May 2007, **MARY ANNE TETANICH**, who was born at Charleston, South Carolina 29 September 1959, formerly wife of Donald Allen Hutson, and daughter of George and Ethel Jean (Smoak) Tetanich.[2158]

Grenville Winthrop graduated from Greenwich High School, Greenwich, Connecticut, and New England College (1989). Mary Anne Tetanich was educated at Trident Technical College (1979).

118. **DUDLEY**[12] **WINTHROP** (*Beekman*[11], *Nathaniel Thayer*[10], *Frederic*[9], *Robert*[8], *Thomas Charles*[7], *Francis Bayard*[6], *John Still*[5], *John*[4], *Waitstill*[3], *John*[2-1]) was born 18 February 1972. He married in October 2005, **JENNIFER LOUISE SNEE**, who was born 28 August 1974, daughter of Thomas and Diane M. (Carter) Snee.[2159]

Dudley Winthrop graduated from the Potomac School, McLean, Virginia, and Middlebury College (1994). Jennifer Louise Snee was educated at Sherwood High School, Olney, Maryland, and Wake Forest University (1996).

Children of Dudley[12] and Jennifer Louise (Snee) Winthrop:[2160]

    i.   KATHARINE TAYLOR[13] WINTHROP, b. 23 Nov. 2007.

    ii. SERAFINA MARGARET WOOD WINTHROP, b. 4 Dec. 2009.

[2157] *Summer Social Register 1997 Dilatory Domiciles May 1997*, 78; Winthrop, *Descendants of Robert Winthrop & Kate Wilson Taylor, 1833–2000*, 47; *Harvard and Radcliffe Class of 1986 Twentieth Anniversary Report* (Cambridge, Mass.: Printed for the Class, 2006), 489; questionnaire from John Winthrop, Jr., 2013.

[2158] Questionnaire from Grenville Winthrop 2014.

[2159] *Daily Press*, 4 September 2005.

[2160] *Wake Forest Magazine* 55 [March 2008]: 54; 57 [June 2010]: 57.

119. **MARIANA LOWELL**[12] **BARZUN** (*Serita*[11] *Winthrop, Nathaniel Thayer*[10], *Frederic*[9], *Robert*[8], *Thomas Charles*[7], *Francis Bayard*[6], *John Still*[5], *John*[4], *Waitstill*[3], *John*[2-1]) was born at New York, New York 5 March 1969. She married at Rhinebeck, New York 1 May 1999, **JONATHAN LEE MENSCH**, who was born at Ithaca, New York 14 October 1969, son of Steven Harold and Elizabeth Vance (Birchell) Mensch.[2161]

Mariana Lowell Barzun graduated from the Buckingham, Browne, and Nichols School, Cambridge, Massachusetts, and Trinity College (1991). Jonathan Lee Mensch was educated at the Park School, Amherst, New York; Kenyon College (1992); and New York University (2000 and 2002). In 2016, Mariana Barzun Mensch was Director of Parent Giving and Assistant Campaign Chair at Vassar College, and Jonathan Mensch was managing partner at Great Jones Asset Management.

Children of Jonathan Lee and Mariana Lowell[12] (Barzun) Mensch, born at New York:[2162]

    i. ELIZABETH LOWREY[13] MENSCH, b. 18 Sept. 2001.
    ii. CLAIRE WINTHROP MENSCH, b. 8 July 2003.

120. **MATTHEW WINTHROP**[12] **BARZUN** (*Serita*[11] *Winthrop, Nathaniel Thayer*[10], *Frederic*[9], *Robert*[8], *Thomas Charles*[7], *Francis Bayard*[6], *John Still*[5], *John*[4], *Waitstill*[3], *John*[2-1]) was born at New York, New York 23 October 1970. He married at the Cathedral of the Assumption, Louisville, Kentucky 18 September 1999, **BROOKE LEE BROWN**, who was born at Louisville 18 June 1972, daughter of Owsley and Christina Sim (Lee) Brown.[2163]

Matthew Winthrop Barzun graduated from St. Paul's School, Concord, New Hampshire, and Harvard College (1992). Brooke Lee Brown was educated at the Westover School, Middlebury, Connecticut, and Lake Forest College (1994). After Harvard, Matthew Barzun joined CNET as its fourth employee. He rose to the level of executive vice president and chief strategy officer, then left to start his own consulting firm. According to a profile in *The Telegraph*, as an "activist

---

[2161] Steward and Child, *The Descendants of Judge John Lowell of Newburyport, Massachusetts*, 337; questionnaires from Mariana Barzun Mensch and Serita Winthrop 2013.

[2162] Steward and Child, *The Descendants of Judge John Lowell of Newburyport, Massachusetts*, 338; questionnaire from Mariana Barzun Mensch 2013.

[2163] Steward and Child, *The Descendants of Judge John Lowell of Newburyport, Massachusetts*, 338; http://en.wikipedia.org/wiki/Matthew_Barzun.

in the Democratic Party from a young age, he shot to prominence as a fundraiser in the 2008 Obama campaign, when he was credited with pioneering low-cost, large-scale events which drew in thousands of supporters." In 2009, he was named U.S. Ambassador to Sweden, serving until 2011, and in 2012, he served as national finance chair of President Obama's reelection campaign. In July 2013, he was named U.S. Ambassador to Great Britain,[2164] serving until January 2017.

A 2013 profile in *The Guardian* offered these insights about the new ambassador (and the signal his appointment should be sending):

> The 42-year-old Barzun carries the influence of [his time in Silicon Valley] in his leadership style and forward-leaning approach to diplomacy. He does not accept problems as fixed and unalterable...
>
> With the nomination of Matthew Barzun, the United Kingdom does not just get a U.S. ambassador, it gets an Obama ambassador. In the vernacular of Barzun's Kentucky, it gets a big dog that can hunt in the tall grass.[2165]

Children of Matthew Winthrop[12] and Brooke Lee (Brown) Barzun:[2166]

    i.   JACQUES MARTIN[13] BARZUN, 2ND, twin, b. at Charleston, W.V. 22 Sept. 2001.

    ii. ELEANOR CONLEY BARZUN, twin, b. at Charleston 22 Sept. 2001.

    iii. CHARLES WINTHROP BARZUN, b. at Louisville 3 Oct. 2005.

121. LUCY[12] BARZUN (*Serita*[11] *Winthrop, Nathaniel Thayer*[10], *Frederic*[9], *Robert*[8], *Thomas Charles*[7], *Francis Bayard*[6], *John Still*[5], *John*[4], *Waitstill*[3], *John*[2-1]) was born Lucretia Mott Barzun at Boston, Massachusetts 14 May 1973. She married at Rhinebeck, New York 30 September 2006, ROBERT DONNELLY, who was born at Hartlepool, Durham, England 22 July 1967, son of Kevin and Margaret A. (Kennedy) Donnelly.[2167]

[2164] Alex Spilius, "Matthew Barzun: profile of the new American ambassador to Britain," 10 July 2013, http://www.telegraph.co.uk/news/worldnews/us-politics/10171389/Matthew-Barzun-profile-of-the-new-American-ambassador-to-Britain.html.

[2165] Alec Ross, "Who is Matthew Barzun," 10 July 2013, http://www.theguardian.com/commentisfree/2013/jul/10/matthew-barzun-us-ambassador-britain-obama.

[2166] Steward and Child, *The Descendants of Judge John Lowell of Newburyport, Massachusetts*, 338.

[2167] Steward and Child, *The Descendants of Judge John Lowell of Newburyport, Massachusetts*, 338; notes by Lucy Barzun Donnelly 2013.

Lucy Barzun graduated from St. Paul's School, Concord, New Hampshire, and Georgetown University (1995). Robert Donnelly was educated at the University of Newcastle (1989) and the University of Texas. Lucy Barzun Donnelly's first production credit was for *Pieces of April* (2003), for which Patricia Clarkson was nominated for an Academy Award. Her production of *Grey Gardens* (2009) won Emmy and Golden Globe awards for best television production of 2009 and garnered further awards and nominations for cast and crew members.[2168]

Child of Robert and Lucy[12] (Barzun) Donnelly:[2169]

   i. JACK BARZUN[13] DONNELLY, b. at Los Angeles, Calif. 20 Nov. 2008.

122. **CHARLES LOWELL**[12] **BARZUN** (*Serita*[11] *Winthrop, Nathaniel Thayer*[10], *Frederic*[9], *Robert*[8], *Thomas Charles*[7], *Francis Bayard*[6], *John Still*[5], *John*[4], *Waitstill*[3], *John*[2-1]) was born at Boston, Massachusetts 19 March 1975. He married at Cranberry Isles (Great Cranberry Island), Maine 14 July 2012, **EMILY BRADFORD LITTLE,** who was born at New York, New York 22 March 1985, daughter of Carl von Kienbusch Little and Margaret Ann Beaulac.[2170]

Charles Lowell Barzun graduated from St. George's School, Newport, Rhode Island; Harvard College (1997); and the University of Virginia (2005). Emily Bradford Little was educated at Mount Desert High School, Mount Desert, Maine; the University of Maine (2009); and Georgetown University (2013). After college, Charles L. Barzun traveled in South America ("mostly teaching English in Argentina and backpacking through Peru, Ecuador, and Colombia"); in 2002, he was living in California and working for CNET: "However, I suspect that by the time this Report is published I will already have left San Francisco. I am hoping to return to school next fall, and right I now I really have very little idea of where I'll be next year or what I'll be doing a few years from now."[2171] Later in 2002, he entered the law school at the University of Virginia, where in 2016 he was Armistead M. Dobie Professor of Law.

[2168] https://en.wikipedia.org/wiki/Lucy_Barzun_Donnelly; http://www.imdb.com/name/nm1198914/?ref_=fn_al_nm_1.

[2169] Steward and Child, *The Descendants of Judge John Lowell of Newburyport, Massachusetts,* 338.

[2170] *The New York Times,* 10 June 1984; *Fence Viewer,* 21 July 2011; Steward and Child, *The Descendants of Judge John Lowell of Newburyport, Massachusetts,* 184; questionnaires from Charles Lowell Barzun and Mariana Barzun Mensch 2013.

[2171] *Harvard and Radcliffe Class of 1997 Fifth Anniversary Report* (Cambridge, Mass.: Printed for the Class, 2002), 19–20.

Child of Charles Lowell[12] and Emily Bradford (Little) Barzun:[2172]

    i. MARIA MARGARET[13] BARZUN, b. at Charlottesville, Va. 29 May 2013.

123. **ELIAS DUNN**[12] **WINTHROP** (*Nathaniel Thayer*[11-10], *Frederic*[9], *Robert*[8], *Thomas Charles*[7], *Francis Bayard*[6], *John Still*[5], *John*[4], *Waitstill*[3], *John*[2-1]) was born at Randolph, Vermont 12 August 1975.[2173]

Elias Dunn Winthrop graduated from Hampshire College in 2002.

Child of Elias Dunn[12] Winthrop and Shannon Victoria Wetmore, who was born 20 October 1972:[2174]

    i. DESMOND CHRISTOPHER O'MEARA[13] WINTHROP, b. at Morristown, Vt. 4 May 2001.

124. **EMMA O'MEARA**[12] **WINTHROP** (*Nathaniel Thayer*[11-10], *Frederic*[9], *Robert*[8], *Thomas Charles*[7], *Francis Bayard*[6], *John Still*[5], *John*[4], *Waitstill*[3], *John*[2-1]) was born at Duxbury, Vermont 12 May 1978. She married at Plainfield, Vermont 28 August 2004, **PETTER MORITZ BAY-HANSEN**, who was born at Montreal, Quebec, Canada 28 June 1970, son of Christopher and Laila (Pettersen) Bay-Hansen.[2175]

Emma O'Meara Winthrop was educated at Montpelier High School, Montpelier, Vermont; Olympia State College (2000); and Union Institute and University (2012).

Children of Petter Moritz Bay-Hansen and Emma O'Meara[12] Winthrop:[2176]

    i. SOREN NATHANIEL[13] BAY-HANSEN, b. at Berlin, Vt. 15 July 2007.
   ii. PETRA JEANNETTE BAY-HANSEN, b. at Burlington, Vt. 31 Dec. 2010.

125. **DANIEL**[12] **WINTHROP** (*Nathaniel Thayer*[11-10], *Frederic*[9], *Robert*[8], *Thomas Charles*[7], *Francis Bayard*[6], *John Still*[5], *John*[4], *Waitstill*[3], *John*[2-1]) was

---

[2172] Questionnaire from Charles Lowell Barzun 2013.

[2173] *Vermont Birth Records, 1909–2008*; *Harvard and Radcliffe Class of 1974 Thirtieth Anniversary Report* (2004), 344; notes by Eli Winthrop 2013.

[2174] Department of Health Vermont Certificate of Live Birth 01092297; *Harvard and Radcliffe Class of 1974 Thirtieth Anniversary Report* (Cambridge, Mass.: Printed for the Class, 2004), 344.

[2175] Department of Health Vermont License and Certificate of Marriage 04003514; *Harvard and Radcliffe Class of 1974 Thirtieth Anniversary Report*, 344; notes by Emma O'Meara Winthrop 2013.

[2176] Department of Health Vermont Certificate of Live Birth 07003240; notes by Martha Dunn Winthrop 2015.

born at Duxbury, Vermont 3 May 1980. He married at Christ Church, Montpelier, Vermont 15 February 2014, **MICHELE LYNN CRONAN**, who was born at Hanover, New Hampshire 27 April 1977, daughter of Michael Patrick and Tina Marie (Peters) Cronan.[2177]

Daniel Winthrop was educated at Montpelier High School, Johnston State College, and Evergreen State College.

Child of Daniel[12] and Michelle Lynn (Cronan) Winthrop:[2178]

    i.   JASPER FELIX[13] WINTHROP, b. at Hanover 14 June 2014.

126. **ANNE MARINA**[12] **VAN NOTTEN** (*Henriette Albertine*[11] *van Roijen, Jan Herman*[10] *van Roijen, Albertina Taylor*[9] *Winthrop, Robert*[8], *Thomas Charles*[7], *Francis Bayard*[6], *John Still*[5], *John*[4], *Waitstill*[3], *John*[2-1]) was born at Rotterdam (South Holland), the Netherlands 2 August 1960. She married at Amsterdam (North Holland) 31 December 1987, **JOHANNES PAULUS ALOYSIUS MARIE PETIT**, who was born at Eindhoven (North Brabant), the Netherlands, son of Johannes Baptistes Gerardus and Louise Catharina Maria (van Heijst) Petit.[2179]

Marina van Notten was educated at the European School of Brussels, Uccles, Belgium; Bryn Mawr College; and the University of Groningen (1984). Johannes Paulus Aloysius Marie Petit graduated from the United World College of the Atlantic, St. Donat's, Glamorganshire, Wales; the University of Groningen; and the University of Pennsylvania (1984).

127. **HENRIETTE DIGNA ALBERTINA WINTHROP**[12] **VAN NOTTEN** (*Henriette Albertine*[11] *van Roijen, Jan Herman*[10] *van Roijen, Albertina Taylor*[9] *Winthrop, Robert*[8], *Thomas Charles*[7], *Francis Bayard*[6], *John Still*[5], *John*[4], *Waitstill*[3], *John*[2-1]), twin, was born at New York, New York 10 August 1962. She married at Wassenaar (South Holland), the Netherlands 23 September 1992, **REINDERT CARL FRANS EDUARD HOUBEN**, who was born at The Hague (South Holland) 19 August 1962, son of Piet Hein Houben and Barones Theresia Maria Ludovica van Voorst tot Voorst.[2180]

[2177] *Vermont Birth Records, 1909–2008*; notes by Daniel Winthrop 2013 and Martha Dunn Winthrop 2015.

[2178] Notes by Martha Dunn Winthrop 2015.

[2179] Winthrop, *Descendants of Robert Winthrop & Kate Wilson Taylor, 1833–2000*, 29, 49; http://gw.geneanet.org/kooler?lang=en;pz=louise+elisabeth;nz=koole;ocz=1;alwsur n=yes;p=henriette+albertina;n=van+royen; http://gw.geneanet.org/kooler?lang=en; pz=louise+elisabeth;nz=koole;ocz=1;alwsurn=yes;p=johannes+paulus+aloysius+mar ie;n=petit; questionnaire from Henriette Albertina van Roÿen van Notten 2013.

[2180] Winthrop, *Descendants of Robert Winthrop & Kate Wilson Taylor, 1833–2000*, 29, 49;

Henriette Digna van Notten graduated from St. Mark's School, Southborough, Massachusetts; Georgetown University (1984); and the University of Leiden (1988). Reindert Carl Frans Eduard Houben was educated at the United World College of the Atlantic, St. Donat's, Glamorganshire, Wales; the University of Leiden (1988); and Solvay Brussels School of Business and Economics (1992).

Children of Reindert Carl Frans Eduard and Henriette Digna Albertina Winthrop[12] (van Notten) Houben:[2181]

  i. FRANCESCA DIGNA ALBERTINA[13] HOUBEN, b. at London, England 23 May 2002.

  ii. DANTE REINDERT HENRI HOUBEN, b. at Amsterdam (North Holland) 30 Nov. 2005.

128. **ARIANE SIGRID**[12] **VAN NOTTEN** (*Henriette Albertine*[11] *van Roijen, Jan Herman*[10] *van Roijen, Albertina Taylor*[9] *Winthrop, Robert*[8], *Thomas Charles*[7], *Francis Bayard*[6], *John Still*[5], *John*[4], *Waitstill*[3], *John*[2-1]), twin, was born at New York, New York 10 August 1962. She married at Amsterdam (North Holland), the Netherlands 9 September 1996, **FREDERIK HAROLD FENTENER VAN VLISSINGEN**, who was born at Hilversum (North Holland) 17 December 1968, son of Frederik Hendrik and Marianne (Gleichman) Fentener van Vlissingen.[2182]

Children of Frederik Harold and Ariane Sigrid[12] (van Notten) Fentener van Vlissingen, born at Amsterdam:[2183]

  i. FREDERIK HENDRIK[13] FENTENER VAN VLISSINGEN, b. 15 Nov. 1997.

  ii. DAVID NELSON FENTENER VAN VLISSINGEN, b. 15 Aug. 1999.

  iii. LIVIA LLOYD FENTENER VAN VLISSINGEN, b. 18 Oct. 2001.

---

http://gw.geneanet.org/edriessen?lang=fr&m=N&v=houben; http://gw.geneanet .org/kooler?lang=en;pz=louise+elisabeth;nz=koole;ocz=1;alwsurn=yes;p=henrie tte+albertina;n=van+royen; notes by Henriette Digna van Notten 2013; questionnaire from Henriette Albertina van Roÿen van Notten 2013.

[2181] Winthrop, *Descendants of Robert Winthrop & Kate Wilson Taylor, 1833–2000*, 49; http://www.geneaservice.nl/ar/2007/ar-460.html.

[2182] http://heirsofeurope.blogspot.com/2010/12/fentener-van-vlissingen.html; http://gw.geneanet.org/kooler?lang=en;pz=louise+elisabeth;nz=koole;ocz=1;al wsurn=yes;p=henriette+albertina;n=van+royen.

[2183] http://heirsofeurope.blogspot.com/2010/12/fentener-van-vlissingen.html.

129. **Isabelle Fernande**[12] **van Notten** (*Henriette Albertine*[11] *van Roijen, Jan Herman*[10] *van Roijen, Albertina Taylor*[9] *Winthrop, Robert*[8], *Thomas Charles*[7], *Francis Bayard*[6], *John Still*[5], *John*[4], *Waitstill*[3], *John*[2-1]) was born at Ixelles (Brussels) Belgium 28 June 1964. She married 5 February 1992, **David Michael Rosenberg**, who was born at Bethesda, Maryland 16 January 1965, son of Robert Gordon and Lynn Sue (Abrahamson) Rosenberg.[2184]

Isabelle Fernande van Notten graduated from the European School of Brussels, Uccles, Belgium; the University of York (1985); and the University of Sussex (1987). David Michael Rosenberg was educated at Brookline High School, Brookline, Massachusetts; Princeton University (1986); and Boston University (1993).

130. **Jan Herman**[12] **van Roijen** (*Jan Herman Robert Dudley*[11] *van Roijen, Jan Herman*[10] *van Roijen, Albertina Taylor*[9] *Winthrop, Robert*[8], *Thomas Charles*[7], *Francis Bayard*[6], *John Still*[5], *John*[4], *Waitstill*[3], *John*[2-1]) was born at The Hague (South Holland), the Netherlands 27 December 1964. He married at The Hague 5 (*civil*) / Reformed Church, Voorschoten (South Holland) 13 July 1996 (*religious*), **Sophie Charlotte Egbertine van der Kuip**, who was born at Quito, Ecuador 25 September 1967, daughter of Egbert Johan and Else Ada Nelly (Zilvold) van der Kuip.[2185]

Dr. Herman van Roijen graduated from Ashbury College, Ottowa, Ontario, Canada, and the University of Utrecht (1994). Sophie van der Kuip was educated at St. Bonifatius' College, Utrecht, and the University of Utrecht.

Children of Jan Herman[12] and Sophie Charlotte Egbertina (van der Kuip) van Roijen, first two born at Rotterdam (South Holland):[2186]

  i. Jan Herman Marnix[13] van Roijen, b. 9 Sept. 1999.
  ii. Deirdre Else Carolina van Roijen, b. 21 Aug. 2001.
  iii. Christiaan Willem Egbert van Roijen, b. at Tilburg (North Brabant), the Netherlands 19 Oct. 2004.

[2184] Winthrop, *Descendants of Robert Winthrop & Kate Wilson Taylor, 1833–2000*, 29, 49; http://gw.geneanet.org/kooler?lang=en;pz=louise+elisabeth;nz=koole;ocz=1;al wsurn=yes;p=henriette+albertina;n=van+royen; http://gw.geneanet.org/kooler?l ang=en;pz=louise+elisabeth;nz=koole;ocz=1;alwsurn=yes;p=david+michael;n=r osenberg; questionnaire from Henriette Albertina van Roÿen van Notten 2013.

[2185] http://www.lichtenbelt.com/genealogie/lichtparenteel/tekst.htm; notes by Dr. Herman van Roijen 2013; questionnaire from and notes by Sophie van der Kuip van Roijen 2014.

[2186] Winthrop, *Descendants of Robert Winthrop & Kate Wilson Taylor, 1833–2000*, 50; http://www.lichtenbelt.com/genealogie/lichtparenteel/tekst.htm; questionnaire from Sophe van der Kuip van Roijen 2014.

131. **ANNE**[12] **VAN ROIJEN** (*Jan Herman Robert Dudley*[11] *van Roijen, Jan Herman*[10] *van Roijen, Albertina Taylor*[9] *Winthrop, Robert*[8], *Thomas Charles*[7], *Francis Bayard*[6], *John Still*[5], *John*[4], *Waitstill*[3], *John*[2-1]) was born at Jakarta, Indonesia 7 May 1966. Her partner is **JAN PIETER DE KOK**, who was born at Rotterdam (South Holland), the Netherlands 15 January 1952, son of Jan Pieter and Henriëtte (Korpel) de Kok.[2187]

Children of Jan Pieter de Kok and Anne[12] van Roijen:[2188]

152   i.   NATHALYA GALADRIEL[13] DE KOK, b. at The Hague (South Holland) 12 July 1990.

ii.   GARION ERINDALE DE KOK, b. at The Hague 27 Aug. 1991.

iii. APHRAEL TREVIZENT DE KOK, b. at The Hague 15 Oct. 1992.

iv.   CEDRIC ANAKHA DE KOK, b. at The Hague 11 Feb. 1995.

v.   EHLANA POLGARA DE KOK, b. at The Hague 22 Jan. 1998.

vi.   IZABELLA SEPHRENIA DE KOK, b. at The Hague 9 Dec. 1999.

Adopted child of Jan Pieter de Kok and Anne[12] van Roijen:[2189]

vii. PERSIJN VAN DER LINDE, b. at Rheden (Gelderland), the Netherlands 19 Nov. 2004.

132. **THEODORA HELENA WILHELMINA**[12] **VAN ROIJEN** (*Jan Herman Robert Dudley*[11] *van Roijen, Jan Herman*[10] *van Roijen, Albertina Taylor*[9] *Winthrop, Robert*[8], *Thomas Charles*[7], *Francis Bayard*[6], *John Still*[5], *John*[4], *Waitstill*[3], *John*[2-1]) was born at Ukkel (Brussels), Belgium 16 October 1968. She married at Wassenaar (South Holland), the Netherlands 15 May 1999, **FRANK VAN DEN MERKENHOF**, who was born at Haarlem (North Holland) 17 August 1958.[2190]

133. **JONKHEER JAN DERCK**[12] **VAN KARNEBEEK** (*Digna Anne*[11] *van Roijen, Jan Herman*[10] *van Roijen, Albertina Taylor*[9] *Winthrop, Robert*[8], *Thomas Charles*[7], *Francis Bayard*[6], *John Still*[5], *John*[4], *Waitstill*[3], *John*[2-1]) was born at The Hague (South Holland), the Netherlands 12 April 1967. He married at Nijmegen (Gelderland), the Netherlands 13 December 1998, **JACQUELINE THŸSSEN**, who was born at Nÿmegen 26 April 1966, daughter of Guus and Elisabeth (Burger) ThŸssen.[2191]

[2187] Notes by Anne van Roijen and Jan Pieter de Kok 2014.

[2188] Notes by Anne van Roijen and Jan Pieter de Kok 2014 and 2015.

[2189] Notes by Anne van Roijen and Jan Pieter de Kok 2014.

[2190] http://www.lichtenbelt.com/genealogie/lichtparenteel/tekst.htm; questionnaire from Carolina Reuchlin van Roijen 2014.

[2191] http://www.kloek-genealogie.nl/Block3.htm; questionnaire from Digna Anne van

Jonkheer Jan Derck van Karnebeek was educated at Cincinnati Country Day School, Cincinnati, Ohio; the University of Utrecht (1991); and INSEAD (1993). Jacqueline Thÿssen graduated from the University of Amsterdam in 1992. Jan Derck van Karnebeek has spent his entire professional career at Heineken NV; in 2015, he was named the company's Chief Commercial Officer.[2192]

Children of Jonkheer Jan Derck[12] van Karnebeek and Jacqueline Thÿssen:[2193]

    i. Jonkheer Herman Adriaan[13] van Karnebeek, b. at Hong Kong 4 April 1999.

    ii. Jonkvrouwe Philine Digna Iris van Karnebeek, b. at Bratislava, Slovakia 7 Aug. 2000.

    iii. Jonkvrouwe Alexine van Karnebeek, b. at Bratislava 6 Dec. 2001.

    iv. Jonkvrouwe Juliette Emilie Marie van Karnebeek, b. at Hilversum (North Holland) 30 March 2005.

134. Jonkvrouwe Emilie Thelma[12] van Karnebeek (*Digna Anne*[11] *van Roijen, Jan Herman*[10] *van Roijen, Albertina Taylor*[9] *Winthrop, Robert*[8], *Thomas Charles*[7], *Francis Bayard*[6], *John Still*[5], *John*[4], *Waitstill*[3], *John*[2-1]) was born at Rheden (Gelderland), the Netherlands 7 March 1969. She married at Diever (Drenthe), the Netherlands 27 June 1998, Jeroen Henk Leonard Pit, who was born at Vianen (Utrecht), the Netherlands 20 May 1968 and died at Amsterdam (North Holland) 5 February 2012, son of Ari and Marianne Leonie (Boer) Pit.[2194]

Jonkvrouwe Emilie Thelma van Karnebeek graduated from Cincinnati Country Day School, Cincinnati, Ohio, and the University of Groningen (1993). Jeroen Henk Leonard Pit was educated at the University of Amsterdam.

Roÿen van Karnebeek 2013.

[2192] http://www.bloomberg.com/research/stocks/people/person.asp?person Id=54468686&privcapId=410350.

[2193] http://www.kloek-genealogie.nl/Block3.htm; questionnaire from Digna Anne van Roÿen van Karnebeek 2013.

[2194] http://www.kloek-genealogie.nl/Block3.htm; questionnaires from Digna Anne van Roÿen van Karnebeek 2013 and Emilie van Karnebeek Pit 2014.

Children of Jeroen Henk Leonard Pit and Jonkvrouwe Emilie Thelma[12] van Karnebeek, born at Amsterdam:[2195]

    i. ISABELLE ANNE[13] PIT, b. 8 Oct. 1999.

    ii. OLIVIER ADRIAAN PIT, b. 3 April 2001.

    iii. ROEMER ALEXANDER PIT, b. 15 June 2003.

135. **JONKVROUWE CLARA DIGNA MALOUT**[12] **VAN KARNEBEEK** (*Digna Anne*[11] *van Roijen, Jan Herman*[10] *van Roijen, Albertina Taylor*[9] *Winthrop, Robert*[8]*, Thomas Charles*[7]*, Francis Bayard*[6]*, John Still*[5]*, John*[4]*, Waitstill*[3]*, John*[2-1]) was born at Zwolle (Overijssel), the Netherlands 26 September 1972. She married at Amsterdam (North Holland), the Netherlands 31 December 2003, **RODERICK FRANCIS ARTHUR HOUBEN**, who was born at The Hague (South Holland) 14 March 1970, son of Philippus Josephus Ignatius Maria and Margaretha Maria Josepha (van Acker) Houben.[2196]

Children of Roderick Francis Arthur Houben and Jonkvrouwe Clara Digna Malout[12] van Karnebeek:[2197]

    i. PHILIP DEGI ALEXANDER[13] HOUBEN, b. at The Hague 10 Jan. 2005.

    ii. CEDRIC QUINTEN DICKY HOUBEN, b. at Amsterdam 31 Aug. 2006.

136. **JORIS WILLEM PETER**[12] **VAN ROIJEN** (*Willem Joris Winthrop John*[11] *van Roijen, Jan Herman*[10] *van Roijen, Albertina Taylor*[9] *Winthrop, Robert*[8]*, Thomas Charles*[7]*, Francis Bayard*[6]*, John Still*[5]*, John*[4]*, Waitstill*[3]*, John*[2-1]) was born at The Hague (South Holland), the Netherlands 10 June 1975. He married at the Dutch Reformed Church, Wassenaaer (South Holland) 28 August 2005, **MARIE-ANNE ODINK**, who was born at Nijkerk (Gelderland), the Netherlands 19 October 1977, daughter of Reinhold and Ellen Marie (van der Hoeven) Odink.[2198]

Joris Willem Peter van Roijen graduated from the Rijnlands Lyceum, Wassenaar, and the University of Amsterdam (2002).

[2195] http://www.kloek-genealogie.nl/Block3.htm; questionnaires from Digna Anne van Roÿen van Karnebeek 2013 and Emilie van Karnebeek Pit 2014.

[2196] http://www.kloek-genealogie.nl/Block3.htm; http://gw.geneanet.org/edriesse n?lang=fr&m=N&v=houben ; questionnaire from Digna Anne van Roÿen van Karnebeek 2013.

[2197] http://www.kloek-genealogie.nl/Block3.htm; questionnaire from Digna Anne van Roÿen van Karnebeek 2013.

[2198] Winthrop, *Descendants of Robert Winthrop & Kate Wilson Taylor, 1833–2000*, 29; notes by Joris Willem Peter van Roijen and Marie-Anne van Roijen-Odink 2013; questionnaires from Willem Joris Winthrop John van Roijen 2013 and Joris Willem Peter van Roijen 2015; notes by Willem Joris Winthrop John van Roijen 2014.

Children of Joris Willem Peter[12] and Marie-Anne (Odink) van Roijen:[2199]

   i.   Anne Juliette Emilie[13] van Roijen, b. at Amsterdam (North Holland) 17 Sept. 2006.

  ii.   Willem Joris Christopher van Roijen, b. at New York, N.Y. 27 March 2008.

 iii.   Berend Robert Reinhold van Roijen, b. at Greenwich, Conn. 16 Aug. 2011.

137. **Robert Dudley**[12] **van Roijen** (*Willem Joris Winthrop John*[11] *van Roijen, Jan Herman*[10] *van Roijen, Albertina Taylor*[9] *Winthrop, Robert*[8], *Thomas Charles*[7], *Francis Bayard*[6], *John Still*[5], *John*[4], *Waitstill*[3], *John*[2-1]) was born at The Hague (South Holland), the Netherlands 17 September 1979. He married at Wassenaar (South Holland) 31 January 2009, **Emilie Ploeg**, who was born at Oegstgeest (South Holland) 22 August 1978, daughter of Geert Arjen and Jerphia (Fabery de Jonge) Ploeg.[2200]

Robert Dudley van Roijen graduated from the Rijnlands Lyceum, Wassenaar, and the University of Groningen (2005). Emilie Ploeg was also educated at the University of Groningen.

Children of Robert Dudley[12] and Emilie (Ploeg) van Roijen, born at Amsterdam (North Holland):[2201]

   i.   Olivier Willem Geert[13] van Roijen, b. 6 Feb. 2010.

  ii.   Anique Sophia van Roijen, b. 26 March 2012.

 iii.   Hebe Hermy van Roijen, b. 16 Feb. 2014.

[2199] Questionnaires from Willem Joris Winthrop John van Roijen 2013 and Joris Willem Peter van Roijen 2015; notes by Willem Joris Winthrop John van Roijen 2014.

[2200] Winthrop, *Descendants of Robert Winthrop & Kate Wilson Taylor, 1833–2000*, 29; notes by Joris Willem Peter van Roijen and Marie-Anne van Roijen-Odink 2013; questionnaire from Willem Joris Winthrop John van Roijen 2013.

[2201] Questionnaire from Willem Joris Winthrop John van Roijen 2013.

THE THIRTEENTH GENERATION

138. JOSHUA ELIAS[13] MORSE (*Jeffrey Birt*[12] *Morse, Thomas Spurr*[11] *Morse, Kate*[10] *Winthrop, Grenville Lindall*[9], *Robert*[8], *Thomas Charles*[7], *Francis Bayard*[6], *John Still*[5], *John*[4], *Waitstill*[3], *John*[2-1]) was born at Richmond, Massachusetts 29 November 1978.[2202]

Joshua Elias Morse graduated from the Darrow School, New Lebanon, New York, and Emerson College (2002).

Child of Joshua Elias[13] Morse and Melissa Andrus:[2203]

    i.   JACKSON[14] MORSE, b. at Great Barrington, Mass. 19 Dec. 2006.

139. LUCAS TYLER[13] MORSE (*Peter Darwin*[12] *Morse, Thomas Spurr*[11] *Morse, Kate*[10] *Winthrop, Grenville Lindall*[9], *Robert*[8], *Thomas Charles*[7], *Francis Bayard*[6], *John Still*[5], *John*[4], *Waitstill*[3], *John*[2-1]) was born at Columbus, Ohio 26 August 1980. He married at the King Plow Arts Center, Atlanta, Georgia 26 October 2013, AMANDA LOUISE JONES, who was born at Hartford, Connecticut 17 February 1980, daughter of Robert Lee and Queen Ann (Alajian) Jones.[2204]

Lucas Tyler Morse graduated from Sabino High School, Tucson, Arizona; Johnson & Wales University in Denver (2009); and Chamberlain College of Nursing (2015). Amanda Louise Jones was educated at Georgia State University (2003 and 2006).

Child of Lucas Tyler[13] and Amanda Louise (Jones) Morse:[2205]

    i.   ASHTON LEE[14] MORSE, b. at Atlanta, 15 May 2015.

[2202] Winthrop, *Descendants of Robert Winthrop & Kate Wilson Taylor, 1833–2000*, 31; notes by Joshua Elias Morse 2013; notes by Amy Bradford Morse 2014.

[2203] Notes by Joshua Elias Morse 2013 and Amy Bradford Morse 2014.

[2204] Notes by Amy Bradford Morse 2014; questionnaire from Lucas Tyler Morse 2014.

[2205] Notes by Lucas Tyler Morse 2017.

140. **James Thomas**[13] **Morse** (*Peter Darwin*[12] *Morse, Thomas Spurr*[11] *Morse, Kate*[10] *Winthrop, Grenville Lindall*[9]*, Robert*[8]*, Thomas Charles*[7]*, Francis Bayard*[6]*, John Still*[5]*, John*[4]*, Waitstill*[3]*, John*[2-1]) was born at Tucson, Arizona 8 February 1987. He married there 9 March 2012, **Amanda Elizabeth Moody**, who was born at Safford, Arizona 2 April 1988, daughter of John Edward and Laurie Jo (Bingham) Moody.[2206]

James Thomas Morse graduated from the University of Arizona (2010 and 2012).

141. **Sarah Livingston**[13] **Hicks** (*Edward Livingston*[12] *Hicks, Elizabeth Stuyvesant*[11] *Kean, Robert Winthrop*[10] *Kean, Katharine Taylor*[9] *Winthrop, Robert*[8]*, Thomas Charles*[7]*, Francis Bayard*[6]*, John Still*[5]*, John*[4]*, Waitstill*[3]*, John*[2-1]) was born at Philadelphia, Pennsylvania 22 August 1982. She married at Santa Fe, New Mexico 23 June 2012, **Joseph Wayne Dean**, who was born at Miami, Florida 11 June 1974, son of Carl Patrick and Arlene Jo (Vail) Dean.[2207]

Dr. Sarah Livingston Hicks was educated at the Friends' Central School, Wynnewood, Pennsylvania; Hampshire College (2006); and the University of New Mexico (2015). Joseph Wayne Dean graduated from Golden High School, Golden, Colorado, and the University of Massachusetts, Amherst (2004).

Children of Joseph Wayne and Sarah Livingston[13] (Hicks) Dean, born at Albuquerque, New Mexico:[2208]

    i.   Oren Livingston[14] Dean, b. 17 Sept. 2013.

    ii   Petra Vail Dean, b. 15 May 2016.

142. **Eliza Joy**[13] **Niles** (*Cynthia Montgomery*[12] *Hicks, Elizabeth Stuyvesant*[11] *Kean, Robert Winthrop*[10] *Kean, Katharine Taylor*[9] *Winthrop, Robert*[8]*, Thomas Charles*[7]*, Francis Bayard*[6]*, John Still*[5]*, John*[4]*, Waitstill*[3]*, John*[2-1]) was born 15 June 1978. She married 2 September 2007, **Chad Hoskins**.[2209]

Dr. Eliza Joy Niles graduated from the Hackley School, Tarrytown, New York; Georgetown University (2000); and George Washington

---

[2206] Notes by Amy Bradford Morse 2014.

[2207] Winthrop, *Descendants of Robert Winthrop & Kate Wilson Taylor, 1833–2000*, 34; questionnaire from Sarah Hicks Dean 2014.

[2208] Notes by Sarah Hicks Dean 2017.

[2209] http://familytreemaker.genealogy.com/users/c/u/t/Mikey-B-Cutting/GENE2-0012.html; notes by Dr. Eliza Niles Hoskins 2013.

University (2004). Chad Hoskins was educated at Georgetown (1999), Columbia University (2004), and the University of Pennsylvania (2006).

Children of Chad and Eliza Joy[13] (Niles) Hoskins:[2210]

    i. HALEY ELIZABETH[14] HOSKINS, b. 2 July 2009.

    ii. HORACE JACKSON HOSKINS, b. 6 Nov. 2011.

143. **JULIA KEAN**[13] **NILES** (*Cynthia Montgomery*[12] *Hicks, Elizabeth Stuyvesant*[11] *Kean, Robert Winthrop*[10] *Kean, Katharine Taylor*[9] *Winthrop, Robert*[8], *Thomas Charles*[7], *Francis Bayard*[6], *John Still*[5], *John*[4], *Waitstill*[3], *John*[2-1]) was born 31 March 1980. She married 15 July 2011, **SEAN EASTON**.[2211]

Julia Kean Niles was educated at the Hackley School, Tarrytown, New York, and Colorado College.

Children of Sean Easton and Julia Kean[13] Niles:[2212]

    i. KODIAK NILES[14] EASTON, b. 7 Aug. 2010.

    ii. AVA LUNA EASTON, b. 26 Feb. 2013.

144. **PHILIP EDWARD PATTERSON**[13] **KEAN** (*Robert Winthrop*[12-10] *Kean, Katharine Taylor*[9] *Winthrop, Robert*[8], *Thomas Charles*[7], *Francis Bayard*[6], *John Still*[5], *John*[4], *Waitstill*[3], *John*[2-1]) was born at Morristown, New Jersey 23 August 1982. He married in Sonoma County, California 30 March 2013, **STEFANIE COLEMAN**, who was born at Sydney, New South Wales, Australia 1 June 1983, daughter of Keith James and Cathy Lee (Allen) Coleman.[2213]

Philip Edward Patterson Kean graduated from the Lawrenceville School, Lawrenceville, New Jersey, and the College of Charleston (2005). Stefanie Coleman was educated at Sydney Church of England Girls' Grammar School, Darlinghurst, New South Wales, and the University of Sydney (2005).

Child of Philip Edward Patterson[13] and Stefanie (Coleman) Kean:[2214]

    i. ALICE LIVINGSTON[14] KEAN, b. at New York, N.Y. 21 June 2016.

[2210] Notes by Dr. Eliza Niles Hoskins 2013.

[2211] http://familytreemaker.genealogy.com/users/c/u/t/Mikey-B-Cutting/GENE2-0012.html; notes by Julia Kean Niles 2013.

[2212] Notes by Julia Kean Niles 2013.

[2213] http://law.onecle.com/tax/2003/kean.tcm.wpd03.html; Social Security Death Index; notes by Philip Edward Patterson Kean 2013; questionnaire from Robert Winthrop Kean, 3rd, 2014; notes by Stefanie Coleman Kean 2015.

[2214] Notes by Stefanie Coleman Kean 2016.

145. **Christina Dear**[13] **Kean** (*Robert Winthrop*[12-10] *Kean, Katharine Taylor*[9] *Winthrop, Robert*[8], *Thomas Charles*[7], *Francis Bayard*[6], *John Still*[5], *John*[4], *Waitstill*[3], *John*[2-1]) was born at New York, New York 4 September 1984.[2215]

Christina Dear Kean graduated from Blair Academy, Blairstown, New Jersey, and Temple University (2006).

Child of Christina Dear[13] Kean:[2216]

    i. Michael David Tarantula[14] Kean, b. at Hoboken, N.J. 6 March 2009.

146. **Jesse Carow**[13] **Kean** (*Peter Stuyvesant*[12] *Kean, Robert Winthrop*[11-10] *Kean, Katharine Taylor*[9] *Winthrop, Robert*[8], *Thomas Charles*[7], *Francis Bayard*[6], *John Still*[5], *John*[4], *Waitstill*[3], *John*[2-1]) was born at Belleville, New Jersey 5 March 1978. He married 8 September 2007, **Dawn Allison Sticklor**, who was born at Boston, Massachusetts 21 December 1976, daughter of Howard and Marilyn (Lauer) Sticklor.[2217]

Jesse Carow Kean graduated from Phillips Academy, Andover, Massachusetts; Georgetown University (2000); and Fordham University (2008).

Children of Jesse Carow[13] Kean and Dawn Allison Sticklor, born at New York, New York:[2218]

    i. Laila Miriam[14] Kean, b. 2 May 2008.
   ii. Violet Alexandra Kean, b. 20 Feb. 2011.

147. **Hallie Elizabeth**[13] **Kean** (*Peter Stuyvesant*[12] *Kean, Robert Winthrop*[11-10] *Kean, Katharine Taylor*[9] *Winthrop, Robert*[8], *Thomas Charles*[7], *Francis Bayard*[6], *John Still*[5], *John*[4], *Waitstill*[3], *John*[2-1]) was born at Livingston, New Jersey 2 May 1983. She married at New York, New York 10 January 2004, **Joshua Council**, from whom she was divorced.[2219]

[2215] Questionnaire from Robert Winthrop Kean, 3rd, 2014.

[2216] Notes by Christopher Kean 2014; questionnaire from Robert Winthrop Kean, 3rd, 2014.

[2217] Winthrop, *Descendants of Robert Winthrop & Kate Wilson Taylor, 1833–2000*, 35; notes by Christopher Kean and Jesse Carow Kean 2014.

[2218] Notes by Christopher Kean and Jesse Carow Kean 2014.

[2219] Winthrop, *Descendants of Robert Winthrop & Kate Wilson Taylor, 1833–2000*, 35, 53; notes by Hallie Elizabeth Kean 2013 and Jesse Carow Kean 2014.

Child of Joshua Council and Hallie Elizabeth[13] Kean:[2220]

    i. JACOB KEAN[14] COUNCIL, b. at Morristown, N. J. 29 April 2004.

Child of Chris Rex and Hallie Elizabeth[13] Kean:

    ii. MAYA EMIKO[14] REX, b. 16 Aug. 2014.

148. **ADAM**[13] **KEAN** (*Alexander Livingston*[12] *Kean, Robert Winthrop*[11-10] *Kean, Katharine Taylor*[9] *Winthrop, Robert*[8], *Thomas Charles*[7], *Francis Bayard*[6], *John Still*[5], *John*[4], *Waitstill*[3], *John*[2-1]) was born at Pequannock, New Jersey 22 June 1973. He married 29 April 2000, **CAROLINA DA SILVA MONZA**, who was born at Rio de Janeiro, Brazil 2 December 1974, daughter of Celso da Silva Monza and Janice Martins.[2221]

    Children of Adam[13] Kean and Katrina Patterson:[2222]

    i. CASSIDY[14] KEAN, b. at Jacksonville, Fla. 26 Nov. 1993; she was educated at Blair Academy, Blairstown, N.J., and the Johnston Center for Integrative Studies.
    ii. MARY JANE KEAN, b. at Coconut Grove, Fla. 17 Oct. 1996.

    Children of Adam[13] Kean and Carolina da Silva Monza:[2223]

    iii. GIULIA MONZA[14] KEAN, b. at Rio de Janeiro 20 Aug. 2000.
    iv. IAN MONZA KEAN, b. at Hackettstown, N.J. 8 July 2003.

149. **THEODORA WINTHROP**[13] **HIGGINSON** (*Thomas Lee*[12] *Higginson, Jr.*, *Theodora*[11] *Winthrop, Robert*[10], *Frederic*[9], *Robert*[8], *Thomas Charles*[7], *Francis Bayard*[6], *John Still*[5], *John*[4], *Waitstill*[3], *John*[2-1]. Also *Thomas Lee*[13] *Higginson, Jr., Theodora*[12] *Winthrop, Robert*[11] *Winthrop, Dorothy*[10] *Amory, Charles Walter*[9] *Amory, Anna Powell Grant*[8] *Sears, David*[7] *Sears, Anne*[6] *Winthrop, John Still*[5]) was born at Washington, D.C. 26 January 1987. She married at "Claybrook," Rectortown, Virginia 3 October 2015, **BENJAMIN OSTLER HANNA**, who was born at Keene, New York 22 January 1986, son of Thomas Russell and Elke (Ostler) Hanna.[2224]

[2220] Winthrop, *Descendants of Robert Winthrop & Kate Wilson Taylor, 1833–2000*, 53.

[2221] Winthrop, *Descendants of Robert Winthrop & Kate Wilson Taylor, 1833–2000*, 35, 54; notes by Adam Kean and Carolina da Silva Monza 2013; notes by Alexander Livingston Kean and Carolina da Silva Monza 2014.

[2222] Winthrop, *Descendants of Robert Winthrop & Kate Wilson Taylor, 1833–2000*, 54; notes by Alexander Livingston Kean 2014.

[2223] Winthrop, *Descendants of Robert Winthrop & Kate Wilson Taylor, 1833–2000*, 54; notes by Carolina da Silva Monza 2014.

[2224] Steward, *The Sarsaparilla Kings*, 126, 140–41; Steward and Child, *The Descendants of*

Theodora Winthrop Higginson graduated from the Groton School, Groton, Massachusetts, and the University of Virginia (2010 and 2011). Benjamin Ostler Hanna was educated at Middlebury College (2008) and Boston College (2015).

150. **MIRANDA CLAIRE**[13] **RIDEMAN** (*Elizabeth*[12] *Higginson, Theodora*[11] *Winthrop, Robert*[10], *Frederic*[9], *Robert*[8], *Thomas Charles*[7], *Francis Bayard*[6], *John Still*[5], *John*[4], *Waitstill*[3], *John*[2-1]. Also *Elizabeth*[13] *Higginson, Theodora*[12] *Winthrop, Robert*[11] *Winthrop, Dorothy*[10] *Amory, Charles Walter*[9] *Amory, Anna Powell Grant*[8] *Sears, David*[7] *Sears, Anne*[6] *Winthrop, John Still*[5]) was born at Boston, Massachusetts 23 August 1983. She married at 90 Dwinell Street, West Roxbury (Boston) 20 June 2015, **JONATHAN EVERETT TRAHAN**, who was born at New Haven, Connecticut 24 November 1970, son of George Peter and Constance Jean (Caras) Trahan.[2225]

Miranda Claire Rideman graduated from the Foxcroft School, Middleburg, Virginia; Boston University (2005); and Northeastern University (2009). Jonathan Everett Trahan was educated at Hopkins Grammar Day–Prospect Hill School, New Haven, and Roger Williams College (1993).

151. **AURELIA ANNE**[13] **HIGGINSON** (*Robert Winthrop*[12] *Higginson, Theodora*[11] *Winthrop, Robert*[10], *Frederic*[9], *Robert*[8], *Thomas Charles*[7], *Francis Bayard*[6], *John Still*[5], *John*[4], *Waitstill*[3], *John*[2-1]. Also *Robert Winthrop*[13] *Higginson, Theodora*[12] *Winthrop, Robert*[11] *Winthrop, Dorothy*[10] *Amory, Charles Walter*[9] *Amory, Anna Powell Grant*[8] *Sears, David*[7] *Sears, Anne*[6] *Winthrop, John Still*[5]) was born at Santa Fe, New Mexico 21 March 1985. She married at "Tide Rock," Middletown, Rhode Island 10 August 2013, **SPENCER LAUDER BEANE**, who was born at Laconia, New Hampshire 9 April 1982, son of Dana Scott and Rebecca Anne (Miller) Beane.[2226]

Aurelia Anne Higginson graduated from Santa Fe Country Day School, Middlebury College (2007), and Tufts University (2014). Spencer Lauder Beane was educated at the Sant Bani School, Sanbornton, New Hampshire; Rensselaer Polytechnic Institute (2008); and Tufts (2011).

Judge John Lowell of Newburyport, Massachusetts, 398; notes by Henry Lee Higginson 2013 and Feroline Burrage Higginson 2015.

[2225] Steward, *The Sarsaparilla Kings*, 126, 141; Steward and Child, *The Descendants of Judge John Lowell of Newburyport, Massachusetts*, 399; notes by Theodora Winthrop Hooton and Jonathan Everett Trahan 2015.

[2226] Steward, *The Sarsaparilla Kings*, 126, 141; Steward and Child, *The Descendants of Judge John Lowell of Newburyport, Massachusetts*, 399; questionnaire from Aurelia Higginson Beane 2014.

152. **Nathalya Galadriel**[13] **de Kok** (*Anne*[12] *van Roijen, Jan Herman Robert Dudley*[11] *van Roijen, Jan Herman*[10] *van Roijen, Albertina Taylor*[9] *Winthrop, Robert*[8]*, Thomas Charles*[7]*, Francis Bayard*[6]*, John Still*[5]*, John*[4]*, Waitstill*[3]*, John*[2-1]) was born at The Hague (South Holland), the Netherlands 12 July 1990.[2227]

Child of Nathalya Galadriel[13] de Kok:[2228]

i. **Amyra Undómiel**[14] **de Kok**, b. at Kruisland (Brabant), the Netherlands 27 June 2008.

[2227] Notes by Jan Pieter de Kok and Anne van Roijen 2014.
[2228] Notes by Jan Pieter de Kok and Anne van Roijen 2014.

BIBLIOGRAPHY

ARTICLES (*see also* Journals *and* Serials)

"The William Amory House," *Proceedings of the Brookline Historical Society*, vol. 3 (1904)

E.G. Chamberlain, "Gov. Winthrop's Outing to Doublet Hill in 1631," *Appalachia*, vol. 13 (1914)

James Lawrence Chew, "The Houses of Old New London," *Records and Papers of the New London County Historical Society*, 1st series, vol. 4 (1893)

John Frederick Dorman III, "Descendants of Ann Clark[,] Wife of Owen Gwathmey," *The Filson Club History Quarterly*, vol. 27 (1953)

Hervé Douxchamps et Henry Hoff, "La Souche Stiers," *Le Parchemin: Bulletin Belge d'entr'aide & de documentation héraldique, généalogique, onomastique*, vol. 35 (1985)

George Folsom, "Memoir of Hon. Thomas Lindall Winthrop, LL.D.," *Archaeologia Americana: Transactions and Collections of the American Antiquarian Society*, vol. 3 (1857)

Charles Fraser, "Fraser Family Memoranda," *The South Carolina Historical and Genealogical Magazine*, vol. 5 (1904)

Peter J. Gomes, "Best Sermon: Pilgrim's Progress," *The New York Times Magazine*, 18 April 1999

Larry D. Gragg, "A Puritan in the West Indies: The Career of Samuel Winthrop," *The William and Mary Quarterly*, third series, vol. 50 (1993)

"Diary of Joshua Hempstead," *Collections of the New London County Historical Society*, vol. 1 (1901)

E.S. Holden, "The Fifth Satellite of Jupiter," *Publications of the Astronomical Society of the Pacific*, vol. 4 (1892)

James Mascarene Hubbard, "Boston's Last Town Meetings and First City Election," *The Bostonian Society Publications*, vol. 6 (1910)

John Hull, "Some Passages of God's Providence," *Archaeologia Americana: Transactions and Collections of the American Antiquarian Society,* vol. 3 (1857)

R.G. Lang, ed., *Two Tudor Subsidy Rolls for the City of London 1541 and 1582, London Record Society Publications,* vol. 29 (1993)

Theodore B. Lewis, "Land Speculation and the Dudley Council of 1686," *The William and Mary Quarterly,* third series, vol. 31 (1974)

Lilian J. Redstone, "'First Ministers' Account' of the Possessions of the Abbey of St. Edmund," *Proceedings of the Suffolk Institute of Archaeology and Natural History,* vol. 13 (1909)

Arthur M. Schlesinger, "Colonial Appeals to the Privy Council, II," *Political Science Quarterly,* vol. 28 (1913)

J. Hammond Trumbull, ed., "Note-book Kept by Thomas Lechford, Esq., Lawyer, in Boston, Massachusetts Bay," *Archaeologia Americana: Transactions and Collections of the American Antiquarian Society,* vol. 7 (1885)

BLOGS

Journal of the History of Ideas (jhiblog.org)
    9 February 2015, Frederic Clark, "Annotations and Generations"

http://www.christopherlong.co.uk/pub/fourcade.html

New York Society Library's Library Blog (nysoclib.org/blog)
    20 March 2015, Frederic Clark, "Erudition and Encyclopedism:
    Adam Winthrop Reads Conrad Gesner's Mithridates"

Vita Brevis (http://vita-brevis.org/)

BOOKS (*see also* Serials)

Truman Abbe and Hubert Abbe Howson, *Robert Colgate the Immigrant: A Genealogy of the New York Colgates. . . .* (New Haven, Conn.: The Tuttle, Morehouse and Taylor Company, 1941)

Andrew N. Adams, comp., *A Genealogical History of Robert Adams of Newbury, Mass., and His Descendants, 1635-1900* (Rutland, Vt.: The Tuttle Co., Printers, 1900)

George Adlard, *The Sutton-Dudleys of England and the Dudleys of Massachusetts in New England* (London: John Russell Smith, 1862)

Charles Allyn, ed., *The Battle of Groton Heights,* rev. ed. (New London, the author, 1882)

Thomas C. Amory, *Life of James Sullivan, with Selections from His Writings,* 2 vols. (Boston: Phillips, Sampson and Co., 1859)

Robert Charles Anderson, *The Great Migration Begins: Immigrants to New England, 1620–1633,* 3 vols. (Boston: New England Historic Genealogical Society, 1995)

——, *The Winthrop Fleet: Massachusetts Bay Company Immigrants to New England, 1629–1630* (Boston: New England Historic Genealogical Society, 2012)

James N. Arnold, *Vital Record of Rhode Island, 1636-1850, First Series,* 21 vols. (Providence: Narragansett Historical Publishing Co., 1891–1912)

Algernon Aikin Aspinwall, *The Aspinwall Genealogy* (Rutland, Vt.: The Tuttle Co., 1901)

John Osborne Austin, *The Genealogical Dictionary of Rhode Island* (Albany, N.Y.: Joel Mussell's Sons, 1887)

Charles Edward Banks, *The Planters of the Commonwealth* (Boston: Houghton Mifflin, 1930)

——, *The Winthrop Fleet of 1630* (Boston, 1930; rep. Baltimore: Genealogical Publishing Co., 1999)

Walter Barrett, *The Old Merchants of New York City,* 2nd series (New York: Carleton, Publisher, 1863)

John Russell Bartlett, ed., *Records of the Colony of Rhode Island and Providence Plantations,* 10 vols. (Providence: A. Crawford Greene, 1862)

Charissa Taylor Bass, *Taylor-Snow Genealogy, In Memory of Oscar Taylor and Malvina Snow Taylor* (Freeport, Ill.: C.T. Bass, 1935)

Helen Beach, *The Descendants of Jacob Sebor, 1709–1793, of Middletown, Connecticut* (1923)

Charles H. Bell, *History of the Town of Exeter, New Hampshire* (Exeter, 1888)

Thomas Williams Bicknell et al., *The History of the State of Rhode Island and Providence Plantations,* 5 vols. (New York: American Historical Society, 1920)

Biographical Catalogue of the Trustees, Teachers and Students of Phillips Academy, Andover, 1778–1830 (Andover, Mass.: The Andover Press, 1903)

J. Leander Bishop, *A History of American Manufactures from 1608 to 1860,* 2 vols. (Philadelphia: Edward Young & Co., 1864)

S. Leroy Blake, *The Later History of the First Church, New London* (New London, Conn.: Day Publishing, 1900)

George Madison Bodge, *Soldiers in King Philip's War* (Boston: the author, 1906)

Henry Bond, *Genealogies of the Families and Descendants of the Early Settlers of Watertown, Massachusetts,* 2nd ed., 2 vols. (Boston: New England Historic-Genealogical Society, 1860)

The Boston Directory (Boston: John West, 1798)

Francis J. Bremer, *John Winthrop: America's Forgotten Founding Father* (New York: Oxford University Press, 2003)

Francis J. Bremer and Tom Webster, eds., *Puritans and Puritanism in Europe and America,* 2 vols. (Santa Barbara, Calif.: ABC Clio, 2006)

Thomas Bridgman, *Memorials of the Dead in Boston* (Boston: Benjamin B. Mussey & Co., 1853)

L. Vernon Briggs, *History and Genealogy of the Cabot Family, 1475–1927,* 2 vols. (Boston: Charles E. Goodspeed & Co., 1927)

John R. Brodhead, ed., *Documents Relative to the Colonial History of the State of New-York,* 15 vols. (Albany: Weed, Parsons and Co., 1853)

Charles H. Browning, *Americans of Royal Descent,* 2nd ed. (Philadelphia: Porter & Coates, 1891)

Calendar of N.Y. Colonial Manuscripts Indorsed Land Papers, 1643–1803 (Albany: Weed, Parsons & Co., 1864)

Doris Buffett, *An Obscure Family: The Buffetts in America* (Fredericksburg, Va., 2012)

Knute Emil Carlson, *Relations of the United States with Sweden* (Allentown, Pa.: H. Ray Haas & Co., 1921)

Helen Graham Carpenter, *The Reverend John Graham of Woodbury, Connecticut, and His Descendants* (Chicago: Monastery Hill Press, 1942)

Frances Manwaring Caulkins, *History of New London* (New London, Conn.: the author, 1852)

Joshua Lawrence Chamberlain, *The Passing of the Armies: An Account of the Final Campaign of the Army of the Potomac, Based upon Personal Reminiscences of the Fifth Army Corps* (New York: G.P. Putnam's Sons, 1915)

Mellen Chamberlain, *A Documentary History of Chelsea,* 2 vols. (Boston: Massachusetts Historical Society, 1908)

Marquis de Chastellux, *Travels in North-America in the Years 1780, 1781 and 1782,* 2nd ed., 2 vols. (London: G.G.J. and J. Robinson, 1787)

Arthur H. Chester, *Trinity Church in the City of Boston* (Cambridge, Mass.: John Wilson and Son, 1888)

Peter Wilson Coldham, *American Migrations, 1765–1799* (Baltimore: Genealogical Publishing Co., 2000)

College of Physicians and Surgeons in the City of New York, Medical Department of Columbia College: Catalogue of the Alumni, Officers and Fellows, 1807–1891 (New York: Bradstreet Press, 1891)

Complete Regular Army Register of the United States for One Hundred Years (1779–1879) (Washington, D.C.: T.H.S. Hamersly, 1881)

A *Comprehensive Catalogue of the Correspondence and Papers of James Monroe*, 2 vols. (Westport, Conn.: Greenwood Press, 2001)

Ethel Colby Conant, ed., *Vital Records of Augusta, Maine, to the Year 1892*, 2 vols. (Auburn, Me.: Maine Historical Society, 1934)

John J. Currier, *History of Newburyport, Mass., 1764-1905* (Newburyport: the author, 1906)

William T. Davis, *Bench and Bar of the Commonwealth of Massachusetts*, 2 vols. (Boston: The Boston History Company, 1895)

John Ross Delafield, *Delafield: The Family History of Brig. Gen. John Ross Delafield*, 2 vols. (New York: Privately printed, 1945)

Franklin Bowditch Dexter, ed., *Ancient Town Records: New Haven Town Records, 1649–1769*, 3 vols. (New Haven, Conn.: New Haven Colony Historical Society, 1917)

——, *Biographical Sketches of the Graduates of Yale College*, 6 vols. (New York: Henry Holt & Co., 1911–12)

Allegra di Bonaventura, *For Adam's Sake: A Family Saga in Colonial New England* (New York: Liveright Publishing Corp., 2013)

Samuel G. Drake, *The History and Antiquities of Boston* (Boston: Luther Stevens, 1856)

William Dugdale, *Monasticon Anglicanum: A New Edition*, 6 vols. (London: James Bohn, 1846)

William Duncan, *The New-York Directory and Register for the Year 1794* (New York: T. and J. Swords, 1794)

Robert J. Dunkle and Ann S. Lainhart, eds., *Deaths in Boston 1700 to 1799*, 2 vols. (Boston: New England Historic Genealogical Society, 1999)

——, *Inscriptions and Records of the Old Cemeteries of Boston* (Boston: New England Historic Genealogical Society, 2000)

——, *John Haven Dexter's Memoranda of the Town of Boston in the 18th & 19th Centuries* (Boston: New England Historic Genealogical Society, 1997)

——, *Records of the Churches of Boston* (Boston: New England Historic Genealogical Society, 2002)

Richard S. Dunn, *Puritans and Yankees: The Winthrop Dynasty of New England, 1630–1717* (Princeton, N.J.: Princeton University Press, 1962)

Richard S. Dunn and Laetitia Yeandle, eds., *The Journal of John Winthrop, 1630–1649* (Cambridge, Mass.: Belknap Press of Harvard University, 1996)

Benjamin W. Dwight, *The History of the Descendants of John Dwight of Dedham, Mass.,* 2 vols. (New York: John F. Trow & Son, 1874)

Bryan Edwards, *The History, Civil and Commercial, of the British Colonies in the West Indies,* 3rd ed., 3 vols. (London: John Stockdale, 1801)

William C. Endicott, *Memoir of Samuel Endicott with a Genealogy of His Descendants* (Boston, 1924)

J. Farmer and J.B. Moore, eds., *Collections, Historical and Miscellaneous: and Monthly Literary Journal,* 3 vols. (Concord, N.H., 1823)

John Farmer, *A Genealogical Register of the First Settlers of New England* (Lancaster, Mass.: Carter, Andrews & Co., 1829)

Joseph B. Felt, *The Annals of Salem from Its First Settlement* (Salem, Mass.: W. & S. B. Ives, 1827)

——, *History of Ipswich, Essex and Hamilton* (Cambridge, Mass.: Charles Folsom, 1834)

Henry L. Ferguson, *Fishers Island, N.Y. 1614-1925* (New York: Privately printed, 1925)

Ralph E. Forbes, *The Forbes Family* (Milton, Mass.: the author, 1934)

Peter Force, ed., *Tracts and Other Papers Relating Principally to the Origin, Settlement and Progress of the Colonies in North America,* 4 vols. (Washington, privately printed, 1838; rep. New York: Peter Smith, 1947)

Samuel A. Forman, *Dr. Joseph Warren: The Boston Tea Party, Bunker Hill and the Birth of American Liberty* (Gretna, La.: Pelican Publishing, 2011)

J.W. Fortescue, ed., *Calendar of State Papers, Colonial Series, America and West Indies,* 44 vols. (London, 1899)

Joseph Foster, ed., *London Marriage Licences 1521–1869* (London: Bernard Quaritch, 1887)

Augustus Theodore Francis, comp., *History of the 71st Regiment, N.G., N.Y.* (New York: The Veterans Association, 1919)

General Catalogue of Bowdoin College and the Medical School of Maine, 1794-1916 (Brunswick, Me., 1912)

Joshua R. Giddings, *History of the Rebellion: Its Authors and Causes* (New York: Follett, Foster & Co., 1864)

Anna Glover, *Glover Memorials and Genealogies: An Account of John Glover of Dorchester and His Descendants* (Boston: David Clapp & Son, 1867)

Gravestone Inscriptions and Records of Tomb Burials in the Granary Burying Ground, Boston, Mass. (Salem, Mass.: The Essex Institute, 1918)

Isaac J. Greenwood, *Captain John Manley, Second in Rank in the United States Navy, 1776–1783* (Boston: C.E. Goodspeed & Co., 1915)

James W. Hagy, *People and Professions of Charleston, South Carolina, 1782–1802* (Baltimore: Genealogical Publishing Co., 1999)

Charles Hale, ed., *Connecticut Newspaper Notices,* 68 vols. (Hartford: Connecticut State Library, 1941)

Edward Everett Hale, Jr., ed., *Note-book kept by Thomas Lechford, esq., lawyer, in Boston, Massachusetts Bay, from June 27, 1638, to July 29, 1641* (Cambridge, Mass.: J. Wilson & Son, 1885)

Edward Doubleday Harris, *An Account of Some of the Descendants of Capt. Thomas Brattle* (Boston: D. Clapp and Son, 1867)

Harvard College class reports, various

Charles H. Haswell, *Reminiscences of an Octagenarian of the City of New York (1816 to 1860)* (New York: Harper & Brothers, 1896)

Ebenezer Hazard, ed., *Historical Collections; Consisting of State Papers and Other Authentic Documents, Intended as Materials for an History of the United States of America,* 2 vols. (Philadelphia: T. Dobson, 1794)

William Herbert, *History of the Twelve Great Livery Companies,* 2 vols. (London: the author, 1836)

Andrew Hilen, ed., *The Letters of Henry Wadsworth Longfellow,* 6 vols. (Cambridge, Mass.: Harvard University Press, 1982)

Charles J. Hoadly, ed., *The Public Records of the Colony of Connecticut,* 15 vols. (Hartford: Case, Lockwood and Brainard, 1868)

Daniel Hodas, *The Business Career of Moses Taylor: Merchant, Finance Capitalist and Industrialist* (New York: New York University Press, 1975)

Matthew Holland, *Bonds of Affection* (Washington, D.C.: Georgetown University Press, 2007)

James Camden Hotten, *The Original List of Persons of Quality* (London, 1874; rep. Boston: New England Historic Genealogical Society, 2012)

Alice R. Huger Smith and D.E. Huger Smith, *Charles Fraser* (Charleston, S.C.: Garnier, 1967)

F.A. Inderwick, ed., *A Calendar of the Inner Temple Records,* 3 vols. (London, 1896–1919)

Henry F. Jenks, *Catalogue of the Boston Public Latin School* (Boston: The Boston Latin School Association, 1886)

Clare Jervey, *Inscriptions on the Tablets and Gravestones in St. Michael's Church and Churchyard, Charleston, S.C.* (Columbia, S.C.: The State Company, 1906)

Laura Winthrop Johnson, *The Life and Poems of Theodore Winthrop,* Edited by His Sister (New York: Henry Holt and Co., 1884)

John W. Jordan, ed., *Colonial and Revolutionary Families of Pennsylvania,* 3 vols. (New York: The Lewis Publishing Co., 1911)

Elizabeth Dennistoun Kane, *Story of John Kane of Dutchess County, New York* (Philadelphia: J. B. Lippincott Co., 1921)

Robert Winthrop Kean, *Fourscore Years: My First Twenty-four* (privately printed, 1974)

Charles P. Keith, *The Provincial Councillors of Pennsylvania Who Held Office Between 1733 and 1776* (Philadelphia, 1883)

Howard A. Kelly, *A Cyclopedia of American Medical Biography,* 2 vols. (Philadelphia: W.B. Saunders, 1912)

Gertrude Selywn Kimball, ed., *The Correspondence of the Colonial Governors of Rhode Island, 1723–1775,* 2 vols. (Boston: Houghton, Mifflin and Co., 1902)

Robert Means Lawrence, *The Descendants of Major Samuel Lawrence of Groton, Massachusetts, with some mention of allied families* (Cambridge, Mass.: Printed at the Riverside Press, 1904)

Laws of the Commonwealth of Massachusetts, Vol. 13 (Boston: Dutton & Wentworth, 1836), 121.

Lawrence H. Leder, *Robert Livingston, 1654–1728, and the Politics of Colonial New York* (Chapel Hill, N.C.: University of North Carolina Press, 1961)

Charles H. Lincoln, ed., *Narratives of the Indian Wars, 1675–1699* (New York: Charles Scribner's Sons, 1913)

John William Linzee, *The Linzee Family of Great Britain and the United States. . . .,* 2 vols. (Boston: Privately printed, 1917)

Henry Cabot Lodge, *Early Memories* (New York: Charles Scribner's Sons, 1913)

David Longworth, *American Almanac, New-York Register and City Directory* (New York, 1815)

The Manifesto Church: Records of the Church in Brattle Square, Boston (Boston: The Benevolent Fraternity of Churches, 1902)

Charles William Manwaring, *A Digest of the Early Connecticut Probate Records,* Vol. 1, Hartford District, 1635–1700 (Hartford: R.S. Peck: 1904)

Nathan Washington Marston, *The Marston Genealogy in Two Parts* (South Lubec, Me., 1888)

Cotton Mather, *Hades Look'd Into: Sermon at the Funeral of the Honourable Wait Winthrop Esq.* (Boston: T. Crump, 1717)

Samuel B. May, *The Descendants of Richard Sares (Sears) of Yarmouth, Mass. 1638-1888* (Albany, N.Y.: Joel Munsell's Sons, 1890)

Lawrence Shaw Mayo, *The Winthrop Family in America* (Boston: The Massachusetts Historical Society, 1948)

Memorial of St. Mark's Church in the Bowery (New York, 1899)

R. Burnham Moffat, *The Barclays of New York: Who They Are and Who They Are Not – and Some Other Barclays* (New York: Robert Grier Cooke, 1904)

Samuel Eliot Morison, *The Founding of Harvard College* (Cambridge, Mass.: Harvard University Press, 1935)

——, *Massachusettensis de conditoribus, or Builders of the Bay Colony* (Boston: Houghton Mifflin, 1930)

Charles Mosley, ed., *Burke's Peerage, Baronetage & Knightage, 107th ed.,* 3 vols. (Wilmington, Del.: Burke's Peerage Ltd., 2003)

Beamish Murdoch, *A History of Nova Scotia, or Acadie,* 2 vols. (Halifax: John Barnes, 1866)

David Savile Muzzey, *The United States of America: Through the Civil War,* 2 vols. (Boston: Ginn and Co., 1922)

Sylvanus Chace Newman, *Rehoboth in the Past: An Historical Oration Delivered on the Fourth of July 1860* (Pawtucket, R.I.:, Robert Sherman, 1860)

Arthur Percival Newton, *The Colonising Activities of the English Puritans* (New Haven, Conn.: Yale University Press, 1914)

John Nichols, *The History and Antiquities of the County of Leicester,* 4 vols. (London, 1795–1811)

Sybil Noyes, *Charles T. Libby, and Walter G. Davis, Genealogical Dictionary of Maine and New Hampshire* (Portland, Me.: The Southward Press, 1928)

E.B. O'Callaghan, *The Documentary History of the State of New-York,* 4 vols. (Albany: Weed, Parsons & Co., 1849)

Obituary Record of the Graduates of Bowdoin College and the Medical School of Maine (Lewiston, Me.: Journal Printshop, 1911)

Official Records of the Union and Confederate Armies, First Series (Washington, D.C.: National Archives, 1959)

Fitch Edward Oliver, *The Diaries of Benjamin Lynde and of Benjamin Lynde, Jr.* (Boston, 1880)

——, *The Diary of William Pynchon of Salem* (Boston: Houghton, Mifflin and Co., 1890)

Vere Langford Oliver, *The History of the Island of Antigua,* 3 vols. (London: Mitchell and Hughes, 1899)

Sidney Perley, *The History of Salem, Massachusetts,* 2 vols. (Salem, Mass.: the author, 1924)

Richard D. Pierce, ed., *The Records of the First Church in Salem, Massachusetts 1629-1736* (Salem, Mass.: Essex Institute, 1974)

Porcellian Club 1791–2016 (Cambridge, Mass.: the Club, 2016)

Portrait and Biographical Record of Randolph, Jackson, Perry and Monroe Counties, Illinois (Chicago: Biographical Publishing Co., 1894)

Temple Prime, *Some Account of the Bowdoin Family,* 2nd ed. (New York, 1894)

——, *Some Account of the Bowdoin Family, with a notice of the Erving family,* 3rd ed. (New York: DeVinne Press, 1900)

——, *Some Account of the Temple Family,* 3rd ed. (New York, 1896)

——, *Some Account of the Temple Family: Appendix* (New York, 1899)

Private and Special Statutes of the Commonwealth of Massachusetts, 21 vols. (Boston: Wells and Lilly, 1805-1912)

The Probate Records of Essex County, Massachusetts, 3 vols. (Salem, Mass.: The Essex Institute, 1920)

Edmund Quincy, *Life of Josiah Quincy,* 6th ed. (Boston: Little, Brown and Co., 1874)

Quinquennial Catalogue of the Officers and Graduates of Harvard University, 1636–1915 (Cambridge, Mass.: Harvard University Press, 1915)

Steven Rappaport, *World Within Worlds: The Structure of Life in Sixteenth-Century London* (Cambridge: Cambridge University Press, 1988)

The Record of the Royal Society of London (London: Oxford University Press, 1912)

Records Relating to the Early History of Boston, Containing Boston Marriages from 1752 to 1809, Vol. 30 (Boston: Municipal Printing Office, 1903)

The Records of the Town of Cambridge (formerly Newtowne) Massachusetts, 1630-1703 (Cambridge, 1901)

The Register Book of the Lands and Houses in the "New Towne" and the Town of Cambridge (Cambridge, Mass., 1896)

Report of the d'Hauteville Case: The Commonwealth of Pennsylvania, at the suggestion of Paul Daniel Gonsalve Grand d'Hauteville, versus David Sears, Miriam C. Sears, and Ellen Sears Grand d'Hauteville (Philadelphia: Printed by William S. Martien, 1840)

A Report of the Record Commissioners Containing Boston Births, Baptism, Marriages and Deaths, 1630-1699, Report of the Record Commissioners, Vol. 9 (Boston: Rockwell and Churchill, 1883)

A Report of the Record Commissioners of the City of Boston Containing Boston Births from A.D. 1700 to A.D. 1800 (Boston: Rockwell and Churchill, 1894)

A Report of the Record Commissioners of the City of Boston, Containing the Boston Marriages from 1700 to 1751, Vol. 28 (Boston: Municipal Printing Office, 1898)

Cuyler Reynolds, ed., *Genealogical and Family History of Southern New York and the Hudson River Valley,* 3 vols. (New York: Lewis Historical Publishing Co., 1914)

Daniel Ricketson, *The History of New Bedford, Bristol County, Massachusetts* (New Bedford, Mass.: the author, 1858)

Oliver Ayer Roberts, *History of the Military Company of the Massachusetts, now called The Ancient and Honorable Artillery Company of Massachusetts, 1637–1888,* 4 vols. (Boston: Alfred Mudge & Son, 1895–1901)

Samuel Forbes Rockwell, *Davis Families of Early Roxbury and Boston* (North Andover, Mass: Andover Press, 1932)

James Swift Rogers, *James Rogers of New London, Ct., and His Descendants* (Boston: the author, 1902)

James Savage, *A Genealogical Dictionary of the First Settlers of New England,* 4 vols. (Boston: Little, Brown & Co., 1860–62)

——, ed., *The History of New England from 1630 to 1649, by John Winthrop, Esq.,* 2 vols. (Boston: Little, Brown & Co., 1853)

Charles M. Selleck, *Norwalk* (Norwalk, Conn.: the author, 1896)

William A. Shaw, *The Knights of England: A Complete Record from the Earliest Time to the Present Day of the Knights in all the Orders of Chivalry,* 2 vols. (London: Sherratt and Hughes, 1906)

Thomas Townsend Sherman, *Sherman Genealogy: Including Families of Essex, Suffolk, and Norfolk, England. . . .* (New York: T. A. Wright, 1920)

Evelyn Philip Shirley, *Hanley and the House of Lechmere* (London: Pickering and Co., 1883)

Nathaniel B. Shurtleff, ed., *Records of the Governor and Company of the Massachusetts Bay in New England, 1628-1686,* 5 vols. in 6 (Boston: W. White, printer to the Commonwealth, 1853–54)

John Langdon Sibley et al., *Biographical Sketches of Graduates of Harvard University,* 18 vols. (Cambridge and Boston, Mass., 1873–1999)

Sixty-fifth Annual Report of the Trustees of the Perkins Institution and Massachusetts School for the Blind for the year ending August 31, 1896 (Boston: Press of George H. Ellis, 1897)

R.H. Raymond Smythies, *Historical Records of the 40th (2nd Somersetshire) Regiment* (Devonport, Devonshire: A.H. Swiss, 1894)

Edwin M. Snow et al., comps., *Alphabetical Index of the Births, Marriages and Deaths, Recorded in Providence, Rhode Island,* 31 vols. (Providence, 1879–1945)

Social Register, various cities

Kathleen A. Staples and Madelyn Shaw, *Clothing through American History: The British Colonial Era* (Santa Barbara, Calif.: Greenwood, 2013)

The Statutes of the Realm, 11 vols. (London: Great Britain Records Commission, 1810–28)

Sven Stelling-Michaud, ed., *Le Livre du Recteur de l'Académie de Genève,* 6 vols. (Geneva, Switzerland: Librairie Droz, 1972–80)

Raymond Phineas Stern, *The Strenuous Puritan: Hugh Peter, 1598–1660* (Urbana, Ill.: The University of Illinois, 1954)

Scott C. Steward, *The Descendants of Dr. Nathaniel Saltonstall of Haverhill, Massachusetts* (Boston: Newbury Street Press, 2013)

———, *The Sarsaparilla Kings: A Biography of Dr. James Cook Ayer and Frederick Ayer, with a record of their family* (Cambridge, Mass.: Privately printed, 1993)

Scott C. Steward and John Bradley Arthaud, eds., A *Thorndike Family History: Descendants of John and Elizabeth (Stratton) Thorndike* (Boston: Newbury Street Press, 2000)

Scott C. Steward and Christopher C. Child, *The Descendants of Judge John Lowell of Newburyport, Massachusetts* (Boston: Newbury Street Press, 2011)

Scott Campbell Steward and Newbold Le Roy 3rd, *The Le Roy Family in America, 1753-2003* (Laconia, N.H.: Peter E. Randall, 2003)

John E. Stillwell, *Historical and Genealogical Miscellany: Early Settlers of New Jersey and Their Descendants,* 5 vols. (New York, 1932)

Charles Stimpson, Jr., *Stimpson's Boston Directory* (Boston: Stimpson & Clapp, 1831–35)

Frances Mary Stoddard, *An Account of a Part of the Sufferings and Losses of Jolley Allen* (Boston: Franklin Press, 1883)

Sword's Pocket Almanack (New York: T. and J. Swords, 1832)

David Langdon Tappan, *Tappan-Toppan Genealogy: Ancestors and Descendants of Abraham Toppan of Newbury, Massachusetts, 1606–1672* (Arlington, Mass: the author, 1915)

Ellery Kirke Taylor, *The Lion and the Hare: Being the Graphic Pedigree of over One Thousand Descendants of John Winthrop, 1588–1649* (1939)

Robert N. Toppan and Alfred Goodrick, eds., *Edward Randolph, Including His Letters and Official Papers from the New England, Middle and Southern Colonies in America,* 7 vols. (Boston: The Prince Society, 1909)

W. B. Trask et al., eds., *Suffolk Deeds,* 14 vols. (Boston, 1880–1906)

Trial by a Court Martial of Lieut. Col. Grenville Temple Winthrop on Charges Preferred Against Him by Adjutant Gen. William H. Sumner in Pursuance of Orders from His Excellency Levi Lincoln, Governor of the Commonwealth of Massachusetts (Boston: Carter, Hendee & Co., 1832)

Trinity Church in the City of Boston, Massachusetts (Boston: Merrymount Press, 1933)

Benjamin Trumbull, *A Complete History of Connecticut,* 2 vols. (New Haven, Conn.: Maltby, Goldsmith & Co., 1818)

J. Hammond Trumbull, ed., *Plain Dealing or News from New England, by Thomas Lechford* (Boston: J.K. Wiggin & Wm. Parsons Lunt, 1867)

——, *The Public Records of the Colony of Connecticut,* 15 vols. (Hartford: Brown & Parsons, 1850)

Joseph Hopkins Twichell, ed., *Some Old Puritan Love Letters: John and Margaret Winthrop, 1618–1638* (New York: Dodd, Mead, 1893)

D.T. Valentine, *Manual of the Corporation of the City of New York* (New York: Edmund Jones & Co., 1862)

Florence Van Rensselaer, *The Livingston Family in America and Its Scottish Origins* (New York, 1949)

John Adams Vinton, *The Giles Memorial* (Boston: Henry W. Dutton & Son, 1864)

Vital Records of Cambridge, Massachusetts to the Year 1850, 2 vols. (Boston: New England Historic Genealogical Society, 1914)

Vital Records of Gloucester, Massachusetts to the End of the Year 1849, 3 vols. (Topsfield, Mass.: Topsfield Historical Society, 1917)

Vital Records of New Haven, 1649–1850, 2 vols. (Hartford: The Connecticut Society, 1924)

Vital Records of Roxbury, Massachusetts, to the End of the Year 1849, 2 vols. (Salem, Mass.: The Essex Institute, 1925)

Vital Records of Salem, Massachusetts to the End of the Year 1849, 6 vols. (Salem: The Essex Institute, 1916)

Vital Records of Salisbury, Massachusetts to the End of the Year 1849 (Topsfield, Mass.: Topsfield Historical Society, 1915)

Vital Records of Wenham, Massachusetts to the Year 1849 (Salem, Mass.: The Essex Institute, 1904)

A Volume Relating to the Early History of Boston Containing the Aspinwall Notarial Records from 1644 to 1651 (Boston: Municipal Printing Office, 1903)

Edward Warren, *The Life of John Collins Warren, M.D., Compiled Chiefly from His Autobiography and Journals,* 2 vols. (Boston: Ticknor & Fields, 1860)

John Collins Warren, *Genealogy of Warren and Some Historical Sketches* (Boston: John Wilson and Son, 1854)

Thomas Warren, *A History and Genealogy of the Warren Family* (London: the author, 1902)

Henry F. Waters, *Genealogical Gleanings in England,* 3 vols. (Boston: New England Historic Genealogical Society, 1901)

Thomas Franklin Waters, *A Sketch of the Life of John Winthrop the Younger, Founder of Ipswich, Massachusetts, in 1633,* in *Publications of the Ipswich Historical Society,* vol. 7 (1889)

Marston Watson, *Royal Families: Americans of Royal and Noble Descent,* 3 vols., 2nd ed. (Baltimore: Genealogical Publishing Co., 2002-7)

William Way, *History of the New England Society of Charleston, South Carolina* (Charleston: The Society, 1920)

Glenn Weaver, *The History of Trinity College* (Hartford: Trinity College Press, 1967)

Lyman Horace Weeks, *Prominent Families of New York,* rev. ed. (New York: The Historical Company, 1898)

H. Barbara Weinberg and Carrie Rebora Barratt, eds., *American Stories: Paintings of Everyday Life, 1765-1915* (New Haven, Conn.: Yale University Press, 2009)

Dorothy B. Wexler, *Reared in a Greenhouse: The Stories – and Story – of Dorothy Winthrop Bradfo*rd (New York and London: Garland Publishing, 1998)

Walter Muir Whitehill, ed., *Captain Joseph Peabody, East Indian Merchant of Salem (1757-1844),* comp. by William Crowninshield Endicott (Salem, Mass.: Peabody Museum, 1962)

Zachariah G. Whitman, *The History of the Ancient and Honorable Artillery Company,* 2nd ed. (Boston: John H. Eastburn, 1842)

Alicia Crane Williams, *Early New England Families, 1641–1700,* Vol. 1 (Boston: New England Historic Genealogical Society, 2015)

H. Wilson, comp., *Trow's New York City Directory for the Year Ending May 1, 1857* (New York: John F. Trow, 1856)

——, *Trow's New York (City) Directory* (New York: John F. Trow, 1860)

James Grant Wilson and John Fiske, eds., *Appleton's Cyclopædia of American Biography,* 6 vols. (New York: D. Appleton and Co., 1889)

——, *Appleton's Cyclopaedia of American Biography,* rev. ed., 7 vols. (New York: D. Appleton and Co., 1898)

Justin Winsor, ed., *The Memorial History of Boston,* 4 vols. (Boston: James R. Osgood & Co., 1881)

John Winthrop, *Descendants of Robert Winthrop & Kate Wilson Taylor, 1833-2000* (Privately printed, 2006)

Robert C. Winthrop, *Addresses and Speeches on Various Occasions* (Boston: Little, Brown and Co., 1852)

——, *Addresses and Speeches on Various Occasions, from 1852 to 1867* (Boston: Little, Brown and Co., 1867)

——, *Life and Letters of John Winthrop, Governor of the Massachusetts-Bay Company at Their Emigration to New England, 1630,* 2 vols. (Boston: Ticknor and Fields, 1864)

——, *Reminiscences of Foreign Travel: A Fragment of Autobiography* (Privately printed, 1894)

——, *A Short Account of the Winthrop Family* (Cambridge, Mass.: John Wilson and Son, 1887)

Robert C. Winthrop, Jr., *A Few Words in Defence of an Elderly Lady: A Difference of Opinion Concerning the Reasons Why Katharine Winthrop Refused to Marry Chief Justice Sewall* (Boston: Privately printed, 1885)

——, *A Memoir of Robert C. Winthrop Prepared for the Massachusetts Historical Society* (Boston: Little, Brown and Co., 1897)

———, *Some of Account of the Early Generations of the Winthrop Family in Ireland* (Cambridge: John Wilson and Son, 1883)

Missy Wolfe, *Insubordinate Spirit: A True Story of Life and Loss in Earliest America, 1610–1665* (Guilford, Conn.: Globe Pequot, 2012)

J. Walter Wood, *William Wood (Born 1656) of Earlsferry, Scotland, and Some of His Descendants and Their Connections* (New Haven, Conn.: Tuttle, Morehouse & Taylor Co., 1916)

Walter W. Woodward, *Prospero's America: John Winthrop, Jr. and the Creation of New England Culture, 1606–1676* (Chapel Hill, N.C.: University of North Carolina Press, 2010)

David B. Yoffie and Mary Kwak, *Judo Strategy: Turning Your Competitors' Strength to Your Advantage* (Boston: Harvard Business School Press, 2001)

CD-ROMS

Robert J. Dunkle and Ann S. Lainhart, *Records of the First Church in Boston* (Boston: New England Historic Genealogical Society, 2001)

DATABASES

AmericanAncestors.org

    Boston, MA: Church Records

    Records of the Churches of Boston

- Robert J. Dunkle and Ann S. Lainhart, *Deaths in Boston 1700 to 1799*
- ———, *"The Records of Baptisms, Marriages and Deaths, The King's Chapel, Boston"*
- ———, *"Records of the Old South Church in Boston"*

Ancestry.com

    1911 England Census

    California Birth Index, 1905–1995

    Connecticut Death Index, 1949–2012

    England & Wales, Civil Registration Birth Index, 1837–1915

    England & Wales, Civil Registration Birth Index, 1916–2005

    England & Wales, Civil Registration Marriage Index, 1916–2005

    London, England, Church of England Marriages and Banns, 1734–1921

    Massachusetts Town and Vita Records, 1620–1988

    Minnesota Birth Index, 1900–1934

U.S. Social Security Applications and Claims Index, 1936–2007

World War II Draft Registration Cards, 1942

FamilySearch.org

District of Columbia Deaths, 1874–1961

England, Cornwall and Devon Parish Registers, 1538–2010

"Parish Registers for Hanley-Castle, 1538-1966"

"Parish Registers for St. Andrew Undershaft Church, London, 1558-1901"

Findagrave.com, various

greenwood.com

Thomas C. Winthrop family burial records (Charles F., Clarence, Eugene, Gen. Frederick, Georgianna M., Gertrude, and Thomas C. Winthrop)

DTB Rotterdam Stadstrouw [Rotterdam City Archive Weddings], online at *digitalestamboom.nl*

JOURNALS (*see also* Articles)

The American Genealogist, 88 vols. to date (1922–)

Vol. 11 (1934), Donald Lines Jacobus, "James, Mellowes and Ingoldsby Family Connections"

The American Journal of Science and Arts, 316 vols. to date (1818–)

Vol. 47 (1844), "Ancient Catalogue of Objects of Natural History"

Americana, 37 vols. (1909–43)

Vol. 11 (1916), Arthur Wentworth Hamilton Eaton, "Chapters in the History of Halifax, Nova Scotia"

Annals of Surgery, 265 vols. to date (1885–)

Vol. 229 (1999), Francis D. Moore, "John Collins Warren and His Act of Conscience"

Amherst College Bulletin, 106 vols. to date (1911–)

Vol. 3 (1914), "Obituary Record 1914"

The Connecticut Nutmegger, 49 vols. to date (1968–)

Vol. 31 (1998), Sherry S. Stancliff, "The Elizabeth Reade Winthrop Tombstone Affair (or the Tale of Three Tombstones)"

The Essex Antiquarian, 13 vols. (1897–1909)

Vol. 13 (1909), Sidney Perley, ed., "Descendants of William Browne of Salem"

The Gentleman's Magazine and Historical Chronicle, 120 vols. (1730–1850)

    Vol. 102 (1832), "Obituary: Vice-Admiral Winthrop"

Great Migration Newsletter, 25 vols. (1990–2016)

    Vol. 4 (1993), Robert Charles Anderson, "Even the Best of Families. . . ."

The Harvard Graduates' Magazine, 42 vols. (1892–1934)

    Vol. 4 (1895), "News from the Classes"

    Vol. 20 (1911–12)

The Herald and Genealogist, 8 vols. (1863—74)

    Vol. 2 (1865), "The Dudleys of Massachusetts"

New England Ancestors, 10 vols. (2000–9)

    Vol. 5 (2004), Timothy G. X. Salls, ed., "Record of the Gilbert Aspinwall family, 1708-1982"

The New England Historical and Genealogical Register, 171 vols. to date (1847–)

    Vol. 3 (1849), "Marriages and Deaths"

    Vol. 4 (1850), Lemuel Shattuck, "Genealogical Memoir of the Descendants of Edward Winslow, Governor of Plymouth Colony"

    Vol. 5 (1851)

    Vol. 7 (1853), Andrew Johonnot, "The Johonnot Family"

    Vol. 7 (1853), Samuel Sewall, "New England Chronology"

    Vol. 7 (1853), John A. Vinton, "Memoir of the Lindall Family"

    Vol. 8 (1854), "Bradstreet's Journal"

    Vol. 10 (1856), "Governor Thomas Dudley and His Descendants"

    Vol. 10 (1856), W.H. Whitmore, "An Account of the Temple Family"

    Vol. 11 (1857), Frances Manwaring Caulkins, "Ancient Burial Ground at New London, Conn."

    Vol. 14 (1860), "Founders of New England"

    Vol. 14 (1860), "Marriages and Deaths: Elizabeth Bowdoin Temple Tappan"

    Vol. 18 (1864), William H. Whitmore, "Notes on the Winthrop Family and Its English Connections Viz.: The Family of Forth, Clopton, Tyndale and Fones"

    Vol. 23 (1869), John W. Dean, "Rev. Joseph or Josse Glover"

    Vol. 25 (1871), John H. Sheppard, "Reminiscences of Lucius Manlius Sargent"

    Vol. 26 (1872), "Hon. David Sears"

    Vol. 27 (1873), "Deaths"

    Vol. 30 (1876), "Memoranda from the Rev. William Cooper's Interleaved Almanacs"

Vol. 33 (1879)

Vol. 35 (1881), "Correspondence of Benedict Arnold"

Vol. 46 (1892)

Vol. 50 (1896)

Vol. 52 (1898), J. Henry Lea, "The English Ancestry of the Families of Batt and Byley of Salisbury, Mass."

Vol. 60 (1906), Henry Herbert Edes, "Robert Charles Winthrop, Jr., A.M."

Vol. 67 (1913)

Vol. 69 (1915), Elizabeth French, "Winthrop"

Vol. 75 (1921), J. Gardner Bartlett, "Leaders in the Winthrop Fleet, 1630"

Vol. 76 (1922), Thomas Amory Lee, "Old Boston Families, Number Six: The Lee Family"

Vol. 84 (1930), John Boyle, "Boyle's Journal of Occurrences in Boston, 1759–1778"

Vol. 86 (1932), "Memoirs: Frederic Winthrop"

Vol. 103 (1949), Milton Rubicam, "A Winthrop-Bernadotte Pedigree"

Vol. 111 (1957), George E. McCracken, "Early Cogans English and American"

Vol. 121 (1967), C. Edward Egan, Jr., "The Hobart Journal"

Vol. 150 (1996), Craig Partridge, "Elizabeth Herbert, Wife of (1) John White and (2) George Corwin"

Vol. 151 (1997), Wayne H.M. Wilcox, "Captain Thomas Hawkins, Shipwright, of London and Dorchester, Massachusetts and Three Generations of Descendants"

The New-England Magazine, 9 vols. (1831–35)

Vol. 3 (1832), "Reminiscences of a Retired Militia Officer"

The New Republic, 4 March 2004

The New York Genealogical and Biographical Record, 148 vols. to date (1870–)

Vol. 4 (1873), Benjamin W. Dwight, "The Descendants of Rev. Benjamin Woolsey, of Dosoris (Glen Cove), L.I."

Vol. 11 (1880), J.J. Latting, "Genealogical Fragments: Feake"

Vol. 16 (1885), Benjamin W. Dwight, "Rogers Lineage"

Vol. 47 (1916), Robert H. Kelby, comp., "New York Marriage Licenses"

Vol. 51 (1920), John R. Totten, "Christophers Family"

Vol. 71 (1940), "Records of St. Mark's Church in the Bowery, New York City"

Vol. 75 (1944), "Records of Trinity Church Parish, New York City"

Vol. 78 (1947), "Records of Trinity Church Parish, New York City"

Vol. 82 (1951), "Records of Trinity Church Parish, New York City"

Vol. 86 (1955), George E. McCracken, "The Feake Family of Norfolk, London, and Colonial America"

Vol. 87 (1956), George B. Kinkead, "Gilbert² Livingston and Some of his Descendants"

Vol. 97 (1966), Donald Lines Jacobus, "That Winthrop Woman Again!"

The North American Review and Miscellaneous Journal, 302 vols. to date (1815–1940, 1964–)

Vol. 7 (1818)

Notes and Queries: A Medium of Inter-Communication for Literary Men, Artists, Antiquaries, Genealogists, etc., 228 vols. in 14 series to date (1849–)

5th series, vol. 12 (1885), William M. Sargent, "Richard Wharton"

Reformation, 21 vols. to date (1996–)

Vol. 1 (1996), W.R. Cooper, "Richard Hunne"

St. Andrew's Magazine, Winter 1998

The Utah Genealogical and Historical Magazine, 31 vols. (1910–40)

Vol. 24 (1933), "The Ancestry of Thomas Richards"

Wake Forest Magazine, March 2008 and June 2010

MANUSCRIPTS

Connecticut Vital Records (compiled under the direction of Lucius Barnes Barbour)

"New London Births–Marriages–Deaths, 1646–1854" (Hartford, 1919)

"Middletown Births–Marriages–Deaths, 1651–1854," in 2 vols. (Hartford, 1923)

Hedwiga Regina Shober Gray diary [1860–1884], 25 vols. (R. Stanton Avery Special Collections, NEHGS)

"Index of Marriages in Massachusetts Centinel and Columbia Centinel 1784–1840," 8 vols. (bound typescript at NEHGS)

Spencer P. Mead, "Abstract of Probate Records for the District of Stamford, County of Fairfield, and State of Connecticut, 1729-1848," 2 vols. (typescript, 1924)

Robert Winthrop, "Draft history of Robert Winthrop & Co.," 1973

NEWSPAPERS

American (New York), 9 January 1822, 10 December 1828

American (Providence), 20 June 1809

American Apollo (Boston), 5 October 1792

Boston Commercial Gazette, 23 September 1830

Boston Daily Advertiser, 22 March 1819

Boston Evening-Post, 9 May 1768

Boston Evening Transcript, 17 September 1852, 31 August 1875, 20 July 1907, 7 May 1938

The Boston Gazette and Country Journal, 13 December 1762, 3 June 1765

The Boston Globe, 31 July 2000, 15 June 2003, 14 November 2010

Boston News-Letter, 3 July 1704, 18 November 1717, 7 April 1718, 22 August 1723, 5 August 1725, 28 November 1746

Boston Traveler, 26 July 1825

The Brewster Standard (New York), 15 November 1979

Centinel of Freedom (Newark, N.J.), 23 July 1844

Charleston Courier, 21 November 1825, 29 July 1828

City Gazette (Charleston, S.C.), 3 October 1798, 23 June 1804, 9 July 1817

Columbia Herald (S.C.), 14 February 1785

Columbian Centinel (Boston), 22 January 1812, 12 January 1820, 15 September 1827

Commercial Advertiser (New York), 21 August 1841, 10 January 1844, 19 March 1844, 2 November 1861

Connecticut Gazette, 1 May 1789, 3 July 1794, 13 April 1797, 12 March 1806, 20 April 1814

Connecticut Gazette, and the Commercial Intelligencer, 24 February 1802

The Connecticut Gazette; and the Universal Intelligencer, 14 June 1776, 14 December 1781

Connecticut Journal, 6 November 1776

Connecticut Courant (Hartford), 12 August 1828

The Connecticut Journal, and New-Haven Post-Boy, 1 February 1771

Constitution (Middletown, Conn.), 17 February 1847, 12 May 1847

Daily Advertiser (New York), 9 August 1799

Daily Atlas (Boston), 5 May 1856

Daily National Intelligencer (Washington, D.C.), 9 September 1843

Daily Press, 4 September 2005

Episcopal Watchman (Hartford), August 1828

Evening Post (New York), 27 September 1823, 15 February 1825, 28 April 1827, 26 December 1831, 22 November 1850, 31 March 1851, 28 April 1873

The Guardian (London), 29 February 1996, 27 May 2005

The Independent (London), 20 May 2005

Independent Chronicle (Boston), 25 February 1811, 9 June 1814

Ipswich Chronicle (Massachusetts), 30 August 2000

The Miami Herald, 1 May 2012

The New-England Courant, 26 August 1723

New-England Palladium (Boston), 20 May 1817

New London Daily Chronicle News, 6 September 1848

The New-London Gazette, 2 March 1770

New-York Daily Advertiser, 17 May 1817

New-York Daily Gazette, 19 October 1791

New-York Gazette, 9 August 1799

New York Herald, 9 March 1869, 21 August 1873

New York Post, 9 June 1818

The New York Review of Books, 28 February 2002

The New York Times, 25 June 1859, 13 June 1861, 3 August 1863, 15 January 1871, 4 June 1873, 3 September 1874, 23 December 1888, 3 June 1892, 28 January 1893, 17 February 1898, 3 December 1900, 8 August 1902, 21 January 1903, 8 October 1903, 13 March 1904, 3 May 1904, 18 May 1904, 17 August 1906, 16 April 1912, 27 February 1916, 19 October 1920, 9 January 1921, 10 November 1921, 17 July 1923, 7 September 1924, 8 September 1924, 21 January 1925, 29 May 1925, 8 June 1925, 16 August 1925, 14 September 1925, 13 September 1926, 11 December 1926, 10 April 1928, 25 October 1928, 11 December 1928, 3 August 1930, 2 September 1931, 22 September 1932, 1 September 1933, 29 March 1934, 21 April 1934, 4 July 1935, 9 October 1936, 1 June 1938,

22 June 1938, 11 November 1940, 24 November 1940, 23 November 1941, 28 December 1941, 31 December 1941, 26 April 1942, 30 October 1942, 20 January 1943, 29 January 1943, 31 July 1943, 25 August 1943, 17 October 1943, 4 March 1944, 8 April 1947, 31 August 1947, 13 November 1947, 22 November 1947, 11 January 1948, 27 June 1948, 27 July 1948, 12 September 1948, 22 February 1949, 5 May 1949, 25 October 1949, 26 March 1950, 17 June 1951, 23 May 1952, 26 June 1952, 11 June 1953, 10 March 1955, 12 March 1955, 26 April 1955, 13 August 1955, 24 September 1956, 24 November 1956, 22 September 1957, 26 April 1958, 6 July 1958, 18 November 1958, 25 January 1959, 13 March 1960, 22 September 1960, 16 August 1962, 2 March 1964, 13 March 1964, 9 September 1966, 11 September 1966, 4 June 1967, 18 March 1969, 12 June 1969, 13 June 1969, 21 December 1969, 28 June 1970, 9 July 1970, 13 September 1970, 31 October 1971, 2 July 1972, 11 August 1975, 4 January 1976, 15 August 1976, 30 March 1979, 23 March 1980, 6 June 1980, 24 September 1980, 1 February 1981, 17 June 1981, 7 July 1981, 28 November 1981, 20 January 1982, 21 March 1982, 10 October 1982, 19 June 1983, 7 August 1983, 11 September 1983, 16 October 1983, 10 June 1984, 11 June 1984, 8 September 1985, 3 October 1985, 7 November 1985, 1 March 1986, 29 January 1988, 2 October 1988, 16 October 1988, 11 February 1989, 18 June 1989, 24 September 1989, 7 May 1990, 17 March 1991, 20 March 1991, 21 July 1991, 25 December 1991, 8 July 1992, 7 February 1993, 21 February 1993, 23 May 1993, 31 July 1994, 11 September 1994, 13 November 1994, 19 May 1995, 7 September 1995, 15 June 1996, 6 July 1997, 10 August 1997, 2 May 1999, 30 September 1999, 31 October 1999, 10 September 2000, 10 December 2000, 17 December 2002, 23 July 2004, 18 December 2005, 5 February 2006, 9 May 2009, 29 May 2011, 24 September 2011, 29 April 2012, 31 January 2013, 18 May 2014, 31 August 2014, 12 April 2016

The New York Times Magazine, 18 April 1999

New York Tribune, 6 November 1861, 29 October 1863, 30 April 1867

Newport Mercury, 6 December 1828

Norwich Aurora, 8 September 1860

The Norwich Packet, or The Country Journal, 22 September 1785

Philadelphia Inquirer, 18 February 1842

Poulson's American Daily Advertiser (Philadelphia), 14 January 1812

Providence Gazette, 10 June 1786

The Putnam County Courier (New York), 22 April 1966

The Salem News (Mass.), 10 August 2011

Sentinel and Witness (Middletown, Conn.), 17 December 1828

South Carolina Gazette, 19 January 1785

Spectator (New York), 26 November 1849, 21 April 1851

[Springer's] Weekly Oracle (New London, Conn.), 17 September 1798

The Telegraph (London), 21 May 2005

The Times (London), 21 May 2005

The Wall Street Journal, 30 July 2004

The Washington Post, 31 March 1979, 5 June 1993, 20 November 2002, 21 May 2014

Weekly Messenger (Boston), 16 August 1821

SERIALS (*see also* Articles)

Collections of the Connecticut Historical Society, 31 vols. (1860–1967)
    Vol. 5 (1896)
    Vol. 23 (1930)

Collections of the Massachusetts Historical Society, 89 vols. in seven series to date (1792–)
    3rd series, vol. 2 (1830)
    3rd series, vol. 7 (1838)
    3rd series, vol. 8 (1843), James Savage, "Gleanings for New England History"
    3rd series, vol. 8 (1843), Groton parish register
    3rd series, vol. 9 (1846), "Memoir of James Bowdoin"
    3rd series, vol. 10 (1849)
    4th series, vol. 2 (1854), "Memoir of the Late Thomas L. Winthrop"
    4th series, vol. 6 (1863)
    4th series, vol. 7 (1865)
    5th series, vol. 1 (1871)
    5th series, vol. 5 (1878)
    5th series, vol. 6 (1879), et seq., "Diary of Samuel Sewell"
    5th series, vol. 7 1882)
    5th series, vol. 8 (1882)
    6th series, vol. 2 (1888)
    6th series, vol. 3 (1889)

   6th series, vol. 5 (1892)

   6th series, vol. 9 (1897)

   7th series, vol. 2 (1902)

   7th series, vol. 3 (1902)

   7th series, vol. 10 (1915)

Collections of the New–York Historical Society, 85 vols. to date (1868–)

   Vol. 3 (1871)

   Vol. 23 (1890)

   Vol. 62 (1930)

Dictionary of Literary Biography, 375 vols. to date (1980–)

   Vol. 24 (1984), *American Colonial Writers, 1606–1734*, Everett Emerson, "John Winthrop"

   Vol. 30 (1984), *American Historians, 1607–1865*, Francis J. Bremer, "John Winthrop"

   Vol. 200 (1999), *American Women Prose Writers to 1820*, Rosemary Fithian Guruswamy, "Margaret Tyndal Winthrop"

The Essex Institute Historical Collections, 129 vols. (1869–1993)

   Vol. 41 (1905), Eugene Tappan, ed., "Essex County Estates Administered in Suffolk County, Prior to 1701"

The National Cyclopaedia of American Biography, 63 vols. (1898–1984)

   Vol. 7 (1897), "Moses Taylor"

   Vol. 18 (1922), "John Kean"

   Vol. C (1930), "Hamilton Fish Kean"

   Vol. 46 (1963), "Hamilton Fish Kean"

   Vol. L (1972), "Robert Winthrop"

[New Hampshire] State Papers Series, 40 vols. (1867–1943)

   Vol. 31 (1907), Albert Stillman Batchellor, ed., *Probate Records of the Province of New Hampshire, Vol. 1, 1635–1717*

Oxford Dictionary of National Biography, 60 vols. + 2 supplemental vols. (Oxford: Oxford University Press, 2004)

   Vol. 2, Peter Speak, "Terence Edward Armstrong (1920–1996)"

   Vol. 13, Peter Elmer, "John Cotta (1575?–1627/8)"

   Vol. 14, Cosmo Russell, "Dunstan Michael Carr Curtis (1910–1983)"

   Vol. 45, Roger Lubbock, "John Sleigh Pudney (1909–1977)"

   Vol. 59, James P. Walsh, "Fitz John Winthrop (1639?–1707)"

   Vol. 59, Francis J. Bremer, "John Winthrop (1588-1649)"

Vol. 59, Walter W. Woodward, "John Winthrop (1606–1676)"

Proceedings of the American Antiquarian Society, 118 vols. (1843–2008)

New series, vol. 14 (1902), George H. Haynes, "'The Tale of Tantiusques': An Early Mining Venture in Massachusetts"

Proceedings of the Massachusetts Historical Society, 109 vols. (1791–1997)

1st series, vol. 5 (1861), Capt. Israel Stoughton to Dr. Stoughton, undated

2nd series, vol. 2 (1886)

2nd series, vol. 2 (1886), Robert C. Winthrop, Jr., "Memoir of the Hon. David Sears, A.M."

2nd series, vol. 5 (1889), John Pierce, "Some Notes on the Commencements at Harvard University, 1803–1848"

2nd series, vol. 6 (1890), Robert C. Winthrop, "Thomas Lyon, His Family and Connections"

2nd series, vol. 7 (1892)

2nd series, vol. 12 (1898)

2nd series, vol. 20 (1906), Charles Francis Adams, "Memoir of Robert C. Winthrop, Jr."

3rd series, vol. 2 (1909)

5th series, vol. 8 (1882)

Vol. 2 (1880)

Vol. 12 (1873)

Vol. 13 (1875), "Mem. of a Voyage from Boston to London, by John Still Winthrop"

Vol. 16 (1879)

Vol. 17 (1880)

Vol. 18 (1881)

Vol. 32 (1899), "Remarks by Mr. R. C. Winthrop, Jr."

Vol. 53 (1920)

Vol. 65 (1934), Henry Adams, "Frederic Winthrop: A Memoir"

Vol. 80 (1969), Malcolm Freiberg, "The Winthrops and Their Papers"

Publications of the Colonial Society of Massachusetts, 88 vols. to date (1895–)

Vol. 24 (1923), William C. Lane, "Early Silver Belonging to Harvard College"

Vol. 26 (1927), Viola F. Barnes, "Richard Wharton, A Seventeenth Century New England Colonial"

Vol. 31 (1935), William C. Lane, "Early Silver Belonging to Harvard College"

Vol. 39 (1961), Richard D. Pierce, ed., "The Records of the First Church of Boston, 1630-1868"

Vol. 56 (1982), Andrew Oliver and James Bishop Peabody, eds., "The Records of Trinity Church, Boston, 1728-1830"

The Publications of the Harleian Society, Register Series, 89 vols. (1877–1953)

Vol. 63 (1933), A.M. Bruce Bannerman, ed., *Registers of St. Matthew, Friday Street, London, 1538 to 1812, and the United Parishes of St. Matthew and St. Peter, Cheap, 1754 to 1812*

Joseph James Muskett, ed., *Suffolk Manorial Families: Being the County Visitations and Other Pedigrees,* 2 vols. (Exeter, Devon: William Pollard & Co., 1900–8)

Vol. 1 (1900), "Goodwin of Bull's Hall"

——, *Suffolk manorial families, being the county visitations and other pedigrees, with extensive additions,* 4 vols. (Boston and Exeter: 1894–1910)

Vol. 1 (1894–96), with Robert C. Winthrop, Jr., *Evidences of the Winthrops of Groton, co. Suffolk, England, and of families in and near that county, with whom they intermarried*

Winthrop Papers, 6 vols. (Boston: Massachusetts Historical Society, 1929–92)

INDEX

Page numbers in bold refer to the photo insert.

CREDITS

EVERY effort has been made to trace the copyright holders of the works published herein. If proper copyright acknowledgment has not been made, please contact the publisher and we will correct the information in future printings.

Reproduced with permission from the Massachusetts Historical Society, *Winthrop Family Papers*, 7, 53, 92, 95, 97, 100, 101, 123, 124, 125, 143, 145, 147, 158, 172, 203.

By permission of Oxford University Press, USA, *John Winthrop: America's Forgotten Founding Father*, 4, 5, 7, 8, 10, 11, 16, 17, 18, 22, 23, 24, 30, 41, 42, 43, 44, 45, 47, 49, 51, 53, 54, 58.

Reproduced with permission from the New England Historic Genealogical Society, *Great Migration Newsletter*, 57, 59, 78.

Reproduced with permission from the New England Historic Genealogical Society, R. Stanton Avery Special Collections, 200, 211, 214, 215, 216, 217, 218, 220, 221, 232, 243, 246, 252, 269.

Courtesy of the *Ipswich Chronicle*, "Burial site of first settler may be revealed," 82.

Reproduced with permission from Dorothy B. Wexler, *Reared in a Greenhouse: The Stories—and Story—of Dorothy Winthrop Bradford*, x, 163, 208, 210, 217, 227, 236, 237, 238, 239, 240, 241, 243, 256, 257, 258, 260, 261, 262, 263, 267, 268, 269, 270, 285, 286, 288, 293, 294, 297, 298, 299, 300, 301, 302, 309, 310, 311, 316, 338.

Reproduced from *Fourscore Years: My First Twenty four*, 237, 238, 239, 240, 241, 257, 258, 259, 267, 268, 292.

Reproduced from the *New York Times*, "Ex-Senator Kean of New Jersey Dies," 258, 259.

Reproduced from the *New York Times*, "Winthrop Sisters in Dual Elopement," 285, 286, 287.